25 Years 2025-2001

ICSE

CHAPTERWISE TOPICWISE
QUESTION BANK

Biology

Class 10

25 Years 2025-2001

ICSE

CHAPTERWISE TOPICWISE

QUESTION BANK

Biology

Class 10

Authors

Madhubala Sharma

Venus Kataria

arihant

SUCCESS AND NOTHING LESS

arihant
SUCCESS AND NOTHING LESS

ARIHANT PRAKASHAN
(School Division Series)

ADMINISTRATIVE & PRODUCTION OFFICES

Regd. Office
'Ramchhaya' 4577/15, Agarwal Road, Darya Ganj, New Delhi -110002
Tele: 011- 47630600, 43518550

Head Office
Kalindi, TP Nagar, Meerut (UP) - 250002, Tel: 0121-7156203, 7156204

SALES & SUPPORT OFFICES

Agra, Ahmedabad, Bengaluru, Bareilly, Chennai, Delhi, Guwahati, Hyderabad, Jaipur, Jhansi, Kolkata, Lucknow, Nagpur & Pune.

PO No : TXT-XX-XXXXXXX-X-XX

Published By Arihant Publications (India) Ltd.

For further information about the books published by Arihant, log on to www.arihantbooks.com or e-mail at info@arihantbooks.com

PRICE ₹270.00

Follow us on

Achieving 99+

Marks in Board Exams

Achieving 99+ marks in board exams is definitely an ambitious goal, but with the right approach and these 7 tips from toppers, you can definitely increase your chances of success!

Here are the 7 Topper Tips to ace your board exams:

1. Master the art of consistency

Consistency builds understanding and confidence, both crucial for excelling in exams.

2. Build a winning study strategy

Create a personalised timetable that prioritises subjects based on your strengths and weaknesses.

3. Befriend the syllabus

Focus on high-weightage topics and prioritise mastering core concepts before moving on to advanced ones.

4. Embrace active learning

Explain concepts to yourself or in study groups to solidify understanding.

5. Conquer the past

Solve Past years' papers and Sample Papers under timed conditions to practice time management and understand paper pattern.

6. Seek help, when needed!

Don't hesitate to clarify doubts with teachers, tutors, or study groups. Asking questions strengthens your understanding and prevents confusion.

7. Prioritise well-being

Eat nutritious meals, get enough sleep, and regular exercise practice stress management techniques like meditation to stay calm and focused during exams.

These tips are just a starting point, and you can personalise them to fit your learning style and preferences.

Description of

Newly Added Features

01

Cell Cycle, Cell Division and Structure of Chromosome

TREND ANALYSIS 4 YEARS

		Average No. of Questions Across all Sets				
		Types of Questions	2024	2023	2020	2019
TOPIC 01	Cell Cycle and Cell Division	1 Mark	-	4	-	1
		2 Marks	-	1	-	2
		3 Marks	1	-	-	-
		4 Marks	-	-	-	-
		5 Marks	-	-	-	1
TOPIC 02	Chromosomes	1 Mark	1	1	-	2
		2 Marks	-	1	-	-
		3 Marks	-	-	-	-
		4 Marks	-	-	-	-
		5 Marks	-	-	-	-

Trend Analysis

At the start of each chapter, Trend Analysis is given to indicate the types of questions asked from different topics of the chapter. This feature helps students to know the importance of different topics of the given chapter from exam point of view and helps them to prepare accordingly.

Key Idea

'Key Idea' is given with selected questions with the purpose to help students to get the approach 'to answer the question'. This feature help students to develop the systematic approach to answer difficult/complex questions.

50. Complete the following process to show how the oxygen in the air reaches a mesophyll cell of the leaf ?

Oxygen in air ⟶ [ ] ⟶ [ ] ⟶ Mesophyll cell.

ICSE 2004

KEY idea

Exchange of gases occurs through stomata.

Ans. The oxygen in air reaches the stomata from which air enters to substomatal space and then to mesophyll cells.

Oxygen in air ⟶ Stoma ⟶ Air space ⟶ Mesophyll cell.

34. Differentiate between cell wall and cell membrane with reference to permeability. **ICSE Specimen 2023**

Ans.

Cell wall is fully permeable to smaller molecules with the size of 30-60 kDa.	**Cell membrane** is semi-permeable and control the movement of the substance into and outside the cell.

Concept Enhancer Cell membrane is present in both plant and animal cells. This is living in nature and made up of lipid, protein and carbohydrate. Cell wall is present in plant cell only. This is non-living in nature and made up of cellulose (plant cell), chitin (fungi) and peptidoglycan (bacteria).

Concept Enhancer

Concept Enhancer gives the brief description of the concept, which has been used to answer the question. This feature provides revision of important concept along with practice of question solving.

Dream, Believe, Achieve

Insights from ICSE Toppers

"Board exams are way easier than you think. It's easy to score if you study regularly for even an hour. Consistency is key,"

ANONDEE SAHA

ICSE Topper (99.6%)

Before the boards, my school had given all students a month to study and I tried my best to study 8-9 hours every day.

I relied on revising the syllabus of each subject at least twice during this period and went through past years' question papers and extra questions that my teachers had sent.

DIVYANSH AGARWAL

ICSE Topper (99.40%)

He dedicated time to solving topic-wise papers from the last 10 years, providing valuable practice before his final revision. A planned approach and schedule help to prepare and cover the syllabus better.

For excelling in the boards I would like to advice students to study regularly from DAY 1. They should refer to previous years Board question papers and should always have a positive attitude and should be confident. But not overconfident

MUSKAN PATHAN

ICSE Topper (99.4%)

"I studied everything independently, which gave me a better understanding of what topics I needed to improve. I studied only 1.5 to 2 hours daily but stayed consistent and regular,"

MIHIKA SANJANWALA

ICSE Topper (99%)

NILOTMA SINGH

ICSE Topper (99.6%)

"I had started preparing, chapter by chapter, right from the beginning of the academic session as we had weekly tests on every topic that was covered in class. However, the hard-core preparation started only in late November 2022 which was about three months prior to the board examination.,"

Previous Years Papers guide me to a great extent as they helped me understand the scope and area of the questions that could be asked. The specimen papers were extremely helpful as we had undergone a change in examination pattern this year.

"While my primary schooling in Shanghai (China) taught me to be a global citizen, my higher secondary schooling at Greenwood High (Bannerghatta) elevated my inquisitiveness and curiosity on various subjects,"

"Personally, POMODORO technique, a time-management method based on 25-minute stretches of focused work broken by five-minute breaks, helped me immensely not only to organise myself better but also to cover a vast syllabus with the least fatigue,"

SHIVANI NEELAMRAJU

ICSE Topper (99.40%)

Please Note that all the information is collected from different websites.

Contents

ICSE Chapterwise Question Bank 2025-2001

Latest Syllabus

Class X (2026)

There will be one paper of two hours duration of 80 marks and Internal Assessment of practical work carrying 20 marks.
The paper will be divided into two sections, Section I (40 marks) and Section II (40 marks).

Basic Biology

(i) Cell Cycle and Cell Division

Cell cycle – Interphase (G_1, S, G_2) and Mitotic phase.

Cell Division:

- Mitosis and its stages.
- A basic understanding of Meiosis as a reduction division (stages not required).
- A brief idea of homologous chromosomes and crossing over leading to variations.
- Significance and major differences between mitotic and meiotic division.

(ii) Structure of Chromosome

Basic structure of chromosome with elementary understanding of terms such as chromatin, chromatid, gene structure of DNA and centromere.

(iii) Genetics: Mendel's Laws of Inheritance and Sex Linked Inheritance of Diseases

- The three laws of Mendel.
- Monohybrid cross – phenotype and genotype.
- Dihybrid cross – Only phenotype.
- The following terms to be covered: Gene, allele, heterozygous, homozygous, dominant, recessive, mutation, variation, phenotype, genotype.
- Sex determination in human beings.
  Sex linked inheritance of diseases to include only X-linked like haemophilia and colour blindness.

Plant Physiology

(i) Absorption by roots, imbibition, diffusion and osmosis; Osmotic pressure, root pressure; turgidity and flaccidity; Plasmolysis and deplasmolysis; The absorption of water and minerals; Active and Passive transport (in brief); The rise of water up to the xylem; Forces responsible for ascent of sap.

- Understanding of the processes related to absorption of water by the roots.
- Characteristics of roots, which make them suitable for absorbing water.
- Structure of a single full-grown root hair.
- A general idea of Cohesive, Adhesive forces and transpirational pull.
- Experiments to show the conduction of water through the xylem.

(ii) Transpiration - process and significance. Ganong's potometer and its limitations.
The factors affecting rate of transpiration. Experiments on transpiration. A brief idea of guttation and bleeding.

- Concept of transpiration and its importance to plants
- Experiments related to transpiration:
  (a) Loss in weight of a potted plant or a leafy shoot in a test tube as a result of transpiration.
  (b) Use of cobalt chloride paper to demonstrate unequal rate of transpiration in a dorsiventral leaf.
- Mechanism of stomatal transpiration on the basis of potassium ion exchange theory.
- Adaptations in plants to reduce transpiration.
- A brief idea of guttation and bleeding.

(iii) Photosynthesis: The process and its importance to life in general; Experiments to show the necessity of light, carbon dioxide, chlorophyll, formation of starch and release of oxygen; carbon cycle.

- The Process and Significance of Photosynthesis.
- The internal structure of chloroplast to be explained to give an idea of the site of light and dark reactions.
- Opening and closing of stomata based on potassium ion exchange theory.
- Overall balanced chemical equation to represent photosynthesis.
- Introduction of the terms "Photochemical" for light phase and "Biosynthetic" for dark phases.
- Light reaction - activation of chlorophyll followed by photolysis of water, release of O_2, formation of ATP (photophosphorylation) and NADPH.
- Dark reaction - only combination of hydrogen released by NADP with CO_2 to form glucose. (detailed equations are not required).
- Adaptations in plants for photosynthesis.
- Experiments with regard to the factors essential for photosynthesis; emphasis on destarching and the steps involved in starch test.
- A diagrammatic representation of carbon cycle.

(iv) Chemical coordination in Plants: A general study of plant growth regulators; Tropic movements in Plants.

- A brief idea of the physiological effects of Auxins, Gibberellins, Cytokinins, Abscisic acid and Ethylene in regulating the growth of plants.
- A basic understanding of the tropic movements in plants with reference to – Phototropism, Geotropism, Hydrotropism, Thigmotropism and Chemotropism (supported with suitable examples).

Human Anatomy and Physiology

(i) Circulatory System: Blood and lymph, the structure and working of the heart, blood vessels, circulation of blood (Only names of the main blood vessels entering and leaving the heart, liver and kidney will be required). Lymphatic system.

- Composition of blood (Structure and functions of RBC, WBC and platelets).
- Brief idea of tissue fluid and lymph.

- Increase in efficiency of mammalian red blood cells due to absence of certain organelles; Reasons for the same.
- A brief idea of blood coagulation.
- Structure and working of the heart along with names of the main blood vessels entering and leaving the heart, the liver and the kidney.
- Concept of systole and diastole; Concept of double circulation.
- Brief idea of pulse and blood pressure.
- Blood vessels: artery, vein and capillary to be explained with the help of diagrams to bring out the relationship between their structure and function.
- Brief idea of the lymphatic organs: Spleen and tonsils.
- ABO blood group system, Rh factor.
- Significance of the hepatic portal system.

(ii) Excretory System: A brief introduction to the excretory organs; Parts of the urinary system; Structure and function of the kidneys; Blood vessels associated with kidneys; Structure and function of nephron.

- A brief idea of different excretory organs in the human body.
- External and internal structure of the kidney;
- Parts of the urinary system along with the blood vessels entering and leaving the kidney; Functions of various parts of the urinary system (emphasis on diagram with correct labelling). A general idea of the structure of a kidney tubule/nephron.
- A brief idea of ultra-filtration (emphasis on the diagram of Malpighian capsule); Selective reabsorption and tubular secretion in relation to the composition of blood plasma and urine formed.

(iii) Nervous system: Structure of Neuron; central, autonomous and peripheral nervous system (in brief); brain and spinal cord; reflex action and how it differs from voluntary action.

Sense organs – Eye: Structure, functions, defects and corrective measures: Ear: Parts and functions of the ear.

- Parts of a neuron.
- Various parts of the external structure of the brain and its primary parts: Medulla oblongata, cerebrum, cerebellum, thalamus, hypothalamus and pons; their functions.
- Reference to the distribution of white and gray matter in Brain and Spinal cord.
- Voluntary and involuntary actions – meaning with examples.
- Diagrammatic explanation of the reflex arc, showing the pathway from receptor to effector.
- A brief idea of the peripheral and autonomic nervous system in regulating body activities.
- Differences between natural and acquired reflex.
- External and Internal structure and functions of the eye and ear and their various parts.
- A brief idea of stereoscopic vision, adaptation and accommodation of eye.

- Defects of the eye (Myopia, hyperopia hypermetropia, presbiopia, astigmatism and cataract) and corrective measures (Diagrams included for myopia and hyperopia only).
- The course of perception of sound in human ear.
- Role of ear in maintaining balance of the body.

(iv) Endocrine System: General study of the following glands: Adrenal, Pancreas, Thyroid and Pituitary. Endocrine and Exocrine glands.

- Differences between Endocrine and Exocrine glands.
- Exact location and shape of the endocrine glands in the human body.
- Hormones secreted by the following glands: Pancreas: insulin and glucagon; Thyroid: only thyroxin; Adrenal gland: Cortical hormones and adrenaline; Pituitary: growth hormone, tropic hormones, ADH and oxytocin.
- Effects of hypo Secretion and hyper Secretion of hormones.
- A brief idea of feedback mechanism with reference to TSH.

(v) The Reproductive System: Organs, fertilisation, functions of placenta in the growth of the embryo, Menstrual cycle.

- Functions of male and female reproductive organs and male accessory glands. An idea of secondary sexual characters.
- Structure and functions of the various parts of the sperm and egg.
- Explanation of the terms: Fertilisation, implantation, placenta, gestation and parturition.
- A brief idea of the role of placenta in nutrition, respiration and excretion of the embryo; Its endocrinal function.
- Functions of Foetal membranes and amniotic fluid.
- Menstrual cycle, outline of menstrual cycle.
- Role of Sex hormones: Testosterone, oestrogen and progesterone in reproduction.
- Identical and fraternal twins: Meaning and differences only.

Population

Population explosion in India; need for adopting control measures - Population control.

- Main reasons for the sharp rise in human population in India and in the world.
- A brief explanation of the terms: Demography, population density, birth rate, death rate and growth rate of population.
- Problems faced due to population explosion: Unemployment, over exploitation of natural resources, low per capita income, price rise, pollution, unequal distribution of wealth.
- Methods of population control: Surgical methods – Tubectomy and vasectomy.

Human Evolution

Basic introduction to Human evolution and Theories of evolution: Lamarck's theory of inheritance; Darwin's theory of evolution by natural selection.

- A brief idea of human ancestors – Australopithecus, Homo habilis, Homo erectus, Neanderthals, Cro-Magnon and Homo sapiens sapiens (Modern Man) with reference to the following characteristics:
  - Bipedalism
  - Increasing Cranial capacity
  - Reduction of size of canine teeth
  - Forehead and brow ridges
  - Development of chin
  - Reduction in body hair
  - Height and Posture
- Lamarck's theory of inheritance of acquired characteristics – with reference to use of organs (e.g.: neck and forelimbs of giraffe) and disuse of organs (e.g.: vestigial organs in humans like wisdom teeth, vermiform appendix, pinnae).
- Darwin's theory of Natural selection: Survival of the fittest - e.g. adaptation of peppered moth.

Pollution

(i) Types and sources of pollution; major pollutants.

- Air: Vehicular, industrial, burning garbage, brick kilns.
- Water: Household detergents, sewage, industrial waste, oil spills.
- Thermal pollution.
- Soil: Industrial waste, urban commercial and domestic waste, chemical fertilisers.
- Biomedical waste – used and discarded needles, syringes, soiled dressings, etc.
- Radiation: X-rays; radioactive fallout from nuclear plants.
- Noise: Motor vehicles, Industrial establishments, Construction sites, Loudspeakers, etc.

(ii) Biodegradable and Non-biodegradable Wastes

Biodegradable wastes: Meaning and example; paper, vegetable peels, etc.

Non-biodegradable wastes: meaning and example; plastics, glass, styrofoam, etc. Pesticides like DDT, etc.

(iii) Effects of pollution on climate, environment, human health and other organisms; control measures.

- Brief explanation of: Greenhouse effect and Global warming, Acid rain, Ozone layer depletion.
- Measures to Control Pollution:

- Use of unleaded petrol / CNG in automobiles , Switching of engines at traffic signal lights , Social forestry,
- Setting of sewage treatment plants , Ban on polythene and plastics, Organic farming
- Euro Bharat vehicular standard. (A brief idea of the above measures)

- A brief mention of "Swach Bharat Abhiyan"- A National Campaign for Clean India.

Internal Assessment of Practical Work

The practical work is designed to test the ability of the candidates to make an accurate observation from specimens of plants and animals.

Plant Life

(i) Observation of permanent slides of stages of mitosis.

(ii) Experiments demonstrating:

- Diffusion: using potassium permanganate in water.
- Osmosis: Thistle funnel experiment and potato osmoscope,
- Absorption: using a small herbaceous plant.

(iii) Experiments on Transpiration

- demonstration of the process using a Bell jar.
- demonstration of unequal transpiration in a dorsiventral leaf using cobalt chloride paper.
- demonstration of uptake of water and the rate of transpiration using Ganong's potometer.

(iv) Experiments on Photosynthesis:

- to show the necessity of light, carbon dioxide and chlorophyll for photosynthesis.
- to show the release of O_2 during photosynthesis using Hydrilla / Eelodea.

Animal Life

(i) Identification of the structures of the urinary system, heart and kidney (Internal structure) and brain (External view) through models and charts

(ii) The identification of different types of blood cells under a microscope.

(iii) Identification of the internal structure of the ear and eye (Through models and charts).

(iv) Identification and location of selected endocrine glands: Adrenal, pancreas, thyroid and pituitary glands with the help of a model or chart.

Analysis of Pupil Performance: ICSE Biology Class X

The document 'Analysis of Pupils' Performance' in ICSE Class 10 & ISC Class 12 Examination, is prepared by Research Development and Consultancy Division (RDCD) of the Council for the Indian School Certificate Examination (CISCE). The purpose of this document is to provide feedback to schools in terms of strengths and weaknesses of the candidates in handling the examination.

TOPICS FOUND DIFFICULT / CONFUSING BY STUDENTS

- Parts of eyeball and their functions.
- Gases causing depletion of ozone layer.
- Difference between carbaminohaemoglobin and carboxyhaemoglobin.
- Discoveries of Mendel, Watson and Crick, Lamarck and Darwin.
- Parts of brain and their functions.
- Experiments on photosynthesis and significance of photosynthesis.
- Number of cranial and spinal nerves.
- Chromosomes in sperm.
- Disorders caused due to hypo and hypersecretion of hormones.
- Genetic diseases.
- Abbreviations.
- Difference between stimulus and tropic movement.
- Location of testis and corpus callosum.
- Functions of blood vessels and male accessory glands.
- Diagram of stomatal apparatus.
- Organism for industrial melanism.
- Monohybrid and dihybrid cross.
- Placement of cytons and axons in brain and spinal cord.
- Fertilisation and implantation in female reproductive system.

SUGGESTIONS FOR STUDENTS

- Read the scope and syllabus prescribed for ICSE Biology.
- Revise the topics repeatedly for better understanding of concepts.
- Prepare a list of abbreviations you come across the syllabus, absorb them mentally.
- Learn the keywords/biological terms/definitions with conceptual clarity.
- Practise drawing neat and labelled diagrams.
- Give importance to biological and technical terms.
- Revise previous years question papers.
- Use the 15 minutes reading time to understand and assimilate the questions.
- Read the rubric attentively and choose the questions as per the rubrics, plan and organise your thoughts accordingly to give your best.
- Follow carefully the instructions given for each question.
- Attempt only the number of questions asked for in the question paper.
- Write the correct question number before answering.
- Be methodical and organised while answering.
- Do not separate the subsections of the question.
- Write in a neat and legible handwriting.
- Be confident and rely only on yourself.

01

Cell Cycle, Cell Division and Structure of Chromosome

TREND ANALYSIS 4 YEARS

Average No. of Questions Across all Sets

Topic	Types of Questions	2024	2023	2020	2019
TOPIC 01 Cell Cycle and Cell Division	1 Mark	–	4	–	1
	2 Marks	–	1	–	2
	3 Marks	1	–	–	–
	4 Marks	–	–	–	–
	5 Marks	–	–	–	1
TOPIC 02 Chromosomes	1 Mark	1	1	–	2
	2 Marks	–	1	–	–
	3 Marks	–	–	–	–
	4 Marks	–	–	–	–
	5 Marks	–	–	–	–

TOPIC 1

Cell Cycle and Cell Division

Cell

It is the structural and functional unit of life. However, a brief revision about basics of cell is required to further study about cell cycle and cell division.

Basic features of cells are as given below

- All organisms including humans, are made up of cells.
- All cells arise from pre-existing cells.
- Organisms may be unicellular (made up of single cell), e.g. bacteria, yeast, etc., or multicellular (made up of more than single cell), e.g. humans, plants, etc.

The above basic features are also collectively called as **cell theory** that were given by **Schleiden** and **Schwann**.

Each and every cell in an organism possess three essential parts as given below

3 essential parts of cell

Cell membrane	Cytoplasm	Nucleus
– Present in both plant and animal cell. – Semipermeable.	– Semi-liquid part present between cell membrane and nuclear membrane. – Contains organelles, e.g. ER, mitochondria, etc.	– Present in centre of cell. – Contains genetic material.

Cell Cycle

It is an orderly sequence of events taking place in a cell leading to its division. It is also known as a period between the growth of the cell and its division into daughter cells. The cell cycle is divided into two main phases.

These are

1. **Interphase** (Resting Phase)

It is the period between two successive cell divisions, i.e. an interval between the end of one cell division to the beginning of next cell division. It is also known as the interphase or **resting phase.**

Interphase itself is divided further into three main stages, depending upon its synthetic activities as described below

(i) **G_1-phase** (First growth phase) In this phase, cell grows in size and becomes metabolically active. It grows continuously and prepare itself for DNA replication, synthesis of RNA and proteins takes place.

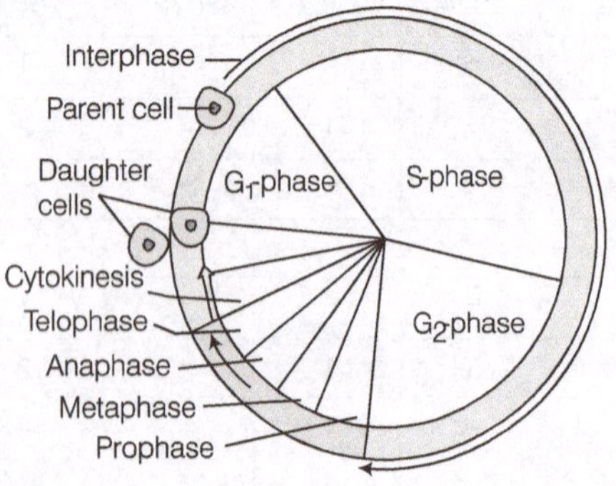

Fig. 1.1 Cell cycle

(ii) **S-phase** (Synthesis phase) It is the phase in which actual synthesis or DNA replication takes place. The chromosomes are duplicated, i.e. each chromosome contains two sister chromatids.

(iii) **G_2-phase** (Second growth phase) It is also known as **pre-mitotic phase**. During this phase the synthesis of only RNA and proteins continue as they are required for mitosis.

2. **M-phase**

Following the interphase, cell enters into the M-phase. It starts with the division of nucleus, i.e. karyokinesis and usually ends with the division of cytoplasm, i.e. cytokinesis.

Cell Division

It is essential for maintaining life of the organisms on the Earth. It forms new cells for growth, repair, replacement and reproduction.

There are two types of cell division.

I. Mitosis II. Meiosis

I. Mitosis

- In this division, one parent cell (diploid) divides into two identical daughter cells (diploid).
- It occurs only in somatic or body cells, e.g. cells of skin, hair and muscle cells, etc. So it is also known as **somatic cell division**.
- Chromosomes in mitosis are replicated and are distributed equally into the two daughter nuclei. Thus, both parent cell and the daughter cells have equal number of chromosomes at the end of division. Therefore, it is also known as **equational division**.

Stages of Mitosis

These are broadly divided into two stages

1. **Karyokinesis** (Division of Nucleus)

It refers to the division of nucleus into two daughter nuclei of about same size having same number of chromosomes as present in parent cell.

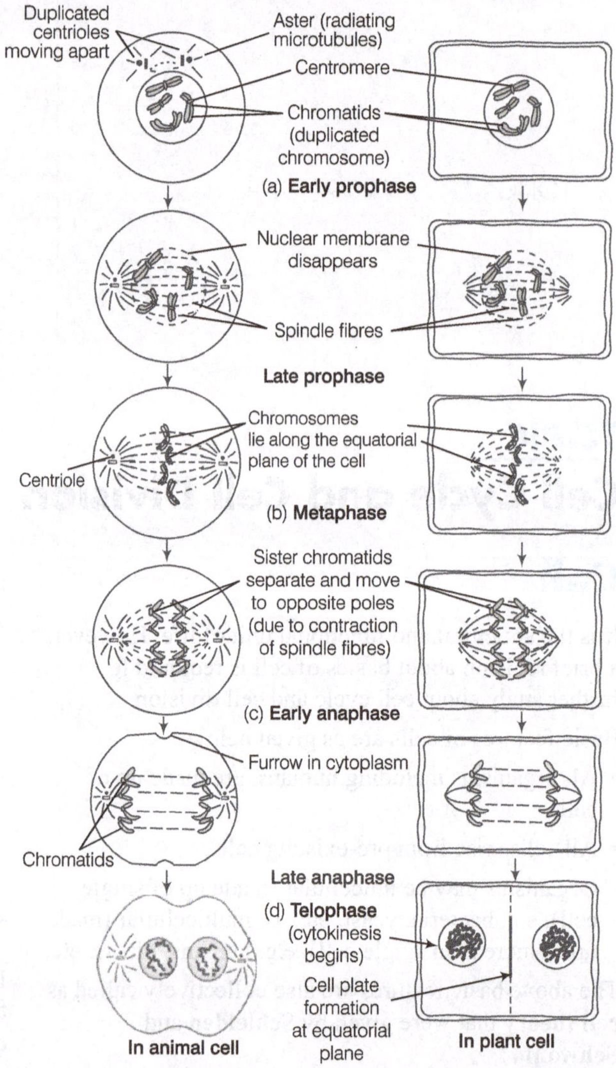

Fig. 1.2 Different stages of mitosis

There are four main stages of karyokinesis

(i) **Prophase**

- Longest and most complex phase.
- Nuclear membrane and nucleolus disappear.
- Centrioles radiate astral rays and move apart to opposite poles.
- Spindle fibre appear between two centrioles.

(ii) **Metaphase**

- Next phase after prophase.
- Chromosomes get attached to spindle.
- Chromosomes arrange at equator in one plane known as **metaphasic plate**.

(iii) **Anaphase**

- Shortest phase of mitosis.
- Chromosomes split and move to opposite poles.

(iv) **Telophase**

- It is end phase of mitotic division.
- Spindle fibres disappear.
- Nuclear membrane, Golgi complex and nucleolus reappear.

2. **Cytokinesis** (Division of Cytoplasm)

- Soon after the karyokinesis, i.e. all the changes mentioned previously in the mitosis, division of cytoplasm (cytokinesis) occurs.
- The process of cytokinesis occur differently in plant and animal cells.

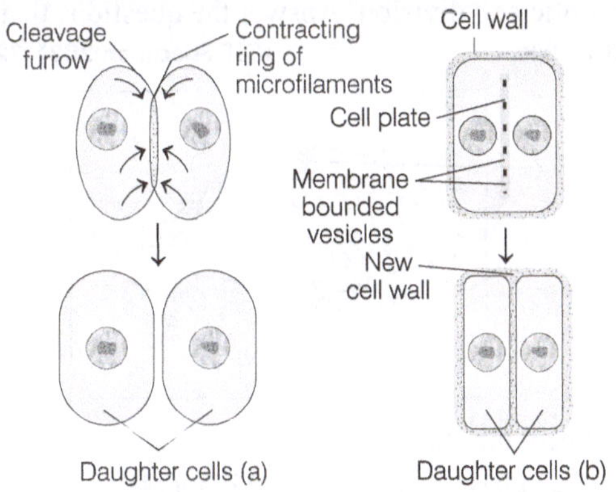

Fig. 1.3 Cytokinesis : (a) in animal cells (by cell furrowing), (b) in plant (by cell plate formation) cells

- In **plant cells**, formation of cell plate takes place at the equatorial plane of the spindle which further grows from the centre to periphery and form two daughter cells.
- In **animal cells** a furrow appears on the periphery that deepens and finally splits the cell into two, producing two daughter cells.

Significance of Mitosis

- Maintain the number of chromosomes as that of parents (in this way it maintains genetic stability).
- Helps in repair or healing of injured and worn out tissues and also replacement of old and dead cells, e.g. skin cells.
- Also help in growth of multicellular organisms.

Differences between Mitosis of Plant and Animal Cells

Animal cell	Plant cell
Asters are formed.	Asters are not formed.
Occurs nearly in all tissues.	Occurs mainly at meristems.
Centrioles present at spindle poles.	Centrioles are absent at spindle poles.
Cytokinesis is by cell furrowing.	Cytokinesis is by the formation of cell plate.

II. **Meiosis** (Reduction Division)

- It is a type of cell division in which the chromosome number is reduced in such a way that each daughter cell receives only half set of chromosomes number present in the parent cell.
- Hence, meiosis is also known as the **reduction division** which results in the production of four cells (haploid).
- It takes place in reproductive cells (germ cells or sex cells) in human and animals in their testes and ovaries, of males and females, respectively.
- It is completed in two stages, i.e. meiosis-I and meiosis-II which takes place in rapid succession, one after another.

Significance of Meiosis

- It produces gametes.
- Helps in maintaining constant number of chromosomes in species.

- Also responsible for producing variations in species and due to these variations, evolution takes place. These variations occur due to crossing over phenomenon.

Differences between Mitosis and Meiosis

Mitosis	Meiosis
It occurs in somatic cells.	It occurs in reproductive cells or germ cell.
Two daughter cells are produced.	Four daughter cells are produced.
Daughter cells receive full set of chromosomes, i.e. diploid ($2n$) number of chromosomes.	Daughter cells receive only half the number of chromosomes, i.e. haploid (n) number of chromosomes.
It occurs for growth and replacement.	It occurs only for gamete formation.
Only single nuclear division occurs.	Two nuclear divisions occur.

PYQs Previous Years' Questions

1 Mark Questions

Multiple Choice Questions

1. The sex chromosome in a human ovum is **ICSE 2023**
   (a) X-chromosome
   (b) Y-chromosome
   (c) Both X and Y-chromosomes
   (d) Either X or Y-chromosome

Ans. (a) X-chromosome

2. Haploid number of chromosomes are found in **ICSE 2023**
   (a) nephrons (b) neurons (c) skin cells (d) sperms

Ans. (d) Sperms

3. During the synthesis phase of the cell cycle, more of **ICSE 2023**
   (a) RNA is synthesised
   (b) RNA and proteins are synthesised
   (c) DNA is synthesised
   (d) Glucose is synthesised

Ans. (c) DNA is synthesised

4. The number of chromosomes in a human skin cell are **ICSE Specimen 2023**
   (a) 22 (b) 23 (c) 44 (d) 46

Ans. (d) 46

5. State the exact location of the spindle fibres **ICSE Specimen 2021-22 Sem. I**
   (a) between the two centrioles
   (b) between the two centrosomes
   (c) between chromatid and centromere
   (d) between the two centromeres

Ans. (a) between the two centrioles

6. The cell component visible only during cell division **ICSE Specimen 2021-22 Sem. I**
   (a) chromosome (b) chromoplast
   (c) chromatin (d) centriole

Ans. (a) chromosome

7. During meiosis .... daughter cells are formed. **ICSE Specimen 2021-22 Sem. I**
   (a) 4 (b) 2 (c) 8 (d) 6

Ans. (a) 4

8. Given below is a diagram representing a stage during mitotic cell division. Answer the questions that follows **ICSE Specimen 2021-22 Sem. I**

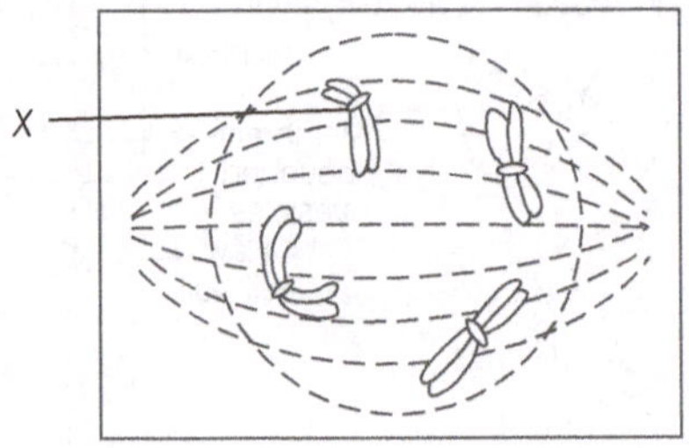

(i) Identify the stage.
   (a) Telophase (b) Prophase
   (c) Metaphase (d) Anaphase

Ans. (b) Prophase

(ii) Label part marked '*X*'.
   (a) Centriole (b) Centrosome
   (c) Centromere (d) Chromatid

Ans. (c) Centromere

(iii) Name the stage that follows the one shown here.

(a) Interphase (b) Anaphase

(c) Telophase (d) Metaphase

Ans. (d) Metaphase

(iv) What is the diploid number of chromosomes shown in the diagram?

(a) 6 (b) 2 (c) 4 (d) 8

Ans. (c) 4 diploid number of chromosomes.

(v) Mention one important feature of this stage.

(a) Nucleolus reappears

(b) Nuclear membrane reappears

(c) Nuclear membrane disappears

(d) Chromosomes align on the equator

Ans. (c) Nuclear membrane disappears

9. After mitosis, a female human cell will have **ICSE 2021-22 Sem. I**

(a) 44 + XX chromosomes (b) 22 + X chromosomes

(c) 22 + Y chromosomes (d) 44 + XY chromosomes

Ans. (a) 44 + XX chromosomes

10. At the end of ...., cytokinesis is completed. **ICSE 2021-22 Sem. I**

(a) metaphase (b) prophase

(c) interphase (d) telophase

Ans. (d) telophase

11. Replication of DNA in the cell cycle occurs during the **ICSE 2021-22 Sem. I**

(a) G_1-phase (b) Anaphase

(c) S-phase (d) G_2-phase

Ans. (c) S-phase

12. Explain the term 'karyokinesis'. **ICSE 2021-22 Sem. I**

(a) It is the division of nucleus during cell division

(b) It is the division of cytoplasm during cell division

(c) It is the division of centrosome

(d) It is the division of nucleolus

Ans. (a) It is the division of nucleus during cell division.

13. Mention the exact location of 'aster'. **ICSE 2021-22 Sem. I**

(a) Around the centrioles in the plant cells

(b) Around the centrioles in animal cells

(c) Around the chromatids in animal cells

(d) Around the chromatids in plant cells

Ans. (b) Around the centrioles in animal cells.

14. Mention the exact location of 'centrioles'.

(a) Found only in plant cells **ICSE 2021-22 Sem. I**

(b) Found inside nucleus

(c) Found only in animal cells

(d) Found in animal and plant cells

Ans. (c) Found only in animal cells.

15. Synthesis phase in the cell cycle is called so, because of the synthesis of more **ICSE 2017**

(a) RNA

(b) RNA and proteins

(c) DNA

(d) Glucose

Ans. (c) DNA

16. Chromosomes get aligned at the center of the cell during **ICSE 2015**

(a) metaphase (b) anaphase

(c) prophase (d) telophase

Ans. (a) Metaphase

Very Short Answer Type Questions

17. Name the organelle that forms the aster during cell division. **ICSE 2023**

Ans. Centrosome

18. Given below are five sets of terms. In each case arrange and rewrite each set so as to be in a logical sequence.
One is done as an example for you.
Example Large intestine, Stomach, Mouth, Small intestine, Oesophagus.
Ans. Mouth, Oesophagus, Stomach, Small intestine, Large intestine.

Metaphase, Interphase, Anaphase, Prophase, Telophase **ICSE Specimen 2019, 2004**

Ans. Interphase, Prophase, Metaphase , Anaphase, Telophase.

19. Choose the **odd** one out from the given term and name the **category** to which the others belong.

Example Nose, Tongue, Arm, Eye
Answer **Odd term**-Arm, **Category** - Other are sense organs.
Centrosome, Cell wall, Cell membrane, Large vacuoles **ICSE 2018**

Ans. **Odd term** Centrosome
Category Components of plant cells.

20. Given below are groups of terms. In each group the first pair indicates the relationship between the two terms. Rewrite and complete the second pair on a similar basis.

Example Oxygen : Inspiration : : Carbon dioxide : Expiration

Cytoplasm : Cytokinesis : : Nucleus : .... **ICSE 2017**

Ans. Cytoplasm : Cytokinesis : : Nucleus : Karyokinesis

21. Name the exchange of chromatid parts between the maternal and the paternal chromatids of a pair of homologous chromosomes during meiosis.

Ans. Crossing over **ICSE 2016**

22. Given below is the group of five terms, arrange and rewrite the terms in the correct order, so as to be in a logical sequence.Metaphase, telophase, prophase, anaphase, cytokinesis. **ICSE 2013**

Ans. The correct order, so as to be in a logical sequence is prophase, metaphase, anaphase, telophase, cytokinesis.

23. Briefly explain the term cytokinesis in plant cells. **ICSE 2013**

Ans. Cytokinesis is the division of cytoplasm that occurs after division of nucleus. In plant cells, formation of cell plate takes place at the equatorial plane of the spindle. This cell plate grows from centre to periphery to form two daughter cells.

24. Given below are the sets of five terms, rewrite the terms in a logical sequence as directed at the end of the statement.
Karyokinesis, S-phase, Cytokinesis, G_1-phase, G_2-phase (cell cycle). **ICSE 2012**

Ans. The correct sequence, so as to be in a logical sequence is
G_1-phase, S-phase, G_2-phase, Karyokinesis, Cytokinesis.

25. Name the type of cell division which occurs in the cells of reproductive organs. **ICSE 2010**

Ans. Meiosis is the type of cell division which occurs in the cells of reproductive organs.

26. State whether the following statement is true or false. If false, rewrite the correct form of the statement by changing the first and last word only.
Mitosis is the type of cell division occur in the cells of injured parts of the body. **ICSE 2010**

Ans. The statement is true.

27. State whether the following statement is true or false. If false, write the correct form of the statement by changing the first or last word only.
The resting stage of mitosis is called interphase. **ICSE 2009**

Ans. The statement is true.

28. Give the specific function of the centrosome found in the body of animals. **ICSE 2009**

Ans. The specific function of the centrosome found in the body of animals is to initiate cell division.

29. Name a membrane that disappears during late prophase. **ICSE 2008**

Ans. Nuclear membrane disappears during late prophase.

30. Give one point of difference between the following on the basis of what is given in the bracket?
Karyokinesis and cytokinesis (explain the term). **ICSE 2007**

Ans. Difference between karyokinesis and cytokinesis is as follows

Karyokinesis	Cytokinesis
It is the division of nucleus that occurs during cell division.	It is the division of cytoplasm that takes place soon after karyokinesis.

31. Name the organelle which initiates the cell division in animal cell. **ICSE 2007**

Ans. Centrosome helps in the initiation of cell division in an animal cell.

32. State whether the following statement is true or false. If false, rewrite the correct form of the statement by changing either the first or the last word only.
Cytokinesis is a division of cytoplasm. **ICSE 2004**

Ans. The statement is true.

2 Marks Questions

33. Differentiate between karyokinesis and cytokinesis. **ICSE 2023**

Ans. Differences between karyokinesis and cytokinesis are

Karyokinesis	Cytokinesis
It means the process of division of the nucleus.	It means the process of division of cytoplasm.
The nucleus gets divided into two daughter nuclei.	The cytoplasm, cell organelles and the nuclei divide and are passed onto daughter cells equally.
It can occur with or without cytokinesis.	It is dependent on karyokinesis.

34. Differentiate between cell wall and cell membrane with reference to permeability. **ICSE Specimen 2023**

Ans.

Cell wall is fully permeable to smaller molecules with the size of 30-60 kDa.	**Cell membrane** is semi-permeable and control the movement of the substance into and outside the cell.

Concept Enhancer Cell membrane is present in both plant and animal cells. This is living in nature and made up of lipid, protein and carbohydrate. Cell wall is present in plant cell only. This is non-living in nature and made up of cellulose (plant cell), chitin (fungi) and peptidoglycan (bacteria).

35. Give one difference between each of the following pairs on the basis of what is given in the brackets Metaphase and Anaphase (position of chromatids) **ICSE Specimen 2019**

Ans. Difference between metaphase and anaphase is

Metaphase	Anaphase
Chromosomes are lined up and each sister chromatid is connected to a spindle fibre during metaphase.	Sister chromatids (now called chromosomes) are driven towards opposite poles during anaphase.

36. Give the biological / technical terms for the following.

(i) The stage of cell division in which the nuclear membrane disappears and the chromosomes become short and thick. **ICSE Specimen 2019**

(ii) The repeating components of each DNA strand lengthwise.

Ans. (i) Prophase

(ii) Polynucleotide

37. Give reason for the following

Gametes have a haploid number of chromosomes. **ICSE Specimen 2017**

Ans. Gametes have a haploid number of chromosomes because they are formed by meiotic cell division. During meiosis, the chromosome number is reduced in such a way that each daughter cell receives only half set of chromosomes as of the parent cell.

38. State whether the following statements are true or false. If false, rewrite the correct form of the statement by changing the first or last word only.

(i) Lysosomes is a part of the cell in which chromosomes are present.

(ii) Centromere is the organelle of the cell that initiates cell division. **ICSE 2011**

Ans. Both statements are false and can be corrected as

(i) **Nucleus** is a part of the cell in which chromosomes are present.

(ii) **Centrosome** is the organelle of the cell that initiates cell division.

39. Mention the difference between mitosis and meiosis with reference to

(i) Number of daughter cells formed at the end of the cell division.

(ii) The chromosome number of daughter cells formed. **ICSE 2008**

Or Distinguish between the following on the basis of what is given in the bracket? Mitosis and meiosis (number of daughter cell formed). **ICSE 2007**

Ans. Refer to table on page no. 4.

40. Column 'B' is a list of items related to ideas in Column 'A'. Match the term in Column 'B' with the suitable idea given in Column 'A'. **ICSE 2008**

Column A	Column B
Chromosomes become arranged in a horizontal plane at the equator.	Anaphase
Daughter chromosomes move to opposite poles of the spindle.	Prophase
Chromosomes become visible as fine, long threads.	Telophase
Chromosomes lose their distinctiveness and gradually become transformed into chromatin network.	Metaphase

Ans. Correct matches are given below

Column A	Column B
Chromosomes become arranged in a horizontal plane at the equator.	Metaphase
Daughter chromosomes move to opposite poles of the spindle.	Anaphase
Chromosomes become visible as fine, long threads.	Prophase
Chromosomes lose their distinctiveness and gradually become transformed into chromatin network.	Telophase

Diagram Based Questions

41. The diagram given below represents a stage in mitosis. **ICSE 2024 (3M)**

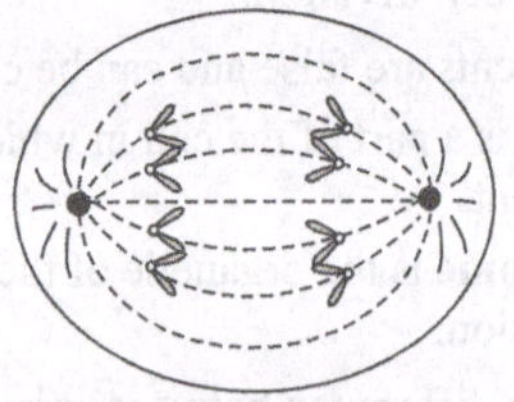

(i) Identify the stage given above.

(ii) Give one reason to support your answer in (a).

(iii) Mention the number of chromosomes given in the diagram.

Ans. (i) Anaphase

(ii) During anaphase the centromere of each chromosome splits into two, resulting into two sister chromatids. It leads to the migration of daughter chromosomes towards respective poles.

(iii) 8

42. Given below is a diagram representing a stage during the mitotic cell division. Answer the following questions. **ICSE Specimen 2023 (3M)**

(i) Identify the stage.

(ii) Give a suitable reason for your answer in (i).

(iii) Name the stage that follows the one shown in the diagram.

Ans. (i) Late prophase

(ii) As nuclear membrane disappeared

(iii) Metaphase

Concept Enhancer At metaphase stage, chromosomes are distinguishable when viewed via microscope. Metaphase chromosomes are used in karyotyping, laboratory technique for identifying chromosomal abnormalities.

43. Given below is a diagram representing a stage during the mitotic cell division. Study the diagram and answer the following questions. **ICSE 2019 (5M)**

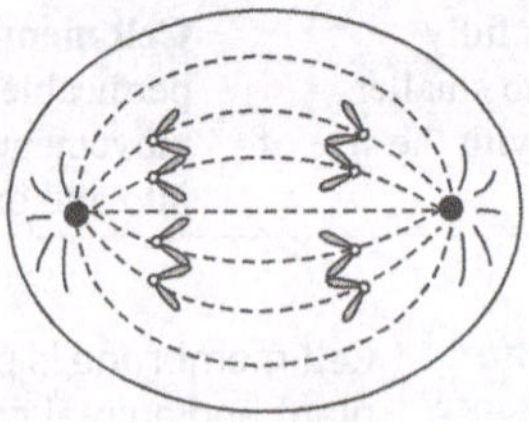

(i) Identify the stage by giving a suitable reason.

(ii) Is it a plant or an animal cell? Give a reason to support your answer.

(iii) Draw a neat, labelled diagram of the stage which follows the one shown in the question.

(iv) How many chromosomes will each daughter cell have after the completion of the above division?

(v) Name the four nitrogenous bases.

Ans. (i) **Anaphase** During this phase, the splitting of chromosomes take place. This splitting occurs due to the division of centromere which attaches two sister chromatids.

(ii) Animal cell as it contains centrosomes.

(iii) Telophase

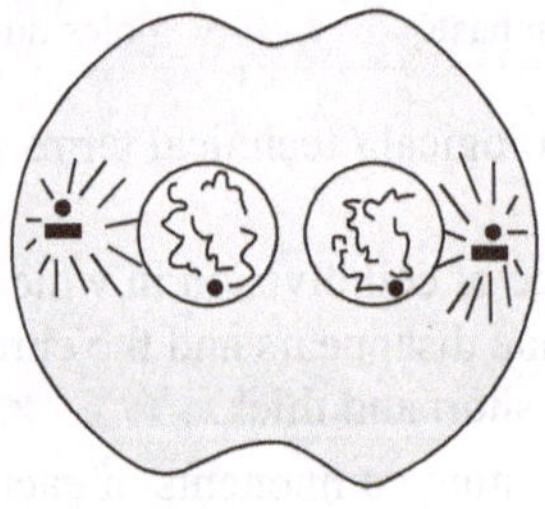

In animal cell

(iv) Two sets of chromosomes in each daughter cell.

(v) Adenine Guanine
Cytosine Thymine

44. Draw a diagram of the nucleus of a cell, having chromosome number 6, as it would appear in the metaphase stage of mitosis and label the following parts **ICSE 2018 (2M)**

(i) Aster

(ii) Acromatic spindle

(iii) Chromatid

(iv) Centromere

Ans. Diagram showing metaphase stage of mitosis in the nucleus of a cell, having chromosome number 6 is given below

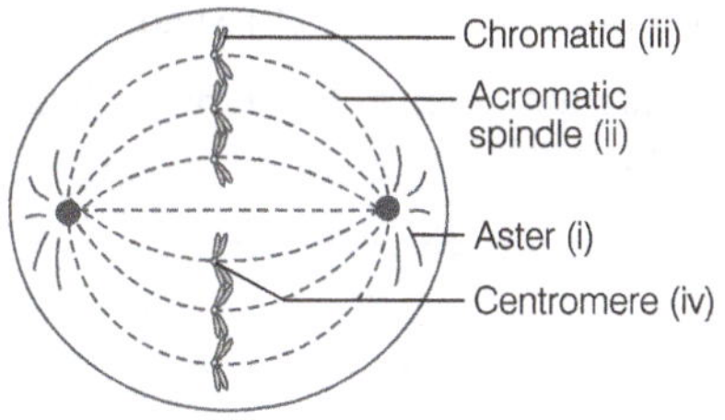

45. The diagram given below represents a stage during cell division. **ICSE 2018 (5M)**

Study the same and answer the questions that follows

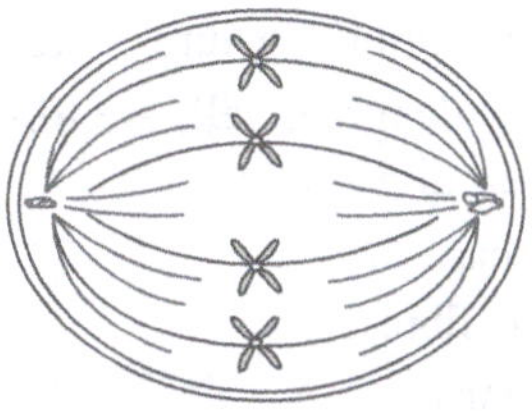

(i) Identify whether it is a plant cell or an animal cell.
Give a reason in support of your answer.

(ii) Name the stage depicted in the diagram.
What is the unique feature observed in this stage?

(iii) Name the type of cell division that occurs during
1. replacement of old leaves by new ones.
2. formation of gametes.

(iv) What is the stage that comes before the stage shown in the diagram?

(v) Draw a neat and labelled diagram of the stage mentioned in (iv) above, keeping the chromosome number constant.

Ans. (i) The given cell is an animal cells as it contains centrosome.

(ii) The stage depicted in the diagram is metaphase.
The unique feature observed in this stage is that chromosomes are aligned on equatorial region.

(iii) (1) Mitosis (2) Meiosis

(iv) Late prophase

(v)

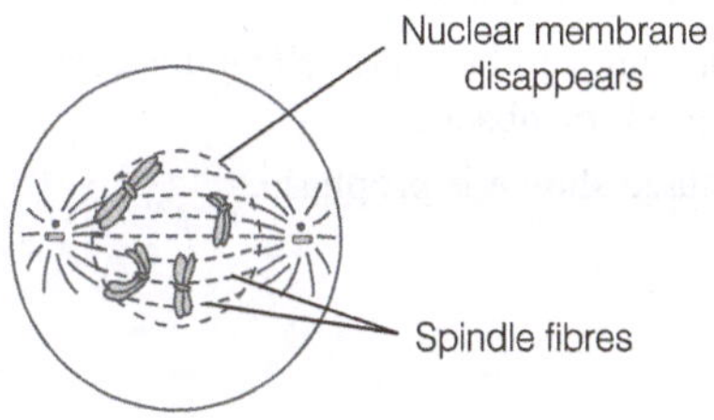

46. The given diagram represents a stage during mitotic cell division in an animal cell.
ICSE Specimen 2017, 2007 (5M)

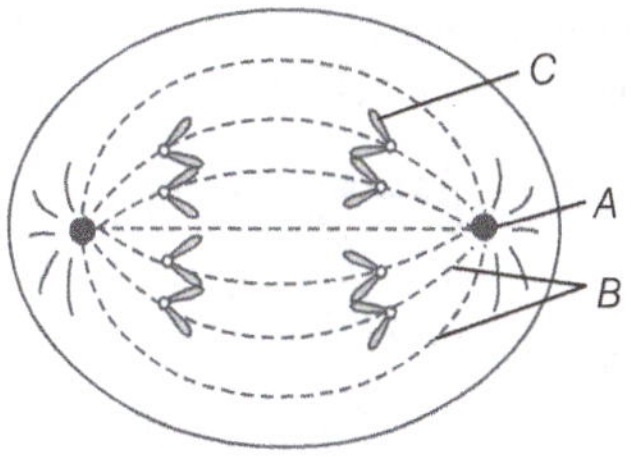

(i) Identify the stage. Give a reason to support your answer.

(ii) Name the parts labelled *A*, *B* and *C*.

(iii) What is the chromosome number of the cell shown?

(iv) Draw a neat and labelled diagram of the cell as it would appear in the next stage. Name the stage.

Ans. (i) This diagram represents anaphase stage of the mitotic division. In this, centromere divides separating sister chromatids of each chromosome. They are now drawn apart and move towards opposite poles.

(ii) Different labelled parts are as follows
A – Centriole, *B*– Spindle fibres, *C* – Chromatids

(iii) Chromosomes number of the cell shown is four.

(iv) For figure refer to answer no.43 (iii). The stage that comes next after the stage shown in the diagram is telophase.

47. Study the given diagram which represents a stage during the mitotic cell division and answer the questions that follows **ICSE 2017 (5M)**

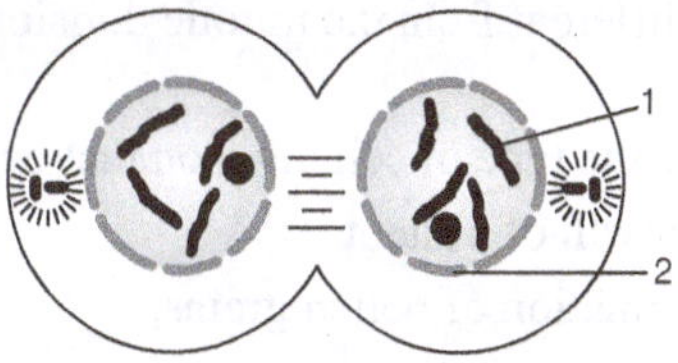

(i) Identify the stage giving suitable reasons.

(ii) Name the parts numbered 1 and 2.

(iii) What is the technical term for the division of nucleus?

(iv) Mention the stage that comes before the stage shown in the diagram. Draw a neat and labelled diagram of the stage mentioned.

(v) Which is the cell division that results in half the number of chromosomes in daughter cells?

Ans. (i) In the given figure, the two sets of daughter chromosomes have reached to opposite poles as well as reformation of nuclear membrane has also started. Therefore, it is telophase of mitotic division.

(ii) 1–Chromosomes, 2–Nuclear membrane (appearing)

(iii) Karyokinesis is the technical term which is used for the division of nucleus.

(iv) Telophase is preceded by anaphase. A diagram of anaphase is given below

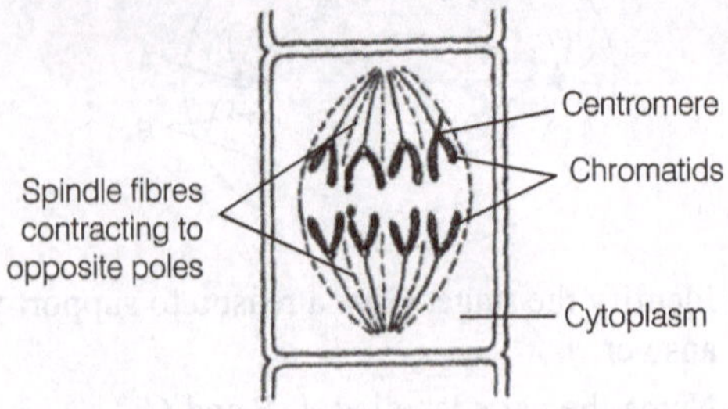

(v) During meiosis, the chromosome number is reduced in such a way that each daughter cell receives only half the number of chromosomes present in the parent cell.

48. The given diagram shows a stage during mitotic division in an animal cell. **ICSE 2016 (5M)**

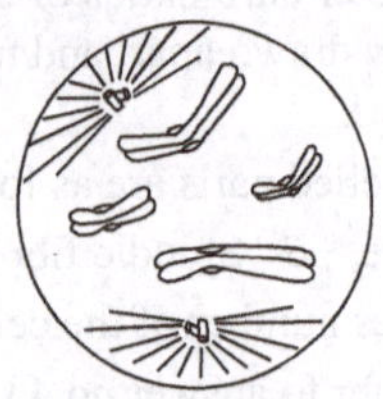

(i) Identify the stage. Give a reason to support your answer.

(ii) Draw a neat and labelled diagram of the cell as it would appear in the next stage. Name the stage.

(iii) In what two ways is mitotic division in an animal cell different from the mitotic division in a plant cell?

(iv) Name the type of cell division that occurs during

(a) growth of a shoot.

(b) formation of pollen grains.

Ans. (i) **Late prophase** Chromosome start coming in the centre of the cell. Nuclear membrane, nucleolus disappears and centriole appears which reaches at opposite pole of the cell.

(ii) **Metaphase**

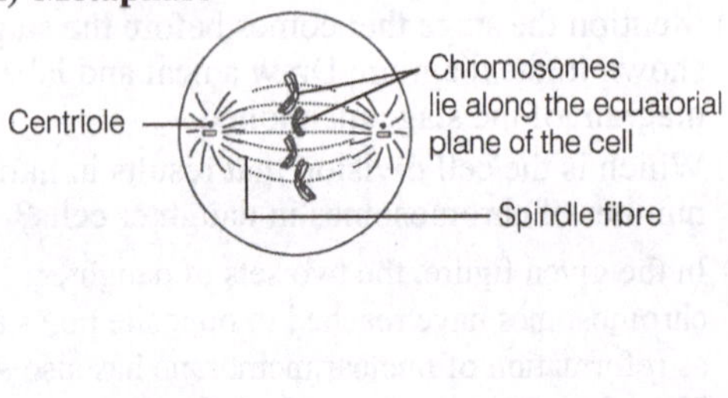

(iii) In animal cell the two daughter cells separate by growing furrow while in plant, cell separate by cell plate formation.

(iv) (a) Mitosis (b) Meiosis

49. The diagram given below represents a certain stage of mitosis. **ICSE 2015 (4M)**

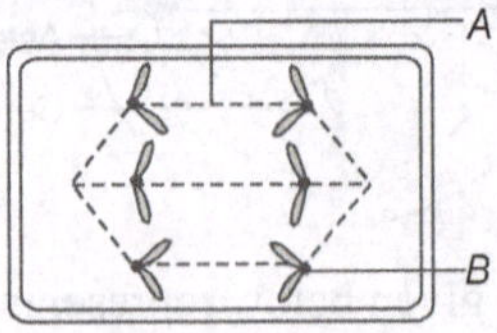

(i) Identify the stage of cell division.

(ii) Name the parts labelled *A* and *B*.

(iii) What is the unique feature observed in this stage?

(iv) How many daughter cells are formed from this type of cell division?

Ans. (i) Late anaphase

(ii) *A*– Spindle fibre

B– Centromere

(iii) Unique feature of this stage is that the chromosome get divided into sister chromatids that move towards the opposite poles.

(iv) Two daughter cells are formed from this kind of cell division.

50. Given below is a diagram representing a stage during mitotic cell division. Study it carefully and answer the questions that follows **ICSE 2014 (5M)**

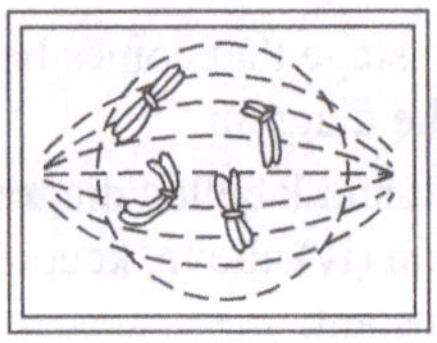

(i) Is it a plant cell or an animal cell? Give a reason to support your answer.

(ii) Identify the stage shown.

(iii) Name the stage that follows the one shown here. How is that stage identified?

(iv) How will you differentiate between mitosis and meiosis on the basis of the chromosome number in the daughter cells?

Ans. (i) It is a plant cell because cell wall is present and centrioles are absent.

(ii) The stage shown is prophase.

(iii) The stage that follows the one shown here, (prophase) is metaphase.
It is identified by the position of chromosomes that are arranged at the equator attached to the spindle fibre.

(iv) In mitosis, the chromosome number in daughter cell is same as that of the mother cell, i.e. diploid parent cell gives rise to two diploid ($2n$) daughter cells. In meiosis the chromosome number is halved in the daughter cell, i.e. the diploid mother cell gives rise to four haploid (n) daughter cells.

51. Draw a well-labelled diagram to show the anaphase stage of mitosis in a plant cell having four chromosomes. **ICSE 2013 (2M)**

Ans. Anaphase stage of mitosis in plant cell is given below

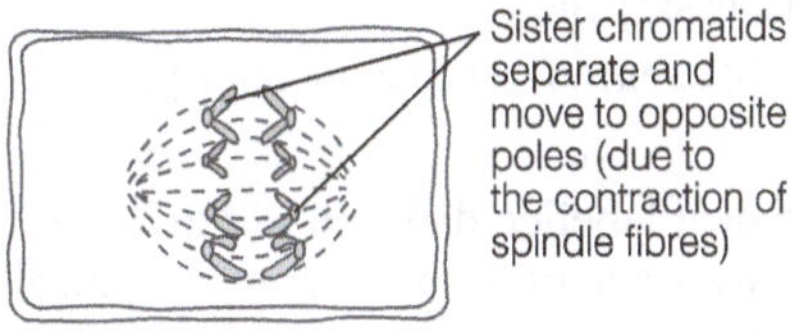

52. Draw a well-labelled diagram to show the metaphase stage of mitosis in an animal cell having four chromosomes. **ICSE 2012 (2M)**

Ans. Metaphase stage of mitosis in animal cell is given below

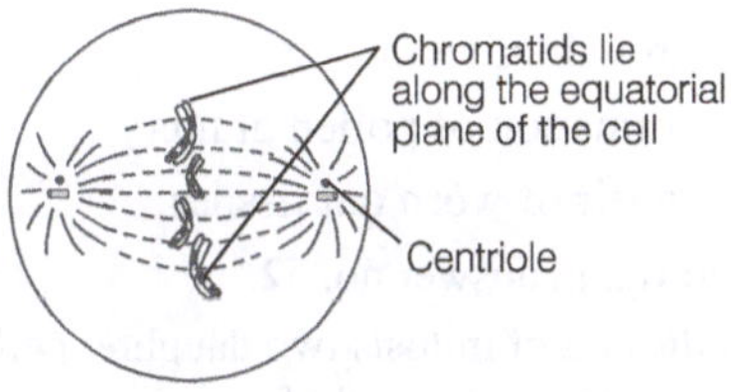

53. The diagram represents a stage during cell division. Study the same and then answer the questions that follows **ICSE 2011 (5M)**

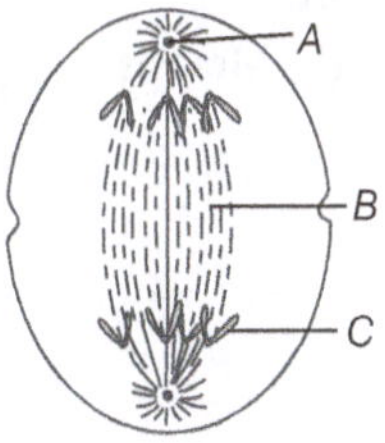

(i) Name the parts labelled A, B and C.

(ii) Identify the above stage and give a reason to support your answer.

(iii) Mention where in the body this type of cell division occurs.

(iv) Name the stage prior to this stage and draw a diagram to represent the same.

Ans. Different parts can be labelled as

(i) A – Centriole
B – Spindle fibres
C – Chromatid

(ii) The above stage is late anaphase because the sister chromatids are seen at the poles.

(iii) This type of cell division occurs in the body cells.

(iv) The stage prior to anaphase is metaphase.
(Refer to fig. in answer no. 52)

54. There is a diagram representing a stage during mitotic cell division in an animal cell. **ICSE 2010 (5M)**

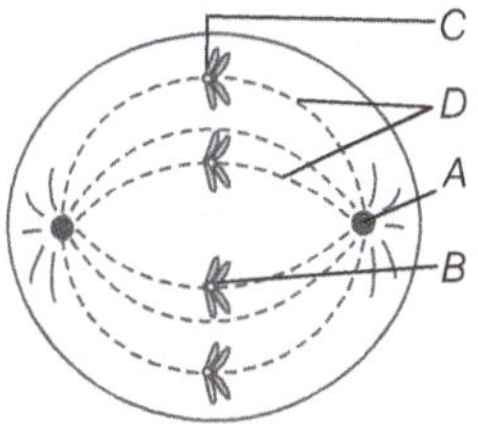

(i) Identify the above stage. Give a reason to support your answer.

(ii) Name the parts labelled A, B, C and D.

(iii) What is the function of part C ?

(iv) Name the stage that comes just after the stage shown in the diagram. Draw a well-labelled diagram of this stage.

Ans. (i) The above stage is metaphase because chromosomes are thick and short and are present at equatorial plate.

(ii) Different labelled parts are as follows
A – Centriole,
B – Chromatid,
C – Centromere,
D – Spindle fibres.

(iii) The part 'C', i.e. centromere keeps the two sister chromatids together. It regulates the exact distribution of genetic information during mitosis.

(iv) The stage that comes just after the stage shown in the diagram is anaphase. For figure refer to answer no. 51.

55. The diagram represents a stage in cell division. **ICSE 2009 (5M)**

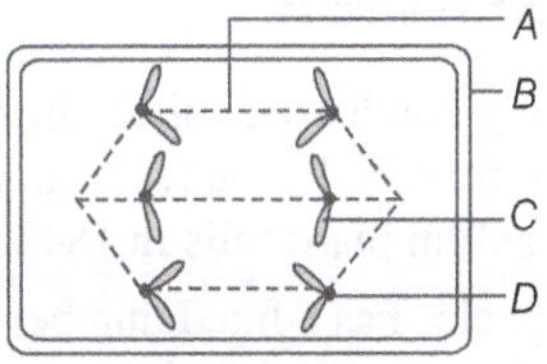

Study the same and answer the questions that follows

(i) Identify the stage of cell division.

(ii) Name the parts labelled A, B, C and D.

(iii) What is the unique feature observed in this stage?
(iv) Where does this type of cell division usually occur?
(v) How many daughter cells are formed from this type of cell division?
(vi) Is the dividing cell shown a plant or an animal cell? Give a reason to support your answer.

Ans. (i) The stage of cell division shown is anaphase.
(ii) Different labelled parts are as follows

A – Spindle fibre   *B* – Cell wall
C – Chromatid   *D* – Centromere

(iii) Unique feature of this stage is that chromosome get divided into sister chromatids that move towards the opposite poles.
(iv) This type of cell division usually occurs in somatic (body) cells.
(v) Two daughter cells are formed from this kind of cell division.
(vi) Dividing cell shown here is a plant cell because cell wall is clearly visible (which is a unique feature of only plant cells).

56. Given below is a diagram representing a stage during mitotic cell division in an animal. **ICSE 2003 (5M)**

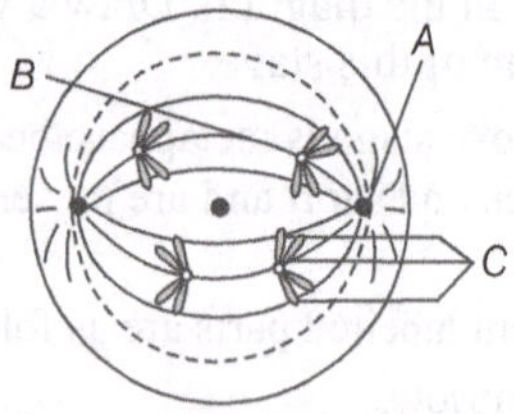

(i) Identify the above stage. Give a reason to support your answer.
(ii) Name the cell organelle that forms the aster.
(iii) Name the parts labelled *A*, *B* and *C*.
(iv) Name the stage that follows this stage of mitosis. How can this stage be identified?
(v) Mention two points of difference between mitosis and meiosis with regard to
(a) number of daughter cells formed.
(b) the chromosome number in the daughter cells.

Ans. (i) Given stage in the figure is prophase because nuclear membrane is disappearing.
(ii) Organelle that forms aster is known as centrosome.
(iii) Different labelled parts are as follows:
A – Centrosome, *B* – Spindle fibres,
C – Sister chromatids.
(iv) Stage that follows prophase is metaphase. Metaphase can be identified easily because chromosomes are arranged at the equatorial or metaphasic plate.
(v) For difference refer to table on page no. 4.

5M ICSE 2003

57. Draw a neat labelled diagram to show the metaphase stage of mitosis in an animal cell having chromosomes. **2M ICSE 2001**
(i) How many daughter cells are formed at the end of mitosis and at the end of meiosis?
(ii) Name the type of cell division that occurs during
(a) growth of shoot
(b) formation of pollen grains
(c) repair of worn out tissues.

Ans. Refer to fig. in answer no. 52.
(i) At the end of mitosis two daughter cells are formed and at the end of meiosis four daughter cells are formed.
(ii) Types of cell division that occurs during the following cases are
(a) Mitosis (b) Meiosis (c) Mitosis

TOPIC 2
Chromosomes

These are the highly condensed coiled chromatin fibres. They were first discovered by the Swiss botanist **Karl Wilhelm von Nageli** in plant cells in 1842.

Each and every species has a fixed number of chromosomes and every cell of that species has the same number of chromosome, e.g. human being have 46 chromosomes, (i.e. 23 pairs).

Homologous chromosomes are the pair of corresponding chromosomes having same shape, size and structure. In a pair, these come from each parent.

Structure of Chromosomes

- Each chromosome when present in the condensed form, consists of two exactly similar rod-like structures called **chromatids**.

- Both chromatids are joined by a point of attachment known as **centromere** (primary constriction) which is located at a particular site in the chromosome and helps in attachment of the spindle fibres to the chromosome.
- During cell division when the contraction of spindle fibre occurs, centromere divides into two, thus pulling the two sister chromatids towards opposite poles.
- **Chromatin** is a thread-like structure, located in the nucleus of the cell. It exist in the form called 'chromatin' when the cell is not dividing, but forms chromosomes when cell divides. Chromatin mainly consist of DNA and protein (histones).
- The complete structure of a negatively charged DNA wrapped around the positively charged histone octamer is called **nucleosome**.

Genes

These are the segments of DNA that act as the units of heredity. Each gene has two alternative forms called **allele**, which has different effect for a particular trait or a character.

Structure of DNA

- The double stranded helical structure of DNA (Deoxyribonucleic Acid) is the chemical basis of gene which acts as a genetic material in most living organisms.
- It is made up of two polynucleotide chains.
- Each single polynucleotide chain has repeated nucleotides which are made up of three basic components.
- These are as follows
  (i) Nitrogenous bases, a nitrogen containing organic compound.
  (ii) Sugar (mainly pentose). (iii) Phosphate group.

Nitrogenous bases are of following two main types

(a) **Purine** has double ring structure containing two bases, i.e. Adenine (A) and Guanine (G).

(b) **Pyrimidine** has single ring structure also containing two bases, i.e. Cytosine (C) and Thymine (T).

These bases are present in a DNA molecule forming two complementary polynucleotide chains of DNA molecule.

Double Helix Model of DNA

This model of DNA was given by **Watson** and **Crick** in 1953. They proved that each DNA molecule has two polynucleotide chains that run anti-parallel to each other and are helically coiled over each other at same axis.

Purine of one polynucleotide chain always pairs with the pyrimidine of another polynucleotide chain. The complementary nitrogenous bases are joined by hydrogen bonds.

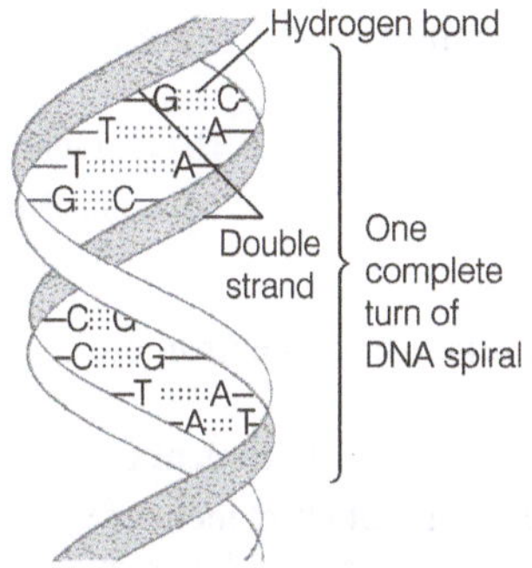

Fig. 1.4 Diagrammatic representation of double helical structure of DNA

Thus, adenine always pairs with the thymine with **two hydrogen bonds** and cytosine always pairs with guanine with **three hydrogen bonds.**

PYQs Previous Years' Questions

1 Mark Questions

Multiple Choice Questions

1. Duplicated chromosomes are joined at a point termed **ICSE 2024**

   (a) centrosome (b) centromere
   (c) centriole (d) chromatid

Ans. (a) centrosome

2. Chromosomes **ICSE Specimen 2021-22 Sem. I**

   (a) are the carriers of heredity
   (b) are the controlling centre of the cell
   (c) are the site for various chemical reactions
   (d) are intracellular digestion

Ans. (a) are the carriers of heredity

3. The alternative forms of the same gene occupying the same position on homologous chromosomes. **ICSE Specimen 2021-22 Sem. I**

   (a) Chromatids
   (b) Alleles
   (c) Autosomes
   (d) Centromere

Ans. (b) Alleles

4. The complex molecule consisting of a DNA strand and a core of histones. **ICSE Specimen 2021-22 Sem. I**

(a) Centrosome (b) Nucleotide
(c) Nucleosome (d) Chromosome

Ans. (c) Nucleosome

5. A pair of corresponding chromosomes of the same shape and size but one from each parent **ICSE Specimen 2021-22 Sem. I**

(a) autosomes (b) sex chromosomes
(c) homologous chromosomes (d) analogous chromosome

Or

A pair of corresponding chromosomes of the same shape and size and derived one from each parent is named as **ICSE 2019, 2017**

Ans. (c) homologous chromosomes

6. The basic units of heredity are .... **ICSE 2021-22 Sem. I**

(a) chromosomes (b) chromatids
(c) genes (d) centrosome

Ans. (c) genes

7. State the function of 'centromere'. **ICSE 2021-21 Sem. I**

(a) It is the point of attachment of two sister chromatids
(b) It is the point of attachment of two centrioles
(c) It is the point of attachment of two centrosomes
(d) It is the point of attachment between two daughter nuclei

Ans. (a) It is the point of attachment of two sister chromatids.

8. The nitrogenous base adenine always pair with .... **ICSE 2021-22 Sem. I**

(a) thymine (b) guanine
(c) cytosine (d) thiamine

Ans. (a) thymine

9. A cell has five pairs of chromosomes. After mitotic division, the number of chromosomes in the daughter cells will be **ICSE Specimen 2019**

(a) five (b) ten (c) twenty (d) fourty

Ans. (b) Ten

10. The cell component visible only during cell division

(a) Mitochondria (b) Chloroplast **ICSE 2013**
(c) Chromosome (d) Chromatin

Ans. (c) Chromosome

Very Short Answer Type Questions

11. Expand the biological abbreviation of DNA. **ICSE 2023, 2014, 2007**

Ans. Deoxyribonucleic Acid is the full form of DNA.

12. Correct the statement by changing the underlined word.

Nitrogen bonds are present between the complementary nitrogenous bases of DNA. **ICSE 2018**

Ans. Hydrogen

13. Give appropriate biological or technical term for

'The complex consisting of a DNA strand and a core of histones.' **ICSE 2018**

Ans. Nucleosome

14. Given below are groups of terms. In group the first pair indicates the relationship between the two terms. Rewrite and complete the second pair on a similar basis.

Example: Oxygen : Inspiration : : Carbon dioxide : Expiration

Adenine : Thymine : : Cytosine : .... **ICSE 2017**

Ans. Adenine : Thymine : : Cytosine : Guanine

15. In each set of terms given below, there is an odd one and cannot be grouped in the same category to which the other three belong. Identify the odd term in each set and name the category to which the remaining three belong.

Example Ovary, Fallopian tube, Ureter, Uterus

Answer Odd term Ureter.

Category Other are part of female reproductive system.

Thymine, Cytosine, Adenine, Pepsin **ICSE 2016**

Ans. **Odd term** Pepsin

Category Other are nitrogenous base.

16. State the exact location of centromere. **ICSE 2016**

Ans. In centre of chromosomes

17. Give the biological/technical term for

'The repeating components of each DNA strand lengthwise.' **ICSE 2016**

Or Give technical term for the repeated units of DNA molecule. **ICSE 2014**

Ans. Polynucleotides

18. Give example of a nitrogenous base in DNA. **ICSE 2014**

Ans. Adenine is an example of nitrogenous base found in DNA.

19. Write the names of four nitrogenous bases in a DNA molecule. **ICSE 2013**

Ans. Four nitrogenous bases of DNA molecule are

(a) Adenine
(b) Guanine } Purines

(c) Cytosine
(d) Thymine } Pyrimidines

20. Identify and name the following process/term from the statement given below.
Chromosomes that appear thread like. **ICSE 2009**

Ans. Chromatin fibres/materials are the chromosomes that appear thread-like.

21. Name the specific part of a chromosome that determines hereditary characteristics. **ICSE 2008**

Ans. Gene is the specific part of chromosome that determines heredity characteristics.

22. Name the structure responsible to transmits characteristics from parent to offspring. **ICSE 2002**

Or

Given below is the functional activity of structure in the body of living organism. Name the structure responsible for the same acts as a bearer of heredity units. **ICSE 2002**

Ans. The structure responsible to transmit characteristics from parent to offspring is chromosome.

23. With reference to cell division explain the following terms.
Chromatid, centromere and haploid. **ICSE 2001**

Ans. Each single unit of chromosome is called chromatid. Centromere is the point of contact between the two homologous chromatids.

Haploid refers to the half the number of chromosomes (n) present in cell as compared to parent cell $(2n)$.

2 Marks Question

24. Mention the two pairs of nitrogenous bases which pair with each other with hydrogen bonds.

Ans. Adenine pairs with thymine and cytosine pairs with guanine.

> **Concept Enhancer** The adenine always pair with thymine with two hydrogen bonds and cytosine always pair with guanine with three hydrogen bonds.

Diagram Based Questions

25. Draw a duplicated chromosome and label its parts. **ICSE 2014 (3M)**

Ans.

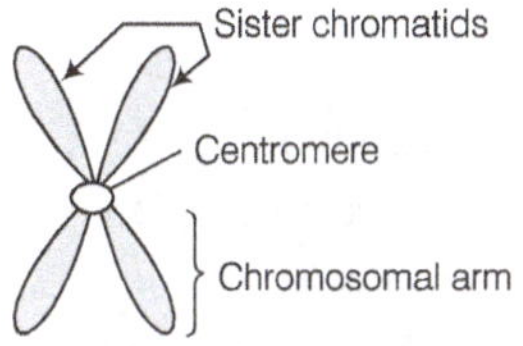

26. There is a diagram of a double helical structure of DNA. **ICSE 2010 (3M)**

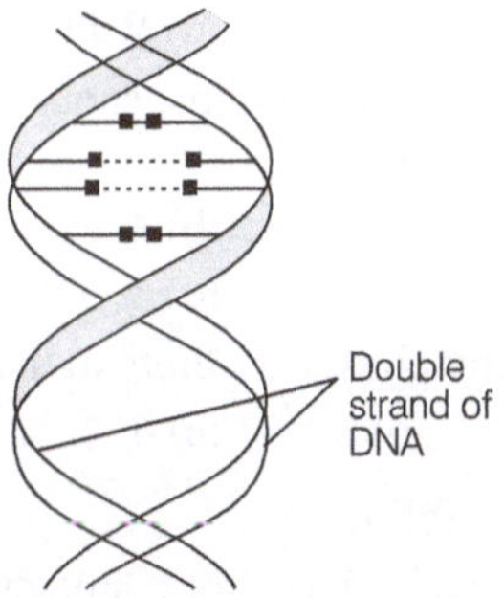

(i) Name the four nitrogenous bases that form a DNA molecule.

(ii) Give the full form of DNA.

(iii) Name the unit of heredity.

Ans. (i) Adenine, guanine, thymine and cytosine are four nitrogenous bases that form a DNA molecule.

(ii) The full form of DNA is Deoxyribonucleic Acid.

(iii) Genes are the unit of heredity.

CHAPTER TEST

Section-A

01 Mark Questions

1 Select the correct answer to the questions from the given options.

(i) The most prominent feature of life is
(a) cell cycle
(b) cell division
(c) arrangement of cells
(d) cell lysis

(ii) Chromatin is mainly made up of
(a) protein (b) protein and DNA
(c) DNA (d) RNA

(iii) Which German scientist first discovered chromosomes in animals?
(a) Paul Ehrlich (b) Friedrich Loeffler
(c) Robert Koch (d) Walther Flemming

(iv) How many types of nitrogenous bases are discovered in the DNA?
(a) 3 (b) 4
(c) 6 (d) 8

(v) How many phases are there in the interphase?
(a) 4 (b) 3 (c) 6 (d) 8

2 (i) Name the following
(a) A cell which undergoes through the process of growth and division in a systematic sequence of events.
(b) The phase which is considered as the first stage in mitosis.
(c) Another name of resting phase of mitosis.
(d) A type of cell division that is responsible for producing sex cells.

(ii) Arrange and rewrite the terms in each group in the correct order so as to be in a logical sequence beginning with the term that is underlined.
(a) Prophase, Anaphase, Telophase, Metaphase,
(b) G_1-phase, G_2-phase, M-phase, S-phase
(c) Volume of cytoplasm increase, RNA and necessary protein synthesised, DNA synthesised, cytokinesis.
(d) DNA, Chromosome, Nucleosome, Chromatin fibre.

(iii) Match the items given in Column I with most appropriate ones in Column II and rewrite the correct matching pairs.

Column I		Column I	
A.	Prophase	1.	Plant cell
B.	Metaphase	2.	Sister chromatids separate and move to opposite poles
C.	Anaphase	3.	Centrioles moves apart and reach opposite poles
D.	Telophase	4.	Chromosome lined in one plane at equator
E.	Cell plate formation	5.	Nuclear membrane reappear

(iv) Choose the odd one out from the following terms and name the category to which others belong.
(a) Adenine, Thymine, Anaphase, Guanine
(b) Prophase, Telophase, Metaphase, Interphase
(c) DNA, RNA, Protein, Metaphase
(d) G_1, S, M-phase, G_2-phase

(v) State the exact location of the following structures.
(a) DNA (genetic material)
(b) Spindle fibres
(c) Centromere
(d) Gene

02 Marks Questions

3 What are chromosomes ? Write its significance.

4 State two differences between centrosome and centromere.

5 List three sub-stages of interphase.

6 Write the significance of mitosis.

7 Define gene. Write its significance.

03 Marks Questions

8 State the reason why new cells are required to be produced?

9 Write briefly about the two types of cell division.

10 Write any three points of difference between mitosis in animal and plant cell.

11 Write the significance of meiosis.

12 Draw a labelled diagram to show the anaphase stage of mitosis in an animal cell having 4 chromosomes.

Section-B

Diagram Based Questions

13 Study the diagrams given below and answer the quesitons that follows

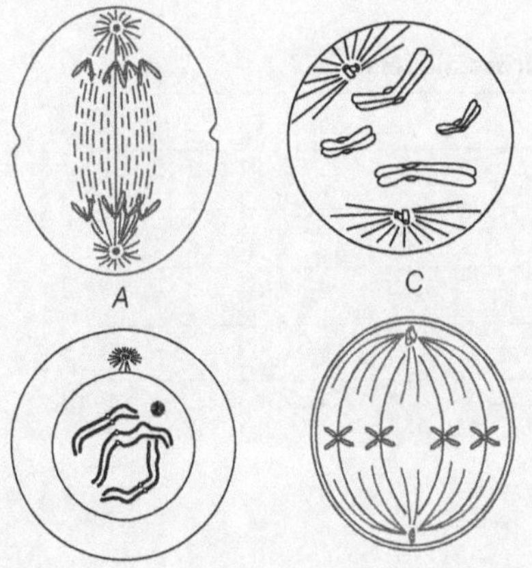

(i) Write the type of division occurring in it (mitosis or meiosis).

(ii) Write the correct sequence with the name and special features of the stages.

(iii) In which stage centriole moves to opposite poles?

14 Answer the following questions on the basis of figure '*A*'

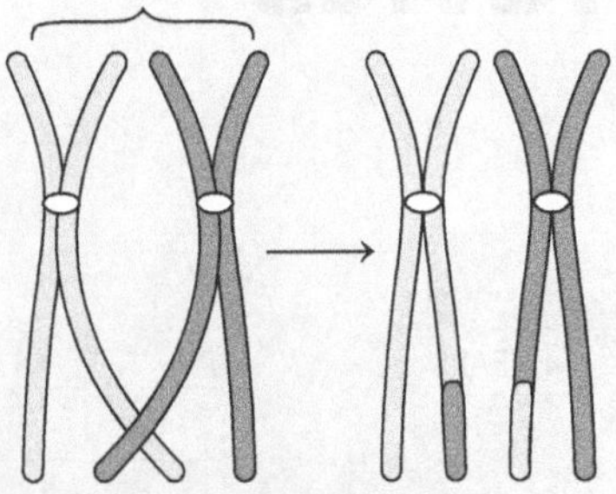

Fig. *A*

(i) Name the phenomenon this figure is representing. Write the phase in which this phenomenon occur.

(ii) Explain the term homologous chromosome.

(iii) Write the significance of phenomenon represented in figure *A*.

Answers

1. (i) (b), (ii) (b), (iii) (d), (iv) (b), (v) (b)

02 Genetics

TREND ANALYSIS 4 YEARS

Average No. of Questions Across all Sets

	Types of Questions	2024	2023	2020	2019
Genetics	1 Mark	3	2	–	–
	2 Marks	–	2	–	–
	3 Marks	1	–	–	–
	4 Marks	–	–	–	–
	5 Marks	–	–	–	1

Genetics is the branch of biology that deals with the study of inheritance as well as variation of characters from parents to offsprings.

The transmission of characters (both similarities and differences) from parents to progeny, i.e. from one generation to the next is called **inheritance**.

Variation may be defined as the degree of differences in characteristics among the individuals of a species.

Gregor Johann Mendel

- He was the first to conduct experiments for the purpose of understanding the pattern of inheritance of characters in living beings. His findings on genetics are known as Mendel's laws of inheritance. Therefore, he is also known as the **Father of Genetics**.
- He recognised that a factor in gametes (genotype) is responsible for the appearance of particular character (phenotype) in the offspring.
- This Mendelian factor is now known as **gene**. Before describing Mendel's experiments for understanding the transmission of characteristics from parents to their offspring, we should know the meaning of some terms.

Some Important Genetic Terms

(i) **Gene** is a portion (or sequence) of DNA that codes for a known cellular function or process. These are also called the unit of inheritance containing the information required to express a trait.

(ii) **Allele** is one of a number of alternative forms of the same gene. Alleles refer to a pair of genes responsible for particular characteristics in an individual.

(iii) **Homozygous** or **pure condition** appears when organisms have two similar genes or alleles for a particular character in a homologous pair of chromosomes, e.g. TT or tt.

(iv) **Heterozygous** or **hybrid condition** appears when organisms contain two different alleles for a particular character in a homologous pair of chromosome, e.g. Tt.

Note Pure strains are made up of same type of alleles. Hybrid strains are made up of different types of alleles.

(v) **Dominant allele** is one of the gene of an allelic pair which can express itself even in the presence of an alternative gene, i.e. in heterozygous condition.

(vi) **Recessive allele** is the gene of an allelic pair which can express itself only in the presence of another identical gene, i.e. in homozygous condition. It is the suppressed allele of a gene.

(vii) **Phenotype** are the physical or observable characteristics of an organism which are genetically controlled.

(viii) **Genotype** is the genetic make up of an organism, i.e. the characters which are not visually observable.

Mendel's Experiment

Mendel conducted breeding experiments on garden pea plant (*Pisum sativum*) for complete seven years (1856-1863). He selected garden pea plant because many varieties of peas were easily available with contrasting pair of characters.

He conducted artificial pollination/ cross pollination using several true breeding pea lines.

Monohybrid Cross

It is a type of cross which is performed by taking only one pair of contrasting character or one feature at a time.

For example, when a cross between pure tall plant (TT) and pure dwarf plant (tt) was done, i.e. taking only one character (i.e. height of plant), it was observed that in the first filial generation (F_1), all tall plants were produced masking the effect of another. After self-pollination, in second filial generation (F_2) both the traits, i.e. tallness and dwarfness were expressed in the ratio 3 : 1.

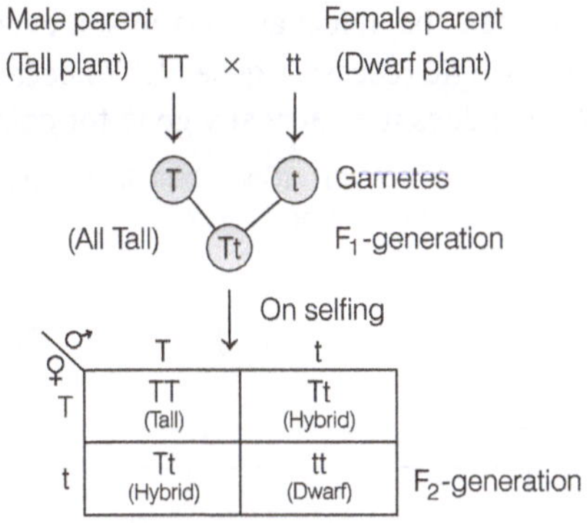

Fig. 2.1 Phenotype 3 : 1 (Tall : Dwarf)
Genotype 1 : 2 : 1 (TT : Tt : tt)

Dihybrid Cross

It is a type of cross, which is performed by taking two pairs of contrasting characters or two features at a time. For example, when a cross between a plant having round, yellow seeds (RRYY) and a plant having wrinkled, green seeds (rryy) was done, only round, yellow seeds were produced in F_1-generation (as round, yellow were dominant alleles).

Further when F_1 were self-pollinated, four different types of seed combinations were obtained in F_2-generation.

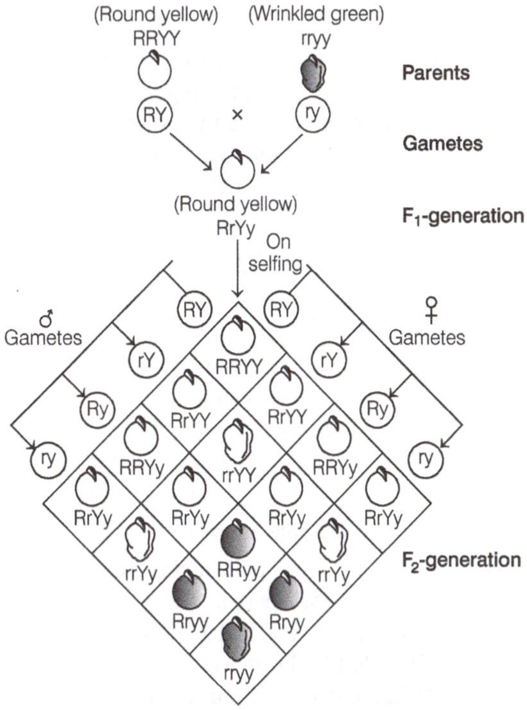

Phenotypic Ratio Round yellow : Round green : Wrinkled yellow : Wrinkled green = 9 : 3 : 3 : 1

Genotypic Ratio 1 : 2 : 2 : 4 : 1 : 2 : 1 : 2 : 1

Fig. 2.2 Dihybrid cross

Mendel's Laws of Inheritance

On the basis of the inferences of monohybrid crosses, Mendel proposed two general rules to consolidate his understanding of inheritance in monohybrid crosses.

These rules are called **Principle or laws of inheritance**, i.e. law of dominance and law of segregation. Law of independent assortment was proposed on the observation of dihybrid crosses.

These laws are as follows

(i) **Law of dominance** (First law) This law states that when two alternative forms of trait or character are present in an organism, only one factor expresses itself in F_1-progeny. This factor is called **dominant factor**, while the other factor which remains hidden is called **recessive factor**. It explains the expression of a gene in a cross and 3 : 1 ratio is obtained in F_2-generation.

(ii) **Law of segregation** (Second law) During gamete formation, the alleles for each gene segregate from each other so that each gamete carries only one allele for each gene.

(iii) **Law of independent assortment** (Third law) According to this law, when two pairs of contrasting characters are combined in a hybrid, segregation of one pair of character is independent to the another pair of character at the time of gamete formation.

Sex-Determination in Human Beings

In humans, 23 pairs of chromosomes are present. These are classified into two main types such as

(i) **Autosome** It is a chromosome that is not an allosome, i.e. not sex chromosome. These are exactly similar chromosomes in both males and females (22 pairs). These are found in somatic cells.

(ii) **Sex-chromosome** It is a pair of chromosome which determines the sex of a person. There are two types of sex-chromosomes, one is called X-chromosome and the other is called Y-chromosome occurring in pairs and are designated as 23rd pair of chromosomes. In males it is XY and in females it is XX.

Mechanism of Sex-Determination

- The sex determining mechanism in human beings is XX-XY type. In human beings, male gamete (sperm) contains either X or Y-chromosome, while female gamete (egg) contains only X-chromosome.
- The sex of a child depends upon the kind of sperm that fertilises the egg during fertilisation.

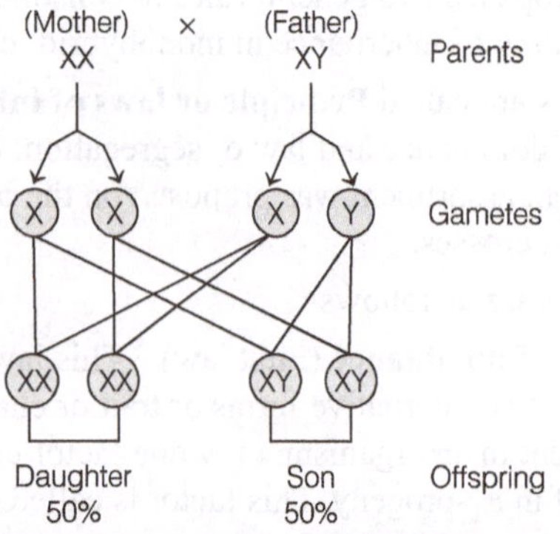

- In case, the sperm carrying X chromosome, fertilises the egg X, then the resulting child will be female XX, if the sperm carrying Y chromosome fertilises the egg (X) then the resulting child will be male XY. This can be shown by the following cross

Sex-linked Inheritance

- It is the appearance of a trait or a character due to the presence of an allele either on the X or Y-chromosome. Certain disorders in human beings are transferred to the next generation because they are associated with the inheritance of changed or altered genes or chromosomes. These are called **genetic disorders**.
- These disorders, when occur due to change in sex-chromosomes are known as sex-linked inherited diseases.
- **Colour blindness** and **haemophilia** are the common sex-linked inherited diseases found in human beings. These defects occur due to occurrence of recessive genes on the X-chromosome. These diseases follow ***criss-cross* inheritance**, a phenomenon of transmission of sex-linked gene from mother to son and from father to the daughter.
- Some common examples showing *criss-cross* inheritance are as follows

1. Colour Blindness

This cross shows that, the daughter of a colourblind father will be colourblind only if the mother is carrier of the disease. Whereas, the defect appears in son even in the presence of a single recessive gene (X^cY) because Y-chromosome does not carry any gene for colour vision.

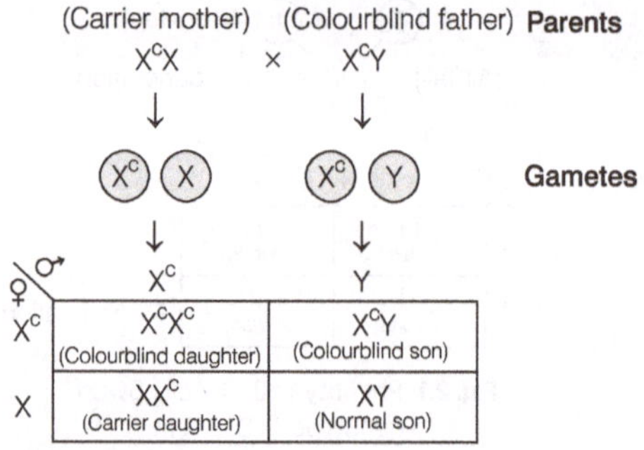

2. Haemophilia

This cross shows that the disease is transmitted from unaffected carrier female to some of the male offsprings. The possibility of a female becoming a haemophilic is extremely rare because mother of such a female has to be atleast carrier and father should be haemophilic.

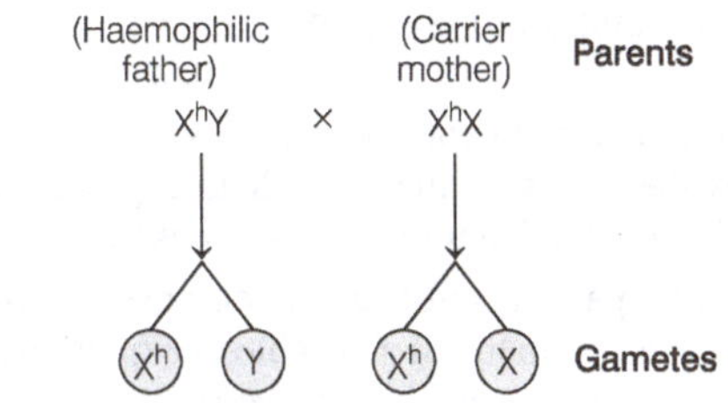

♀ \ ♂	X^h	Y
X^h	X^hX^h (Haemophilic daughter)	X^hY (Haemophilic son)
X	X^hX (Carrier daughter)	XY (Normal son)

Genotypic ratio 1 : 1 : 1 : 1

Mutation

- A sudden and inheritable change in the nucleotide sequences of the genome of an individual which ultimately changes the genotype of an organism.
- These mutations may or may not induce any phenotypic characteristics of an organism.
- The agents which cause mutation are called **mutagens**. They can be physical and chemical factors such as ultraviolet (UV) radiation, certain chemicals, etc.
- The mutation can be of two main types
  (i) **Gene mutation** (Change in the sequence of DNA)
  (ii) **Chromosomal mutation** (Change in the number or arrangement of the chromosomes).

PYQs Previous Years' Questions

1 Mark Questions

Multiple Choice Questions

1. A zygote which has Y-chromosome inherited from the father will develop into a **ICSE 2024**

(a) will depend on the chromosome inherited form the mother
(b) girl
(c) either boy or a girl
(d) boy

Ans. (d) boy

2. Four friends P, Q, R and S were discussing the examples of genetic disorders. The examples they quoted were as follows **ICSE 2024**

P. Colour blindness and malaria
Q. Albinism and cholera
R. Haemophilia and colour blindness
S. Haemophilia and albinism

Who gave the correct examples?

(a) P and Q
(b) R and S
(c) P and R
(d) Q and S

Ans. (b) R and S

3. A male gorilla has 48 chromosomes in each of its body cells. How many chromosomes will each of the sperms have? **ICSE 2024**

(a) 24 (b) 48 (c) 12 (d) 16

Ans. (a) 24

4. Define the term mutation. **ICSE 2023**

Or State the function of 'mutation'. **ICSE 2021-22 Sem. I**

(a) It is a sudden change in one or more genes in an organism's cells, which is heritable
(b) It is a change in the number of centrosomes in an organism's cells, which is heritable
(c) It is a change in the structure of cell membrane in an organism's cells, which is heritable
(d) It is a change in the shape of cells, which is heritable

Ans. (a) It is a sudden change in one or more genes in an organism's cells, which is heritable.

5. A pair of corresponding chromosome of the same shape and size but one from each parent. **ICSE Specimen 2021-22 Sem. I**

(a) Autosomes
(b) Sex chromosomes
(c) Homologous chromosome
(d) Analogous chromosome

Ans. (c) Homologous chromosome

6. The alternative forms of same gene occupying the same position on homologous chromosomes. **ICSE Specimen 2021-22 Sem. I**
(a) Chromatids (b) Alleles
(c) Autosomes (d) Centromere

Ans. (b) Alleles

7. Law of segregation **ICSE Specimen 2021-22 Sem. I**
(a) the two members of a pair of factors join during the formation of gametes
(b) the two members of a pair of factors separate during the formation of gametes
(c) the two members of a pair of factors separate during the formation of gametes
(d) the two members of a pair of factors separate during the process of germination

Ans. (b) The two chromosomes of a pair of factors separate during the formation of gametes.

8. Chromosomes **ICSE Specimen 2021-22 Sem. I**
(a) the carrier of heredity
(b) the controlling centre of cell
(c) the site for various chemical reactions
(d) intracellular digestion

Ans. (a) The carrier of heredity

9. The type of gene, which in the presence of a contrasting allele is not expressed. **ICSE 2021-22 Sem. I**
(a) Homozygous (b) Heterozygous
(c) Dominant (d) Recessive

Ans. (d) Recessive

10. The genotype of a person who cannot roll his tongue is .... **ICSE 2021-22 Sem. I**
(a) Rr (b) RR
(c) rr (d) RRr

Ans. (c) rr

11. Genes **ICSE 2021-22 Sem. I**
(a) are present on cell wall
(b) are present on chloroplast
(c) are present on chromosomes
(d) are present on centrosomes

Ans. (c) Present on chromosomes

12. A homozygous pea plant having purple flowers is crossed with a homozygous pea plant bearing white flowers. The phenotypic ratio of the offspring obtained in F_2- generation is **ICSE 2021-22 Sem. I**
(a) 2 : 1 (b) 1 : 1
(c) 1 : 2 : 1 (d) 3 : 1

Ans. (d) 3 : 1

13. State the function of law of dominance. **ICSE 2021-22 Sem. I**
(a) Out of a pair of contrasting alleles present together, only the recessive allele is able to express itself while the dominant remains suppressed
(b) Out of a pair of contrasting alleles present together, only the dominant allele is able to express itself while recessive remains suppressed
(c) Out of a pair of contrasting alleles present together, both the dominant and recessive cannot express themselves
(d) Out of a pair of contrasting alleles present together, both the dominant and recessive can express themselves

Ans. (b) Out of a pair of contrasting alleles present together, only the dominant allele is able to express itself while recessive remains suppressed.

14. After mitotic cell division, a female human cell will have **ICSE 2014**
(a) 44 + XX-chromosome (b) 44 + XY-chromosome
(c) 22+ X-chromosome (d) 22+ Y-chromosome

Ans. (a) 44 + XX-chromosomes

15. The recessive gene is one that expresses itself in **ICSE 2013**
(a) heterozygous condition (b) homozygous condition
(c) F_2-generation (d) Y-linked inheritance

Ans. (b) Homozygous condition.

Very Short Answer Type Questions

16. Name a genetic disorder in which the blood does not clot. **ICSE 2023**

Ans. Haemophilia

17. Name the following.
The suppressed allele of a gene. **ICSE Specimen 2023**

Ans. Recessive allele

18. Define gene. **ICSE Specimen 2023**

Ans. It is a unit of hereditary information that occupies a fixed position (locus) on a chromosome.

19. Give the biological/technical terms for the following
The repeating components of each DNA strand lengthwise. **ICSE Specimen 2019**

Ans. Gene.

20. Name the number of chromosomes present in a nerve cell of a human being. **ICSE 2018**

Ans. Like any other somatic cell, human nerve cell also contains 46 (23 pairs) chromosomes.

21. Give appropriate biological or technical terms for

'The condition in which a pair of chromosome carries similar alleles of a particular character.'

Ans. Homozygous condition **ICSE 2018**

22. Give technical terms for the following
Alternative form of a gene on a pair of homologous chromosomes. **ICSE Specimen 2017**

Ans. Alleles

23. Given below are groups of terms. In each group the first pair indicates the relationship between the two terms. Rewrite and complete the second pair on a similar basis.
Example Oxygen : Inspiration : : Carbon dioxide : Expiration

TT : Homozygous : : Tt : ....

ICSE 2017

Ans. TT : Homozygous : : Tt : Heterozygous

24. Give appropriate biological/technical terms for

'The suppressed allele of a gene.' **ICSE 2017**

Or

Give the biological term for the suppressed allele of a gene. **ICSE 2012**

Ans. Recessive allele

25. Give reasons for the following. **ICSE Specimen 2017**
Gametes have a haploid number of chromosome.

Ans. Gametes are produced as a result of meiosis during which the chromosome number is reduced to half and each daughter cell receives half set of chromosomes.
Therefore, gametes have a haploid number of chromosome.

26. Choose the odd one out from the given term and name the category to which the others belong.

Example Ovary, Fallopian tube, Ureter, Uterus
Answer **Odd term**-Ureter.

Category-Part of female reproductive system

Typhoid, Haemophilia, Albinism, Colour blindness
ICSE 2016

Ans. **Odd term**–Typhoid

Category–Genetic disorders (diseases)

27. Differentiate between the pair on the basis of what is mentioned within bracket.
Human skin cell and human ovum (Number of chromosomes). **ICSE 2016**

Ans. Human skin cell–46 chromosomes and human ovum–23 chromosomes.

28. Give the biological/technical term for

'An alteration in the genetic material that can be inherited.' **ICSE 2016**

Or Give the technical term for the sudden heritable change in the gene. **ICSE 2014**

Ans. Mutation

29. Give scientific reasons of colour blindness is more common in men than in women. **ICSE 2016**

Ans. Colour blindness is a sex-linked disease. It is more common in males than in females as genes responsible for colour blindness are located on X-chromosome. Males possess only one X-chromosome. One defective X-chromosome is enough to cause colour blindness.
Whereas in case of females, since there are two X-chromosomes, the trait is not effective rendering females as carriers of the disease.

30. Name the cross between two parents having one pair of contrasting characters. **ICSE 2015**

Ans. Monohybrid cross

31. Rewrite and complete the sentence by inserting the correct word in the space indicated.

..... is the scientific name of garden pea, which Mendel used for his experiments. **ICSE 2015**

Ans. *Pisum sativum* is the scientific name of garden pea, which Mendel used for his experiments.

32. State Mendel's law of dominance. **ICSE 2015, 2002**

Ans. Mendel's law of dominance states that when two alternative forms of trait of character are present in an organism, only one factor expresses itself in F_1-progeny. This factor is called dominant factor, while the other factor which remains suppress is called recessive factor. It explains the expression of a gene in a cross and 3 : 1 ratio is obtained in F_2- generation.

33. Name the type of gene, which in the presence of a contrasting allele is not expressed. **ICSE 2014, 2004**

Ans. Recessive gene is not expressed in the presence of a contrasting dominant allele.

34. Explain the term monohybrid cross. **ICSE 2014**

Ans. Refer to text on page no. 19.

35. Name the physical expression of genes in an individual. **ICSE 2013**

Ans. Phenotype is the physical expression of genes in an individual.

36. Briefly explain the term gene. **ICSE 2013, 2003**

Ans. Refer to text on page no. 18.

37. Briefly explain the term allele. **ICSE 2012**

Ans. Refer to text on page no. 18.

38. Given below is set with four terms. In the set, a term is an odd one that cannot be grouped in the same category to which the other three belong. Identify the odd one in the set and name the category to which the remaining three belong. Haemophilia, colour blindness, albinism, night blindness. **ICSE 2012**

Ans. The difference between set, odd one and category are given below

Set	Odd one	Category
Haemophilia, colour blindness, albinism, night blindness	Night blindness (It is caused due to nutritional deficiency)	Sex-linked diseases

39. Rewrite and complete the following sentence by inserting the correct word in the space indicated

Phenotype is the observable characteristic which is .... controlled. **ICSE 2011**

Ans. Phenotype is the observable characteristic which is **genetically** controlled.

40. Write down the difference between the following pair as indicated within the bracket

Monohybrid and dihybrid cross (phenotypic ratio). **ICSE 2011**

Ans. Phenotypic ratio in F_2-generation of monohybrid cross is **3 : 1**.

While, phenotypic ratio in F_2-generation of dihybrid cross is **9 : 3 : 3 : 1**.

41. State whether the following statement is true or false. If false, rewrite the correct form of the statement by changing the first or last word only.

Chromosomes other than the pair of sex-chromosome are called alleles. **ICSE 2010**

Ans. The statement is false. It can be corrected as chromosomes other than the pair of sex-chromosome are called **autosomes.**

42. Give one point of difference between the following on the basis of what is given in the bracket?

Genotype and phenotype (definition). **ICSE 2010, 2004**

Ans.

Genotype	Phenotype
It is the genetic makeup of an organism.	It is the physical or observable characteristics of an organism.

43. Identify and name the term from the statement given below

A pair of chromosomes carrying dissimilar alleles for a particular character. **ICSE 2009**

Ans. A pair of chromosomes carrying dissimilar alleles of a particular character is called **heterozygous.**

44. Name the two sex-linked diseases in male. **ICSE 2009**

Ans. Colour blindness and haemophilia are the two sex-linked diseases in males.

45. Give the dihybrid ratio. Name and state the law which explains the same. **ICSE 2008**

Ans. The dihybrid ratio is 9 : 3 : 3 : 1.

Based on the observation in dihybrid crosses Mendel proposed **Law of independent assortment** (third law) which states that when two pairs of contrasting characters are combined in a hybrid, segregation of one pair of character is independent of the another pair of character at the time of gamete formation.

46. Name the pair of genes responsible for a particular characteristics in an individual **ICSE 2007**

Ans. The pair of genes responsible for a particular characteristics in an individual are called alleles.

47. Distinguish between on the basis of what is given in the bracket.

Pure strains and hybrid strains (definition). **ICSE 2007**

Ans. Difference between pure strains and hybrid strains are

Pure strains	Hybrid strains
These are made up of same type of alleles.	These are made up of different types of alleles.

48. Name the genetic constitution of an organism. **ICSE 2003**

Ans. Genotype is known as the genetic constitution of an organism.

49. What is a dihybrid ratio? **ICSE 2002**

Ans. The ratio of each phenotype (or appearance) in the F_2-generation obtained in a dihybrid cross is called dihybrid ratio, i.e. 9 : 3 : 3 : 1.

50. Define phenotype. **ICSE 2002**

Ans. Refer to text on page no. 19.

51. What are autosomes? **ICSE 2002**

Ans. Refer to text on page no. 20.

2 Marks Questions

52. State Mendel's law of segregation.

Ans. Refer to text on page no. 20. **ICSE 2023, 2014, 2009**

53. A pure breeding red flower variety of pea plant (RR) is crossed with a pure breeding white flower variety of pea plant (rr). Draw a Punnett square to find out the phenotypic and genotypic ratios of the progeny belonging to the F_2-generation. **ICSE 2023**

Ans.

Parents Red flower RR × White flower rr

Gametes (R) (R) × (r) (r)

Rr (All red flowres)

↓ on selfing

Rr × Rr

F_2

♀ \ ♂	R	r
R	RR	Rr
r	Rr	rr

Phenotypes of ratio F_2 3 Red : 1 White

Genotypes of ratio F_2 1 RR : 2 Rr : 1 rr

54. State Mendel's law of segregation.

Ans. Refer to text on page no. 20. **ICSE Specimen 2023**

55. Colour blindness is generally seen in males. Explain.

Ans. Refer to answer no. 29. **ICSE Specimen 2023**

56. In a certain species of animals black fur (B) is dominant over brown fur (b).
Predict a genotype and phenotype of the offspring when both parents are Bb or have heterozygous black fur. **ICSE 2014**

Ans.

(Black Fur) Bb × (Black Fur) Bb Parents

(B) (b) × (B) (b) Gametes (on selfing)

♀ \ ♂	B	b
B	BB (Pure black)	Bb (Hybrid black)
b	Bb (Hybrid black)	bb (Pure brown)

Phenotypes 3 Black : 1 Brown

Genotypes 1 Pure black : 2 Hybrid black : 1 Pure brown

3 Marks Questions

57. Given below is a schematic representation of the inheritance of the shape of seeds of garden pea. Answer the questions that follows: **ICSE 2024**

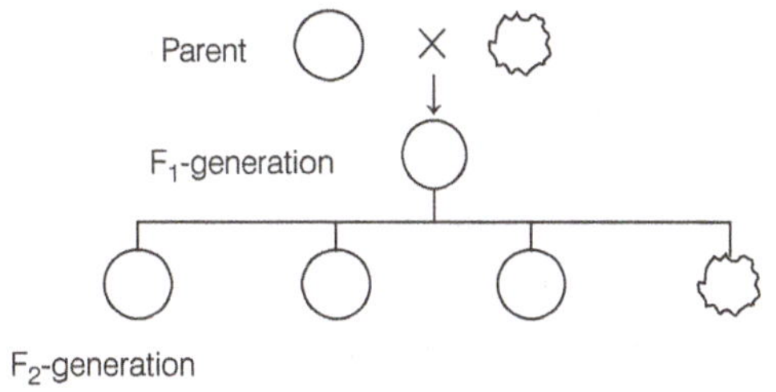

(i) Which is the dominant and recessive allele of the trait ?

(ii) What does the ratio 3 : 1 in the F_2-generation represent?

(iii) State Mendel 's law of dominance.

Ans. (i) Dominant allele is R. Recessive allele is r.

(ii) The ratio 3 : 1 in the F_2-generation represents the phenotypic ratio, i.e. that 3 - plants have round seeds and 1 - plant has wrinkled seeds.

(iii) **Mendel's Law of Dominance** In a single individual, when two different alleles of a unit factor or gene responsible for a single character are present, then one allele is dominant over the other.

58. Explain the following terms

(i) Monohybrid cross (ii) Gene

(iii) Phenotype **ICSE 2009**

Ans. (i) Refer to text on page no. 19.

(ii) Refer to text on page no. 18.

(iii) Refer to text on page no. 19.

56. Explain briefly.

(i) Mutation (ii) Allele **ICSE 2007**

Ans. (i) Refer to text on page no. 21.

(ii) Refer to text on page no. 18.

5 Marks Questions

60. A homozygous purple flower variety of pea plant (PP) is crossed with white flower variety of pea (pp). Answer the questions that follows. **ICSE Specimen 2019**

(i) Mention the phenotype and genotype of the F_1-generation of offspring.

(ii) If the offspring of the F_1-generation are crossed, what will be the phenotypic and genotypic ratios of the F_2-generation?

(iii) State Mendel's law of dominance.

(iv) What is the scientific name of pea plants?

(v) Name two genetic diseases in humans.

Ans. (i) Phenotype-Purple flower

Genotype-Pp

(ii) F_1 self-crossed

F_1 Pp × Pp

F_2 PP Pp Pp pp

Phenotypic ratio 3:1

Genotypic ratio 1 : 2 : 1

(iii) Refer to text on page no. 19.

(iv) *Pisum sativum*

(v) (a) Thalassemia

(b) Sickle-cell anaemia

61. In Mendel's experiments, tall pea plants (T) are dominant over dwarf pea plants (t). **ICSE 2019**

(i) What is the phenotype and genotype of the F_1-generation if a homozygous tall plant is crossed with a homozygous dwarf plant?

(ii) Draw a Punnett square board to show the gametes and offspring when both the parents are heterozygous for tallness.

(iii) What is the phenotypic ratio and genotypic ratio of the above cross in (ii)?

(iv) State Mendel's law of dominance.

(v) What is a dihybrid cross ?

Ans. (i) Phenotype- All tall plants were produced. Genotype - Tt (tall plants).

(ii)

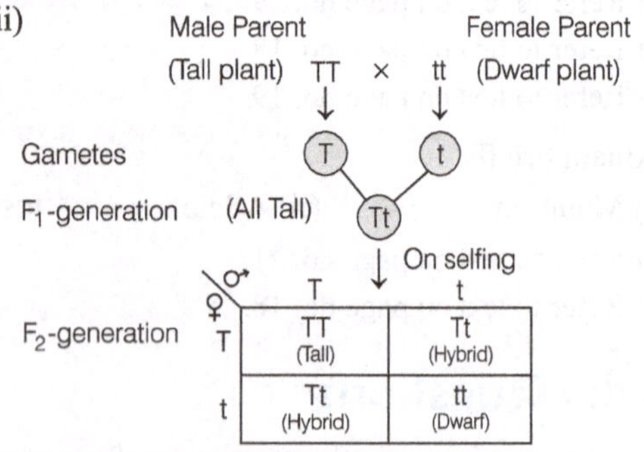

Thus, when both parents are heterozygous the offspring will be as above.

(iii) Phenotypic ratio – 3 : 1 (Tall : Dwarf)

Genotypic ratio – 1 : 2 : 1 (TT : Tt : tt)

(iv) Refer to text on page no. 19.

(v) **Dihybird cross** This type of cross performed by taking two pairs of contrasting characters at a time.

62. A pea plant which is homozygous for green pods which are inflated (GGII) is crossed with a homozygous plant for yellow pods which are constricted (ggii). Answer the following questions.

(i) Give the phenotype and genotype of the F_1-generation.

Which type of pollination has occurred to produce F_1-generation?

(ii) Write the phenotypic ratio of the F_2-generation.

(iii) Write the possible combinations of the gametes that can be obtained if two F_1-hybrid plants are crossed.

(iv) State Mendel's law of 'segregation of gametes'.

(v) What is the scientific name of the plant which Mendel used for his experiments on inheritance? **ICSE 2018**

Ans. (i) **Phenotype** - All plants are green and inflated.

Genotype - GgIi.

F_1-generation is produced by cross-pollination between parent plants.

(ii) Phenotypic ratio of F_2-generation is 9 : 3 : 3 : 1.

(iii) GI, Gi, gI, gi

(iv) **Law of segregation** states that during gamete formation, the alleles for each gene segregate from each other, so that each gamete carries only one allele for each gene.

(v) *Pisum sativum.*

63. In a homozygous pea plant, axial flowers (A) are dominant over terminal flowers (a).

(i) What is the phenotype and genotype of the F_1-generation if a plant bearing pure axial flowers is crossed with a plant bearing pure terminal flowers?

(ii) Draw a Punnett square board to show the gametes and offsprings when both the parent plants are heterozygous for axial flowers.

(iii) What is the phenotypic ratio and genotypic ratio of the above cross shown in (ii)?

(iv) State Mendel's law of dominance.

(v) Name two genetic disorders commonly seen in human males. **ICSE 2017**

Ans. (i) If a plant bearing pure axial flowers (AA) is crossed with a plant bearing pure terminal flowers (aa), the phenotype of flower of F_1-generation will be axial flowers while the genotype will be Aa.

(ii) The Punnett square representing the given cross is as follows

(Aa) × (Aa) Parents

Gametes ♂ / ♀	A	a
A	AA (Axial)	Aa (Axial)
a	Aa (Axial)	aa (Terminal)

(iii) **Phenotypic ratio** - 3(axial) : 1 (terminal)

Genotypic ratio - 1(AA) : 2(Aa) :1(aa).

(iv) **Law of dominance** (First law) This law states that when two alternative forms of a trait or character are present in an organism, only one factor express itself in F_1-progeny. This factor is called **dominant factor,** while the other factor which remains hidden is called **recessive factor**. It explains the expression of a gene in a cross and 3 : 1 ratio is obtained in F_2-generation.

(v) Colour blindness and haemophilia are the two genetic disorders commonly seen in human males.

64. A homozygous tall plant (T) bearing red coloured (R) flowers is crossed with a homozygous dwarf (t) plant bearing white (r) flowers.

(i) Give the genotype and phenotype of the plants of F_1-generation.

(ii) Mention the possible combinations of the gametes that can be obtained from the F_1 hybrid plant.

(iii) State the Mendel's law of independent assortment.

(iv) Mention the phenotypes of the offspring obtained in F_2 - generation.

(v) What is the phenotypic ratio obtained in F_2 -generation? **ICSE 2016, 2007**

Ans. (TTRR) × (tt rr)

Tall and red coloured flower ↓ Dwarf and white coloured flower

Tt Rr

(i) Genotype - TtRr, Phenotype - Tall and Red coloured flower.

(ii) (TR) (tR) (Tr) (tr)

(iii) **Law of Independent Assortment** (Third Law)

Based on the observation in dihybrid crosses Mendel proposed third law. According to this law, when two pairs of contrasting characters are combined in a hybrid, segregation of the members of one pair of character into the gamete is independent to the members of the another pair of character at the time of gamete formation.

(iv) a. Tall and red flower

b. Dwarf and red flower

c. Tall and white flower

d. Dwarf and white flower

(v) 9 : 3 : 3 : 1

65. In a homozygous plant round seeds (R) are dominant over wrinkled seeds (r)

(i) Draw a Punnett square to show the gametes and offspring when both the plants have heterozygous round seeds (Rr).

(ii) Mention the phenotype and genotype ratios of the offspring in F_2-generation.

(iii) Name the sex chromosomes in human males and females.

(iv) Briefly explain the term 'mutation'.

(v) What is the number of chromosomes in the gametes of human beings? **ICSE 2015**

Ans. (i)

	R	r
R	RR	Rr
r	Rr	rr

(ii) **Phenotypic ratio** 3:1(Round : Wrinkled)

Genotypic ratio 1 : 2 : 1 (RR : 2 (Rr) : rr)

(iii) Sex chromosomes in human males is XY and in females is XX.

(iv) Mutation is defined as a sudden and inheritable change in the nucleotide sequences of the genome of an individual which ultimately changes the genotype of an organism.

Concept Enhancer Mutation contributes to variation in a population. Cancer is the most common genetic disease occurs due to mutation.

(v) The number of chromosomes in the gametes of human beings are 23.

66. A homozygous plant having round (R) and yellow (Y) seed is crossed with homozygous plant having wrinkled (r) and green (y) seeds

(i) Give the scientific name of the plant on which Mendel conducted his hybridisation experiments.

(ii) Give the genotype of the F_1-generation.

(iii) Give the dihybrid phenotypic ratio and the phenotype of the offspring of the F_2-generation when two plants of the F_1-generation are crossed.

(iv) Name and state the law which explains the dihybrid ratio.

(v) Give the possible combinations of gametes that can be obtained from F_1-hybrid. **ICSE 2014**

Ans. (i) *Pisum sativum* (pea) is the scientific name of the plant on which Mendel conducted his hybridisation experiments.

(ii) Genotype of the F_1-generation is RrYy.

(iii) Ratio of F_2-generation 9 : 3 : 3 : 1

Phenotypes of F_2-generation are

9 Round and yellow, 3 Round and green,
3 Wrinkled and yellow, 1 Wrinkled and green.

(iv) Law of independent assortment explain the dihybrid ratio. Refer to text on page no. 20.

(v) The possible combination of gametes that can be obtained from F_1-hybrid will be RY, Ry, rY, ry.

Diagram Based Questions

67. Given below is a schematic diagram showing Mendel's experiment on sweet pea plants having axial flowers with round seeds (AARR) and terminal flowers with wrinkled seeds (aarr).

Study the same and answer the questions that follow.

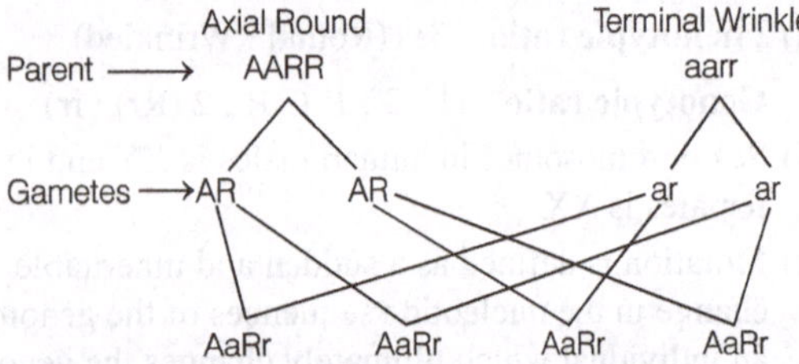

(i) Give the phenotype of F_1-progeny.

(ii) Give the phenotypes of F_2-progeny produced upon by the self-pollination of F_1-progeny.

(iii) Give the phenotypic ratio of F_2-progeny.

(iv) Name and explain the law introduced by Mendel on the basis of the above observation. **ICSE 2013 (5M)**

Ans. (i) Phenotype of F_1-progeny is axial flowers with round seeds.

(ii) Phenotype of F_2-progeny axial round (9), axial wrinkled (3), terminal round (3) and terminal wrinkled (1).

(iii) Phenotypic ratio of F_2-progeny is 9 : 3 : 3 : 1.

(iv) Mendel introduced the law of independent assortment on the basis of above observation. Refer to text on page no. 20.

68. (i) State Mendel's law of dominance.

(ii) A pure tall plant (TT) is crossed with a pure dwarf plant (tt).

Draw Punnett squares to show (i) F_1-generation (ii) F_2-generation.

(iii) Give the phenotype of the F_2-generation.

(iv) Give the phenotypic and genotypic ratio of the F_1 and F_2-generation.

(v) Name any one X-linked disease found in humans. **ICSE 2010 (5M)**

Ans. (i) Refer to text on page no. 19.

(ii) Punnett square showing cross between TT and tt is given below

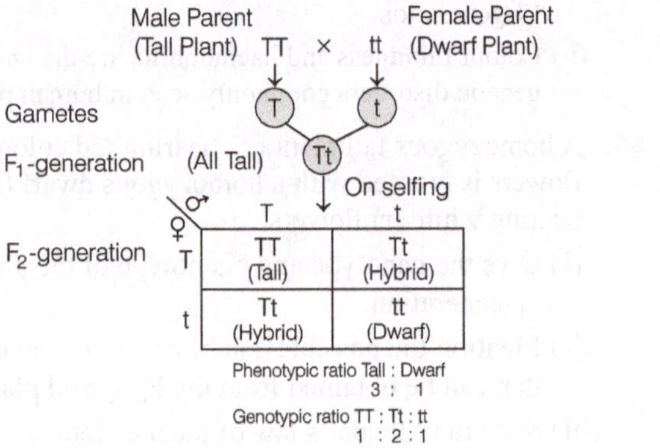

(iii) Phenotype of the F_2- generation is

3 Tall : 1 Dwarf

(iv) **F_1-generation**

Phenotypes – All tall

Genotype– Tt

F_2-generation

Phenotypic ratio – 3 : 1

(Tall : Dwarf)

Genotypic ratio – 1 : 2 : 1

(Tall : Hybrid tall : Dwarf)

(v) X-linked disease found in human is haemophilia.

CHAPTER TEST

Section-A

01 Mark Questions

1 Select the correct answers to the questions from the given options.

(i) What is the probability that the male progeny will be a boy?

(a) 50% (b) 56%

(c) 47% (d) None of these

(ii) The number of pairs of sex chromosomes in the zygote of a human being is

(a) 2 (b) 3

(c) 1 (d) 4

(iii) If a round, green seeded pea plant (RRyy) is crossed with a wrinkled yellow seeded pea plant (rrYY) the seeds produced in F_1-generation are

(a) round and green (b) round and yellow

(c) wrinkled and green (d) wrinkled and yellow

(iv) Which of the following decides the sex of the child?

(a) Male gamete, i.e. sperm

(b) Female gamete, i.e. ovum

(c) Both sperm and ovum

(d) Mother

(v) Which of the following disease shows *criss-cross* inheritance ?

(a) Haemophilia

(b) Sickle-cell anaemia

(c) Colour blindness

(d) Both (a) and (c)

2 (i) Name the following.

(a) Carriers of heredity

(b) Sudden change in gene

(c) Sickle-shaped RBCs production occur

(d) Alternative forms of a character

(ii) Mention the following statements are 'True' or False.

(a) Thalassemia follows the criss-cross inheritance.

(b) Albinism is a disorder occur due to total absence of pigment in skin.

(c) Humans have 46 pairs of chromosomes.

(d) Mother's genetic makeup is responsible for the gender of progeny.

(e) The chromosome as a whole can be either dominant or recessive.

(iii) Match the items given in Column I with the most appropriate once in Column II and rewrite the correct matching pairs.

	Column I		Column II
A.	Thalassemia	1.	Haemophilia
B.	*Criss-cross* inheritance	2.	UV rays
C.	Mutagen	3.	Phenotype
D.	Expressed character	4.	Genotype
E.	Combination of genes	5.	Defective haemoglobin

(iv) Given below are groups of terms. In each group, the first pair indicates the relationship between the two terms. Rewrite and complete the second pair on a similar bases.

(a) TT: Homozygous : : Tt: ....

(b) Character: Trait : : Gene: ....

(c) Colour blindness: Sex chromosomes : : Thalassemia: ....

(d) Skin cells : 46 : : Ovum : ....

(v) Give appropriate technical term for the following.

(a) A pair of corresponding chromosomes of same size and shape, one from each parent.

(b) The chromosome which determine the gender of an individual.

(c) An image of complete set of chromosome.

(d) Transmission of genetically based characteristics from parents to offspring.

(e) Alternative form of a character.

02 Marks Questions

3 Differentiate between genotype and phenotype.

4 State the law of independent assortment.

5 Explain dihybrid cross with example.

6 Define mutation with example.

7 What is *criss-cross* inheritance?

03 Marks Questions

8 List the application of Mendel's law.

9 Differentiate between homozygous and heterozygous cross.

10 State three Mendel's laws of inheritance.

11 Explain sex-linked inheritance. Give example of the genetic disorder which occur do to it.

12 Give three reasons why Mendel had selected garden pea for his experiments?

Section-B

Diagram Based Questions

13 Study the following cross and then answer the questions that follows

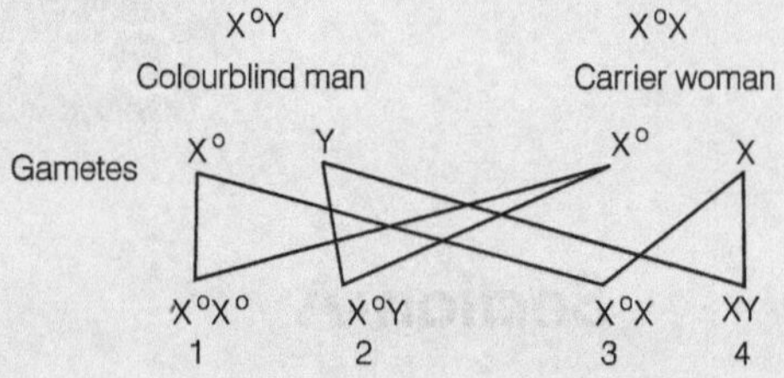

(i) Give the phenotype of the offspring numbered 1, 2, 3, 4.

(ii) Give the phenotypic and genotypic ratio of the above cross.

(iii) Name and state Mendel's law that explain the above cross.

14 Draw a Punnett square for finding out the proportion of different genotypes in the progeny of a genetic cross between

(i) A pure round yellow (RRYY) pea plant with a pure wrinkled, green (rryy) pea plant.

(ii) Red flower variety of pea (RR) with white flower variety of pea (rr).

Answers

1. (i) (a), (ii) (c), (iii) (b), (iv) (a), (v) (d)

03

Absorption by Roots

TREND ANALYSIS 4 YEARS

	Average No. of Questions Across all Sets				
	Types of Questions	2024	2023	2020	2019
TOPIC 01 Plant-Water Relation	1 Mark	2	1	–	1
	2 Marks	1	2	–	–
	3 Marks	–	1	–	–
	4 Marks	–	–	–	–
	5 Marks	–	–	–	–
TOPIC 02 Absorption of Water and Minerals	1 Mark	1	1	–	–
	2 Marks	–	–	–	–
	3 Marks	–	–	–	–
	4 Marks	–	–	–	–
	5 Marks	–	–	–	–

The absorption of water and minerals from the soil takes place *via* roots of plant which is further conducted to all parts of the plant body through xylem.

TOPIC 1

Plant-Water Relation

Water is essential for plants in order to perform processes like photosynthesis, transpiration, transportation and for providing mechanical stiffness as well.
Apart from water, plants also require mineral nutrients which are absorbed from the soil by roots. These nutrients are required as constituents of the cell and cell organelles and also for the synthesis of different compounds in the cell.

Roots

- These are branched parts at the lower end of a plant.
- Plants absorb water through roots from the soil, this is the most important and life-supporting function of the roots. However, the area of the roots where most absorption of water and minerals takes place is the **root hair zone**.
- **Root hairs** are thin-walled, extensions of the outer (epidermal) cells of roots present at the tip of the root.
- Root hairs have vacuoles filled with cell sap (a liquid material). They are surrounded by two layers, i.e. cell wall and cell membrane.
- As soil water is hypotonic (when compared to the cell sap present in the root hair) it leads to diffusion of water molecules from soil to the root hairs.

- Water and minerals absorbed by the roots of the plants are further conducted into the stem for their supply to the upper parts of the plant like leaves, fruits, flowers, etc.

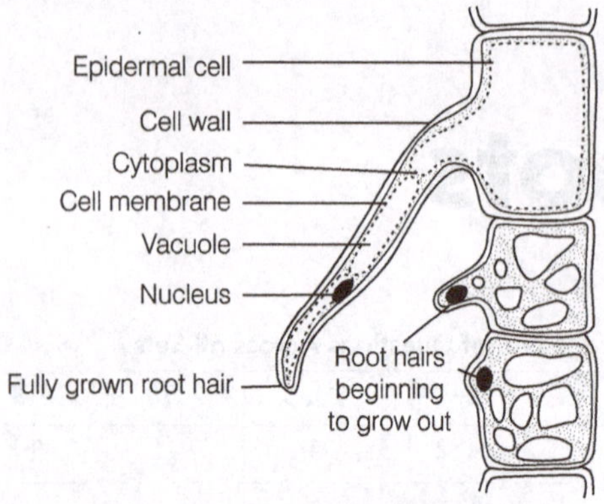

Fig. 3.1 Root hair showing various parts

Characteristics of Roots

Roots possess the following characteristics in order to draw water from soil

- Plants have extensive root system which grows rapidly in soil.
- Root hairs provide large surface area. This increases the area of absorption of water.
- Cell sap of root hairs have higher concentration than the surrounding water.
- Cell wall of root hairs is thin and permeable so as to allow the movement of water molecules and dissolved substances freely.

Process of Water and Mineral Absorption

The entire process of absorption is the result of some important processes such as imbibition, diffusion, osmosis, plasmolysis, etc.

1. Imbibition

- It is a special phenomenon by which water or any other liquid is adsorbed by the living or dead cells by surface attraction.
- It is a type of diffusion by which water moves along the diffusion gradient. Thus, hydrophilic (or water loving) substances have the tendency to imbibe water or moisture which causes them to swell up, e.g. swelling up of dry seeds, wooden doors, etc. on exposure to moist air/water.
- The solid particles which imbibe water or any other liquid are called **imbibants**, while the liquid which is imbibed is called **imbibate**.
- Transpiraiton of water from stomata occurs by diffusion.
- It helps in ascent of sap *via* root hairs.

2. Diffusion

- It is a process by which the molecules of a substance, i.e. solvent or solute, gas, liquid, etc., move from a region of higher concentration to a region of lower concentration.
- The diffusing particles in a medium exert a pressure which is directly proportional to their concentration. This pressure is known as **diffusion pressure**.
- Imbibition distributes ions and molecules into the protoplasm. Transpiration of water from stomata occurs by diffusion.

3. Osmosis

- It is defined as the movement or diffusion of water molecules from the region of their higher concentration to the region of their lower concentration through a semipermeable membrane (a membrane that allows only certain molecules to pass through it, e.g. egg membrane, plasma membrane, etc).
- Osmosis takes place spontaneously in response to a driving force. It is a passive process, i.e. does not require any input of energy. Discovery of osmosis was done by **Pfeffer**.
- Osmosis can be of following two types, depending upon the concentration of the cell and the surrounding medium
  - (i) **Exosmosis** It is the **outerward movement** of water molecules through the semipermeable membrane when the medium surrounding the cell is more concentrated. In this condition, cell shrinks and becomes **flaccid**.
  - (ii) **Endosmosis** It is the **inward movement** of water molecules through the semipermeable membrane when the medium surrounding the cell is less concentrated or diluted than the medium inside the cell. In this condition, cell swells up and becomes turgid.

    Absorption of water from soil by root hairs is due to osmosis.

Osmotic Pressure (OP)

It is lowest possible pressure required to prevent the entry of pure solvent in the solution by means of semipermeable membrane.

Tonicity of a Solution

Osmosis gets affected by the environment in which it takes place, i.e. the tonicity of a solution. It is determined by the relative concentration of the solution which determines the direction of the diffusion.

Types of solutions based on the tonicity, solutions are divided into three main types

(i) **Hypotonic solution** It is the solution having lower solute concentration (outside the cell) than the fluids inside the cell. In this case, endosmosis takes place, i.e. water moves into the cell and cell swells up.

(ii) **Isotonic solution** It is the solution in which the relative concentration of water molecules and the solute on either sides is equal, i.e. inside and outside of the cell membrane. In this case, size of cell remains same.

(iii) **Hypertonic solution** It is the solution having higher solute concentration (outside the cell) than the fluids (inside the cell). In this case, exosmosis takes place, i.e. water moves out of the cell and cell gets shrink.

4. Turgidity

- It is the condition of a cell in which it becomes distended or bulged due to the entry of water by endosmosis. Such a cell is known as **turgid cell**, e.g. reversal of wilting when plant cell gets water.
- Two kinds of pressure are generated by a turgid cell which are as follows
  (i) **Turgor Pressure** (TP) It is the pressure exerted by the protoplasm against the cell wall in a turgid cell.
  (ii) **Wall Pressure** (WP) It is the back pressure exerted by the cell wall against the protoplasm of a fully turgid cell.
- The opening and closing of stomata is regulated by turgidity of the guard cells.

Note Both TP and WP are equal and opposite to each other

5. Flaccidity

It is the condition of a cell in which it looses water from its cytoplasm due to exosmosis. Such cell is known as flaccid cell, e.g. wilting property of leaves when plant is exposed to the Sun.

6. Plasmolysis

- It is the phenomenon which occurs when water moves out of the cell when placed in a hypertonic solution by the process of osmosis.
- Due to plasmolysis, plant cell loses its original appearance, i.e. protoplasm shrinks and plasma membrane is pulled away from the cell wall.
- This makes the cell to look flaccid in appearance.
- It is used in killing bacteria that grow on or contaminate food items, such as meat, pickles, etc., by adding large amount of salt or sugar in it. In such conditions, the bacteria die due to the loss of water from their cell body.

7. Deplasmolysis

- It is exactly the reverse of plasmolysis in which the protoplasm of the cell returns to its original position when favourable conditions are provided, i.e. placed in pure water or hypotonic solution.
- This again makes the cell to become normal (turgid) and attain its original shape and size, e.g. if a plant cell is placed in salt solution, it becomes plasmolysed but if the same cell is placed in tap water, its original state will reappear, i.e. it will become deplasmolysed.

Types of Absorption

Absorption of water by roots takes place by the following two processes

1. Passive Absorption or Passive Transport

It is the mechanism of movement of substances into root cells simply by diffusion, i.e. without the expenditure of energy, from the region of higher concentration to the region of their lower concentration.

2. Active Absorption or Active Transport

- It is the mechanism of transport of molecules (ions) against a concentration gradient, i.e. from the region of lower concentration to the higher concentration, with the help of energy in the form of ATP.
- Direction of molecules in active transport is just opposite to that of diffusion.
- Nutrient molecules such as potassium, zinc, nitrates, sulphates, etc., do not pass through the cell membrane because of their higher concentration inside the root cells. Thus, these molecules are forcibly carried inside the cell, against their concentration gradient.

PYQs Previous Years' Questions

1 Mark Questions

Multiple Choice Questions

1. Osmosis takes place when there is **ICSE 2024**
   (a) a freely permeable membrane
   (b) a cell wall
   (c) a selectively permeable membrane
   (d) an impermeable membrane

Ans. (c) a selectively permeable membrane

2. Deplasmolysis occurs when a plasmolysed cell is placed in **ICSE Specimen 2023**
   (a) concentrated salt solution
   (b) tap water
   (c) concentrated sugar solution
   (d) hypertonic salt solution

Ans. (b) tap water

3. Marine fish when placed in tap water bursts because of **ICSE Specimen 2023**

Or Marine fish when placed in tap water bursts because of .... **ICSE Specimen 2021-22 Sem.I, 2017**
   (a) endosmosis (b) exosmosis
   (c) diffusion (d) plasmolysis

Ans. (a) endosmosis

4. Active transport **ICSE Specimen 2021-22 Sem. I**
   (a) passage of water from its lower to higher concentration through a cell membrane without any expenditure of energy
   (b) passage of ions from its lower to higher concentration through a cell membrane without any expenditure of energy
   (c) passage of water from its lower to higher concentration through a cell membrane using energy from the cell
   (d) passage of ions from its lower to higher concentration through a cell membrane using energy from the cell

Ans. (d) Passage of ions from its lower to higher concentration through a cell membrane using energy from the cell.

5. Root hair **ICSE Specimen 2021–22 Sem. I**
   (a) extension of cortex (b) extension of epithelium
   (c) extension of epidermis (d) extension of endodermis

Ans. (c) Extension of epidermis

6. The pressure exerted by the cell contents on the cell wall.

Or

Name the pressure exerted by cell contents on a plant cell wall. **ICSE Specimen 2021–22 Sem. I, 2000**
   (a) Turgor pressure (b) Partial pressure
   (c) Wall pressure (d) Osmotic pressure

Ans. (a) Turgor pressure

7. When a cell is placed in a .... solution it becomes plasmolysed. **ICSE 2021-22 Sem. I**
   (a) distilled water (b) hypertonic
   (c) isotonic (d) hypotonic

Ans. (b) hypertonic

8. State the function of 'cell wall'. **ICSE 2021-22 Sem. I**
   (a) Regulates entry of solutes in plant cells
   (b) Regulates entry of solutes in animal cells
   (c) Gives rigidity and shape to plant cells
   (d) Gives rigidity and shape to animal cells

Ans. (c) Give rigidity and shape to plant cells.

9. Plasmolysis identifies the process of **ICSE Specimen 2017**
   (a) imbibition (b) diffusion
   (c) active transport (d) osmosis

Ans. (d) osmosis

10. A plant cell may burst when
   (a) turgor pressure equalises wall pressure
   (b) turgor pressure exceeds wall pressure
   (c) wall pressure exceeds turgor pressure
   (d) None of the above **ICSE 2016**

Ans. (b) turgor pressure exceeds wall pressure.

11. The space between the cell wall and plasma membrane in plasmolysed cell is filled with **ICSE 2000**
   (a) isotonic solution (b) hypotonic solution
   (c) hypertonic solution (d) water

Ans. (c) hypertonic solution

Very Short Answer Type Questions

12. Name the following
   Unicellular outgrowths from the epidermis of roots. **ICSE 2024**

Ans. Root hair

13. Briefly explain the term osmosis.
ICSE Specimen 2021-22 Sem. I

Ans. Osmosis is the process of movement of water molecules from a region of their higher concentration to a region of their lower concentration through a semipermeable membrane.

14. Rewrite the sentence by inserting the correct word in the space indicated.
Wooden doors swell up in rainy reason due to .... **ICSE Specimen 2021-22 Sem. I**

Ans. Imbibition

15. Give one difference on the basis of what is given in the brackets.
Turgid cell and Plasmolysed cell (tonicity of the surrounding solution) **ICSE Specimen 2019**

Ans. Difference between turgid cell and plasmolysed cell is

Turgid cell	Plasmolysed cell
It is the condition of a cell in which cell becomes bulged due to entry of water by endosmosis.	It is condition of cell when water comes out of the cell when placed in a hypertonic solution by the process of exosmosis.

16. Give suitable biological reason for the statement given below.
Root hairs become flaccid and drop when excess fertilisers are added to the moist soil around them.
ICSE 2019

Ans. When fertilisers are added to the moist soil around root hairs, it will form hypertonic solution, resulting the protoplasm to shrink. Hence, the root hairs also become limp or flaccid.

17. Correct the statement by changing the underlined word.
The cell sap of root hair is <u>hypotonic</u>. **ICSE 2018**

Ans. The cell sap of root hair is hypertonic.

18. Give appropriate biological or technical term for 'Movement of molecules of a substance from their higher concentration to their lower concentration when they are in direct contact.' **ICSE 2018, 2009**

Ans. Diffusion.

19. Differentiate between the given pair on the basis of what is indicated in bracket.
Hypotonic solution and hypertonic solution (Condition of a plant cell when placed in them). **ICSE 2018**

Ans. When a plant cell is placed in hypotonic solution, it becomes turgid due to endosmosis.

While, when it is placed in hypertonic solution, it becomes flaccid or plasmolysed due to exosmosis.

20. Movement of water molecules across the cell membrane from hypertonic to hypotonic solution.

Ans. Reverse osmosis. **ICSE Specimen 2017**

21. Give reason for the following.
Plant begin to die when excess of soluble fertilisers are added to soil. **ICSE Specimen 2017, 2007**

Ans. Fertilisers along with soil water act as a hypertonic solution. This leads to exosmosis, i.e. movement of water molecules from plant. Thus, the plants begin to die.

22. Name the process by which root hairs absorb water from the soil. **ICSE 2017, 2001**

Or Mention the process by which water enters into root hair cell. **ICSE 2001**

Ans. **Osmosis** is the process by which root hairs absorb water from the soil.

23. The statement given below is incorrect. Rewrite the correct statement by changing the underlined word of the statement.

Free movement of solutes in and out of cell takes place across the <u>cell membrane</u>. **ICSE 2017**

Ans. Free movement of solutes in and out of cell takes place across the **cell wall**.

24. Differentiate between the given pair on the basis of what is mentioned in bracket.

Active transport and diffusion (Significance in plants) **ICSE 2017**

Ans. Difference between active transport and diffusion is

Active transport	Diffusion
Uptake of mineral ions into root cells occurs through active transport.	Exchange of gases (CO_2 and O_2) between the plant interior and exterior occurs through diffusion.

25. Give the biological/technical term for

'The process of uptake of mineral ions against the concentration gradient using energy from the cell.'
ICSE 2016, 2015

Ans. Active transport.

26. Differentiate between the given pair on the basis of what is mentioned within brackets.

'Diffusion and osmosis (Definition) **ICSE 2015**

Ans. **Diffusion** It is the process by which molecules move from a region of high concentration to the region of low concentration.

Osmosis It is the process of movement region of water molecules from the region of higher water concentration to the region of lower concentration through a semipermeable membrane.

27. Explain the term turgor pressure. **ICSE 2015**

Ans. **Turgor pressure** The pressure exerted by water inside the cell against the cell wall is called turgor pressure.

When a plant cell stores ions, sugars and other solutes in its vacuole, this causes an influx of water. The influx of water results in a large turgor pressure exerted on the plant cell wall.

28. Differentiate between the following pair on the basis of what is mentioned within bracket.

Turgor pressure and Wall pressure (Explain). **ICSE 2014, 2008**

Ans. Turgor pressure is the pressure exerted by the protoplasm against the cell wall. While, wall pressure is the back pressure exerted by the cell wall on the protoplasm.

29. Give biological reason why wooden frames of doors get jammed during the monsoon season. **ICSE 2013**

Ans. Wooden frames of doors get jammed during monsoon season due to the process of imbibition.

In this process, water is adsorbed to the surface of hydrophilic colloids. As wood has a strong affinity for water (hydrophilic), they adsorb or imbibe water or moisture from their surroundings and get swelled up.

30. Name the phenomenon by which living or dead plant cells absorb water by surface attraction. **ICSE 2012**

Ans. Imbibition is the phenomenon by which living or dead plant cells or cell materials adsorb water by surface attraction.

31. Give the biological term for a membrane which allows the passage of molecules selectively. **ICSE 2012**

Ans. Plasma membrane is selectively permeable membrane which allows the passage of molecules selectively.

32. Give reason why potato cubes when placed in water become firm and increase in size. **ICSE 2011**

Ans. Potato cubes when placed in water become firm and increase in size.

This happens because water acts as a hypotonic medium, thus water enters into potato cells due to endosmosis making them firm and large in size (turgid).

33. Explain the term turgidity. **ICSE 2010**

Ans. Turgidity is the condition of a cell in which it becomes distended or bulged due to the entry of water by endosmosis.

34. Explain the term diffusion. **ICSE 2010, 2002**

Ans. Diffusion is the process of movement of water molecules from a region of their higher concentration to a region of their lower concentration.

35. Rewrite the completed explanation by inserting the key word in the space indicated by '∧'.

Osmosis is the movement of water molecules from a region of their higher concentration to a region of their lower concentration through a '∧' membrane. **ICSE 2008**

Ans. Osmosis is the movement of water molecules from a region of their higher concentration to a region of their lower concentration through a **semipermeable membrane**.

36. Give the biological term of the process of mixing of two different substances/molecules. **ICSE 2008**

Ans. Diffusion is the biological term for the process of mixing of two different substances/molecules.

37. Name a solution whose concentration is greater than that of cell sap. **ICSE 2007**

Ans. A solution whose concentration is greater than that of cell sap is known as **hypertonic solution**.

38. Define hypotonic solution. **ICSE 2006**

Ans. Hypotonic solution is the solution that has lower solute concentration (outside the cell) than that inside the cell sap (fluids inside the cell).

39. Give the biological reason why marine fishes burst when thrown under tap water. **ICSE 2005**

Ans. Marine fishes burst when thrown under tap water because their cells exist best in hypertonic solution or salty water. When put in tap water or hypotonic solution their cells show endosmosis and thus, swell and burst.

40. Give biological reason for 'On sprinkling common salt on grass growing in a lawn, the grass is killed.' **ICSE 2004**

Ans. Sprinkling salt makes soil hypertonic, hence, grass loses water due to exosmosis and thus, gets killed.

41. Define the term active transport giving one example. **ICSE 2003**

Ans. Active transport is the movement of molecules (or ions) from lower concentration to higher concentration against a concentration gradient using energy in the form of ATP (Adenosine Triphosphate), e.g. uptake of mineral ions into root cells.

42. Give one reason for 'Wilted lettuce leaves if kept in cold water become crisp'. **ICSE 2003**

Ans. Leaves of wilted lettuce are flaccid in nature due to the loss of water. When these leaves are kept in cold water, the water enters the cell making them turgid. Hence, they become crisp.

43. Answer the following briefly.

Plants growing in fertilised soil are often found to wilt if the soil is not adequately watered, why? **ICSE 2000**

Ans. If the soil is fertilised and not well-watered, the concentration of the soil solution will be very high and water begins to move from the root hair cells to soil due to exosmosis. If this process continues for a long time plasmolysis takes place and leads to wilting of plants.

2 Marks Questions

44. Mention two adaptations in roots for absorption of water from the soil. **ICSE 2024**

Ans. (i) The root hair represents a large surface area in contact with the soil particles.

(ii) The root hair can penetrate between soil particles.

45. What is active transport? **ICSE Specimen 2023**

Ans. Active transport is defined as a process that involves the movement of molecules from a region of lower concentration to a region of higher concentration against a gradient with the help of energy in the form of ATP.

46. What is a semipermeable membrane? Name the semipermeable membrane present in a plant cell. **ICSE Specimen 2023**

Ans. A membrane through which only smaller molecules like water can pass but not the bigger molecules like solutes, is known as semipermeable membranes.

Cell membrane or Plasma membrane is a living, thin, delicate, elastic, selectively permeable membrane made up of proteins and lipids, present in both plant and animal cell.

47. Explain the term plasmolysis. Give one application of this phenomenon in our daily lives. **ICSE 2017, 2005**

Ans. (i) Refer to text on page no. 33.

(ii) One of the applications of plasmolysis includes addition of salt to pickles to preserve them for longer duration.

48. Complete the following.

Rewrite the sentence by inserting the correct word in the space indicated

(i) Wooden doors swell up in rainy season due to ....

(ii) .... is the phenomenon of contraction of the cytoplasm from the cell wall. **ICSE 2011**

Ans. (i) Wooden doors swell up in rainy season due to **imbibition**.

(ii) **Plasmolysis** is the phenomenon of contraction of the cytoplasm from the cell wall.

4 Marks Question

49. Potato cubes of 1 cm^3 in size were placed in two containers, one containing water, the other containing concentrated sugar solution. After about 24 hours when the cubes were examined, those placed in water were found to be firm and had increased in size by a few millimetres. Those placed in concentrated sugar solution were found to be soft and had decreased in size. Use the above information to answer the questions that follows.

(i) Account for the firmness and increase in size of the potato cubes which were placed in water.

(ii) Account for the softness and decrease in size of the potato cubes which were placed in the sugar solution.

(iii) Name and define the physical process being investigated in this experiment. **ICSE 2001**

Ans. (i) The cubes of potato were firm and had increased in size because of the entry of water into the cell due to endosmosis.

(ii) The cubes that were placed in sugar solution were soft and had decreased in size due to the movement of water to outside from the cell, i.e. exosmosis.

(iii) The physical process being investigated in this experiment is called osmosis. It is the passage of water from a region of their higher concentration to a region of their lower concentration through a semipermeable membrane.

Diagram Based Questions

50. Study the diagram given below and answer the questions that follows **ICSE Specimen 2023 (3M)**

(i) Name the process being studied in the above experiment.

(ii) What will you observe with regard to the level of water when this setup is placed in bright sunlight?

(iii) Mention one adaptation found in plants to overcome the process of guttation.

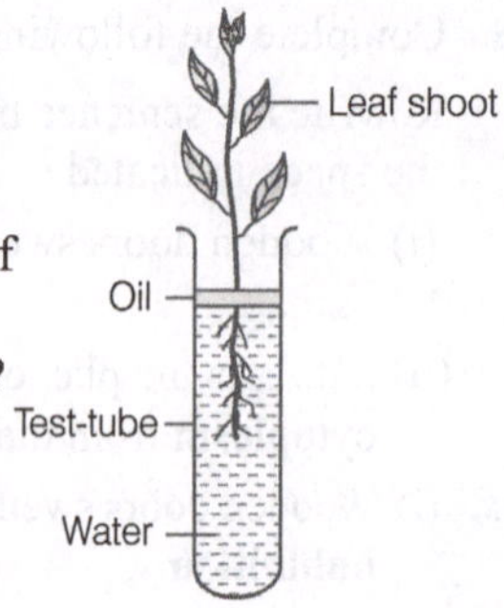

Ans. (i) Absorption of water by roots.

(ii) The level of water remain same as there is a layer of oil on the surface of water so there is no loss of water from test tube.

(iii) The plant can develop thick cuticle on the surface of leaves.

51. The diagram given below represents a plant cell after being placed in a strong sugar solution. Study the diagram and answer the questions that follows

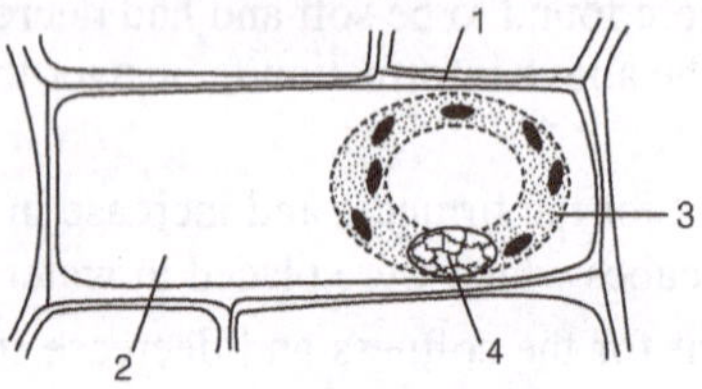

(i) What is the state of the cell shown in the diagram?

(ii) Name the structure that acts as a selectively permeable membrane.

(iii) Label the parts numbered 1 to 4 in the diagram.

(iv) How can the above cell be brought back to its original condition? Mention the scientific term for the recovery of the cell.

(v) State any two features of the above plant cell which is not present in animal cells. **ICSE 2017 (5M)**

Ans. (i) The cell shown in the figure is plasmolysed.

(ii) Plasma membrane acts as a selectively permeable membrane.

(iii) 1–Cell wall, 2–Hypertonic solution
3–Plasma membrane 4–Nucleus

(iv) The cell can be returned back to its original condition, if it is placed in a hypotonic medium or pure water for sometime. The scientific term for the recovery of the cell is deplasmolysis.

(v) The two features of the given plant cell which are not present in animal cell are
- the presence of cell wall.
- the presence of chloroplast.

52. A candidate in order to study the process of osmosis has taken 3 potato cubes and put them in 3 different beakers containing 3 different solutions. After 24 hours in the first beaker, the potato cube increased in size, in the second beaker, the potato cube decreased in size and in the third beaker, there was no change in the size of the potato cube. The following diagram shows the result of the same experiment.

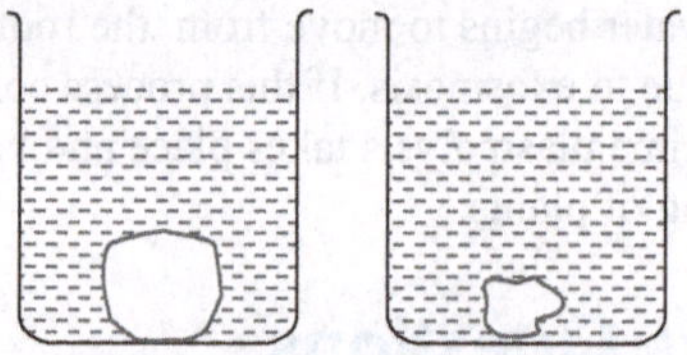

(a) Size increased (b) Size decreased

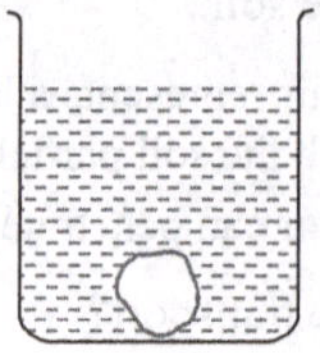

(c) Size remains same

(i) Give the technical terms for the solutions used in beakers, *a*, *b* and *c*.

(ii) In beaker *c*, the size of the potato cube remains the same. Explain the reason in brief.

(iii) Write the specific feature of the cell sap of root hairs which helps in absorption of water.

(iv) What is osmosis?

(v) How does a cell wall and a cell membrane differ in their permeability? **ICSE 2014 (5M)**

Ans. (i) The technical terms for the solutions used in beakers (*a*), (*b*) and (*c*) are
(a) Hypotonic solution
(b) Hypertonic solution
(c) Isotonic solution

(ii) In beaker *c*, the concentration of water and solute is same in solution as the potato cube. Due to which no osmosis occurs and the size of potato cube remains the same.

(iii) The concentration of cell sap is higher in the root hair as compared to soil water. Thus, endosmosis takes place facilitating the absorption of water.

(iv) Osmosis is a process of diffusion of water molecules from higher concentration to lower concentration through a semipermeable membrane.

(v) Cell wall is freely permeable, while cell membrane is semipermeable.

Concept Enhancer Cell wall is fully permeable to smaller molecules with the size of 30-60 KDa, cell membrane controls the movement of the substance into and outside the cell.

53. The figure given alongside shows the epidermal cells of an onion bulb. This cell was then transferred to a drop of sugar solution.

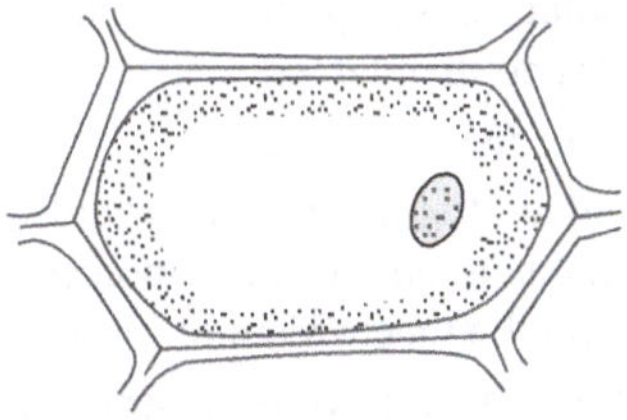

(i) Draw a well-labelled diagram of the epidermal cell as it would appear after immersion in a strong sugar solution.

(ii) What scientific term is used for the changes as shown in (i) above?

(iii) What should be done to restore the cell back to its original condition?

(iv) Give the scientific term for the recovery of the cell as a result of the step taken in (iii) above.

(v) Define the term osmosis. **ICSE 2013 (5M)**

Ans. (i)

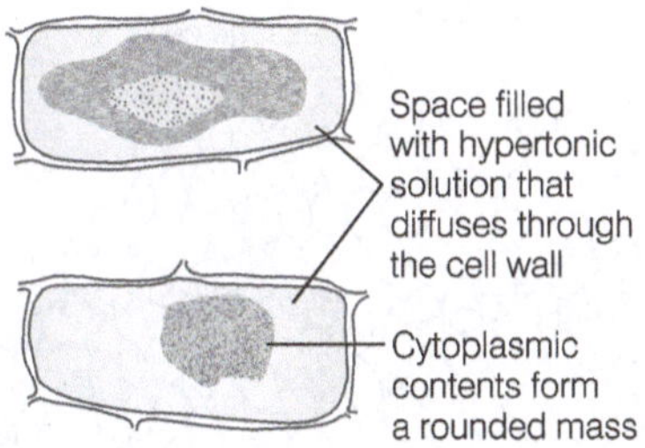

(ii) The scientific term used for the above change shown in figure is plasmolysis.

(iii) To restore the cell back to its original condition, it must be placed in hypotonic solution immediately after it gets plasmolysed.

(iv) The scientific term used for the recovery of the cell as a result of the step taken in (iii) above is deplasmolysis.

(v) Refer to text on page no. 32.

54. Given alongside is the diagram of a cell as seen under the microscope after been placed in a solution.

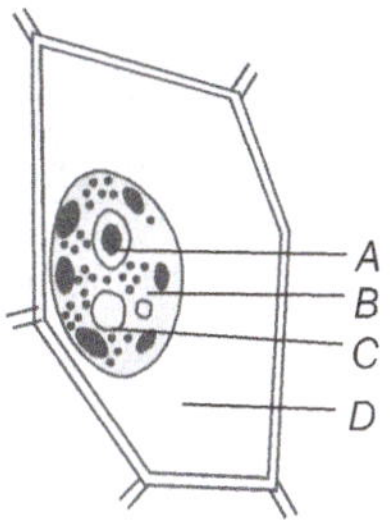

(i) What is the technical term used for the state/condition of the cell given?

(ii) Give the technical term for the solution in which the cell was placed.

(iii) Name the parts numbered *A* to *D*.

(iv) Is the cell given plant cell or an animal cell? Give two reasons in support of your answer as evident from the diagram.

(v) What would you do to bring this cell back to its original condition? **ICSE 2011(5M)**

Ans. (i) Given cell is plasmolysed in nature.

(ii) Cell was placed in the hypertonic solution.

(iii) *A* — Nucleus, *B* — Chloroplast
C — Vacuole, *D* — Hypertonic solution

(iv) The cell given is plant cell because
(a) of the presence of cell wall.
(b) chloroplast is clearly seen in the cytoplasm.
(c) centrosome is not present there.

(v) The cell can be returned back to its original condition, if it will be placed in a hypotonic medium or pure water for sometime.

55. The diagram alongside represents a layer of epidermal cells showing a fully grown root hair. Study the diagram and answer the questions that follows.

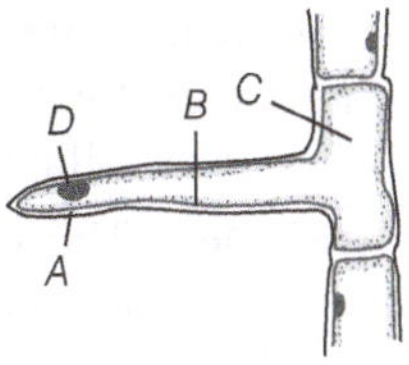

(i) Name the parts labelled *A*, *B*, *C* and *D*.

(ii) The root hair cell is in a turgid state. Name and explain the process that caused this state.

(iii) Mention one distinct difference between the parts labelled *A* and *B*. **ICSE 2011 (3M)**

Ans. (i) Different parts can be labelled as
A — Cell wall of root hair.
B — Cell membrane of root hair.
C — Cytoplasm.
D — Nucleus.

(ii) The soil medium is hypotonic, thus endosmosis will occur due to which the root hair cell turns turgid. Endosmosis is the inward movement of water molecules through the semipermeable membrane when the medium surrounding the cell is less concentrated or diluted than the medium inside the cell.

(iii)

A (Cell wall)	B (Cell membrane)
It is freely permeable.	It is semipermeable.

56. Given alongside is the diagram of an apparatus setup to study a very important physiological process.

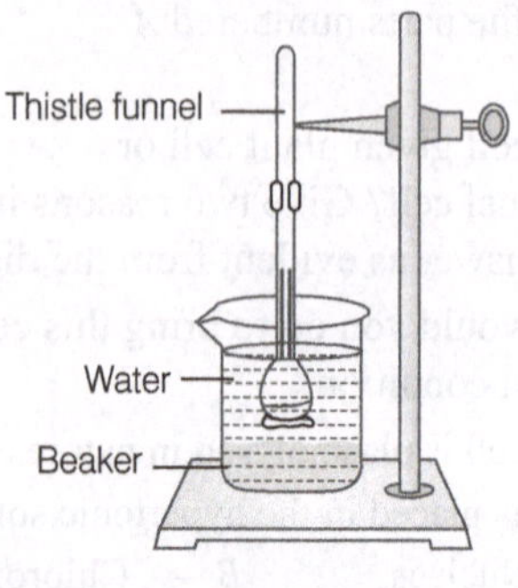

(i) Name the process being studied through the given experiment.

(ii) Explain the process.

(iii) What change would you observe in the thistle funnel containing sugar solution after about 10 minutes?

(iv) Is sugar solution hypertonic or hypotonic?

(v) Name the part of the plant cell which is represented by the sugar solution.

(vi) Explain why much salt is added to pickles.

ICSE 2010 (5M)

Ans. (i) Osmosis is the process being studied through the given experiment.

(ii) Refer to text on page no. 32.

(iii) After about 10 minutes, the sugar solution in the thistle funnel will rise up.

(iv) Sugar solution is hypertonic in nature as it is more concentrated than water.

(v) Cell sap of the root hair.

(vi) Salt is added to pickles as it provides hypertonic medium due to which water molecules move out of the cell by the mechanism of plasmolysis. This allows pickles to be preserved for longer duration.

TOPIC 2

Absorption of Water and Minerals

The processes like diffusion, osmosis, etc. can only transport substances over short distances. For long distance transport, the same job is done by the vascular tissues.

There are generally two types of vascular tissues in plants which are mainly responsible for transport of water, minerals and food.

These are as follows

(i) **Xylem** This is mainly responsible for the transport of water and minerals from roots to aerial parts of the plant.

(ii) **Phloem** This is mainly responsible for the transport of organic and inorganic substances such as food, etc. from leaves to other parts of the plant.

Ascent of Sap

It is the upward movement of water from roots to the upper parts of the plant (such as leaves and other growing points) by the stems. It occurs through the tracheary elements of xylem.

Path followed by water during transport is given below

Root hair → Cortex cells → Endodermis → Passage cells → Xylem vessels.

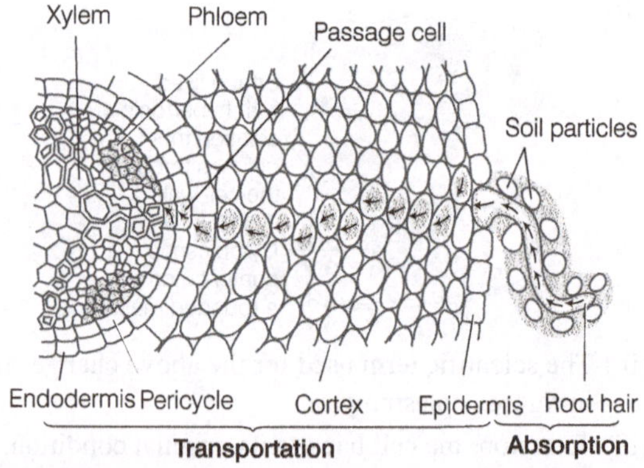

Fig. 3.2 Diagram showing cross-section of a part of a root indicating cell-to-cell conduction of water from a root hair to xylem by arrows

Many theories have been put forward to explain the upward movement of water (ascent of sap).

Some of the theories are as follows

1. Root Pressure Theory

It is the pressure that develops in the xylem of roots mainly in cortical cells due to inflow of water. It pushes the water and minerals in the upward direction. Root pressure develops largely due to osmotic phenomenon.

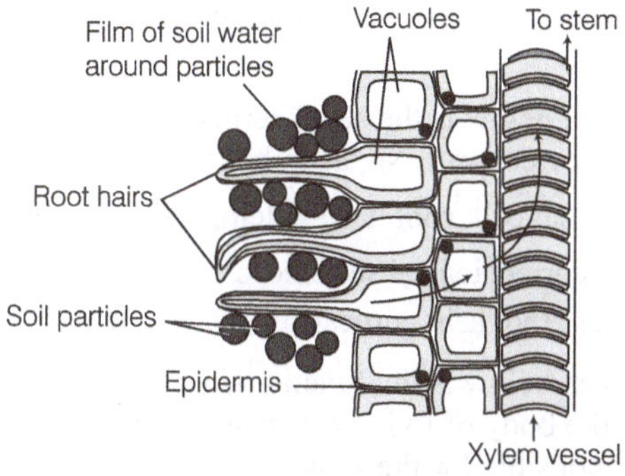

Fig. 3.3 Root pressure builds up due to osmosis and turgidity of root cells, and up into the xylem vessels

The root pressure is maximum during early morning of spring and rainy season when the level of evaporation is low. It is measured by an instrument called **manometer**.

This theory is not applicable in case of tall plants.

2. Transpirational Pull Theory

Also known as cohesion-tension theory. This theory is based on the following phenomenon concepts

(i) **Continuous water column** Plants have a continuous water column in their xylem channels from roots to the leaves, from where water is lost through the process of transpiration.

(ii) **Cohesion** Water molecules stick together by a strong force of attraction called cohesive force. This mutual attraction is due to the presence of H-bonds between adjacent water molecules.

(iii) **Adhesion** Water molecules also stick to the walls of xylem vessels due to adhesive property of water to cell wall material. This is called adhesive force.

Cohesion and adhesion ensure that the water column is not broken. Water is lost from the leaf cells (mesophyll) to the intercellular space as a result of transpiration and this develops a strong negative water potential.

This negative pressure exerts an upward pull over the water column. This pull is known as **transpirational pull** which is transmitted upto the roots in search of more water.

Experiment to Show that Xylem Conducts Water

Take a young medium-sized balsam plant. Wash it and place it in a beaker containing an eosin dye solution (pink) in water. It is to be noted that the roots should be completely submerged in the solution.

The set up is allowed to stand for about 3-4 hrs. Take the plant out of the solution after the period of 3-4 hrs and wash it in tap water. Cut and make a Transverse Section (TS) of the stem, leaves or roots. Examine them under a microscope. You will notice that the xylem vessels have taken the stain indicating that the solution moves through xylem.

PYQs Previous Years' Questions

1 Mark Questions

Multiple Choice Questions

1. The pressure developed in the roots due to the continuous inward movement of water by cell to cell osmosis. **ICSE 2021-22 Sem. I**

(a) Root pressure (b) Wall pressure
(c) Turgor pressure (d) Air pressure

Ans. (a) Root pressure.

2. A shoot from a balsam plant is kept in a beaker containing eosin solution (pink). The pink colour will be distinctly seen in the **ICSE 2021-22 Sem. I**

(a) xylem (b) phloem
(c) epidermis (d) cortex

Ans. (a) xylem

3. Xylem tissue **ICSE 2021-22 Sem. I**

(a) conducts water and minerals in leaves
(b) does not conduct water and minerals in stems
(c) conducts food and nutrients to roots
(d) conducts food and nutrients to all part of the plant

Ans. (a) conducts water and minerals in leaves.

Very Short Answer Type Questions

4. Arrange and rewrite the terms in each group in the correct order to be in a logical sequence beginning with the term that is underlined:

Water vapour, <u>Soil water</u>, Leaves, Ascent of sap **ICSE 2024**

Ans. Soil water, Ascent of sap, Leaves, Water vapour.

5. Arrange and rewrite the terms in each group in the correct order so as to be in a logical sequence beginning with the term that is underlined. **ICSE Specimen 2023**

Xylem, <u>Soil water</u>, Cortical cells, Root hair

Ans. Soil water, Root hair, Cortical cells, Xylem.

6. Rewrite the correct terms in the correct order so, as to be in a logical sequence.

Endodermis, cortex, soil water, xylem, root hair. **ICSE Specimen 2023, 2013, 2010, 2008, 2006**

Ans. The correct logical sequence is

Soil water, root hair, cortex, endodermis, xylem.

7. Correct the statement by changing the underlined word <u>Xylem</u> transports starch from the leaves to all parts of the plant body. **ICSE 2018**

Ans. Phloem.

8. Given below is a set of terms arranged in logical sequence, representing a process or a function. Of these, one term is incorrect. Identify the incorrect term and replace it with the correct term.

Soil water → root hair → cells of cortex → epidermis → xylem. **ICSE 2017, 2007**

Ans. **Incorrect term** Epidermis

Correct term Endodermis

9. Given below is an example of a certain structure and its special functional activity. On a similar pattern fill in the blanks with suitable functions.

Example: Chloroplast and Photosynthesis
Xylem and .... **ICSE 2015**

Ans. Upward water transport in plants.

10. Explain the term root pressure. **ICSE 2009**

Ans. The pressure generated by the cortical cells of the root which pushes the water and minerals into the xylem vessels of the root for upward conduction of water upto stem level is known as root pressure.

11. Write the name of the organ that transports water from the soil to other parts of the plant. **ICSE 2007**

Ans. Xylem transports water from soil to other parts of the plant.

12. Given below is the set of terms, rewrite the terms in the correct order so, as to be in a logical sequence.

Cortical cell, root hair, xylem, water, veins. **ICSE 2004**

Ans. The correct logical sequence is

Water, root hair, cortical cell, xylem, veins.

13. Given below is the functional activity of a structure in the body of living organisms. Name the structure responsible for the same.
Transports manufactured food from leaves to other parts of the plant. **ICSE 2002**

Ans. Phloem transports manufactured food from leaves to other parts of the plant.

2 Marks Question

14. Name the following

(i) The tissue responsible for ascent of sap in plants.
(ii) The pressure which is responsible for the movement of water molecules across the cortical cells of the roots. **ICSE 2003**

Ans. (i) Xylem tissue is responsible for ascent of sap in plants.

(ii) Osmotic pressure is responsible for the movement of water molecules across cortical cells of the roots.

Concept Enhancer It is seen that snails are killed by sprinkling salt on them. This is due to the process of osmosis that they end up loosing water as the liquid inside them tends to dilute the salt concentration outside.

5 Marks Question

15. The following paragraph is related to absorption of water from the soil. Copy and complete the following paragraph by selecting the correct word from those given in the box. You may use the term only once. **ICSE Specimen 2019, 2017**

exosmosis, hypertonic, osmosis, isotonic, hypotonic, cortical cells, endosmosis

Water enters the root hair from the soil by the process of ..... . This is because the solution in the soil is ....., whereas the cell sap in the root hair cell is .... The water then passes through the ..... cells by cell to cell ..... and reaches the xylem of the root.

Ans. Water enters the root hair from the soil by the process of **endosmosis**. This is because the solution in the soil is **hypotonic**, whereas the cell sap in the root hair cell is **hypertonic**. The water then passes through the **cortical cells** by cell to cell **osmosis** and reaches the xylem of the root.

Diagram Based Questions

16. The figure given below is a diagrammatic representation of a part of the cross section of the root in the root hair zone. Study the same and then answer the questions that follows.

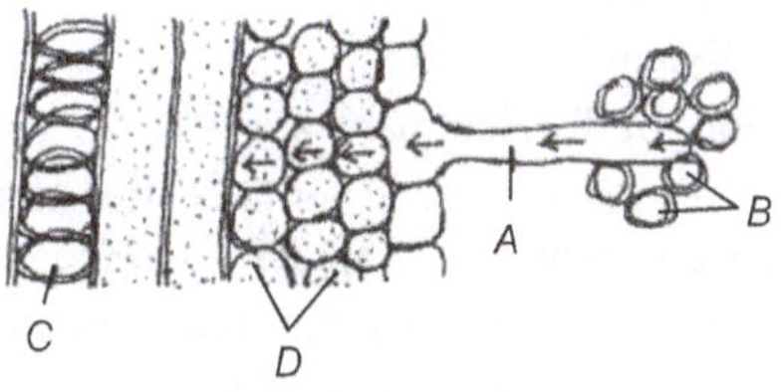

(i) Name the parts indicated by the guidelines *A* to *D*.

(ii) Which is the process that enables the passage of water from the soil into the root hair?

(iii) Name the pressure that is responsible for the movement of water in the direction indicated by the arrows. Define it.

(iv) Due to an excess of this pressure sometimes drops of water are found along the leaf margins of some plants especially in the early mornings. What is the phenomenon called?

(v) Draw a well-labelled diagram of the root hair cell as it would appear if an excess of fertiliser is added to the soil close to it. **ICSE 2016 (5M)**

Ans. (i) *A*–Root hair

B–Water molecules

C–Xylem

D–Cortex

(ii) Endosmosis

(iii) Osmotic pressure (Refer to text on page no. 32)

(iv) Guttation

(v)

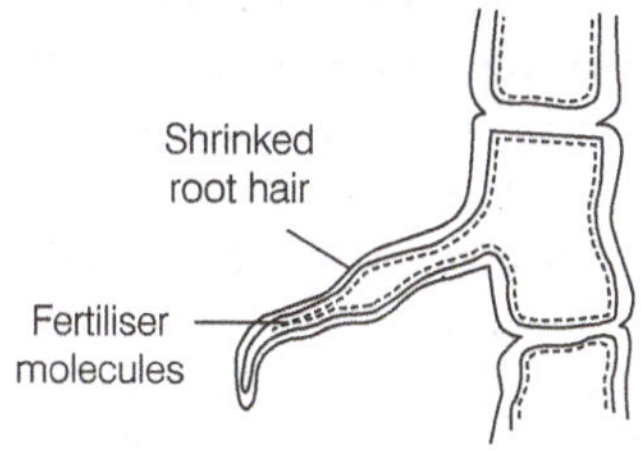

Diagram showing shrinking/ loosening/ flaccid condition of root hair

17. Given below are the diagrams of plant cells as seen under the microscope after having been placed in two different solutions.

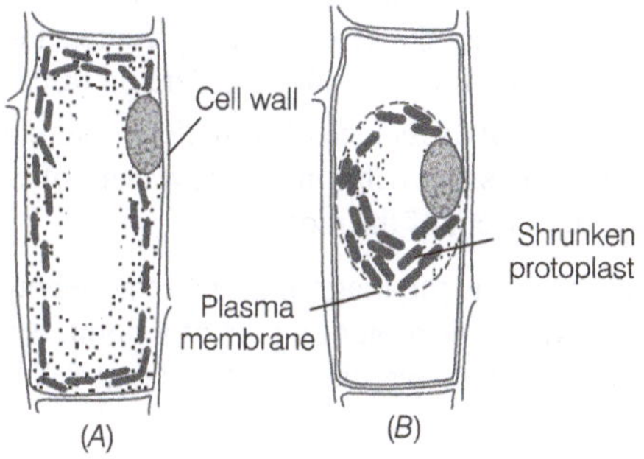

(i) What is the technical term for the condition of

(a) cell (*A*)

(b) cell (*B*) ?

(ii) From the solutions given in brackets (water, strong sugar solution, 1% salt solution) name the solution into which

(a) cell (*A*) was placed

(b) cell (*B*) was placed before being viewed under the microscope

(iii) Under what conditions in the soil will root hair cell resemble

(a) cell (*A*)

(b) cell (*B*) ?

(iv) Name the pressure responsible for the movement of water from the root hair cell to the xylem of the root. How is it setup?

(v) Name the pressure that helps in the movement of water up the xylem of the root. **ICSE 2008 (5M)**

Ans. (i) The technical term used for the condition shown by cell (*A*) is turgid and for the condition shown by cell (*B*) is plasmolysed or flaccid.

(ii) Cell (*A*) was placed in water solution whereas, cell (*B*) was placed in strong sugar solution before being viewed under the microscope.

(iii) The root hair cell will resemble cell (*A*) in the condition when the field is overflooded. The root hair cell will resemble cell (*B*) in case of excessive application of fertilisers in the fields.

(iv) Root pressure is responsible for the movement of water from the root hair cell to the xylem of the root. This pressure is built up due to cell to cell osmosis in the root tissues.
As one turgid cell presses the next cell, the force of the flow of water increases inward. When the water reaches the xylem vessels, it enters the pores of their thick walls with considerable force.

(v) Cell to cell difference of osmotic pressure and turgor pressure helps in the movement of water up the xylem of the root.

18. Given below is the diagrammatic representation of the transverse section of a part of a plant. Study the same and answer the questions that follows

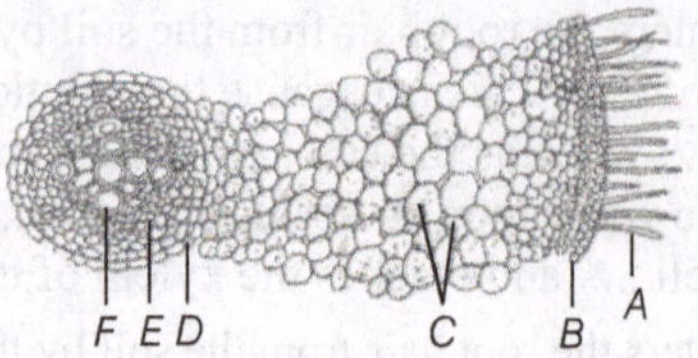

(i) Name the part of the plant that is shown.
(ii) Label the parts *A* to *F*, indicated in the diagram.
(iii) Write the functions of parts *C* and *E*. **ICSE 2005 (3M)**

Ans. (i) Part of the plant shown in the figure is the internal structure of a root.

(ii) Different parts can be labelled as

A — Root hair
B — Epidermis
C — Cortex
D — Endodermis
E — Phloem
F — Xylem

(iii) Functions of different parts are

Part *C* (Cortex) The cells of the cortex store food and also conduct water from epidermis to the inner tissues.

Part *E* (Phloem) Phloem transports organic food made in leaves to storage organs of the plant.

CHAPTER TEST

Section-A

01 Mark Questions

1 Select the correct answers to the questions from the given options. (Do not copy the question, write the correct answer only)

(i) The structure which increase the area of absorption of water is

(a) root epidermis (b) root cap
(c) root hair (d) endodermis

(ii) Wooden frames of doors get jammed during the monsoon because of

(a) osmosis (b) diffusion
(c) imbibition (d) exosmosis

(iii) When plant cell is placed in a medium containing concentrate solution the plant cell becomes

(a) turgid (b) flaccid
(c) deplasmolysed (d) cell remain same

(iv) Under what conditions there will be no net flow of water in a system? (TP= Turgor pressure, WP=Wall pressure)

(a) TP>WP (b) WP>TP
(c) TP=WP (d) TP ⋝ WP

(v) The mechanism of transport of molecules (ions) against a concentration gradient with the expenditure of energy is called

(a) diffusion
(b) passive absorption
(c) active absorption
(d) imbibition

2 (i) Name the following

(a) Area of the roots where most absorption of water and minerals takes place.

(b) Water absorbed by solid particles without formation of solution.

(c) Instrument used to measure osmotic strength of solution.

(d) Movement of molecules of a substance from their higher concentration to lower concentration when they are in direct contact.

(ii) Arrange and rewrite terms in each group in the correct order so as to be in a logical sequence beginning with term that is underlined.

(a) <u>Root cap</u>, Zone of cell maturation, Zone of cell elongation, Zone of cell division.

(b) <u>Water,</u> Cortical cell, Root hair, Xylem, Veins.

(c) <u>Epidermis,</u> Pericycle, Endodermis, Cortex, Xylem.

(d) <u>Soil,</u> Root hair, Epidermis, Secondary cortex, Endodermis, Pericycle.

(iii) Match the items given in Column I with the most appropriate ones in Column II and rewrite the correct matching pairs.

Column I	Column II
A. Absorption of water	1. Xylem
B. Transpiration	2. Imbibition
C. Transportation of water	3. Stomata
D. Swelling of dry seeds	4. Root hairs

(iv) Choose the odd one out from the following terms and name the category to which the other belong.

(a) Swelling of dry seeds, Swelling of wooden doors, Swelling of plant cell, Swelling of raisins.

(b) Root hair, Xylem, Water, Phloem

(c) Starch, Mesophyll cell, Chloroplast, Phloem, Xylem

(d) Diffusion, Imbibition, Active absorption, Passive absorption

(v) State the exact location of the following structures.

(a) Root cap
(b) Root hair
(c) Stomata

02 Marks Questions

3 Define imbibition. Give one example.

4 What is diffusion? Write the significance of diffusion.

5 What is osmosis?

6 What do you mean by osmotic pressure?

7 Define cohesion and adhesion.

03 Marks Questions

8 Differentiate between diffusion and osmosis.

9 What do you mean by hypotonic, isotonic and hypertonic solution.

10 Explain root pressure theory.

11 Differentiate between plasmolysis and deplasmolysis. Give example of each.

12 Explain in brief the role of root in absorption of water and minerals.

Section-B

Diagram Based Questions

13 The diagram is showing a stem girdled by removing a ring of bark, leaving the xylem intact. A bulge develops above the girdle in a few weeks.

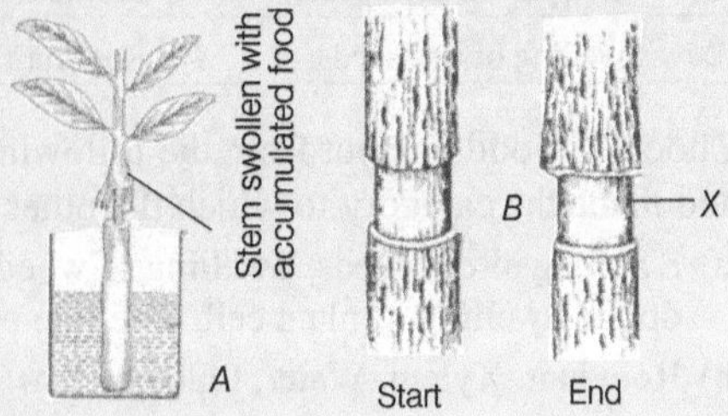

(i) Which part of the stem of the plant is removed in the form of a girdle or ring?

(ii) Which part of plant continue to get a supply of water through the deeper located xylem?

(iii) Identify the labelled '*X*'.

(iv) In this experiment, which part dies first?

14 A cell '*P*' after immersion in a '*X*' solution showing the successive stages of protoplasm. Study the diagram and answer the questions that follow

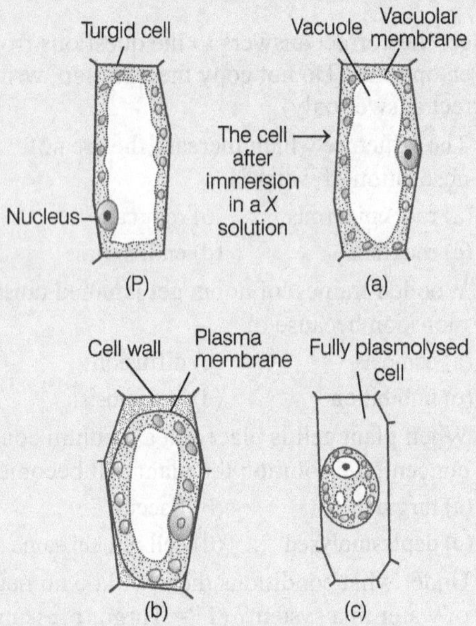

(i) Name the solution '*X*'.

(ii) Identify the turgid cell and flaccid cell.

(iii) Define plasmolysis.

Answers

1. (i) (c), (ii) (c), (iii) (b), (iv) (c), (v) (c)

04

Transpiration in Plants

TREND ANALYSIS 4 YEARS

Average No. of Questions Across all Sets

	Types of Questions	2024	2023	2020	2019
Transpiration in Plants	1 Mark	1	3	–	–
	2 Marks	1	2	–	–
	3 Marks	–	–	–	–
	4 Marks	–	–	–	–
	5 Marks	–	–	–	1

Transpiration is the evaporative loss of water by the aerial parts of plants (such as leaves, etc.) in the form of water vapour. It is a vital process both plants and environment and consequently for humans.

Transpiration can be of following types depending on the parts of the plant

(i) **Cuticular Transpiration** This occurs through cuticle of leaves and stems of plants.

(ii) **Lenticular Transpiration** This occurs through the open structures present on the bark of the woody stems known as lenticels.

(iii) **Stomatal Transpiration** This occurs through stomata present in leaves. It is the type of transpiration which contribute mainly in the loss of water from plants (more than 95%), while the other two types play role in gaseous exchange.

Structure of Stomata

- These are the minute pores found in the epidermal layer of leaves and green stems. Each stoma (Pl. stomata) is surrounded by two **guard cells**.
- Apart from transpiration stomata also help in exchange of gases, i.e. O_2 and CO_2 in the leaves. During the day time, stomata are open for intake of CO_2 to take part in photosynthesis.
- Stomata vary in number in various types of plants.
- In **isobilateral leaves** (mostly in monocots), same number of stomata are found on the upper and the lower surfaces, whereas in **dorsiventral leaves** (mainly found in dicot plants), the number of stomata are very few on upper surface in comparison to those found on lower surface.

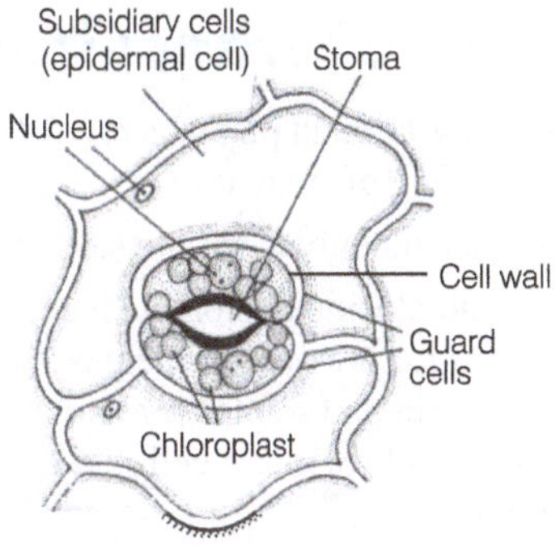

Fig. 4.1 Stomata

Mechanism of Stomatal Transpiration

- A large number of spongy mesophyll cells present in the leaves (between the upper and lower epidermis) have their surfaces exposed to the intercellular spaces.
- The intercellular spaces communicate through stomata with the outer atmosphere and give off some water in the form of water vapours.
- The osmotic diffusion of water from xylem vessels (in leaves) maintains the turgidity of mesophyll cells.
- Water tends to evaporate from these cells thus, saturating the air in the intercellular spaces.
- The water from the intercellular spaces get diffused into the other connecting intercellular spaces and finally reaches to the sub-stomatal space.
- From here it escapes out through the stomata.
- This complete movement of water vapour from the cell surface to the outer atmosphere occurs through the process of diffusion.

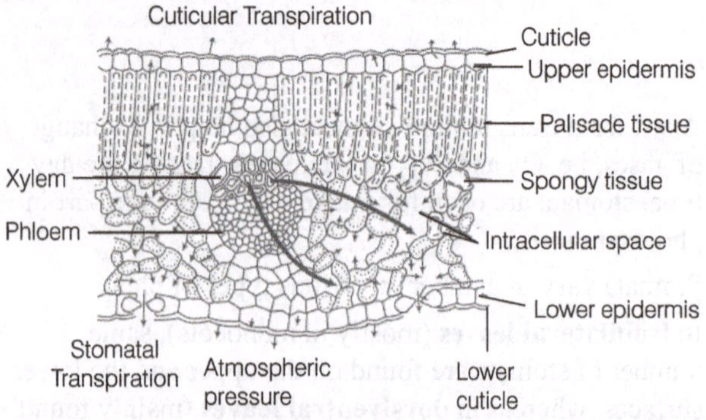

Fig. 4.2 Vertical section of leaf indicating diffusion of water vapour through stomata

Regulation of Transpiration

- Process of transpiration in plants is regulated by the opening and closing of stomata.
- Transpiration occurs only when the stomata are open.
- This opening and closing of stomata is regulated by the change in the turgor pressure of the guard cells or by the amount of water and solutes present in the guard cells. The inner walls of guard cells are thick and elastic in nature.
- The opening and closing of stomata can be understand by the following theory

Potassium Ion Exchange Theory

- According to the potassium ion exchange theory, the guard cells become turgid when K^+ gradient is setup in the cells (during day time). This causes the stomatal pores to open up and transpiration occurs.
- At night, reverse happens, i.e. the K^+ ions leak out, turning the guard cells flaccid. Thus, closing the stomatal pores.
- The process of opening and closing of stomata is outlined below

Opening of stomata	**Closing of stomata**
During day/light	During night/dark
⇓	⇓
Accumulation of K^+ ions by the guard cells	Loss of K^+ ions by the guard cells
⇓	⇓
Increased solute concentration of guard cells	Decreased solute concentration in them
⇓	⇓
This decreases water potential in them	This increases water potential in them
⇓	⇓
Endosmosis of water in guard cells	Exosmosis of water in guard cells occur
⇓	⇓
Leads to increased turgidity and thus stretching outer wall	Decreases turgidity making guard cell flaccid
⇓	⇓
Stoma open	Stoma close

Factors Affecting the Rate of Transpiration

The rate of transpiration can be affected by following factors

External Factors

(i) **Temperature** Transpiration increases with increase in temperature and *vice-versa*.

(ii) **Humidity** If air is humid, transpiration will be reduced.

(iii) **Intensity of sunlight** Transpiration is more in high intensity, i.e. in day light.

(iv) **Carbon dioxide concentration** Transpiration decreases with the increase in CO_2 concentration (above 0.03%).

(v) **Velocity of wind** Transpiration increases with the velocity of wind.

Internal Factors

(i) **Leaf area** Larger leaves lose more water than smaller ones.

(ii) **Age of plants** Rate of transpiration is slow at the seedling stage, maximum at maturity and gradually decreases near senescence (ageing).

(iii) **Water content of leaves** The leaves wilt to reduce transpiration if the water content of leaves decreases due to insufficient absorption of water by roots.

Significance of Transpiration

Transpiration acts as a significant phenomenon for the plants.

Some major advantages of transpiration are given below

- Helps in exchange of gases in the plants.
- Provides cooling effect.
- Increases the upward movement of water into xylem.
- Influences the movement of minerals along with water absorption.
- Maintains the shape and structure of plant parts by keeping the cells turgid.
- Controls the rate of absorption of water by roots through transpiration pull.

Disadvantages of Transpiration

If excess amount of transpiration occurs, it may lead to

- wilting of plants which can be lethal at times.
- premature falling of leaves.
- also reduce the production of flowers and fruits.

Adaptations in Plants to Reduce Excessive Transpiration

Many plants that grow in unfavourable conditions, i.e. dry, humid climate have evolved a number of permanent adaptations in order to reduce the rate of transpiration. Some of them are given below

- Presence of sunken stomata (e.g. *Nerium*).
- Presence of thick cuticle on leaves (e.g. Banyan).
- Presence of reduced number of stomata.
- Presence of narrower leaves (e.g. *Nerium*).
- Loss of leaves (e.g. *Cactus*, xerophytes).
- Reducing the exposed surface area (e.g. Lavender).

Direct Loss of Water by Plants

Some plants have the property of loosing water in form of liquid directly and not as water vapour. This can occur in the following two ways

1. Guttation

- It occurs during warm humid conditions, i.e. when the amount of root pressure is high and rate of transpiration is low.
- Many herbaceous plants (such as grass, rose, strawberry, banana, tomato etc.) tend to loose small quantities of water in the form of drops from the **hydathodes** (water glands, i.e. pores present along leaf margin).
- These tiny drops appear mainly along the margins or tips of the leaves especially during the early morning time. Thus, guttation is the process by which the sap escapes from leaf tips. .

2. Bleeding

The exudation of cell sap from any injured or cut part of a plant due to increased root pressure is called bleeding.

Differences between Transpiration and Guttation

Transpiration	Guttation
Loss of water in the form of water vapour.	Loss of water in the form of water droplets.
Occurs in the presence of sunlight.	Does not require sunlight, seen in early morning.
Water loses through stomata, lenticels and cuticles.	Water loses through hydathodes.
Provides cooling effect to the plant body.	Does not provide any cooling effect.
May cause wilting of leaf cells by affecting turgidity.	Does not affect turgidity of leaf cells.

Experiments for Transpiration

Various experiments are performed in order to demonstrate the process of transpiration. Some of them are described below

Experiment 1

Experiment to measure the loss in weight due to transpiration

- Take two test-tubes A and B filled with water. Insert a leafy shoot only (no roots) in test-tube 'A'.

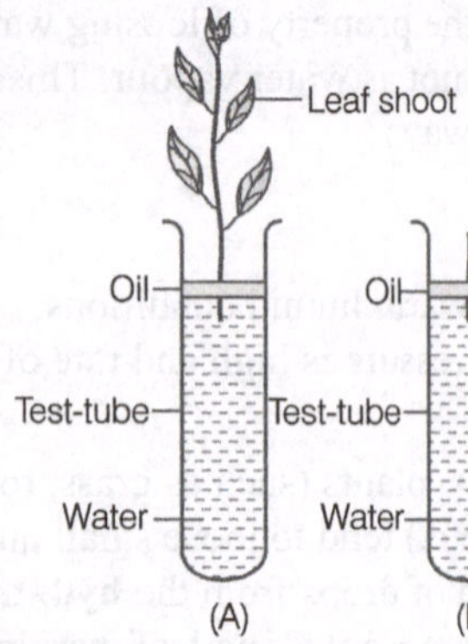

Fig. 4.3 Experiment to show loss in weight by transpiration

- Pour some oil on the surface of both test-tubes to prevent any loss of water due to evaporation.
- Weigh both the test-tubes separately and allow the set-up to stand for few hours in sunlight.
- After few hours, weigh the test-tubes again.
- You will notice that test-tube 'A' has lost some weight.
- This is because shoot of the plant inserted in test-tube 'A' has lost water in the form of water vapour by transpiration, while test-tube 'B' has same weight as there was no plant in it. Due to this, no transpiration has taken place.

Experiment 2

Experiment to show the process of transpiration

- Take two medium-sized well watered potted plants A and B (with broad leaves).
- Cover the pot completely with a polythene bag and tie the mouth firmly around the base of stem. Now, cover the entire set-up under a bell jar.
- Keep a piece of dry cobalt chloride paper by the side of the plant inside the bell jar (B).
- Take a third bell jar without plant containing a piece of cobalt chloride paper (C).
- Now, place all the three bell jars in the Sun for some time.
- After some time, following observation can be made
  (i) 'A' shows water vapour condensing on its inner walls.
  (ii) 'B' also show similar condensation and simultaneously, the blue cobalt chloride paper would turn pink.
  (iii) 'C' does not change at all or there are no water drops on the jar's inner walls. This jar is a control which proves that there was no moisture in the air as there was no plant in it.

These jars give double visual proof of transpiration due to following reasons

(a) Condensation of water vapour into droplets.
(b) Change of colour in cobalt chloride paper from blue to pink is due to the presence of water.

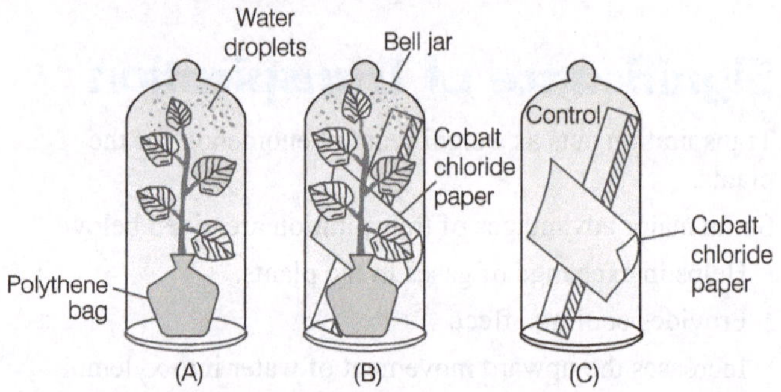

Fig. 4.4 An experiment to demonstrate the process of transpiration in plants

Experiment 3

Experiment to show the unequal rate of transpiration in a dorsiventral leaf.

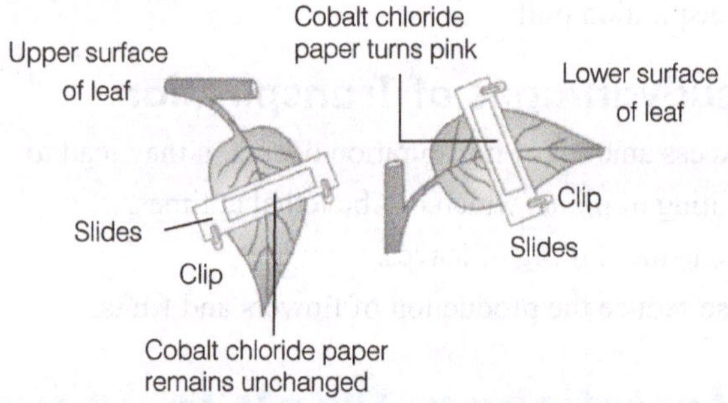

Fig. 4.5 An experiment to demonstrate unequal rate of transpiration in a dorsiventral leaf

- Take a dorsiventral leaf.
- Attach dry cobalt chloride paper to both the surfaces of leaf with the help of the clips.
- The leaf should remain attached to the plant.
- It is observed that the cobalt chloride paper present on the upper surface of leaf does not turn pink or turns pink in a much longer time whereas the cobalt chloride paper present on the lower surface of leaf turns pink much faster.
- Thus, the experiment proves that unequal rate of transpiration occurs in a dorsiventral leaf.

Experiment 4

Experiment to measure the rate of transpiration by the use of Ganong's potometer

- Take Ganong's potometer (a device used to measure the rate of water uptake by a leafy shoot).
- To initiate the experiment, cut a twig of a suitable plant with a sharp knife and fix it into the upper end of the apparatus.
- Fill the entire apparatus with water (it is to be noted that there should be no air spaces in between).

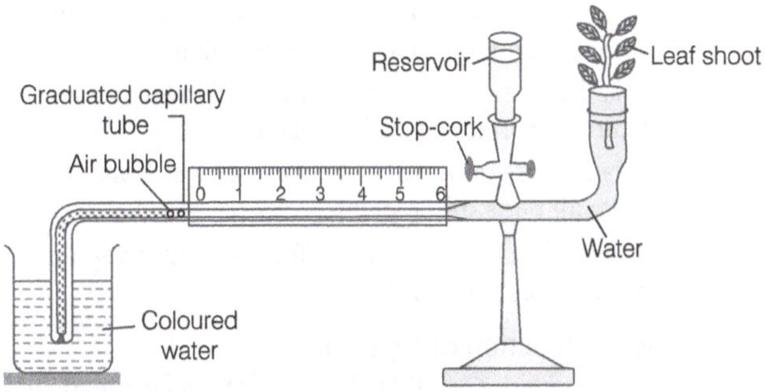

Fig. 4.6 Ganong's potometer for measuring water uptake

- Introduce an air bubble into the horizontally graduated capillary tube (dipped inside the beaker). By introducing the air bubble, the rate of water uptake can be easily calculated.
- This can be done by noting the movement of the air bubble over a fixed distance on the scale of the capillary tube.
- The reservoir in the apparatus helps to bring the air bubble back to its original position. This can be done by releasing some more water into the capillary tube by opening the stop-cork.
- Leave the apparatus undisturbed for some time.
- After few hours you will observe that the air bubble has started moving through the horizontal capillary tube of potometer.
  This can be easily detected by noting the readings given on the capillary tube scale.
- This experiment shows that as the process of transpiration proceeds, a suction force is set-up which pulls the water from the beaker and makes the bubble to move along.Some limitations of potometer are given below
  (i) Introducing the air bubble into the capillary tube is difficult.
  (ii) Amount of water lost during transpiration is not measured.
  (iii) Position of air bubble may get affected due to the change in the outside air temperature.

PYQs Previous Years' Questions

1 Mark Questions

Multiple Choice Questions

1. The process in which water is lost from the margins of strawberry leaves is **ICSE 2024**
   (a) osmosis
   (b) imbibition
   (c) diffusion
   (d) guttation

Ans. (d) cobalt chloride paper

2. The paper used to demonstrate unequal transpiration in a dicot leaf is **ICSE 2023**
   (a) filter paper
   (b) litmus paper
   (c) starch paper
   (d) cobalt chloride paper

Ans. (d) cobalt chloride paper

3. Ganong's potometer is used to study **ICSE Specimen 2023**
   (a) Photosynthesis
   (b) Rate of uptake of water
   (c) Exosmosis
   (d) Guttation

Ans. (b) Rate of uptake of water

4. Explain the term guttation. **ICSE Specimen 2023, 2021-22 Sem. I, 2007**
   (a) The loss of water in the form of water droplets from the surface of the leaf
   (b) The loss of water in the form of water droplets through the stomata
   (c) The loss of water in the form of water vapour along the leaf margin
   (d) The loss of water in the form of water droplets along the leaf margin

Ans. (d) Guttation is the process by which plant loses water in the form of droplets through pores (hydathodes).

5. The factor that does not affect the rate of transpiration. **ICSE Specimen 2021-22 Sem. I**

(a) Intensity of light (b) Velocity of wind
(c) Carbon dioxide (d) Oxygen

Ans. (d) Oxygen

6. State the exact location of stomata. **ICSE Specimen 2021-22 Sem. I**

(a) More on the upper surface of the dorsiventral leaves
(b) More on the lower surface of the dorsiventral leaves
(c) Both upper and lower surface of the dorsiventral leaves
(d) None of the above

Ans. (b) More on the lower surface of the dorsiventral leaves

7. State the function of

(i) Guard cells **ICSE Specimen 2021-22 Sem. I**

(a) regulate the closing of stomata
(b) regulate the opening and closing of stomata
(c) regulate the opening of stomata
(d) regulate the process of photosynthesis

(ii) Xylem

(a) translocation of food from the leaves to the other parts of the plant
(b) conduction of food
(c) conduction of water and food
(d) conduction of water and minerals from the root to the other parts of the plant

(iii) Hydathode

(a) helps in transpiration
(b) helps in guttation
(c) helps in imbibition
(d) helps in transportation of water

Ans. (i) (b) (ii) (d) (iii) (b)

8. Permanently open structures seen on the barks of old woody stems **ICSE 2021-22 Sem. I**

(a) Stomata (b) Hydathodes
(c) Lenticels (d) Epidermal pores

Ans. (c) Lenticels

9. Transpiration is useful to the plant because it **ICSE 2021-22 Sem. I**

(a) creates a suction force for absorption of water from the soil
(b) helps in photophosphorylation
(c) synthesises glucose
(d) splits water molecules

Ans. (a) Creates a suction force for absorption of water from the soil.

10. Mention the exact location of guard cells. **ICSE 2021-22 Sem. I**

(a) Around the root hairs (b) Around the lenticels
(c) Around the thylakoids (d) Around the stoma

Ans. (d) Around the stoma

11. Explain the term 'transpiration'. **ICSE 2021-22 Sem. I**

(a) It is the loss of water in the form of droplets from the aerial parts of the plant
(b) It is the loss of water in the form of water vapour from the underground parts of the plant
(c) It is the loss of water in the form of water vapour from the aerial parts of the plant
(d) It is the loss of water in the form of water vapour from all parts of the plant

Ans. (c) It is the loss of water in the form of water vapour form the aerial parts of the plant

12. State the function of 'hydathodes'. **ICSE 2021-22 Sem. I, Specimen 2019**

(a) Transpiration (b) Absorption of water
(c) Photosynthesis (d) Guttation

Ans. (d) Guttation

13. State the function of the cuticle on leaves. **ICSE 2021-22 Sem. I**

(a) Prevents photosynthesis
(b) Reduces transpiration
(c) Protects leaves from grazing animals
(d) Gives colour to leaves

Ans. (b) Reduces transpiration

14. Which one of the following does not affect the rate of transpiration? **ICSE 2021-22 Sem. I**

(a) Light (b) Humidity
(c) Wind (d) Age of the plant

Ans. (d) The rate of transpiration is not affected by the age of plant.

15. Choose the correct answer from the options given below.

The rate of transpiration will be fastest when the day is **ICSE Specimen 2019**

(a) hot, humid and windy
(b) cool, humid and windy
(c) hot, humid and still
(d) hot, dry and windy

Ans. (d) hot, dry and windy

Very Short Answer Type Questions

16. Name the following. **ICSE 2023**

The openings on the barks of trees through which transpiration occurs.

Ans. Lenticels

17. Define the term transpiration. **ICSE 2023**

Ans. Transpiration is the process in which water is lost as water vapour from the aerial parts of the plants through stomata.

18. Guttation takes place through ......

Ans. Hydathodes **ICSE Specimen 2021-22 Sem. I**

19. Name the wax-like layer on the epidermis of leaves which reduces transpiration. **ICSE 2018, 2013**

Ans. Cuticle is the water impervious protective layer covering the epidermal cells of leaves and other parts that reduces water loss during transpiration.

20. Choose between the two options to answer the question specified in the brackets for the following.

An example is illustrated below

Example Corolla or calyx (Which is the outer whorl?)

Answer Calyx

Lenticels or stomata (Which one remains open always?) **ICSE 2018**

Ans. Lenticels

21. Mention the exact location of hydathodes. **ICSE 2018, 2011**

Ans. Hydathodes (water glands) are present along leaf margin.

22. State whether the following statement is true or false. If false, rewrite the correct form of the statement by changing the first word only.

Guttation is the loss of water in the form of water droplets from hydathodes. **ICSE 2017**

Ans. True

23. Give biological reasons for

'In some xerophytes leaves are modified into spines.' **ICSE 2017, 2006**

Ans. Xerophytes grow in scarcity of water. So, in order to decrease the rate of transpiration, their leaves are modified into spines or reduced in size.

24. Give appropriate biological/technical term for

'An apparatus that measures the rate of water uptake in a cut shoot due to transpiration.' **ICSE 2017**

Ans. Ganong's potometer

25. State the main function of guard cells. **ICSE 2016**

Ans. The main function of guard cells is to regulate stomatal opening and closing.

26. Due to an excess of the pressure sometimes drops of water are found along the leaf margins of some plants especially in the early mornings. What is the phenomenon called? **ICSE 2016**

Ans. Guttation

27. Mention the exact location of the lenticels sturctures. **ICSE 2015, 2012**

Or State the function of lenticels. **ICSE 2014**

Or Give the exact location and one function of lenticels. **ICSE 2005**

Ans. The exact location of the lenticels is on the bark and roots of woody trees. Lenticels help in facilitating the process of transpiration in woody plants.

28. Rewrite and complete the following sentences by inserting the correct word in the space indicated.

The phenomenon of loss of water through a cut stem or injured part of plant is called .... **ICSE 2015**

Identify/name the following process/term for the statement given below.

Or The loss of water from injured parts of plant. **ICSE 2009**

Or Give the technical/biological term for

The exudation of sap from injured parts of a plant. **ICSE 2008**

Ans. The phenomenon of loss of water through a cut stem or injured part of plant is called bleeding.

29. Identify the odd one in a set given below and name the category to which the remaining three belongs.

Transpiration, photosynthesis, phagocytosis, guttation. **ICSE 2014**

Ans. **Odd term** Phagocytosis

All the other three terms are concerned with different processes in plants.

30. Give scientific reason why balsam plants wilt during mid day even if the soil is well watered. **ICSE 2014**

Or

Account for the given below briefly.

Herbaceous plant growing in well watered solids are found to wilt on a hot day. **ICSE 2008**

Ans. Balsam is a herbaceous plant that loses too much of water by excessive transpiration, i.e. the rate of transpiration is more than the rate of absorption.

So, their stem drops and wilts during the mid day even if the soil is well watered.

31. Give the biological/technical terms for the permanently open structures seen on the bark of an old woody stem. **ICSE 2013**

Ans. **Lenticel** is the biological term used for the permanently open structures seen on the bark of an old woody stem.

32. Differentiate between the transpiration and guttation on the basis of structures involved. **ICSE 2012**

Ans. Refer to text on page no. 49.

33. Given below is a set of five terms. Rewrite the terms in logical sequence as directed at the end of the statement.

Stoma, mesophyll cells, xylem, substomatal space, intercellular space (loss of water due to transpiration). **ICSE 2010**

Ans. The logical sequence is as follows
Xylem, mesophyll cells, intercellular spaces, substomatal space, stoma.

34. Choose the correct answer to the following statement out of the three choices given after the statement.
Loss of water as droplets from hydathodes is called

(i) transpiration
(ii) bleeding
(iii) guttation **ICSE 2010**

Ans. (iii) Loss of water as dropletes from hydathodes (water glands) is called **guttation**.

35. Explain the term bleeding in plants. **ICSE 2010, 2006**

Ans. **Bleeding** is the exudation of cell sap from any injured or cut part of a plant, due to increased root pressure.

36. Account for the leaves of certain plants roll up on a bright sunny day. **ICSE 2010**

Ans. On a bright sunny day, the cells of the leaves lose water due to transpiration and thus lose their turgidity.
This causes the leaves to roll up and thus reduce transpiration.

37. Give the specific function of the hydathodes in the plant body. **ICSE 2009**

Ans. Hydathodes are the structures involved in the guttation process that occurs in the plants.

38. Give the exact location and one function of stoma. **ICSE 2006**

Ans. **Location** Stoma is found on epidermis of the leaves.
Function Stoma helps in the process of transpiration.

39. What is Ganong's potometer used for? Write any two limitations of this apparatus. **ICSE 2005**

Ans. Ganong's potometer is used to measure the rate of transpiration.
Limitations of this apparatus are as follows

(i) Introducing air bubble is difficult.
(ii) Amount of water loss through transpiration cannot be measured.

40. Give the technical term for

'Loss of water in the form of water droplets from the margin of leaves'. **ICSE 2003**

Ans. **Guttation** is the technical term for the loss of water in the form of water droplets from the margin of leaves.

41. Mention where in the guard cells located and state its main function. **ICSE 2001**

Ans. Guard cells are the part of stomatal apparatus found in the epidermis of leaves.
Function They help to regulate the rate of transpiration by opening and closing the stomata.

42. Define transpiration. **ICSE 2001**

Ans. **Transpiration** is the loss of water in the form of water vapour from the aerial parts of plant.

43. List any two advantages of transpiration to a plant. **ICSE 2001**

Ans. Two advantages of transpiration to plants are

(i) It helps in upward movement of water and minerals in the plants.
(ii) It controls the rate of water being absorbed by the roots.

44. Note the relationship between the first two words and suggest the suitable word/words for the fourth place
Stomata : Transpiration : : Hydathodes : ..... **ICSE 2000**

Ans. Stomata : Transpiration :: Hydathodes : Guttation.

2 Marks Questions

45. Mention two advantages of transpiration. **ICSE 2024**

Ans. Two advantages of transpiration are as follows

- Helps in exchange of gases in plants.
- Controls the rate of absorption of water by roots through transpirational pull.

46. State any two adaptations in plants to reduce transpiration. **ICSE 2023**

Ans. Adaptations in plants to reduce transpiration are as follows

- The leaves in the desert plants are modified into spines to decrease the surface area for transpiration.
- A waxy layer called cuticle on the surface of the leaves lowers the transpiration rate.

47. Leaves of certain plants roll up on a hot sunny day. Explain by giving suitable reasons. **ICSE 2023**

Ans. Leaves of some plants roll up on a bright sunny day to reduce the effective surface area for transpiration. The reduced surface area ultimately reduces the rate of transpiration.

48. Give one difference between lenticels and stomata. **ICSE Specimen 2023**

Ans. Difference between lenticels and stomata is

Lenticels	Stomata
Lenticels are permanent open structures present on the bark of old woody stem.	Stomata are minute pores found in the epidermal layer of leaves and green stems. Stomata can be closed and opened.

49. Plants droop on a hot day even though the soil is well watered explain. **ICSE Specimen 2023**

Ans. Refer to answer no. 30.

50. Explain how the rate of transpiration is affected on
(i) a windy day
(ii) a foggy day **ICSE 2010, 2009**

Ans. (i) On a windy day, the rate of transpiration increases because of moving wind which removes the water vapour from surroundings of the leaves.
(ii) On a foggy day, the rate of transpiration decreases, because of high atmospheric moisture (humidity) which lowers the rate of transpiration.
- Wind velocity is directly proportional to the rate of transpiration.
- Increase in relative humidity of atmosphere decreases the rate of transpiration.

51. Mention three adaptations found in plants to reduce transpiration. **ICSE 2009**

Ans. Adaptations found in plants to reduce transpiration are given below
(i) The leaves may be covered with thick cuticle.
(ii) The stomata are sunken or reduced in some plants, specially in xerophytes.
(iii) The leaves may be absent or modified into spines as in most cacti.

Concept Enhancer Xerophytes are a group of plants that are adapted to survive in arid regions like desert and snow-covered areas by conservation of water. Examples are *Cactus*, *Cassia*, pineapple, etc.

52. Complete the following process to show how the oxygen in the air reaches a mesophyll cell of the leaf?

Oxygen in air ⟶ ☐ ⟶ ☐ ⟶ Mesophyll cell.

ICSE 2004

KEY idea
Exchange of gases occurs through stomata.

Ans. The oxygen in air reaches the stomata from which air enters to substomatal space and then to mesophyll cells.
Oxygen in air ⟶ Stoma ⟶ Air space ⟶ Mesophyll cell.

53. Briefly explain how the rate of transpiration is affected by
(i) intensity of light
(ii) humidity of the atmosphere. **ICSE 2001**

Ans. (i) In bright light the rate of transpiration increases as the stomata is wide open. In dim light, rate of transpiration gets lowered as stomata are partially closed.
(ii) The higher humidity, the lower is the rate of transpiration. The lower humidity, higher is the amount of water lost during transpiration as the evaporation rate is increased.

Concept Enhancer Any decrease in the amount of water in the atmosphere creates a gradient, causing water to move from the leaf into the atmosphere.

Diagram Based Questions

54. Given below is the diagram of an experimental setup to study the process of transpiration. Cobalt chloride papers are fixed on the upper as well as lower surface of the leaf. **ICSE 2021-22 Sem. I (5M)**

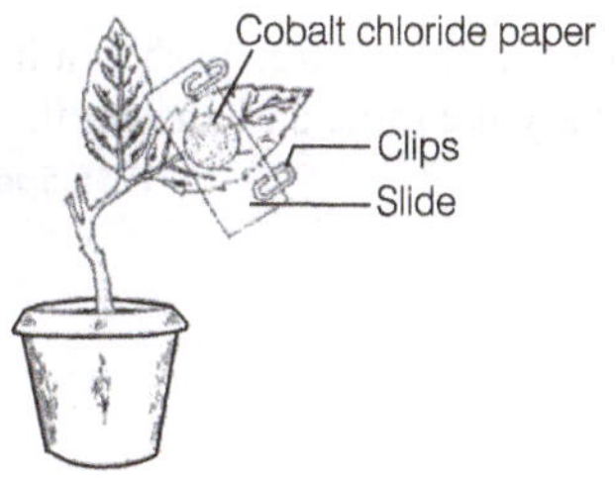

Answer the questions that follow

(i) What is the aim of experiment?

(a) To prove that more transpiration occurs from the lower surface of a dicot leaf

(b) To prove that more transpiration occurs from the upper surface of a dicot leaf

(c) To prove that transpiration is equal to both sides of the leaf

(d) To prove that transpiration does not take place in a dicot leaf

(ii) What is the colour of dry cobalt chloride paper?

(a) Pink (b) Blue

(c) Brown (d) White

(iii) After about an hour, what change if any, would you expect to find in the cobalt chloride paper placed on the upper and lower surface of the leaf?

(a) Upper surface-pink, lower surface-blue

(b) Upper surface-white, lower surface-blue

(c) Upper surface-less pink, lower surface-more pink

(d) Upper surface-more pink, lower surface-less pink

(iv) Two adaptations in plants to reduce transpiration are

(a) narrow leaves, thin cuticle

(b) fewer stomata, broad lamina of leaves

(c) thin cuticle, sunken stomata

(d) narrow leaves, fewer stomata

(v) The rate of transpiration is less when there is

(a) high humidity in the air and low temperature

(b) less humidity in the air and the decrease in atmospheric pressure

(c) bright sunlight and high temperature

(d) more wind and low intensity of sunlight

Ans. (i) (a) To prove that more transpiration occurs from the lower surface of a dicot leaf

(ii) (b) Blue

(iii) (c) Upper surface-less pink, lower surface-more pink

(iv) (d) Narrow leaves, fewer stomata

(v) (a) High humidity in the air and low temperature.

55. An outline sketch of a tree is shown in the diagram below. Study the same and answer the questions that follows. **ICSE Specimen 2019 (5M)**

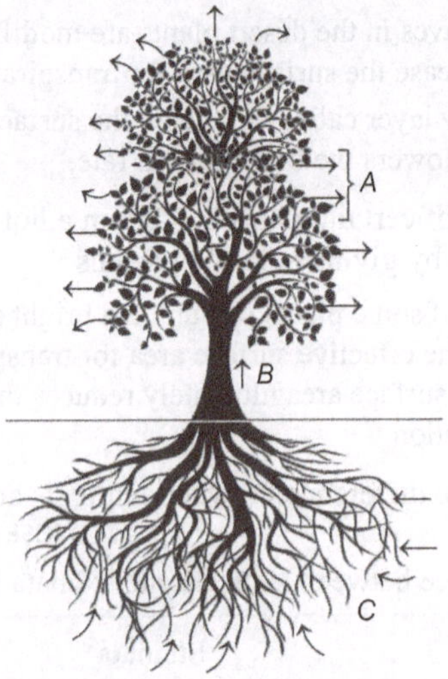

(i) Name the phenomenon that is labelled A in the diagram.

(ii) Explain the phenomenon occurring in A.

(iii) What is the importance of this phenomenon in plants?

(iv) Explain the role of any three external factors that will increase the rate of the phenomenon.

(v) What do the direction of arrows in B and C indicate?

Ans. (i) The label A shows the process of transpiration.

(ii) **Transpiration** is the evaporative loss of water by the aerial parts of plants (such as leaves, etc.) in the form of water vapour.

Transpiration can be of following types depending on the parts of the plant.

- **Stomatal transpiration** This occurs through stomata present in leaves.
- **Cuticular transpiration** This occurs through cuticle of leaves and stems of plants.
- **Lenticular transpiration** This occurs through the open structure present on the bark of the woody stems known as lenticels.

(iii) **Significance of transpiration** Transpiration acts as a significant phenomenon for the plants.

Some major advantages of transpiration are given below

- Helps in exchange of gases in the plants.
- Provides cooling effect.

- Increases the upward movement of water into xylem.
- Also influences the movement of minerals along with water absorption.
- Maintain the shape and structure of plant parts by keeping the cells turgid.
- Control the rate of absorption of water by roots through transpiration pull.

(iv) The rate of transpiration can be increased by following factors.

- **Temperature** Transpiration increases with increase in temperature and *vice-versa*.
- **Velocity of wind** Transpiration increases with the velocity of wind.
- **Leaf area** Larger leaves lose more water than smaller one.

(v) Direction of arrows *B* and *C* indicates upward-movement of water.

56. Given below is an apparatus which was setup to investigate a physiological process in plants. The setup was placed in bright sunlight. Answer the questions that follow **ICSE 2019 (5M)**

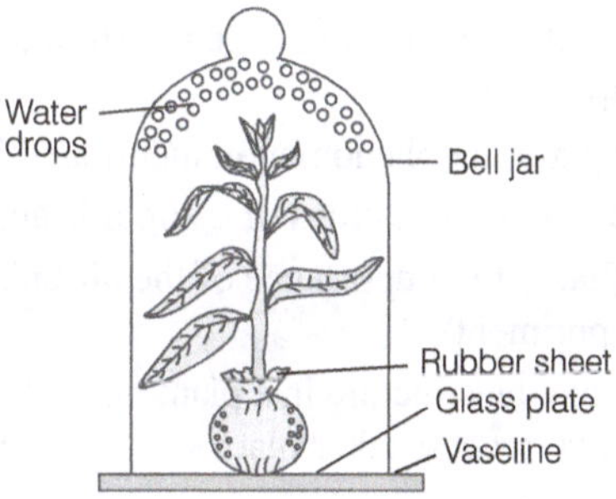

(i) Name the process being studied. Define the process.

(ii) Why was the pot enclosed in a rubber sheet ?

(iii) Mention two external factors which can accelerate the above process.

(iv) List two adaptations in plants to reduce the above process.

(v) Draw a neat, labelled diagram of a stomatal apparatus.

Ans. (i) The process being studied is transpiration. The process of loss of water in the form of vapour from the exposed or aerial parts of a plant (such as leaves, etc.) is called transpiration.

(ii) To prevent the escape of water vapours from the pot.

(iii) (a) Temperature,

(b) Velocity of wind

(iv) Adaptations to reduce the transpiration are

(a) The presence of sunken stomata.

(b) The presence of thick cuticle on leaves.

(v)

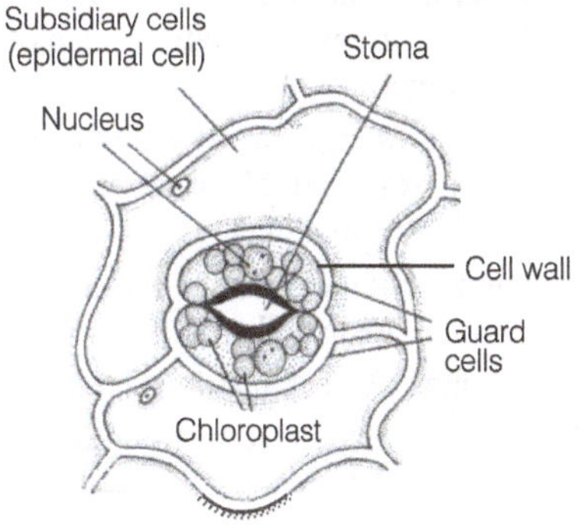

Portion of leaf epidermis showing one single stoma

57. The diagram given below represents a process in plants. The setup was placed in bright sunlight. Answer the following questions.

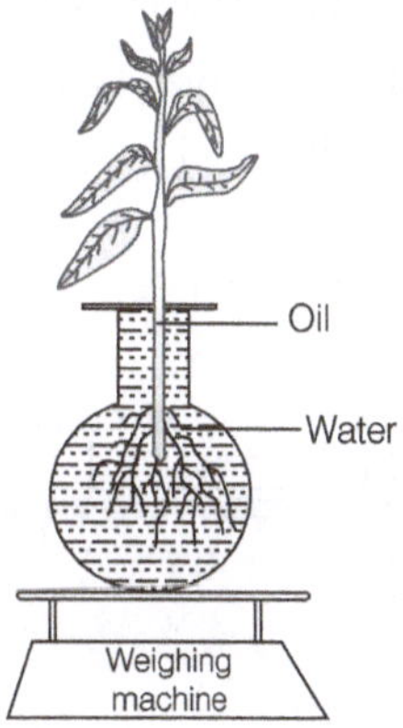

(i) Name the physiological process depicted in the diagram. Why was oil added to the water?

(ii) When placed in bright sunlight for four hours, what do you observe with regard to the initial and final weight of the plant? Give a suitable reason for your answer.

(iii) What happens to the level of water when this setup is placed in

1. Humid conditions? 2. Windy conditions?

(iv) Mention any three adaptations found in plants to overcome the process mentioned in (i).

(v) Explain the term 'guttation'. **ICSE 2018 (5M)**

Ans. (i) The given diagram shows the process of transpiration.

Oil is added to prevent any loss of water due to evaporation.

(ii) We will observe a decrease in the weight of plant due to the loss of water in the form of water vapour by transpiration.

(iii) (a) In humid conditions, there is no or very little decrease in level of water as rate of transpiration is minimum.

(b) Transpiration increases with the increase in velocity of wind. Thus, water level will decrease in windy conditions.

(iv) Adaptations found in plants to overcome excessive transpiration are as follows

(a) Presence of sunken stomata (e.g. *Nerium*).

(b) Presence of thick cuticle on leaves (e.g. banyan).

(c) Loss of leaves or leaves reduced to spines (e.g. *Cactus*, xerophytes).

(v) Guttation is the process of loss of water in the form of water droplets through hydathodes present along leaf margin. It occurs when the amount of root pressure is high and the rate of transpiration is low.

58. Observe the diagram given below and answer the questions that follow.

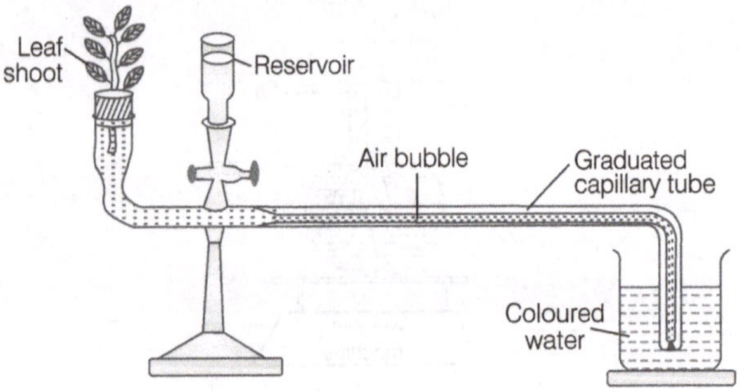

(i) Name the apparatus.

(ii) Mention one limitation of this apparatus.

(iii) Which phenomenon is studied with the help of this apparatus ?

(iv) What is the function of the part marked 'reservoir' ?

(v) What is the role of the air bubble in the experiment ? **ICSE Specimen 2017, 2016, 2007 (5M)**

Ans. (i) The apparatus given in the experiment is Ganong's potometer.

(ii) One limitation of this apparatus is that it is not easy to introduce an air bubble in the capillary tube.

(iii) With the help of this apparatus we can easily measure the rate of transpiration.

(iv) Reservoir helps in bringing back the bubble to its original position.

This can be done by releasing some water into the capillary tube by opening the stop-cork.

(v) By introducing an air bubble in the apparatus, the rate of water uptake can be calculated by noting the movement of air bubble over a fixed distance on the scale.

59. The diagram of an apparatus given below demonstrates a particular process in plants. Study the same and answer the questions that follow.

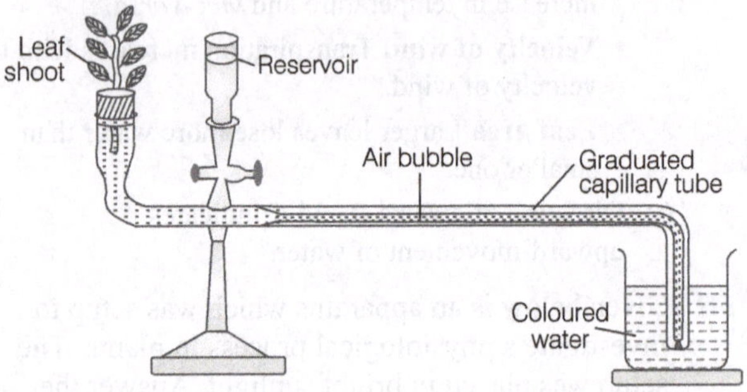

(i) Name the apparatus.

(ii) Which phenomenon is demonstrated by this apparatus?

(iii) Explain the phenomenon mentioned in (ii) above.

(iv) State two limitations of using this apparatus.

(v) What is the importance of the air bubble in this experiment?

(vi) Name the structure in a plant through which the above process takes place. **ICSE 2016 (5M)**

Ans. (i) Ganong's potometer

(ii) The phenomenon demonstrated by this apparatus is transpiration.

(iii) Transpiration is loss of water in the form of water vapours from aerial parts of the plant into the atmosphere.

(iv) Two limitations of using this apparatus are as follows

(a) Introducing the air bubble into the capillary tube is difficult.

(b) Amount of water lost during transpiration is not measured.

(v) The movement of bubble signifies the amount of water lost by transpiration.

(vi) The experiment demonstrate transpiration which takes place through stomata present on the leaves.

60. An apparatus as shown below was set up to investigate a physiological process in plants. The set up was kept in sunlight for two hours. Droplets of water were then seen inside the bell jar. Answer the questions that follow

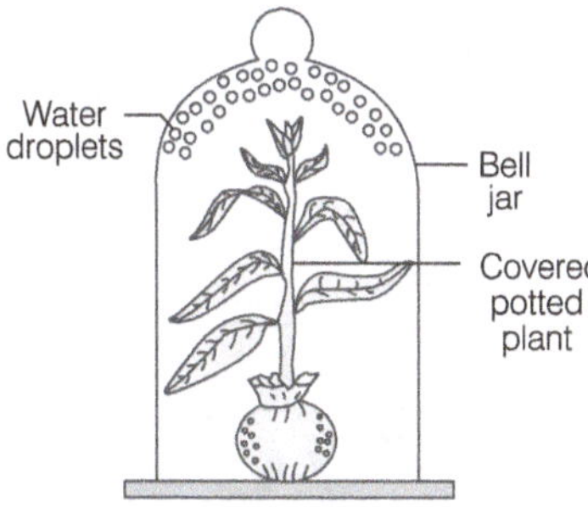

(i) Name the process being studied.
(ii) Explain the process named above in (i).
(iii) Why was the pot covered with a plastic sheet?
(iv) Suggest a suitable control for this experiment.
(v) Mention two ways in which this process is beneficial to plants.
(vi) List three adaptations in plants to reduce the above mentioned process. **ICSE 2015 (5M)**

Ans. (i) Transpiration
(ii) Transpiration is defined as the loss of water in the form of water vapours from the aerial parts of the plant.
(iii) The pot is covered with a plastic sheet so as to prevent the escape of water vapours from the pot.
(iv) The suitable control for the experiment can be similar to an empty plastic sheet (with its mouth tied) kept in the sunlight. This will not show any drops of water.
(v) The two ways in which this process is beneficial to plants are
(a) Upward movement of water and minerals by suction force.
(b) Helps in exchange of gases in the plants.
(vi) The three adaptations in plants to reduce the transpiration are
(a) the presence of sunken stomata
(b) the presence of narrower leaves
(c) the presence of thick cuticle on leaves.

61. Draw a neat diagram of the stomatal apparatus found in the epidermis of leaves and label the stoma, guard cells, chloroplast, epidermal cells, cell wall and nucleus. **ICSE 2004 (2M)**

Ans. Refer to answer no. 56 (v).

62. The figure given below represents an experimental set-up with a weighing machine to demonstrate a particular process in plants. The experimental set-up was placed in bright sunlight. Study the diagram and answer the following questions.

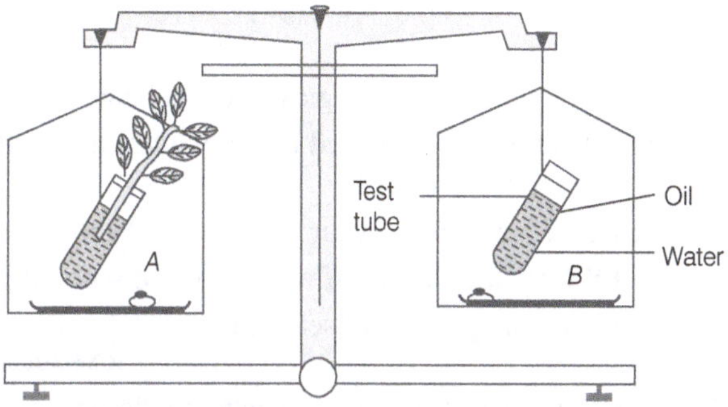

(i) Name the process intended for study.
(ii) Define the above mentioned process.
(iii) When the weight of the test tube (A and B) is taken before and after the experiment, what is observed? Give reasons to justify your observation in 'A' and 'B'.
(iv) What is the purpose of keeping the test tube 'B' in the experimental set-up? **ICSE 2014 (5M)**

Ans. (i) The process intended for study is transpiration.
(ii) Transpiration is the process of loss of water in the form of water vapour from the aerial parts of the plant.
(iii) After the experiment was observed that the test tube 'A' has raised up due to the loss of weight and in test tube 'B', the weight remains unchanged. This happens because in test tube 'A' plant undergoes the transpiration and loses water, while in test tube 'B', no transpiration occurs because there was no plant in the test tube. Also direct evaporation was prevented in test tube 'B' due to the oil present on the surface so, weight remains unchanged.
(iv) Test tube 'B' was kept in the experimental set-up as a control.

63. Study the diagram given below and answer the questions that follow.

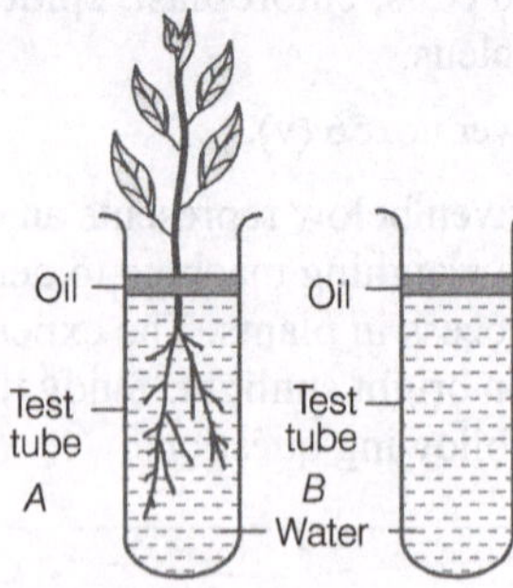

(i) Explain the physiological process being studied.
(ii) What will be observed in the two test tubes after two to three days ?
(iii) Give a reason for your answer in (ii) above.
(iv) Why is the surface of water covered with oil ?
(v) State the purpose of setting up test-tube 'B'.

ICSE 2005 (5M)

Ans. (i) The physiological process being studied is transpiration.
(ii) After 2-3 days the level of water in test-tube 'A' will go down (to a greater extent) as compared to test-tube 'B' in which the level of water remains the same.
(iii) The water in test-tube 'A' was absorbed by roots. It reaches the leaves through the xylem vessels. The process of transpiration is responsible for the loss of water through the leaves.
Therefore, the level of water in test tube 'A' falls down. In test tube 'B', there is no plant so, no transpiration has taken place. Also oil prevents the loss of water by evaporation. Therefore, the level of water remains the same.
(iv) The surface of water is covered with oil in each test-tube in order to prevent loss of water due to evaporation.
(v) Test tube 'B' has been set-up as a control in the experiment which shows that water is absorbed by roots and transpired by a plant in the test tube 'A'.

64. The apparatus shown here is Garreau's potometer designed to demonstrate unequal transpiration from the two surface of a dorsiventral leaf. Before keeping the leaf in between the cups anhydrous calcium chloride ($CaCl_2$) contained in two small vials were weighed and placed in both the cups.

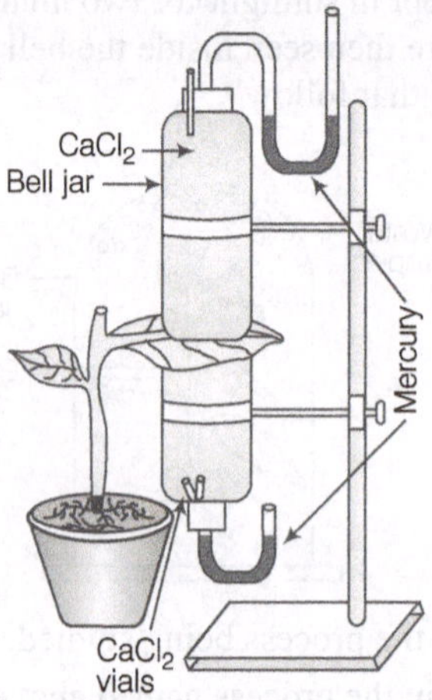

The ends of the cups were closed with corks through which two mercury manometers were connected. After a few hours, $CaCl_2$ vials were taken out and weighed again.
(i) What is the purpose of keeping $CaCl_2$ vials inside the cup ?
(ii) After a few hours $CaCl_2$ vials were taken out and weighed again. Will you expect any difference in weight? If so, give reasons.
(iii) What was the purpose of using a manometer ?
(iv) What do you mean by transpiration?

ICSE 2000 (5M)

Ans. (i) $CaCl_2$ vials were kept in order to absorb moisture, formed due to transpiration from upper and lower surface of the leaf.
(ii) Yes, because $CaCl_2$ vials will absorb water vapours given out from the surface of leaf due to transpiration and will weigh more.
(iii) Manometer has been used to check outside and inside pressures to prevent any possible entry or exit of air.
(iv) The loss of water from aerial parts of the plants in the form of water vapour is called transpiration. This occurs from the cuticle, lenticels and the stomatal parts of the plants. More than 95% loss of water occurs as water vapour from the stomata of leaves. It increases in bright light and decreases in dim light.

CHAPTER TEST

Section-A

01 Mark Questions

1 Select the correct answers to the questions from the given options. Do not copy the question, write the correct answer only

(i) The main function of guard cells is to help with ....

(a) transpiration (b) guttation
(c) transcription (d) evaporation

(ii) Transpiration is regulated by the movements of ....

(a) parenchyma cells (b) guard cells
(c) epithelial cells (d) All of these

(iii) The exudation of xylem sap drops on the edges of leaves is called

(a) transpiration (b) guttation
(c) condensation (d) None of these

(iv) Transpiration occurs through the open structures present on the bark of the woody stems are known as ....

(a) lenticels (b) cuticle
(c) stomata (d) stoma

(v) The rate of transpiration is not affected by

(a) Temperature (b) Humidity
(c) O_2 (d) CO_2

2 (i) Name the following

(a) The phenomenon of loss of water through a cut stem or injured part of plant .

(b) Permanently open structures present on woody bark.

(c) Structure present along the leaf margin through which guttation occurs.

(d) Structure present on leaf epidermis, regulated by ions.

(ii) Arrange and rewrite the terms in each group in the correct order so as to be in a logical sequence beginning with the term that is underlined.

(a) Oxygen in air, air space, stoma, mesophyll cell.

(b) Root pressure, transpiration, absorption of water, stomata.

(c) Lower surface, pink cobalt chloride paper, transpiration, blue cobalt chloride paper.

(d) Turgid guard cell, gases exchange, stomata open, stomata close, dim light.

(iii) Match the items given in Column I with the most appropriate ones in Column II and rewrite the correct matching pairs.

Column I	Column II
A. Hydathodes	1. Woody roots
B. Lenticels	2. Banyan
C. Thick cuticle	3. Leaf margins
D. Leaf spine	4. *Cactus*

(iv) Choose the odd one out from the following terms and name the category to which the others belong:

(a) Stomata, transpiration, gases exchange, starch, storage.

(b) Subsidiary cells, stoma, root hair, guard cell.

(c) Lenticels, stomata, hydathodes, chloroplasts.

(d) Temperature, humidity ,wind velocity, CO_2 concentration, O_2 concentration.

(v) State the exact location of the following structures.

(a) Hydathodes (b) Lenticels
(c) Stomata (d) Mesophyll cells

02 Marks Questions

3 Define transpiration.

4 Give the difference between stomata and hyadathode.

5 What is cuticular transpiration ? Give an example.

6 State two functions of stomata.

7 What is the significance of transpiration?

03 Marks Questions

8 Mention the adaptations in plants to reduce excessive transpiration.

9 Explain the external factors affecting the rate of transpiration.

10 Give four differences between transpiration and guttation.

11 What is guttation ? How it differs from bleeding?

12 Explain the three types of transpiration on the basis of parts involved in the process.

Section-B

Diagram Based Questions

13 The leaves of certain plants exhibit droplets of water along their margins in the morning. Study the diagram and then answer the questions

(i) Name the structure through which droplets of water oozes out.

(ii) Explain the process concerned with this diagram.

(iii) What is the reason of this process?

14 Given below is the diagram of an experimental setup to study the process of transpiration. Study the diagram and answer the following questions.

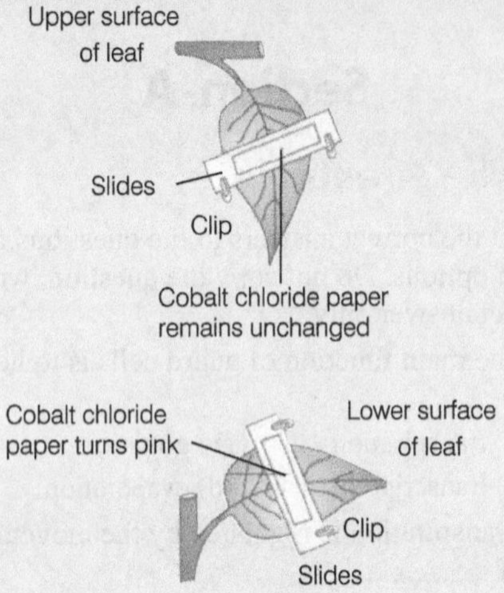

An experiment to demonstrate unequal rate of transpiration in a dorsiventral leaf

(i) What is the aim of experiment?

(ii) On which surface of leaf more transpiration occurs and why?

(iii) Give the significance of transpiration.

Answers

1. (i) (a), (ii) (b), (iii) (b), (iv) (a), (v) (c)

05

Photosynthesis

TREND ANALYSIS 4 YEARS

Average No. of Questions Across all Sets

Topic	Types of Questions	2024	2023	2020	2019
TOPIC 01 Basics of Photosynthesis	1 Mark	3	1	–	1
	2 Marks	–	–	–	–
	3 Marks	1	–	–	–
	4 Marks	–	–	–	–
	5 Marks	–	–	–	–
TOPIC 02 Different Experiments and Factors Affecting Photosynthesis	1 Mark	–	1	–	–
	2 Marks	–	–	–	–
	3 Marks	–	1	–	–
	4 Marks	–	–	–	–
	5 Marks	1	1	–	2

TOPIC 1

Basics of Photosynthesis

It is a process by which plants, some bacteria and some protists fix energy from sunlight to produce sugar in the presence of CO_2 and water with the help of chlorophyll. Over all reaction of photosynthesis can be summarised as follows

$$6CO_2 + 12H_2O \xrightarrow[\text{Chlorophyll}]{\text{Sunlight}} C_6H_{12}O_6 + 6H_2O + 6O_2\uparrow \text{ (byproduct)}$$

Chloroplast : Site of Photosynthesis

- A chloroplast is an oval, minute, double membrane bound cell organelle found typically in plant cells.
- It contains a green pigment called **chlorophyll** which absorbs light energy for photosynthesis.
- Internally, chloroplast contains a liquid proteinaceous ground substance known as **stroma** and a membrane system containing a number of disc-like sacs, known as **thylakoids**.
- At some places the thylakoids arrange themselves to form a stack of coin like structure forming a cylindrical dense granular bodies called **grana** (green in colour).
- Each stack of thylakoid sacs are connected by a structure known as **stromal lamellae**, which helps in keeping the sacs at a distance from each other.

- The chloroplasts mainly occur in chlorenchymatous cells (particularly in mesophyll) of leaves. They are also found in the guard cells of the stomata and in the outer layers of the green stems.

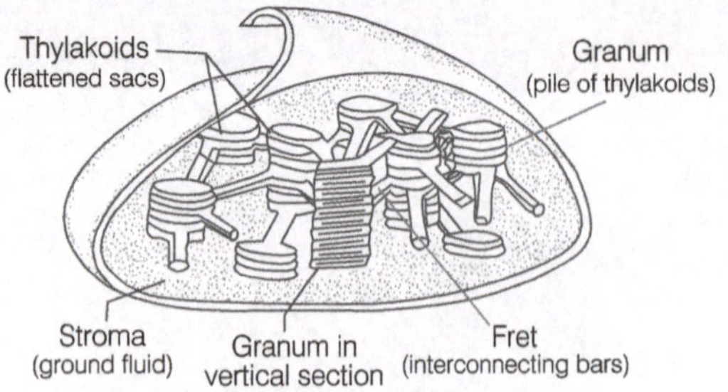

Fig. 5.1 A chloroplast showing internal structure revealed by electron microscope

Opening and Closing of Stomata

- These are the structures mainly responsible for the gaseous exchange in the process of photosynthesis, respiration and transpiration.
- In photosynthesis, they allow plants to exchange gases necessary for cellular processes.
- Stomata open during the day time, in the presence of light to allow CO_2 to diffuse in. On the other hand they get closed when plants are not photosynthesising, i.e. in the absence of light.
- The opening and closing of stomata depends on the turgidity of the guard cells, which have **inner wall** (thick and rigid) and **outer wall** (thin and elastic).

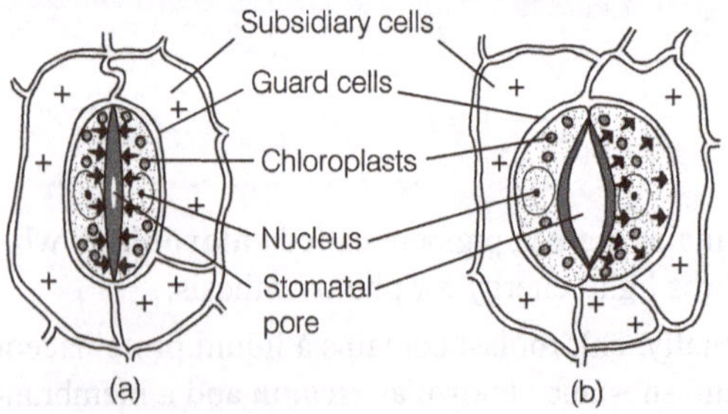

Fig. 5.2 (a) Closed stoma (b) Open stoma

- According to potassium ion (K^+) theory, the opening of stomata is due to the entry of K^+ ions in the guard cells.
- This is aided by the ATP produced by the plant during the daytime (when it photosynthesises) and leads to opening of stomata.
- The stomatal closure, on the other hand, occurs during the night time when no photosynthesis takes place.
- The K^+ ions leak out of the guard cells making the stomata lose its turgidity and thus resulting in closure of stomatal pore. A detailed description of this theory is given in the previous chapter.

Process of Photosynthesis

Photosynthetic process begins when the sunlight falls on the mesophyll cells of the leaf. The light energy is trapped by the chlorophyll present in the layers of mesophyll cells.

During the process, the raw materials, i.e. CO_2 and water together with the solar energy trapped by the chlorophyll, gets converted into chemical energy in the form of food, i.e. glucose and starch.

Phases of Photosynthesis

The process of photosynthesis takes place in the following two main steps

1. **Light Reaction** (Photochemical Phase)

This is a light dependent phase where a quick succession of chemical reactions initiated by light occurs, that is why it is also called photochemical phase.

The light of visible wavelengths, i.e. 400-700 nm are absorbed by chlorophyll molecules present in the **thylakoids** of the chloroplast.

This phase is completed into two main sub-stages

(i) **Photolysis of Water** The process of photolysis get completed into two steps

Step I Activation of chlorophyll The chlorophyll molecule gets activated by absorbing photons of the light energy.

Step II Splitting of water The absorbed energy by the activation of chlorophyll is used in splitting of water molecules into two major components, i.e. hydrogen and O_2.

$$2H_2O \xrightarrow{\text{Energy of 4 photons}} 4H^+ + 4e^- + O_2\uparrow$$

At the end of photolysis, the hydrogen ions (H^+) are picked up by a compound NADP (Nicotinamide Adenine Dinucleotide Phosphate) and gets converted into NADPH.

$$NADP^+ + e^- + H^+ \xrightarrow{\text{Enzyme}} NADPH$$

And the oxygen (O) component is released in the form of O_2 (molecular oxygen).

$$2O \longrightarrow O_2\uparrow$$

(ii) **Photophosphorylation** It is the process in which ADP (Adenosine Diphosphate) is converted into ATP (Adenosine Triphosphate) by the addition of one phosphate (Pi) group, i.e. inorganic phosphate, utilising the energy from the photons.

$$ADP + Pi \longrightarrow ATP$$

2. Dark Reaction (Biosynthetic Phase/Calvin Cycle)

- This is a light independent phase. This reaction takes place in the **stroma** or **matrix** of the chloroplast.
- The dark reaction and light reaction takes place simultaneously with the time gap of less than one thousandth of a second.
- During dark reaction, fixation and reduction of CO_2 occurs, resulting in the formation of carbohydrates by the utilisation of ATP and NADPH produced as the result of light reaction.
- RuBP (Ribulose Bisphosphate) acts as a primary acceptor of atmospheric CO_2 in the beginning of this phase and at the end of the cycle, glucose is synthesised and RuBP is regenerated.
- The overall reaction of this phase is

$$6RuBP + 6CO_2 + 18ATP + 12NADPH + 12e^- \longrightarrow 6RuBP + C_6H_{12}O_6 + 18ADP + 18Pi + 12NADP^+ + 6H_2O$$

- The hydrogen ions combine with CO_2 to form glucose which later is stored in the form of starch by the process of **polymerisation**, (where several molecules of glucose form one molecule of starch).

Adaptations of Leaves for Photosynthesis

Leaves of some plants are adapted in various ways to perform the process of **photosynthesis**. These are as follows

(i) **Presence of more stomata** to allow rapid exchange of gases like (CO_2 and O_2).

(ii) **Arrangement of chloroplasts** on the upper surface of leaves so as to receive maximum amount of light.

(iii) **Large surface area** of leaves for absorbing maximum light.

(iv) **Presence of transparent cuticle and upper epidermis** to allow light to enter freely.

(v) **Thinness of leaves** which reduces the distance between cells so as to facilitate the rapid transport of raw materials like H_2O, CO_2, etc.

(vi) **Arrangement of leaves** at right angle to the sunlight so as to trap the maximum solar radiation.

PYQs Previous Years' Questions

1 Mark Questions

Multiple Choice Questions

1. The process of conversion of ADP to ATP during photosynthesis is called **ICSE 2024, ICSE specimen 2021-22 Sem. I**

(a) polymerisation (b) photophosphorylation
(c) photorespiration (d) photolysis

Or Name the process of conversion of ADP into ATP during photosynthesis. **ICSE 2014**

Ans. (b) Photophosphorylation

2. Expand the abbreviation NADP. **ICSE 2024**

Or NADP is expanded as **ICSE 2021-22 Sem. I**

(a) Nicotinamide Adenosine Dinucleotide Phosphate
(b) Nicotinamide Adenine Dinucleotide Phosphate
(c) Nicotinamide Adenine Dinucleolus Phosphate
(d) Nicotinamide Adenosine Dinucleolus Phosphate

Or

Expand the following biological abbreviation NADP **ICSE 2013**

Ans. (b) Nicotinamide Adenine Dinucleotide Phosphate

3. Which one of the following helps in the opening of stomata? **ICSE 2024**

(a) Cobalt ions (b) Potassium ions
(c) Magnesium ions (d) Aluminium ions

Ans. (b) Potassium ions

4. The site of light reaction in the cells of a green leaf is **ICSE 2023**

(a) nucleus
(b) grana of chloroplast
(c) cytoplasm
(d) stroma of chloroplast

5. Mention the exact location of 'thylakoids'. **ICSE Specimen 2023, 2021-22 Sem. I**

Or Exact location of 'thylakoids'.

(a) In the inner membrane of the chloroplast
(b) Wall of the chloroplast
(c) In the chlorophyll
(d) In the stroma of the chloroplast

Ans. (d) A membrane system containing a number of disc-like sacs known as **thylakoids** which are located in the stroma of in chloroplast.

6. Light dependent phase of photosynthesis in green leaves takes place in **ICSE Specimen 2023**

(a) Grana of chloroplast (b) Stroma of chloroplast
(c) Nucleus of chloroplast (d) Cytoplasm of palisade cells

Ans. (a) Grana of chloroplast

7. The site of dark reaction of photosynthesis **ICSE Specimen 2021-22 Sem. I**

(a) Grana (b) Fret (c) Stroma (d) Stomata

Ans. (c) Stroma

8. Photolysis **ICSE Specimen 2021-22 Sem. I**

(a) splitting of water molecules into hydrogen ions and oxygen in the presence of light in grana
(b) splitting of water molecules into hydrogen ions and oxygen in the presence of light in the stroma
(c) splitting of water molecules into hydrogen ions and oxygen in the absence of light in grana
(d) splitting of water molecules into hydrogen ions and oxygen in the absence of light in stoma

Ans. (a) splitting of water molecules into hydrogen ions and oxygen in the presence of light in grana.

9. Stroma is **ICSE Specimen 2021-22 Sem. I**

(a) site of photolysis of photosynthesis
(b) site of photochemical phase of photosynthesis
(c) site of light dependent phase of photosynthesis
(d) site of light independent phase of photosynthesis

Ans. (d) site of light independent phase of photosynthesis.

10. Explain the term 'photosynthesis'. **ICSE 2021-22 Sem. I**

(a) It is the synthesis from carbon dioxide by non-green plants using light energy
(b) It is the synthesis of glucose by green plants from carbon dioxide using light energy
(c) It is the synthesis of glucose from carbon dioxide and water by non-green plants using light energy
(d) It is the synthesis of glucose from carbon dioxide and water by green plants using light energy

Ans. (d) It is the synthesis of glucose from carbon dioxide and water by green plants using light energy.

11. Complete the sentence given below.
Grana of chloroplast is not the **ICSE 2021-22 Sem. I**

(a) site of light independent phase
(b) site of light dependent phase
(c) site of photolysis
(d) site of photon absorption

Ans. (a) site of light independent phase

12. The individual flattened stacks of membranous structures inside the chromoplasts are known as

(a) grana (b) stroma
(c) thylakoids (d) cristae **ICSE 2016**

Ans. (c) thylakoids

Very Short Answer Type Questions

13. Write the overall chemical equation for photosynthesis. **ICSE Specimen 2023**

Ans. $6CO_2 + 12H_2O \xrightarrow[\text{Chlorophyll}]{\text{Sun light}} C_6H_{12}O_6 + 6H_2O + 6O_2$ (byproduct)

14. Mention two adaptations in leaves to perform photosynthesis. **ICSE Specimen 2023**

Or Mention any three adaptations found in plants to favour the process of photosynthesis. **ICSE Specimen 2023, 2009**

Ans. Adaptations of leaves for photosynthesis

(i) Presence of more stomata to allow rapid exchange of gases like (CO_2 and O_2).
(ii) Large surface area of leaves for absorbing maximum light.

15. Name that part of the chloroplast where the light reaction of photosynthesis takes place. **ICSE Specimen 2023, 2011**

Or

Complete the following statement by filling in the blanks with the appropriate word from the choices given in bracket and rewrite the complete statement.
The site of light reaction in the cells of a leaf is .... (grana, cytoplasm, stroma). **ICSE 2009**

Ans. Light reaction of photosynthesis takes place in the **grana/thylakoids** of the chloroplast.

16. Give the biological/technical terms for the site of photosynthesis in a plant cell. **ICSE Specimen 2019**

Ans. Chloroplasts

17. Give suitable biological reason for the statement given below.
All life on earth is supported by photosynthesis. **ICSE 2019**

Ans. Photosynthesis is important for supporting life on earth in the following ways

- It provides food to all organisms through food chain.
- Photosynthesis gives off oxygen, which acts as a life supporting gas. As a result of photosynthesis, some amount of oxygen produced is used by the plant itself for the process of respiration. But the major amount of O_2 is diffused out into the atmosphere through stomata. Thus, this oxygen which gets diffused out, is not a waste material because it acts as a life supporting gas for other living organisms including humans on earth.
- It helps in maintaining balanced level of O_2 and CO_2 in the atmosphere.
- The fossil fuels like coal, petroleum and natural gas are formed by the decomposition of photosynthetic organisms. (Any 1)

18. Differentiate between the pair on the basis of what is indicated in brackets.

Leaf and liver (form in which glucose is stored) **ICSE 2018**

Ans. Glucose is stored in the form of starch in leaves and as glycogen in liver.

19. Mention the exact function of 'thylakoids'. **ICSE 2017**

Or State the main function of thylakoids. **ICSE 2012**

Ans. Thylakoids are sac-like structure present in the matrix of chloroplasts. They mainly absorb the light energy and carry out the process of light reaction.

20. Explain the term photolysis in photosynthesis. **ICSE 2017, 2009, 2006**

Ans. Photolysis is the splitting of water molecules into proton, electron and oxygen in the presence of chlorophyll and light.

21. Differentiate between the given pair on the basis of what is mentioned in bracket.

NADP and ATP *(expand the abbreviation)* **ICSE 2017**

Ans. Difference between NADP and ATP

NADP	ATP
NADP is Nicotinamide Adenine Dinucleotide Phosphate.	ATP is Adenosine Triphosphate.

22. Briefly explain photophosphorylation. **ICSE 2016**

Or

Define the term photophosphorylation. **ICSE 2003**

Ans. **Photophosphorylation** It is the formation of ATP from ADP and inorganic phosphate in the presence of light. It occurs in light reaction of photosynthesis.

23. State the exact location of the chloroplast. **ICSE 2013**

Ans. Chloroplasts are mainly found in the **mesophyll cells** located between the upper and lower epidermis of the leaves.

24. Differentiate between the following pair on the basis of what is mentioned in bracket?
Photolysis and photophosphorylation. (definition) **ICSE 2013**

Ans. Difference between photolysis and photophosphorylation is

Photolysis	Photophosphorylation
It is a process of splitting of water molecule into two major components, i.e. hydrogen and O_2 in the presence of sunlight by activated photosynthetic pigments.	It is a process of formation of ATP from ADP and inorganic phosphate by the utilisation of energy released by electrons emitted during photolysis of water.

25. Differentiate between the following pair on the basis of what is mentioned in bracket?
Stoma and stroma (describe its structure). **ICSE 2012**

Ans.

Stoma	Stroma
Stoma is the opening of the stomata through which transpired water and respiratory gases pass.	Stroma is the part/region in the chloroplast (matrix), where dark reaction of the photosynthesis takes place.

26. Give one point of difference between the following on the basis of what is given in the bracket.
Light reaction and dark reaction. (site of occurrence) **ICSE 2010**

Ans.

Light reaction	Dark reaction
Light reaction occurs in the thylakoids/ grana of the chloroplast.	Dark reaction occurs in the stroma of the chloroplast.

27. Give the biological/technical term for the process of conversion of several molecules of glucose to one molecule of starch. **ICSE 2010**

Ans. **Polymerisation** is the biological term used for the process of conversion of several molecules of glucose to one molecule of starch.

28. Why is sleeping under a tree at night not advisable? **ICSE 2010, 2003**

Ans. Sleeping under tree at night is not advisable because plants respire at night due to which the atmosphere surrounding the tree is rich in CO_2 which is harmful for us.

29. Name the cell organelle responsible for photosynthesis. **ICSE 2009**

Ans. **Chloroplast** is the cell organelle responsible for the photosynthesis.

30. State whether the following statement is true or false. If false, write the correct form of the statement by changing the first or last word only. Photosynthesis occurs in all the cells of the plant. **ICSE 2009, 2005**

Ans. The given statement is false. The correct statement is **respiration** occurs in all the cells of the plant.

31. Name the ground substance present in a chloroplast.

Ans. **Stroma** is the ground substance present in the chloroplast. **ICSE 2009**

32. Write true or false. Correct the false statement by changing the last word only. Plants that manufacture their own food are called heterotrophs. **ICSE 2008**

Ans. The given statement is false. The correct statement is plants that manufacture their own food are called **autotrophs**.

33. Rewrite the completed explanation by inserting a key word in the space indicated by '^'. Photolysis is the splitting of water molecules into hydrogen ions and hydroxyl ions in the presence of '^' and light. **ICSE 2008**

Ans. Photosynthetic Pigment.

34. Account for the given below briefly
Animals owe their existence to chlorophyll. **ICSE 2008**

Ans. Animals owe their existence to chlorophyll because plants with chlorophyll produce the food used by all the living organisms.

35. Name the following
Cytoplasmic organelle that helps in the manufacture of starch. **ICSE 2007**

Ans. **Chloroplast** is the cytoplasmic organelle that helps in the manufacture of glucose and starch.

36. The dark reaction of photosynthesis is light independent. Write true or false. **ICSE 2007**

Ans. The statement is true.

37. Give reason–Green leaves are thin and broad.

Ans. Green leaves are thin and broad so as to provide the large surface area for trapping light and easy gaseous exchange for photosynthesis to occur. **ICSE 2007**

38. Give the exact location and one function of thylakoids. **ICSE 2005**

Ans. **Location** Thylakoids are found in chloroplast.

Function Refer to answer no. 19.

39. Given below is biological statement which is incomplete and hence, is incorrect. Rewrite the correct form of the statement by inserting a suitable word/words at the right place. Do not delete any word already given in the statement. Under the inserted word/words.
The splitting of water molecules into hydrogen ions and hydroxyl ions is termed as photolysis. **ICSE 2004**

Ans. The splitting of water molecules in the **presence of sunlight and in grana** into hydrogen and hydroxyl ion is termed as photolysis.

40. Write the full form of NADP and ADP. **ICSE 2004**

Ans. **NADP** Nicotinamide Adenine Dinucleotide Phosphate.

ADP Adenosine Diphosphate.

41. Name the part of the chloroplast where the dark reaction of photosynthesis takes place. **ICSE 2003**

Ans. Stroma of chloroplast.

42. Mention the reactants of photosynthesis. **ICSE 2002**

Ans. The reactants of photosynthesis are carbon dioxide and water (in the presence of chlorophyll and sunlight).

43. What do the abbreviation stand for ATP ? **ICSE 2002**

Ans. Adenosine Triphosphate is the full form of ATP.

3 Marks Question

44. Draw a neat labelled diagram fo chloroplast. **ICSE 2024**

Ans. Refer to fig. 5.1 on pg. no. 64.

45. Observe the diagram given below and answer the questions. **ICSE Specimen 2021-22 Sem. I**

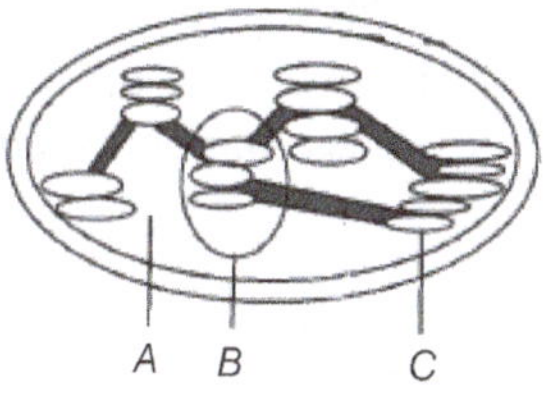

(i) Identify the cell organelle.

(a) Mitochondria (b) Lysosome
(c) Ribosome (d) Chloroplast

(ii) Label the parts marked A, B and C.

A. 1. Granum 2. Stroma 3. Fret 4. Thylakoid
B. 1. Granum 2. Stroma 3. Fret 4. Thylakoid
C. 1. Granum 2. Stroma 3. Fret 4. Thylakoid

(iii) The unit of light absorbed by chlorophyll is ....

(a) proton (b) photon (c) electron (d) neutron

Ans. (i) (d) (ii) A-2, B-1, C-4 (iii) (b)

5 Marks Question

46. Complete the following by filling in the blanks numbered (i–x) with the appropriate word/term.

Photosynthesis involves light reaction and dark reaction. During light reaction, the chlorophyll present in the (i)......... gets activated by absorbing light energy. This energy splits (ii)......... molecules to (iii) .... and oxygen and releases two electrons. This process is called (iv) .... The (v) .... ions are picked up by NADP to form (vi) .... The ADP is converted to (vii) .... This process is called (viii) .... During the dark phase, the compound produced at the end of light reaction reacts with carbon dioxide to form (ix) .... This product is converted to starch. The process is called (x) .... **ICSE 2001**

Ans. Photosynthesis involves light reaction and dark reaction. During light reaction, the chlorophyll present in the (i) **thylakoid** gets activated by absorbing light energy. This energy splits (ii) **water** molecules to (iii) **hydrogen ion** and oxygen and release two electrons. This process is called (iv) **photolysis**. The (v) **hydrogen** ions are picked up by NADP to form (vi) **NADPH$_2$**. The ADP is converted to (vii) **ATP**. This process is called (viii) **photophosphorylation**. During the dark phase, the compound produced at the end of light reaction reacts with carbon dioxide to form (ix) **glucose**. This product is converted to starch. The process is called (x) **polymerisation**.

Diagram Based Question

47. The given diagram is a diagrammatic representation of the internal structure of an organelle found in a plant cell. Study the same and then answer the questions that follow

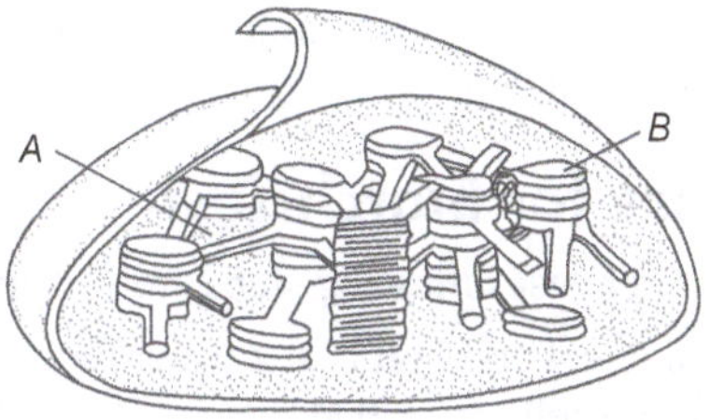

(i) Identify the organelle.

(ii) Name the physiological process occurring in this organelle.

(iii) Mention one way in which this process is beneficial to man.

(iv) Name the phases of the process occurring in the part labelled '*A*' and '*B*'.

(v) A chemical substance 'NADP' plays an active part in one of the phases. Give the expanded form of NADP and state its role in the above process.

(vi) Represent the physiological process mentioned in (ii) above in the form of a chemical equation.

ICSE Specimen 2021-22, Sem. I, 2008 (5M)

Ans. (i) The organelle shown in the diagram is chloroplast.

(ii) Photosynthesis is the process which occurs in the chloroplast.

(iii) Photosynthesis gives food and the life saving gas, i.e. oxygen.

(iv) Phases of the process occurs in parts labelled are

Part A–Dark reaction

Part B –Light reaction.

(v) Nicotinamide Adenine Dinucleotide Phosphate (NADP). It picks up hydrogen ion [H^+] during photolysis of water in light reaction.

(vi) $$\underset{\text{(Carbon dioxide)}}{6CO_2} + \underset{\text{(Water)}}{(12H_2O)} \xrightarrow[\text{Chlorophyll}]{\text{Sunlight}} \underset{\text{(Glucose)}}{C_6H_{12}O_6} + \underset{\text{(Water)}}{6H_2O} + \underset{\text{(Oxygen)}}{6O_2} \uparrow$$

TOPIC 2

Different Experiments and Factors Affecting Photosynthesis

Number of experiments have been performed to prove that various raw materials photosynthesis, i.e. light, CO_2, water, chlorophyll are necessary for photosynthesis.

Before discussing the experiments, it is important to know about the process of destarching and its importance in plants. To destarch the leaves, they are kept in a dark room (with no exposure of natural or artificial light) for 1 or 2 days. By doing this all starch from the storage organs of the leaves will be removed.

Procedure for Starch Test

For doing starch test following steps are performed

(i) Pluck the leaf and boil it in a water for a minute, so that all the cells are killed.

(ii) Remove the leaf from water and boil it into an alcohol to remove its chlorophyll. This will make leaf little hard and brittle.

(iii) Place the same leaf in boiled water again to make it soft.

(iv) Spread the leaf on a tray and add few drops of iodine solution to the boiled leaf.

(v) If the blue-black colour is observed on the leaf, it indicates the presence of starch and if the leaf turns brown in colour it shows the absence of starch.

Some of the experiments based on starch test to prove the process of photosynthesis are given below

Experiment to Show that Sunlight is Necessary for Photosynthesis

- Take a potted plant and destarch it for 48 hrs.
- Cover one of the leaf with black paper (with a design being cut).
- Keep the pot under the sunlight.
- Remove it after 1 hr and test the covered leaf for the presence of starch, by pouring iodine solution on it.
- It will be observed that uncovered leaves and the part of the leaf which was able to get light through the cut design will turn into blue-black colour which indicates the presence of starch, while the portion which was covered with black paper will turn into brown colour (showing absence of starch).
- This experiment thus, proves that the light is an essential requirement for the process of photosynthesis to take place.

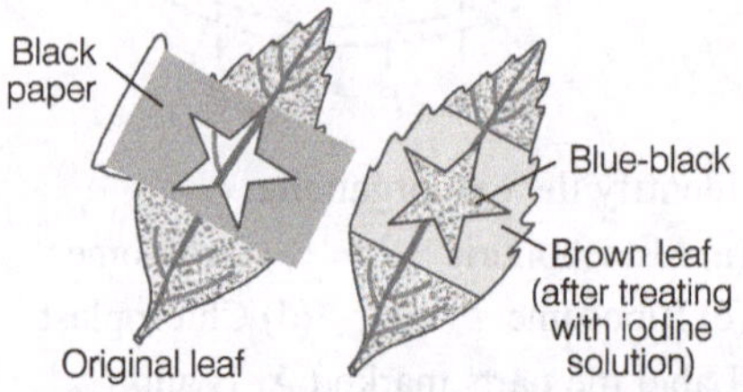

Fig. 5.3 Only the parts of the leaf exposed to sunlight give the iodine test, proving that light is necessary for photosynthesis

Experiment to Show that CO_2 is Necessary for Photosynthesis

- Take destarched potted plant.
- Take wide mouth corked bottle and put in it a strong KOH solution.
- Insert about half of the leaf inside the bottle through the split cork as shown in figure.
- Place the whole apparatus in light and test the leaf for starch after 8 hours.

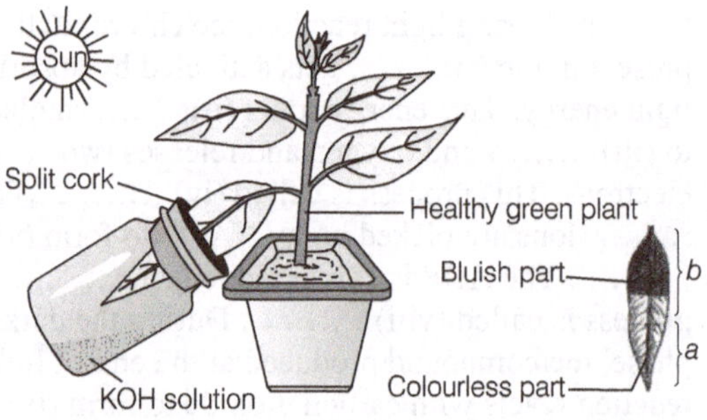

Fig. 5.4 Experiment to prove that carbon dioxide is necessary for photosynthesis

- Portion of the leaf inside the bottle and within cork gives negative test for starch because CO_2 is not present in the bottle.

Note Potassium hydroxide absorbs carbon dioxide.

Experiment to Show that Chlorophyll is Necessary for Photosynthesis

- Take a potted plant with variegated leaves (having different colour zones, i.e. green and non-green areas), e.g. *Croton*, *Coleus,* etc.
- First, destarch the leaves by keeping them in the dark room for about 2-3 days. Then restarch them by keeping the plant in the Sun.
- After few hours of keeping under the Sun, pluck on leaf. Draw the outline on a paper marking the green and non-green areas on the outline.

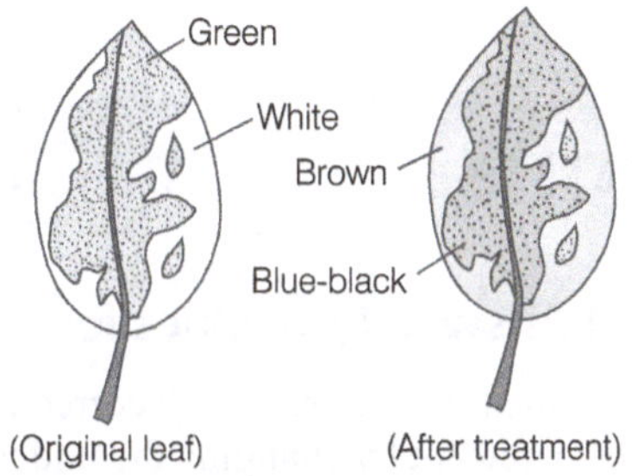

Fig. 5.5 Experiment to show that chlorophyll is necessary for photosyntheis

- Now when you will test the leaf for starch, you will observe that only the areas of leaf which were green will turn into blue-black colour showing the presence of starch, while the non-green area will not.
- This experiment proves that photosynthesis can take place only in the presence of chlorophyll, which is present is the green areas of the leaf.

Experiment to Show that Oxygen is Liberated During Photosynthesis

- Fill the beaker with pond water and keep the water plant, (e.g. *Hydrilla*) into the beaker.
- Cover the plant by a short-stemmed funnel (it is to be noted that funnel should not touch the base of the beaker).
- Now take a test-tube full of water and invert it over the stem of the funnel. Allow the set-up to stand in the sunlight for about few hours.
- After few hours you will observe the presence of bubbles in the inverted test-tube, which will get collected in the form of gas in the test-tube. The gas formed is oxygen.

This demonstrates that O_2 is liberated as a byproduct in photosynthesis.

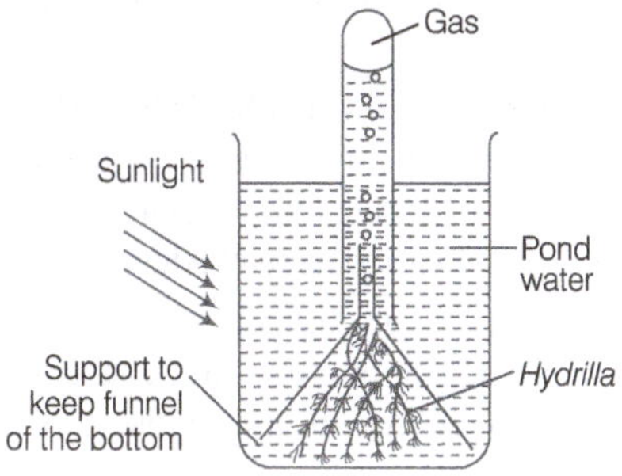

Fig. 5.6 Experiment to show that oxygen is given out during photosynthesis

Importance of Photosynthesis

It is important for supporting life on earth in the following ways

- It provides food to all organisms through the food chain.
- Photosynthesis gives off oxygen which acts as a life supporting gas.
- It helps in maintaining balanced level of O_2 and CO_2 in the atmosphere.

Output of Oxygen

As a result of photosynthesis, some amount of oxygen produced is used by the plant itself for the process of respiration. But the major amount of O_2 is diffused out into the atmosphere through stomata.

Thus, this oxygen which get diffused out is not a waste material because it acts as a life supporting gas for other living organisms including humans on earth.

Carbon Cycle

It is a series of chemical reactions, where carbon is removed from the air, used by living organisms in the form of food and is finally returned to the atmosphere. The steps involved in carbon cycle are

(i) Photosynthetic plants use carbon in the form of CO_2 from the atmosphere to produce carbohydrates (food).

(ii) Carbon through the food chain is passed on to animals including humans.

(iii). By respiration, decay of plant and animal dead bodies, burning of fuel (like coal, petroleum, etc.), and carbon returned back to the atmosphere in the form of CO_2.

Green plants perform photosynthesis by utilising CO_2 and H_2O in the presence of sunlight and chlorophyll. In this process, CO_2 is transformed into simple carbohydrate (sugar) and O_2 is liberated as byproduct.

Carbohydrates (sugar) are further broken into simpler molecules, i.e. glucose, fructose, etc. These glucose molecules provide energy for the synthesis of other biologically important molecules or are converted into other substances.

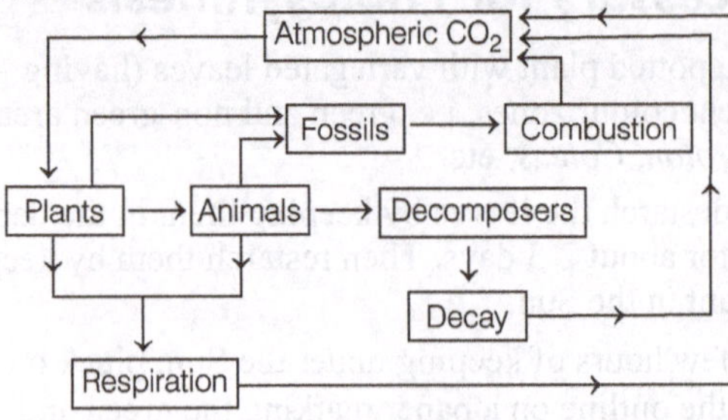

Fig. 5.7 Carbon cycle

PYQs Previous Years' Questions

1 Mark Questions

Multiple Choice Questions

1. The solvent used to dissolve the chlorophyll pigment while testing a leaf for starch. **ICSE Specimen 2021-22 Sem. I**

(a) Soda lime (b) Carbonic acid
(c) Methylated spirit (d) Water

Ans. (c) Methylated spirit

2. A plant with variegated leaves is .... **ICSE Specimen 2021-22 Sem. I**

(a) *Coleus* (b) lotus (c) peepal (d) mango

Ans. (a) *Coleus*

3. Choose the correct answer from the four options given below in the statement.
A plant is kept in a dark cupboard for about 48 hrs before conducting any experiment on photosynthesis to **ICSE 2013, 2002**

(a) remove chlorophyll from the leaves
(b) remove starch from the plant
(c) ensure that no photosynthesis occurs
(d) ensure that the leaves are free from starch

Ans. (b) remove starch from the plant

4. Given below is a statement followed by four choices. Select and rewrite the correct answer.
A destarched plant is one whose **ICSE 2009**

(a) leaves are free from chlorophyll
(b) aerial parts are free from starch
(c) leaves are free from starch
(d) plant is free from starch

Ans. (c) Leaves are free from starch

Very Short Answer Type Questions

5. The statement given below is incorrect. Rewrite the correct statement by changing the underlined words of the statement. The solvent used to dissolve the chlorophyll pigments while testing a leaf for starch is <u>soda lime</u>. **ICSE 2017**

Ans. The solvent used to dissolve the chlorophyll pigments while testing a leaf for starch is alcohol.

6. Give one example for

'An aquatic plant used in the lab to demonstrate O_2 liberation during photosynthesis'. **ICSE 2014**

Ans. *Hydrilla* is an aquatic plant used in the lab to demonstrate O_2 liberation during photosynthesis.

7. Explain the term 'Destarched plant'. **ICSE 2010, 2008**

Ans. Destarched plant is the one which is kept in the dark to remove the starch from the leaves. The process of destarching is done by keeping the plant in dark for 2-3 days.

8. Without changing the first term rearrange the remaining terms in logical sequence.

Destarched plant, iodine added, washed in water, a leaf boiled in alcohol, placed in sunlight (testing the presence of starch). **ICSE 2008**

Ans. Destarched plant $\rightarrow$ placed in sunlight $\rightarrow$ leaf boiled in alcohol $\rightarrow$ washed in water $\rightarrow$ iodine added.

2 Marks Question

9. Enumerate the steps involved in testing a green leaf for the presence of starch. **ICSE 2017, 2005**

Ans. Refer to text on page no. 70.

5 Marks Questions

10. Study the diagram given below and fill in the blanks with suitable words. **ICSE 2024**

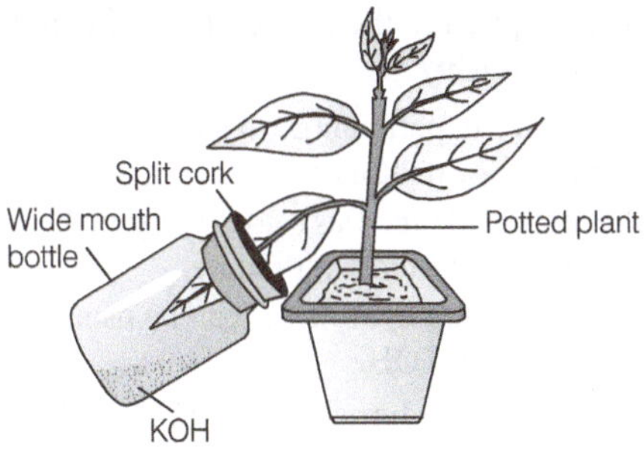

In order to prove that carbon dioxide is necessary for **(a)**.......... a potted plant is placed in dark for 48 hours to **(b)** .... the leaves. A part of a leaf is inserted into a conical flask containing potassium hydroxide solution. This is to absorb **(c)** .... from the flask. The plant is then placed in sunlight for a few hours. The experimental leaf is tested for starch. The part of the leaf that was inside the conical flask turns **(d)** .... whereas the part of the leaf outside turns **(e)**......... in colour.

Ans. (a) Photosynthesis (b) Destarch
(c) Carbon dioxide (d) Colourless
(e) Bluish-black

11. A potted plant with variegated leaves was kept in dark for 24 hours and then placed in bright sunlight. Answer the following questions.

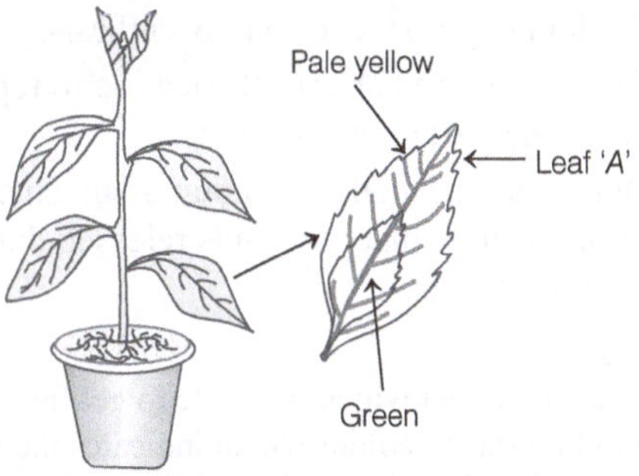

(i) Which aspect of photosynthesis is being tested in the above diagram?
(ii) Why was the plant kept in the dark for 24 hours?
(iii) After the starch test what will be the colour of the yellow and green parts of the leaf? Give reasons to support your answer. **ICSE 2023**

Ans. (i) Sunlight is the important aspect of photosynthesis which is tested here in this experiment.
(ii) The plant was kept in dark to eliminate the starch in the leaves.
(iii) After the starch test the green parts of the leaf will become blue black while the yellow parts lacking chlorophyll will show negative starch test. The green part which contains chlorophyll will be able to synthesise starch while the yellow part lacking chlorophyll will not be able to synthesise starch hence will show negative starch test.

12. Complete the following paragraph by filling in the blanks (i) to (v) with appropriate words

To test a leaf for starch, the leaf is boiled in water to (i) .... It is then boiled in methylated spirit to (ii) .... The leaf is dipped in warm water to soften it. It is placed in a petri dish and (iii) ...... solution is added.
The region of the leaf which contains starch, turns (iv) ...... and the region which does not contain starch, turns (v) .... **ICSE 2018, 2011**

Ans. (i) to kill all cells
(ii) to remove its chlorophyll
(iii) Iodine
(iv) Blue-black
(v) Brown

Diagram Based Questions

13. The diagram given below represents an experiment to demonstrate a particular aspect of photosynthesis. The letter '*A*' indicates a certain condition inside the flask. Answer the questions. **ICSE 2021-22 Sem. I (5M)**

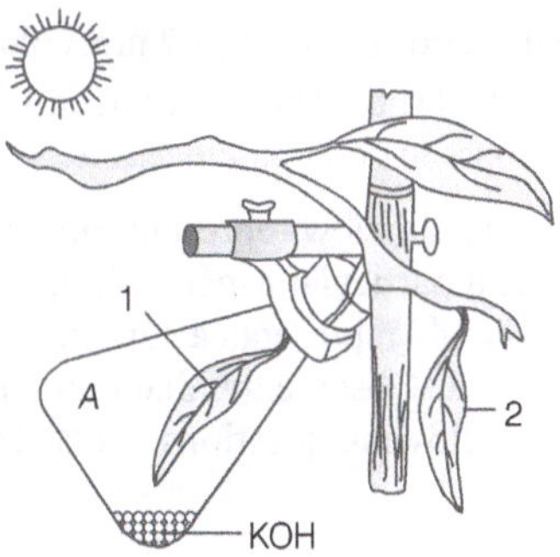

(i) What is the aim of the experiment?
(a) To show that oxygen is released during photosynthesis
(b) To show that photosynthesis occurs in the presence of KOH
(c) To show that chlorophyll is necessary for photosynthesis
(d) To show that carbon dioxide is necessary for photosynthesis

(ii) What is the special condition inside the flask?
(a) Air inside the flask is free of oxygen
(b) Air inside the flask is free of carbon dioxide
(c) Air inside the flask is free of nitrogen
(d) KOH purifies the air inside the flask

(iii) An alternative chemical that can be used instead of KOH is
(a) sodium hydroxide (b) sodium chloride
(c) potassium chloride (d) potassium permanganate

(iv) In what manner do the leaves 1 and 2 differ at the end of the starch test?
(a) Leaf 1 turns brown, leaf 2 turns blue black
(b) Leaf 1 turns blue black, leaf 2 turns brown
(c) Leaf 1 turns purple, leaf 2 remains green
(d) There is no change in the colour of the leaves

(v) What is the important step that should be taken before performing this experiment?
(a) The plant should be placed in dark for 24 hours to destarch the entire plant
(b) The plant should be placed in dark for 24 hours to remove chlorophyll from the leaves
(c) The plant should be placed in dark for 24 hours to destarch the leaves
(d) The plant should be placed in dark for 24 hours for the roots to absorb water

Ans. (i) (d) To show that carbon dioxide is necessary for photosynthesis
(ii) (b) Air inside the flask is free of carbon dioxide
(iii) (a) Sodium hydroxide
(iv) (a) Leaf 1 turns brown, leaf 2 turns blue black
(v) (c) The plant should be placed in dark for 24 hours to destarch the leaves.

14. The figure given below represents an experiment to demonstrate a particular aspect of photosynthesis. The alphabet '*A*' represents a certain condition inside the flask. Observe the diagram and then answer the following questions. **ICSE 2019, 2013 (5M)**

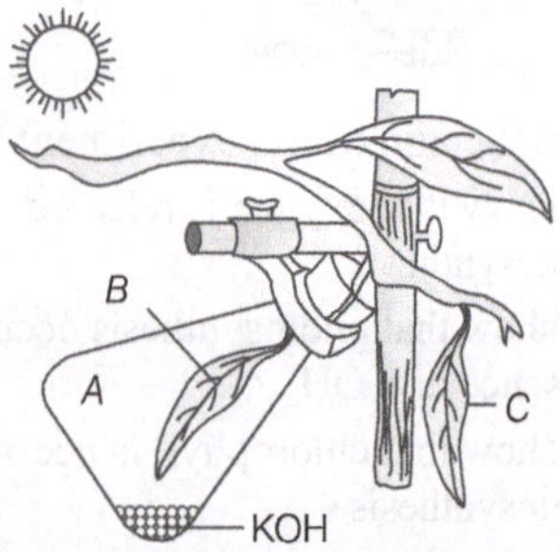

(i) What is the aim of the experiment ?

(ii) What happens to the leaf inside the flask when tested with iodine ?

(iii) Which chemical can be used as an alternative of KOH ?

(iv) What happen to the leaf *B* and leaf *C* at the end of the starch test?

Ans. (i) The aim of experiment is to show that CO_2 is necessary for photosynthesis.
(ii) The leaf inside the flask does not give blue-black colour when tested with iodine.
(iii) NaOH (sodium hydroxide) can be used as an alternative of KOH.
(iv) Leaf *B* does not turned blue-black, while leaf *C* turned blue-black at the end of the starch test.

15. The diagram given below represents an experiment to prove the importance of a factor in photosynthesis. Answer the questions that follow **ICSE 2019 (5M)**

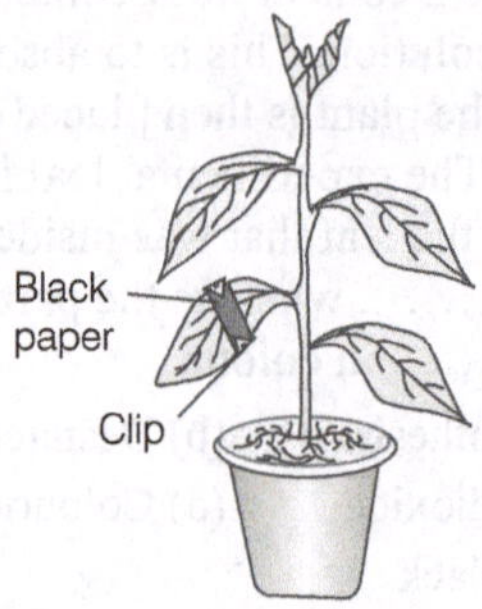

(i) Name the factor studied in this experiment.

(ii) What will you observe in the experimental leaf after the starch test ?

(iii) Explain the process of photosynthesis.

(iv) Give a balanced chemical equation to represent the process of photosynthesis.

(v) Draw a neat, labelled diagram of an experimental setup to show that oxygen is released during photosynthesis.

Ans. (i) Light
(ii) Uncovered leaf which was able to get light will turn into blue-black colour which indicates the presence of starch, while the portion which was covered with black paper will turn into brown colour showing absence of starch.
(iii) Photosynthesis process begins when the sunlight falls on the mesophyll cells of the leaf. The light energy is trapped by the chlorophyll present in the layers of mesophyll cells. During the process, the raw materials, i.e. CO_2 and water together with the solar energy trapped by the chlorophyll gets converted into chemical energy in the form of food, i.e. glucose and starch.

(iv) $6CO_2 + 12\,H_2O \xrightarrow[\text{Chlorophyll}]{\text{Sunlight}}$

$$C_6H_{12}O_6 + 6H_2O + 6O_2 \text{ (byproduct)}$$

(v)

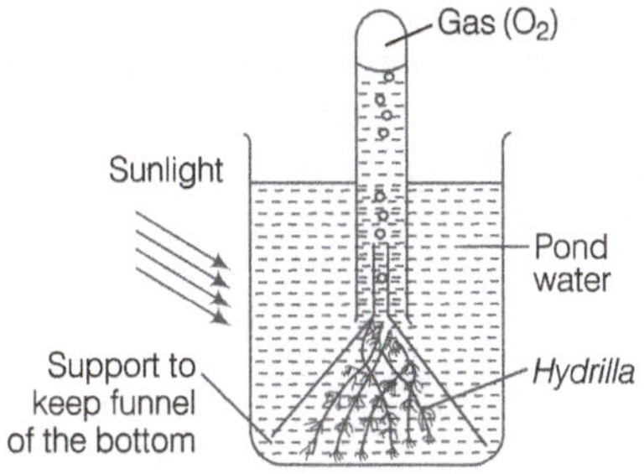

Experiment to show that oxygen is given out during photosynthesis

16. A potted plant with variegated leaves was taken in order to prove a factor necessary for photosynthesis.

The potted plant was kept in the dark for 24 hours and then placed in bright sunlight for a few hours. Observe the diagrams and answer the questions

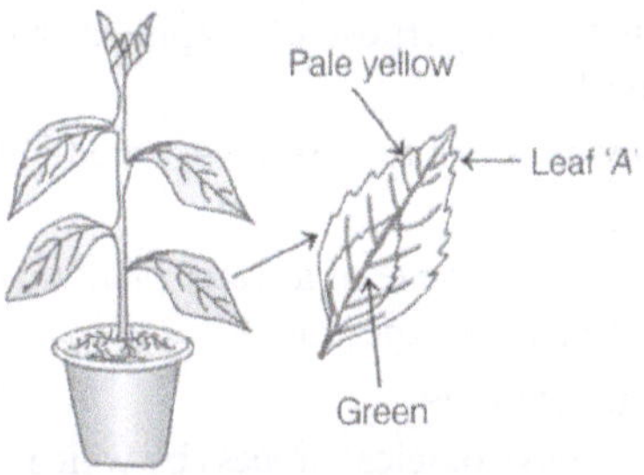

(i) What aspect of photosynthesis is being tested in the above diagram?

(ii) Represent the process of photosynthesis in the form of a balanced equation.

(iii) Why was the plant kept in the dark before beginning the experiment?

(iv) What will be the result of the starch test performed on leaf '*A*' shown in the diagram? Give an example of a plant with variegated leaves.

(v) Draw a neat and labelled diagram of a chloroplast. **ICSE 2018 (5M)**

Ans. (i) The experiment was performed to prove that photosynthesis can take place only in presence of chlorophyll, which is present in the green areas of the leaf.

(ii) $6CO_2 + 12H_2O \xrightarrow[h\,n\text{ (Sunlight)}]{\text{Chlorophyll}} C_6H_{12}O_6 + 6H_2O +$

$$6O_2 \uparrow \text{ (byproduct)}$$

(iii) The plant was kept in the dark before beginning the experiment to destarch the leaves.

(iv) When we test the leaf for starch, we observe that only the green areas of leaf will turn into blue black colour showing the presence of chlorophyll, while the non-green area will not. Examples of plant with variegated leaves are *Croton, Coleus*, etc.

(v)

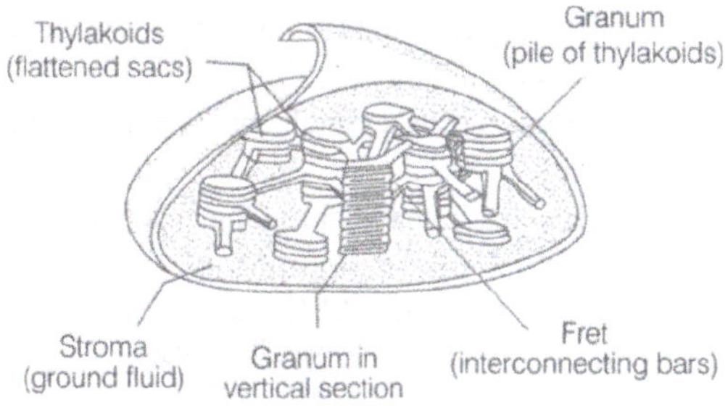

17. The given diagrams represent the relationship between a mouse and a physiological process that occurs in green plants. Study the diagrams and answer the questions that follow

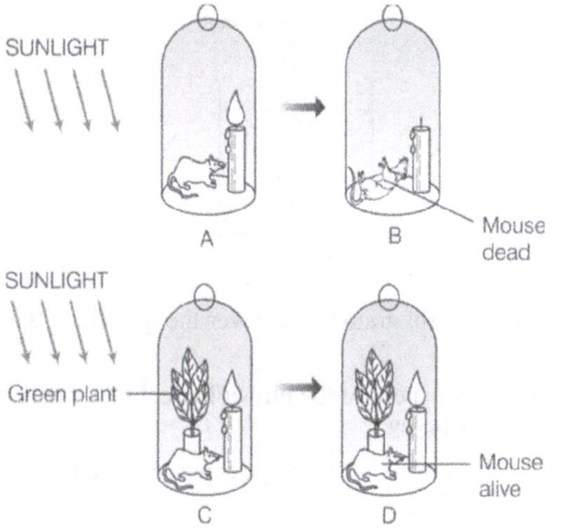

(i) Name the physiological process occurring in the green plant that has kept the mouse alive.

(ii) Explain the physiological process mentioned above.

(iii) Why did the mouse die in bell jar B?

(iv) What is the significance of the process as stated in (i) for life on earth?

(v) Represent the above mentioned physiological process in the form of a chemical equation. **ICSE 2017 (5M)**

Ans. (i) Photosynthesis, occurring in the green plant, has kept the mouse alive.

(ii) Photosynthesis is the process by which plants, some bacteria and some protists use energy from sunlight to produce sugar in the presence of CO_2 and water with the help of chlorophyll.

(iii) The oxygen present in the bell jar *B* was utilised in the burning of candle. Therefore, in the absence of O_2 mouse died.

(iv) Photosynthesis is important for supporting life on earth in the following ways

- It provides food to all organisms through food chain.
- It gives off O_2 which acts as a life supporting gas.
- It helps in maintaining the balanced level of O_2 and CO_2 in the atmosphere.

(v) $$\underset{\text{Carbon dioxide}}{6CO_2} + \underset{\text{Water}}{12H_2O} \xrightarrow[\text{Chlorophyll}]{\text{Sunlight}} \underset{\text{Glucose}}{C_6H_{12}O_6} + \underset{\text{Water}}{6H_2O} + \underset{\text{Oxygen}}{6O_2} \uparrow \text{(byproduct)}$$

18. The following diagram demonstrates a physiological process taking place in green plants. The whole set up was placed in bright sunlight for several hours.

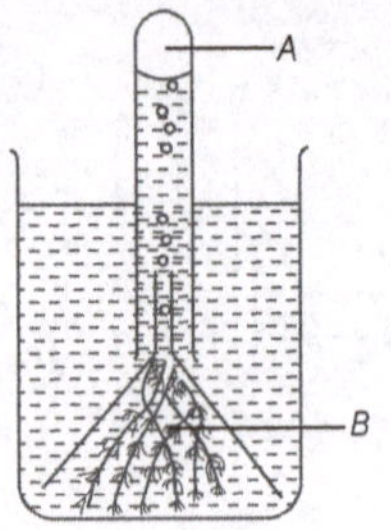

Study the diagram and answer the questions that follow.

(i) What aspect of the physiological process is being examined?

(ii) Explain the physiological process mentioned in (i) above.

(iii) Label the parts numbered *A* and *B* in the diagram.

(iv) Write a well–balanced chemical equation for the physiological process explained in (ii) above.

(v) What would happen to the rate of bubbling of the gas if a pinch of sodium bicarbonate is added to the water in the beaker? Explain your answer.

ICSE 2016 (5M)

Ans. (i) The aspect of physiological process examined here is release of O_2 in photosynthesis.

(ii) It is the manufacturing of sugar (glucose) and oxygen by plants in the presence of sunlight with the help of chlorophyll, H_2O and CO_2.

(iii) A-Oxygen in test tube. B-Green plant Hydrilla.

(iv) $$6CO_2 + 12H_2O \xrightarrow[\text{Sunlight}]{\text{Chlorophyll}} C_6H_{12}O_6 + 6H_2O + 6O_2 \text{ (byproduct)}$$

(v) Addition of $NaHCO_3$ will increase rate of photosynthesis because of increase in CO_2 available in water.

19. The diagram given below shows two test tubes *A* and *B*. Test tube *A* contains a green water plant. Test tube *B* contains both a green water plant and a snail. Both Test tubes are kept in sunlight. Answer the questions that follow

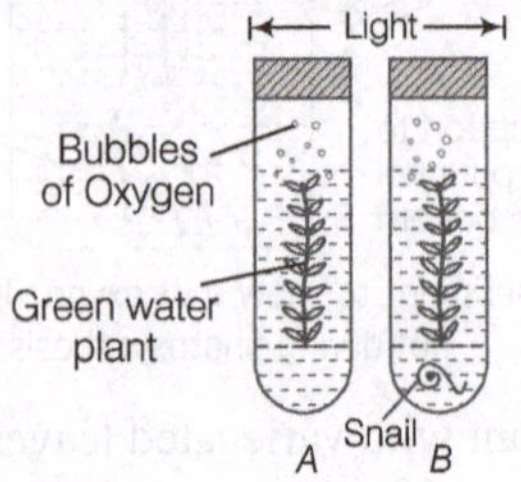

(i) Name the physiological process that releases the bubbles of oxygen.

(ii) Explain the physiological process as mentioned above in (i).

(iii) What is the purpose of keeping a snail in test tube *B*?

(iv) Why does test tube B have more bubbles of oxygen?

(v) Give an example of a water plant that can be used in the above experiment. **ICSE 2015 (5M)**

Ans. (i) Photosynthesis

(ii) It is a physiological process by which chlorophyll bearing cells of the plant prepare glucose in the presence of sunlight using CO_2 and water. O_2 is released as a byproduct during the process.

(iii) Snail while respiring releases carbon dioxide which acts as a precursor for green plant for the process of photosynthesis.

(iv) Test tube *B* has more bubbles of oxygen because the snail which is respiring release carbon dioxide which is used by green plant for the process of photosynthesis and thus due to high rate of photosynthesis, the formation of oxygen will occur more.

(v) *Hydrilla*

20. A potted plant was taken in order to prove a factor necessary for photosynthesis. The potted plant was kept in the dark for 24 hrs. One of the leaves was covered with black paper in the centre. The potted plant was then placed in sunlight for a few hours.

(i) What aspect of photosynthesis was being tested ?

(ii) Why was the plant placed in the dark before beginning the experiment ?

(iii) During the starch test why was the leaf
(a) boiled in water?
(b) boiled in methylated spirit ?

(iv) Write a balanced chemical equation to represent the process of photosynthesis.

(v) Draw a neat diagram of a chloroplast and label its parts. **ICSE 2014 (5M)**

Ans. (i) The aspect that is studied is that sunlight is necessary for photosynthesis.

(ii) Plant is placed in the dark before beginning the experiment to make the leaves free from starch.

(iii) (a) Leaf is boiled in water to kill the cells.
(b) Leaf is boiled in methylated spirit to remove the chlorophyll.

(iv) Refer to answer no. 15 (iv).

(v) Refer to answer no. 16(v).

21. The diagram given below is an experiment conducted to study a factor necessary for photosynthesis. Observe the diagrams and then answer the following questions

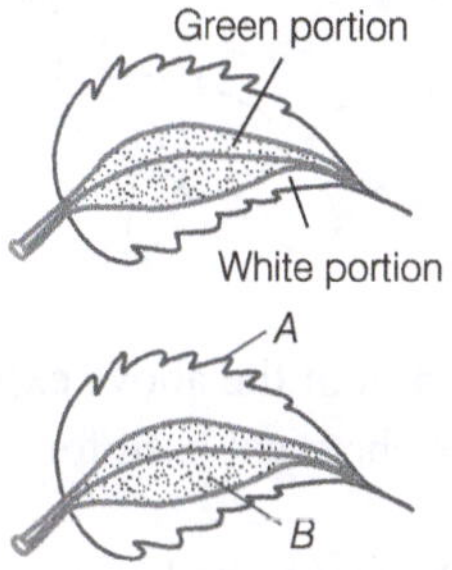

(i) What is the aim of the experiment ?

(ii) Name the test performed on the leaf and the solution used for the test.

(iii) What type of leaf was used for the experiment? Give an example.

(iv) What is the expected result of the above test on the parts labelled *A* and *B* ?

(v) Give a balanced chemical equation to represent the process of photosynthesis. **ICSE 2012 (5M)**

Ans. (i) Aim of the given experiment is to show that chlorophyll is necessary for photosynthesis.

(ii) The test performed on the leaf is starch test and the solution used is iodine solution.

(iii) Variegated leaf (leaf having non-green and green regions) was used for the experiment, e.g. *Coleus* leaf.

(iv) After performing starch test
Part B will turn blue-black with iodine solution.
Part A will turn brown with iodine solution.

(v) Refer to answer no. 15 (iv).

22. The figure given represents an experiment set-up to study a physiological process in plants.

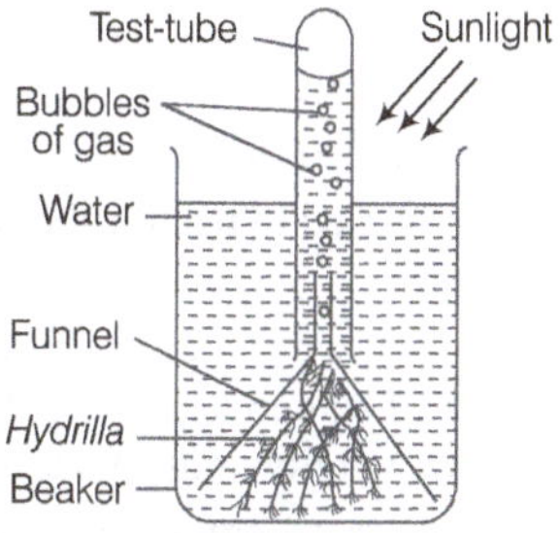

(i) Name the physiological process being studied.

(ii) Explain the process.

(iii) What is the aim of the experiment ?

(iv) Give a well-balanced equation to represent the process. **ICSE 2010 (4M)**

Ans. (i) The physiological process studied is photosynthesis.

(ii) It is a physiological process by which chlorophyll bearing cells of the plant prepare glucose in the presence of sunlight using CO_2 and water. O_2 is released during this process.

(iii) The aim of this experiment is to prove that oxygen is released during photosynthesis.

(iv) Refer to answer no. 15 (iv).

23. The diagram given below represents an experiment conducted to prove the importance of a factor in photosynthesis. Study the same and then answer the questions that follow

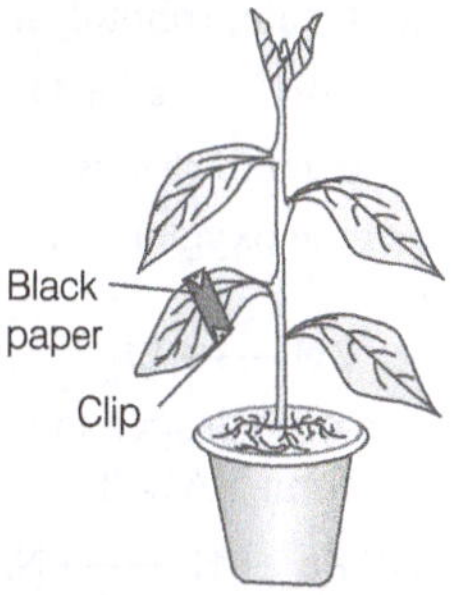

(i) Name the factor being studied in this experiment

(ii) Why was the plant kept in a dark room before conducting the experiment ?

(iii) Why was the experimental leaf then kept in
(a) boiling water? (b) methylated spirit?

(iv) Name the solution used to test for the presence of starch in the leaf.

(v) What will be observed in the experimental leaf at the end of the starch test ? **ICSE 2009 (5M)**

Ans. (i) Sunlight is the factor being studied in the experiment.

(ii) To destarch the leaves.

(iii) Refer to answer no. 20 (iii).

(iv) Iodine solution is used to test for the presence of starch in the leaf.

(v) On treating the leaf with iodine solution it shows that the portion of leaf covered with the strip of black paper does not give positive test for starch. The covered portion of leaf indicates the absence of starch after iodine test because it could not get light to perform photosynthesis. Hence, it is proved that in the absence of light the leaf cannot manufacture the starch.

24. (i) Draw a neat and well-labelled diagram of the chloroplast.

(ii) List the events taking place in the photochemical phase of photosynthesis.

(iii) If you are planning an experiment to show the effect of light on photosynthesis

(a) Will you select white light or green light ? Justify your answer.

(b) Why would you select a destarched plant ?

Ans. (i) Refer to anwer no. 16 (v). **ICSE 2007 (3M)**

(ii) Events that takes place in the photochemical phase of photosynthesis are

(a) Activation of chlorophyll.

(b) Splitting of water (photolysis).

$$2H_2O \xrightarrow[\text{energy of 4 photons}]{} 4H^+ + 4e^- + O_2\uparrow$$

(c) Release of the oxygen component as molecular oxygen.

$$2O \longrightarrow O_2\uparrow$$

(d) Picking up of hydrogen ions by a compound NADP to form NADPH,

i.e. $NADP + e^- + H^+ \longrightarrow NADPH$

(e) Conversion of ADP into energy rich compound (ATP) by adding one inorganic phosphate (P_i).

$$ADP + \underset{\text{(inorganic)}}{\text{Phosphate}} \longrightarrow ATP$$

(iii) (a) We select white light for photosynthesis but not green light because chlorophyll does not absorb all of white light but it does absorb most of it, other than the green.
As, photosynthesis does not occur in green light because chloroplasts (contain chlorophyll) absorbs light in red and in blue part of spectra and thus reflects green light.

(b) We will select a destarched plant because destarching ensures that any starch present after the experiment has been formed under experimental conditions.

25. A healthy *Croton* plant bearing variegated leaves was kept in a dark cupboard to despatch it, after which it was placed in sunlight for a few hours. One of the leaves was then plucked and an outline of the leaf marking the green and the non-green regions was drawn. The leaf was then tested for starch. Using the above information, answer the following questions

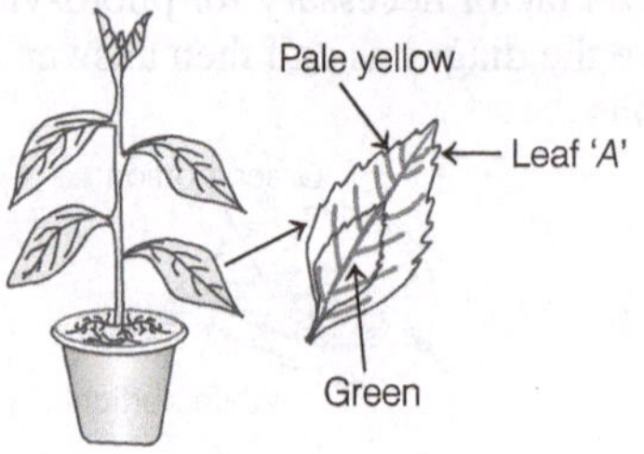

(i) State the aim of the above experiment.

(ii) Name the chemical used for testing the presence of starch.

(iii) Why is the leaf boiled in water and alcohol before testing for the presence of starch?

(iv) What change is seen on the leaf after the starch test?

(v) Give the chemical equation to represent the process of starch formation in plants. **ICSE 2003 (5M)**

Ans. (i) The aim of the experiment is to prove that chlorophyll is necessary for photosynthesis.

(ii) Chemical used for testing the presence of starch is iodine solution.

(iii) Leaf is boiled in water to kill the cells and boiled in alcohol to remove chlorophyll.

(iv) The green parts of the leaf turned blue-black, while non-green parts turned brown.

(v) $$6CO_2 + 12H_2O \xrightarrow[\text{Chlorophyll}]{\text{Sunlight}} C_6H_{12}O_6 + 6H_2O + 6O_2\uparrow \text{ (byproduct)}$$

26. (i) Draw a neat labelled diagram of the experimental set-up to show that green plants give out oxygen during photosynthesis.

(ii) Give the overall chemical equation to represent the process of photosynthesis. **ICSE 2001 (2M)**

Ans. (i) Refer to fig. on page no. 71. (Experiment to show that oxygen is given out during photosynthesis)

(ii) Refer to ans. no.18 (iv).

27. The following diagram is a set-up to demonstrate an experiment. Pondweed was placed in five water-filled tubes. The experiment was set-up as shown in the diagram. The tubes were then left for 24 hrs.

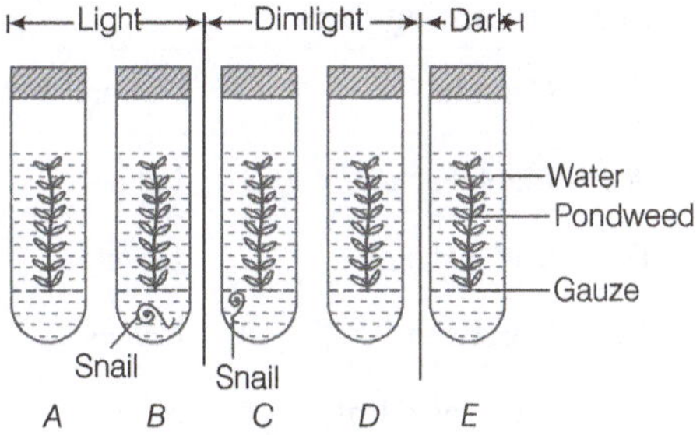

Write the correct answer out of the available choices given under each question

(i) In which tube would you expect the greatest increase in dry weight of the pondweed ?

(a) *A* (b) *B* (c) *C* (d) *D* (e) *E*

(ii) In which tube would you expect to find the plant with the least amount of starch ?

(a) *A* (b) *B* (c) *C* (d) *D* (e) *E*

(iii) The tube in which most oxygen would be found is

(a) *A* (b) *B* (c) *C* (d) *D* (e) *E*

(iv) The tube in which least carbon dioxide would be found is

(a) *A* (b) *B* (c) *C* (d) *D* (e) *E*

(v) The tube in which the plant would survive for the shortest length of time is

(a) *A* (b) *B* (c) *C* (d) *D* (e) *E* **ICSE 2000 (5M)**

Ans. (i) (b) (ii) (e) (iii) (a) (iv) (a) (v) (c)

CHAPTER TEST

Section-A

01 Mark Questions

1 Select the correct answer to the questions from the given options. (Do not copy the question, write the correct answer only)

(i) ....is released as a byproduct of photosynthesis.

(a) CO_2 (b) H_2O_2
(c) O_2 (d) N_2

(ii) Individual disc-like sac present in the stroma of chloroplast is known as

(a) thylakoids (b) grana
(c) stroma (d) stoma

(iii) Dark reaction of photosynthesis occurs in

(a) thylakoids
(b) matrix of chloroplast
(c) inner membrane of chloroplast
(d) grana

(iv) Splitting of water results in release of

(a) H^+, O_2, e^- (b) N, O_2, e^-
(c) H_2O, O, e^- (d) Only O_2

(v) Biosynthetic phase in photosynthesis also called as

(a) light dependent reaction
(b) photochemical reaction
(c) Z- scheme
(d) dark reaction

2 (i) Name the following.

(a) Pile of thylakoids are known as
(b) Two granum in stroma of chloroplast connected to each other by means of
(c) Ion involves in the opening and closing of stomata.
(d) Chemical used in starch test.

(ii) Arrange and rewrite the terms in each group in the correct order so as to be in a logical sequence beginning with term that is underlined.

(a) Light energy, Dark reaction , Photosynthetic pigments, Light reaction.
(b) Light, Electron transfer, ATP, Photolysis.
(c) Destarched plant, Washed in water, Leaf boiled in alcohol, Iodine added.
(d) During night, Decreased solute concentration in Guard cell, Increase water potential, Exosmosis in guard cell, Cell flaccid, Loss of K^+, Stoma close.

(iii) Match the items given in Column I with the most appropriate ones in Column II and rewrite the correct matching pairs.

Column I	Column II
A. Light reaction	1. Iodine
B. Dark reaction	2. Grana
C. Starch test	3. *Coleus*
D. Variegated leaf	4. Stroma

(iv) Choose the odd one out from the following terms and name the category to which other belong.

(a) Fret, Thylakoids, Grana, Stroma, Mesosome
(b) $4H^+$, $4e^-$, O_2, $C_6H_{12}O_6$
(c) Large surface area of leaves, Rapid exchange of gases, Chloroplasts on upper surface of leaves, Low light intensity
(d) Subsidiary cell, K^+ ions, Stoma, Turgidity, Grana.

(v) State the exact location of the following.

(a) Granum
(b) Photolysis of water
(c) Light dependent reaction
(d) Calvin cycle
(e) Release of O_2

02 Marks Questions

3 Define photosynthesis. Give its balanced chemical equation.

4 Explain photolysis of water.

5 State the main function of chloroplast.

6 What is photophosphorylation?

7 Mention the products of photosynthesis.

03 Marks Questions

8 Write about the factors affecting photosynthesis.

9 Explain the role of light in photosynthesis.

10 What controls the opening and closing of stomata ? Explain.

11 Write any four adaptations of leaves for photosynthesis.

Section-B

Diagram Based Questions

12 Stomata are minute openings occurring in large numbers on the lower surface of a leaf. The opening and closing of the stomata occurs on account of the movement of water in and out of the '*X*' cells. Study the figure carefully and answer the following questions.

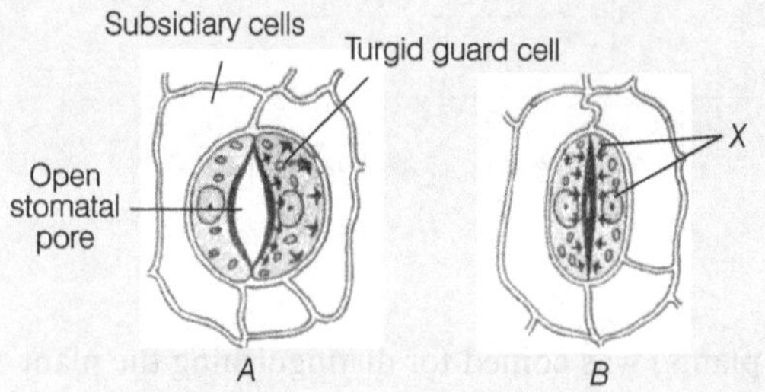

(i) Read the statement and name the '*X*' cells.

(ii) What *A* and *B* represents?

(iii) Which ion helps in stomatal regulation?

(iv) Define subsidiary cells.

13 Diagram showing an experiment conducted to study a factor necessary for photosynthesis. Observe the diagram and then answer the following questions.

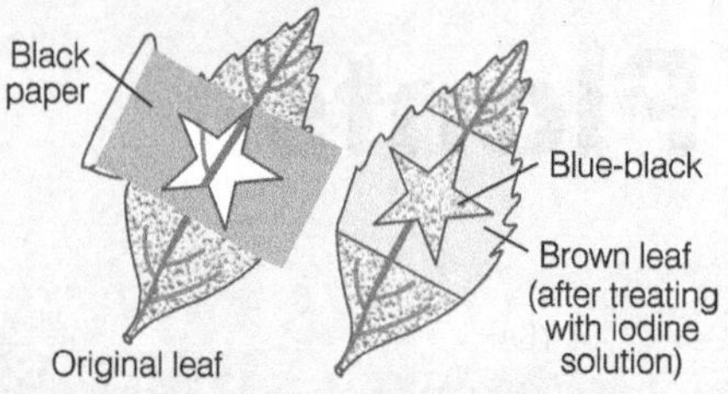

(i) What is the aim of experiment?

(ii) Name the test performed on leaf and solution used for the test.

(iii) Give a balanced chemical equation to represent the process of photosynthesis.

Answers

1. (i) (c), (ii) (a), (iii) (b), (iv) (a), (v) (d)

06

Chemical Coordination in Plants

TREND ANALYSIS 4 YEARS

Average No. of Questions Across all Sets

	Types of Questions	2024	2023	2020	2019
Chemical Coordination in Plants	1 Mark	1	1	–	6
	2 Marks	–	–	–	–
	3 Marks	1	1	–	–
	4 Marks	–	–	–	–
	5 Marks	–	–	–	1

All living organisms (plants or animals) respond and react to changes that occur in their environment by showing certain movements of their body parts. These responses to external stimuli are produced by working of various organs in a systematic and controlled manner which is known as **coordination**.

For control and coordination, animals have both the nervous system and hormones. However, the plants respond to stimuli and coordinate *via* the hormones only. In this chapter, we will study about plant hormones and movement in plants.

Plant Hormones

Cells cannot continuously create and transmit electrical impulses. Thus, most multicellular organisms use another means of communication between different cells that is called the **chemical coordination**.

The chemicals used in such communication are known as **hormones**.

The term 'hormone' was first used by **William Bayliss** and **Ernest Starling** in 1902. The term phytohormone (for plants) was coined for distinguishing the plant hormones from the animal hormones.

The hormones work as messengers (as in animals) to control and coordinate plant movements. They are produced at one location and transported across the plant body for functioning.

Plants respond to production of these hormones by growth. However in certain cases, hormones also negatively affect the plant growth.

In this section, we will study about major plant hormones, their discovery and their physiological functions in plants.

Auxin

It was the first plant growth regulator to be discovered. Auxins are indole compounds. They are produced in the actively growing regions of the plants, i.e. stem and root apices.

From here they migrate to other sites as when required. In plants, the first auxin was isolated from coleoptile tips of oat seedlings by **FW Went. IAA** (Indole Acetic Acid) is the main natural auxin found in plants.

Physiological Effects of Auxin

These are as follows

(i) **Root initiation** Auxin inhibits the elongation of primary root. But, it can stimulate the initiation of lateral and adventitious roots. Auxins are used to induce formation of roots on stem cutting. NAA and IBA are often used for rooting.

(ii) **Flowering** NAA and 2, 4-D are often employed for inducing flowering in litchi and pineapple.

(iii) **Parthenocarpy** Auxins can induce the formation of fruits without involving fertilisation, e.g. banana, tomatoes, etc.

(iv) **Cell elongation** It stimulates the elongation of cell in the shoot and promotes cell enlargement.

(v) **Apical dominance** It is a phenomenon in which apical buds inhibit the growth of lateral buds. Apical buds accomplish this by producing auxins. It inhibits the growth of lateral buds.

(vi) **Cell division** Auxin initiates and promotes cell division in vascular cambium, e.g. NAA.

(vii) **Inhibition of abscission** Natural auxins delay abscission of young fruits and leaves.

Gibberellins

These were first discovered in Japan from a fungus *Gibberella fujikuroi*. This fungus causes foolish seedling disease of rice (Bakanae disease). Almost 100 types of gibberellins have been reported till now. These are denoted as GA_1, GA_2, GA_3 and so on. $GA_3(C_{19}H_{26}O_6)$ is the first discovered and most studied gibberellin.

Physiological Effects of Gibberellins

These are as follows

(i) **Fruit growth** Gibberellins promote growth of fruits. Like it increases length of stalks of bunches of grapes.

(ii) **Malting** Gibberellins (GA_3) are used in breweries. They increase malt production in barley grains.

(iii) **Delayed ripening** Gibberellins cause delay in ripening of citrus fruits.

(iv) **Rapid maturity** Gibberellins cause quicker growth in conifers. Thus, it is used to obtain economically important seeds.

(v) **Breaking seed dormancy** Gibberellin causes mobilisation of food. Due to this, seed and bud dormancy is broken.

(vi) **Elongation of dwarfs** Gibberellins enhance the longitudinal growth of internodes in dwarf plants.

(vii) **Parthenocarpy** Gibberellins are considered more efficient than auxins to produce parthenocarpic fruits.

(viii) **Stem and leaf growth** Gibberellins can stimulate stem elongation, e.g. in sugarcane it elongates stem size.

(ix) **Seed germination** Gibberellins promote seed germination. They stimulate the synthesis of hydrolytic enzymes like amylases, proteases, etc.

Cytokinin

It was discovered by **Skoog** and **Miller** in 1955. It is widely distributed in plants.

Physiological Effects of Cytokinins

These are as follows

(i) **Flowering** Cytokinin induces flowering in plants like in *Lemna* and *Wolffia*. It is also responsible for breaking dormancy.

(ii) **Promotes cell division and organ formation** Cytokinins are essential for cell division.

High auxin to cytokinin ratio favours root development. High cytokinin to auxin ratio favours shoot development.

(iii) **Promotes lateral-bud development in dicots** Cytokinins counter act apical dominance. They promote lateral bud formation even in the presence of apical buds.

(iv) **Development of chloroplast** Cytokinins promote chloroplast formation. They also increase the rate of chlorophyll formation.

(v) **Delay senescence** These also help in delaying senescence (ageing) of leaves and other organs by controlling synthesis of protein and mobilisation of resources or nutrients.

Ethylene

It is the only gaseous hormone of the plants. It causes fruit ripening. All seed bearing plants produce ethylene.

Maximum synthesis of ethylene occurs during the ripening of fruits and tissues undergoing senescence. It is widely utilised in agricultural practices.

Physiological Effects of Ethylene

These are as follows

(i) **Fruit ripening** Ethylene stimulates ripening of fruits such as tomatoes, lemons, oranges, etc. It also increases the rate of respiration. It causes dehiscence of dry fruits.

(ii) **Abscission and senescence** It enhances abscission and senescence of leaves, fruits and flowers.

(iii) **Breaking dormancy** Ethylene is responsible for breaking dormancy of different plant organs, but not of lateral buds.

(iv) **Root and root hair initiation** Ethylene in low concentration promotes growth of roots. It can initiate root hair formation also.

(v) **Flowering** Ethylene usually inhibits flowering. But in some plants (e.g. pineapple and mango), it induces flowering.

Abscisic Acid (ABA)

It is also a growth retarding hormone. ABA is produced when a plant is exposed to stress hence, is also known as **stress hormone.**

It is found in the chloroplasts of leaves. Fruits and seeds contain the highest amount of ABA.

The common stresses include lack of water, saline soils, cold temperature and frost.

Physiological Effects of ABA

These are as follows

(i) **Induces stomatal closure** ABA causes stomata to close during stress conditions.

(ii) **Bud dormancy** ABA induces axillary buds to become dormant during winters.

(iii) **Abscission** It causes abscission in leaves, flowers and fruits.

(iv) **Geotropism in roots** Application of ABA on root results in geotropism.

(v) ABA is applied to green oranges. It is done to turn them yellow.

(vi) ABA in most cases acts in opposition to gibberellins.

Plant Movements

These are changes in the position of plants or their parts. The movements occur in response to some stimulus. Stimulus may be defined as any change in the external environment. The movement of plants is broadly classified into two main types

(i) **Movement independent of growth** This type of movement does not involve growth of the plant, e.g. the 'sensitive' or 'touch-me-not' (chhui-mui) plant (*Mimosa pudica*) shows peculiar response to touch. The leaves of this plant begin to fold up and droop in response to touch.

(ii) **Movement dependent on growth** This type of movement involves the growth of the plant, e.g. when a seed germinates, the root goes down and the stem comes up into the air always.

Tropic Movements

When the stimulus has a particular direction and movement of plant occurs in the direction of the stimulus (either towards the stimulus or in the opposite direction), the movement is called as **tropic movement.**

Types of Tropic Movements

These are based on environmental triggers like light, gravity of earth, water and certain chemicals.

1. Phototropic Movement (stimulus– light)

The movement of the plant part in response to light is called phototropic movement and the phenomenon involved is called **phototropism.**

As the shoot grows towards light, it is known as **positive phototropism** and growth of root away from the light is called **negative phototropism,** e.g. if a plant gets unilateral light, its shoot will bend in the same direction.

Fig. 6.1 Response of the plant to the direction of light

2. Geotropic Movement (stimulus–gravity)

The movement of plant part in response to gravity is called geotropic movement and the phenomenon involved is called **geotropism.**

- When the tip of the stem grows away from the earth's gravitational force, it is known as **negative geotropism** and when the root tips grow towards gravity, it is known as **positive geotropism**.
- Roots always move towards centre of gravity (downward). For example, when bean or gram seed is sown in moist soil, after a few days the stem grows away from the force of gravity and the root grows towards the force of gravity.

Fig. 6.2 Response of the plant to the direction of gravity

3. **Hydrotropic Movement** (stimulus– water)

- It is the growth of the plant in response to water. The phenomenon involved in this is called **hydrotropism**.
- When the plant grows towards the source of water (moisture), the movement is **positively hydrotropic** (e.g. root). This ensures the availability of water to roots.
- When the plant grows away from the source of water (moisture), it is known as **negatively hydrotropic** (e.g. shoot). For example, during seed germination, the roots grow towards the moist soil (upwards) where water is abundantly present.

4. **Thigmotropic movement** (stimulus-touch)

- In thigmotropism, the growth or movement of plants occurs in response to touch.
- For example, the tendrils of plants like sweet pea, grapes, *Cuscuta* are sensitive to touch. When these tendrils come in contact with any support, the part of tendril in contact with the object does not grow as rapidly as other parts of the plant. The tendrils then start to circle around the object and cling to the available support.

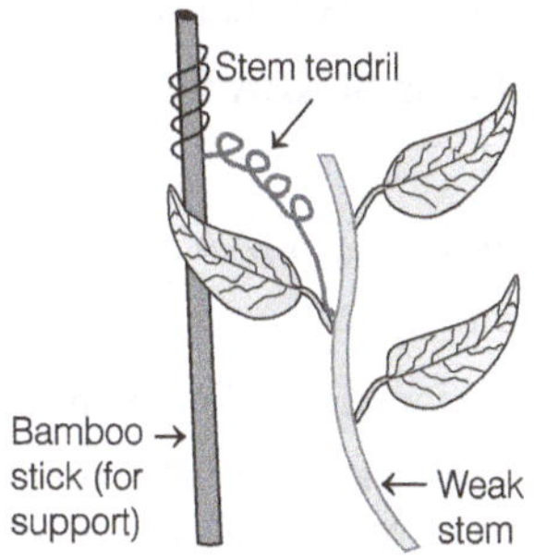

Fig. 6.3 Thigmotropism in plant

5. **Chemotropic movement** (stimulus-chemical)

It is the growth of the plant in response to a chemical stimulus and the phenomenon involved is called **chemotropism**, e.g. growth of pollen tube towards ovules during fertilisation.

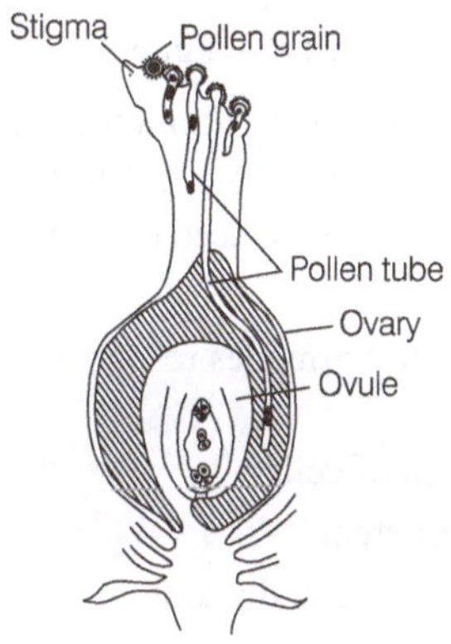

Fig. 6.4 Chemotropism in pollen tube growth

PYQs Previous Years' Questions

1 Mark Questions

Multiple Choice Question

1. Cytokinins are predominantly present in **ICSE Specimen 2023, 2019**

(a) meristematic tissues
(b) permanent tissues
(c) endodermis
(d) epidermis

Ans. (a) meristematic tissues

Very Short Answer Type Questions

2. Name the following.
The tropic movement of plant parts in response to chemicals. **ICSE 2024**

Ans. Chemotropism

3. Name the following. A gaseous plant hormone which promotes ripening of fruits. **ICSE 2023**

Ans. Ethylene.

4. Identify the odd term in each set and name the category to which the remaining belong.
Gibberellin, Auxin, Vasopressin, Abscisic acid. **ICSE 2019**

Ans. Vasopressin, remaining belongs to phytohormone.

5. Give the full form of ABA **ICSE 2019**

Ans. Abscisic Acid.

6. What is the full form of IAA? **ICSE 2019**

Ans. Indole-3-Acetic Acid.

7. State the main functions of cytokinins. **ICSE 2019**

Ans. Main function of cytokinins is to promote cell division and organ formation, e.g. *Lemna* and *Wolffia*.

8. What is parthenocarpy? Give one example. **ICSE 2019**

Ans. Parthenocarpy is the development of fruits without fertilisation, e.g. banana, tomatoes, etc.

Important Questions

9. Name the following.
(i) A hormone which delays fall of leaves.
(ii) A hormone which prevents ageing of plant parts.

Ans. (i) Auxin (ii) Cytokinin

10. Name one plant growth hormone, which retards growth during extremely dry season.

Ans. Abscisic acid makes the seed dormant in extremely dry season.

11. Name the plant hormones responsible for the following.
(i) Elongation of cells
(ii) Growth of stem
(iii) Promotion of cell division
(iv) Falling of senescent leaves

Ans. (i) Auxin (ii) Gibberellin
(iii) Cytokinin (iv) Abscisic acid

12. What do we call the movement of shoot towards light?

Ans. The movement of shoot towards light is called positive phototropism.

13. A young green plant receives sunlight from one direction only. What will happen to its shoot and roots?

Ans. The shoot of the plant bends towards the light, whereas roots bend away from the light.

14. Why are roots known as positively geotropic?

Ans. The roots always grow towards the gravity of the earth, that is why they are positively geotropic.

15. Name any two types of tropic movements.

Ans. The types of tropic movements are
(i) Geotropism, i.e. response to gravity.
(ii) Chemotropism, i.e. response to chemical substances.

16. In what way tropic movements are different from other types of movements?

Ans. The tropic movements are directional with respect to the stimulus received.

17. Give technical terms for the following events.
(i) The movement of roots in response to presence of water/moisture nearby.
(ii) The movement of plant parts towards a chemical substance.

Ans. (i) Hydrotropism
(ii) Chemotropism

18. The electrical-chemical signals are not considered an efficient means of communication in plants? Give reason.

Ans. Unlike animals, where there is a nervous system for conduction of nerve impulses and circulatory system for conduction of hormones, there are no specialised tissues in plants. So, the electrical-chemical signals are not an effective means of communication in plants.

19. How does control and coordination carried out in plants?

Ans. In plants, control and coordination is brought about by means of chemical substances called phytohormones. In addition, environmental factors like water, temperature and light control growth and development.

20. What are plant hormones? Write two important functions of auxin.

Ans. Plant hormones are chemical substances produced naturally in plants. These are capable of translocation and regulation of one or more physiological processes when present in low concentration. Two important functions of auxin hormone are that it promotes cell elongation, root formation, cell division, etc.

21. Name the plant growth regulators which can be used when you are asked to
(i) induce rooting in a twig
(ii) quickly ripen a fruit
(iii) delay leaf senescence
(iv) induce growth in axillary buds

Ans. (i) Auxins (like IAA)
(ii) Ethylene
(iii) Cytokinin
(iv)Cytokinin

22. By giving an example, explain how does a plant respond to an external stimuli?

Ans. Take a healthy potted plant. Keep this plant inside a dark room by the side of an open window. After a few days, it is observed that the plant bends towards the open window (that is, towards light). This shows that the plant give positive response towards light, known as positive phototropism.

2 Marks Questions

Important Questions

23. List the sequence of events that occur when a plant is exposed to unidirectional light, leading to bending of a growing shoot. Also name the hormone and the type of movement.

Ans. A plant placed in unidirectional light shows bending towards the light source. This is known as phototropism. This movement is facilitated by auxin hormone which diffuses towards the shady side. This causes elongation of shoot on shady side.

24. Which of the following movements are tropic? Identify along with names.

(i) Opening of flower
(ii) Roots moving downwards
(iii) Shoots moving towards light
(iv) Twirling of a tendril

Ans. Tropic movements are

(i) Opening of a flower is not tropic movement.
(ii) Roots moving downwards is geotropism. Here the stimulus is gravity.
(iii) Shoots moving towards light is phototropism. Here, the stimulus is light.
(iv) Twirling of a tendril is thigmotropism. Here, the stimulus is touch.

3 Marks Questions

Important Questions

25. List five main natural plant growth regulators. Write a note on discovery, physiological functions and agricultural /horticultural applications of any one of them.

Ans. Five main natural plant growth regulators are auxins, gibberellins, ethylene, cytokinins and ABA.

Auxins

(i) **Discovery** They were first isolated from human urine. They are generally produced by the growing apices of the stems and roots of plants.

(ii) **Physiological functions** They help to initiate rooting in stem cuttings. They are widely used for plant propagation. Auxins promote flowering, e.g. in pineapples.

They help to prevent fruit and leaf drop at early stages, but promote the abscission of older mature leaves and fruits.

(iii) **Agricultural/horticultural applications**
Auxins also induce parthenocarpy, e.g. in tomatoes. They are widely used as herbicides 2, 4-D is used to kill dicotyledonous weeds. It also controls xylem differentiation and helps in cell division.

26. Which parts of the plants produce gibberellins? State two functions of this hormone and mention why it was named gibberellin?

Ans. The major sites of gibberellin production in plants are embryos, roots and young leaves near the shoot tip.

The functions of gibberllins are

(i) They are used in the process of malting in brewing industry to speed up the process. They increase malt production in barley grains.
(ii) Gibberellins delay senescence in plants.

It was named after the fungus, which is the source of it, i.e. *Gibberella fujikuroi.*

27. How are gibberellins useful in agriculture to improve productivity? Give any three points in support of your answer.

Ans. Gibberellins are useful in agriculture in the following ways

(i) Gibberellins increase the length of the stem and increases the yield of sugar in sugarcane.
(ii) Gibberellins promotes seed germination.
(iii) They can cause fruits like apple to elongate and improve in shape.

28. (i) Which plant hormone is present in greater concentration in the areas of rapid cell division?
(ii) Give one example of a plant growth promoter and a plant growth inhibitor.

Ans. (i) Cytokinin is present in greater concentration in the areas of rapid cell division.
(ii) An example of a plant growth promoter is gibberellins and example of a plant growth inhibitor is abscisic acid.

29. Justify by giving any three examples that even plants respond to stimuli.

Ans. Plants also respond to external stimulus perceived by them. They show certain movements of plant parts in response to stimuli like light, gravity, water, etc.

(i) Roots of plants move downwards in response to gravitational force.

(ii) Movement of shoots in plants towards the light.

(iii) Closing of leaves of *Mimosa pudica* plant when touched.

5 Marks Questions

Important Questions

30. 'Plants also perform chemical coordination'. Elaborate.

Ans. Plants also perform chemical coordination for various activities with the help of hormones. These are the chemical compounds released by stimulated cells that diffuse to various locations in plants performing different functions. These hormones produced by plants are also called as phytohormones. Different types of hormones produced by plants are

Plant hormone	Physiological effect
Auxin	Synthesised in the young tip of roots and shoots. It diffuses towards the shady side of plant, which stimulates the cells to grow longer, resulting in bending of shoot towards light.
	Promotes cell elongation and division.
	Plays an important role in formation of roots and seedless fruits.
Gibberellin	Helps in growth of stem and flower.
	Helps in germination of seeds.
Cytokinins	Promote cell division and delay leaf ageing.
	Also stimulate leaf expansion.
Abscisic acid	Growth inhibitor.
	Reverses the growth promoting effects of auxins and gibberellins.
Ethylene	Promotes transverse growth.
	Essential for fruit ripening, promotes senescence and abscission of leaves.

31. Name a hormone which

(i) is gaseous in nature

(ii) is responsible for phototropism

(iii) breaks apical dominance

(iv) is used for killing weeds (dicots)

(v) induces flowering in long day plants

Ans. (i) Ethylene

(ii) Auxin hormone

(iii) Cytokinin hormone

(iv) 2, 4-D (Auxin)

(v) Gibberellin hormone.

32. Mention the factors which prove that phytohormones act together or opposite to each other.

Ans. The factors which prove that phytohormones act together or oppositely are

(i) Cell division is promoted by both auxins and cytokinins acting together.

(ii) Auxins and cytokinins interact to control the differentiation of shoot and root. High auxin to cytokinin ratio favours root development while high cytokinin to auxin ratio favours shoot development.

(iii) Auxins and cytokinins act against each other controlling apical dominance. Auxins cause apical dominance, while cytokinins overcome the same.

(iv) Senescence is prevented by auxins and cytokinins and is stimulated by abscisic acid.

(v) The activity of cambium and fruit growth seems to be promoted by auxins, gibberellins and cytokinins, the same is inhibited by abscisic acid.

(vi) The dormancy of seeds and buds is mostly due to abscisic acid and the same is broken by gibberellins.

(vii) Cytokinins cause opening of stomata, while abscisic acid results in their closure.

33. (i) Define phototropism. Give one example.

(ii) What is meant by positive and negative phototropism?

(iii) What does a plant do in response to water? Identify this phenomenon. Give an example.

Ans. (i) Phototropism is the growth movement shown by plants in response to light, e.g. bending of plant stem placed in a dark room towards the light source.

(ii) When the plant shows growth movements by bending towards the light source, it is called positive phototropism.

When the plant or its parts (like roots) respond to light by growing away from it then it is called negative phototropism.

(iii) A plant when comes in contact with a water source, shows the growth movement towards it.

This phenomenon is known as hydrotropism, e.g. the roots of plants always go towards the water, even if it means going against the pull of gravity.

34. The response of a plant when gravity is the external stimulus is called as geotropism. How are plant parts sensitive to gravity? Explain.

Ans. Gravity is the force applied by earth to pull all things downward. The response of plants to this gravity is called geotropism. The roots of plants always tend to grow downward in response to gravity. This ensures that they will have soil and water availability(positive geotropism).

The stems of plants always grow upwards (negative geotropism). This ensures the availability of light. Both these movements of plants are considered as geotropism.

Diagram Based Questions

35. Ali has some pea plants in his garden which need a support to grow as seen in the picture given below. **ICSE 2024 (3M)**

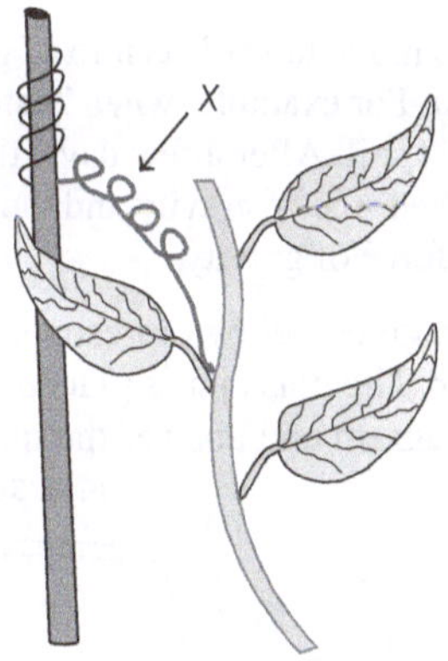

(i) Name the phenomenon depicted by the shoot in the given figure.

(ii) Define the above phenomenon.

(iii) Write the name of the part marked *X*.

Ans. (i) Thigmotropism

(ii) Thigmotropism can be defined as the movement of plant part in response to stimulus of contact.

(iii) Stem tendril.

36. Study the diagram given below and answer the questions that follow **ICSE 2023 (3M)**

(i) Name the phenomenon depicted by the shoot in the above diagram.

(ii) Which plant hormone plays an important role in the above movement?

(iii) Complete and rewrite the given statement by filling in the correct terms:
Shoots show positive .... whereas, roots show positive ....

Ans. (i) The phenomenon depicted by the shoot in the above diagram is phototropism.

(ii) Auxin plays an important role in phototropism.

(iii) Shoots show positive **phototropism** whereas, roots show positive **geotropism**.

37. The diagram given below shows a type of tropism. Answer the questions that follow **ICSE Specimen 2023 (3M)**

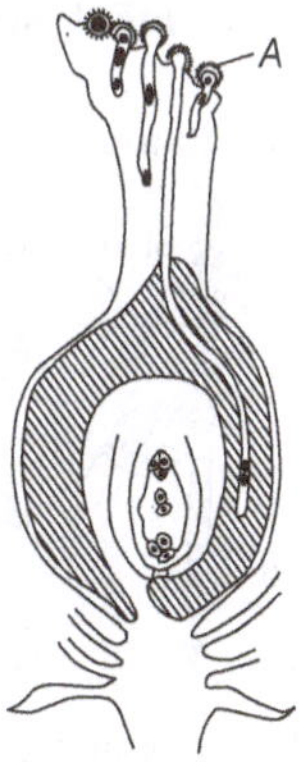

(i) Name the type of tropism.

(ii) Define the above mentioned tropism.

(iii) Give an example of a stimulant that helps in the growth of the part marked *A*.

Ans. (i) Chemotropism.

(ii) It is the growth of plant organ in response to a chemical and the phenomenon involved is called chemotropism.

(iii) Chemical.

38. Given below is an experimental setup to demonstrate a particular tropic movement in germinating seeds. Study the diagram and answer the questions that follows **ICSE 2019 (5M)**

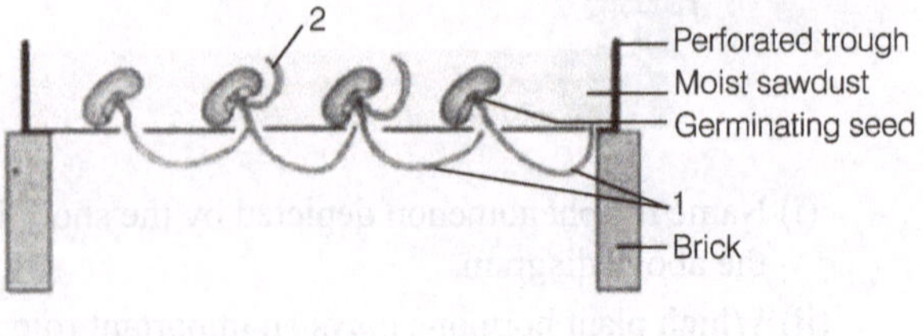

(i) Label the parts 1 and 2.

(ii) Name the tropic movement shown by part 1.

(iii) Part 1 is affected by two stimuli. Name them. Which one of the two is stronger ?

(iv) What is thigmotropism? Give one example.

(v) What is meant by 'positive' and 'negative' tropic movement in plants ?

Ans. (i) Part 1 - Radicle
Part 2- Plumule

(ii) **Positive geotropism** when the root tips grows towards gravity, it is known as positive geotropism.

(iii) Gravity and water are two stimuli which affect part 1. **Water** is considered as stronger factor.

(iv) **Thigmotropic movement** (stimulus-touch) In thigmotropism, the growth or movement of plants occurs in response to touch.

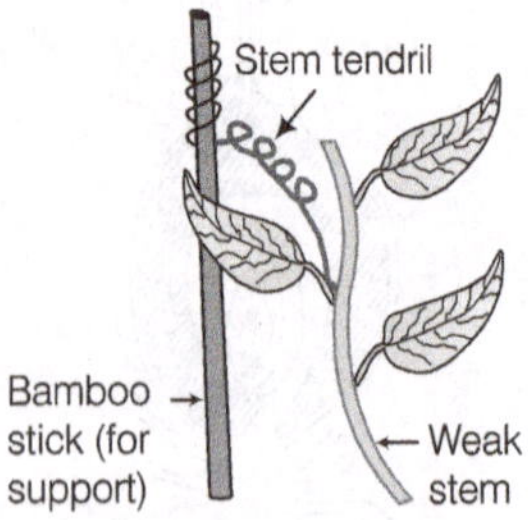

Thigmotropism in plant

For example, the tendrils of plants like sweet pea, grapes, *Cuscuta* are sensitive to touch. When these tendrils come in contact with any support, the part of tendril in contact with the object does not grow as rapidly as other part of the plant. The tendrils then start to circle around the object and cling to the available support.

(v) **Geotropic movement** (stimulus–gravity) The movement of plant part in response to gravity is called geotropic movement and the phenomenon involved is called **geotropism.**
When the tip of the stem grows away from the earth's gravitational force, it is known as **negative geotropism** and when the root tips grow towards gravity, it is known as **positive geotropism.**

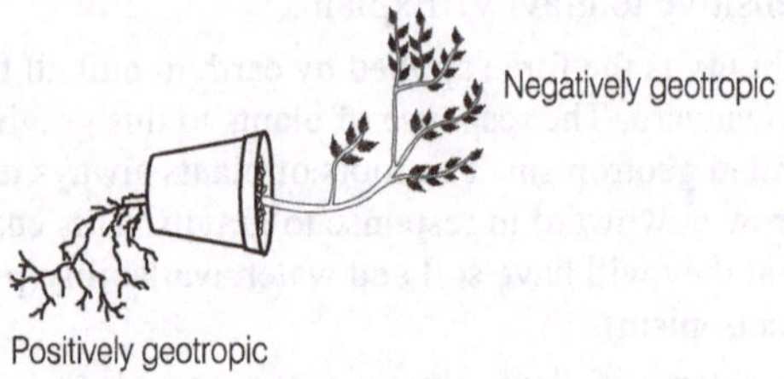

Response of the plant to the direction of gravity

Concept Enhancer Hydrotropism is stronger than geotropism. Roots grow in the direction of gravity and water. The growth of roots towards water overcoming the force of gravity suggests that roots are positively hydrotropic than geotropic. This implies that water is a more effective stimulus than gravity.

Roots always move towards centre of gravity (downwards). For example, when bean or gram seed is sown in moist soil. After a few days, the stem grows away from the force of gravity and the root grows towards the force of gravity.

39. The diagram given below represents a plant growing in a glass jar. The glass jar is placed near a window. Study the diagram and answer the questions that follows. **ICSE Specimen 2019 (5M)**

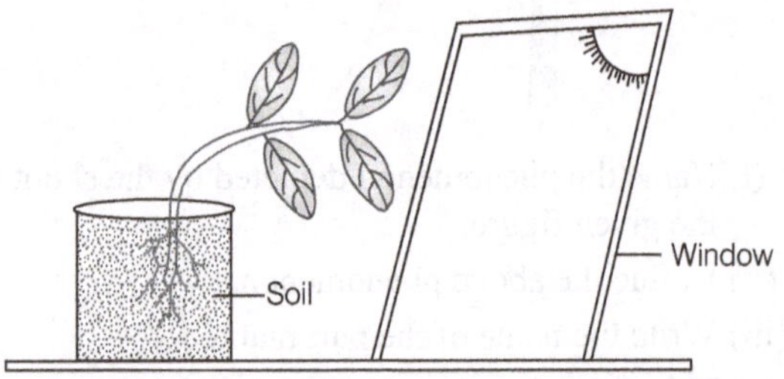

(i) Name the tropic movements shown by the shoot and roots.

(ii) What is the stimulus that made the shoot bend towards the window?

(iii) Which plant hormone caused the above effect?

(iv) Explain the role of the hormone in bending the shoot towards the window.

Ans. (i) Phototropic movements are shown by shoot and geotropic movements are shown by roots.

(ii) Light.

(iii) Auxin

(iv) Auxin present in area receiving light moves towards the shady side of the stem and causes elongation of that part. Thus, shoot appears bend towards light.

Important Questions

40. Demonstrate using an activity the geotropism in plants. **(3M)**

Ans. Take a few seeds of bean or gram and sow them in moist soil in a glass beaker. In three or four days, the seeds will sprout. Each seed will give rise to a tiny seedling. Water the seedlings regularly. Observe their growth for 8-9 days.

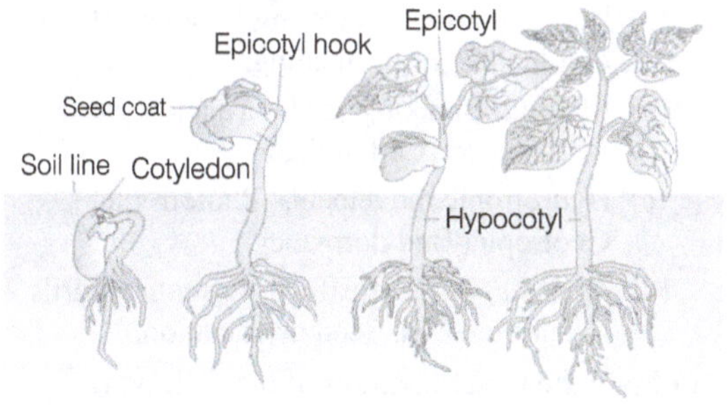

Geotropism

Notice the increase in the length of the stem growing away from the force of gravity and that of the roots growing towards the force of gravity. The growth in the stem shows negative (away) response to gravity, while the root shows positive (towards) response to gravity.

41. A tropism is a plant movement that is determined by the direction of an environmental stimulus. When the stimulus is received by the plant, specific part of the plant shows response in the form of growth movements.

This is due to unequal growth on its two sides by the action of phytohormone. Two pictures *A* and *B* given below are showing different kinds of tropic movements. Select the correct option.

(a) *A* – Thigmotropism *B* – Hydrotropism

(b) *A* – Phototropism *B* – Geotropism

(c) *A* – Phototropism *B* – Thigmotropism

(d) *A* – Chemotropism *B* – Chemotropism **(2M)**

Ans. (b) *A* – Phototropism, because it shows the response of a plant towards light.

B – Geotropism because it shows the growth of roots towards earth and shoots in air.

42. Through an experimental set-up, demonstrate how, hydrotropism occurs in plants? **(2M)**

Ans. The growth of plant parts towards or away from water is called hydrotropism. It is shown in the diagram given below

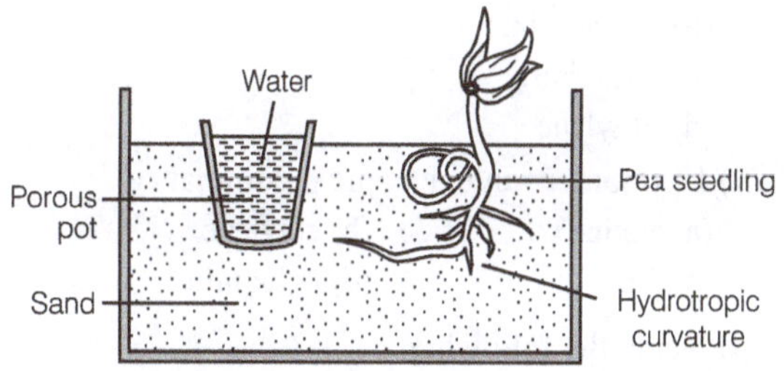

Concept Enhancer The plant roots grows towards the source of water, this movement is positively hydrotropic. The stem grows away from the source of water this movement is negatively hydrotropic.

CHAPTER TEST

Section-A

01 Mark Questions

1 Select the correct answer to the questions from the given options. (Do not copy the question, write the correct answer only).

(i) *Gibberella fujikuroi* is a

(a) bacteria (b) fungi

(c) virus (d) protozoan

(ii) IAA is associated with

(a) gibberellins (b) cytokinins

(c) auxin (d) ethylene

(iii) Which of the following is used to kill dicotyledonous weeds?

(a) 2, 4-D (b) GA_3

(c) Kinetin (d) NAA

(iv) Hormone associated with malt production in barley grains.

(a) Auxin

(b) Gibberellins

(c) Cytokinin

(d) Ethylene

(v) Hormone counteract apical dominance

(a) auxin (b) ethylene

(c) ABA (d) cytokinin

2 (i) Name the following.

(a) Scientist associated with discovery of auxin.

(b) Hormone breaking seed dormancy.

(c) Scientist associated with discovery of cytokinin.

(d) Stress hormone.

(ii) Arrange and rewrite terms in each group in the correct order so as to be in a logical sequence begining with the term that is underlined.

(a) <u>Positive phototropism</u>, Light, Shoot

(b) <u>Negative geotropism</u>, Shoot, Young shoot tip

(c) <u>*Gibberella*</u>, GA_3, Bakanae disease

(d) <u>Leaf expand</u>, Leaf fold, Stimulus

(iii) Match the items given in Column I with the most appropriate ones in Column II and rewrite the correct matching pairs.

	Column I		Column II
A.	Thigmotropic	1.	Shoot
B.	Negative geotropic	2.	Auxin
C.	Cell division	3.	Pea tendrils
D.	Flowering in pineapple	4.	Cytokinin
E.	Fruit ripening	5.	ABA
		6.	Ethylene

(iv) Choose the odd one out from the following terms and name the category to which the others belong.

(a) Root initiation, Flowering in pineapple, Apical dominance, Fruit ripening.

(b) Malting, Breaking seed dormancy, Seed germination, Cell division.

(c) Hydrotropic movements, Phototropic, Geotropic, Bud dormancy.

(d) *Mimosa pudica*, Leaflets, *Cuscuta* tendrils, Grapes tendrils, Seed germination.

(v) State the exact location of the following structures

(a) Auxin (b) Gibberellin

(c) Ethylene (d) Abscisic acid

02 Marks Questions

3 What are the physiological effects of auxin ?

4 What are tropic movements ? Name any two tropic movements in plants.

5 Define thigmotropic movements in plant. Give one example.

6 What are the physiological effects of ethylene ?

7 What do you mean by phytohormone?

03 Marks Questions

8 Explain in brief about discovery of gibberellins.

9 Define phototropic movement. Draw a diagram of plant responses to the direction of light.

10 Write any five physiological functions of cytokinin.

11 Define hydrotropic movements. Draw a diagram of plant showing hydrotropic movement.

12 Write the physiological effects of ABA.

Section-B

Diagram Based Questions

13 Thigmotropic movement of plants occurs in response to touch. Study the diagram and answer the questions that follows.

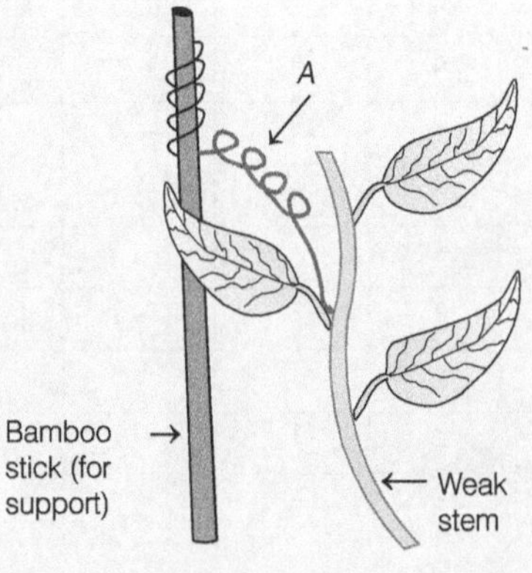

(i) Name the part labelled as *A*.

(ii) Name any two plants in which part *A* is present.

(iii) What do you mean by movement independent of growth?

(iv) Name the plant which show peculiar response to touch.

14 The diagram given below shows the type of tropic movement. Study the diagram and answer the following questions.

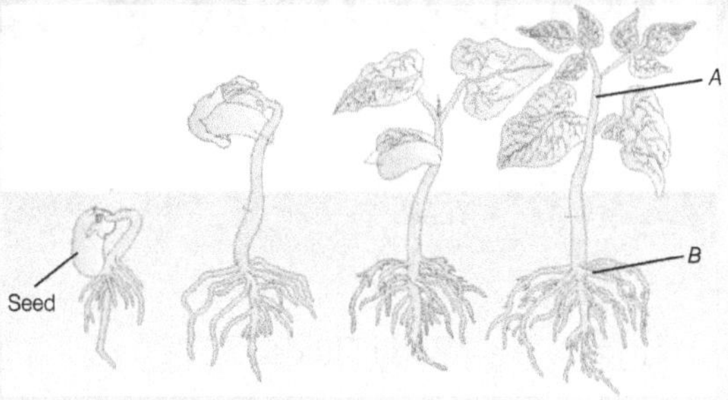

(i) Name and explain the type of tropic movement shown in figure.

(ii) Identify the part labelled as *A* and *B*.

(iii) Name the hormone that helped in the germination of seed.

(iv) Hormone associated with breaking seed dormancy.

Answers

1. (i) (b), (ii) (c), (iii) (a), (iv) (b), (v) (d)

07

Circulatory System

TREND ANALYSIS 4 YEARS

		Average No. of Questions Across all Sets				
		Types of Questions	2024	2023	2020	2019
TOPIC 01	Body Fluids	1 Mark	4	1	–	–
		2 Marks	1	1	–	–
		3 Marks	–	–	–	–
		5 Marks	–	–	–	–
TOPIC 02	Circulatory System	1 Mark	4	3	–	3
		2 Marks	1	–	–	–
		3 Marks	–	1	–	–
		4 Marks	–	–	–	–

TOPIC 1

Body Fluids

- The flow of the fluids inside the body is known as **circulation** and the organs involved in it together constitute the **circulatory system.**
- All living organisms, including human beings have some kinds of **fluids** circulating in their bodies. These fluids have the ability to pick up substances and distribute them to various parts of the body.
- There are three main types of body fluids found in human beings such as blood, tissue fluid and lymph. These are described as follows

Blood

It is a fluid connective tissue which is found circulating inside the body. The blood is bright red in colour with a pH of about 7.3-7.5, i.e. slightly alkaline in nature. The blood is composed of following two main components.

I. Plasma

- It is the liquid portion of the blood, slightly yellow in colour. It constitutes about 50-60% of the total blood.
- It mainly consists of water, proteins, inorganic salts and other substances such as glucose, urea, hormones, etc.
- **Serum** is the fluid that is left out liquid part when the fibrinogen proteins are removed from plasma.

II. Blood Corpuscles

The blood corpuscles are the cellular elements of the blood constituting about 45% of the blood. These include erythrocytes (RBCs), leucocytes (WBCs) and thrombocytes (platelets).

1. **Erythrocytes** (RBCs)

- These are the cellular components of blood containing haemoglobin. These are the most abundant type of cells found in the blood.

- RBCs are biconcave disc-like structures. It extremely small in size of about 7 μm, due to which they move easily through the capillaries in the body.
- Mature RBCs are enucleated, i.e. they lack nucleus and endoplasmic reticulum which makes them more flexible. This increases their surface area to volume ratio for carrying more oxygen.
- RBCs lack mitochondria which means that red cells cannot use oxygen by themselves instead, all the oxygen absorbed from the lungs is transported to all other tissues.
- RBCs are red in colour due to the presence of a red coloured pigment called **haemoglobin.** It acts as an oxygen carrier molecule. It has an iron containing part called **haem** and a protein called **globin**.
- Haemoglobin has ability to combine readily with oxygen to form **oxyhaemoglobin**, an unstable compound which readily gives up oxygen to the body tissues.
- The average lifespan of a mature RBC is only 120 days after which it get destroyed in the spleen (known as graveyard of RBCs).
- **Function** Its major function is to carry and transport respiratory gases to the tissues.

2. **Leucocytes** (WBCs)

- These are the most active and motile constituents of blood.
- They differ from RBCs as they are nucleated (have nucleus) and lack the coloured pigment (haemoglobin).
- WBCs are irregular in shape and are generally short lived, i.e. only 12-14 days.
- Leucocytes also show the property of **diapedesis**, i.e. oozing out as they have the ability to move out of capillaries into the tissues.

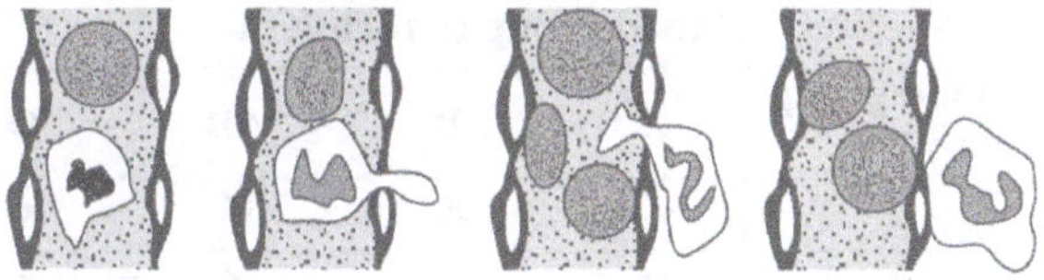

Fig. 7.1 A WBC oozing out of the blood vessel (diapedesis)

Different types of white blood cells (leucocytes) after staining

Two major categories of WBCs	Cell type	Distinguishin g features	Functions
Granular	Neutrophils (62%)	Nucleus with 3-4 lobes. Granules stain with neutral dyes.	Engulf bacteria (phagocytosis)
	Eosinophils (2.3%) (count increases during allergic reactions	Nucleus with 2 lobes. Granules stain dark red with eosin (acid dye).	Engulf bacteria. Secrete antitoxins, is associated with allergy.
	Basophils (0.4%)	Nucleus large indistinctly lobed. Granules stain with basic dyes, i.e. methylene blue.	Release chemicals (such as histamine) for inflammation which dilate blood vessels.
Agranular	Lymphocytes (30%)	Smallest type of WBC. It has single large nucleus.	Produce antibodies.
	Monocytes (5.3%)	Large kidney-shaped nucleus. Transform into macrophages at the site of infection.	Ingest germs.

- **Functions** The major function of leucocytes is that they act as a defence mechanism for body. They have the ability of phagocytosis (e.g. neutrophils engulf thc foreign particle mainly bacteria).
- Some types of WBCs help in reducing inflammation caused by injury or trauma (e.g. monocytes, neutrophils). WBCs also produce antibodies that help in killing foreign particles or germs, e.g. lymphocytes.

3. **Thrombocytes** (Blood platelets)

- These are minute oval or round, enucleated structures found floating in the blood. Their lifespan is about 3-5 days and get destroyed in the spleen alongwith RBCs.
- **Function** Their main function is to help in clotting or coagulation of blood.

Blood Clotting

- It is a mechanism of formation of a clot when an injury or trauma occurs.
- It has been seen that when a blood vessel is cut during an injury, blood does not continue to flow for a longer time, instead it stops flowing after sometime.

- If somebody fails to exhibit this property of clotting, that person will continue to bleed when he/she gets injured as he/she may lack of one or the other factor that normally control clotting of blood. This can even lead to the death of that person.
- Blood clotting is a complex process which involves a series of steps to get completed. These are as follows

Injured tissue cells and platelets release thromboplastin (factor X)

↓

Thromboplastin with the help of Ca^{2+} (present in the plasma) converts prothrombin (inactive) into thrombin (active)

↓

Thrombin acts as an enzyme and along with Ca^{2+} it reacts with soluble fibrinogen and convert it into fibrin (insoluble form), a solid substance that forms threads.

↓

These threads traps RBCs and finally form a clot

Functions of Blood

It performs the following important functions

- Helps in the transportation of respiratory gases (i.e. O_2, CO_2, etc).
- Helps in healing the wounds.
- Maintains body pH, water and ionic balance.
- Fights against infections by forming body immunity.
- Helps in transportation of hormones from endocrine glands to target organs.

Blood Groups

There are two main types of blood grouping systems, i.e. ABO and Rh system. These are described below

1. ABO System

This is the most common system found in human beings described by **Karl Landsteiner**.

- According to this system, blood is classified into four main types, i.e. A, B, AB and O blood groups.
- This grouping is mainly based on the type of antigens and antibodies present on the surface of red blood corpuscles.

The representation of different antigens and antibodies are depicted in the table given below

Blood group	Antigen present	Antibody present
A	A	b
B	B	a
AB	A and B	—
O	—	a and b

Blood Transfusion

- It is a mechanism of injecting blood from a healthy person into the body of the patients (undergoing operation or any other injury).
- The person who gives blood is known as **donor**, while a person receiving blood from a healthy person is known as **recipient**.
- A person with blood group 'O' is known as **universal donor** (as it lacks antigen) and can donate blood to the persons with any blood groups, i.e. A, B, AB and O.
- A person with blood group 'AB' is known as **universal recipient** (as it has all known antigens) and can receive blood from every other blood groups, i.e. A, B, AB and O.
- But before transfusion of blood from one person to another, it is necessary to match the type of blood groups between the two, in order to avoid clumping of blood or destruction of RBCs.
- Thus, it is important to match the compatibility (matching) and incompatibility (mis-matching) in ABO blood system.
- This can be easily understood by the table given below

Summary of ABO Blood Group Matching (Compatibility)

Blood group of donor	Blood group of recipient			
	A	B	AB	O
A	✓	✗	✓	✗
B	✗	✓	✓	✗
AB	✗	✗	✓	✗
O (Universal donor)	✓	✓	✓ Universal recipient	✓

2. Rh System

- It is another type of blood group system found in human beings.
- The blood of most people contains a unique factor known as Rh-factor (it was named after it was first discovered in **Rhesus monkey**).
- Rh-factor is based on the presence or absence of an antigen on the surface of RBCs.
- Thus, the person having Rh-antigen on their RBCs are called **Rh-positive** (Rh +ve), while person who does not have Rh-antigen on their RBCs are called **Rh-negative** (Rh–ve).
- It is also necessary to test–Rh-factor before transfusing blood as if a Rh +ve blood is transfused into Rh –ve person, the recipient will develop an antibody in response for Rh-antigen.
- Due to this during second transfusion, the antibody produced by first transfusion will cause a reaction with the transfused blood, which may even cause death of that individual.

Tissue Fluid (Extracellular fluid)

- During blood flow through the capillaries, plasma and leucocytes from the blood get leaked out through their walls and accumulate in the intercellular spaces. This fluid is known as tissue fluid.
- Far off cells of the body which are not in contact with capillaries, use or absorb O_2 and other substances from this fluid and inturn give off CO_2 and other wastes back to it. Net complete amount of tissue fluid enters into the lymphatic vessels.

Lymph

Tissue fluid after entering the lymph vessels is known as lymph. It only flows in lymphatic vessels and lymph organs.

Function Its major function is to supply O_2, absorption of fats from intestine and also acts as a defence mechanism.

Examination of a Blood Smear

A blood smear or a blood film can be easily prepared in the laboratory by following the common procedure. After preparing the film, it is viewed under the microscope.

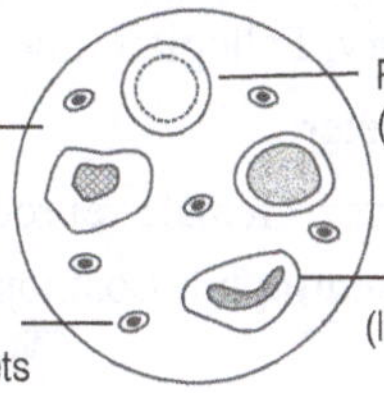

Note The slide must be dried before examining. Different components of blood, i.e. RBCs, WBCs, blood platelets, plasma, etc., all can be observed in the slide.

PYQs Previous Years' Questions

1 Mark Questions

Multiple Choice Questions

1. The lifespan of an RBC is **ICSE 2023**

(a) 120 days (b) 220 days
(c) 20 days (d) 2 days

Ans. (a) 120 days

2. A muscular wall is absent in **ICSE Specimen 2021-22 Sem. II**

(a) capillary
(b) vein
(c) venule
(d) arteriole

Ans. (a) capillary

Very Short Answer Type Questions

3. Choose the odd one out from the following terms and name the category to which the others belong .
Prothrombin, Thrombin, Fibrinogen, Albumin

Ans. **Odd term** : Albumin **ICSE 2024**

Category : Others are blood clotting factors.

4. Name the mineral elements required for clotting blood. **ICSE 2024**

Ans. Ca^{2+}

5. Briefly explain the term diapedesis. **ICSE 2024, 2014, 2006, 2000**

Ans. **Diapedesis** is the process by which white blood cells squeeze out through the walls of capillaries to reach at the site of infection.

6. Choose the odd one out from each of the following sets, giving the reason for your choice.
Basophils, Neutrophils, Monocytes, Eosinophils.

Ans. **Odd one** Monocytes **ICSE 2024, 2005**

Category Rest all are granulocyte.

7. Given below are five sets of terms. In each case arrange and rewrite each set so as to be in a logical sequence. One is done as an example for you.
Example : Large intestine, Stomach, Mouth, Small intestine, Oesophagus.
Ans : Mouth, Oesophagus, Stomach, Small intestine, Large intestine.
Posterior vena cava, Renal artery, Aorta, Renal vein, Kidney **ICSE Specimen 2019**

Ans. Aorta, Renal artery, Kidney, Renal vein, Posterior vena cava

8. Identify the odd term in each set and name the category to which the remaining 3 belong.
Example : Ovary, Fallopian tube, Ureter, Uterus

Odd term : Ureter

Category : Parts of female reproductive system.

(i) Basophil, Neutrophil, Eosinophil, Lymphocyte. **ICSE Specimen 2019, 2017**

(ii) Pulmonary vein, Hepatic vein, Renal vein, Post caval **ICSE Specimen 2019**

Ans. (i) **Odd term** : Lymphocyte

Category : Other are granulocytes..

(ii) **Odd term** : Pulmonary vein

Category : Others are deoxygenated blood carrying blood vessels.

9. Give one difference between each of the following pairs on the basis of what is given in the brackets.
Mitral valve and Aortic semilunar valve (location)

Ans. Difference between Mitral valve and Aortic semilunar valve is **ICSE Specimen 2019**

Mitral valve	Aortic semilunar valve
It is located between the left atrium and left ventricle.	It is located between the left ventricle and aorta.

10. Give appropriate biological or technical terms for 'Squeezing out the white blood cells from the capillaries into the surrounding tissues.' **ICSE 2018**

Or Give the biological/technical terms for.

'WBCs squeeze through the walls of the capillaries into the tissue.' **ICSE 2012**

Ans. Diapedesis

11. Name the following
The respiratory pigment found in erythrocytes. **ICSE Specimen 2017**

Or

Name the respiratory pigment present in erythrocytes. **ICSE 2004**

Or

Name the iron containing pigment in erythrocytes. **ICSE 2000**

Ans. Haemoglobin

12. Give technical term for the following.
Plasma devoid of fibrinogen. **ICSE Specimen 2017**

Ans. Serum

13. Given below are sets of five terms each. Rewrite the terms in correct order in a logical sequence.

Example Large intestine, Stomach, Mouth, Small intestine, Oesophagus.

Answer Mouth → Oesophagus → Stomach → Small intestine → Large intestine.

Fibrin, Platelets, Thromboplastin, Fibrinogen, Thrombin. **ICSE 2017**

Ans. Platelets → Thromboplastin → Thrombin → Fibrinogen → Fibrin
(Mechanism of blood clotting)

14. Give appropriate biological/technical terms for

'Cellular components of blood containing haemoglobin.' **ICSE 2017**

Ans. Erythrocytes

15. Choose the correct answer from the four options given below.

The mineral ion needed for the formation of blood clot is **ICSE 2016**

(a) potassium (b) sodium
(c) calcium (d) iron

Ans. (c) Calcium

16. State the main function of lymphocytes of blood. **ICSE 2016**

Ans. Lymphocytes keep away infection by producing antibodies against foreign particles.

17. Give scientific reasons for the given statement.

Mature erythrocytes within human lack nucleus and mitochondria. **ICSE 2016**

Or 'A mature mammalian erythrocyte lacks nucleus and mitochondria.' **ICSE 2011**

Ans. Refer to text on page no. 95.

18. Rewrite and complete the sentence by inserting the correct word in the space indicated.
Oxygen combines with haemoglobin present in RBC and forms .... **ICSE 2015**

Ans. Oxygen combines with haemoglobin present in RBC and forms oxyhaemoglobin.

19. Differentiate between the given pair on the basis of what is mentioned within bracket.
RBC and WBC (Shape) **ICSE 2015**

Ans. **RBCs** They are biconcave disc-shaped and have no nucleus.
WBCs They are amoeboid in shape but have a nucleus.

20. Give the technical term for the fluid portion of blood. **ICSE 2014**

Ans. **Plasma** is the technical term for the fluid portion of blood.

21. Name the mineral element essential for the clotting of blood. **ICSE 2012, 2011**

Ans. Calcium is the mineral element essential for the clotting of the blood.

22. State the main function of thrombocytes. **ICSE 2011, 2008**

Ans. Thrombocytes help in blood clotting by producing thromboplastin.

23. Write down the difference between the pair as indicated within the bracket.
Erythrocytes and leucocytes (function). **ICSE 2011**

Ans. **Erythrocytes** transport respiratory gases.
Leucocytes produce antibodies and protect the body from disease causing germs.

24. Give the technical or biological term for
The process by which white blood cells engulf harmful microbes. **ICSE 2008, 2000**

Ans. **Phagocytosis** is the process by which WBCs engulf harmful microbes.

25. State whether the statement is true or false. If false, write the correct statement by changing the first word only. Iron is the mineral element responsible for the clotting of blood. **ICSE 2006**

Ans. This statement is false. For correct statement refer to answer no. 21.

26. Give one reason for : Erythrocytes are biconcave discs and lack nucleus. **ICSE 2006, 2004, 2002**

Ans. RBCs/erythrocytes are biconcave disc-like structures that lack nucleus to provide large volume surface for the absorption and transport of oxygen.

27. Given below are certain biological statements which are incomplete and hence incorrect. Rewrite the correct form of the statement by inserting a suitable word/words at the right place. Do not delete any word already given in the statement. Underline the inserted word/words.
The process of movement of corpuscles through capillary walls. **ICSE 2004**

Ans. Diapedesis is the process of movement of **white blood cells** through capillary walls into the extra cellular fluid.

28. Give one point difference between the pair on the basis of what is indicated in bracket.
Red blood corpuscles and White blood corpuscles (origin). **ICSE 2004**

Ans. Difference between RBC and WBC is

RBC	WBC
These are originated in the bone marrow of long bones.	These are originated in the lymph nodes.

29. State whether the following statement is true or false. Correct and rewrite the false statement by changing either the first or the last word. Platelets which disintegrate in the injured tissue cells release prothrombin. **ICSE 2004**

Ans. The statement given is false. Platelets which disintegrate in the injured tissue cells release **thromboplastin**.

30. Differentiate between blood plasma and serum. **ICSE 2003**

Ans. Difference between blood plasma and serum is

Blood Plasma	Serum
It is the liquid portion of the blood excluding blood corpuscles.	It is known as the blood plasma without protein (fibrinogen) in it.

31. Given below is the functional activity of specific structures in the body of living organisms. Name the structure responsible for the transport of oxygen to the cells of the human body. **ICSE 2002**

Ans. **Red blood cells** transport oxygen to the cells of the human body.

32. Choose the correct answer from the four options given below.
Agranulocytes are **ICSE 2000**
(a) lymphocytes and monocytes
(b) lymphocytes and basophils
(c) eosinophils and basophils
(d) eosinophils and monocytes

Ans. (a) Lymphocytes and monocytes are the type of agranulocytes.

33. Given below is an example of a certain structure and its special functional activity kidney and excretion. Erythrocyte and ..... **ICSE 2000**

Ans. Erythrocytes and gaseous exchange.

34. Select the correct answer out of the four available choices given under each question.
The chief function of lymph nodes in mammals is to **ICSE 2000**

(a) produce WBCs (b) produce hormones
(c) destroy old RBCs (d) destroy pathogen

Ans. (a) Lymph nodes in mammals produce WBCs.

2 Marks Questions

35. Why are RBCs efficient in their functions though they lack nucleus and mitochondria? **ICSE 2024**

Ans. Refer to text on page no. 95.

36. Mention any two functions of blood. **ICSE 2023**

Ans. Functions of blood are
Transportation of oxygen from the lungs to the tissues.
Transportation of digested food from the small intestine to the tissues and cells around the body.

37. Give the location of pericardial fluid. What is its function? **ICSE Specimen 2021-22 Sem. II**

Ans. This fluid is present in pericardial cavity between the inner and outer pericardial.Pericardial fluid helps to reduce friction within the pericardium by lubricating the epicardial surface and allowing the membranes to glide over each other with each heart beat.

38. Given below is the diagram of a human blood smear. Label the parts numbered 1, 2 and 3. **ICSE Specimen 2021-22 Sem. II**

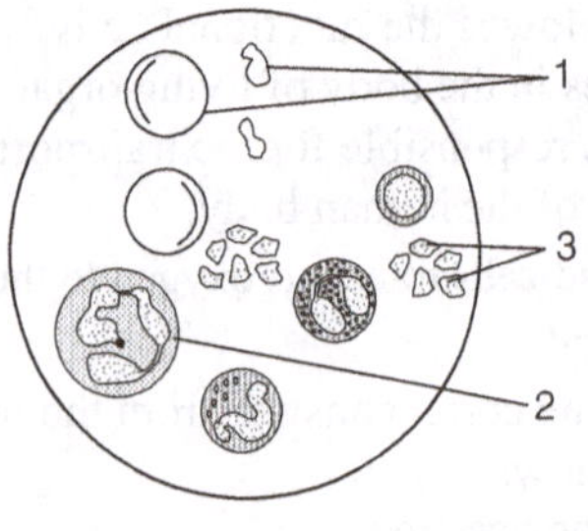

Ans. 1- RBCs 2-WBCs 3-Platelets

39. Name the substance that initiates blood clotting. What is the mineral element essential to form a blood clot? **ICSE Specimen 2021-22 Sem. II**

Ans. Platelets, Calcium

40. A mature mammalian erythrocyte lacks nucleus and mitochondria but is efficient in its functioning. Explain by giving suitable reasons.

Ans. Refer to text on page no. 95. **ICSE 2021-20 Sem. II**

41. Differentiate between the following pairs on the basis of what is given in brackets. **ICSE Specimen 2017, 2006**
(i) Lymphocytes and Neutrophils (structure of nucleus).
(ii) Plasma and Serum (composition).

Ans. (i)

Lymphocytes	Neutrophils
These are small cells with round and large nuclei and little cytoplasm.	These are most abundant WBCs with multilobed nuclei.

(ii) **Plasma** mainly consists of water, proteins, inorganic salts and other fibrinogen substances such as glucose, urea, hormones, fibrinogen, etc.
Serum is the fluid that is left out liquid part when the fibrinogen proteins are removed from plasma.

42. Draw a diagram of the different blood cells as seen in a smear of human blood. **ICSE 2014**

Ans. Refer to figure on page no. 97.

3 Marks Question

43. Mention one function for each of the following.
(i) Lymphocytes (ii) Thrombocytes
(iii) Neutrophils **ICSE 2021-22 Sem. II**

Ans. Functions are as follows
(i) **Lymphocytes** These are agranular leucocytes that produce antibodies.
(ii) **Thrombocytes** These are also known as platelets. Their main function is to help in blood coagulation.
(iii) **Neutrophils** These destroy the bacteria by engulfing them (phagocytosis) thus, boosting the immune response.

Diagram Based Questions

44. Study the diagrams given below and answer the questions that follows **ICSE Specimen 2019 (5M)**

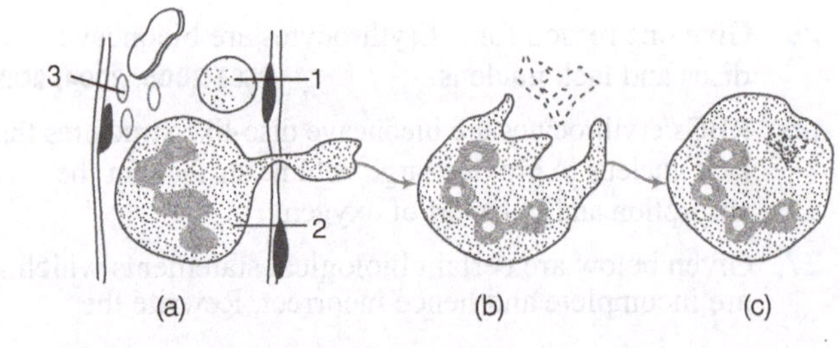

(i) Name the cells numbered 1, 2 and 3.

(ii) Identify the phenomenon occurring in (a). Explain the phenomenon.

(iii) Mention two structural differences between 1 and 2.

(iv) Name the process occurring in (b) and (c).

(v) State the importance of this process in the human body.

Ans. (i) The cell numbered as 1 is RBC, 2 is WBC and 3 is platelets.

(ii) The phenomenon occurring in part (a) is diapedesis, i.e. the movement of leucocytes from blood capillaries into the tissues. Here, it differentiates to form macrophages and dendritic cells.

(iii) Structural differences between 1 (RBC) and 2 (WBC) are

Part 1 (RBC)	**Part 2** (WBC)
Biconcave in shape	Amoeboid in shape
Nucleus absent	Nucleus present

(iv) Phagocytosis is the process occurring in (b) and (c).

(v) During this phenomenon, the WBC engulfs the disease causing germs that enter the body and thus, defend our body from these organisms.

45. Given below is a diagram of a human blood smear. Study the diagram and answer the questions that follow

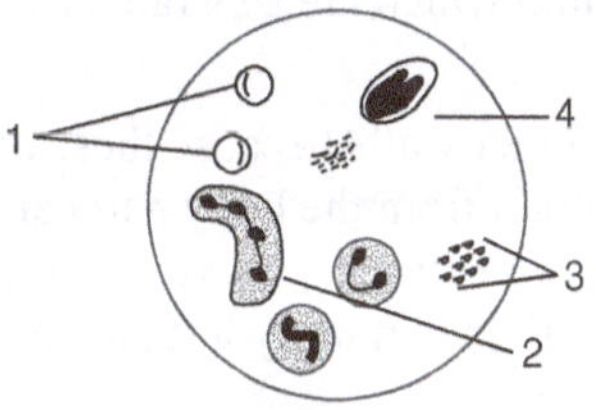

(i) Name the components numbered '1' to '4'.

(ii) Mention two structural differences between the parts '1' and '2'.

(iii) Name the soluble protein found in part '4' which forms insoluble threads during clotting of blood.

(iv) What is the average lifespan of the component numbered '1'?

(v) Component numbered '1' do not have certain organelles but are very efficient in their function. Explain. **ICSE 2018 (5M)**

Ans. (i) (1) RBC (2) WBC (3) Platelets (4) Plasma

(ii) Structural differences between RBC and WBC are as follows

RBC	**WBC**
Biconcave in shape.	Amoeboid in shape.
Nucleus absent.	Nucleus present.

(iii) Plasma contains a soluble protein fibrinogen.

During blood clotting, soluble fibrinogen converts into fibrin (insoluble form) in the presence of enzyme thrombokinase and Ca^{2+} ion.

(iv) The average lifespan of RBC is 120 days.

(v) Mature RBCs are enucleated, i.e. they lack nucleus and endoplasmic reticulum which makes them more flexible thus, increasing their surface area to volume ratio for carrying more oxygen. They lack mitochondria which means that red cells cannot use oxygen by themselves instead all the oxygen absorbed from the lungs is transported to all other tissues.

46. Study the following diagram carefully and then answer the questions that follow

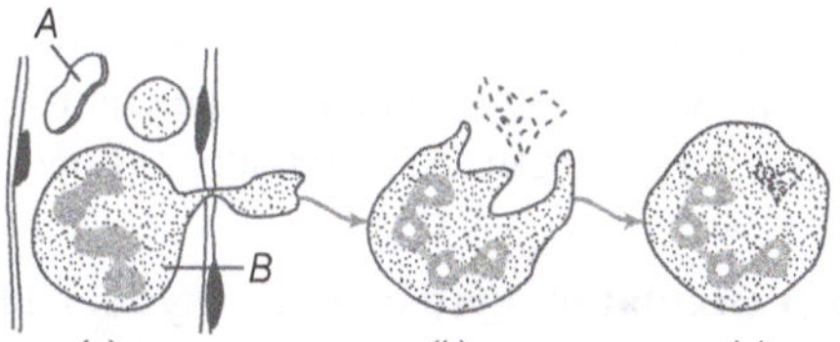

(a) (b) (c)

(i) Name the cell labelled *A*.

(ii) Identify the phenomenon occurring in (*a*).

(iii) Mention two structural differences between *A* and *B*.

(iv) Name the process occurring in (*b*) and (*c*) and state the importance of this process in the human body. **ICSE 2011 (5M)**

Ans. (i) Cell labelled as *A* in the diagram is red blood cells.

(ii) The phenomenon occurring in part (*a*) is **diapedesis.**

(iii) Refer to ans. 45 (ii).

(iv) **Phagocytosis** is the process occurring in (*b*) and (*c*).

During this phenomenon, the WBC engulfs the disease causing germs that enter the body and thus, defend our body from them.

47. Given alongside is diagram of a smear of human blood. Study the same and then answer the questions that follow

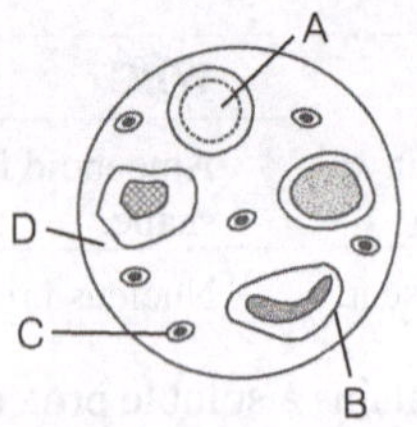

(i) Name the parts *A*, *B*, *C* and *D* indicated by guidelines.

(ii) Mention two structural differences between the parts labelled '*A*' and '*B*'.

(iii) What is the main function of the parts labelled *A*, *B*, *C*?

(iv) What is the lifespan of the part labelled '*A*'?

(v) Name a soluble protein found in '*D*' which helps in the clotting of blood. **ICSE 2002 (5M)**

Ans. (i) The part *A*, *B*, *C* and *D* indicated in the diagram are

A – Erythrocytes *B* – Leucocytes

C – Thrombocytes *D* – Plasma

(ii) Refer to ans. 45 (ii).

(iii) The main function of part *A*, *B* and *C* are

A–Transport oxygen as oxyhaemoglobin (erythrocytes) to the body tissues.

B–Defend the body against disease causing germs (leucocytes).

C–Initiate clotting of blood (thrombocyte).

(iv) Lifespan of the part labelled *A*, i.e. RBCs is 120 days.

(v) Soluble protein found in *D*, i.e. plasma which helps in the clotting of blood is fibrinogen.

TOPIC 2

Circulatory System

In living beings circulatory system is comprised of a heart (a muscular pumping organ) and blood vessels, i.e. arteries, veins and capillaries. Depending upon the circulatory patterns in different organisms, circulatory system is of two types. These are

(i) **Open circulatory system** In this system, blood is pumped from the heart through blood vessels but then it leaves the blood vessels and enters into the body cavities. The blood pressure is low and generally the blood (called haemolymph) has low cellularity, e.g. arthropods, molluscs, protochordates, etc.

(ii) **Closed circulatory system** In this system, the flow of blood occurs inside the tubular vessels and the blood contains a respiratory pigment haemoglobin, e.g. humans, birds, earthworms, etc.

The Heart

- It is the main pumping organ found in the thoracic cavity in human beings, i.e. between the two lungs and above the diaphragm. It is about the size of our close fist.
- It protected by a double membranous covering known as **pericardium.**
- The space between the two pericardial membranes is filled with **pericardial fluid.** This protects the heart from any mechanical injury and shocks and also helps in reducing friction.
- Human heart is comprised of four main chambers.

These are as follow

1. Two Atria (sing. atrium)

- These are the upper two chambers of the heart, i.e. left and right atrium which are separated by **inter-atricular septum.**
- They have thinner walls because these are meant to receive the blood from the body parts and pump it into their respective ventricles, i.e. right atrium pump blood into right ventricle, similarly left atrium into left ventricle.
- They are also known as **auricles.**

2. Two Ventricles

- These are the lower two chambers of the heart, i.e. left and right ventricles which are separated by **inter-ventricular septum.**
- They have thicker muscular walls than auricles because they are meant to pump blood to larger distances.
- A septum called **atrio-ventricular septum** is present in between the right atria and left ventricles. It separates or prevents the mixing of oxygenated and deoxygenated blood.
- At the corner of right auricle near the opening of vena cava. A band of muscles is present known as Sino-Atrial

node (SA node), which generates impulse that spreads in all directions. It is also called as **pacemaker**.

- Another band of muscular tissue called Atrio-Ventricular node (AV node) is also present in the lower side of right atrium which strengthen the signals generated by SA node. It is also called **pacesetter**.

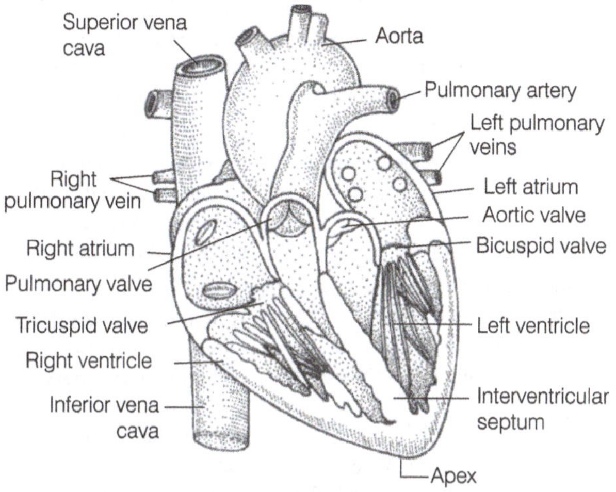

Fig. 7.2 Heart

Different Valves of Heart

Valves are the muscular flaps meant to prevent back flow of blood. There are four types of valves present in the heart.

Different Valves of Human Heart

Tricuspid valve	It is located at the aperture between the right auricle and right ventricle and is also known as right atrio-ventricular valve.
Mitral (bicuspid) valve	It is located at the aperture between the left auricle and left ventricle and is also known as left atrio-ventricular valve.
Pulmonary semilunar valve	The opening of right ventricle into the pulmonary artery is provided with the pulmonary semilunar valve.
Aortic semilunar valve	It is located at the point of origin of aorta from left ventricle.

Note Chordae tendinae are located on the inner surface of the ventricles.Their main function is to keep the cuspid valves in position

Blood Vessels

These are the branched tubes which extends from heart to all parts of the body. There are three main types of blood vessels which carry blood towards and away from the heart. These are as follows

(i) **Artery** It is a blood vessel whose function is to carry blood away from the heart and towards any other organ. The flow of blood is in spurts in arteries.

An artery is comprised of thick walls and narrow central lumen (core). Arteriole is the smallest final branch of artery which further breaks up into the capillaries.

(ii) **Vein** It is a type of blood vessel which carries blood away from the organs and towards the heart. The flow of blood in veins is found to be uniform. It is comprised of thinner walls and a larger central lumen than arteries. Veins contain a thin pocket type valve towards the heart which help them to prevent back flow of blood.

(iii) **Capillary** It is a narrow tube-like blood vessel, comprised of single layer of endothelial cells. Capillaries have the ability of contracting and dialating with the decrease and increase in the blood supply to various body parts.

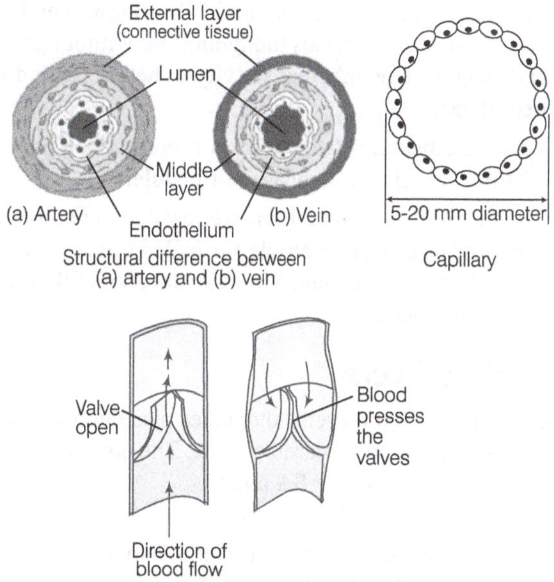

Fig. 7.3 Valves in a vein regulate the flow of blood in the direction of the heat

Blood Vessels Entering the Heart

(i) **Anterior** (superior) **vena cava** brings deoxygenated blood from the upper portion of the body, i.e. from head, chest, arms, etc., into right atrium.

(ii) **Posterior** (inferior) **vena cava,** brings blood from the lower portion of the body, i.e. from abdomen and legs into the right atrium.

(iii) **Pulmonary veins** (two from each lung), brings oxygenated blood to the left atrium.

Note Coronary artery supplies oxygenated blood to the walls of heart.

Blood Vessels Leaving the Heart

(i) **Pulmonary artery,** carries deoxygenated blood to the lungs for purification (oxygenation). It arises from right ventricle.

(ii) The aorta, is the largest artery in human body which carries oxygenated blood to all other body parts. It arises from left ventricle.

Pulse

- Counting of pulse is indirectly the counting of the heartbeat. Rate of pulse increases during stress, emotions or doing physical exercise.
- The heart regularly and rhythmically contracts and relaxes at short intervals thoughout life without pause and fatigue. This inherent activity of heart is called its **heartbeat**.
- Each heartbeat has two phases, i.e. contraction phase or **systole** and relaxation phase or **diastole.**
- The rate of throbbing felt in arteries due to pumping action of heart (left ventricle) is called **pulse**. Its rate is about 72 times per minute in man and about 80 times per minute in women.

Cardiac Cycle

The sequence of the events that takes place in heart during one heartbeat is called cardiac cycle. The command for heartbeat starts from the SA node.

It is comprised of following phases

- In atrial systole, the artia contract due to the wave of contraction, stimulated by the SA node.
- Ventricular systole in which both ventricles contract, forcing blood through the capillary artery to the lungs and through the aorta to rest of the body.
- Atrial diastole in which atria relax.
- Ventricular diastole in which ventricles relax, and become ready to fill with blood from atria as the next cycle begins.

Differences between Artery Systole and Ventricular Systole

Atrial systole	Ventricular systole
This is a contraction phase which initiates with the contraction of atrial muscles. ↓ This opens the vena cava and inturn closes the pulmonary vein. ↓ Blood through tricuspid and mitral valve enters the ventricles. This closes pulmonary and aortic semilunar valves. ↓ Production of a 'Dup' sound occurs preventing the back flow of blood into ventricles.	During this phase the contraction of ventricular muscles takes place. ↓ Tricuspid and mitral valves get closed (with a jerk) and produce a sound called 'Lubb'. ↓ Blood through semilunar valves passes into aorta and pulmonary artery and then enters into atria through the openings of vena cava and pulmonary vein.

Heart Sounds

- Heart produces the following two sounds in short succession followed by a small gap.
- The first sound called **Lubb** is produced due to the sharp closure of tricuspid and mitral valves at the start of ventricular systole.
- The second sound called **Dupp** is produced due to the closure of aortic semilunar valve and pulmonary semilunar valve at the beginning of ventricular diastole, which prevents the backflow of blood into ventricles.
- Human heartbeats around 72 times in one minute. Adult women has higher rate of heart beat, i.e. 78-82 beat per minute than men, i.e. 70-72 heartbeat per minute.

Blood Pressure

- It is the pressure exerted by the arteries on their walls, while the blood is flowing through them.
- The rise of blood pressure during contraction of heart is called **systolic pressure.**
- And the fall of blood pressure during relaxation of heart is known as **diastolic pressure.** The normal blood pressure for an adult is 100-140 mm Hg (systolic pressure) and 60-80 mm Hg (diastolic pressure).

- A rise in blood pressure is called **hypertension** (above the normal level) and decrease in blood pressure is called **hypotension** (below the normal level).

Types of Blood Circulation

Blood in human beings flows twice in the heart before it completes one round. It is comprised of one short flow, i.e. pulmonary circulation and another long flow, i.e. systemic circulation. Due to this reason the blood flow in humans is known as **double circulation.**

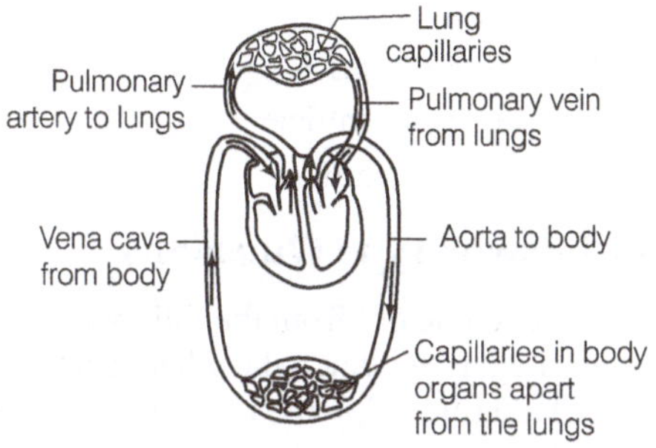

(i) **In pulmonary circulation**, deoxygenated blood is collected from the heart (right ventricle) by pulmonary artery and oxygenated blood is returned to the heart (left atrium) through pulmonary veins.

(ii) **In systemic circulation**, oxygenated blood from the heart (left ventricle) is carried to different body parts of the body through aorta and deoxygenated blood is carried into the heart (right atrium) through vena cava.

Hepatic Portal System

The veins from the stomach and intestine instead of carrying blood directly to posterior vena cava, first enter the liver as a combined hepatic portal vein. This further breaks up into small capillaries and form a hepatic vein that joins to the posterior vena cava.

Significance

- Hepatic portal system acts like a store to regulate the quantity of nutrients flowing in the blood, i.e. it helps in storing excess of nutrients in liver and allowing remaining required amount of nutrients to flow in the blood.
- It allows the required amount of nutrients like heparin, fibrinogen, prothrombin and vitamin-A to flow in the blood.
- Also, if certain poisons are absorbed through food, the detoxification of food occurs in the liver.

Main Blood Vessels of Liver and Kidney

- Hepatic artery (from aorta into liver) and hepatic portal vein (from stomach and intestine into liver) are the blood vessels that enter the liver.
- Hepatic vein (from the liver into posterior vena cava) leaves the liver.
- Renal artery (from aorta into kidney) enters the kidney.
- Renal vein (from kidney into posterior vena cava) leaves the kidney.

Lymphatic System

This system of human comprises of lymph, lymphatic capillaries, lymphatic vessels, lymphatic ducts and lymphatic nodes. It also comprises of lymphatic organs and glands.

- **Lymph** is the tissue fluid after entering the lymph vessels.
- **Lymphatic capillaries** lie close to the blood capillaries, but differ from them to the extent that they end blindly.
- **Lymphatic vessels** The lymphatic capillaries unite to form larger lymphatic vessels.
- **Lymphatic ducts** Lymph vessels of left and right side of the body combines to form a thoracic duct or left lymphatic duct and right lymphatic duct, respectively.
- **Lymphatic nodes** These are located along the length of lymphatic vessels.

Lymphatic Organs and Glands

The tonsils on the sides of the neck are lymph glands.

The spleen is a large lymphatic organ. It is reddish brown in colour. Spleen is found in the abdomen behind the stomach and above the left kideny. It acts as a blood reservoir, produce lymphocytes and destroy worn-out red blood cells.

PYQs Previous Years' Questions

1 Mark Questions

Multiple Choice Questions

1. If a person has a heart attack, what must be done immediately? **ICSE 2024**

   P. Loosen his/her clothing

   Q. Make him/her lie down in an airy room

   R. Rush him/her to the hospital

   S. Engage him/her in a conversation

   (a) P and Q (b) P and S (c) R and S (d) P, Q and R

Ans. (d) P, Q and R

2. The heart sound 'Dup' is produced when **ICSE 2023**

   (a) semilunar valves open

   (b) atrioventricular valves close

   (c) semilunar valves close

   (d) atrioventricular valves open

Ans. (c) semilunar valves close

3. Oxygenated blood to liver is supplied by **ICSE 2023**

   (a) hepatic artery (b) hepatic vein

   (c) inferior vena cava (d) hepatic portal vein

Ans. (a) hepatic artery

4. The mineral element in haemoglobin is

   (a) manganese (b) iron **ICSE 2021-22 Sem. II**

   (c) sodium (d) calcium

Ans. (b) iron

5. Pericardium covers the **ICSE 2021-22 Sem. II**

   (a) heart (b) brain (c) spinal cord (d) eyeball

Ans. (a) heart

6. The blood vessel that carries oxygenated blood is **ICSE 2021-22 Sem. II**

   (a) pulmonary artery (b) pulmonary vein

   (c) renal vein (d) hepatic vein

Ans. (b) pulmonary vein

7. While recording the pulse rate, where exactly does a doctor press on our wrist ? **ICSE 2019**

   (a) Nerve (b) Vein (c) Artery (d) Capillary

Ans. (c) Artery

8. A muscular wall is absent in **ICSE 2019**

   (a) capillary (b) venule (c) arteriole (d) vein

Ans. (a) Capillary

9. Choose the correct answer from the four options given below.

   Pulse wave is mainly caused by the **ICSE 2013**

   (a) systole of atria

   (b) diastole of atria

   (c) systole of the left ventricle

   (d) systole of the right ventricle

Ans. (c) systole of the left ventricle.

Very Short Answer Type Questions

10. Choose the odd one out from the following terms and name the category to which the others belong .

    Tonsils, Glomerulus, Spleen, Lymph nodes **ICSE 2024**

Ans. **Odd term** : Glomerulus

Category : Others are lymphatic organs.

11. Choose the odd one out from the following terms and name the category to which the others belong

    Pulmonary artery, Renal artery, Coronary artery, Hepatic artery **ICSE 2024**

Ans. **Odd term** : Coronary artery

Category : Others supply blood to various organs oxygenated blood.

12. Mention two structural differences between an artery and a vein. **ICSE 2024, ICSE Specimen 2021-22 Sem. II**

Ans. Differences between an artery and vein are

Artery	Vein
It carry blood away from heart towards any organ.	It carry blood towards the heart.
It has narrow lumen.	It has broad lumen.

13. State the exact location of papillary muscles. **ICSE 2023**

Ans. Papillary muscles of the heart are pillar-like muscles found within the cavity of the ventricles, attached to their walls.

14. What is the contraction phase of auricles called? Name the two valves that open during this phase. **ICSE Specimen 2021-22 Sem. II**

Ans. Atrial systole.

Bicuspid and tricuspid value.

15. State the main function of coronary artery. **ICSE 2019, 2011, 2006**

Ans. Coronary arteries supply oxygenated blood to the heart muscles.

16. Choose the **odd** one out from the following terms given and name the **category** to which the others belong
Example Nose, tongue, arm, eye

Answer Odd term-Arm, Category - Sense organs

Lumen, muscular tissue, connective tissue, pericardium **ICSE 2018**

Ans. **Odd term** Pericardium

Category Components of blood vessels.

17. Name the blood vessel which supplies blood to the liver. **ICSE 2018**

Ans. Hepatic artery is the blood vessel that supplies oxygenated blood to the liver.

18. Choose between the two options to answer the question specified in the brackets for the following An example is illustrated below
Example Corolla or calyx (Which is the outer whorl?) **Answer** Calyx
Blood in the pulmonary artery or pulmonary vein (Which one contains less oxyhaemoglobin?)

Ans. Pulmonary artery **ICSE 2018**

19. Mention the exact location of pulmonary semilunar valve. **ICSE 2018, 2013**

Ans. The opening of right ventricle into the pulmonary artery is provided with the pulmonary semilunar valve.

20. Give appropriate biological or technical terms for
The relaxation phase of the heart. **ICSE 2018**

Ans. Diastole

21. Give biological reasons for
'The left ventricle of the heart has a thicker wall than the right ventricle.' **ICSE 2017**

Ans. The right ventricle pumps deoxygenated blood to the lungs and blood flow is for a short distance. On the other hand, left ventricle pumps oxygenated blood to the various body parts and blood flow is for a longer distance. Therefore, the wall of left ventricle is thicker than the right ventricle to provide more strength for the same.

22. Given below are group of terms. In each group the first pair indicates the relationship between the two terms. Rewrite and complete the second pair on a similar basis.Example : Oxygen : Inspiration ::
Carbon dioxide : Expiration
Foetus : Amnion :: Heart : .... **ICSE 2017**

Ans. Pericardium

23. Give one difference on the basis of what is given in the brackets.

Beginning of ventricular systole
and the end of ventricular systole (type of heart sound) **ICSE 2011, 2006**

Ans.

Beginning of ventricular systole	End of ventricular systole
In beginning of ventricular systole sound produced is Lubb.	In end of ventricular systole sound produced is Dupp.

24. State the exact location of chordae tendinae. **ICSE 2016**

Or Give the exact location and one function of chordae tendinae **ICSE 2005**

Ans. (i) **Location** : Chordae tendinae is found at right ventricle.

(ii) **Function**: Its main function is to keep the cuspid valves in position.

25. Differentiate between the pair on the basis of what is mentioned within bracket.

Lubb and dupp (Name of the valves whose closure produce the sound) **ICSE 2016**

Ans. **Lubb** Mitral and tricuspid valve

Dupp Aortic and pulmonary semilunar valve

26. Give scientific reasons for given statement.

Blood flows in arteries with spurts and high pressure. **ICSE 2016**

Or Give biological reasons for the blood in the arteries flows in spurts. **ICSE 2005**

Ans. Blood in the artery flows in spurts because flow of blood is under pressure and also because arteries have elastic walls.

27. Name the vein that carries oxygenated blood.

Ans. Pulmonary vein **ICSE 2015**

28. Mention the exact location of bicuspid valve.

Ans. The exact location of bicuspid valve is between left atrium and left ventricle. **ICSE 2015**

29. Give the biological/technical terms for

'The sound produced when the atrio-ventricular valves close in the heart.' **ICSE 2015**

Ans. Lubb

30. Explain the term pulse. **ICSE 2015**

Or Briefly explain the pulse. **ICSE 2012**

Ans. Pulse is the rhythmical throbbing of the arteries as blood is propelled through them. It is typically observed in the wrist or neck.

31. Name the protective covering of the heart. **ICSE 2014**

Ans. **Pericardium** is the protective covering of heart.

32. State the exact location of the tricuspid valve. **ICSE 2014**

Ans. **Tricuspid valve** is found between the right auricle and right ventricle.

33. Differentiate between the following pair on the basis of what is given in the bracket.

Bicuspid valve and tricuspid valve. (function) **ICSE 2013**

Ans. Difference between bicuspid valve and tricuspid valve is

Bicuspid valve	Tricuspid valve
It guards the opening of auriculo-ventricular valves when blood rushes from left auricle into left ventricle.	It guards the opening of auriculo- ventricular valves when blood rushes from right atrium to right ventricle.

34. Give biological reasons for the wall of the ventricle is thicker than the auricles. **ICSE 2013**

Ans. Ventricles have thicker walls than auricles because they are meant to pump blood with pressure to make blood reach to larger distances.

35. Name the phase of cardiac cycle in which the auricles contract. **ICSE 2012**

Ans. Auricular systole is the phase of cardiac cycle in which auricles contract.

36. Give the exact location of the mitral valve. **ICSE 2012, 2011**

Ans. **Mitral valve** is found between the left auricle and left ventricle.

37. Rewrite the following sentence by inserting the correct word in the space indicated. The blood vessel that begins and ends in capillaries is the .... **ICSE 2011**

Or The blood vessel that begins and ends in capillaries is the .... (hepatic artery, hepatic portal vein, hepatic vein). **ICSE 2001**

Ans. The blood vessel that begins and ends in capillaries is the **hepatic portal vein.**

38. Given below is a group of five terms, arrange and rewrite the terms in the correct order so, as to be in a logical sequence. Aorta, hepatic vein, hepatic portal veins, stomach, liver. **ICSE 2006**

Ans. The logical sequence is

Aorta $\rightarrow$ stomach $\rightarrow$ hepatic portal vein $\rightarrow$ liver $\rightarrow$ hepatic vein.

39. Name the phase of the cardiac cycle in which the ventricles relax. **ICSE 2005**

Ans. **Ventricular diastole** is the phase of cardiac cycle in which the ventricles relax.

40. Choose the odd one out from the set, giving the reason for your choice.

Mitral valve, sino-atrial node, aorta, pulmonary vein. **ICSE 2005**

Ans. **Odd one** Sino-atrial node, it is the structure present in the right side of the heart and rest of all others are found in the left side of the heart.

41. Given below is set of terms, arrange and rewrite the terms so as to be in logical sequence.
Right auricle, pulmonary vein, post and pre-vena cava, lungs, right ventricle, pulmonary artery, left auricle. **ICSE 2005**

Ans. The logical sequence is

Post and pre vena cava $\rightarrow$ Right auricle $\rightarrow$ Right ventricle $\rightarrow$ Pulmonary artery $\rightarrow$ Lungs $\rightarrow$ Pulmonary vein $\rightarrow$ Left auricle.

42. Give one point difference between the following pair on the basis of what is indicated in bracket?
Pleura and Pericardium. (location) **ICSE 2004**

Ans.

Pleura	Pericardium
It lines each lung and the wall of the chest cavity.	It surrounds the heart and the proximal ends of the aorta, vena cava and the pulmonary artery.

43. Give one point difference between the following pair on the basis of what is indicated in bracket?
Bicuspid valve and Tricuspid valve. (place where it is present) **ICSE 2004**

Ans.

Bicuspid	Tricuspid
It is located at the aperture between the left auricle and left ventricle.	It is located at the aperture between the right auricle and right ventricle.

44. State whether the given statement is true or false. Correct and rewrite the false statement either the first word or the last word only.

'Dupp' is the first heart sound. **ICSE 2004**

Ans. The statement is false. **Lubb** is the first heart sound produced.

45. Name the blood vessel which carries oxygenated blood to the liver. **ICSE 2003**

Ans. Hepatic artery is the blood vessel which carries oxygenated blood to liver.

46. Name the phase of contraction of the chambers of the heart. **ICSE 2003**

Ans. **Systole** is the phase of contraction of chambers of the heart.

47. Name the valve present in between the chambers of the right side of the human heart. **ICSE 2002**

Ans. Refer to answer no. 32.

48. Give one point difference between the following pair on the basis of what is indicated in bracket? Artery and vein. (type of blood flowing through) **ICSE 2002**

Ans. Arteries carry oxygenated blood, while veins carry deoxygenated blood except pulmonary vein.

49. Name the phase of the cardiac cycle in which the auricles contract. **ICSE 2002**

Ans. Atrial systole

50. Why are veins provided with valves? **ICSE 2001**

Ans. Veins are provided with valves because the blood in them flow at low pressure and these prevent the back flow of blood.

51. Complete the statement by filling in the blank with the appropriate word from the choices given the bracket. You must rewrite the complete statement.

The pulse beat per minute of a normal human adult is ...., (72, 82, 78. **ICSE 2001**

Ans. The pulse beat of a normal human adult is 72 beat/min.

2 Marks Questions

52. Give the exact location of

(i) Pericardium

(ii) Bicuspid valve **ICSE 2024**

Ans. (i) Pericardium is a double layered protective covering of heart.

(ii) Bicuspid valve is located between the left atrium and left ventricle.

53. Give the exact location of pulmonary semilunar valve. When does it close? **ICSE 2021-20 Sem. II**

Ans. Pulmonary semilunar valve is located between the right ventricle and the pulmonary artery. These are closed during atrial systole.

Concept Enhancer In atrial systole vena cava opens for the entry of deoxygenated blood from all parts of the body.

54. What are the two types of blood circulation in humans? **ICSE 2021-22 Sem. II**

Ans. Refer to text on page no. 105.

55. Give the biological/technical term for the following.

(i) The vein which drains the blood from the intestine to liver. **ICSE 2016**

(ii) Blood vessels carrying blood to the left atrium. **ICSE 2016**

Ans. (i) Hepatic portal vein (ii) Pulmonary vein

56. From where to where do the following blood vessels carry blood?

(i) Hepatic vein (ii) Hepatic portal vein **ICSE 2013**

Ans. (i) Hepatic vein carries blood from liver to posterior vena cava.

(ii) Hepatic portal vein carries blood from intestine to liver.

Diagram Based Questions

57. The diagram below depicts the human heart in one of its phases. Answer the questions that follow **ICSE 2023 (3M)**

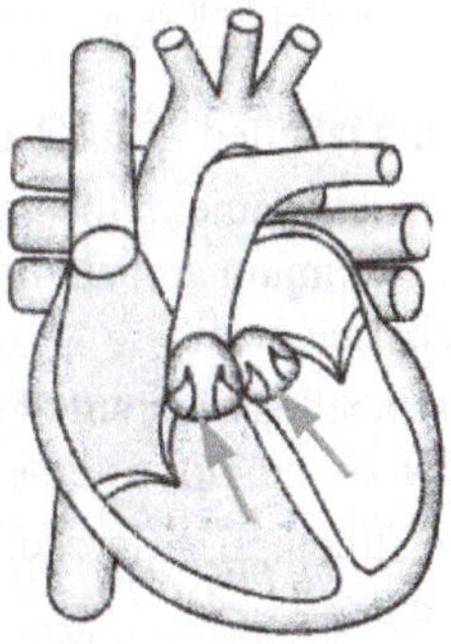

(i) Which part of the heart is in the contraction phase?

(ii) Give a suitable reason to justify your answer in (i).

(iii) Distinguish between systole and diastole.

Ans. (i) Here in this diagram ventricles are the contracting part of the heart.

(ii) The blood is moving into the respective arteries (Pulmonary artery and dorsal aorta) because the ventricles are contracting.

(iii) Differences between systole and diastole are

Systole	**Diastole**
It happens when the heart muscle contracts and the blood moves to the aorta and pulmonary artery.	It happens when the heart muscle relaxes between two contractions and the heart is filled with blood.
Systole reduces the volume of the heart as all the blood gets pumped out.	Diastole increases the heart volume and makes it normal as the blood comes back in.

58. Given below is a diagrammatic representation of a certain part of the process of circulation of blood in man. Study the same and then answer the questions that follow **ICSE 2017 (4M)**

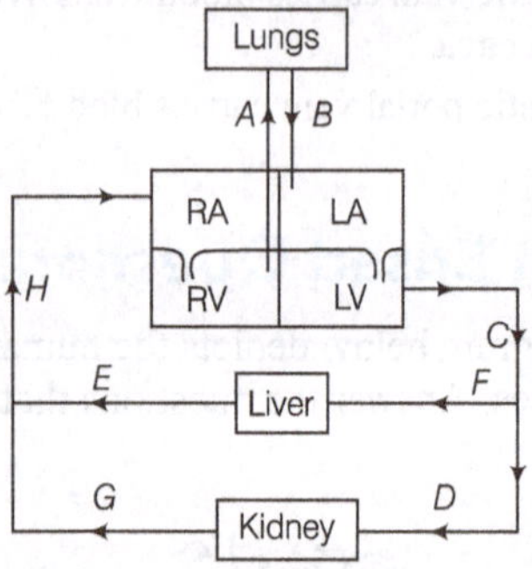

(i) Name the parts labelled *A, B, D* and *F*.

(ii) Give the label and name of the vessel which contains the maximum amount of urea a few hours after a protein rich meal.

(iii) Draw a neat, labelled diagram of the cross sectional view of the blood vessel labelled *C*.

(iv) Mention two structural differences between blood vessels '*C*' and '*H*'.

Ans. (i) The different labelled parts are

A– Pulmonary artery *B*– Pulmonary vein

D– Renal artery *F*– Hepatic artery

(ii) Blood vessel *E*, i.e. hepatic vein contains the maximum amount of urea few hours after a protein rich meal.

(iii) Blood vessel *C* is aorta Its diagrammatic representation is given below

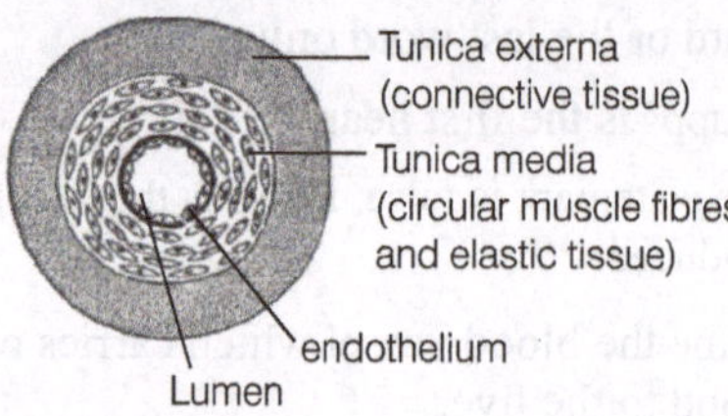

(iv) Two structural differences between *C* and *H* vessels are

Blood vessel *C* (aorta)	**Blood vessel *H*** (Vena cava)
It has thick muscular wall.	It has thin muscular wall.
The valves are absent in its interior wall.	The valves are present in its interior wall.

59. The given diagram represents a section of the human heart. Answer the questions that follows

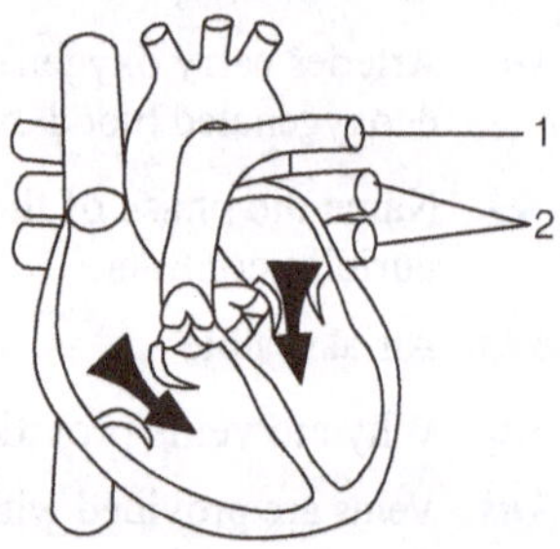

(i) Which parts of heart are in the diastolic phase? Give a reason to support your answer.

(ii) Label the parts numbered 1 and 2 in the diagram. What type of blood flows through them?

(iii) What causes the heart sounds 'LUBB' and 'DUPP'?

(iv) Name the blood vessels that supply oxygenated blood to the heart muscles.

(v) Draw neat labelled diagrams of a cross section of an artery and a vein. **ICSE 2017 (5M)**

Ans. (i) In the given figure, ventricles are in diastolic phase. The tricuspid and bicuspid valves are open. It occurs only when pressure in the ventricles falls. As a result blood flows from the atria into the ventricles.

(ii) 1–**Pulmonary artery** It carries deoxygenated blood to the lungs for purification.

2–**Pulmonary veins** They bring oxygenated blood to the left atrium.

(iii) 'Lubb' sound is produced when tricuspid and mitral valves get closed, while 'Dupp' sound is produced when pulmonary and aortic semilunar valves get closed.

(iv) Blood vessel that supplies blood to the walls of the heart is 'coronary artery'.

(v)

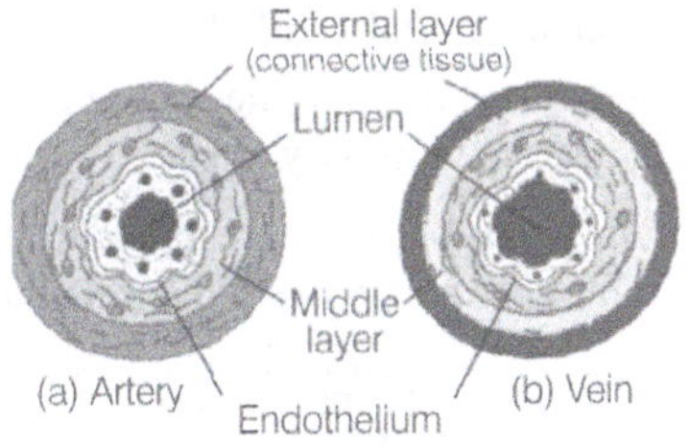

Cross Section of
(a) artery and (b) vein

60. The diagrams given below are cross sections of blood vessels.

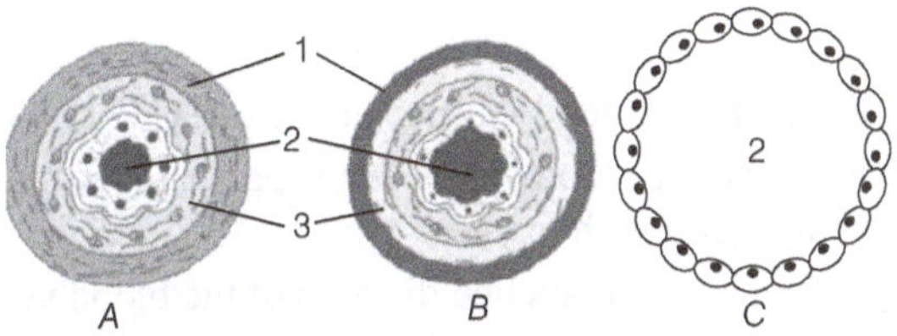

(i) Identify the blood vessels *A*, *B* and *C*.

(ii) Name the parts labelled 1 to 3.

(iii) Name the type of blood that flows through *A*.

(iv) Mention one structural difference between *A* and *B*.

(v) In which of the above vessels does exchange of gases actually take place? **ICSE 2015 (5M)**

Ans. (i) *A* - Artery, B - Vein, C - Capillary

(ii) 1 - Tunica adventitia (External layer-connective tissue)
2 - Lumen
3 - Tunica media (Middle layer)

(iii) *A* (artery) carries fully oxygenated blood.

(iv) The structural difference between *A* and *B* is

A (Artery)	**B** (Vein)
They have narrow lumen and valves are absent.	They have wider lumen and valves are present.

(v) *C*-Capillaries are involved in the exchange of gases.

61. The diagram given below represents the human heart in one phase of its functions. Study the diagram carefully and answer the questions that follow

(i) Name the phase.

(ii) Which part of the heart is contracting in this phase? Give a reason to support your answer.

(iii) Name the parts labelled 1 to 4.

(iv) Which type of blood flows through 2?

(v) State the function of the part numbered 5.

(vi) Name the membrane that covers the heart.

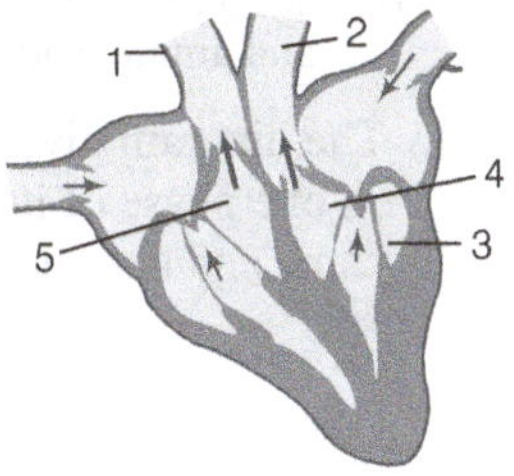

ICSE 2015 (6M)

Ans. (i) Ventricular systole

(ii) **Ventricular muscles** The lower part consisting of the right and left ventricles are contracting in this phase as the blood is seen to be flowing in the pulmonary artery and main aorta while the bicuspid and tricuspid valves are closed.

(iii) 1 - Pulmonary artery 2 - Aorta
3 - Left atrio-ventricular valve 4 - Left atrium

(iv) Oxygenated blood flow through aorta.

(v) Right atrium (5 has thin muscular walls. It carries deoxygenated blood.

(vi) The membrane that covers the heart is pericardium.

62. The diagram given below represents the simplified pathway of the circulation of blood. Study the same and answer the questions that follow

(i) Name the blood vessels labelled *A* and *B*.

(ii) State the function of blood vessels labelled *E* and *H*.

(iii) What is the importance of the blood vessel labelled *F*?

(iv) Which blood vessel will contain a high amount of glucose and amino acids after a meal?

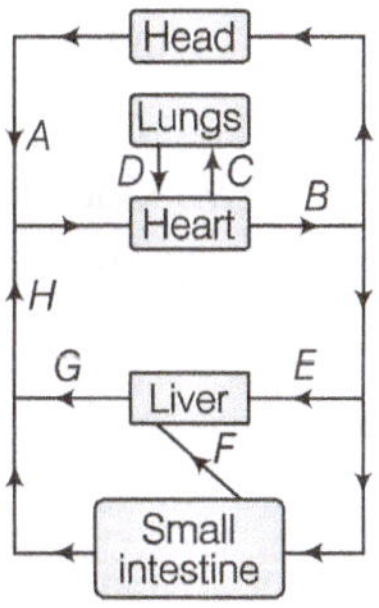

ICSE 2014 (5M)

Ans. (i) Bood vessels labelled as *A* and *B* are
A– Vein *B*– Artery

(ii) Function of different blood vessels labelled as *E* is to regulate quantity of nutrient flowing in blood and *H* carries the blood from liver to heart.

(iii) Blood vessel *F* is called hepatic portal vein. It carries deoxygenated blood from intestine to liver.
This blood contains excess glucose, some toxic substances, etc. which are sent to liver where they are detoxified and the excess glucose is converted to glycogen and stored.
This prevents these substances from directly entering the heart and damaging the vital organs including heart.

(iv) Blood vessel *F* will contain high amount of glucose and amino acid after a meal.

63. The diagram given below represents the human heart in one phase of its functional activities. Study the same and answer the questions that follow.

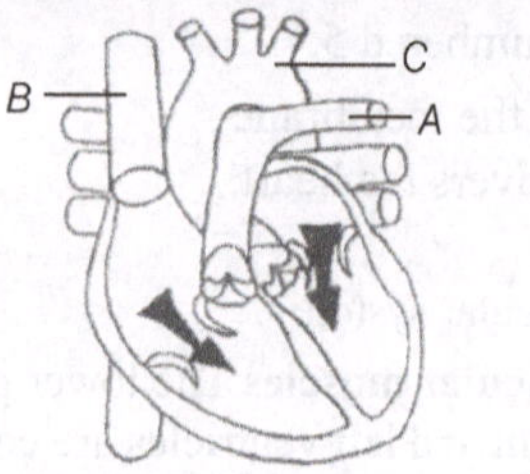

(i) Name the phase.

(ii) Label the parts *A*, *B* and *C*.

(iii) Which part of the heart is contracting in this phase? Give a reason to support your answer.

ICSE 2013, 2001 (3M)

Ans. (i) The phase is atrial systole.

(ii) The parts *A*, *B* and *C* in the given figure are labelled as

A– Pulmonary artery,
B– Superior vena cava, *C*– Aorta

(iii) Upper chambers, i.e. both the atria are contracting in this phase because blood is flowing downwards (towards the ventricles).

64. The diagram given below show the cross-section of two kinds of blood vessels.

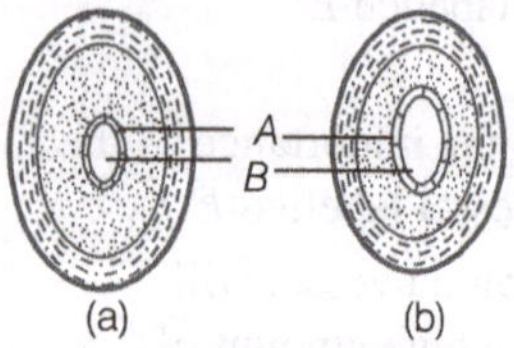

(i) Identify the blood vessels *a* and *b*. In each case give a reason to support your answer.

(ii) Name the parts labelled *A* and *B*.

(iii) When are the sound 'Lubb' and 'Dup' produced during a heartbeat?

(iv) Name the blood vessel that

(a) begins and ends in capillaries.

(b) supplies blood to the walls of the heart.

ICSE 2012 (5M)

Ans. (i) Blood vessels labelled as *a* is artery because it has narrow lumen and thick muscular wall and *b is* vein because it has wide lumen and thin muscular wall.

(ii) The parts labelled *A* and *B* in the diagram are endothelium and lumen respectively.

(iii) 'Lubb' sound is produced when tricuspid and mitral valves get closed, while 'Dup' sound is produced when pulmonary and aortic semilunar valves get closed.

(iv) (a) Blood vessels that begins and ends in capillaries is 'hepatic portal vein'.

(b) Blood vessel that supplies blood to the walls of the heart is 'coronary artery'.

65. The diagram given below represents circulation in the human body. Answer the questions that follow

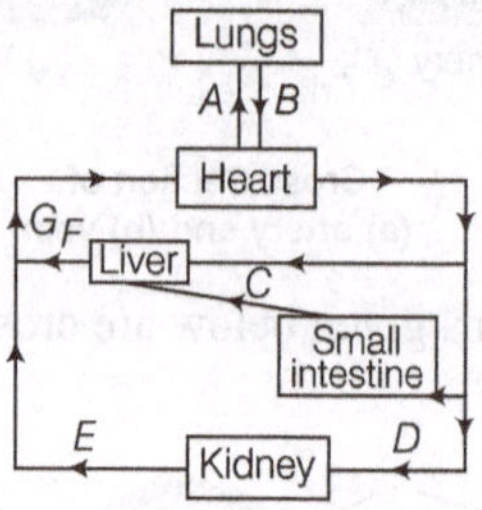

(i) Name the blood vessels labelled *A*, *C*, *F* and *G*.

(ii) Name the blood vessel that supplies the walls of the heart with oxygen.

(iii) Draw a neat labelled diagram of the blood vessel labelled '*B*' as seen in a cross-section.

(iv) Mention one structural difference between blood vessels numbered *D* and *E*. **ICSE 2011 (5M)**

Ans. (i) Blood vessels labelled as *A*, *C*, *F* and *G* are

A – Pulmonary artery, *C* – Hepatic portal vein
F – Hepatic vein *G* – Posterior vena cava.

(ii) The bood vessels that supplies the walls of the heart with O_2 is coronary artery.

(iii) Blood vessel labelled as '*B*' is vein.

Refer to fig. on page 103.

(iv) Structural difference between blood vessels labelled *D* (renal artery) and *E* (renal vein) is

D (Renal artery)	***E*** (Renal vein)
Has thick muscular wall with narrow lumen.	Has thin muscular wall with wide lumen.

66. Given below is a schematic representation of the circulatory system in man.

Study the same and answer the questions that follow

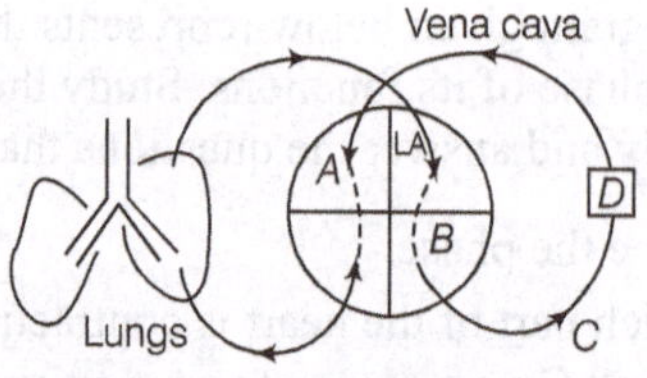

(i) Label the parts A to D indicated in the diagram.

(ii) Give one difference between the parts A and B based on

(a) their structure

(b) the nature of blood flowing through them.

(iii) What is the specific name of the type of blood circulation that takes place between the heart and the lungs?

(iv) Name the valve found at the beginning of the part labelled C. **ICSE 2006 (5M)**

Ans. (i) Parts labelled as A to D in the diagram are

A – Right auricle
B – Left ventricle
C – Aorta
D – Body organ

(ii) Difference between the parts A and B are

	Part-*A* (Right auricle)	**Part-*B*** (Left ventricle)
Structure	Thin muscular walls.	Thick muscular walls.
Nature of blood flowing through them	Receives deoxygenated blood.	Receives oxygenated blood.

(iii) The specific name of the type of blood circulation that takes place between heart and lung is **pulmonary circulation.**

(iv) Valve found at the beginning of part labelled as C is **aortic semilunar valves.**

67. Given below is a diagrammatic representation of a certain part of the process of circulation of blood in man. Study the same and then answer the questions that follow.

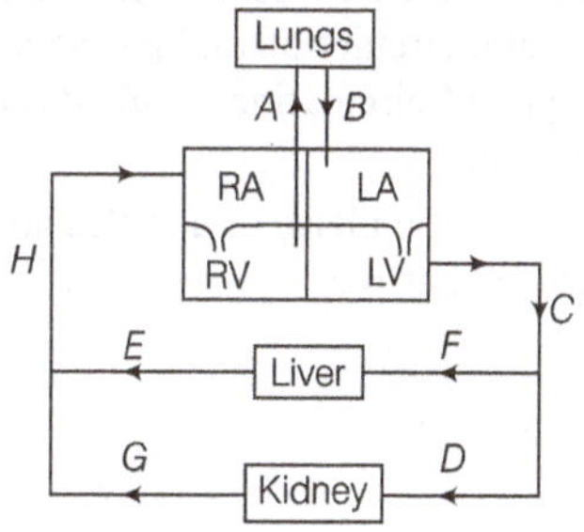

(i) Name the parts labelled A, B, D and F.

(ii) Give the number and name of vessel which contains the maximum amount of urea a few hours after a protein rich meal.

(iii) Mention two structural difference between blood vessels 'C' and 'H'. **ICSE 2004 (3M)**

Ans. The parts labelled as A, B, D and F are

(i) A – Pulmonary artery
B – Pulmonary vein
D – Renal artery
F – Hepatic artery

(ii) Vessel E named as hepatic vein will contain the maximum amount of urea few hours after the protein rich meal.

(iii) Two structural differences between blood vessels C and H are

Blood vessel C (Aorta)	**Blood vessels** H (Vena cava)
Lumen is small.	Lumen is large.
Valves are absent.	Valves are present.

68. The diagram given represents a certain category of blood vessels showing the role of a special structure in their walls.

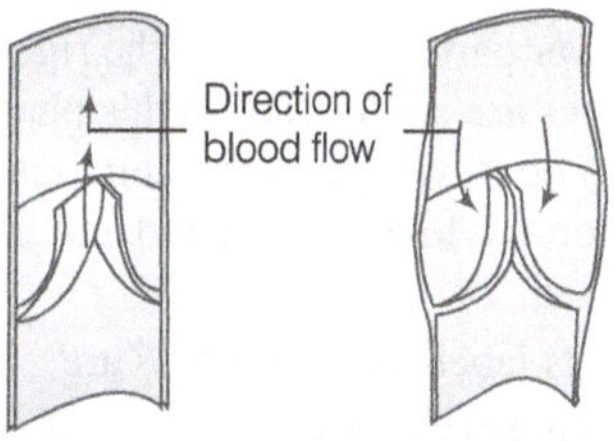

(i) Name the kind of blood vessels shown.

(ii) Name the structure shown inside the blood vessels.

(iii) Describe the role of these structures.

(iv) Are these structures present in any other kind of blood vessel? If yes, name it.

(v) Towards which side of the figure (top or bottom) is the heart located? **ICSE 2003 (5M)**

Ans. (i) The blood vessel shown in the figure is vein.

(ii) The structure inside the blood vessels are valves.

(iii) Valves are present to prevent the back flow of blood in veins.

(iv) Yes, these are also present in the heart at the openings of aorta and pulmonary artery.

(v) The heart is located towards the top side of the figure.

69. The below diagram represents the human heart in one phase of its activity. Study the same then answer the questions that follow.

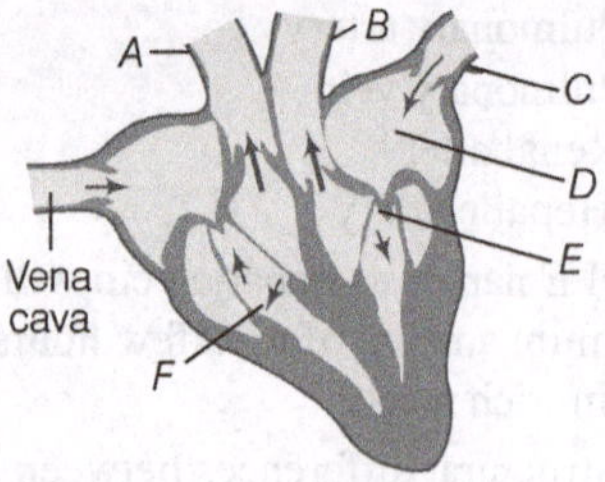

(i) Name the phase.

(ii) Which parts of the heart are contracting in this phase?
Give a reason to support your answer.

(iii) Name the parts labelled from *A* to *F*.

(iv) What type of blood flows through the parts marked '*A*' and '*B*'?

(v) How many valves are closed in this phase?

ICSE 2001 (5M)

Ans. (i) The phase shown in figure is venticular systole.

(ii) The lower part consisting of the right and left ventricles are contracting in this phase as the blood is seem to be flowing into the pulmonary artery and main aorta, while the bicuspid and tricuspid valves are closed.

(iii) The parts labelled from *A* to *F* are

A – Pulmonary artery

B – Main aorta

C – Pulmonary vein

D – Left auricle

E–Bicuspid valve

F–Right ventricle

(iv) In part *A* deoxygenated blood from heart is flowing to lungs. In part *B* (pulmonary vein) carries oxygenated blood from the heart to all other body parts.

(v) Two valves, i.e. the bicuspid and tricuspid valves leading from the auricle to the ventricles are closed during systole to prevent the back flow of blood into the auricles.

70. Given below is a simple diagram of the circulation of blood in a mammal showing the main blood vessels, the heart, lungs and body tissues. The blood vessel labelled *F* contains deoxygenated blood and the valve leading to it has three semi-lunar pockets.

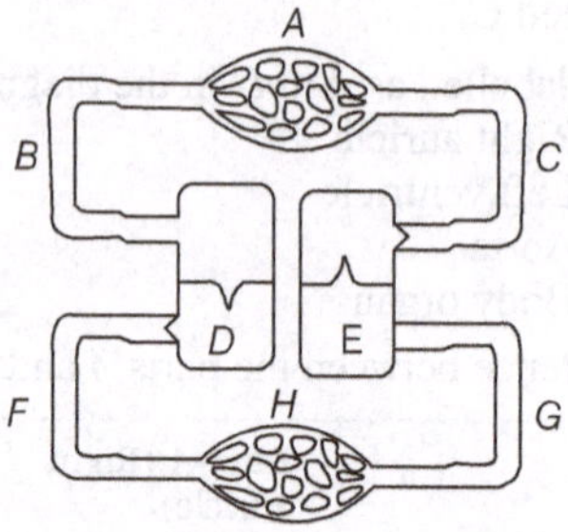

(i) Name the blood vessels or organs marked by numbers *A* to *H*.

(ii) What do you mean by 'double circulation' of blood in mammals?

(iii) What is diastole?

ICSE 2000 (3M)

Ans. Blood vessels or organs marked from number *A* to *H* are

(i) *A*–Lung *B*–Vena cava

C– Pulmonary vein *D*–Right ventricle

E–Left ventricle *F*–Pulmonary artery

G–Aorta *H*–Body tissues

(ii) For one complete circulation, blood has to pass from the heart through two separate pathways, i.e. systematic circulation and pulmonary circulation. This type of circulation is called double circulation.

(iii) The relaxation phase of auricles and ventricles is known as diastole.

CHAPTER TEST

Section-A

01 Mark Questions

1 Select the correct answer to the questions from the given options. (Do not copy the question. Write the correct answer only)

(i) Contraction in auricles of heart is called as
(a) diastole (b) systole
(c) heartbeat (d) hypertension

(ii) Rate of human heartbeat is around .... times/minute.
(a) 52 (b) 40
(c) 72 (d) 62

(iii) The covering of heart is known as
(a) pericardium (b) pleura
(c) peritoneum (d) plasma membrane

(iv) The chambers of the heart which receive oxygenated blood from pulmonary vein are known as
(a) septa (b) ventricle
(c) venule (d) auricles

(v) Another name of mitral valve is
(a) pulmonary semilunar valve
(b) bicuspid valve
(c) aortic semilunar valve
(d) tricuspid valve

2 (i) Name the following.
(a) WBCs engulf microbes by the process called.
(b) Blood vessels which supply blood to kidney.
(c) The type of blood cell that has no nucleus, mitochondria, ER
(d) The yellow coloured fluid part of blood.
(e) The respiratory pigment present in RBCs.

(ii) Arrange and rewrite the terms in each group in correct order so as to be in a logical sequence beginning with the term that is underlined.
(a) Injured tissue, thrombin, thrombokinase, prothrombin, fibrin, fibrinogen
(b) Deoxygenated blood, right ventricle, right auricle, lungs, pulmonary artery.
(c) Artery, arterial capillaries, arteriole, venous capillaries, venule.
(d) O, A/B , AB [hint on the basis of antibodies in plasma]
(e) Oxygenated blood, left ventricle, left auricle, aorta.

(iii) Match the items given in Column I with the most appropriate once in Column II and rewrite the correct matching pairs.

	Column I		Column II
A.	RBC	1.	Oxygenated blood
B.	Vein	2.	Phagocytosis
C.	WBC	3.	0.85 sec
D.	Cardiac cycle	4.	Biconcave, enucleated
E.	Artery	5.	Deoxygenated blood

(iv) Choose the odd one out from the following terms and name the category to which others belong.
(a) Neutrophils, Eosinophils, Monocytes, RBC
(b) Prothrombin, Fibrinogen, Thrombokinase, Aorta.
(c) Artery, Vein, Aorta, RBC.
(d) Tricuspid valve, Mitral valve, Haemoglobin, Aortic semilunar valve.
(e) AB, Hb, O, B

(v) State the exact location of following structures.
(a) SA node
(b) Aortic semilunar valve
(c) Tricuspid valve
(d) Haemoglobin
(e) Pericardium

02 Marks Questions

3 Write the function of blood plasma.

4 Write the difference between artery and vein.

5 Name two major circulation of blood in human body.

6 Define pulse.

7 Name two main lymphatic organs in humans.

03 Marks Questions

8 Write the sequence of steps of blood clotting.

9 What is meant by double circulation?

10 Explain the reason why a matured mammalian RBC lacks nucleus and mitochondria.

11 Write the functions of tonsils and spleen.

12 Explain the following terms.

(i) Rh factor (ii) Serum

(iii) Lymph

Section-B

Diagram Based Questions

13 Given below are different kinds of blood cells observe them and answer the following questions.

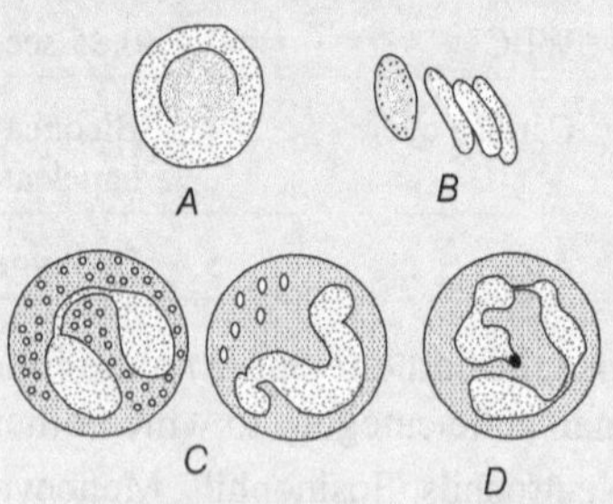

(i) Which kind of blood cells are involved in releasing chemicals responsible for inflammation?

(ii) State the function of cells labelled as *A*.

(iii) Which blood cells are involved in coagulation?

14 The following simplified diagram refers to the outline plan of the circulation of blood in a mammal. Study the diagram and write the number and the name of the blood vessel in each case as mentioned ahead.

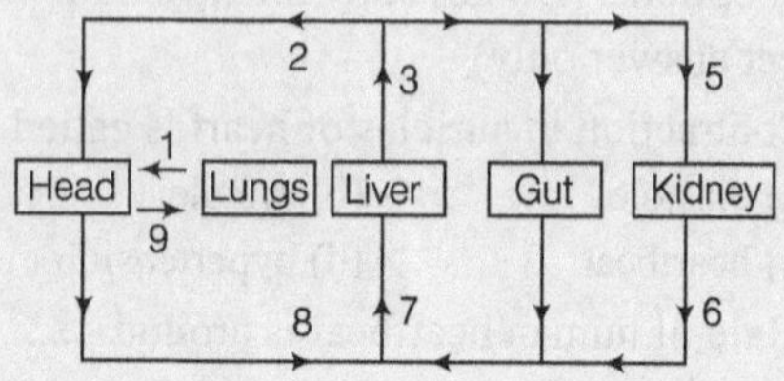

(i) Several hours after a meal containing a lot of protein, which vessel will contain the highest concentration of urea?

(ii) Which vessel would contain the highest concentration amino acids and glucose soon after a meal?

Answers

1. (i) (b), (ii) (c), (iii) (a), (iv) (d), (v) (b)

08

Excretory System

TREND ANALYSIS 4 YEARS

Average No. of Questions Across all Sets

	Types of Questions	2024	2023	2020	2019
TOPIC 01 Basis of Excretion and Excretory Organs	1 Mark	3	1	–	3
	2 Marks	–	1	–	–
	3 Marks	–	–	–	–
	5 Marks	–	–	–	1
TOPIC 02 Urine Formation and Osmoregulation	1 Mark	1	1	–	–
	2 Marks	–	–	–	–
	3 Marks	–	1	–	–
	5 Marks	–	–	–	–

Various metabolic reactions occurring inside the body, whether **anabolic** (constructive, i.e. formation of complex molecules from simple ones) or **catabolic** (destructive, i.e. breakdown of complex molecules into simpler forms) release energy and form some substances that are not required by the body. These substances are called **waste products** and they need to be removed from the body at earliest possible time, as they can be toxic to the body.

TOPIC 1

Basis of Excretion and Excretory Organs

Excretion is the phenomenon of removal of harmful metabolic waste products mainly nitrogenous wastes from the body. It plays an important role in maintaining homeostatic conditions of the body.

Waste products produced are mainly organic and metabolic wastes. The organic wastes include CO_2 while the nitrogenous wastes include urea, uric acid and ammonia.

In human beings, process of excretion is brought about by the following four organs

(i) **Kidneys** These are the primary excretory organs which excrete urea as a waste product in the form of urine.

(ii) **Skin** It bears several sweat glands under the layer of skin. These glands secrete sweat which carries small amount of nitrogenous wastes with it. Sweating is mainly concerned with the process of maintaining thermoregulation, i.e. providing cooling effect to the body.

(iii) **Lungs** These are meant to excrete out carbon dioxide (a waste product) during expiration (breathing out).

(vi) **Liver** It removes urea, bile pigments and other toxins and is known as a detoxifying gland. Urea is synthesised from amino acids in the liver.

Human Excretory System

The excretory system in humans consist of a pair of kidney, a pair of ureter, a urinary bladder and a urethra.

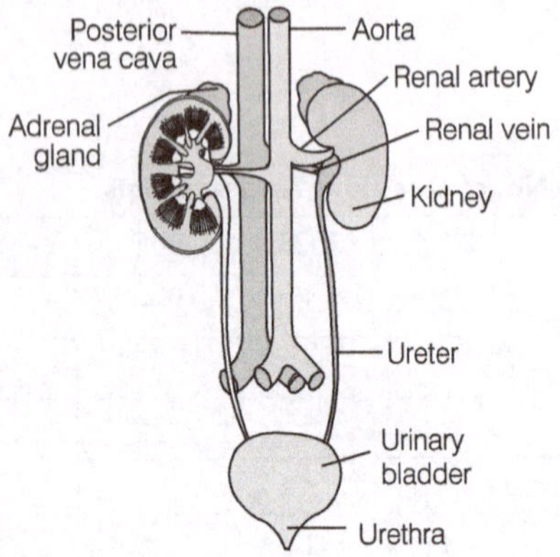

Fig. 8.1 Excretory system in human

Kidneys

These are two bean-shaped structures, located on either sides of the backbone in the abdominal cavity.

Right kidney is slightly lower than left kidney because liver takes much space of right sides and pushes it down.

External Structure of Kidney

- The outer surface of kidney is convex and the inner surface is concave.
- At the inner concave surface, a notch type structure called hilum is present through which renal vein and renal artery pass in and out of the kidney, respectively.
- The kidneys are covered by three layers which protect them from external shocks and injuries.

Internal Structure of Kidney

- Internally, each kidney is made up of two main regions, i.e. **outer cortex** and **inner medulla.**
- The medulla is composed of a finely striped substance being arranged in several conical projections called renal or medullary pyramids.
- Apex of each pyramid projects inward towards the pelvis.
- Each kidney is composed of enormous number of microscopic tubules called nephrons or renal tubules, which are functional units of the kidney.

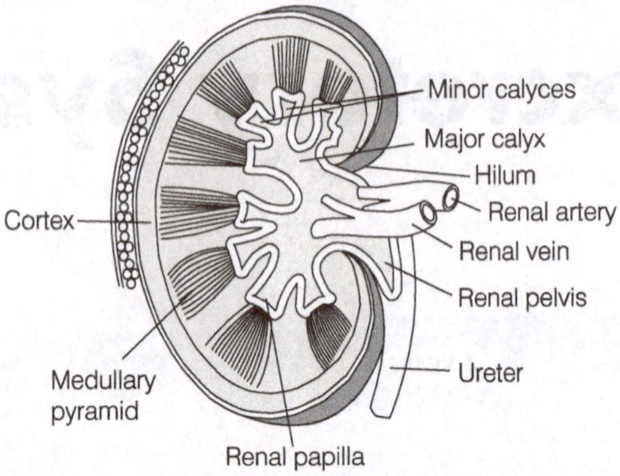

Fig. 8.2 Longitudinal section of a kidney

Nephron (Renal Tubule)

Each nephron consists of two parts, the Malpighian body or renal corpuscle and renal tubules.

(i) **Malpighian Body** The glomerulus along with Bowman's capsule is known as Malpighian body. It filters out large solutes from the blood and delivers small solutes for modification into the renal tubule.

Bowman's capsule is a single-celled, thick-walled, cup-like structure and glomerulus is a tuft of capillaries formed by afferent arteriole (a fine branch of renal artery).

(ii) **Renal Tubules** The Bowman's capsule leads into a coiled part of nephron called renal tubule. These tubules are attached to each Bowman's capsule and are long and thin with three distinct regions.

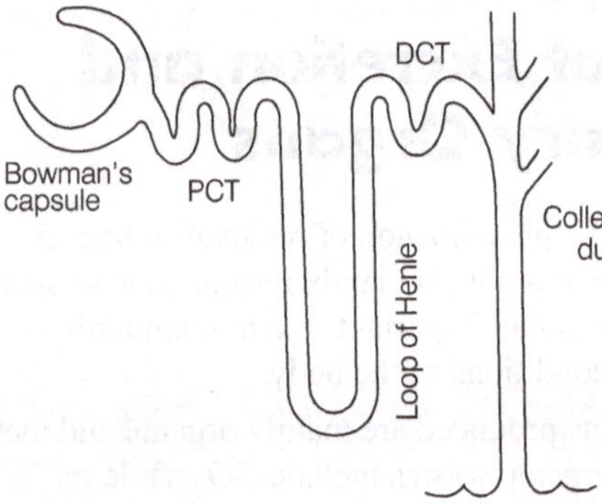

Fig. 8.3 Basic structures of a renal tubule

(a) **Proximal Convoluted Tubule** (PCT) It is the starting point of the convoluted region which makes few coils and is found behind the neck of Malpighian body.

PCT along with Bowman's capsule lies in the cortex region of the kidney giving it a dotted appearance because it is dark in colour.

(b) **Henle's Loop** It is a U-shaped (or hairpin-shaped) region of renal tubule that runs in the medulla region of kidney. It has a descending loop that ends into the medulla and an ascending limb that extends back from medulla into the cortex.

(c) **Distal Convoluted Tubule** (DCT) It is considered as the end part of renal tubule lying in the cortex region of the kidney. It further opens up into a **collecting duct**.

It is meant to receive the waste products pouring it into the pelvis of kidney as urine.

Blood Vessels (In and Out) of Renal Tubules

- A pair of renal artery branches off from dorsal aorta and enters into the kidneys.

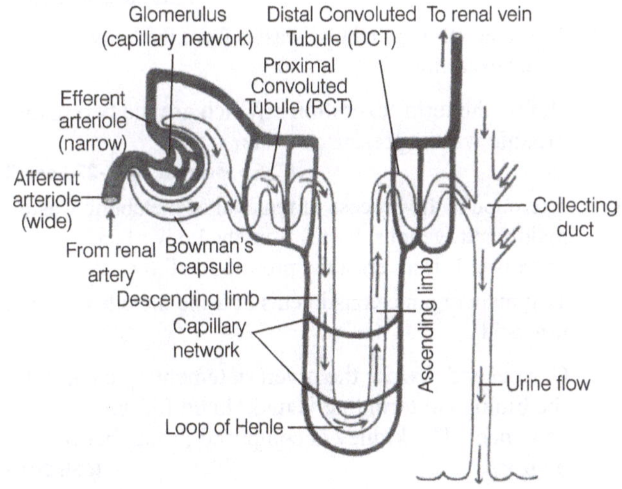

Fig. 8.4 A single renal tubule (nephron) showing the flow of urine

- Renal artery further gives rise to arterioles, which enters the Bowman's capsule and supply blood to the glomerulus. These are known as afferent arterioles.
- The capillaries forming the glomerulus reunite together and emerge out from the Bowman's capsule. This forming an efferent arteriole, carrying blood away from the glomerulus.
- Efferent arteriole emerges out of the glomerulus and breaks up into a secondary capillary network (vasa recta) which further joins to form venules.
- These venules join to form a renal vein that opens into the posterior vena cava.

Functions of Kidney

- Help in regulating water and electrolyte balance.
- Help in excreting metabolic waste products.
- Help in regulating pH of the blood.
- Also help in regulation of arterial pressure.

Ureter

- These are the paired tubular structures arising from the pelvis of each kidney.
- The urine produced in the kidneys constantly flows through these ureters and collects into the urinary bladder.
- The valves present in the ureters prevent the backflow of urine during contraction of bladder.

Urinary Bladder

It is a thin-walled, pear-shaped sac which is meant to store urine temporarily, till the person is not having an urge to urinate.

Urethra

- It is a membranous tube through which urine emptied from bladder is conducted to the exterior.
- The urethral sphincters keep the urethra closed and open only at the time of urination.

PYQs Previous Years' Questions

1 Mark Questions

Multiple Choice Questions

1. Urine is carried from kidney to urinary bladder by **ICSE Specimen 2023, 2013**
   (a) uterus (b) urethra
   (c) umbilical cord (d) ureter

Ans. (d) ureter

2. Loop of Henle lies in **ICSE Specimen 2021-22 Sem. II**
   (a) medulla (b) cortex (c) pelvis (d) ureter

Ans. (a) medulla

3. The main nitrogenous waste formed in the human body. **ICSE 2021-22 Sem. II**
   (a) Uric acid (b) Urea (c) Ammonia (d) Creatinine

Ans. (b) Urea

4. The structure that stores urine temporarily is **ICSE 2021-22 Sem. II**
   (a) ureter (b) urethra
   (c) urinary bladder (d) kidneys

Ans. (c) Urinary

5. The nephron discharge their urine at the **ICSE 2016**
   (a) urinary bladder (b) urethra
   (c) renal pelvis (d) renal pyramid

Ans. (c) renal pelvis

Very Short Answer Type Questions

6. Name the following:
   The main nitrogenous waste formed in the body.

Ans. Urea **ICSE 2024**

7. Arrange and rewrite the terms in each group in the correct order to be in a logical sequence beginning with the term that is underlined: **ICSE 2024**

   Loop of Henle, Distal convoluted tubule, <u>Bowman's capsule</u>, Proximal convoluted tubule.

Ans. Bowman's capsule, Proximal convoluted tubule, Loop of Henle, Distal convoluted tubule.

8. Differentiate between afferent arteriole and efferent arteriole (diameter). **ICSE 2024**

Ans. (i) Afferent arterioles deliver blood to the glomerulus of the nephron and efferent arterop;es carruy blood away from the glomerulus.

(ii) The average diameter of afferent arteriole is much larger than efferent arteriole due to which blood pressure in the efferent arteriole is higher than the blood pressure in the afferent arteriole.

9. Given below is the set with four terms in which one term is odd and cannot be grouped in the same category to which the other three belong.

   Identify the odd one in the set and name the category to which the remaining three belong.

   Urethra, Uterus, Urinary bladder, Ureter.

Ans. **Odd term** Uterus **ICSE 2023, 2014**

Category Remaining all are the parts of excretory system.

10. Name the following. **ICSE Specimen 2023**

    The knot-like mass of blood capillaries in Bowman's capsule.

Ans. Glomerulus

11. Define excretion. **ICSE Specimen 2023**

Ans. The removal of metabolic wastes from the body is called excretion.

12. Define the term 'excretion'. Which are the two main organic wastes present in urine? **ICSE Specimen 2021-22 Sem. II**

Ans. Excretion is the process of removal of metabolic waste mainly nitrogenous wastes from the body of an organism. It is an essential process in all forms of life.

Two main organic constituents of urine include urea and uric acid.

13. Correct and rewrite the given statement by changing the biological term that is underlined for the statement. The kidney is composed of number of <u>neurons</u>. **ICSE 2019**

Ans. Nephrons

14. Mention the exact function of the nephron. **ICSE Specimen 2019**

Ans. The exact function of nephron is to filter your blood and return the needed substance to your blood and remove wastes.

15. Given below are five sets of terms. In each case arrange and rewrite each set so as to be in a logical sequence.
    One is done as an example for you

Example Large intestine, Stomach, Mouth, Small intestine, Oesophagus.
Ans. Mouth, Oesophagus, Stomach, Small intestine, Large intestine.

Posterior vena cava, Renal artery, Aorta, Renal vein, Kidney **ICSE Specimen 2019**

Ans. Aorta, Renal artery, Kidney, Renal vein, Posterior vena cava.

16. Choose between the two options to answer the question specified in the bracket for the following. An example is illustrated below

Example Corolla or calyx (Which is the outer whorl?)
Ans. Calyx
Blood in the renal artery or renal vein (Which one has more urea?) **ICSE 2018**

Ans. Blood in the renal artery has more urea.

17. Differentiate between the given pair on the basis of what is indicated in bracket.

Ureter and Urethra (Function) **ICSE 2018**

Ans. Difference between ureter and urethra on the basis of its function is

Ureter	Urethra
It transports urine from the kidney to urinary bladder.	It transports urine from urinary bladder to the exterior or outside of our body.

18. Name the organ which produces urea. **ICSE 2017, 2012, 2005**

Ans. Urea is produced in the liver. It is a metobolite product of CO_2 and amino acid.

19. Differentiate between the pair on the basis of what is mentioned in bracket. Renal cortex and Renal medulla (Parts of the nephrons present) **ICSE 2017**

Ans. Difference between renal cortex and renal medulla is

Renal Cortex	Renal Medulla
Malpighian body, Proximal Convoluted Tubule (PCT) and Distal Convoluted Tubule (DCT) are found in renal cortex.	Henle's loop is found in renal medulla.

20. State the exact location of proximal convoluted tubule. **ICSE 2016**

Ans. Cortex region of kidney.

21. Give the biological/technical term for

'The removal of nitrogenous wastes from the body.'

Ans. Excretion **ICSE 2016**

22. Mention the exact location of the loop of Henle. **ICSE 2015**

Ans. Henle's loop is a U-shaped region of renal tubule that runs in the medulla region of the kidney. It has a descending loop that ends into the medulla and an ascending limb that extends back from medulla into the cortex.

23. Write special functional activity of the ureter. **ICSE 2013**

Ans. Ureter carries urine from kidney to the urinary bladder.

24. Differentiate between the following about what is given in the bracket?

Bowman's capsule and Malpighian capsule. (Parts included) **ICSE 2013**

Ans. Difference between Bowman's capsule and Malpighian capsule is

Bowman's Capsule	Malpighian Capsule
It is a cup-shaped structure that indi cates the beginning of nephron.	It is comprised of glomerulus and Bowman's capsule.

25. The renal cortex has a dotted appearance, why? **ICSE 2013**

Ans. Renal cortex is dark in colour and the presence of numerous nephrons in a highly coiled manner gives this region a dotted appearance.

26. Given below is the set of five terms, rewrite the terms in logical sequence as directed at the end of each statement.

Renal vein, renal artery, afferent arteriole, efferent arteriole, glomerulus (Pathway of blood through glomerulus). **ICSE 2012**

Ans. Logical sequence for pathway of blood through glomerulus is as follows

Renal artery, Afferent arteriole, Glomerulus, Efferent arteriole, Renal vein.

27. Name the structural and functional unit of the kidney. **ICSE 2011**

Ans. Nephron is known as the structural and functional unit of the kidney.

28. State whether the given statement is true or false. If false, rewrite the correct form of the statement by changing the first or last word only.
Urethra carries urine from kidney to the urinary bladder. **ICSE 2011**

Ans. The given statement is false. Correct statement is **Ureter** carries urine from kidney to the urinary bladder.

3 Marks Question

29. Draw a neat diagram of a longitudinal section of human kidney and label renal cortex and renal medulla on the diagram. **ICSE 2021-22 Sem. II, 2005**

Ans. Refer to fig. on page no. 118.

Diagram Based Questions

30. The diagram given below represents an organ system in the human body. Study the same and answer the questions that follows. **ICSE 2019 (5M)**

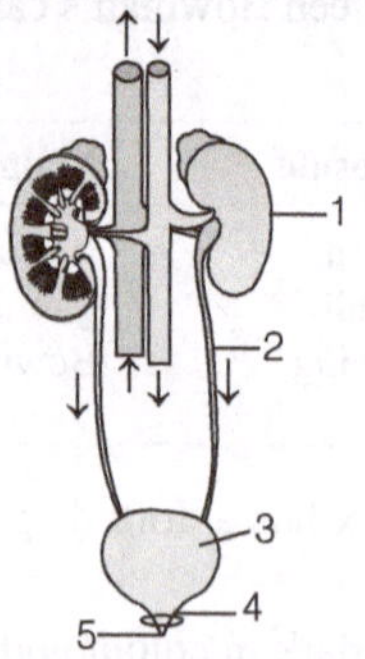

(i) Identify the system.

(ii) Label the parts marked 2 and 4. Mention the function of part 5.

(iii) Name the structural and functional units of the part marked as 1.

(iv) What is the fluid that accumulates in part 3 ? Which is the main nitrogenous waste present in it ?

(v) Draw a neat, labelled diagram showing the longitudinal section of part 1.

Ans. (i) Excretory system in human.

(ii) Part-2—Ureter
Part-4 —Sphincter muscles
Part-5 is urethra → It is the passage through which urine and semen are excreted out of the body.

(iii) Nephron is known as the structural and functional unit of kidney.

(iv) Urinary bladder contains the urine untill it is released out. Urea is the main nitrogenous waste present in urine.

(v)

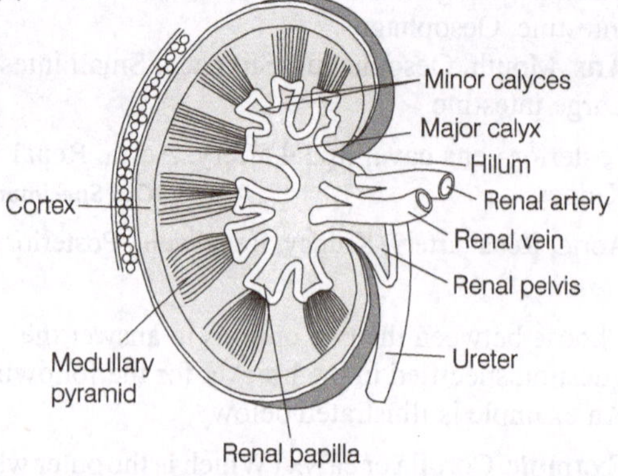

Longitudinal section of a kidney

31. The diagram given below shows the excretory system of a human being. Study the same and then answer the questions that follows

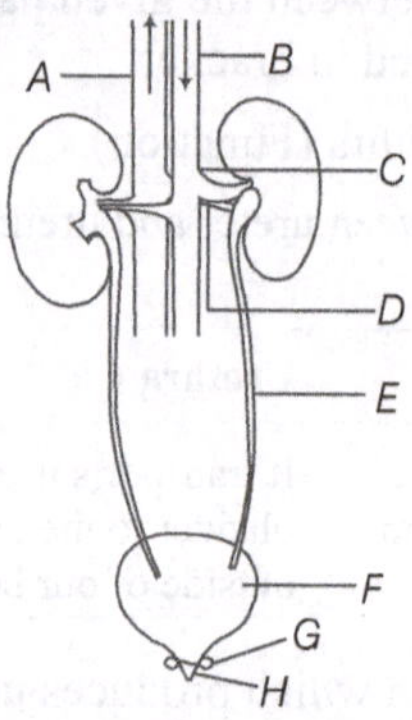

(i) Name the parts labelled as *A*, *B*, *C* and *D*.

(ii) Give the main function of the parts labelled as *E*, *F*, *G* and *H*.

(iii) Name the endocrine gland, which could be added in the diagram and state its location/position. **ICSE 2012 (5M)**

Ans. (i) Different parts in the diagram are labelled as

A – Posterior vena cava *B* – Aorta
C – Renal artery *D* – Renal vein

(ii) Main functions of the parts laballed as *E*, *F*, *G* and *H* are

E — **Ureter** Carries urine from kidneys to urinary bladder.

F — **Urinary bladder** Stores the urine till it is released out.

G — **Sphincter muscles** Guards the urethra.

H — **Urethra** Passage through which urine is excreted out from the body.

(iii) **Adrenal gland** is an endocrine gland which is located above each kidney in the form of a cap.

TOPIC 2

Urine Formation and Osmoregulation

Uropoiesis

The process of formation of urine is called uropoiesis. Formation of urine is comprised of the following three steps

1. **Ultrafiltration** (Glomerular Filtration)

It is the very first step in the process of formation of urine which involves the filtration of blood in the glomerulus.

- During ultrafiltration, the blood flows under a great pressure through glomerulus. This is because the efferent (outgoing) arteriole is narrow in diameter than the afferent (incoming) arteriole.
- Due to this high pressure, the liquid portion of the blood is filtered out from glomerulus and passes into the Bowman's capsule to enter into the renal tubule.
- This fluid (which is entering in renal tubule) is now known as **glomerular filtrate** which includes water, urea, glucose, salts and other plasma solutes.

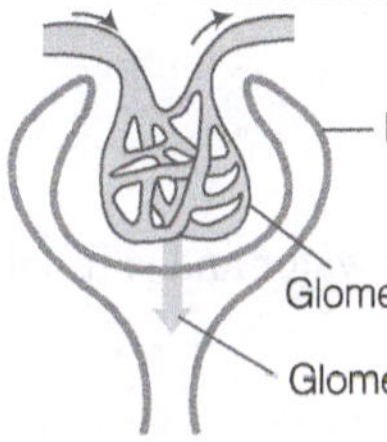

Fig. 8.5 Diagrammatic sketch of one Malpighian capsule (Bowman's capsule + glomerulus)

2. **Selective Reabsorption**

This is the second step in urine formation

- During this step, the glomerular filtrate in the form of dilute solution enters the renal tubule and various materials present in the filtrate are reabsorbed.
- As the filtrate passes down the tubule some amount of water is reabsorbed along with other useful substances such as water, salts, amino acids, glucose, etc., to the extent without affecting the normal concentration of the blood.
- Depending upon the types of molecules being reabsorbed, movement into and out of the epithelial cells in different segments of nephron occur either by passive transport or by active transport.
  These are described as follows
  - **Water** and **urea** are reabsorbed by passive transport (i.e. water is reabsorbed by osmosis and urea by simple diffusion).
  - **Glucose** and **amino acids** are reabsorbed by active transport.
  - The **reabsorption of Na^+** occurs both by passive and active transport.

3. **Tubular Secretion**

It is the last step in the formation of urine

- The substances such as K^+, Na^+, H^+ and certain chemicals which are not removed by filtration are removed by this process.
- They are instead passed into the distal convoluted tubule by the activity of cells of tubular walls, i.e. reabsorption and secretion.

Urine

- The filtrate left behind after the completion of all steps is known as **urine**. It is expelled out from the urethra (in the penis in males and directly to exterior in females) under the impulse of nervous system.
- This process of expelling out of urine is known as **urination** or **micturition**.
- Urine is a clear yellow fluid having pH around 6-8 (slightly acidic in nature). The colour of urine is yellow due to the presence of **urochrome**, a pigment found by breakdown of haemoglobin.
- The colour and pH of urine may vary with the diet of a person.

Composition of Urine

Normally urine constitutes of about 95% water and 5% solid wastes (including organic and inorganic substances).

Constituents of urine (in gm/L of urine) are listed in the table given below

Composition of Urine

Organic (g/L)	**Inorganic** (g/L)
Urea 2.3	NaCl 9.0
Uric acid 0.7	KCl 2.5
Creatinine 1.5	Ammonia 0.6
Other 2.6	Others 2.5

Abnormal Urine

Any deviation in colour, constitution, smell, pH or other factors from the normal urine is called **abnormal urine.**

Disorders of Excretory System

Malfunctioning of kidneys can lead to several disorders of the excretory system.

Glycosuria	This occurs mainly when glucose passes with urine due to diabetes mellitus, i.e. lack of insulin hormone in the body.
Diuresis	This occurs due to the lack of Antidiuretic Hormone (ADH) due to which the production of urine is increased.
Kidney stones	This occurs due to the accumulation of calcium oxalate crystals in the kidney.
Gout	This occurs when the uric acid is crystallised and gets deposited in the joints.
Haematuria	This occurs mainly due to the infection in the urinary tract. During this condition, the formation of kidney stone or tumour occurs and also blood passes with urine.

Osmoregulation

- It is the phenomenon of regulating the composition of water and salts in the body while removing wastes from the blood.
- It can be described as the phenomenon of regulating osmotic pressure of the blood which helps in maintaining the composition of the body fluid static, also known as **homeostasis.**
- During summer, as the temperature is high, we loose a considerable amount of water through perspiration. Due to this more water is absorbed by the kidneys, thus, making the urine more concentrated.

PYQs Previous Years' Questions

1 Mark Questions

Multiple Choice Question

1. The pale yellow colour of normal human urine is due to the pigment **ICSE 2023, Specimen 2021-22 Sem. II**

(a) melanin (b) anthocyanin
(c) urochrome (d) haemoglobin

Ans. (c) urochrome

Very Short Answer Type Questions

2. Define the term ultrafiltration. **ICSE 2024**

Ans. The filtration of blood in glomerulus part of a nephron under high pressure is called ultrafiltration.

3. Correct the statement by changing the underlined word.

Normal pale yellow colour of the urine is due to the presence of the pigment <u>melanin</u>. **ICSE 2018**

Ans. Urochrome

4. Give appropriate biological or technical term for 'Process of maintaining water and salt balance in the blood.' **ICSE 2018**

Ans. Osmoregulation

5. Choose the odd one out of the terms given and name the category to which the others belong.

Bile, Urea, Uric acid, Ammonia **ICSE 2017**

Ans. **Odd term** - Bile

Category - Rest three are the types of excretory material in human body.

6. Give biological reason for the statement.

There is frequent urination in winter than in summer. **ICSE 2017**

Ans. During winter, the surrounding temperature is very low. Thus, the loss of water through perspiration is very slow. Moreover, to keep the body temperature constant, the blood capillaries in the skin get constricted and the blood pressure is increased.

The result is that the body gets warmed up. In order to maintain the blood pressure normal, the excess water along with wastes is excreted mostly in the form of urine. This is the reason for frequent urination during winter.

7. State true or false
Nephrons are the basic unit of brain. **ICSE 2015**

Ans. False

8. Explain the selective reabsorption. **ICSE 2015**

Ans. **Selective reabsorption** It is a process that takes place in the Proximal Convoluted Tubules (PCT) of the kidney. In this, certain substances like glucose, amino acids, vitamins, water, etc. which are filtered out of the blood during ultrafiltration are absorbed.

9. Give reason. Urine is slightly thicker in summer than in winter. **ICSE 2011, 2004**

Ans. In summer as the temperatures is high so considerable amount of water is lost due to perspiration. Due to which more water is absorbed by the kidneys. Thus, making the urine more concentrated.

10. Glucose is normally not found in urine. Explain briefly. **ICSE 2006**

Ans. The glomerular filtrate contains lots of glucose, salt, etc. which are useful to us. In the proximal convoluted tubule of the nephron, all the glucose is reabsorbed in the blood by the process of selective reabsorption. Therefore, glucose is normally not found in urine.

11. Explain the term osmoregulation. **ICSE 2005**

Ans. Osmoregulation is the regulation of osmotic pressure of the blood (regulating water and salt) which helps in maintaining the composition of the body fluid static.

12. Name the two main stages of urine formation. **ICSE 2005**

Ans. The two main stages of urine formation are
(i) Ultrafiltration (ii) Selective reabsorption

2 Marks Question

13. Briefly describe the formation of glomerular filtrate. **ICSE 2005**

Ans. The diameter of the efferent arteriole is narrower than the afferent arteriole. Due to which, a hydrostatic pressure is created in the blood flowing through the glomerulus which forces the liquid part of the blood into the Bowman's capsule.

This filtration under high pressure is called ultrafiltration. The liquid which enters into the Bowman's capsule is called glomerular filtrate.

3 Marks Questions

14. Draw neat and labelled diagram of Malpighian capsule. **ICSE 2023, 2015**

Ans.

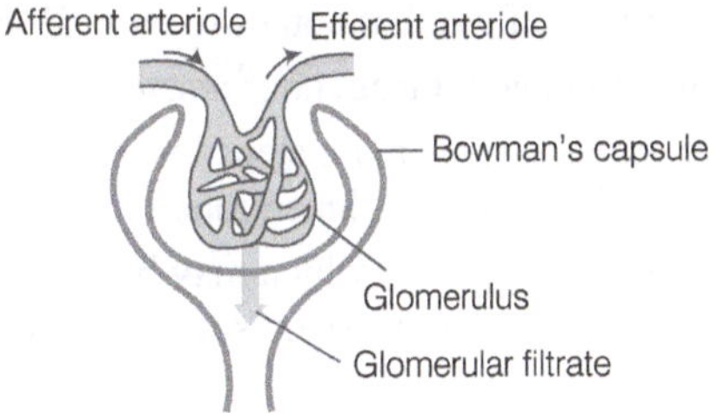

Malpighian capsule

15. Mention the three major steps involved in the production of urine. **ICSE 2021-22 Sem. II**

Ans. For the major steps involved in the production of urine refer to text on page 123.

16. (i) Draw a neat diagram of a single Malpighian capsule (body) and label the following parts.
Glomerulus, Bowman's capsule, afferent arteriole and efferent arteriole.
(ii) Name and explain the process that occurs in the glomerulus. **ICSE Specimen 2017, 2003**

Ans. (i) Refer to answer no. 14.
(ii) **Ultrafiltration** is the process that occurs in the glomerulus. It is defined as the filtration of blood that takes place under high pressure.

Diagram Based Questions

17. The diagram given below is that of a structure present in a human kidney.
Study the same and answer the questions that follows

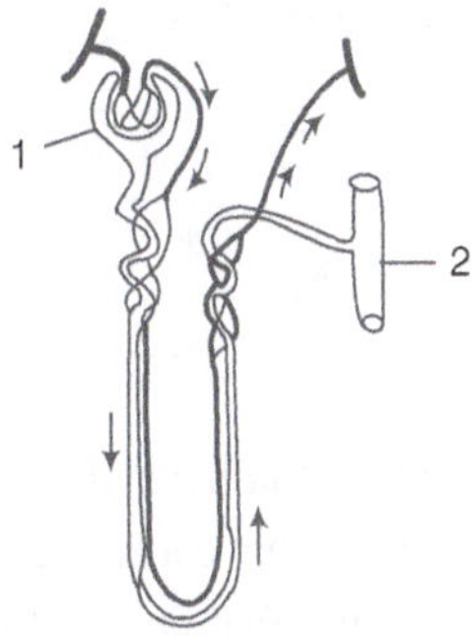

(i) Name the structure represented in the diagram.

(ii) What is the liquid entering part '1' called? Name two substances present in this liquid that are reabsorbed in the tubule.

(iii) What is the fluid that comes to part '2' called? Name the main nitrogenous waste in it.

(iv) Mention the three main steps involved in the formation of the fluid mentioned in (iii).

(v) Name the substance which may be present in the fluid in part '2' if a person suffers from diabetes mellitus. **ICSE 2018 (5M)**

Ans. (i) Nephron.

(ii) Glomerular filtrate.

Glucose, amino acids,salts, etc. get reabsorbed from the filtrate as it passes down the tubule.

(iii) Urine

Urea is the main nitrogenous waste (2.6 g/L) present in urine.

(iv) Three main steps of urine formation are

(a) Ultrafiltration (Glomerular filtration)

(b) Selective reabsorption

(c) Tubular secretion

(v) The urine of a person suffering from diabetes mellitus contains glucose in it. This condition is called as glycosuria.

18. The diagram given below shows a section of a human kidney. Study the diagram carefully and answer the questions that follows.

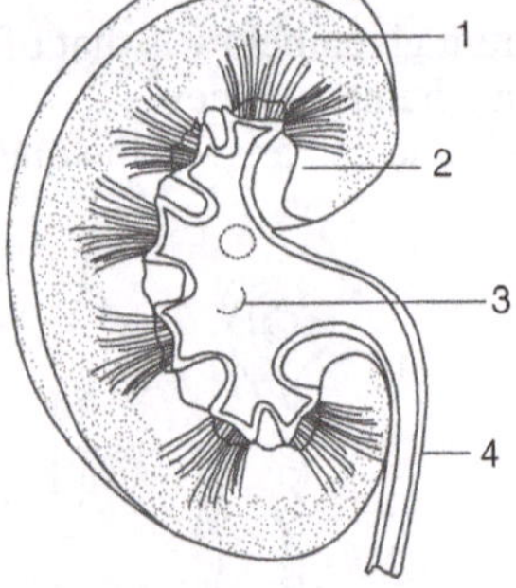

(i) Label the parts numbered 1 to 4.

(ii) Why does part 2 have a striped appearance?

(iii) What is the fluid that passes down part 4? Name the main nitrogenous waste present in it.

(iv) Mention the structural and functional unit of the kidney.

(v) Name the two major steps in the formation of the fluid mentioned in (iii). **ICSE 2015 (5M)**

Ans. (i) 1 – Cortex 2 – Medulla

3 – Pelvis 4 – Ureter

(ii) Medulla have a striped appearance due to the arrangement of several conical projections called renal or medullary pyramids.

(iii) Urine is the fluid that passes down from part 4 (ureter). The main nitrogenous waste in urine is urea.

(iv) Nephron

(v) The two major steps in the formation of the fluid (urine) are

1. Ultrafiltration
2. Selective reabsorption

19. The diagram given below represents a nephron and its blood supply. Study the diagram and answer the following questions.

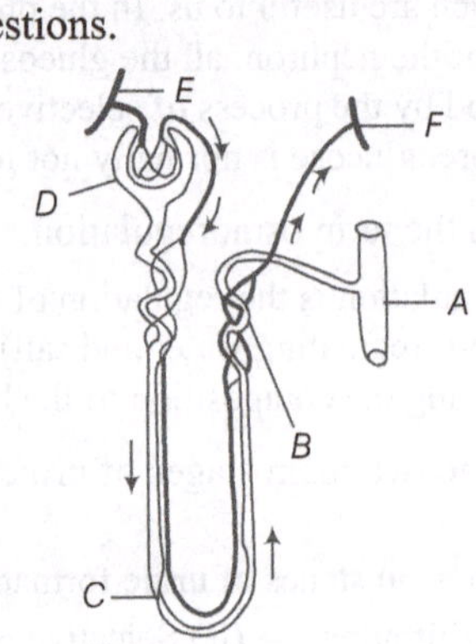

(i) Label parts *A*, *B*, *C* and *D*.

(ii) State the reason for the high hydrostatic pressure in the glomerulus.

(iii) Name the blood vessel which contains the least amount of urea in this diagram.

(iv) Name the part of the nephron which lies in the renal medulla. **ICSE 2014 (5M)**

Ans. (i) Different parts in the diagram are labelled as

A — Collecting duct

B — Distal convoluted tubule

C — Loop of Henle

D — Bowman's capsule

(ii) The diameter of the efferent arteriole is narrower than the afferent arteriole. Due to which, a hydrostatic pressure is created in the blood flowing through the glomerulus which forces the liquid part of the blood into the Bowman's capsule.

(iii) Blood vessel that contains the least amount of urea in this diagram is efferent arteriole, that joins renal vein.

Concept Enhancer The blood vessel which contain highest amount of urea is hepatic vein.

(iv) Loop of Henle is the part of renal tubule that lies in medulla region of the kidney.

19. Given below is the diagram of a part of the nephron of the kidney. Study the same and answer the questions that follows

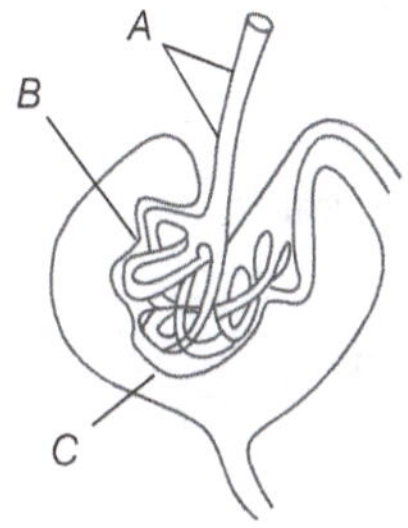

(i) Name the parts labelled A, B and C.

(ii) What is the collective term used for B and C?

(iii) Why is the right kidney at a slightly lower level than the left?

(iv) Explain the term homeostasis. What is the role of the kidney in this? **ICSE 2006 (5M)**

Ans. Different parts in the diagram can be labelled as

(i) A — Afferent arteriole

B — Glomerulus

C — Bowman's capsule.

(ii) The collective term used for part B and C is Malpighian capsule.

(iii) Right kidney is placed slightly at lower level than the left because the liver takes much space of the right side.

Concept Enhancer Right kidney is 2-8 cm lower than the left kidney.

(iv) Homeostasis is the phenomenon of keeping the same level of composition of the body fluids. By the process of osmoregulation, kidney helps in maintaining the osmotic concentration of the body and also helps in removing extra water or salts from the body.

CHAPTER TEST

Section-A

01 Mark Questions

1 Select the correct answer to the question from the given options.

(i) Which of the following is a main excretory product of human body?

(a) Urea (b) Amino acids
(c) Haemoglobin (d) Plasma

(ii) The total amount of urine output per day by a normal human being is

(a) 0.5 to 1.0 L/day
(b) 3-4 L/day
(c) 4-5 L/day
(d) 1 to 1.5 L/day

(iii) The stable condition of body is maintained with the help of

(a) internal process (b) excretion
(c) reproduction (d) external process

(iv) Which of the following organs come under the category of excretory organs?

(a) Kidney (b) Liver
(c) Skin (d) All of these

(v) The loop of Henle play an important role in the process of absorbing

(a) water and sodium ions
(b) salt and glucose
(c) fructose and sucrose
(d) sugar and iodine

2 (i) Name the following.

(a) The excretory product of human beings.
(b) Excretory unit of the kidney.
(c) The blood vessel which enters in the glomerulus.
(d) Name the part which transfer urine from kidney to urinary bladder.

(ii) Arrange and rewrite the terms in each group in the correct order so as to be in a logical sequence beginning with the term that is underlined.

(a) Ultrafiltration, Urine, Tubular secretion, Reabsorption.
(b) Glomerulus, DCT, PCT, Loop of Henle
(c) Afferent arteriole, Efferent arteriole, Glomerulus, Bowman's capsule
(d) Efferent arteriole, Renal vein, Vasa recta, Posterior vena cava.

(iii) Match the items given in Column I with the most appropriate ones in Column II and rewrite the correct matching pairs.

	Column I		Column II
A.	Uric acid	1.	Diabetes insipidus
B.	Urea	2.	Gout and kidney stones
C.	Urine	3.	Skin
D.	Sweat	4.	Nitrogenous waste excreted by kidney
E.	ADH	5.	1 to 1.5 L/ day
		6.	Ureter
		7.	Ammonia

(iv) Choose the odd one out from the following terms and name the category to which others belong.

(a) Urea, Ammonia, Uric acid, Urine
(b) CO_2, Water, Excess salts, Blood
(c) Ultrafilteration. Tubular secretion, Reabsorption, Osmoregulation
(d) Sodium chloride, Potassium chloride, Ammonia, Urea

(v) State the exact location of the following structures.

(a) Nephron (b) Urinary bladder
(c) Sweat glands (d) Loop of Henle

02 Marks Questions

3 Explain the external structure of the kidney.

4 Why is blood in glomerulus under high pressure?

5 Define osmoregulation.

6 Which substance are reabsorbed in DCT and PCT.

7 What happens to glucose which enters in the nephron along with the filtrate?

03 Marks Questions

8 Write the functions of human kidney.

9 Draw a neat labelled diagram of kidney.

10 Write a short note on excretion.

11 What are the three stages in urine formation ? Write the functions of different part of nephron in urine formation.

12 Give a biological reason for the following statement. Deficiency of ADH cause diabetes insipidus.

Section-B

Diagram Based Questions

13 With reference to the given figure. Answer the following questions.

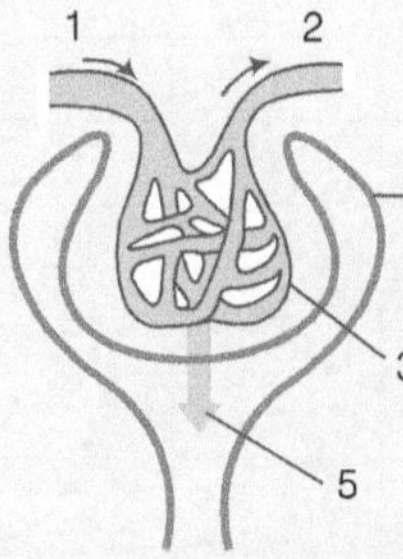

(i) Write the name of parts labelled as 1-5.

(ii) Write the significance of structural difference between 1 and 2.

(iii) Write the stage of urine formation takes place in given figure.

14 The given figure is of human kidney. Answer the following question with reference to it.

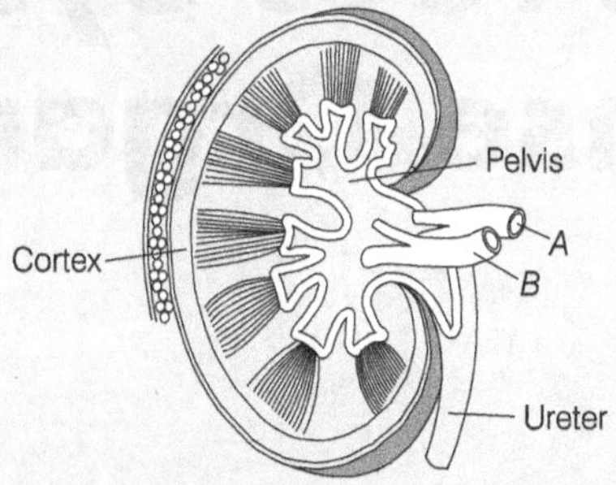

(i) Write two difference in the composition of blood. following through blood vessel *A* and *B*.

(ii) Explain the reason behind the dotted appearance of cortex of kidney.

(iii) Which part of the nephron runs in medulla region of the kidney.

Answers

1. (i) (a), (ii) (d), (iii) (b), (iv) (d), (v) (a)

09 Nervous System and Sense Organs

TREND ANALYSIS 4 YEARS

		Average No. of Questions Across all Sets			
	Types of Questions	2024	2023	2020	2019
TOPIC 01 Basics of Nervous System	1 Mark	2	–	–	3
	2 Marks	–	–	–	–
	3 Marks	–	–	–	–
	5 Marks	–	–	–	–
TOPIC 02 Human Nervous System	1 Mark	1	3	–	3
	2 Marks	–	2	–	–
	3 Marks	–	–	–	–
	5 Marks	–	–	–	1
TOPIC 03 Sense Organs	1 Mark	3	1	–	8
	2 Marks	1	1	–	–
	3 Marks	1	–	–	–
	5 Marks	–	–	–	1

In animals including humans, control and coordination are provided by the integration of nervous system and endocrine system. Nervous system is an organised system which keeps us informed about the world through sense organs. It enable us to think, remember, react and to figure out things and control the reflex actions of our body.

TOPIC 1

Basics of Nervous System

Neurons

The neural system consists of highly specialised cells called neurons. A neuron is the structural and functional unit of nervous system. These are the longest cells in the human body. Human neural system has about 100 billions neurons. Fully formed neurons never divide and once a neuron is dead, it cannot be replaced.

Structure of Neurons

- Each neuron or nerve cell is comprised of following three parts
  (i) **Cell body or Cyton** It contains granular cytoplasm (due to the presence of Nissl's granules), nucleus and cell membrane.
  The cytoplasm has cell organelles like mitochondria, Golgi apparatus, ribosomes, lysosomes, etc., except centrosomes because nerve cells does not have the ability to divide.
  (ii) **Dendrites** (dendron) These are usually shorter, tapering and branched cytoplasmic projections of the cell body. They also contain Nissl's granules. They conduct nerve impulses towards the cell body.
  (iii) **Axon** It is a single, usually very long process originating from the cell body.
- In most neurons, axon is surrounded by a myelin sheath. The gaps between the two adjacent myelin sheath are called **nodes of Ranvier**.
- The terminal portions of the axons have swollen bulb-like structure called **synaptic knob** which store certain chemicals called **neurotransmitters**.
- The axon transmit impulses away from the cell body to a synapse or to a neuromuscular junction.

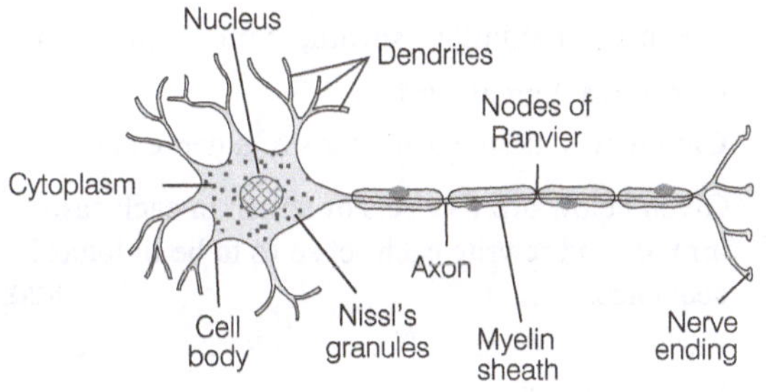

Fig. 9.1 Structure of typical neuron

Types of Neuron

They are of following three main types

(i) **Sensory neuron** is the one which transmits information to the main nervous system, i.e. brain and spinal cord.
(ii) **Motor neuron** is the one which transmits information from the main nervous system to effectors such as muscles and glands.
(iii) **Relay** (association or connecting) **neuron** is the one which serves as a link between the sensory and motor neuron. These are found in brain and spinal cord mainly.

Nerves

A nerve is a bundle of nerve fibres, i.e. axons of separate neurons being enclosed in a tube-like sheath. Nerves emerge out from the brain and spinal cord and branch out to usually all parts of the body.

Mixing of impulses is prevented by the myelin sheath of each axon which acts like an insulation material.

Nerves are of following three main types

(i) **Sensory nerves** consists of only sensory fibres.
(ii) **Motor nerves** consists of only motor fibres.
(iii) **Mixed nerves** consists of both sensory and motor fibres.

Transmission of a Nerve Impulse

- The transmission of all information in the body has a general scheme of flow.
- All the information from the environment is detected by the **receptors** (sense organs) in the body.
- The neurons of the receptors transfer this information to the effectors for the appropriate response.
- The information acquired at the end of the dendrite neuron causes a chemical reaction that produces an electrical impulse.
- That electrical impulse travels from the dendrite to the cell body (cyton) and then along the axon to its end.
- At the end of axon, the electrical impulse causes the release of some chemicals. These chemicals cross the gap (synapse) and start a similar electrical impulse in a dendrite of next neuron.
- A similar synapse finally allows delivery of such impulses from one cell to other cells, such as muscle cells of gland.
  Thus, the complete pathway followed by the nerve impulse in the body is given below

Stimulus → Neuron of a receptor → Dendrite → Cell body → Axon → Axon terminal → Effector

Synapse

It is the point of contact between the nerve endings of one neuron and the dendrites of another neuron, separated by a fine gap.

This is actually a gap in which neurotransmitters (the chemicals such as acetylcholine) are released when the impulse reaches the terminal end of an axon.

These neurotransmitters sets a nerve impulse in the dendrites and travel across the special receptors on the membrane of the next nerve ending.

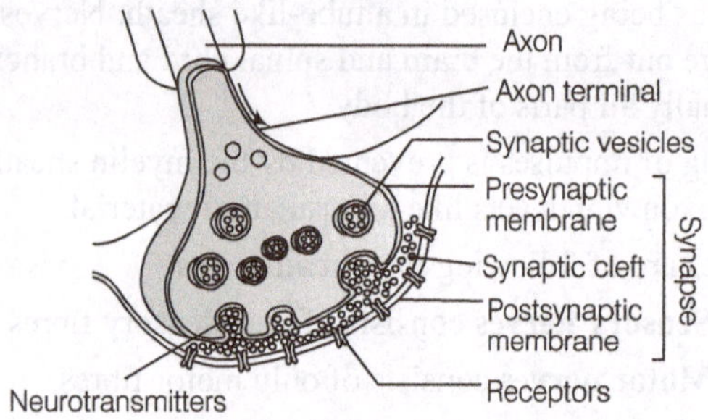

Fig. 9.2 Synapse

Limitations of the Use of Electrical Impulse

It is an excellent means to transmit information during fast responses to stimulus. But there are certain limitations to the use of electrical impulses.

These are as follows

- The electrical impulse is limited to only those cells that are connected by nervous tissue, i.e. not each and every cell in the animal body.
- Once an electrical impulse is generated and transmitted in a cell, the cell will take sometime to reset its mechanism before it can generate and transmit a new impulse.

PYQs Previous Years' Questions

1 Mark Questions

1. Arrange and rewrite the terms in each group in the correct order to be in a logical sequence beginning with the term that is underlined:

   Effector, Receptor, Motor neuron, Sensory neuron. **ICSE 2024**

Ans. Receptor, Sensory neuron, Motor neuron, Effector.

2. Name the type of nerve which has the fibres of both sensory and motor neurons. **ICSE 2024**

Ans. Mixed nerves have the fibres of both sensory and motor neurons.

3. Given below are five sets of terms. In each case arrange and rewrite each set so as to be in a logical sequence.

   Synapse, Axon endings, Cyton, Node of Ranvier, Dendrite **ICSE 2019**

Ans. Dendrite, Cyton, Node of Ranvier, Axon endings, Synapse.

4. Identify the odd term in the set given below and name the category to which the remaining three belong.

   Axon, dendron, photon, cyton **ICSE 2019**

Or Cyton, photon, axon, dendron **ICSE 2014**

Ans. **Odd term** Photon

Category All others are parts of a neuron.

5. Briefly explain synapse. **ICSE 2019, 2016**

Or

Briefly explain the term synapse. **ICSE 2012**

Ans. **Synapse** It is the junction point of the two adjacent neurons, between axon ending of one neuron with dendrite of other.

6. Choose the **odd** one out from the given terms and name the **category** to which the others belong.

   Example Nose, tongue, arm, eye

   Answer Odd term-Arm, Category - Sense organs

   Dendrites, medullary sheath, axon, spinal cord

Ans. **Odd term** Spinal cord **ICSE 2018**

Category All others are parts of a nerve cell

7. Given below are five sets of terms. In each case, arrange and rewrite each set so as to be in logical sequence. **ICSE 2017**

   Association neuron, effector, motor neuron, receptor, sensory neuron.

Ans. Receptor, sensony neuron, association neuron, motor neuron, effector

8. Mention the exact location of myelin sheath. **ICSE 2017**

Ans. **Myelin sheath** It surrounds axon of the neuron.

9. Name the cell body of a nerve cell. **ICSE 2013**

Ans. **Cyton** is known as the cell body of a nerve cell.

10. Which chemical is found in human brain, write its special functional activity? **ICSE 2013**

Ans. Neurotransmitters helps in conduction of nerve impulse.

11. Choose the correct answer to the following statements out of the three choices given after each statement. **ICSE 2010**

A point of contact between two neurons is termed

(i) synapsis (ii) neuromotor junction (iii) synapse

Ans. (iii) Synapse is the point of contact between two neuron.

12. Name the neurotransmitter stored at the terminal end of the axon. **ICSE 2009**

Ans. Acetylcholine is a neurotransmitter stored at the terminal end of the axon.

13. Give the technical/biological term for 'The point of contact between two neurons'. **ICSE 2008, 2000**

Ans. The point of contact between two neurons is synapse.

2 Marks Question

14. Draw a neat diagram of a neuron and label any two parts. **ICSE 2021-22 Sem. II**

Or Draw a well labelled diagram of a neuron and name the following parts **ICSE 2012**

(i) Node of Ranvier (ii) Nissl's granules

(iii) Cyton

Ans. Refer to fig. on page no. 131 (Structure of a typical neuron)

5 Marks Questions

15. (i) Draw a well labelled diagram of a neuron showing the following parts

Dendrites, axon, node of Ranvier and myelin sheath.

(ii) State the function of sensory neuron and a motor neuron.

(iii) What is a nerve made up of? **ICSE 2010**

Ans. (i) Refer to fig. on page no. 131 (Structure of a typical neuron

(ii) Functions of different neurons are given below

(a) **Sensory neuron** brings the impulse from the receptor organ, to the brain or spinal cord.

(b) **Motor neuron** brings the impulse from the brain or spinal cord to all effector organs.

(iii) A nerve is made up of a bundle of nerve fibres, i.e. axons of separate neurons enclosed in tube-like sheath.

16. Draw neat and labelled diagrams of a myelinated neuron. **ICSE 2015**

Ans. Refer to fig. on page no.131 (Structure of a typical neuron)

TOPIC 2

Human Nervous System

It is divided into two main divisions, i.e. central nervous system and peripheral nervous system.

Central Nervous System (CNS)

CNS is known as the integrating and command centre of the nervous system. It is comprised of mainly two parts, i.e. brain and spinal cord.

1. Brain

It is known as the central information processing system of animal body including humans. In proportion to the size of the body, brain in humans is known to be the largest among all animals. It is considered as the most delicate organ, thus it is well protected in a box-like structure known as **cranium** (brain box) or **the skull**.

Protective Covering of the Brain

The brain is protected by the three membranous coverings known as **meninges**. These are given below

(i) **Duramater** It is the tough fibrous outer most covering of the brain.

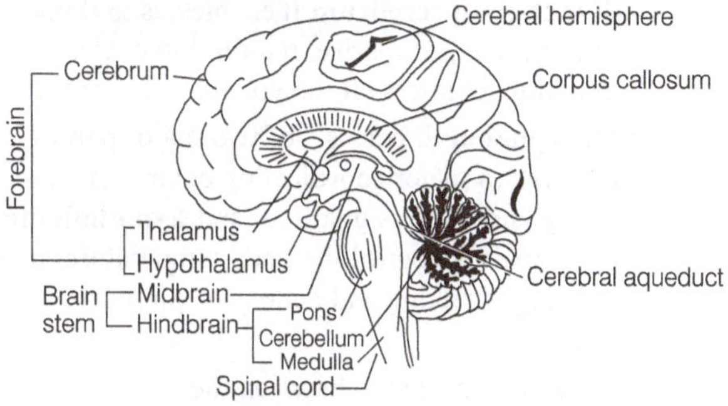

Fig. 9.3 Structure of brain

(ii) **Arachnoid mater** It is the middle very thin and delicate layer of the brain. The space between the arachnoid and piamater is filled with **cerebrospinal fluid**, a clear, colourless fluid found in brain and spine. It acts as a cushion for the brain cortex and provides mechanical protection and nourishment to the brain.

(iii) **Piamater** It is the innermost thin and very delicate membrane, which is in contact with the brain tissue.

Parts of Brain

Human brain is divisible into three main parts

(i) **Forebrain** It is the largest part of the brain and is divided into olfactory lobe, cerebrum and diencephalon.

(a) **Olfactory lobe** These are paired lobes and functionally related to smell.

(b) **Cerebrum** It is the largest, most complex and developed part of the human brain.

- It is divided into two main parts (halves) known as **cerebral hemispheres**. Each cerebral hemisphere is hollow from the interior and has two regions, i.e. **outer cortex** and **inner medulla**.
- The outer (cortex) portion is grayish in colour containing all the cell bodies of the neuron. It is also known as **grey matter**.
- The large grooves formed by the layers of gray matter are called **gyri** and the small folds in it are called **sulci**. The inner (medulla) portion is composed of **white matter** which mainly consists of axons of the neurons.
- The two cerebral hemispheres are interconnected to each other by a sheet of fibres known as **corpus callosum**. It is meant to transfer information from one cerebral hemisphere to the another.
  Function of cerebrum It enables us to think, invent, plan, memorise, reason, logic, etc. It mainly controls all the voluntary actions.

(c) **Diencephalon** It consists of two major parts – **thalamus** (a major coordinating centre for sensory and motor signalling) and **hypothalamus** (which mainly control the body temperature, urge for eating, drinking and actions of pituitary gland).

(ii) **Midbrain** It is located in between the thalamus/hypothalamus (of forebrain) and pons (of hindbrain). It is the small tubular part of the brain which helps to relay information for vision and hearing.

(iii) **Hindbrain** It further consists of following three main parts

(a) **Cerebellum** It is the much smaller region of the brain than the cerebrum and is also known as little brain.

- Cerebellum is situated just at the base, under the cerebrum of forebrain.
- It is also composed of outer cortex and inner medulla consisting of grey and white matter respectively.
  Function of cerebellum It coordinates the muscular activity and maintain the balance of the body.

(b) **Pons** It is located below the cerebellum and is responsible for carrying impulses from cerebellum to cerebrum. It also helps in regulation of breathing movements.

(c) **Medulla Oblongata** It is the lower most portion of the hindbrain situated at the base of the skull. It continues behind as the spinal cord.
Function of medulla oblongata It's main function is to control the activities like respiration, gastric secretions, etc.

Functions of Human Brain

- It coordinates all the activities of the body.
- It stores information, so that behaviour of human being can be modified according to past experience.
- It receives information carrying impulses from all the sensory organs of the body.
- It correlates the various stimulus from different sense organs and produces appropriate response.
- It responds to the impulses.

2. Spinal Cord

- It is a long tube-like structure extending from the medulla of the brain to the almost complete length of the backbone.
- It also contains the gray and the white matter but in opposite forms as brain (gray matter in the inner side and the white matter of the outer side).
- Inside the spinal cord there is a **central canal** which runs entirely with the length of the spinal cord and is continuous with the cavities of the brain.
- **Function of spinal cord** It conducts impulses to and from the brain. It controls most of the reflex activities of the brain. It also acts as a means of communication between the spinal nerves and the brain.

Peripheral Nervous System (PNS)

This system of brain mainly consists of all the nerves which transmits impulses to and from the central nervous system.

It is sub-divided into two main divisions such as

1. **Somatic Nervous System** (SNS)

- It contains nerves that relay information in the form of impulses from CNS to the skeletal muscles.
- On the basis of their origin, nerves of SNS are further categorised as, **cranial nerves** (arise from brain) and **spinal nerves** (arise from spinal cord).
- There are 10 pairs of cranial nerves and 10 pairs of spinal nerves in fishes and amphibians and 12 pairs of cranial nerves and 31 pairs of spinal nerves in humans.

2. **Autonomous Nervous System** (ANS)

It consists of **sympathetic** and **parasympathetic** nervous system and control the involuntary actions of the internal organs.

The difference in functions of sympathetic and parasympathetic nervous system are given below

Functions of Sympathetic Nervous System	**Functions of Parasympathetic Nervous System**
Vasoconstriction in general and vasodilation (brain, heart, lungs and skeletal muscles)	Vasodilation of coronary vessel
Dilates pupil	Constricts pupil
Increases lacrimal glands secretion	Inhibits lacrimal glands secretion
Inhibits salivary glands and digestive glands	Stimulates salivary gland and digestive gland
Accelerates heart beat	Retards heart beat
Dilates trachea, bronchi and lungs	Constricts trachea, bronchi and lungs
Inhibits gut peristalsis	Stimulates gut peristalsis
Contracts sphincter	Relaxes sphincter
Relaxes urinary bladder	Contracts urinary bladder
Increases adrenal secretion	Inhibit adrenal secretion
Blood sugar increases by glucagon	Blood sugar decreases by insulin
Increases sweat secretion	Inhibits sweat secretion

Different Actions in the Body

Our body perform various actions which are categorised into two main categories.

Involuntary Actions (Reflexes)	**Voluntary Actions**
Mainly self-protective due to environment.	Fulfilment of a desired goal.
Initiated by some stimulus (touch, pain, pressure, heat, light, etc).	Initiated by a willing thought.
Involve muscles and glands.	Involves only muscle.
Commands originate mostly in the spinal cord and autonomic nervous system and a few in the brain as well. e.g. shivering in cold non stop heart beat, etc.	Commands originate in brain. e.g. running, walking writing, etc.

Reflex Action and Reflex Arc

- A reflex action, differently known as reflex is an involuntary or instantaneous movement in response to a stimuli, e.g. coughing, blinking of eyes, sneezing, etc.
- In reflex action the message is passed straight to the motor neuron through a relay neuron.
- The reflex actions are mainly controlled by spinal cord and not by the brain. This is because on their way to the brain, nerves from all over the body meet in spinal cord.
- **Reflex arc** is the nervous pathway taken by nerve impulses in a reflex action. It is the route of an electrical impulse in a reflex action.
- This general pathway is depicted below

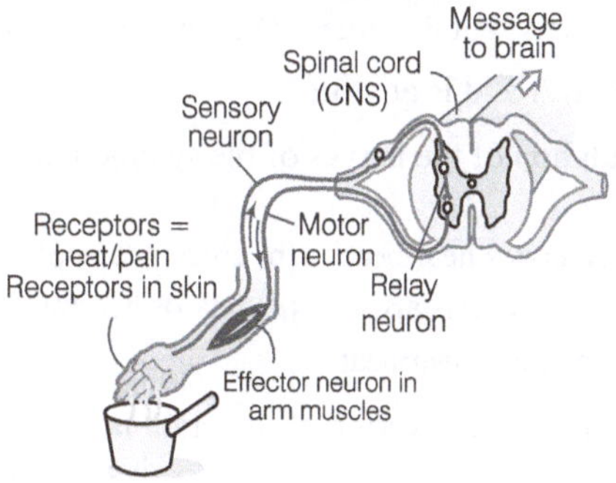

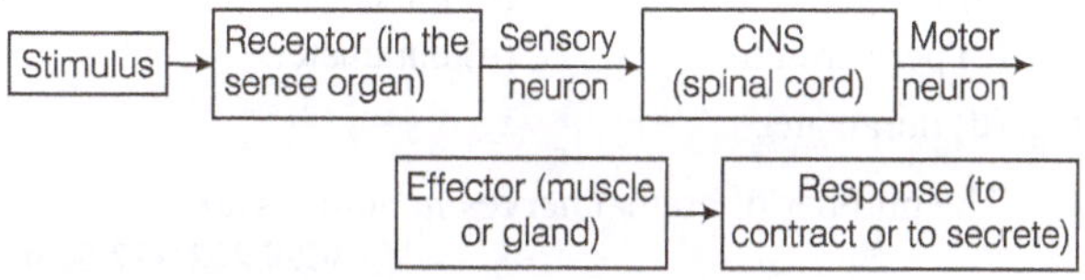

Types of Reflexes

Reflexes are categorised into following two categories

(i) **Natural** (unconditioned) **reflexes** (ii) **Conditioned** (acquired) **reflexes**

Differences between Conditioned and Unconditioned Reflexes

Natural Reflex (inherited)	**Conditioned Reflex** (Acquired)
Inborn (inherited) requiring no previous experience.	Developed by experience or learning.
Directly related to the stimulus.	Brought about by a condition totally different from the direct initial stimulus.
Similar in all humans (similar among all individuals of any one species).	Differs in different individuals, subjected to learning and experience.
e.g. Coughing of eyes, breast sneezing etc.	e.g. Applying brieaks of vehicles playing music instrument, etc.

Importance of Reflex Action

- It enables the organism for an immediate response to a harmful stimulus.
- It reduces the overloading in brain.
- It increases the chances of survival of an organism.

PYQs Previous Years' Questions

1 Mark Questions

Multiple Choice Questions

1. **Assertion** (A) Sympathetic nervous system prepares the body for violent action against abnormal conditions.
Reason (R) Sympathetic nervous system accelerates heartbeat. **ICSE 2024**
Which of the following is correct?
(a) Both A and R are true (b) A is true, R is false
(c) A is false but R is true (d) Both A and R are false

Ans. (a) Both A and R are true

2. Stimulation of the nerves of the sympathetic nervous system **ICSE 2023**
(a) accelerates heartbeat (b) constricts pupil of eyes
(c) increases peristalsis (d) retards heartbeat

Ans. (a) accelerates heartbeat

3. The outermost covering of the brain is **ICSE Specimen 2023**
(a) arachnoid (b) piamater
(c) pericardium (d) duramater

Ans. (d) duramater

4. The number of cranial nerves in humans are **ICSE 2021-22 Sem. II**
(a) 12 (b) 31 pairs
(c) 31 (d) 12 pairs

Ans. (d) 12 pairs

5. Which one of the following is not a simple reflex? **ICSE Specimen 2021-22 Sem. II**
(a) Coughing (b) Blinking
(c) Eating (c) Swallowing

Ans. (d) Swallowing

6. The number of spinal nerves in a human being are **ICSE Specimen 2021-22 Sem. II, 2018**
(a) 31 pairs (b) 10 pairs
(c) 21 pairs (d) 30 pairs

Ans. (a) 31 pairs

7. Learning is related to **ICSE Specimen 2019**
(a) cerebrum (b) cerebellum
(c) medulla oblongata (d) hypothalamus

Ans. (a) cerebrum

8. Which one of the following is mainly associated with the maintenance of the posture?
(a) cerebrum (b) cerebellum
(c) thalamus (d) pons **ICSE 2015**

Ans. (b) cerebellum

9. Which of the following is not a natural reflex action? **ICSE 2014**

(a) Knee-jerk
(b) Blinking of eyes due to strong light
(c) Salivation at the sight of food
(d) Sneezing when any irritant enters the nose

Ans. (c) Salivation at the sight of food

10. Choose the correct answer from the four options given below

The ventral root ganglion of the spinal cord contains cell bodies of the **ICSE 2013**

(a) motor neuron (b) sensory neuron
(c) intermediate neuron (d) association neuron

Ans. (a) motor neuron

11. Choose the correct answer from the four options given below each statement. **ICSE 2012**

A reflex arc in man is best described as movement of stimuli from

(a) receptor cell, sensory neuron, relaying neuron, effector muscles.
(b) receptor cell, efferent nerve, relaying neuron, muscles of the body.
(c) receptor cell, spinal cord, motor neuron, relaying neuron.
(d) receptor cell, synapse, motor neuron, relaying neuron.

Ans. (a) receptor cell, sensory neuron, relaying neuron and effector muscles.

Very Short Answer Type Questions

12. What is reflex action? **ICSE 2023**

Or Briefly explain reflex action. **ICSE 2016, 2012, 2010, 2007**

Ans. **Reflex action** It is an involuntary action of any organ or part of the body in response to a particular stimulus without involvement of brain.

13. State the exact location of duramater. **ICSE Specimen 2023**

Ans. The duramater is a membrane that envelops the arachnoid mater.

14. Given below are sets of five terms each. Rewrite the terms in correct order in a logical sequence.

Example Large intestine, Stomach, Mouth, Small intestine, Oesophagus.

Answer Mouth → Oesophagus → Stomach → Small intestine → Large intstine.

Receptor, Spinal cord, Effector, Motor neuron, Sensory neuron. **ICSE 2023, 2017**

Or

Spinal cord, motor neuron, receptor, effector, sensory neuron. **ICSE 2013**

Ans. Receptor → Sensory neuron → Spinal cord → Motor neuron → Effector (Reflex pathway)

15. Choose the odd one out from the following terms and name the category to which the others belong.

Spinal cord, Cerebrum, Pons, Cerebellum **ICSE Specimen 2023**

Ans. (c) **Odd Term** Pons

Category Other three are major parts of brain.

16. Mention the exact location of corpus callosum. **ICSE Specimen 2023, 2013, 2019**

Ans. Corpus callosum is the region that connects the left and right cerebral hemisphere of forebrain.

17. Give the biological/technical term for the following The quick actions which are involuntary and controlled by the spinal cord. **ICSE Specimen 2019**

Ans. Reflex action

18. How are the cyton and axons placed in the brain and the spinal cord? **ICSE 2019**

Ans. **Cyton in Brain** The cerebral cortex is the outer folded part of the brain. It is also known as grey matter which contains all the cell bodies and dendrites of nerve cell.

Axons in Brain The inner portion is composed of white matter mainly consists of axons of the neurons.

In spinal cord, grey matter is present in the inner side and white matter on outer side.

19. Correct and rewrite the statement given below by changing the biological term that is underlined. Maintaining balance of the body and coordinating muscular activities is carried out by the <u>cerebrum</u>.

Ans. Cerebellum. **ICSE 2019**

20. State the main functions of medulla oblongata. **ICSE 2019**

Ans. Medulla oblongata is located in the brain stem, anterior to (in front of) the cerebellum. It helps to regulate breathing, heart and blood vessel function, digestion, sneezing and swallowing.

21. Correct the statements by changing the underlined words

'The outermost layer of meninges is <u>piamater</u>.' **ICSE 2018**

Ans. The outermost layer of meninges is duramater.

22. Given below is a set with four terms each. In each set one term is odd. Choose the odd one out of the following terms given and name the category to which the others belong **ICSE 2017, 2016**

Set	Odd One	Category
Sneezing, coughing, blinking, typing		

Ans.

Set	Odd One	Category
Sneezing, coughing blinking, typing	typing	Other belong to natural reflex action.

23. The statement given below is incorrect. Rewrite the correct statement by changing the underlined word of the statement.

Gyri and sulci are the folds of cerebellum. **ICSE 2017, 2006**

Ans. Gyri and sulci are the folds of **cerebrum**. Cerebellum only contains gyri not sulci.

24. Give scientific reasons for

'Injury to medulla oblongata leads to death'. **ICSE 2017, 2016, 2007**

Ans. Any damage to the medulla oblongata may lead to the death of a person. The projecting process of the vertebra axis in the neck pierces the medulla under heavy shock as a result of which involuntary actions such as breathing and heartbeat are stopped.

25. Name the part of the brain that carries impulses from one hemisphere of the cerebellum to the other.

Ans. Pons varoli **ICSE 2016**

26. Name the part of the brain associated with memory. **ICSE 2014**

Ans. Cerebrum is the part of brain associated with the memory.

27. State the main function of cerebrospinal fluid. **ICSE 2014**

Or Name the fluid that provides protection and nourishment to the cells of the brain. **ICSE 2007**

Ans. Cerebrospinal fluid provide mechanical protection and nourishment to brain.

28. Differentiate between the following pairs on the basis of what is mentioned within brackets?

Spinal nerves and cranial nerves. (number of nerves)

Ans. **Spinal nerves** are 31 in pairs. **ICSE 2014**

Cranial nerves are 12 in pairs.

29. Give scientific/biological reasons for

'A person after consuming alcohol walks clumsily'.

Or

'An alcoholic person walks unsteadily when drunk'. **ICSE 2014, 2010**

Ans. An alcoholic person when drunk walks clumsily because of the effect of alcohol on cerebellum. This is because cerebellum is mainly responsible for the muscular coordination.

30. Differentiate between the following pair on the basis of what is mentioned in bracket?

Cerebrum and spinal cord. (arrangement of nerve cell) **ICSE 2013, 2010, 2004**

Ans. Differences between cerebrum and spinal cord are

Cerebrum	Spinal Cord
Gray matter is found on the outer side which contains cell bodies of the neurons whereas, white matter remains towards the inner side which mainly contains the axons (nerve fibre) of the neuron.	White matter lies towards the outer side containing axons and gray matter lies towards the inner side containing the cell body of motor (efferent and association neuron).

31. Give biological reasons for.

The hand automatically shows the direction to turn a cycle without thinking. **ICSE 2013**

Ans. It is conditioned reflex which is learnt by the brain due to prior learning. As the brain is already conditioned it remembers to automatically direct the hand to show direction while turning a cycle.

32. Given below is the set with four terms, in which one term is an odd one and cannot be grouped in the same category to which the other three belong. Identify the odd one in the set and name the category to which the remaining three belong.

Cerebrum, cerebellum, thalamus, hypothalamus. **ICSE 2012**

Ans.

Set	Odd One	Category
Cerebrum, cerebellum, thalamus, hypothalamus	Cerebellum	All others are the part of forebrain

33. Give the technical term for the protective covering of brain and spinal cord. **ICSE 2012**

Or Name the biological term given to the protective membranes of the brain. **ICSE 2009, 2008**

Ans. **Meninges** is the technical term for the protective covering of brain and spinal cord.

34. Given below is the biological statement which incomplete/incorrect. Rewrite the correct form of the statement by inserting a suitable word/words at the right place. Do not delete any word already given in the statement. Underline the inserted word/words.
A reflex action in a spontaneous response to a stimulus. **ICSE 2004**

Ans. A reflex action is a spontaneous **involuntary** response to a stimulus.

2 Marks Questions

35. What are the two functions of cerebellum? **ICSE 2023**

Ans. (i) Two functions are coordinates the muscular activities of the body.
(ii) It maintains the balance of the body.

36. State the function of medulla oblongata with a suitable example. **ICSE 2023, 2011**

Ans. The function of medulla oblongata is the control the activities of internal organs, e.g. peristaltic movement of the alimantary canal, movement of breathing, etc.

37. How are cyton and axon arranged in the spinal cord? **ICSE 2021-22 Sem. II**

Ans. The arrangement of cytons and axons is just opposite to that in brain.
In the spinal cord, cyton lies inside and forms the grey matter whereas axon lies outside forming white matter.

38. Name the part of the human brain which is concerned with the following
(i) Seat of memory
(ii) Coordinates muscular activity **ICSE 2012**

Ans. (i) Part associated with seat of memory is **cerebrum** of the brain.
(ii) The part that coordinates muscular activity is **cerebellum** of the brain.

39. During a street fight between two individuals, mention the effects on the following organs by the autonomous nervous system, in the table given below (one has been done for you as an example). **ICSE 2011**

Organ	Sympathetic Nervous System	Parasympathetic Nervous System
Lungs	Dilates bronchi and bronchioles	Constricts bronchi and bronchioles
Heart		
Pupil of the eye		
Salivary gland		

Ans. Refer to 'table of comparison between the function of SNS and PNS' on page no. 135.

40. State whether the following statements are true or false. If false, rewrite the correct form of the statement by changing the first or last word only.
Dilation of the pupil is brought about by the sympathetic nervous system. **ICSE 2010**

Ans. The statement is true.

41. Given below is the sets of five terms each. Rewrite the terms in logical sequence as directed at the end of the statement. Motor neuron, receptor, sensory neuron, effector, association neuron (pathway of a nerve impulse). **ICSE 2010**

Ans. The correct pathway of nerve impulse is receptor, sensory neuron, association neuron, motor neuron, effector.

42. In the given set there is one odd term which does not match to the category. Pick out the odd one and also write down the category of the group to which the remaining three belong. **ICSE 2010**

Blinking, knitting without looking, smiling, blushing, crying.

Ans.

Odd One	Category
Knitting without looking	All others are the type of simple reflex

43. State whether the following statement is true or false. If false, write the correct form of the statement by changing the first or last word. All voluntary actions are controlled by the cerebellum. **ICSE 2009**

Ans. The statement is true.

44. Given below is the question followed by four choices select and rewrite the correct answer to the given statement from the choices given below
The cerebral hemispheres in mammals are connected by **ICSE 2009**

(i) corpus luteum (ii) hypothalamus
(iii) pons Varolii (iv) corpus callosum

Ans. (iv) The cerebral hemispheres are connected by corpus callosum in mammals.

45. Give the exact location and one function of each of the meninges. **ICSE 2005**

Ans. **Meninges** are located as the covering of brain and spinal cord. Its function is to provide protection to the brain and spinal cord. Refer to text on page no. 133.

46. Given below is the set of terms in each case. Arrange and rewrite the set of term so as to be in a logical sequences. Dorsal root ganglion, receptor, effector, ventral root ganglion, associated neuron. **ICSE 2005**

Ans. The correct logical sequence is receptor, dorsal root ganglion, associated neuron, ventral root ganglion, effector.

47. Give one point of difference between the following pair on the basis of what is indicated in bracket.

Medulla oblongata and cerebellum (function). **ICSE 2005**

Ans.

Medulla Oblongata	Cerebellum
It control the activities of the internal organs.	It helps in maintaining the body balance.

48. A group is given there is one example which does not fit into the category write down the category of the group and identify

Coughing, sneezing, eating, blinking. **ICSE 2003**

Ans.

Odd One	Category
Eating	All others are the type of simple reflex

49. The part of the human brain that controls body temperature. **ICSE 2002**

Ans. Hypothalamus is the part of human brain that controls temperature.

50. Choose the correct answer to the following

Cerebellum is the part of the brain which is responsible for

(a) interpreting sensations.

(b) conducting reflexes in the body.

(c) maintaining posture and equilibrium.

(d) controlling, thinking, memory and reasoning. **ICSE 2002**

Ans. (c) Cerebellum is the part of the brain which is responsible for maintaining posture and equilibrium.

51. Given below is set of items belonging to a common category. Complete the filling in the category and the odd one in the blanks. **ICSE 2002**

Set	Category	Odd One
Pleura, pericardium, meninges, spinal cord.		

Ans.

Odd One	Category
Spinal cord	All others are related to the protective covering of visceral organs.

52. Given below is the type of structure found in humanbrain write its special functional activity in the blank given Cerebellum .... **ICSE 2000**

Ans. Cerebellum controls and coordinates the muscles of balancing organs.

53. Choose the odd one in the following series

Pons, cerebellum, medulla oblongata, cerebrum.

Ans. **Odd one** Cerebrum. **ICSE 2000**

54. Give the biological /technical terms for the following

(i) The fluid present between the layers of meninges.

(ii) The change in an organism resulting due to stimulus. **ICSE 2000**

Ans. (i) **Cerebrospinal fluid** is present between the layers of meninges.

(ii) **Reflex action** is the change in an organism that results due to the stimulus.

3 Marks Questions

55. Define the term synapse.

How are cytons and axons of neurons placed in the cerebrum? **ICSE 2021-22 Sem.II**

Ans. Synapse is the junction point of the two adjacent neurons, between axon ending of one neuron with dendrite of other.

For placing of cyton and axons in cerebrum Refer to text on page no. 134.

56. Name the three membranous coverings of the human brain. **ICSE 2021-22 Sem.II**

Ans. Refer to text on page no. 133.

57. What is a reflex action? Name the two types of reflexes. **2021-22 Sem.II**

Ans. Refer to text on page no. 135-136.

5 Marks Questions

58. Match the items given in Column A with the most appropriate ones in Column B and rewrite the correct matching pairs : **ICSE 2019**

	Column A		Column B
(i)	Cranial nerves	–	Testosterone
(ii)	Leydig cells	–	Natural reflex
(iii)	Acetylcholine	–	12 pairs
(iv)	Spinal nerves	–	Prolactin
(v)	Sneezing	–	Neurotransmitter
		–	18 pairs
		–	31 pairs
		–	Conditioned reflex

Ans.

	Column A	Column B
(i)	Cranial nerves	12 pairs
(ii)	Leydig cells	Testosterone
(iii)	Acetylcholine	Neurotransmitter
(iv)	Spinal nerves	31 pairs
(v)	Sneezing	Conditioned reflex

59. State whether the following actions are 'voluntary action, simple reflex or conditioned reflex' **ICSE 2008**

(i) Blinking (ii) Cleaning the table

(iii) Playing on the keyboard

(iv) Salivating when food is put in the mouth.

Ans. Refer to text on page no. 135.

Diagram Based Questions

60. Mohan is fond of playing basketball. His concentration is on shooting the ball into the opponent s basket as given in the picture.

(i) Which part of the brain helps Mohan to concentrate in putting the ball into the basket?

(ii) Name the sense organ that helps to gauge the distance between the ball and the basket.

(iii) Name the part of the brain that co-ordinates all the voluntary muscles of his body. **ICSE 2024 (3M)**

Ans. (i) Cerebrum helps Mohan to concentrate in putting the ball into the basket.

(ii) Eyes help to gauge the distance between the ball and the basket.

(iii) Cerebellum is the part of the brain that co-ordinates all the voluntary muscles of the body.

61. The diagram given below is that of a human brain. Answer the questions that follow.

(i) Label the parts numbered 2-3.

(ii) State any one function of the part numbered 1.

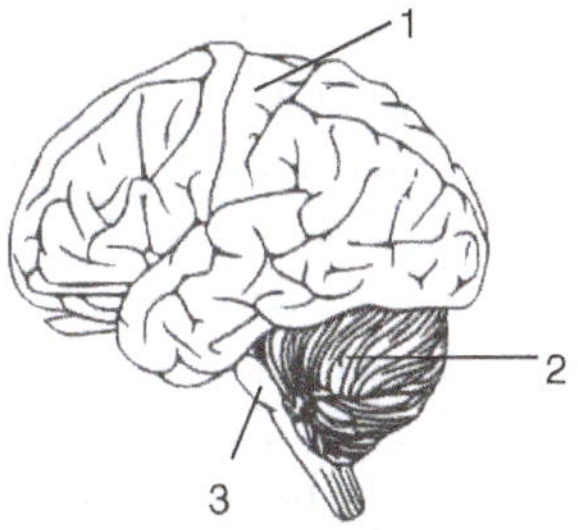

ICSE 2021-22 Sem. II (3M)

Ans. (i) 2-Cerebellum, 3-Pons

(ii) 1-Cerebrum, it enables us to think, invent, plan, memorise, reason, logic, etc. It mainly controls all the voluntary actions.

62. The diagram given below shows the internal structure of a spinal cord depicting a phenomenon. Study the diagram and answer the questions.

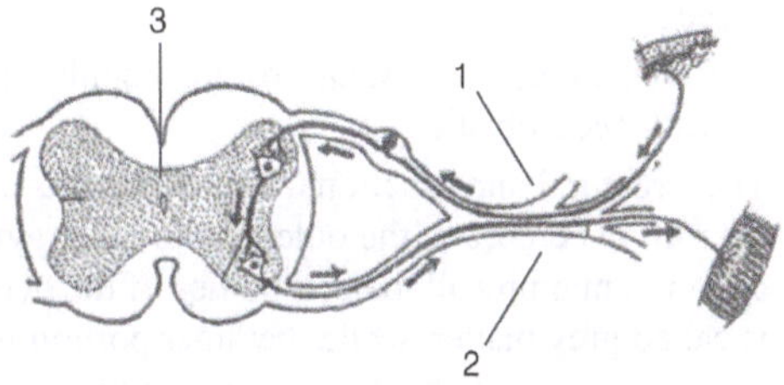

(i) Name the phenomenon that is depicted in the diagram. Define the phenomenon.

(ii) Give the technical term for the points of contact between the two nerve cells.

(iii) Name the parts numbered 1, 2 and 3.

(iv) How does the arrangement of neurons in the spinal cord differ from that of the brain?

(v) Mention two ways by which the spinal cord is protected in our body. **ICSE 2018 (5M)**

Ans. (i) The given figure shows the phenomenon of reflex action. Refer to text on page no. 135.

(ii) Synapse

(iii) (1) Sensory neuron (2) Motor neuron
(3) Grey matter

(iv) Arrangement of grey and white matter in spinal cord is opposite to that found in brain. Grey matter is in the inner side and the white matter is on the outer side in spinal cord.

(v) The spinal cord is well-protected by three membranous coverings known as meninges and cerebrospinal fluid.

63. The given diagram is an external view of the human brain. Study the same and answer the questions that follows.

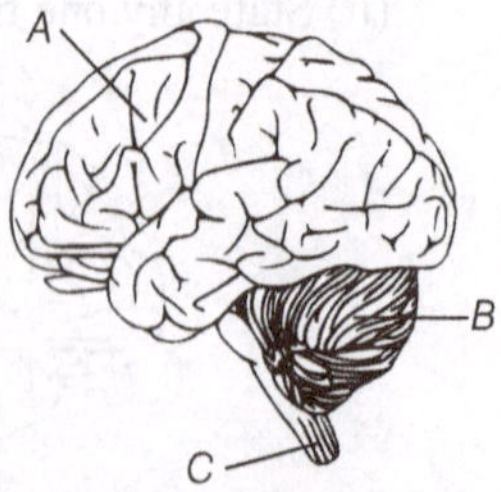

(i) Name the parts labelled *A*, *B* and *C* in the diagram.

(ii) State the main functions of the parts labelled *A* and *B*.

(iii) What are the structural and functional units of the brain? How are the parts of these units arranged in *A* and *C* ?

(iv) Mention the collective term for the membranes covering the brain.

(v) What is the function of cerebrospinal fluid?

ICSE 2017 (5M)

Ans. (i) *A* – Cerebrum, *B* – Cerebellum and *C* – Spinal cord.

(ii) *A* (Cerebrum) – Site of controlling memory, reasoning, thinking, perception, emotions and speech.

B (Cerebellum) – Maintains posture, equilibrium and muscular coordination.

(iii) The structural and functional unit of brain is called neuron. In cerebrum, the outer portion is grayish in colour containing all the cell bodies of the neuron. It is called grey matter, while the inner portion is composed of white matter which mainly consists of axons of the neurons. Spinal cord also contains grey and white matter, but in opposite form as brain (grey matter – inner side and white matter outer side).

(iv) The collective term used for the membranes covering the brain is meninges.

(v) Cerebrospinal fluid provides mechanical protection and nourishment to brain.

64. The diagram given below is a representation of a phenomenon pertaining to the nervous system. Study the diagram and answer the following questions

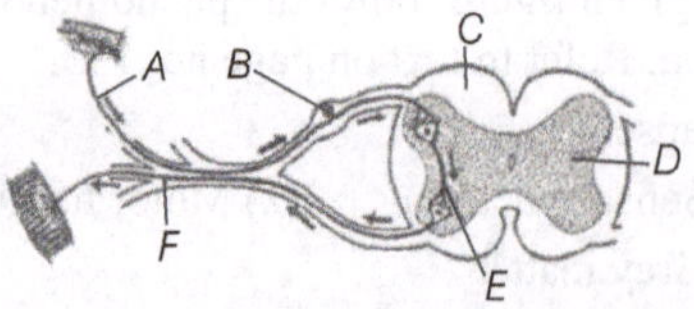

(i) Name the phenomenon that is being depicted.

(ii) Give the technical term for the point of contact between the two nerve cells.

(iii) Name the parts *A*, *B*, *C* and *D*.

(iv) Write the functions of parts *E* and *F*.

(v) How does the arrangement of neurons in the spinal cord differ from that of the brain?

ICSE 2014 (5M)

Ans. (i) The phenomenon depicted is reflex action.

(ii) Synapse is the technical term used for the point of contact between two nerve cells.

(iii) Different parts are labelled as

A – Sensory/Afferent neuron

B – Dorsal ganglion/dorsal root

C – White matter

D – Grey matter

(iv) Function of the *E* (synapse) is to relay transmit the impulse from sensory neuron to the motor neuron.

Function of the *F* (Motor neuron/Efferent neuron) is to relay transmit the command to the effector muscle or glands.

(v) Arrangement of the neurons in the spinal cord differ from the brain in the following ways.

- **In brain** Grey matter is found on the outside and white matter on the inner side.
- **In spinal cord** White matter is found on the outerside and grey matter on inner side.

65. Classify the following actions as simple reflex or conditioned reflex

(i) Playing a guitar.

(ii) Removing your hand suddenly when pricked by a thorn.

(iii) Applying sudden brakes when a dog crosses the path.

(iv) Blinking of eyelids on exposure to light.

(v) Tying one's shoe lace. **ICSE 2009**

Ans. Refer to text on page no. 136 under types of reflexes.

66. The diagram given below depicts the cross-section of the spinal cord. Study the same and then answer the questions that follows.

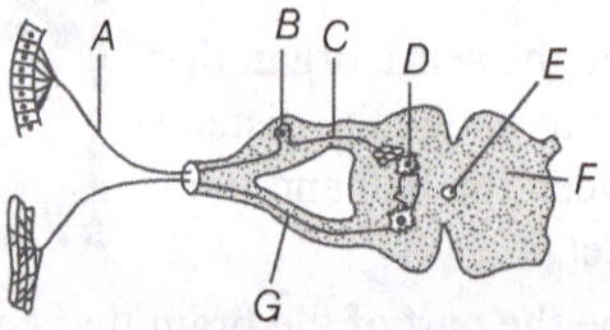

(i) Name the process that is being depicted.

(ii) Name the parts labelled *B*, *E* and *F*.

(iii) Name the cells in contact with the part labelled '*A*'.

(iv) What is the function of the parts labelled *C*, *D* and *G*? What is the technical term given to the pathway represented by *C*, *D* and *G*?

(v) How does the arrangement of cells in the spinal cord differ from that in the brain? **ICSE 2008 (5M)**

Ans. (i) The process depicted by this diagram is known as reflex action.

(ii) Labelled parts are given below

B – Dorsal root ganglion

E – Central canal

F – Grey matter.

(iii) The cells in contact with the part labelled as '*A*' are known as receptor cells.

(iv) Functions of the labelled parts *C*, *D* and *G* are

C–Afferent (sensory) nerve fibre carry the stimulus from receptor organ to the spinal cord.

D–Synapse is space between sensory and motor neuron. It is a place where incoming sensory impulse generates an outgoing motor impulse.

G–Effector neuron carries away the impulse generated by the association neuron in the centre to the effector organ (muscle or gland).

Technical term given to the pathway represented by *C*, *D* and *G* is 'reflex arc'.

(v) In spinal cord, the grey matter lies on the inner side and the white matter lies on the outer side. This arrangement is just reversed in the brain.

67. The diagram given below is the external view of the human brain. Study the same and answer the questions that follows.

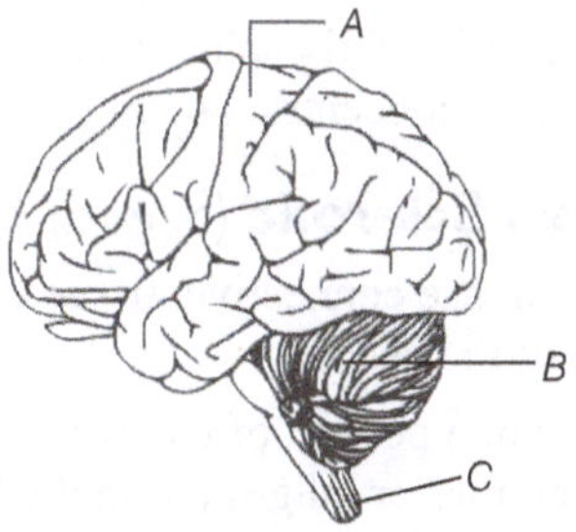

(i) Name the parts labelled *A*, *B* and *C*.

(ii) State the main functions of the parts labelled *A* and *B*.

(iii) How are the brain cells arranged in the part labelled '*A*'?

(iv) What is the structural and functional unit of the nervous system?

(v) Name the fluid that surrounds the brain. State its function. **ICSE 2006 (5M)**

Ans. (i) *A*–Cerebrum *B*–Cerebellum, *C*–Medulla oblongata.

(ii) *A*–Cerebrum is associated with memory, intelligence and sensation.

B–Cerebellum is associated with voluntary muscular movements and maintenance of equilibrium.

(iii) In cerebrum, brain cells are densely packed in the outer region. Gray matter found outside and white matter is inside.

(iv) The structural and functional unit of brain is neuron.

(v) Fluid that surrounds the brain is called cerebrospinal fluid.

Functions

(a) It protects CNS against mechanical shock and injury.

(b) It maintains a constant pressure inside the cranium.

Concept Enhancer The cerebrospinal fluid performs vital functions like, providing nourishment waste removal and protection to the brain.

68. The following diagram represents the human brain as seen in an external view. Study the same and then answer the questions that follows

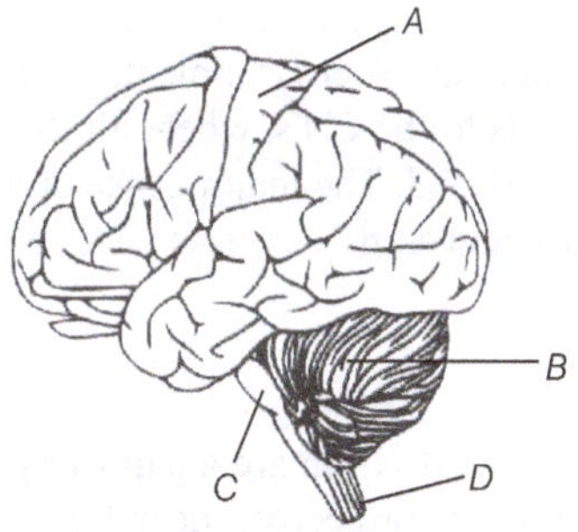

(i) Name the part labelled *A*, *B*, *C* and *D*.

(ii) Mention the difference in the arrangement of the nerve cells in the parts marked '*A*' and '*D*'.

(iii) What is the main function of the parts marked '*C*' and '*D*'?

(iv) Name the sheet of nerve fibres that connect the two halves of the part labelled. **ICSE 2002 (5M)**

Ans. Parts labelled from *A* to *D* are

(i) *A*– Cerebrum *B*– Cerebellum

C–Medulla oblongata *D*– Spinal cord.

(ii) In part *A*–Gray matter found outside and white matter is inside.

In part *D* –White matter is outside and gray matter is inside.

(iii) Different functions are as follows

C–Medulla oblongata, controls all the involuntary movements of internal organs, e.g. breathing movements of lungs, beating of heart.

D–Spinal cord, performs reflex action below the neck.

(iv) Corpus callosum is the sheet of nerve fibres that connects the two halves of the parts labelled *A* (cerebral hemispheres).

69. The diagram shows a section of the human brain. Answer the questions that follow.

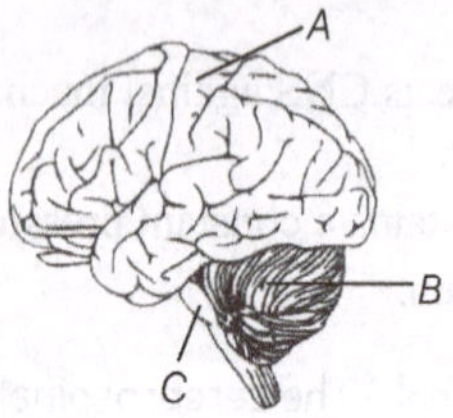

(i) Name the parts labelled *A*, *B* and *C*.

(ii) Give the main function of each of the parts *A*, *B* and *C*.

(iii) Name the three protective membranes covering the brain.

(iv) Name the basic unit of the brain.

Ans. Labelled parts from *A* to *C* are

(i) *A* – Cerebrum *B* – Cerebellum

C – Medulla oblongata

(ii) **Cerebrum** is the site of controlling memory, reasoning, thinking, perception, emotions and speech.

Cerebellum maintains posture, equilibrium and muscular coordination.

Medulla oblongata contains the centre for cardiac, respiratory and vasomotor activities. It also coordinates reflexes for swallowing, coughing, sneezing and vomiting.

(iii) Three protective membranes covering the brain are duramater, arachnoid and piamater.

(iv) The basic unit of brain is called neuron.

TOPIC 3

Sense Organs

These are the organs that enable us to detect all types of changes that occurs in the environment. These organs send appropriate signals to the CNS, where all the inputs are processed and analysed. The major sense organs includes eye, ear, tongue, nose and skin.

The Eye

The organ of sight and vision are a pair of eyes in humans. The eyes are located in the protective, deep bony cavities of the skull known as **eye sockets** or **orbits** on the front side of the head.

Main components of eye are given below

(i) **Eyebrows** As the protective covering because they prevent eyes from rainwater or perspiration from entering into the eyes.

(ii) **Eyelids** both upper and lower are the movable part of the eyes which prevent falling of larger particles into the eyes.

(iii) **Tear glands** (lacrimal glands) are located at the upper sideward portion of the orbit and secrete tears.

They contain an enzyme (lysozyme) which has an antiseptic property and help in killing germs (like bacteria) which enter the eyes.

Structure of Eye : Eyeball

Human eye ball is nearly spherical in structure. It consists of three concentric layers

Outermost Sclerotic (Sclera) Layer

- It contains dense connective tissue which maintains the shape of the eyeball.
- The front white portion of the eye is the sclerotic layer which further bulges out in the front and becomes transparent.
  This transparent portion covers the coloured part of the eye and is known as **cornea**.
- Cornea lacks blood vessels and is the only portion in eye which remains alive upto 40 hrs after the death of a person. Thus, it can be easily removed and replaced soon incase of eye donations.

Middle Choroid Layer

- It is the layer which is richly supplied with blood vessels in order to provide nourishment to the eyes. It is located beneath the sclera.
- It is thin over the posterior part of the eye, but becomes thick over the anterior part of eye to form **ciliary body**.
- Smooth muscles of ciliary body holds the lens in position by suspensory ligament and also helps in altering the shape of the lens.

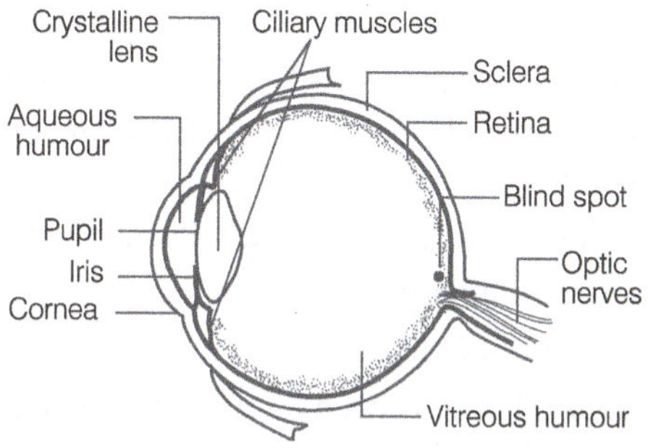

Fig. 9.4 Human eye

- It also contains a dark coloured pigment called **melanin** which helps in preventing light rays from reflecting and scattering inside the eye.
- The eyeball contains a transparent crystalline structure called **lens**. Smooth muscles of ciliary body holds the lens in position.
- **Iris** is the extension of the choroid layer which forms a pigmented circle of muscular diaphragm attached to the ciliary body in front of the lens.
- **Pupil** is the aperture surrounded by the iris. The movement of muscle fibres of iris controls the size of the pupil.

Inner Layer

- **Retina** is the innermost layer of the eye which is most sensitive layer to light.
- It consists of two type of photoreceptor cells known as **rods** and **cones**. Both of these cells contain different photopigments.
- **Rods cells** are the cells which are sensitive to dimlight but does not respond to colour. On the other hand **cones cells** are the cells which are sensitive to bright light and respond to colour.

Other Structures Present in Eye

Besides sclera, choroid and retina, there are other structure present in the eye. These are

(i) **Yellow Spot** As the distribution of rods and cones is not uniform inside the retina. Yellow spot is the area which contains the maximum number of photoreceptor cells (mainly cones), therefore it is known as the region of brightest vision. It is also called **fovea centralis**.

(ii) **Blind Spot** It is the spot found at the lateral side of the yellow spot. It does not contain any photoreceptor cells thus, this is known as the region of no vision.

Contents (Chambers) of the Eye

The eye contains two chambers

(i) **Aqueous Humour** The space between the cornea and lens is called the aqueous or front chamber, which contains a thin watery fluid called aqueous humour. It helps in keeping the lens moist.

(ii) **Vitreous Humour** The space between the lens and retina is called the vitreous chamber, which is filled with a transparent gel-like substance called the vitreous humour. It helps to protect retina. It also helps in maintaining the shape of the eye ball.

Mechanism of Vision

- The vision in human eyes is the binocular vision.
- An image is formed on the retina by successive refractions at the cornea, the aqueous humour, lens and vitreous humour.
- A real, diminished and inverted image of the object is formed on the retina.
- The light-sensitive cells get activated upon illumination and generate electrical signals. These signals are sent to the brain *via* the optic nerves.
- The brain interprets these signals and finally, processes the information so that we perceive objects.

Accommodation (Power of Accommodation)

It is the ability or the property of the eye lens to focus both near and distant objects by adjusting its focal length.

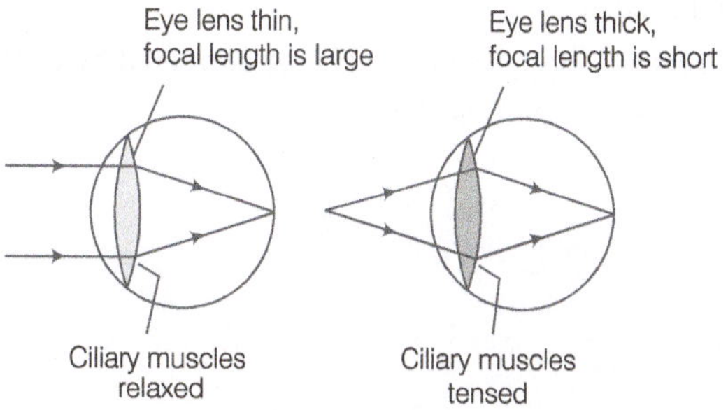

Persistence of Vision

The time for which impression or sensation of an object continues in the eye is called persistence of vision. The minimum time for which we should view an object so that its clear image is formed on retina is 1/16th of a second.

Common Defects of the Eye

The defects due to which the person cannot see the object distinctly and comfortably, are called **defects of vision**. The main defects of vision are as follows

Myopia (Short Sightedness)

- It is the defect in which a person cannot see distant objects clearly but can see near by objects clearly. In this case, image forms before retina (and not on the retina).
- **Causes** Far point nearer than infinity. Decrease in focal length of the lens.
- **Correction** This defect can be corrected by using concave lens of appropriate power.

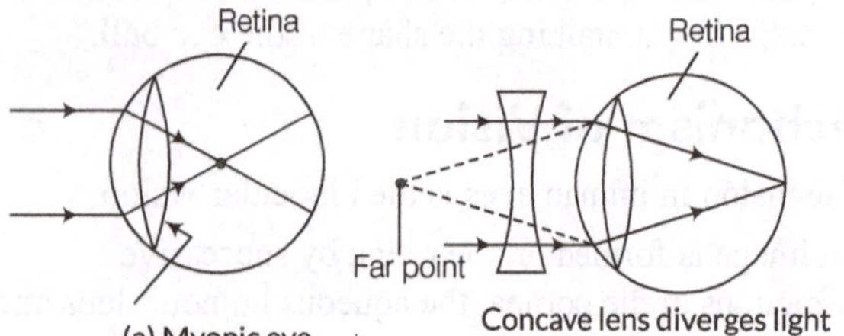

(a) Myopic eye (too much convergence)

(b) Correct eye (myopia and its correction)

Hypermetropia (Long Sightedness)

- It is the defect in which a person cannot see nearby objects clearly but can see distant objects clearly. A person with this defect has the near point farther away from normal near point. In this, image forms beyond retina.
- **Causes** This defect arises due to following reasons
- Focal length of eye lens become large.
- Eyeball become too short so that the image is formed behind retina.
- **Correction** Hypermetropia can be corrected by using convex lens of appropriate power.

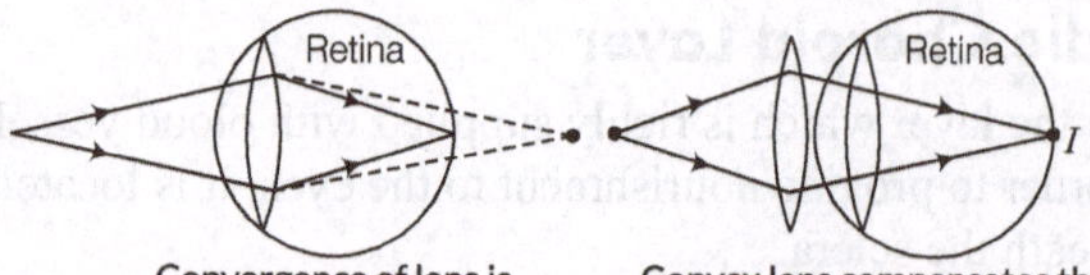

(a) Hypermetropic eye (b) Correct hypermetropic eye

Presbyopia (Old Age Long Sightedness)

- It is the condition found more commonly in old age people. In this defect, one cannot read comfortably and clearly.
- For most people, the near point gradually precedes away. Sometimes, a person may suffer from both myopia and hypermetropia.
- **Causes** This defect arises due to following reasons
  - Weakness of ciliary muscles.
  - Hardening of eye lens.
- **Correction** This defect can be corrected by using bifocal lenses (consisting of both convex and concave lenses).

Astigmatism

- It is the defect, in which eye is unable to focus objects both in horizontal and vertical lines clearly.
- **Causes** Imperfect shape (not perfect spherical) of cornea, or lens or even of both.
- **Correction** This defect can be corrected by using cylindrical lens.

Cataract

- It is the condition in which crystalline lens of eye becomes milky and cloudy due to the growth of membrane over it. It generally occurs among people at an old age.
- This causes partial or complete loss of vision. It is possible to restore vision in this condition through the cataract surgery.

Stereoscopic Vision

It is the phenomenon of simultaneous focusing of an object in both eyes, whose images by a kind of overlapping in the brain gives the three dimensional effect.

The Ear

Human ear is concerned with two functions, sensory functions (such as hearing) and maintenance of body balance. The ears are located on both side of the head.

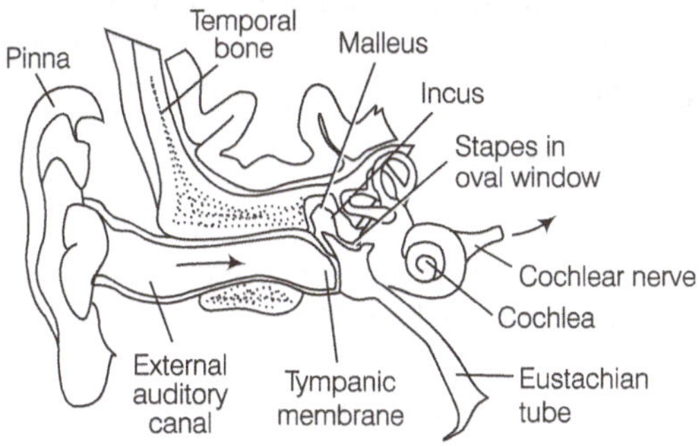

Fig. 9.5 Human ear

Structure of Ear

Each ear is divided into three main divisions such as

(i) **Outer** (external) **ear** This portion of ear mainly consists of **pinna** and **auditory canal** leading to the eardrum.

(ii) **Middle ear** This portion of the ear contains three ossicles bones called **malleus** (hammer), **incus** (anvil) and **stapes** (stirrup) which are attached to each other in chain like fashion.

One end of hammer is attached to the ear drum (tympanic membrane) and the free end of stirrup is attached to oval window of inner ear. It opens into the **eustachian tube** which connects with the pharynx and maintains the pressure on either sides of the ear drum. An infection in throat may also lead to ear infections due to this connection.

(iii) **Inner ear** It is also called membranous labyrinth which consist of two main parts. These are

(a) **Cochlea** It is a coiled portion of the labyrinth and has around two and half turns. Its inner winding cavity is divided into three parallel canals separated by membranes out of which the middle canal contains areas which has auditory sense cells called **organ of Corti**.

It is provided with the hair cells. The impulse from the cochlea of the ear are transmitted to the brain through **auditory nerve**.

(b) **Semicircular canals** These are the set of three semicircular, inter connected tubes located inside each ear. Each canal is filled with the fluid called **endolymph** and contains motion sensor cells within the fluid.

Note Vestibular apparatus of inner ear comprises of three semi-circular canals and the otolith organ consisting of the saccule and utricle.

Mechanism of the Hearing

Sound waves ⟶ External ear ⟶ Ear drum vibrates ⟶ Vibrations transmitted to ear ossicles and then to oval window
↓
The fluid of cochlea generate waves in the lymph.
↓
Basilar membrane ripples ⟶ Bending of hair cells, press against tectorial membrane ⟶ Nerve impulse generated in afferent neurons
↑
Impulse transferred to auditory cortex of brain
↑
Sound is recognised

Role of Ear in Maintaining Balance

Inner ear along with chochlea are connected with semicircular canals, which are usually three tiny tubes that are interconnected, their job is to help to maintain the body's balance. The semicircular canals are filled with fluid that is the essential liquid in the ear for balance.

PYQs Previous Years' Questions

1 Mark Questions

Multiple Choice Questions

1. The ear ossicle that transports sound vibrations to the inner ear **ICSE 2024**

(a) stapes (b) malleus (c) incus (d) cochlea

Ans. (a) stapes

2. Adjusting the focal length of the eye lens to view objects at different distances is done by **ICSE 2024**

(a) cornea (b) iris
(c) ciliary muscles (d) sclera

Ans. (c) ciliary muscles

3. Vitrous humour is present between ICSE 2023
(a) cornea and iris (b) lens and retina
(c) iris and lens (d) cornea and lens

Ans. (b) lens and retina

4. Choose the correct answer from the four options in the given statement. The part of the human eye where rod cells and cone cells are located is the ICSE Specimen 2023, 2012
(a) retina (b) cornea
(c) choroid (d) sclera

Ans. (a) retina

5. Organ of Corti is present inside the ICSE Specimen 2023, 2021-22 Sem. II
(a) cochlea (b) semicircular canals
(c) sacculus (d) utriculus

Ans. (a) cochlea

6. The pigmented circular area seen in front of the eye ICSE 2021-22 Sem. II
(a) cornea (b) lens
(c) iris (d) ciliary muscles

Ans. (c) Iris

7. The circular opening in the centre of iris ICSE 2021-22 Sem. II
(a) lens (b) cornea
(c) sclera (d) pupil

Ans. (d) pupil

8. Aqueous humour is present between the ICSE 2018
(a) lens and retina (b) iris and lens
(c) cornea and iris (d) cornea and lens

Ans. (d) cornea and lens

Very Short Answer Type Questions

9. Arrange and rewrite the terms in each group in the correct order to be in a logical sequence beginning with the term that is underlined:
Pupil, <u>Aqueous humour</u>, Retina, Vitreous humour. ICSE 2024

Ans. Aqueous humour, Pupil, Vitreous humour, Retina.

10. State the main function of vitreous humour.

Or State two functiond of vitreous humour. ICSE 2023 Specimen, 2011

Ans. **Vitreous humour** is the jelly-like substance which gives round shape to the eyeball. It also helps to protect retina.

11. Arrange and rewrite the terms in each group in the correct order so as to be in a logical sequence begining with term that is underlined. ICSE Specimen 2023
(i) <u>Tympanum</u> Incus, malleus, stapes
(ii) <u>Aqueous humour</u> Optic nerve, retina, lens

Ans. (i) Tympanum Malleus, incus, stapes
(ii) Aqueous humour Lens, retina, optic nerve

12. Name the part of internal ear related to static balance of body. ICSE Specimen 2019

Ans. Sacculus

13. Give the biological/technical term for the following

Or

The defected vision in which some parts of objects are seen in focus while the other are blurred. ICSE 2019

An eye defect in which the cornea becomes uneven. ICSE 2010

Ans. **Astigmatism** is an eye defect in which cornea becomes uneven.

14. Name the layer of the eyeball that provides nourishment to the eye. ICSE 2019

Ans. Middle choroid layer

15. Correct and rewrite the given statement by changing the biological term that is underlined below.
The part of the eye which can be donated from a clinically dead person is the <u>retina</u>. ICSE 2019

Ans. Cornea

16. Mention the exact location of incus. ICSE 2019

Or

State the exact location of incus. ICSE 2013

Ans. **Middle ear** It contains three ossicles bones called malleus (hammer), incus (anvill) and stapes (stirrup) which are attached to each other in chain-like fashion.

17. State the main function of tears. ICSE 2019

Ans. Major functions of the tears are washing away irritating materials to prevents microbial infection, healing, damages, nourishes cornea, etc.

18. Which part of the human ear gives 'dynamic balance' and 'static balance' to the body? ICSE 2019

Ans. The sensory cells in semicircular canal of ear are concerned with dynamic balance. Whereas utriculus and sacculus helps in give static balance.

19. Explain how the human eye adapt itself to bright light and dim light. ICSE 2019

Ans. **Pupil** is an aperture surrounded by the iris. The movement of muscle fibres of iris controls the size of pupil and regulates the amount of light entering the eye.

Due to this adjustment, we blink our eyes when see bright light or not able to see when enters a dim light room because pupil takes time to adjust its size according to the amount of light.

20. Name the layer of the eyeball that forms the transparent cornea. **ICSE 2018**

Ans. The transparent cornea is the continuation of sclera layer of eyeball.

21. Name the kind of lens required to correct myopia.

Ans. Myopia can be corrected by using **concave lens** of appropriate power. **ICSE 2017**

22. State whether the following statements are true or false. If false, rewrite the correct form of the statement by changing the first word only **ICSE Specimen 2017**

Cones are photoreceptor cells that are sensitive to dim light.

Ans. False, rods are photoreceptor cells that are more sensitive to dim light.

23. Name the tube which connects the cavity of the middle ear with the throat. **ICSE Specimen 2017**

Ans. Eustachian tube

24. Differentiate between the given pair on the basis of what is mentioned within bracket. **ICSE Specimen 2017**

Rod cells and cone cells (Pigment) **ICSE 2016**

Or Differentiate between the given pair on the basis of what is mentioned within bracket.

Rods and cones of retina (Type of pigment) **ICSE 2015**

Or Give one point difference between the rod and cone cells (pigment) **ICSE 2004**

Ans. **Rods** It contains a pigment called rhodopsin.

Cones It contain a pigment called idopsin.

25. Given below are sets of five terms each. Rewrite the terms in correct order in a logical sequence.

Example Large intestine, Stomach, Mouth, Small intestine, Oesophagus.

Answer Mouth → Oesophagus → Stomach → Small intestine → Large intestine.

Cochlea, Malleus, Pinna, Stapes, Incus. **ICSE 2017**

Ans. Pinna → Malleus → Incus → Stapes → Cochlea

(Route of sound waves in hearing process)

26. Choose the odd one out of the term given and name the category to which the others belong.

Aqueous humor, Vitreous humor, Iris, Central canal **ICSE 2017**

Ans. **Odd term** - Central canal

Category - Rest three are present in eye.

27. Given below term. In this pair indicate the relationship between the two term. Rewrite and complete the second pair on a similar basis.

Example: Oxygen : Inspiration : : Carbon dioxide : Expiration

Eye : Optic nerve : : Ear : .... **ICSE 2017, 2006**

Ans. Eye : Optic nerve : : Ear : **Auditory nerves**

28. Give appropriate biological/technical term

'The antiseptic substance in tears'. **ICSE 2017, 2006**

Ans. Lysozyme.

29. In each set of terms given below, there is an odd one and cannot be grouped in the same category to which the other three belong. Identify the odd term in each set and name the category to which the remaining three belong.

Example Ovary, Fallopian tube, Ureter, Uterus
Odd term-Ureter
Category-Part of female reproductive system

Malleus, Iris, Stapes, Incus **ICSE 2016**

Ans. **Odd term**–Iris

Category–Bones of middle ear.

30. State the exact location of ciliary body. **ICSE 2016, 2014**

Ans. The exact location of ciliary body is anterior part of the eye.

31. State the main function of Eustachian tube. **ICSE 2016**

Ans. The main function of Eustachian tube is that it connects middle ear with pharynx. It also helps to maintain equal air pressure on either sides of the ear drum or tympanum.

32. Briefly explain power of accommodation.

Or

Explain accomodation of eye. **ICSE 2016, 2008**

Ans. **Power of accommodation** The adjustment of the eye to enable it to focus at various distances is called power of accommodation.

33. Mention the exact location of organ of Corti. **ICSE 2015**

Ans. The exact location of organ of Corti is in the mammalian cochlea.

34. Rewrite and complete the following sentence by inserting the correct word in the space indicated.

A fluid that occupies the larger cavity of the eyeball behind the lens is .... **ICSE 2008, 2015**

Ans. A fluid that occupies the larger cavity of the eyeball behind the lens is **vitreous humour**.

35. What is the function of ear ossicles? **ICSE 2015**

Ans. Ear ossicles are present in the middle ear of humans. They receive the sound vibrations from vibrating tympanum and convey them along the three ossicles. These serve to magnify the vibrations.

36. Name the ear ossicle which is attached to the tympanum. **ICSE 2014**

Ans. Malleus/hammer is the ear ossicle which is attached to the tympanum.

37. State the function of the suspensory ligament of the eye. **ICSE 2014**

Ans. Suspensory ligament of the eyes helps in holding the lens in position.

38. State the exact location of yellow spot. **ICSE 2014**

Ans. Yellow spot is located exactly behind the lens on the retina of the eye

39. Differentiate between near vision and distant vision (shape of the eye lens). **ICSE 2014**

Ans. For **near vision** lens must be more concave/too curved.

For **distant vision** lens must be less convex/too flat.

40. Give technical term for the nerve which transmits impulses from the ear to the brain. **ICSE 2014**

Ans. **Auditory nerve** is the one which transmits impulses from the internal ear to the brain.

41. Given below is the set of four terms in which one is odd and cannot be grouped in the same category to which other three belongs. Identify the odd one in each set and name the category to which remaining three belongs.

Haemoglobin, glucagon, iodopsin, rhodopsin.

Ans. **Odd one** Glucagon **ICSE 2014**

Category Rest all others are pigments found in the body.

42. Mention the exact function of iris. **ICSE 2013**

Ans. Iris is responsible for colour of the eyes.

43. Given below is the set with four terms with one odd term that cannot be grouped in the same category to which the other three belong.

Identify the odd one and name the category to which the remaining three belong.

Semicircular canals, cochlea, tympanum, utriculus. **ICSE 2013**

Ans.

Odd	Category
Tympanum	All others are the different parts of inner ear

44. Give biological reasons for throat infections can lead to ear infections. **ICSE 2013, 2008**

Ans. Refer to text on page no. 147 (Under middle ear)

45. Oval window, tympanum, cochlea, auditory canal, ear ossicle (correct path through which a vibration of sound is transferred in the human ear). **ICSE 2012, 2008, 2006**

Ans. Correct path through which a vibration of sound is transferred in the human ear is

Auditory canal → Tympanum → Ear ossicles → Oval window → Cochlea.

46. Give the biological/technical term for

Eye lens losing flexibility resulting in a kind of long sightedness in elderly people. **ICSE 2012, 2008**

Ans. Presbyopia is the technical term used for the kind of long sightedness in elderly people in which eye lens loses flexibility.

47. Give the biological term for the structure that carries visual stimuli from retina to the brain. **ICSE 2012**

Ans. Optic nerve carries visual stimuli from the retina to the brain.

48. Give the exact location of organ of Corti. **ICSE 2011**

Ans. **Organ of Corti** is located in the endolymph present in the middle canal of cochlea.

49. Account for the following.

One feels blinded for a short time while, coming out of a dark room. **ICSE 2010, 2009**

Ans. When we come out from a dark room we feel dazzling effect for a very short period. It is called as light adaptation. This happens because the diameter of pupil is reduced to allow less light to enter the eyes.

50. Given below is the set of five terms, rewrite the terms in logical sequence as directed at the end of the statement. Pupil, yellow spot, cornea, lens, aqueous humour (correct path of entry of light into the eye from an object). **ICSE 2010**

Ans. Correct path of light entering the eye from an object is cornea → aqueous humour → pupil → lens → yellow spot.

51. Given one point of difference between the following on the basis of what is given in the bracket

Myopia and hypermetropia (cause of the defect). **ICSE 2010**

Ans.

Myopia	Hypermetropia
In this eye ball is lengthened from front to back. The lens becomes too curved.	In this eye ball is shortened from front to back. The lens becomes too flat.

52. Explain the term cataract. **ICSE 2010**

Ans. **Cataract** is the eye condition in which the lens turns opaque and vision is cut down even to total blindness.

53. Give the specific function of the Eustachian tube found in the body of animal. **ICSE 2009**

Or Given below is the particular structure write its special functional activity. **ICSE 2008**

Eustachian tube and ....

Ans. Eustachian tube helps to maintain equal air pressure on either sides of the eardrum or tympanum.

54. Given below is the set of term. Without changing the first term rearrange the remaining four so, as to be in logical sequence as per the directions given in bracket. **ICSE 2008, 2006**

Ans. The correct route through which vibra-tions of sound enter the ear is pinna → auditory canal→ tympanum→ear ossicles → cochlea.

55. State whether the following statement is true or false. If false, write the correct statement by changing the incorrect word only.
Rods are responsible for vision in the dark. **ICSE 2007**

Ans. The statement is true.

56. Name the organ or structure that is responsible for protecting the eye from sweat. **ICSE 2007**

Ans. Eyebrows are responsible for protecting the eye from sweat, rain water, etc.

57. Explain the term stereoscopic vision. **ICSE 2007**

Ans. Refer to text on page no. 146.

58. Name the eye defect caused due to the shortening of the eyeball from front to back. **ICSE 2006**

Ans. Hyperopia

59. Differentiate between the following pair on the basis of what is given in bracket?

Choroid and sclerotic layers of the eye (function). **ICSE 2006**

Ans.

Choroid Layer	Sclerotic Layer
Through its blood supply, it nourishes retina.	Gives shape to the eyeball.

60. Give the exact location and one function of the pinna. **ICSE 2006**

Ans. Pinna is a part of the external ear. Its function is to collects sound waves and pass them on to middle ear.

61. Differentiate between the following pair on the basis of what is given in bracket?

Dynamic balance and static balance (definition). **ICSE 2006**

Ans.

Dynamic Balance	Static Balance
The balance which is achieved by the stimulation of endolymph present in the semicircular canals is called dynamic balance.	The balance which is achieved through the gravity receptors located in the utriculus and sacculus is called static balance.

62. Given below is the set of terms. Arrange and rewrite the set of terms so, as to be in logical sequence.

Yellow spot, conjunctiva, pupil, cornea, lens, vitreous humour, aqueous humour. **ICSE 2005**

Ans. The correct logical sequence is
Conjunctiva, cornea, aqueous humour, pupil, lens, vitreous humour, yellow spot.

63. Name the part of the eye responsible for its shape. **ICSE 2003**

Ans. Vitreous humour is the part of an eye responsible for its shape.

64. Given below is the type of structure found in the ear. Write the special functional activity of it in the blank given. Organ of Corti and ....

Ans. Organ of Corti and **hearing**. **ICSE 2000**

65. Choose the odd one in each of the following series.

Myopia, hypermetropia, xerophthalmia, astigmatism. **ICSE 2000**

Ans. **Odd one** Xerophthalmia.

2 Marks Questions

66. Which parts of the ear are responsible for

(i) static equilibrium?

(ii) dynamic equilibrium? **ICSE 2024**

Ans. (i) Utriculus and sacculus (ii) Semicircular canals

67. Distinguish between semicircular canals and utriculus based on their function. **ICSE 2023**

Ans. Refer to answer no. 84 and 86.

68. We cannot distinguish colours in dimlight. Explain giving suitable reasons. **ICSE Specimen 2021-22 Sem. II**

Or

Give scientific reasons for the following statement. We cannot distinguish colours in moonlight. **ICSE 2014**

Ans. As moonlight is a dimlight during which cone cells of our eyes do not function well therefore, the colour is not well perceived. It is only rod cells that function in moonlight.

69. From where the following nerves arise.

(i) Optic nerve **ICSE Specimen 2021-22 Sem. II**

(ii) Auditory nerve

Ans. (i) Refer to answer no. 47.

(ii) Refer to answer no. 40.

70. Which is the light sensitive layer of the eyeball? Where exactly is the image formed on this layer? **ICSE 2021-22 Sem. II**

Ans. Retina is the light sensitive layer of the eye and the exact image is formed on the yellow spot (Fovea centralis). It is the point where brightest and most clear image of object is formed.

71. Name the nerve that transmits impulses to the brain from **ICSE 2021-22 Sem. II**

(i) Ear (ii) Eye

Ans. (i) Ear–Auditory nerve

(ii) Eye –Optic nerve

72. Choose between the two options to answer the question specified in the brackets for the following. An example is illustrated below

Example Corolla or calyx (Which is the outer whorl?) **Answer** Calyx

(i) Perilymph or endolymph (Which one surrounds the organ of Corti ?) **ICSE 2018**

(ii) Sclerotic layer or choroid layer (Which one forms the iris?) **ICSE 2018**

Ans. (i) Endolymph (ii) Choroid

73. Mention the exact location of the following

(i) Lacrimal gland **ICSE 2018**

(ii) Malleus **ICSE 2018**

Ans. (i) Lacrimal glands or tear glands are located at the upper sideward portion of the orbits (eye sockets).

(ii) Malleus is an ear ossicle (bone) present in the middle ear. Its one end is attached to eardrum.

74. Mention the exact location of the following.

(i) Semicircular canals **ICSE 2017**

(ii) Eustachian tube **ICSE 2017**

Ans. (i) **Semicircular canals** These are located in the inner ear.

(ii) **Eustachian tube** It is found in the middle ear.

Concept Enhancer Eustachian tubes connect middle ear to the back of our throat. They help drain the fluid and also equalize the air pressure inside the ears.

75. Given below is an example of a certain structure and its special functional activity. On a similar pattern fill in the blanks with suitable functions.

Example: Chloroplast and Photosynthesis

(i) Ciliary body and ....

(ii) Eustachian tube and .... **ICSE 2015**

Ans. (i) Accommodation, aqueous humour production.

(ii) Protect, aerate and drain the middle ear and mastoid.

76. Give the biological/technical terms for the following:

(i) A thin membrane covering the entire front part of the eye. **ICSE 2015**

(ii) The lens of eye losing flexibility resulting in a kind of long-sightedness in middle aged people.

Ans. (i) Cornea (ii) Presbyopia **ICSE 2015**

77. Write the function of the following

(i) Suspensory ligaments ....

(ii) Semicircular canals .... **ICSE 2010**

Ans. Suspensory ligaments hold lens in position.

Semicircular canals balances the body.

78. Give the biological/technical term for the following.

(i) The photosensitive pigment present in the cone cells of the retina.

(ii) The fluid present in the anterior part in front of the eye lens. **ICSE 2010**

Ans. (i) **Iodopsin** is the photosensitive pigment present in the cone cells of the retina.

(ii) **Aqueous humour** is the fluid present in the anterior part in front of the eye lens.

79. Name the following.

(i) The photosensitive pigment present in the rod cells of the retina.

(ii) The internal layer of the eye which prevents reflection of light. **ICSE 2009**

Ans. (i) **Rhodopsin** is the photosensitive pigment present in the rod cells of the retina.

(ii) **Choroid** is the middle layer of the eye which nourishes the retina and prevents reflection of light.

80. Differentiate between the following on the basis of what is given in bracket.

(i) Myopia and hypermetropia (condition of eyeball).

(ii) Rods and cones (pigment present). **ICSE 2008**

Ans. (i) Refer to answer no. 51.

(ii)

Rods	Cones
Rhodopsin pigment is present.	Iodopsin pigment is present.

81. Name the following

(i) The tube which connects the cavity of the middle ear with the throat.

(ii) The nerves which transmit impulses from the ear to the brain. **ICSE 2004, 2002**

Ans. (i) **Eustachian tube** is the tube which connects the cavity of the middle ear with the throat.

(ii) **Auditory nerve** is the nerve which transmit impulse from ear to the brain.

82. Mention where in living organisms are the following located and state their main functions.

(i) Ear ossicles (ii) Fovea **ICSE 2001**

Ans. (i) **Ear ossicles** are present in the middle ear of man. They receive the sound vibrations form vibrating tympanum and convey them along the three ossicles. These serve to magnify the vibrations.

(ii) **Fovea** or **yellow spot** present on the retina of the eye. It is the place where the most acute image is formed.

3 Marks Questions

83. A teacher drew the diagram of heart on the blackboard and told the students to copy it in their note books. Mahesh couldn't see the diagram clearly as it appeared blurred to him. **ICSE 2024**

Ans. (i) Myopia

(ii) The image is forms before retina (and not on the retina).

(iii) His spectacles have concave or diverging lens which is used to correct this defect.

84. What are the three main parts of the membranous labyrinth? **ICSE Specimen 2021-22 Sem. II**

Ans. The inner ear or membranous labyrinth has three parts

(i) **Cochlea** It is spiral-shaped and contains sensory organ of hearing.

(ii) **Semi-circular canals** It is a set of three canals arranged at right angles to each other in three different planes.

(iii) **Vestibule** It shows two parts utriculus and sacculus which contain sensory cells for static balance.

85. Give the biological terms for the three tiny bones present in the middle ear. **ICSE 2021-22 Sem. II**

Or Give the biological terms for the three ear ossicles. **ICSE 2021-22 Sem. II**

Ans. The biological terms for the three tiny bones (ossicle bones) present in the middle ear are.

(i) Malleus (hammer) (ii) Incus (anvil)

(iii) Stapes (stirrup)

86. Draw a neat labelled diagram of the membranous labyrinth found in the inner ear. Name the part of the structure that is responsible for static balance in human beings. **ICSE 2017**

Ans. Refer to answer no. 89 (ii).
Utriculus and sacculus (vestibule) are the part of the human ear that is reponsible for static balance in human beings.

5 Marks Questions

87. With reference to the functioning of the eye, answer the questions that follow

(i) What is meant by power of accommodation of the eye?

(ii) What is the shape of the lens during (a) near vision (b) distant vision?

(iii) Name the two structures in the eye responsible for bringing about the change in the shape of the lens.

(iv) Name the cells of the retina and their respective pigments which get activated (a) in the dark (b) in light. **ICSE 2011**

Ans. (i) Refer to text on page no. 145.

(ii) The shape of lens is as follows

(a) During near vision lens is **more convex** or **rounded.**

(b) During distant vision lens is **less** convex or **flat.**

(iii) Ciliary muscles and suspensory ligament are the two structures in the eye responsible for bringing about the change in the shape of lens.

(iv) Different cells of retina and their respective pigments which get activated during different light conditions are

(a) **In the dark** The cells are rods and the pigment is rhodopsin.

(b) **In the light** The cells are cones and the pigment is iodopsin.

88. With reference to the human ear, answer the questions that follow.

(i) Give the technical term for the structure found in the inner ear.

(ii) Name the three small bones present in the middle ear. What is the biological term for them collectively?

(iii) Name the part of the ear associated with (a) static balance (b) hearing (c) dynamic balance.

(iv) Name the nerve, which transmits messages from the ear to the brain. **ICSE 2011**

Ans. (i) Membranous labyrinth is the technical term for the structure found in the inner ear.

(ii) Hammer, anvil and stirrup are the three small bones present in the middle ear.

Ear ossicles is the biological term used for these bones collectively.

(iii) Different parts associated with following are

(a) **For static balance** Utriculus and sacculus.

(b) **For hearing** Cochlea.

(c) **For dynamic balance** Semicircular canals.

(iv) Auditory nerve is responsible to transmit messages from ear to brain.

89. (i) What is meant by power of accommodation of the eye? Name the muscles of the eye responsible for the same.

(ii) Draw a labelled diagram of the inner ear. Name the part of the inner ear that is responsible for static balance in human beings. **ICSE 2005**

Ans. (i) **Power of accommodation of eye** The ability of changing the curvature of the elastic lens due to which the image of an object of different distance is sharply focussed. Ciliary muscles are responsible for accommodation of eye.

(ii) Labelled diagram of human inner ear is given below

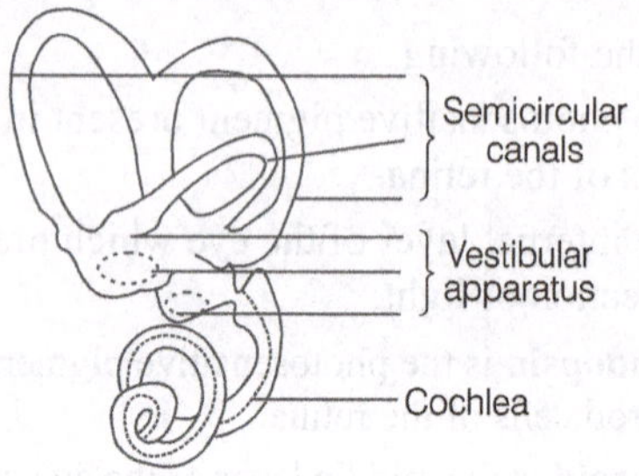

The part of inner ear responsible for static balance is utriculus and sacculus.

90. (i) What is a lacrimal gland?

(ii) In what two ways is yellow spot different from blind spot?

(iii) Name an old-age eye defect. Why is it caused?

(iv) What is meant by power of accommodation of the eye?

(v) Mention the characteristics of the image that falls on the retina of the eye.

(vi) Name the photoreceptors found in the retina of the eye. **ICSE 2002**

Ans. (i) **Lacrimal gland** is a secretory gland present in top right part of the eye. Its secretion is called tears which lubricates the eye and is antiseptic in nature.

(ii) Yellow spot is has more cones and less rod cells. Blind spot foundlateral side of yellow spot. It does not have any photoreceptor cells.

(iii) Presbyopia is a old age eye defect which arises either due to weakness of ciliary muscle or due to hardening of eye lens.

(iv) Refer to text on page no. 145.

(v) The image that falls on the retina of the eye is real, inverted and diminished.

(vi) Rod cells and cone cells are the photoreceptors found in the retina of the eye.

Diagram Based Questions

91. Study the diagram given below and answer the questions that follow **ICSE Specimen 2023 (3M)**

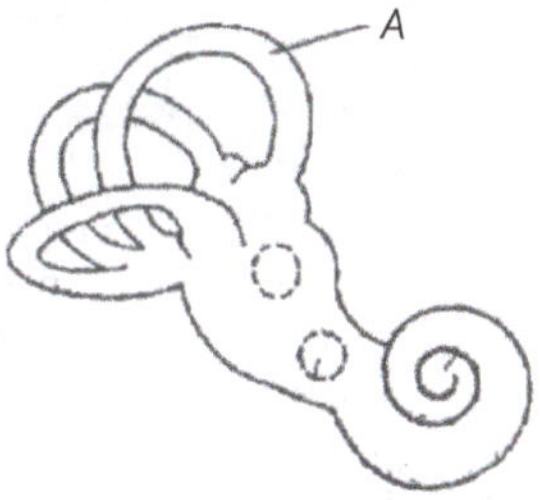

(i) Identify the structure.

(ii) In which part of the ear is it located?

(iii) What is the function of the part marked *A*?

Ans. (i) Membranous labyrinth.

(ii) Membranous labyrinth is found in the inner ear.

(iii) The structure '*A*', i.e. semicircular canal. It sense head rotations arising either from angular acceleration of head or from self-induced movements.

92. Given below is a diagram depicting a defect of the human eye, study the same and then answer the questions that follow

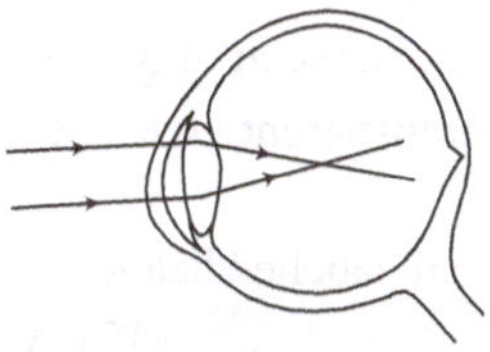

(i) Name the defect shown in the diagram.

(ii) What are the two possible reasons that cause this defect?

(iii) Name the type of lens used to correct this defect.

(iv) With the help of a diagram show how the defect shown above is rectified using a suitable lens.

ICSE Specimen 2021-22 Sem. II, 2016 (5M)

Ans. (i) The defect shown in the diagram is myopia (short sightedness).

(ii) The two possible reasons that cause this defect are as follows

- Image forms before retina
- Caused by excessive curvature of lens

(iii) Concave lens

(iv)

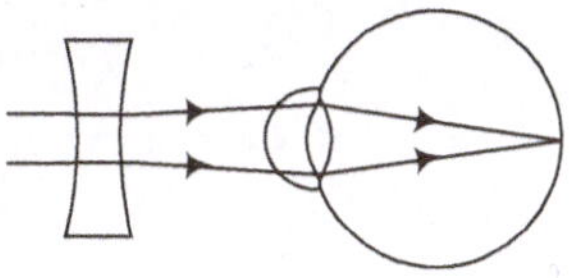

93. Study the diagram given below and answer the questions that follows

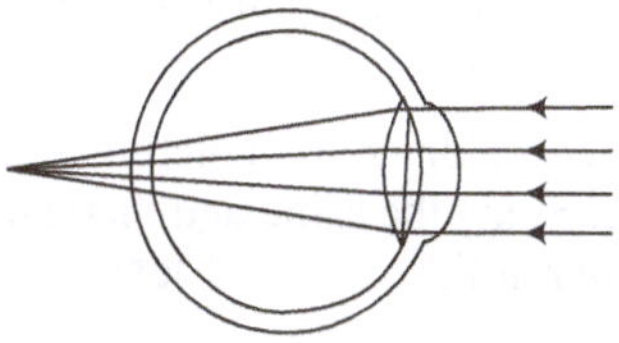

(i) Identify the defect of the eye by mentioning the technical term.

(ii) Mention one reason for this defect.

(iii) Name the type of lens used to correct this defect.

ICSE Specimen 2021-22 Sem. II (3M)

Ans. (i) The defect shown in the diagram is hypermetropia.

(ii) It can be cause due to the following reason.

The eyeball is too short from front to back so that the image is formed behind the retina.

(iii) Hypermetropia can be corrected by using convex lens of appropriate power.

94. Given below is a diagrammatic representation of a defect of the human eye which has been corrected using a suitable lens. Study the diagram and answer the questions that follows **ICSE Specimen 2019 (5M)**

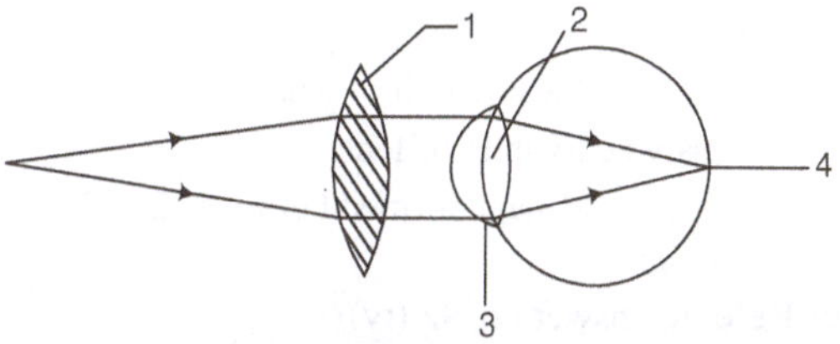

(i) Identify the defect that has been corrected.

(ii) Mention two reasons for the above defect.

(iii) Label the parts numbered 1 to 4.

(iv) State the functions of the parts numbered 3 and 4.

(v) What control maintains the shape of the eyeball?

Ans. (a) (i) The given figure shows the hypermetropia (long sightedness) defect of eye.

(ii) This defect arises due to following reasons.

- Eyeball becomes too short so that the image is formed behind retina.
- The lens is too flat.

(iii) These are as follows

1. Convex lens 2. Lens

3. Cornea 4. Image formed behind retina

(iv) Cornea is transparent portion of sclerotic layer that covers the coloured part of eye.

Retina is the innermost layer of the eye which is sensitive to light.

(v) Vitreous humour control /maintain the shape of the eyeball.

95. Given below is a diagram depicting a defect of the human eye. Study the same and then answer the questions that follows. **ICSE Specimen 2017 (5M)**

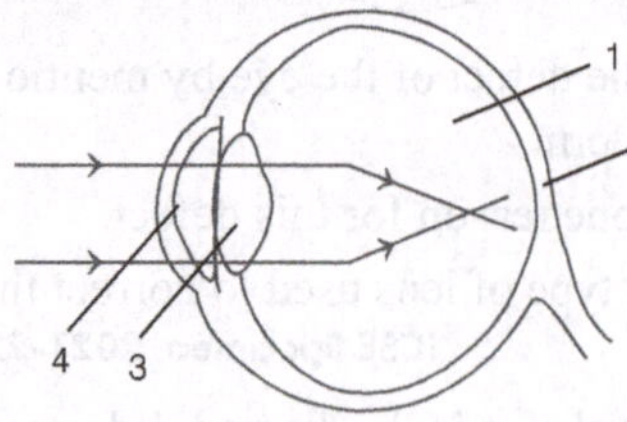

(i) Name the defect shown in the diagram.

(ii) Name two possible reasons for this defect of the eye in human beings.

(iii) Name the parts labelled 1 to 4.

(iv) Draw a labelled diagram to show how the above mentioned defect is rectified using an appropriate lens.

Ans. (i) The defect shown in the diagram is myopia

(ii) The two possible reasons for this defect are as follows

- Decrease in focal length of lens.
- Excessive curvature of lens.

(iii) 1-Eyespot, 2-Image formed before retina, 3-Lens, 4-Cornea

(iv) Refer to answer no. 92 (iv)

96. (i) Draw a well labelled diagram of the membranous labyrinth found in the inner ear.

(ii) Based on the diagram drawn above in (i) give a suitable term for each of the following descriptions.

(a) The sensory cells that help in hearing.

(b) The part that is responsible for static balance of the body.

(c) The membrane covered opening that connects the middle ear to the inner ear.

(d) The fluid present in the middle chamber of cochlea.

(e) The structure that maintains dynamic equilibrium of the body. **ICSE 2016 (5M)**

Ans. (i)

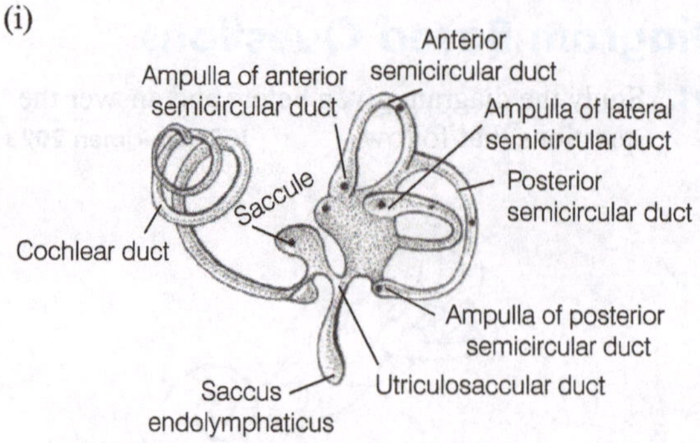

(ii) (a) Organ of Corti

(b) Vestibular apparatus (utriculus and sacculus)

(c) Oval window membrane

(d) Endolymph

(e) Semicircular canals

97. Draw a diagram of the human eye as seen in a vertical section and label the parts which suit the following descriptions relating to the

(i) photosensitive layer of the eye.

(ii) structure which is responsible for holding the eye lens in its position.

(iii) structure which maintains the shape of the eye ball and the area of no vision.

(iv) anterior chamber seen in front of the eye lens.

(v) outermost transparent layer seen in front of the eye ball. **ICSE 2013 (5M)**

Ans. Different parts are labelled below

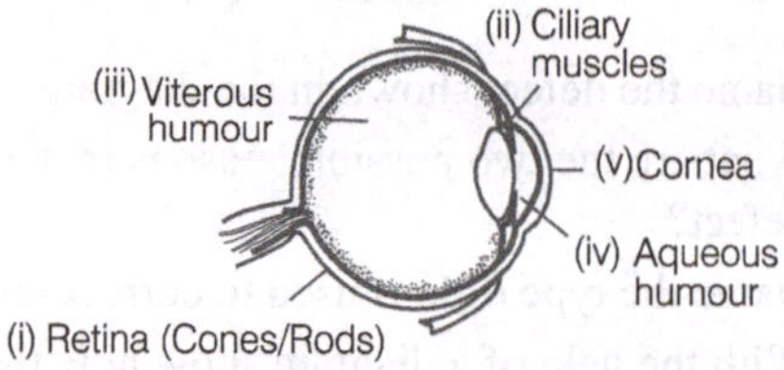

98. Study the following diagram carefully and then answer the questions that follow. The diagram is depicting a defect of the human eye.

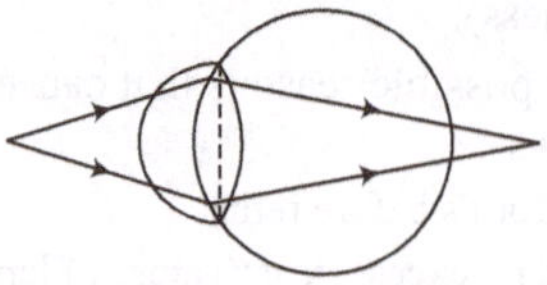

(i) Identify the defect shown in the diagram.

(ii) Give two possible reasons for the above defect.

(iii) Draw a neat labelled diagram to show how the above defect can be rectified. **ICSE 2012 (3M)**

Ans. (i) The defect shown in the diagram is hypermetropia.

(ii) It is caused due to two major reasons

(a) The eyeball is too short from front to back.

(b) The lens is too flat.

(iii) This defect can be rectified by using convex lens as given in the diagram below

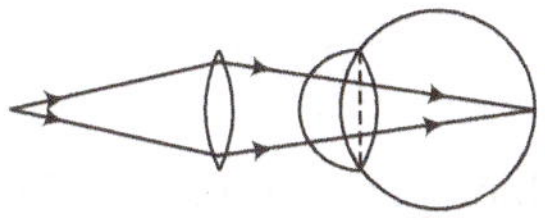

99. The diagram given below represents the structure found in the inner ear. Study the same and then answer the questions that follow

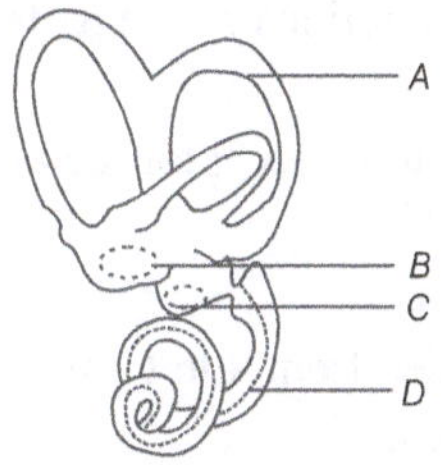

(i) Name the parts labelled A, B, C and D.

(ii) Name the part of the ear responsible for transmitting impulses to the brain.

(iii) Name the part labelled above which is responsible for

(a) static equilibrium

(b) dynamic equilibrium

(c) hearing

(iv) Name the audio receptor cells which pick up vibrations.

(v) Name the fluid present in the inner ear. **ICSE 2009 (5M)**

Ans. (i) Parts labelled from A to D are

A – Semicircular canals.

B – Utriculus

C – Sacculus

D –Cochlea

(ii) **Auditory nerve** is the part of ear responsible for transmitting impulses to the brain.

(iii) (a) Vestibular apparatus (b) Semicircular canals (c) Cochlea

(iv) **Organ of Corti** are the audioreceptor cells which pick up vibrations.

(v) **Endolymph** is the fluid present in the inner ear.

100. Given below is a diagram depicting a defect of the human eye. Study the same and then answer the questions that follow

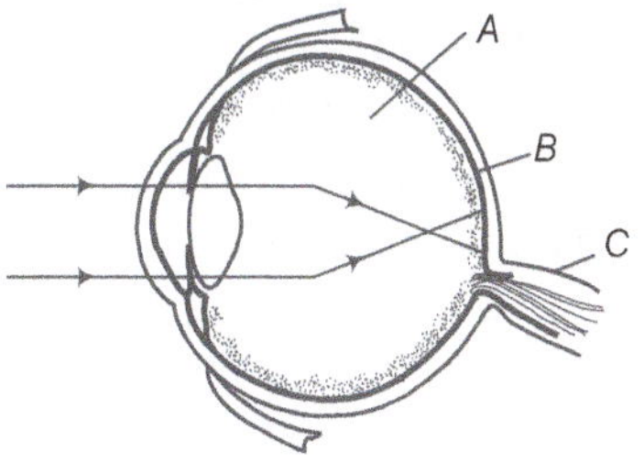

(i) Identify the defect.

(ii) Name the parts labelled A, B and C.

(iii) Give two possible reasons for this eye defect.

(iv) Draw a labelled diagram to show how the above mentioned defect is rectified. **ICSE 2009, 2004 (5M)**

Ans. (i) The defect is myopia.

(ii) Different parts labelled from A to C

A – Vitreous humour

B – Yellow spot

C – Optic nerve

(iii) Two possible reasons for this defect are

(a) The eyeball becomes long from front to back.

(b) The lens becomes too curved/convex.

(iv) This defect can be rectified by concave lens as given below in the diagram.

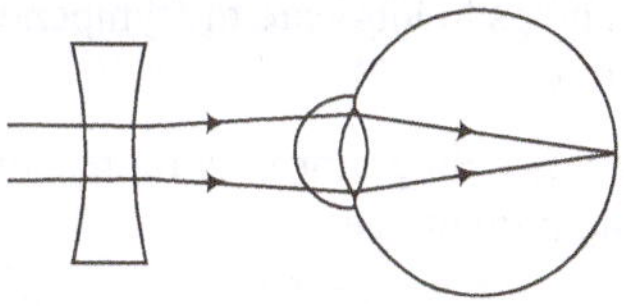

101. Draw a diagram of the human eye as seen in a vertical section and label the part which suits the following functions/description

(i) The layer which prevents reflection of light.

(ii) The structure that alters the focal length of the lens.

(iii) The region of distinct vision.

(iv) The part which transmits the impulse to the brain.

(v) Outermost transparent layer of the eye.

(vi) Fluid in the anterior part of the eye. **ICSE 2008 (5M)**

Ans.

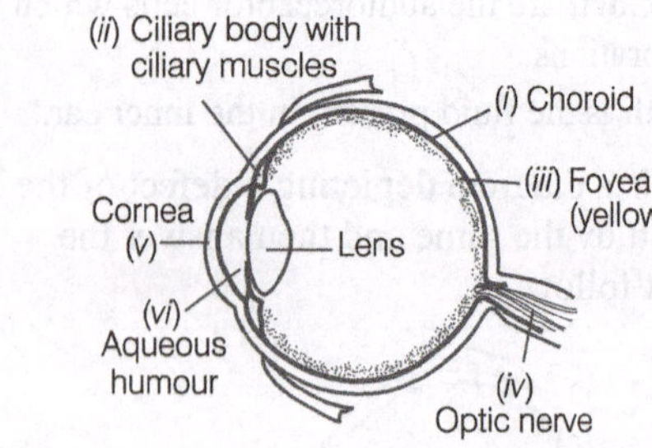

102. Given below is the diagram of the human ear. Study the same and answer the questions that follow

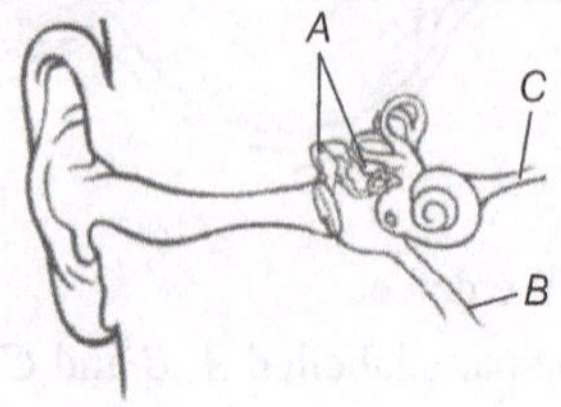

(i) Give the biological term for the part labelled '*A*' and state its function.
(ii) Name the part labelled '*B*' and state its function.
(iii) Name the part labelled '*C*' and state its function.
(iv) Give the function of ear wax. **ICSE 2007 (5M)**

Ans. (i) Part '*A*' is ear ossicles which helps in transmitting the sound waves from external to the internal ear.
(ii) Part '*B*' is called as Eustachian tube which acts as ventilator to equalise pressure of air on both the sides of tympanic membrane that forms the outer boundary of middle ear.
(iii) Part '*C*' is auditory nerve (vestibular and cochlear nerve) which carries hearing impulses to the brain.
(iv) Ear wax helps to lubricate the tympanum for proper functioning.

103. Given below is a diagrammatic representation of a defect of the human eye

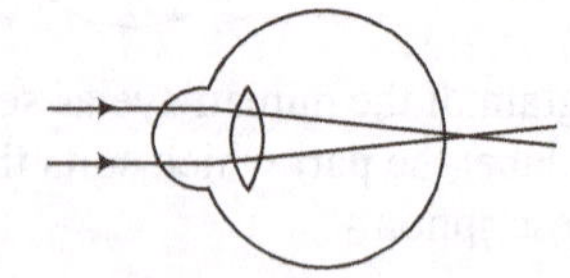

(i) Identify the defect.
(ii) Mention two reasons for the above defect.
(iii) State how the defect can be rectified.
(iv) Name the part of the eye responsible for maintaining the shape of the eyeball. **5M ICSE 2007**

Ans. (i) The defect is hypermetropia because the image is formed behind the retina.
(ii) Refer to answer no. 98 (ii).
(iii) Refer to answer no. 98 (iii).
(iv) Sclera is responsible for shape of the eye ball.

104. Given below is the diagram of a part of the human ear, study the same and then answer the questions that follow

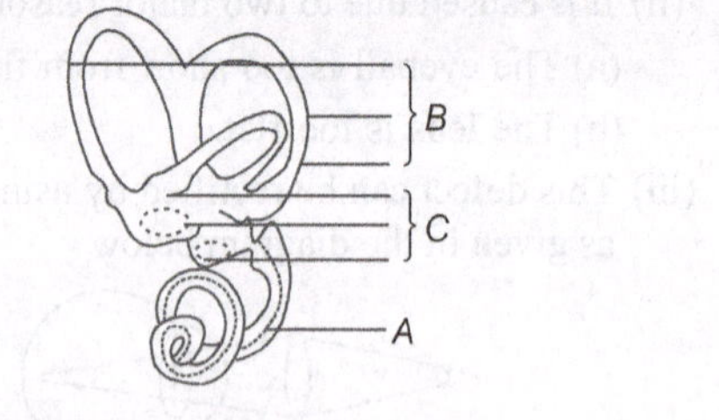

(i) Give the biological term for malleus, incus and stapes.
(ii) Name the parts labelled *A*, *B* and *C* in the diagram.
(iii) State the functions of the parts labelled '*A*' and '*B*'.
(iv) Name the audio receptor region present in the part labelled '*A*'. **ICSE 2003 (5M)**

Ans. (i) ear ossicles.
(ii) Parts labelled from *A* to *C* are
A – Cochlea,
B – Semicircular canals,
C – Vestibular apparatus
(iii) Functions of different parts are
A – Concerned with sense of hearing *B* – Sense of dynamic balance
(iv) Organ of Corti or spiral organ are the audioreceptor region present in the part *A*.

105. The diagram given below refers to the vertical section of the eye of a mammal. Label the parts *A* to *J* to which the guideline points.

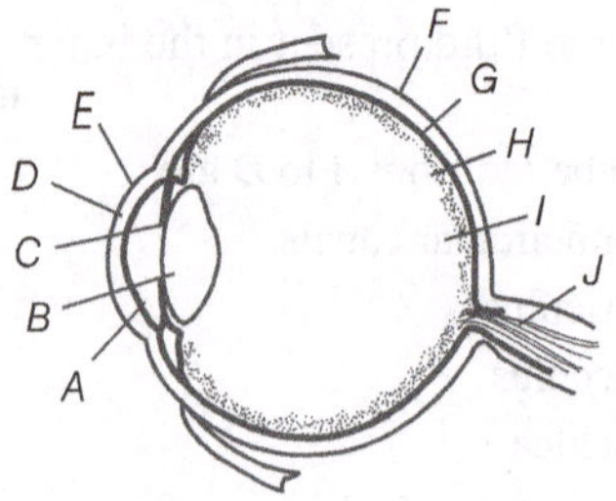

ICSE 2000 (5M)

Ans. *A* – Aqueous humour *B* – Lens
C – Pupil *D* – Cornea
E – Conjuctiva *F* – Sclerotic
G – Choroid *H* – Retina
I – Eyespot *J* – Optic nerve

CHAPTER TEST

Section-A

01 Mark Questions

1 Select the correct answer to the questions from the given options. (Do not copy the question).

(i) A typical neuron is composed of
(a) cell body and dendrite
(b) dendrites and axon
(c) axon and nucleus
(d) cell, axon and dendrites

(ii) Nissl's bodies are mainly composed of
(a) nucleic acid and SER
(b) DNA and RNA
(c) protein and lipids
(d) free ribosomes and RER

(iii) The gap between two adjacent myelin sheath are called
(a) synapse (b) synaptic gap
(c) nodes of Ranvier (d) sheath gap

(iv) The forebrain consists of
(a) cerebrum
(b) thalamus
(c) hypothalamus
(d) All of the above

(v) Which part constitutes the major part of the brain ?
(a) Cerebrum (b) Hypothalamus
(c) Thalamus (d) Cerebellum

2 (i) Name the following.
(a) Largest part of the brain.
(b) Part of brain responsible for thermoregulation.
(c) Part of eye used for donation.
(d) Visible coloured portion of eye.
(e) Region dendrites transmit impulse to

(ii) Arrange and rewrite the terms in each group in the correct order so as to be in a logical sequence beginning with the term that is underlined.
(a) Sound waves, vibrations to ear ossicle, ear drum, nerve impulse
(b) Cornea, vitreous humour, lens, aqueous humour
(c) Light rays, Opsin changes, Focus on retina, Optic nerve
(d) Stimulus, CNS, Effector, Response, Receptor

(iii) Match the items given in Column I with the most appropriate ones in Column II and rewrite the correct matching pairs.

Column I	Column II
A. Glial cells	1. Send signals away from the CNS
B. Sensory neurons	2. Help from blood brain barrier
C. Motor neurons	3. Form inter-connections between neurons and CNS
D. Interneurons	4. Transmit information to the CNS

(iv) Choose the odd one out from the following terms and name the category to which the others belong.
(a) Pinna, Malleus, Incus, Labyrinth, Iris
(b) Sclera, Cornea, Lens, Pupil, Cochlea
(c) Axon, Cyton, Dendrites, Spinal cord
(d) Nose, Tongue, Arm, Eye

(v) State the exact location of
(a) Axon (b) Nissl's bodies
(c) Medulla oblongata (d) Cornea
(e) Cochlea

2/3 Marks Questions

3 Define coordination.

4 Give one difference between optic nerve and auditory nerve.

5 What is hypothalamus? Give its one function.

6 Name three sensory organ.

7 Explain the term synapse.

8 Name three parts is of neuron and give function of each part.

9 Explain the process of transmission of nerve impulse.

10 Explain hindbrain. Give function of human brain.

11 What is the common defects of eye? Explain any one defect of eye.

12 What is astigmatism? Give its cause.

Section-B

Diagram Based Questions

13 The point of contact between the nerve endings of one neuron and the dendrites of another neuron are separated by a fine gap. Study the diagram given below and answer the questions.

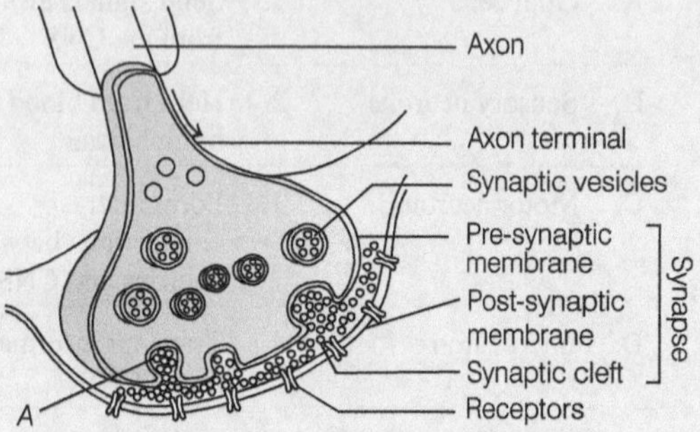

(i) What is shown is this diagram? (one word or oneline)

(ii) Define *A*

(iii) Name the cell body of a nerve cell.

14 Given below is the diagram of spinal reflex action, study the same and then answer the questions that follows.

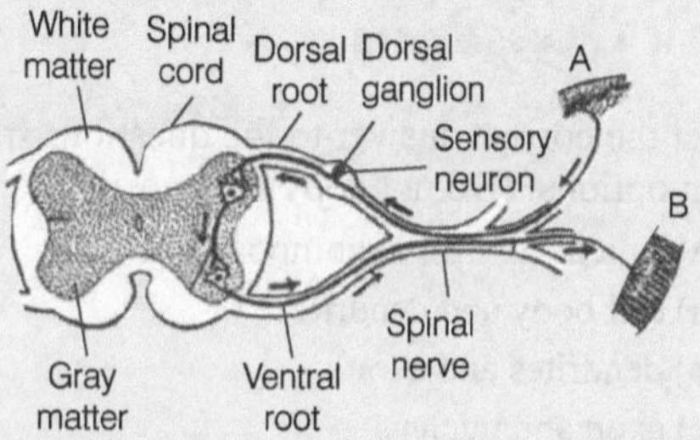

(i) Name the parts labelled as *A* and *B*.

(ii) Explain about the arrangement of neurons in the spinal cord.

(iii) Give two everyday examples of reflex action.

Answers

1. (i) (d), (ii) (d), (iii) (c), (iv) (d), (v) (a)

10

Endocrine System

TREND ANALYSIS 4 YEARS

Average No. of Questions Across all Sets

	Types of Questions	2024	2023	2020	2019
Endocrine System	1 Mark	2	1	–	2
	2 Marks	1	1	–	–
	4 Marks	–	–	–	–
	5 Marks	1	1	–	1

Most multicellular organisms communicate *via* means of certain chemicals called **hormones**. These are poured into the blood and have their effect on target cells or specific organs or tissues of the body. They may be chemically proteins, amino acids or steroids in nature.

These hormones are secreted by the different types of glands and glandular cells which together constitute the endocrine system.

The science associated with the study of structure, mechanism of action, functions, diagnosis and treatment of disorders related to the endocrine glands is known as **Endocrinology**. **Thomas Addison** is the father of endocrinology.

Glands in Humans

There are two types of glands in our body. These are

(i) **Exocrine glands** are those glands which secrete enzymes and have ducts to pour their secretions. Hence, these are called as **duct glands**, e.g. sweat, mammary, salivary, sebaceous glands, etc.

(ii) **Endocrine glands** are those glands which secrete hormones. These glands do not have ducts and their secretions are poured directly into the blood stream to act on a target organ. Hence, are also known as **ductless glands**, e.g. pituitary, pineal, etc. .

Differences between Endocrine and Exocrine Glands

Endocrine glands	Exocrine glands
They do not have ducts.	They have ducts.
They secrete hormones.	They secrete enzymes.
They bring about chemical coordination in the body.	They increase the rate of biochemical reactions.
e.g. Thyroid	e.g. Lacrimal gland secretes tears that lubricates eye surface and kill germs.

Types of Endocrine Glands

- The main endocrine glands in human beings include adrenal gland, pancreas (only endocrine part), thyroid gland, pituitary gland, etc.
- In humans, the complete endocrine system works under the influence of **hypothalamus** which is located below the thalamus of forebrain. Main endocrine glands include

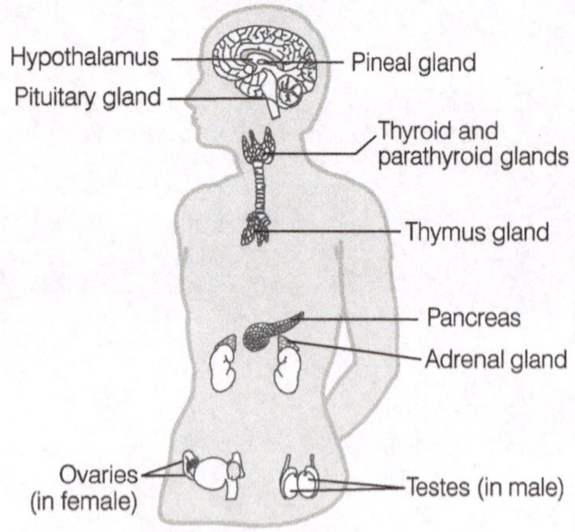

Fig. 10.1 Human endocrine system

Adrenal Glands

These are a pair of small cap-like structure found above each kidney.

Each adrenal gland consists of following two main parts

1. Adrenal Cortex

It is an external, firm and pale-yellowish tissue derived from the mesoderm of embryo. It is formed of three concentric layers, i.e. an inner, a middle and an outer layer.

It secretes many hormones commonly called as **corticoids**. These are given below

(i) **Mineralocorticoids** (Aldosterone) which regulate the metabolism of minerals such as Na^+, K^+ ions in the body.

(ii) **Glucocorticoids** (Cortisol) which regulate the metabolism of carbohydrates, fats and proteins in the body.

(iii) **Sex-corticoids** which act as a precursor of sex hormones in males (testosterone) and females (Estrogen, progesterone). These play a major role in the growth of axial, pubic and facial hair during puberty.

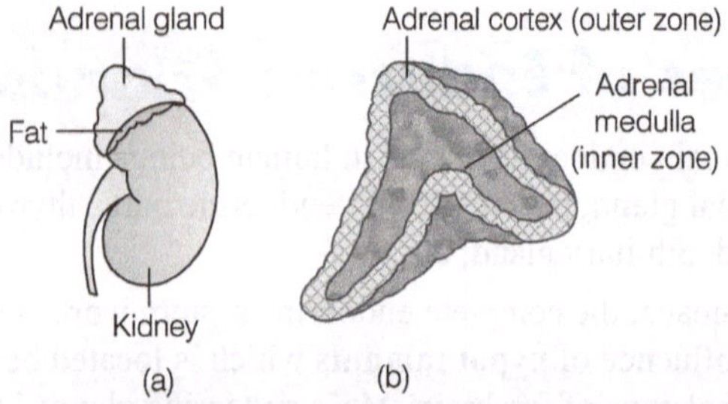

Fig. 10.2 (a) Position (b) Longitudinal section of adrenal gland

2. Adrenal Medulla

The adrenal medulla lies in the centre of the adrenal gland.

It secretes mainly two hormones as given below

(i) **Adrenaline** (epinephrine) is secreted at the time of emergency situation. Thus, it is also known as **emergency hormone** or **hormone** of **fight, fright** and **flight**. It increases heart rate, blood pressure and the supply of blood to muscles stimulating the release of more glucose into the liver.

(ii) **Nor-adrenaline** (nor-epinephrine) regulates blood pressure under normal conditions. It causes constriction of blood vessels (vasoconstriction). It also increases activity of heart.

Pancreas

- It functions both as exocrine (duct) gland and endocrine (ductless) gland. Such a gland is also called **heterocrine gland**. It is situated in the loop of small intestine close to the duodenum part.
- The **exocrine** portion of pancreas secretes pancreatic juice containing enzymes which help in the digestion of food.
- On the other hand, the **endocrine** portion of pancreas has a special group of cells known as **Islets of Langerhans** (found all over the gland).
- It has different types of cells which are responsible for producing different types of hormones. The types of cells are given below
- α-**cells** produce **glucagon** hormone which is responsible for increasing the level of glucose in the blood by stimulating the liver to convert glycogen into glucose.
- β-**cells** produce **insulin** hormone which is responsible for lowering the level of glucose in the blood.
- **Delta cells** secrete somatostatin.

Thyroid Gland

- It is known to be the largest endocrine gland. It is a bilobed structure located in front of the neck just below the **larynx** (voice box).
- The two lobes of thyroid gland are joined by an interconnection known as **isthmus**.
- It mainly secretes the hormone **thyroxine** and **calcitonin** (causes the deposition of Ca^{2+} in bones).
- **Thyroxine hormone** is responsible for regulating the normal basal metabolism of the body. It also influences the general body growth, body temperature, mental

development, etc. It requires iodine in order to be synthesised.

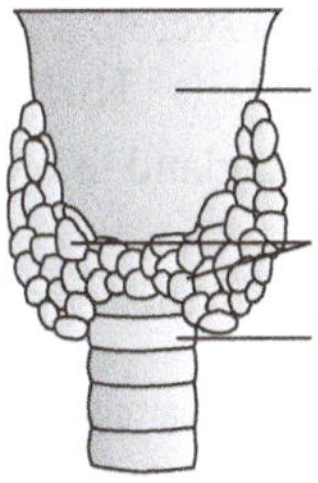

Fig. 10.3 Diagrammatic view of the position of thyroid gland (ventral side)

Pituitary Gland

- It is also known as **master gland** because it controls the activities of all other endocrine glands.
- It is a small pea sized gland found hanging from the base of the midbrain below the hypothalamus.
- Pituitary gland is divided into three major lobes (i.e. anterior, posterior and intermediate pituitary.)

1. Hormones of Anterior Pituitary

Anterior lobe of pituitary gland produces six major hormones. These are given below

(i) **Growth Hormone** (somatotrophin) It is release by somatotropic cells of anterior pituitary gland. GHRH (growth hormone releasing hormone) released by hypothalamus act on somatotropic cells of anterior pituitary gland and stimulates the release of GH.

(ii) **Thyroid Stimulating Hormone** (TSH) It stimulates thyroid gland to produce and release its hormones.

(iii) **Adrenocorticotropic Hormone** (ACTH) It stimulates adrenal cortex to produce its hormones.

(iv) **Follicle Stimulating Hormone** (FSH) It stimulates sperm formation in males and growth of ovarian follicles and secretion of oestrogen in females.

(v) **Luteinizing Hormone** (LH) It stimulates ovulation and secretion of progesterone from **corpus luteum** in females. In males, this hormone is also called ICSH (Interstitial Cell Stimulating Hormone) which induces **Leydig cells** of testes to secrete **testosterone.** (Both FSH and LH stimulates gonadal activity hence, called gonadotrophins).

(vi) **Prolactin** (PRL) It stimulates growth of mammary glands during pregnancy and lactation.Except the growth hormone, all other hormones of anterior pituitary are called **tropic hormones** because they have the ability to stimulate other endocrine glands to produce their specific hormones.

2. Hormones of Posterior Pituitary

The posterior lobe of pituitary stores and releases two main hormones. These are as follow

(i) **Antidiuretic Hormone** (ADH)/**Vasopressin** It acts on kidney to increase reabsorption of water from the renal tubules.

(ii) **Oxytocin** This hormone is secreted in female during later phase of pregnancy. It stimulates uterine contractions during childbirth and milk ejection. Hence, it is also called **birth hormone** or **milk ejection hormone.**

3. Hormone of Intermediate Lobe of Pituitary

It secretes only one hormone, i.e. **Melanocyte Stimulating Hormone** (MSH) which is responsible for pigmentation of skin.

Disorders of Endocrine System

	Anterior pituitary	Posterior pituitary	Thyroid	Adrenal cortex	Adrenal medulla	Pancreatic islets
Hormone secreted	Growth hormone	ADH/Oxytocin	T_3, T_4	Glucocorticoids	Epinephrine Norepinephrine	Insulin
Disorder due to hypersecretion and symptoms	Gigantism (long bones) acromegaly (growth of bone of face)		Exopthalmic goitre (protruding eyes)	Cushing syndrome (obesity. hyperglycemia osteoporosis)	Increased metabolism, Hypertension	
Disorder due to hyposecretion and symptoms	Dwarfism (under growth), Short stature	Diabetes insipidus (Loss of water from urine, person feels thirsty)	Cretinism, Myxoedema, simple goitre (mental retardation, thyroid gland in larynx region enlarges)	Addison's disease (skin pigmentation, loss of energy and weight, hypoglycemia)		Diabetes mellitus, glycosuria

Feedback Mechanism

There are two types of feed back mechanisms.

1. Negative Feedback Control

- It is a closed loop in which synthesis of hormone stops or lowers when its blood level rises above normal.
- **For example,** if the level of glucose rises in the blood, it is detected by beta cells of the pancreas that produce more insulin.
- This promotes absorption of glucose by the cells and its level is brought back to normal. The result is inhibition of insulin.

2. Positive Feedback Control

- It stimulates and enhances the secretion or production of the hormone.
- **For example,** uterine contractions during child birth stimulate the release of oxytocin into the mother's blood. This further intensifies uterine contractions. Thus, causing more oxytocin release.
  Production and release of oxytocin stops after the birth of the baby.

Feedback Control by Thyroid Stimulating Hormone

- Thyroid stimulating hormone stimulates the synthesis and secretion of thyroid hormones from thyroid gland.
- The hypothalamus is stimulated by some external stimulus to produce thyroid releasing hormone. This stimulates anterior pituitary to secrete a specific hormone, i.e. Thyroid Stimulating Hormone (TSH).
- TSH inturn stimulates thyroid gland to produce hormone thyroxine.

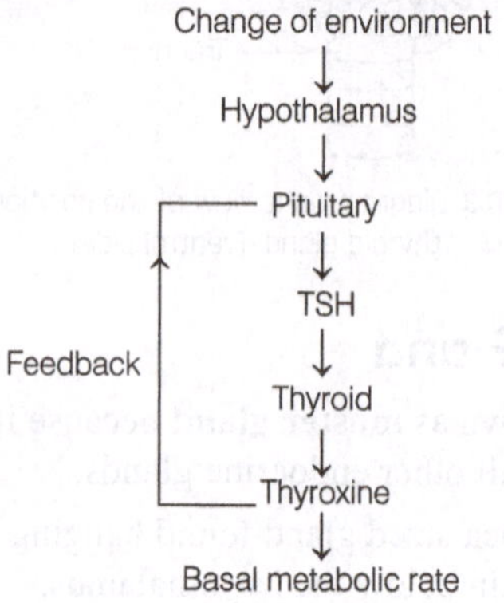

Fig. 10.4 Feedback control by hormone

- If the level of thyroxine in blood is high, it exerts a negative feedback effect on hypothalamus and anterior pituitary.
- If the level of thyroxine is less than normal, it stimulates hypothalamus to produce more Thyroid Stimulating Hormone–Releasing Factors (TSH-RF) (positive feedback). But, if thyroxine is present in more amount, the hypothalamus secretes less TSH-RF (negative feedback).

PYQs Previous Years' Questions

1 Mark Questions

Multiple Choice Questions

1. The hormone that affects urination is **ICSE 2024**

(a) adrenaline (b) vasopressin
(c) oestrogen (d) thyroxine

Ans. (b) vasopressin

2. Alpha cells of pancreas secrete **ICSE 2023**

(a) glycogen (b) glucose
(c) glucagon (d) insulin

Ans. (c) Alpha cells of pancrease secrete glucagon hormone whereas beta cells secrete insulin hormone.

3. Gigantism and acromegaly are due to **ICSE 2021-22 Sem. II, 2016**

(a) hyposecretion of thyroxine
(b) hyposecretion of growth hormone
(c) hypersecretion of thyroxine
(d) hypersecretion of growth hormone

Ans. (d) Hypersecretion of growth hormone

4. Islets of Langerhans are located in **ICSE 2021-22 Sem. II**

(a) liver (b) pituitary gland (c) spleen (d) pancreas

Ans. (d) Islets of Langerhans are present in pancreas and form the endocrine part of the pancreas.

5. Choose the correct answer from the four options given below
Cretinism and myxoedema are due to **ICSE 2014**
(a) hypersecretion of thyroxine
(b) hypersecretion of growth hormone
(c) hyposecretion of thyroxine
(d) hyposecretion of growth hormone

Ans. (c) Cretinism and myxoedema are due to the hyposecretion of **thyroxine**.

6. Choose the correct answer from the four options given below.
A gland which secretes both hormone and enzyme is **ICSE 2013**
(a) pituitary (b) pancreas
(c) thyroid (d) adrenal

Ans. (b) **Pancreas** is the gland which secretes both hormones and enzyme.

Very Short Answer Type Questions

7. Name the mineral elements required for synthesis of thyroxine. **ICSE 2024**

Ans. Iodine

8. Give the exact location of adrenal glands. **ICSE Specimen 2021-22 Sem. II**

Or

State the exact location of adrenal gland. **ICSE 2014**

Ans. Adrenal glands are cap-like structures present on the top of each kidney.

9. Identify the **odd** term and name the **category** to which the remaining three belong.
Example Glucose, starch, cellulose, calcium
Odd term : Calcium
Category : Others are different types of carbohydrates.
Addison's disease, Cushing's syndrome, Acromegaly, Leukemia. **ICSE 2019**

Ans. **Odd term** - Leukemia
Category - Others are result of either hypersecretion or hyposecretion of hormones.

10. Identify the **odd** term and name the **category** to which the remaining three belong.
Insulin, Adrenaline, Pepsin, Thyroxine. **ICSE 2019**

Ans. **Odd term** - Pepsin
Category - Others are the example of amino acid derived hormones.

11. Name the following. **ICSE Specimen 2019**
The hormone that regulates the basal metabolic rate.

Ans. Thyroxine hormone

12. Give appropriate biological or technical terms for this sentence
Hormones which regulate the secretion of other endocrine glands. **ICSE 2018, 2014, 2012**

Or

Give technical term for group of hormones which influence other endocrine glands to produce hormones. **ICSE 2014, 2012**

Ans. Tropic hormones

13. Differentiate between the pair on the basis of what is indicated in brackets.
Leaf and liver (form in which glucose is stored) **ICSE 2018**

Ans. Glucose is stored in the form of starch in leaves and as glycogen in liver.

14. State whether the following statements are true or false. If false, rewrite the correct form of the statement by changing the first word only. **ICSE Specimen 2017**
(i) The beta cells of the pancreas secrete insulin.

Ans. True

15. Name the pituitary hormone which stimulates contraction of uterus during childbirth. **ICSE 2017**

Ans. Oxytocin hormone, secreted from posterior pituitary gland, stimulates the contractions of uterus during childbirth.

16. Choose the odd one out of the term given and name the category to which the others belong.
ACTH, TSH, ADH, FSH **ICSE 2017**

Ans. **Odd term** - ADH
Category- Hormone of posterior pituitary gland.
Rest three are the hormones of anterior pituitary gland.

17. Mention the exact location of Islets of Langerhans. **ICSE 2017**

Ans. **Islets of Langerhans** is the endocrine portion of pancreas, found all over the gland.

18. Give biological reason for
'Some women have facial hair-like beard and moustache.' **ICSE 2017**

Ans. Some women have facial hair-like beard and moustaches due to the hypersecretion of sexcorticoids from adrenal gland. It is known as adrenal virilism in females.

19. In set of terms given below, there is an odd one and cannot be grouped in the same category to which the other three belong. Identify the odd term in the set and name the category to which the remaining three belong.

Example Ovary, Fallopian tube, Ureter, Uterus
Odd term Ureter.
Category Part of female reproductive system.

Cortisone, Somatotropin, Adrenocorticotropic hormone, Vasopressin **ICSE 2016**

Ans. **Odd term** -Cortisone
Category-The remaining three are the pituitary hormones.

20. Complete the following paragraph by filling in the blanks (i) to (v) with appropriate words.

The amount of urine output is under the regulation of a hormone called (i) .... secreted by the (ii) .... lobe of the pituitary gland. If this hormone secretion is reduced, there is an increased production of urine.

This disorder is called (iii) .... Sometimes excess glucose is passed with urine due to hyposecretion of another hormone called (iv) .... leading to the cause of disease called (v) .... **ICSE 2016**

Ans. (i) ADH (ii) posterior
(iii) diabetes insipidus (iv) insulin
(v) glycosuria

21. State the exact location of thyroid gland. **ICSE 2016, 2012**

Ans. The thyroid gland is located in the front of neck region just below the larynx (voice box)

22. Given in the box below are a set of fourteen biological terms. Of these, twelve can be paired into six matching pairs. Out of the six pairs, one has been done for you as an example.

Example : Endosmosis — Turgid cell

Identify the remaining five matching pairs.

Cushing's syndrome, Turgid cell, Iris, Free of red and cone cells, Colour of eyes, Hypoglycemia, Active transport, Acrosome, Addison's disease, Blind spot, Hyperglycemia, Spermatozoa, Endosmosis, Clotting of blood.

Ans. (i) Iris–Colour of eye **ICSE 2016**
(ii) Cushing's syndrome–Hyperglycemia
(iii) Blind spot–Free of rods and cones
(iv) Spermatozoa–Acrosome
(v) Addison's disease–Hypoglycemia

23. Define the term hormone. **ICSE 2024**

Or

Briefly explain hormone. **ICSE 2016**

Ans. **Hormones** are the secretions from specific cells or glands in the body which act as chemical messengers. They are directly released in the blood and control different vital reactions of the body at a very low concentration.

24. Name the form in which glucose is stored in liver. **ICSE 2015, 2014, 2010**

Ans. The form in which glucose is stored in liver is glycogen.

25. Given below is an example of a certain structure and its special functional activity. On a similar pattern fill in the blanks with suitable functions.

Example Chloroplast and Photosynthesis

Thyroid gland and .... **ICSE 2015**

Ans. Make and secrete thyroid hormones.

26. Give the biological/technical terms for the following.

The hormone increasing reabsorption of water by kidney tubules. **ICSE 2015, 2012**

Or

Name the hormone that helps to increase the reabsorption of water from the kidney tubules.

Ans. Antidiuretic hormone (vasopressin).

27. Differentiate between the given pair on the basis of what is mentioned within bracket.
Vasopressin and insulin (Deficiency disorder) **ICSE 2015**

Ans. Difference between vasopressin and insulin are

Vasopressin	Insulin
Hyposecretion of vasopressin causes diabetes insipidus.	Hyposecretion of insulin causes diabetes mellitus.
In this type of diabetes no glucose is present in urine.	In this type of diabetes glucose is present in urine.

28. Name the hormone secreted by Islets of Langerhans. **ICSE 2014**

Ans. **Insulin** and **glucagon** are the hormones secreted by the Islets of Langerhans.

29. Explain the biological abbreviation of TSH. **ICSE 2014**

Ans. **TSH** is abbreviation for Thyroid Stimulating Hormone. It stimulates thyroid gland to produce and release its hormones.

30. Briefly explain the term diabetes insipidus. **ICSE 2013**

Ans. **Diabetes insipidus** is a condition which occurs due to the hyposecretion of antidiuretic hormone or vasopressin from the posterior lobe of pituitary gland. This is characterised by excretion of large amount of urine and subsequent dehydration and thirst.

31. State the function of β-cells of pancreas. **ICSE 2012**

Ans. Beta cells of pancreas secrete insulin that helps to lower the level of glucose in blood.

32. Differentiate between the following pairs on the basis of what is mentioned in bracket.
Diabetes mellitus and diabetes insipidus.
(Reason/cause) **ICSE 2012**

Ans. **Diabetes mellitus** It occurs due to undersecretion of insulin which inturn increases the level of glucose in blood.
Diabetes insipidus It occurs due to the deficiency of ADH (Antidiuretic Hormone)/Vasopressin in which person suffer from loss of water due to frequent urination.

33. Give biological reason for 'Pituitary gland is also known as the master gland'. **ICSE 2012**

Ans. **Pituitary gland** is also known as the master gland because it secretes hormones that regulate activites of other endocrine glands.

34. Differentiate between the following pair according to what is given in the bracket.
Acromegaly and cretinism. (symptoms) **ICSE 2012**

Ans.

Acromegaly	Cretinism
Characterised by long bones of hand and legs which gives a person gorilla-like appearance.	It affects the physical and mental growth of children due to which he/she has retarded growth and mental development.

35. Give the exact location of pituitary gland. **ICSE 2011**

Ans. **Pituitary gland** is located at the base of midbrain below hypothalamus.

36. Given below is the set consisting of five terms. In a set there is a word which is an odd one. Write down the category of the group having identified the odd one out.

Vasopressin, growth hormone, TSH, ACTH, FSH. **ICSE 2010**

Ans.

Odd one	Category
Vasopressin (secreted by posterior pituitary)	All other hormones are secreted by anterior lobe of pituitary gland.

37. State the following statement true or false. If false, write the correct form of statement by changing the first or last word only.

The pituitary gland is both exocrine and endocrine in function. **ICSE 2009**

Ans. The statement is false. The pancreas is both exocrine and endocrine in function.

38. Select and rewrite the correct answer to the given statement from the four choices given below.

Insulin is secreted by **ICSE 2009**

(a) beta cells of pancreas (b) alpha cells of pancreas
(c) delta cells of pancreas (d) None of these

Ans. (a) **Insulin** is secreted by beta cells of pancreas.

39. State whether the following statements is true or false. If false, rewrite the correct statement by changing only the last word of the statement.

The alpha cells of the pancreas secrete insulin. **ICSE 2008**

Ans. The statement is false. The alpha cells of the pancreas secrete **glucagon**.

40. Explain the term tropic hormone. **ICSE 2007**

Ans. Which influence other endocrine glands to produce hormone.

41. Name the hormone that releases glucose into blood. **ICSE 2006**

Ans. **Glucagon** is the hormone that releases glucose in the blood.

42. Given below are the four terms in which one term is odd and cannot be grouped into the category to which the other three belong. Identify the odd one in each set and name the category to which the remaining three belong.

ADH, TSH, NADP, ACTH **ICSE 2006**

Ans.

Set	Odd one	Category
ADH, TSH, NADP, ACTH	NADP (cofactor)	Hormones

43. State whether the following statement is true or false. If false, rewrite the correct statement by changing the first or last word only.
Hormones are secreted directly into the organs. **ICSE 2005**

Ans. The statement is false. Hormones are secreted directly into the blood.

44. Given below is a group of terms, in which one term does not fit into the category of the group to which other three belongs. Write the category of the group and identify the odd one.
Adrenal, liver, thyroid, pituitary **ICSE 2003**

Ans.

Odd one	Category
Liver	All others are endocrine glands.

45. Name the hormone secreted by beta-cells of islets of Langerhans. **ICSE 2001**

Ans. **Insulin** is secreted by the beta cells of islets of Langerhans.

46. Complete the following statements by choosing the correct alternative from the choice given in.
(Myxoedema/simple goitre/exophthalmic goitre) is a disorder caused by excess thyroid hormone. **ICSE 2000**

Ans. **Exophthalmic goitre** is a disorder which is caused by excess production of thyroid hormone.

2 Marks Questions

47. Distinguish between Diabetes mellitus and Diabetes insipidus (endocrine gland concerned). **ICSE 2024**

Ans. Differences between Diabetes mellitus and Diabetes insipidus (endocrine gland concerned) are

Diabetes mellitus	Diabetes insipidus
It is the disorder associated with pancreas.	It is the disorder associated with posterior lobe of pituitary gland.
It is caused due to the deficiency of insulin hormone.	It is caused due to deficiency of vasopressin hormone.

48. State the exact location of the following structures.
(i) Thyroid gland
(ii) Islets of Langerhans **ICSE 2023**

Ans. (i) Thyroid gland is situated in the anterior portion of the neck just below the larynx.
(ii) Refer to answer no. 17.

49. What is adrenal virilism? What causes this condition? **ICSE 2021-22 Sem. II**

Ans. Adrenal virilism is a condition that occurs in females due to the overgrowth of adrenal cortex in a mature female. It results in development of certain male characteristics in female such as beard, moustache, etc.

50. 'Simple goitre is usually seen in people living in the hilly regions'. Give two reasons for the statement. **ICSE 2021-22 Sem. II**

Ans. Simple goitre is a disease caused due to the lack of intake of iodine. In hilly areas, the iodine content of the soil is negligible as compared to people living near coastal areas. Thus, people residing in hilly areas do not get adequate amount of iodine in their diet and suffer from goitre.

51. (i) Name the endocrine gland that secretes thyroxine. Give any one function of thyroxine.
(ii) Give the full form of the abbreviation ACTH. Which gland secretes this hormone? **ICSE 2021-22 Sem. II**

Ans. (i) The endocrine gland that secrete thyroxine is thyroid gland. Thyroxine regulates the basal metabolism and also helps in general growth of the body.
(ii) Full form of ACTH is Adrenocorticotropic Hormone. It is secreted by anterior pituitary gland.

52. Name the homones whose deficiency causes
(i) Diabetes mellitus
(ii) Diabetes insipidus **ICSE 2021-22 Sem. II**

Ans. (i) **Diabetes mellitus** Hyposecretion or deficiency of insulin causes diabetes mellitus.
(ii) **Diabetes insipidus** It is caused by undersecretion/ hyposecretion of ADH or vasopressin.

53. Give the full form of the following abbreviations.
(i) TSH **ICSE Specimen 2021-22 Sem. II**
(ii) ADH

Ans. (i) Thyroid Stimulating Hormone.
(ii) Antidiuretic Hormone.

54. Complete the following table by filling in the blanks (*a*) to (*c*).

Glands	Hormones secreted	Effects of oversecretion
Pancreas	(a)	Hypoglycemia
Thyroid	(b)	(c) ....

ICSE Specimen 2021-22 Sem. II

Ans. (a) –Insulin (b) –T_3, T_4 (Thyroid hormone)
(c) –Exophthalmic goitre

55. Explain the term 'tropic hormone'. Give one example of a tropic hormone. **ICSE Specimen 2021-22 Sem. II**

Ans. Tropic hormone is a group of hormones that stimulate other endocrine glands to produce their specific hormones such as gonadotropic hormones secreted by anterior pituitary and also stimulate gonads to produce certain hormones.

56. Mention three functions of adrenaline. **ICSE Specimen 2021-22 Sem II**

Ans. Three functions of adrenaline are as follows
(i) Increase heart rate.
(ii) Help body in fight, fear and flight situation.
(iii) Dilates pupil.

57. Rewrite the correct form of statement by changing the underline word.
(i) Alpha cells of pancreas secrete insulin. **ICSE 2015**
(ii) Cretinism is caused due to the deficiency of adrenaline. **ICSE 2015**

Ans. (i) Alpha cells of pancreas secrete glucagon.
(ii) Cretinism is caused due to the deficiency of thyroid hormone.

58. Define the following terms giving one example of each.
(i) Hormone (ii) Exocrine gland **ICSE 2003**

Ans. (i) Refer to answer no. 23.
(ii) Exocrine glands are those glands which pour their secretions directly into the tissue/organ with the help of duct, e.g. All salivary glands.

59. Choose the odd one in each of the following series.
(i) Insulin, glucagon, diabetes insipidus, diabetes mellitus.
(ii) Cretinism, myxoedema, goitre, scurvy. **ICSE 2000**

Ans. (i) Odd term is **diabetes insipidus** because it is not related to pancreas.
(ii) Odd term is **scurvy** because it is not a hormonal disorder.

4 Marks Questions

60. Complete the following table by filling in blank space (i) to (viii).

Gland	Substance produced	One important function
Islets of Langerhans	(i)	(ii) ....
(iii)	Adrenaline	(iv) ....
(v)	Thyroxine	(vi) ....
(vii)	LH	(vii) ....

ICSE 2004

Ans.

Gland	Substance produced	One important function
Islets of Langerhans	(i) Insulin	(ii) Decreases sugar level in the body.
(iii) Adrenal	Adrenaline	(iv) Increase heart beat.
(v) Thyroid	Thyroxine	(vi) Regulates basal metabolism.
(vii) Pituitary	LH	(viii) Stimulates production of progesterone.

61. Differentiate between the following pairs
(i) Diabetes mellitus and diabetes insipidus.
(ii) Acromegaly and myxoedema. **ICSE 2004**

Ans. (i)

Diabetes insipidus	Diabetes mellitus
Low secretion of ADH.	Low secretion of insulin.
Patient suffers from loss of water.	Patient suffers from loss of glucose in urine.

(ii)

Acromegaly	Myxoedema
It is caused due to over secretion of growth hormone from pituitary gland in adults.	It is caused due to under secretion of thyroxine from thyroid gland in adults.
Characterised by long bones of hand and legs which gives a person gorilla-like appearance.	Characterised by puffy appearance due to the accumulation of fat in subcutaneous tissue.

62. Complete the following table by filling in the blanks numbered (i) to (viii).

Gland	Hormone secreted	Effect on body
(i)………	(ii)………	Regulates basal metabolism
Pancreas (β-cells)	(iii)………	(iv)………
(v)………	(vi)………	Increases heart beat
(vii)………	Thyroid stimulating hormone	(viii)………

ICSE 2001

Ans.

Gland	Hormone secreted	Effect on body
(i) Thyroid gland	(ii) Thyroxine	Regulates basal metabolism.
Pancreas (β-cells)	(iii) Insulin	(iv) Lowers the blood sugar level in the body.
(v) Adrenal medulla	(vi) Adrenaline	Increases heart beat.
(vii) Anterior pituitary gland	Thyroid stimulating hormone	(viii) Helps thyroid gland to secrete thyroxine.

5 Marks Questions

63. Match the items given in Column I with most appropriate ones in Column II and rewrite the corret matching pairs :

	Column I		Column II
A.	Leydig cells	1.	Lack of thyroxine in children
B.	Stoma	2.	12 pairs
C.	Ova	3.	Testosterone
D.	Cranial nerve	4.	Diffusion of respiratory gases
E.	Cretinism	5.	Haploid cells
		6.	31 pairs
		7.	Diploid cells

ICSE 2024

Ans.

	Column I	Column II
A.	Leydig cells	3. Testosterone
B.	Stoma	4. Diffusion of respiratory gases
C.	Ova	5. Haploid cells
D.	Cranial nerve	2. 12 pairs
E.	Cretinism	1. Lack of thyroxine in children

64. Match the items given in Column I with the most appropriate ones in Column II and rewrite the correct matching pairs.

	Column I		Column II
A.	Hyposecretion of thyroxine in adults	1.	Diabetes insipidus
B.	Hyposecretion of insulin	2.	Myxoedema
C.	Hypersecretion of growth hormone in childhood	3.	Dwarfism
D.	Hyposecretion of ADH	4.	Gigantism
E.	Hypersecretion of thyroxine	5.	Diabetes mellitus
		6.	Exophthalmic goitre
		7.	Cretinism

ICSE Specimen 2023

Ans.

	Column I	Column II
A.	Hyposecretion of thyroxine in adults	1. Cretinism, Myxoedema
B.	Hyposecretion of insulin	2. Diabetes mellitus
C.	Hypersecretion of growth hormone in childhood	3. Gigantism
D.	Hyposecretion of ADH	4. Diabetes insipidus
E.	Hypersecretion of thyroxine	5. Exophthalmic goitre

65. Match the items of Column I with those in Column II and rewrite the correct matching pairs

	Column I		Column II
A.	Diabetes mellitus	1.	Hypersecretion of thyroxine
B.	Diabetes insipidus	2.	Hyposecretion of thyroxine
C.	Cretinism	3.	Hyperglycemia
D.	Insulin shock	4.	Hyposecretion of growth hormone
E.	Exophthalmic	5.	Hypoglycemia
		6.	Hyposecretion of ADH
		7.	Oversecretion of adrenaline

ICSE Specimen 2019

Ans.

A.	Diabetes mellitus	3.	Hyperglycemia
B.	Diabetes insipidus	6.	Hyposecretion of ADH
C.	Cretinism	2.	Hyposecretion of thyroxine
D.	Insulin shock	7.	Oversecretion of adrenalin
E.	Exophthalmic goitre	1.	Hypersecretion of thyroxine

66. Match the items given in Column I with the most appropriate ones in Column II and rewrite the correct matching pairs.

	Column I		Column II
A.	Cretinism	1.	Hypersecretion of adrenal cortex
B.	Diabetes insipidus	2.	Hyposecretion of thyroxine
C.	Exophthalmic goitre	3.	Hyposecretion of growth hormone
D.	Adrenal virilism	4.	Hyposecretion of vasopressin
E.	Dwarfism	5.	Hyposecretion of adrenal cortex
		6.	Hypersecretion of growth hormone
		7.	Hypersecretion of thyoxine

ICSE 2018

Ans. (A) **Cretinism** Hyposecretion of thyroxine

(B) **Diabetes insipidus** Hyposecretion of vasopressin

(C) **Exophthalmic goitre** Hypersecretion of thyroxine

(D) **Adrenal virilism** Hypersecretion of adrenal cortex (sex corticoids)

(E) **Dwarfism** Hyposecretion of growth hormone in childhood

67. Complete the following table by filling in the numbered blanks with an appropriate term/answer.

ICSE Specimen 2017

Gland	Hormone produced	Function
Thyroid	1	2
3	4	Dilates pupil of eye
5	Insulin	6
7	ADH	8
9	10	Conversion of glycogen to glucose

Ans. 1. Thyroxine
2. Basal metabolism
3. Adrenal gland
4. Adrenaline
5. Pancreas
6. Decrease glucose level in blood
7. Posterior pituitary
8. Water reabsorption in nephron (kidney)
9. Pancreas
10. Glucagon

68. Complete the following table by filling in the blanks from (*i*) to (*x*) with appropriate terms.

Gland	Secretion	Function/Effect on body
Thyroid	(i).........	(ii).........
(iii).........	Vasopressin	(iv).........
(v).........	(vi).........	Promotes glucose utilisation by the body cells.
Lacrimal gland	(vii)......	(viii).........
Adrenal medulla	(ix).........	(x).........

ICSE 2013

Ans.

Gland	Secretion	Function/Effect on body
Thyroid	(i) Thyroxine	(ii) Promotes basal metabolism, growth and differentiation.
(iii) Posterior pituitary	Vasopressin	(iv) Increases reabsorption of water from kidneys.
(v) Pancreas	(vi) Insulin	Promotes glucose utilisation by the body cells.
Lacrimal gland	(vii) Tears	(viii) Lubricates eye surface and kills germs.
Adrenal medulla	(ix) Adrenaline	(x) Prepares body for any emergency.

Diagram Based Questions

69. The diagram given below represents an endocrine gland in the human body.

Study the diagram and answer the following questions.

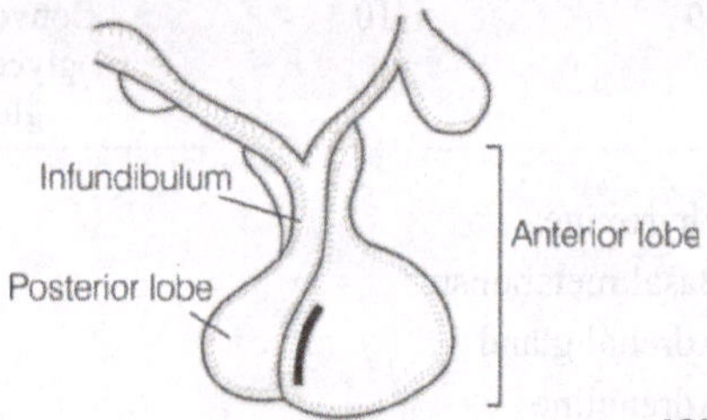

ICSE 1019 (5M)

(i) Identify the endocrine gland. Where it is located ?

(ii) Why is the above gland referred to as the 'master gland' ?

(iii) Name the hormone which in deficiency causes diabetes insipidus. How does this disorder differ from diabetes mellitus ?

(iv) Explain the term 'hormone'. What is the role of tropic hormones in the human body ?

(v) Which lobe of the above gland secretes

1. Oxytocin 2. ACTH

3. Growth hormone

Ans. (i) This endocrine gland is pituitary gland. It is located in the brain between the hypothalamus and pineal gland, just behind the bridge of the nose.

(ii) Pituitary gland is known as master gland because it produces many hormones that travel throughout the body directing certain processes or stimulating other glands to produce other hormones.

(iii) Diabetes insipidus is a condition that results from insufficient production of the Antidiuretic Hormone (ADH) called vasopressin. It characterised by excessive thirst and excretion of large amounts of severely dilute urine. Diabetes mellitus is a group of metabolic disorders characterised by excessive levels of the glucose in the blood.

(iv) Hormones are the chemical regulators that are produced and poured directly into the bloodstream. The site of production and actions are different. Hormones which regulates the secretion of other endocrine glands are known as tropic hormones.

(v) 1. **Oxytocin** It is released into the blood from the posterior lobe of the pituitary gland.

2. **ACTH** Anterior pituitary lobe release adrenocorticotropic hormone to stimulate cortisol production in the adrenal glands.

3. **Growth hormone** Anterior lobe of pituitary gland secretes growth hormone.

70. The given diagram represents the location and structure of an endocrine gland. Study the same and answer the questions that follows.

(i) Name the endocrine gland shown in the diagram.

(ii) Name the secretion of the gland which regulates basal metabolism.

(iii) Name the mineral element required for the synthesis of the above mentioned hormone.

(iv) Name the disease caused due to undersecretion of the above mentioned hormone in children.

(v) Name the disease caused due to hypersecretion of the above mentioned hormone.

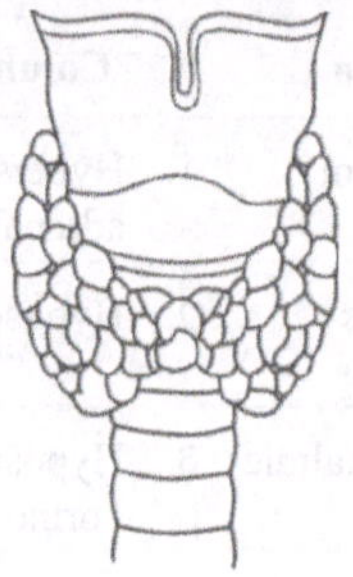

ICSE 2017 (5M)

Ans. (i) The endocrine gland shown in the diagram is thyroid gland.

(ii) Thyroxine hormone, secreted by the thyroid gland which is responsible for the regulation of normal basal metabolism of the body.

(iii) Thyroxine requires iodine in order to be synthesised.

(iv) Undersecretion of thyroxine hormone causes cretinism in children.

(v) Hypersecretion of thyroxine hormone can cause exophthalmic goitre.

71. Given below is the outline of the human body showing the important glands.

(i) Name the glands marked *A* to *D*.

(ii) Name the hormone secreted by part *B*. Give one important function of this hormone.

(iii) Name the endocrine part of the gland labelled as *C*.

(iv) Why is the part labelled *A* called the master gland? Which part of the forebrain controls the gland labelled *A*?

(v) Name the gland that secretes the 'emergency hormone'.

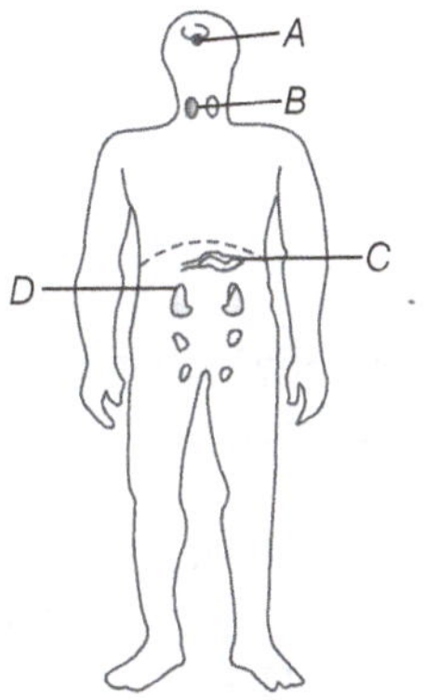

ICSE 2016 (5M)

Ans. (i) *A*–Pituitary *B*–Thyroid
C–Pancreas *D*–Adrenal

(ii) The part '*B*' is represented by thyroid gland. It produces thyroxine which is responsible for regulating the normal basal metabolic rate of the body.

(iii) The part '*C*' represents the Islets of Langerhans (i.e. the endocrine part of the pancreas) which secretes two hormones, namely insulin and glucagon.

(iv) The part labelled '*A*' represents the pituitary gland. Pituitary gland controls the secretions of other endocrine glands of the body. So, it is called as master gland. Its secretions are controlled by hypothalamus.

(v) Adrenal gland produce adrenaline, which is the emergency hormone.

72. Study the diagram given below and answer the questions that follow

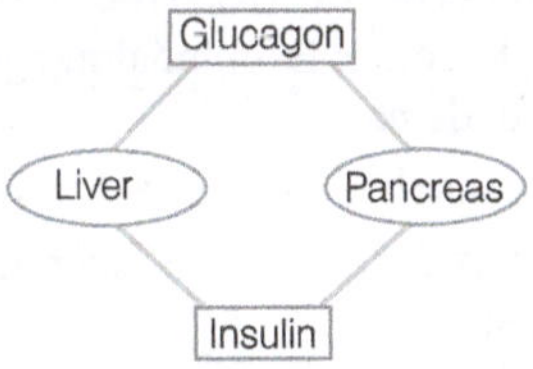

(i) Name the cells of the pancreas that produce
(a) glucagon (b) insulin

(ii) State the main function of
(a) glucagon
(b) insulin

(iii) Why is the pancreas referred to as an exo-endocrine gland?

(iv) Why is insulin not given orally but is injected into the body?

(v) What is the technical term for the cells of the pancreas that produce endocrine hormones?

(vi) Where in the body is the pancreas located?

ICSE 2011 (5M)

Ans. (i) Cells of the pancreas that produces given hormone are as follows
(a) **Glucagon** is produced by alpha cells.
(b) **Insulin** is produced by beta cells.

(ii) Main function of the following hormones is
(a) **Glucagon** It helps to convert glycogen to glucose when blood glucose level falls.
(b) **Insulin** It helps to convert excess amount of glucose to glycogen when there is high level of glucose in blood.

(iii) Refer to text on page no. 162.

(iv) **Insulin** is a protein by composition thus, if it is given orally it will get digested in the stomach and will not be able to perform its function.

(v) **Islets of Langerhans** are the cells of pancreas responsible for the production of endocrine hormones.

(vi) **Pancreas** is located in the abdomen between the loop of small intestine close to duodenum part.

73. Given below is an outline of the human body showing the important glands ICSE 2010 (5M)

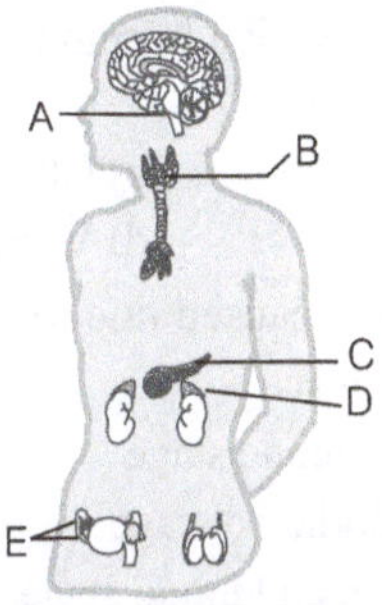

(i) Name the glands marked *A* to *E*.

(ii) Name the hormone secreted by *B* and give one important function of this hormone.

(iii) Name the endocrine cells present in part *C*.

(iv) Name the hormone secreted by part *D* and give one important function of this hormone.

Ans. (i) Different glands labelled from *A* to *E* are
A — Pituitary gland *B* — Thyroid gland
C — Pancreas *D* — Adrenal gland
E — Ovary

(ii) The hormone secreted by part '*B*' is thyroxine.
Function It helps in regulating the normal basal metabolism rate of the body.

(iii) The endocrine cells present in part '*C*' are Islets of Langerhans.

(iv) The hormone secreted by part '*D*' is adrenaline.
Function It prepares body for any emergency situation.

CHAPTER TEST

Section-A

01 Mark Questions

1 Select the correct answer to the question from the given options.

(i) Adrenal gland is cap-like structure situated above

(a) liver (b) anterior pituitary
(c) pancreas (d) kidney

(ii) Which disorder is caused due to hypersecretion of thyroid hormone?

(a) Myxoedema (b) Cretinism
(c) Simple goitre (d) Exophthalmic goitre

(iii) Which gland is called as master gland?

(a) Hypothalamus (b) Thyroid
(c) Pituitary (d) Adrenal

(iv) Deficiency of which hormone results in diabetes insipidus?

(a) Insulin (b) Glycogen
(c) Thyroxine (d) Vasopressin

(v) Acromegaly is caused due to hypersecretion of

(a) GH in adult stage
(b) GH in childhood stage
(c) FSH in childhood stage
(d) Prolactin in childhood stage

2 (i) Name the following.

(a) The hormone that releases glucose in bloodstream.
(b) The hormone produced by thyroid gland.
(c) The gland which produces hormone for emergency condition.
(d) The gland which is known as heterocrine gland.
(e) Cells of pancreas which release insulin hormone.

(ii) Arrange and rewrite the terms in each group in the correct order so as to be in a logical sequence beginning with the term that is underlined.

(a) <u>THRH</u>, Anterior pituitary, Thyroid gland, TSH, Thyroxine
(b) <u>Hypothalamus</u>, Pancreas, Pituitary gland, Adrenal gland
(c) <u>Fear</u>, Glucose release, Adrenaline, Adrenal gland
(d) <u>Low sugar</u>, High sugar, Glucagon, α-cells
(e) <u>Low water level</u>, ADH, Hypothalamus, Posterior pituitary

(iii) Match the items given in Column I with most appropriate ones in Column II and rewrite the correct matching pair.

Column I	Column II
A. Thirst	1. Oxytocin
B. Parturition	2. Insulin
C. β-cells	3. Ovary
D. FSH	4. Vasopressin/ADH
E. Heterocrine gland	5. Adrenal gland
	6. Glucagon
	7. Pancreas

(iv) Choose the odd one out from the following terms and name the category to which the others belong.

(a) Liver, Adrenal gland, Thyroid, Pituitary gland
(b) Pancreas, Insulin, Glucagon, Pituitary gland
(c) FSH, Prolactin, Oxytocin, ACTH, GH
(d) Simple goitre, Exophthalmic goitre, Cretinism, Myxoedema
(e) TSH, Insulin, Sweat, FSH, Prolactin

(v) State the exact location of secretion of following hormones.

(a) Insulin
(b) Gonadotrophic releasing hormone
(c) Oxytocin
(d) Adrenaline
(e) Thyroxine

02 Marks Questions

3 Give the differences between endocrine and exocrine gland.

4 Define endocrinology. Also mention who is considered as father of endocinology?

5 Explain the role of adrenaline and non- adrenaline.

6 Explain the types of feedback mechanism.

7 List the hormones secreted by pancreas with their functions.

03 Marks Questions

8 Give an example of negative feedback mechanism.

9 Why pancreas is called as heterocrine gland?

10 Write the differences between diabetes insipidus and diabetes mellitus.

11 Write the disorders caused by hypo and hyper secretion of thyroid gland with symptoms.

12 Expand the abbereviation.

(i) ACTH (iii) LH

(ii) TSH

Section-B

Diagram Based Questions

13 Study the diagram given below and answer the question that follows

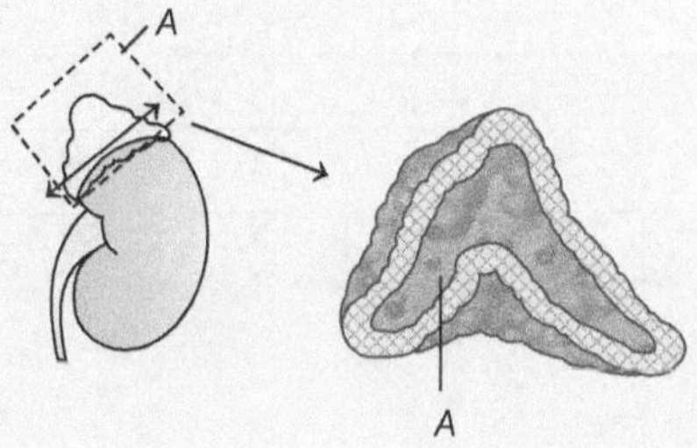

(i) What is shown in the above diagram ?

(ii) Part *A* is removed from a person, mention one condition with which person will suffer?

(iii) Mention the function of the gland shown.

14 Given below is the diagram of disorder caused due to malfunctioning of endocrine system.

(i) Identify the disorders.

(ii) Name the gland responsible for the above disorders.

(iii) Give reason for the causes of above disorders.

Answers

1. (i) (d), (ii) (d), (iii) (c), (iv) (b), (v) (a)

11 Reproductive System

TREND ANALYSIS 4 YEARS

Average No. of Questions Across all Sets

Topic	Types of Questions	2024	2023	2020	2019
TOPIC 01 Basics of Reproduction and Reproductive Organs	1 Mark	–	3	–	3
	2 Marks	–	1	–	–
	3 Marks	1	–	–	–
	4 Marks	–	–	–	–
	5 Marks	–	–	–	1
TOPIC 02 Post-fertilisation Changes	1 Mark	1	1	–	3
	2 Marks	–	1	–	1
	3 Marks	–	–	–	–
	4 Marks	–	–	–	–
	5 Marks	–	–	–	–

TOPIC 1

Basics of Reproduction and Reproductive Organs

Reproduction is the biological process by which organisms produce their offspring. It helps to maintain the continuity of life on Earth. Reproduction therefore, helps in the increase of population of the species. It transfers the characteristics of parents into their offspring. Humans are sexually reproducing **viviparous** (i.e. give birth to young ones) organisms.

They show prominent sexual dimorphism with male and female differing from each other by a number of primary and secondary sex characters.

Reproduction can be of following two major types

(i) **Asexual Reproduction** It is the type of reproduction which produces individuals without the involvement of gametes. It occurs in unicellular and lower organisms, e.g. *Amoeba*, *Paramecium*, *Hydra* and lower plants, etc.

(ii) **Sexual Reproduction** It is the type of reproduction which involves the fusion of gametes, i.e. sex cells of male and female to produce new cell called zygote. It multiplies mitotically to give rise to multicellular organisms like animals and higher plants.

Puberty

- is the process when the reproductive organs start maturing to become fully functional. They become capable of performing sexual reproduction to enable fertilisation.
- In both girls and boys, certain changes take place during this reproductive phase.
- These changes are the signals of sexual maturation and are known as **secondary sexual characters**.

Different Secondary Sexual Characters in Boys and Girls

In Boys	In Girls
Thickness of facial hair growth.	Breast size begins to increase.
Voice begins to crack.	Start of menstruation.
Penis occasionally begins to become enlarged and erect.	Darkening of nipple skin.

Human Reproduction

In human beings, reproduction occurs with the help of organs of the reproductive system. These organs are divided into following two main parts

(i) **Primary Reproductive Organs** These include the gonads of both males (testes) and females (ovaries). These are responsible for producing gametes, i.e. sperms (in males) and eggs (in females).

(ii) **Accessory Reproductive Organs** These include all the structures which help in the process of reproduction.

These parts have distinct roles from fertilisation to growth, development and birth of the baby.

Male Reproductive System

It is located in the pelvic region and comprises of following reproductive parts

Primary Sex Organs

The primary reproductive organs in males are testes where male gametes are produced.

Testes

- These are oval in shape and are found in a thin-walled sac of skin known as **scrotum**, outside the abdomen in order to escape from the high body temperature.
- This is because sperms mature at a temperature of around 2-3°C lower than the normal body temperature. Each testis is divided into 200-300 compartments called **testicular lobules.**
- There are about 250 testicular lobules present in each testis.

An individual lobule of testes contains

1. Seminiferous Tubules

- It is the site of sperm production. The process known as **spermatogenesis.**
- Each seminiferous tubule is lined on its inside by two types of highly specialised cells as given below
  - **Sertoli cells** (nurse cells)
  - **Male germ cells** (spermatogonia)
- The Sertoli cells are tall, pyramidal cells which provide nutrition to the developing germ cells.
- Germinal epithelial cells of seminiferous tubules multiply repeatedly and produce sperm cells.

2. Interstitial Cells (Leydig cells)

- These are the packing tissue found between the coils of the seminiferous tubules. They are responsible for the production of male sex hormone known as **testosterone.**
- Leydig cells are endocrine in function and thus, regulate and maintain male sex characteristics.

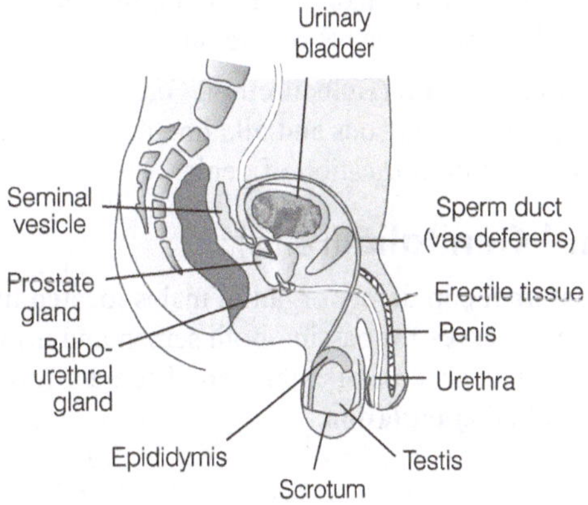

Fig. 11.1 Male reproductive system

Secondary Sex Organ

These are as follows

1. Accessory Duct System

- **Efferent ducts** Sperms after attaining maturity pass down into a small network of tubes which further gives rise to 12-14 ducts known as **efferent ducts.**
- **Epididymis** the efferent ducts join together to form a small tubular knot-like structure called epididymis.

- Sperms are stored inside the epididymis, till they get matured, acquire increased motility and fertilising capacity (i.e. **capacitation**).
- **Vas deferens** Epididymis is continued by the side of testis further giving rise to a highly coiled tube-like structure known as vas deferens.
  It allows the descent of testes from abdomen to scrotum along with their ducts, blood vessels, nerves, etc.
- **Urethra** The two sperm ducts loop over ureters of their side and join urethra (a median duct) at the back of the urinary bladder. It extends through the penis to its external opening called **urethral meatus**.

2. Accessory Glands

The three accessory glands in males are

(i) **Seminal Vesicles** These are a paired lobulated glands found between the posterior surface of urinary bladder and rectum (part of large intestine).

They are responsible for producing a milky fluid known as **semen**, which acts as a medium for transportation of sperms, i.e. it activates sperm inside the sperm duct.

(ii) **Prostate Gland** It is a bilobed structure found surrounding the urethra.

It secretes a white alkaline fluid into the semen to neutralise the acidic pH of vagina.

(iii) **Cowper's Gland** (Bulbourethral Gland) These glands secrete mucous and alkaline fluid into urethra which help in lubrication of penis.

External Genitalia (Penis)

It is the external copulatory organ in males located in front of scrotum. It serves for passing both semen and urine out of the body. The process of expulsion of semen from the urethra is called **ejaculation**.

Semen

The secretions of accessory sex glands and mucus are added to the sperms to form seminal fluid or semen or seminal plasma. These secretions provide medium for the transmission of sperms, give nourishment and activate sperms to keep them viable and motile.

Sperm

A mature sperm cell or spermatozoa is a microscopic, tadpole-shaped structure. It measures about 2.5-3.5 μm in diameter and 60 μm in length. It comprises of three main parts namely

(i) **Head** It is an oval-shaped flat structure. It is composed of a large **nucleus** which contains a genetic material (DNA) and a small cap-like structure known as **acrosome**.

The acrosome secretes an enzyme which facilitates the entry of sperm into the egg. It helps in dissolving the wall of egg cell.

(ii) **Middle Piece** It is cylindrical in shape and is known as power house of the sperm cell because it possess mitochondria that provide energy (in the form of ATP) to the sperm to swim into the female reproductive tract.

(iii) **Tail** It is a long, slender structure which acts as the locomotory organ of the sperm.

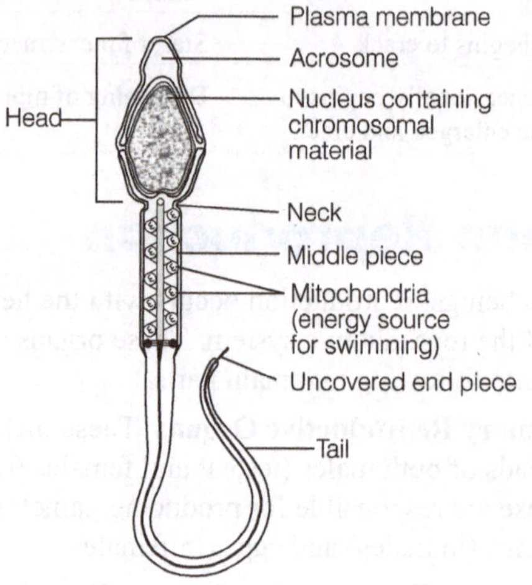

Fig. 11.2 Structure of sperm

Female Reproductive System

The reproductive system of females is comprised of following reproductive parts

Primary Sex Organ

This includes

Ovaries

- These are two small oval-shaped bodies, responsible for producing female gametes, i.e. **ova** (egg cells). These are located near kidneys and stay attached to the lower cavity of abdomen.
- In each ovary, normally one egg matures every month.
- **Oogenesis** is the process of production of mature ovum from the ova producing cells. **Ovulation** is the process in which Graafian follicle ruptures to release the egg cell from the ovary.

A mature egg is contained in a cellular sac-like structure known as **follicle**, which gets enlarged in size and becomes **Graafian follicle.**

The remaining part of Graafian follicle (after release of egg) persists for a short time, after which it gets converted into a yellow mass of endocrine tissue called **corpus luteum**. It is responsible for secreting hormones

(i) **Progesterone** which prepares uterus for pregnancy.

(ii) Oestrogen which is needed for puberty and breast development.

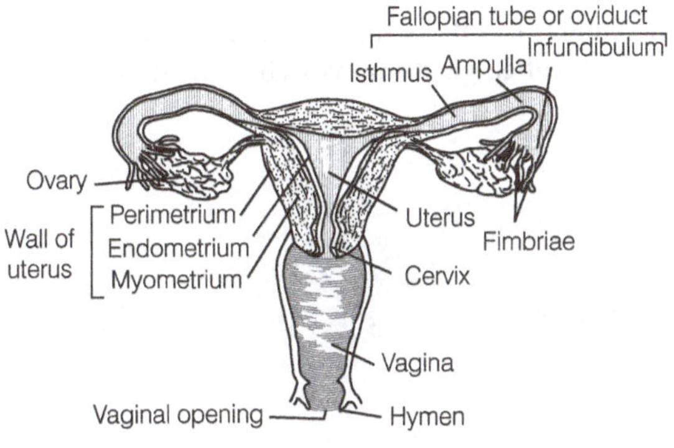

Fig. 11.3 Human female reproductive system

Secondary Sex Organs

These are as follows

1. Accessory Reproductive Structure

The accessory reproductive structures in females are

(i) **Oviducts** (Fallopian Tubes) These are two small tubes, around 10-12 cm long located on either sides of the uterus near the kidney. The cilia of **fimbriae** of oviducts funnel are responsible for picking up and pushing the released egg into the oviduct. At the same time a wave of muscular contraction helps in transporting egg into the uterus.

(ii) **Uterus** It is a hollow pear-shaped organ located in the pelvic cavity between the urinary bladder and rectum. It is also known as **womb** because it is the place where the development of embryo takes place.

(iii) **Vagina** It is a muscular tube-like structure meant to receive male penis during copulation and also acts as a passage for the baby during childbirth. The opening of vagina is normally covered by a membrane called **hymen**.

(iv) **Cervix** (Neck) It is the lower part of the uterus, which is very narrow. The sperms enter into the uterus through this part.

Accessory Glands

A pair of vestibular or **Bartholin's gland** occurs one on each side of the vaginal orifice, which moisten the vagina.

The **mammary** or **milk producing glands** (breast) are present in each normal female. These are responsible for the secretion of milk.

External Genitalia (Vulva)

These include mons pubis, labia majora, labia minora and clitoris.

Menstrual Cycle

It is a series of changes occurring in the wall of uterus (endometrium) of human females that prepares the uterus to receive a fertilised egg.

The first menstruation begins at puberty, i.e. at an age of around 12-13 years known as **menarche** and continues till the age of 40-45 years known as **menopause**.

This complete period from menarche to menopause is known as the **reproductive period** in females.

This period is marked by a characteristic event repeated every month in the form of menstrual flow. It continues from the day of the onset of the flow to the next onset, i.e. after around 27-28 days.

Phases of Menstrual Cycle

The complete period of menstrual cycle is divided into following four main phases

(i) **Menstrual Phase** This is the period that lasts for around 3-5 days. Periodic discharge of blood is seen during this phase due to the shedding of the uterine wall. It is followed by the formation of a new egg in a follicle.

(ii) **Follicular Phase** It lasts for around 5-12 days. This is the period in which secondary follicle changes into Graafian follicle, (as the follicle grows) and again reactivate the wall of uterus (to become thickened and supplied with lot of blood vessels) by producing hormone called **oestrogen**.

(iii) **Ovulatory Phase** In this period, the rupture of Graafian follicle occurs releasing the egg to travel down the oviduct. It occurs on about 13-14th day of the menstrual cycle.

(iv) **Luteal Phase** It continues for around 15-28 days. During this phase uterus lining gets thickened and the remaining part of the Graafian follicle transforms into the corpus luteum an endocrine gland/tissue that produces **progesterone** hormone.

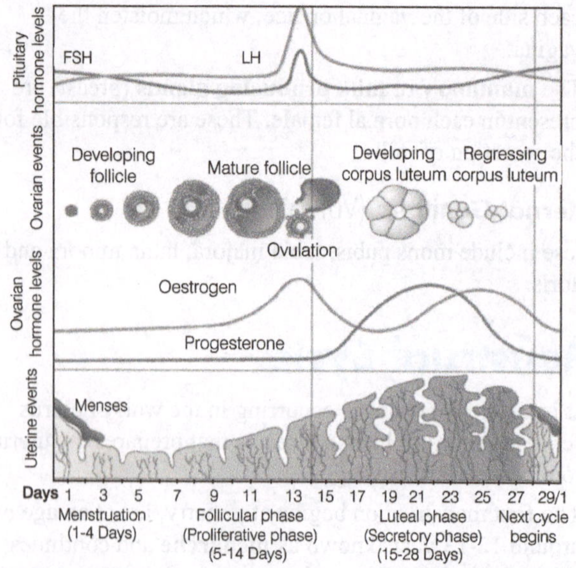

Fig. 11.4 Uterine changes in relation to follicle changes during menstrual cycle

- If there is no fertilisation during this period, the uterus lining again starts shedding on the 28th day.
- If the egg gets fertilised, it gets fixed in the uterus and there will be no menstrual flow because the level of progesterone (hormone secreted by corpus luteum) increases. This further prevents the growth and maturation of another follicle.

Ovum (Egg)

- It is microscopic about 100-130 μm in diameter. It is the female non-motile gamete having the genetic material in the nucleus.
- The ovum possesses three coverings, i.e. inner plasma membrane, oolemma, middle **zona pellucida** and outer cellular **corona radiata**.
- The cytoplasm of ovum is called **ooplasm**. Ovum is alecithal (i.e. yolk is absent) and contains a large haploid nucleus called **germinal vesicle** or **pronucleus.**

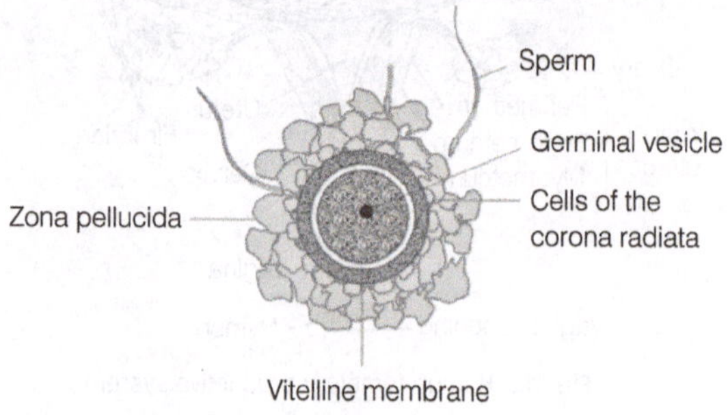

Fig. 11.5 Ovum surrounded by few sperms

- As soon as one sperm enters the ovum (egg), the entry of other sperms is prevented by some chemical barriers.

PYQs Previous Years' Questions

1 Mark Questions

Multiple Choice Questions

1. On which day of the menstrual cycle does ovulation take place? **ICSE Specimen 2023, 2019**
   (a) 1st day (b) 5th day (c) 14th day (d) 28th day

Ans. (c) 14th day

2. Gestation period of human foetus is **ICSE Specimen 2023**
   (a) 40 days (b) 280 days
   (c) 280 weeks (d) 40 months

Ans. (b) 280 days

3. The part that is cut in vasectomy is **ICSE Specimen 2019**
   (a) urethra (b) oviduct
   (c) Fallopian tube (d) vas deferens

Ans. (d) vas deferens

4. Which of the following is not a part of the female reproductive system in human beings? **ICSE Specimen 2017**
   (a) Uterus (b) Ovary
   (c) Ureter (d) Fallopian tube

Ans. (c) Ureter

5. Ovulation occurs **ICSE Specimen 2017**
   (a) at the beginning of menstrual cycle
   (b) in the mid of the menstrual cycle
   (c) at the end of the menstrual cycle
   (d) during any time of the menstrual cycle

Ans. (b) in the mid of the menstrual cycle

6. The site of maturation of human sperms is the ICSE 2014

(a) seminiferous tubule (b) interstitial cells
(c) epididymis (d) prostate gland

Ans. (c) epididymis

7. Given below is the question followed by four choices. Select and rewrite the correct answer to the given statement from four choices given below.

The onset of menstruation in the female is termed as ICSE 2009

(a) ovulation (b) menarche
(c) menopause (d) parthenogenesis

Ans. (b) menarche

Very Short Answer Type Questions

8. Name the following

The permanent stoppage of menstruation in human females around the age of 45 years. ICSE 2023, 2015

Ans. Menopause

9. Arrange and rewrite the terms in each group in the correct order so as to be in a logical sequence beginning with the term that is underlined.

Testis, Urethra, Sperm duct, Epididymis ICSE 2023

Ans. Testis, Epididymis, Sperm duct, Urethra

10. Choose the **odd one out** from the following terms and name the **category** to which the others belong.

Menstrual phase, Telophase, Follicular phase, Luteal phase ICSE 2023

Ans. **Odd term** Telophase

Category Others are stages of menstrual cycle.

11. Mention the exact location of prostate gland. ICSE Specimen 2023, 2017, 2012

Ans. **Prostate gland** It is found in between the urinary bladder and the point where sperm ducts join the urethra.

12. Mention the exact location of testes. ICSE 2019

Ans. Testes are found in a thin-walled sac called scrotum, outside the abdomen in order to escape from high body temperature.

13. State the main functions of seminal vesicles. ICSE 2019

Ans. Seminal vesicles are responsible for producing a milky fluid known as seminal fluid, which acts as a medium for transportation of sperms.

14. Choose the **odd one out** from the given term and name the **category** to which the others belong.
Example Nose, Tongue, Arm, Eye

Answer Odd term-Arm, **Category** - Other are sense organs.
Prostate gland, Cowper's gland, Seminal vesicle, Seminiferous tubules ICSE 2018

Ans. **Odd term** Seminiferous tubules

Category Others are accessory glands of male reproductive system.

15. Mention the exact location of epididymis. ICSE 2018

Ans. Epididymis is a highly coiled structure that lies closely attached to the testis of its side in the scrotal sac.

16. Give appropriate biological or technical terms for

'The onset of menstruation in a young girl'. ICSE 2018, 2013, 2008

Ans. Menarche.

17. Differentiate between the pair on the basis of what is indicated in bracket.

Testosterone and oestrogen (Organ which secretes) ICSE 2018

Ans. Testosterone is secreted by testis, while oestrogen is secreted by ovary.

18. The statement given below is incorrect. Rewrite the correct statement by changing the underlined words of the statement. The Graafian follicle, after ovulation, turns into a hormone producing tissue called corpus callosum. ICSE 2017

Ans. The Graafian follicle, after ovulation, turns into a hormone producing tissue called corpus luteum.
Corpus callosum is a large bundle of myelinated fibres which connects the right and left hemisphere of cerebrum.

19. Give appropriate biological/technical term for

'The accessory gland in human males whose secretion activates the sperms.' ICSE 2017

Ans. Seminal vesicle

20. Differentiate between the pair on the basis of what is mentioned within bracket.

Sperm duct and Fallopian tube (Function) ICSE 2016

Ans. **Sperm duct** It carriers sperms from testis to seminal vesicle.

Fallopian tube Union of male and female gametes takes place in this tube.

21. Give scientific reasons for

'When an ovum gets fertilised, menstrual cycle stops temporarily in a woman.' **ICSE 2016**

Ans. Fertilisation leads to pregnancy in human female. The fertilised egg gets fixed in the uterus and there will be no menstrual flow because the level of progesterone (hormone secreted by corpus luteum) increases (preventing the growth and maturation of another follicle).

22. Given below is an example of a certain structure and its special functional activity. On a similar pattern fill in the blank with suitable function.
Example: Chloroplast and Photosynthesis

Seminiferous tubule and .... **ICSE 2015**

Ans. Sperm production

23. Differentiate between the following on the basis of what is mentioned within brackets.

Corpus callosum and corpus luteum (Function) **ICSE 2014**

Ans. **Corpus luteum** is the remain of Graafian follicle which secretes female sex hormones, e.g. progesterone.

Corpus callosum is the region that connects the left and right cerebral hemisphere of forebrain.

24. State the exact location of seminal vesicle. **ICSE 2014**

Ans. Seminal vesicle is found between the urinary bladder and rectum in males.

25. Select the **odd one out** of the following terms given below. And also write the category for remaining terms. **ICSE 2014**

Cowper's gland, Urethral gland, Lacrimal gland, Seminal vesicles, Prostate gland.

Ans.

Odd one	Category
Lacrimal gland	All others are the parts of male reproductive system.

26. State the main function of a sperm duct.

Ans. Sperm duct is responsible for transmitting sperm from epididymis to the penis for discharge.

27. State the main function of seminiferous tubule. **ICSE 2012**

Ans. Seminiferous tubule in males is responsible for the production of sperms.

28. Given below is the set with four terms in which one term is an odd one and cannot be grouped in the same category to which the other three belongs. Identify the odd one in the set and name the category to which the remaining three belong.

Ovary, Ureter, Fallopian tube and Uterus. **ICSE 2012, 2000**

Ans.

Odd one	Category
Ureter	All others are the parts of female reproductive system.

29. Give the biological/technical term for the phase in the menstrual cycle in which the remnant of follicle in the ovary turns to corpus luteum. **ICSE 2012**

Ans. **Luteal phase** is the phase in the menstrual cycle in which the remnant of follicle turns to corpus luteum in the ovary which produce hormone progesterone.

30. Name the cells of the testes that produce male hormones. **ICSE 2011**

Ans. **Interstitial cells** (Leydig cells) are the cells that produce male hormones.

31. Name the place where fertilisation occurs in the female reproductive system. **ICSE 2010**

Ans. Fertilisation occurs in the Fallopian tube of the female reproductive system.

32. Given below is the set of five terms. Rewrite the terms in logical sequences as directed at the end of each statement.

Vagina, Ovary, Uterus, Oviduct, Cervix. (Pathway of egg after ovulation) **ICSE 2010**

Ans. The logical sequence is
Ovary, Oviduct, Uterus, Cervix and Vagina.

33. Given below is the set of five terms. Without changing the first term rearrange the remaining four, so as to be in logical sequence as per the directions given in the bracket. Seminiferous tubule, penis, urethra, epididymis, vas deferens.(course of passage of sperms in man) **ICSE 2008**

Ans. Sequence of direction for the course of passage of sperm in man is
Seminiferous tubule → Epididymis → Vas deferens → Urethra → Penis.

34. Given below are the particular structures. Write their special functional activity.

(i) Corpus luteum and .... **ICSE 2008, 2000**

(ii) Seminal vesicle and ....

Ans. (i) Corpus luteum and progesterone,

(ii) Seminal vesicle and production of semen, a milky fluid.

35. Name the organ or structure that produce testosterone. **ICSE 2007**

Ans. Interstitial cells of testes produce testosterone.

36. Given below is a set of term in logical sequence, representing a process of a function of these, one term is incorrect. Identify the incorrect term and replace it with the correct term. **ICSE 2007**

Seminiferous tubule → Sperm → Sperm duct → Accessory glands → Semen→ Ureter.

Ans. **Incorrect term** Ureter

Correct term Penis

37. State whether the following statement is true or false. If false, write the correct statement by changing first word only.

Testosterone is an androgen. **ICSE 2006**

Ans. The statement is true.

38. Give the exact location and one function of the following structures. Seminiferous tubules **ICSE 2006**

Ans. **Seminiferous tubules** are located inside the testes.

Function of seminiferous tubule is to produce sperms.

39. Given below is the set of terms, in given case, arrange and rewrite set of terms, so as to be in logical sequence. Graafian follicle, Ostium, Ovum, Uterus, Fallopian tube. **ICSE 2005**

Ans. The logical sequence in the set is
Ostium, Graafian follicle, Ovum, Fallopian tube, Uterus.

40. Name the canal through which testes descend into the scrotum just before birth in a human male child. **ICSE 2004**

Ans. Inguinal canal is the canal through which the testes descend into the scrotum just before the birth in a human male child.

41. Give one point difference between the following pairs on the basis of what is indicated in bracket.
Prostate gland and Cowper's gland (The nature of secretion). **ICSE 2004**

Ans.

Prostate gland	Cowper's gland
Type of accessory gland that secretes a white alkaline fluid into semen to neutralise acidic pH of vagina.	Another type of accessory gland that secrete mucus and alkaline fluid into urethra which helps in lubrication of penis.

42. Given below are the terms. Rewrite the terms in the correct order, so as to be in logical sequance. Luteal phase, Follicular phase, Menstrual phase, Ovulatory phase. **ICSE 2004**

Ans. Logical sequence of phase of menstrual cycle is Menstrual phase, follicular phase, ovulatory phase, luteal phase.

2 Marks Questions

43. What is the significance of the human testes being located in scrotal sacs outside the abdomen? **ICSE 2023**

Ans. The presence of testes outside the abdominal cavity in the scrotum keeps the temperature of testes 2-3 degrees Celsius below the temperature of the body which is important for the production of sperm.

44. Arrange and rewrite the terms in each group in the correct order so as to be in logical sequence beginning with the term that is underlined.
Sperm, Urethra, Sperm duct, Epididymis **ICSE Specimen 2023**

Ans. Sperm, Epididymis, Sperm duct, Urethra.

45. State whether the following statement are true or false. If false, rewrite the correct form of the statement by changing the first word only.

Tubectomy is surgical method of sterilisation in man. **ICSE Specimen 2023, 2017**

Ans. False, vasectomy is surgical method of sterilisation in man.

46. Name the following.

The part of ovary that produces progesterone. **ICSE Specimen 2023, 2017**

Ans. Corpus luteum

47. State the exact location of the following.

(i) Acrosome

(ii) Amnion **ICSE Specimen 2019**

Ans. (i) Acrosome is located in the head region of sperm.

(ii) Amnion is located in uterus around the embryo.

48. Given below are the five sets of terms. In each case arrange and rewrite each set so as to be in a logical sequence. One is done as an example for you

Example Large intestine, Stomach, Mouth, Small intestine, Oesophagus.

Mouth, oesophagus, stomach, small intestine, large intestine.

(i) Graafian follicle, Uterus, Cervical funnel, Fallopian tube, Ovum

(ii) Vagina, Sperm, Uterus, Oviduct, Cervix

ICSE Specimen 2019, 2016

Ans. (i) Ovum → Graafian follicle → Oviducal funnel → Fallopian tube → Uterus.

(ii) Sperm → Vagina → Cervix → Uterus → Oviduct.

49. State the main function of the following.

(i) Leydig cells (ii) Corpus luteum **ICSE 2016**

Ans. (i) **Leydig cells**–Produce testosterone (The male hormone).

(ii) **Corpus luteum**–Produces and secretes progesterone (The female hormone).

50. Give the biological/technical term for the following.

(i) Complete stoppage of menstrual cycle in females.

(ii) The canal through which the testes descend into the scrotum just before the birth of a male baby.

Ans. (i) Menopause **ICSE 2016**

(ii) Inguinal canal

> **Concept Enhancer** Menopause is caused by the loss of ovarian follicular function and a decline in circulating blood oestrogen levels. Usually females who are above 45 years of age attain menopause.

51. Give the technical term for the following.

(i) Thin-walled sac of skin that covers the testes.

(ii) The permanent stoppage of the menstrual cycle in a woman aged 50 years. **ICSE 2016**

Ans. (i) Scrotum is the thin-walled sac of skin that covers testes.

(ii) Menopause is the permanent stoppage of menstrual cycle in a women at aged 50 years.

Diagram Based Questions

52. The diagram given below shows a section of the human ovary. **ICSE 2024 (3M)**

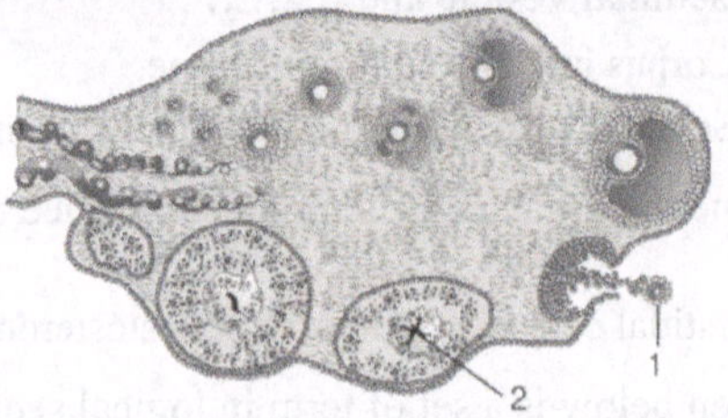

(i) Name the process for the release of the part labelled 1.

(ii) Write the name of the structure marked 2.

Ans. (i) The process is called ovulation.

(ii) The structure marked 2 is corpus luteum.

53. The diagram given below represents a system in the human body. Study the diagram and answer the following questions.

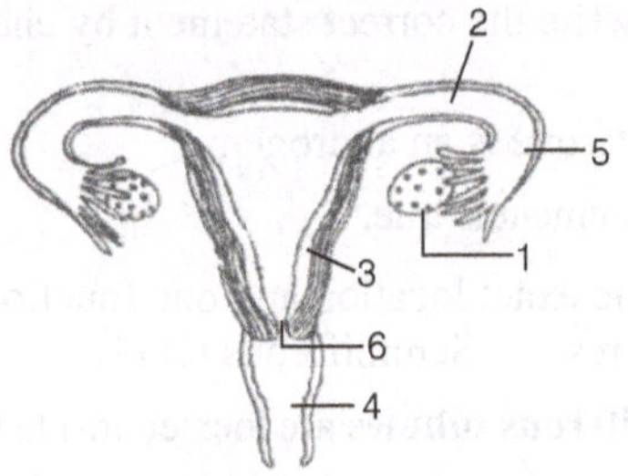

(i) Identify the system.

(ii) Label the parts marked as 5 and 6.

(iii) Name the two hormones secreted by 1.

(iv) Mention the number and the name of the part involved in fertilisation and implantation from the above diagram.

(v) Mention the surgical methods of contraception in

1. Human males

2. Human females **ICSE 2019 (5M)**

Ans. (i) Female reproductive system.

(ii) Part 5- Funnel of oviduct.

Part 6 - Cervix.

(iii) Progesterone, oestrogen.

(iv) Part -2 Fertilisation in Fallopian tube.

Part -3 Implantation occurs in uterus.

(v) **Vasectomy** is a surgical procedure for male contraception.

Tubectomy is a surgical method for female contraception.

54. Given below is the diagram of the male reproductive system and its associated parts in the human body. Study the diagram and answer the questions that follow. **ICSE Specimen 2019 (5M)**

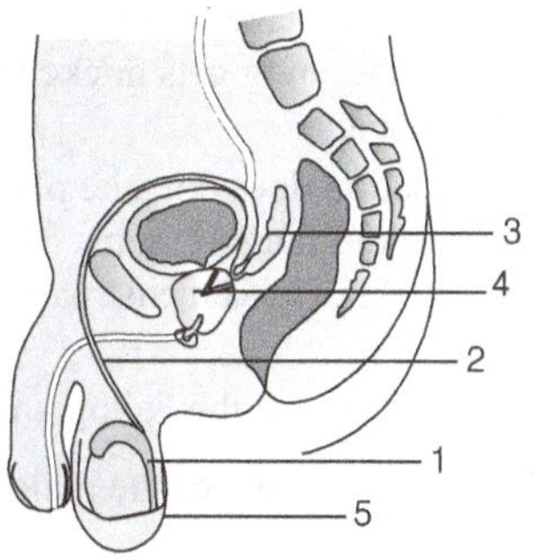

(i) Name the parts labelled as 3-5.

(ii) State the function of the part marked as 2 and 3.

(iii) What is the significance of the part labelled as 5?

(iv) Mention the hormone secreted by the part labelled as 1.

(v) Draw a neat and labelled diagram of a human sperm.

Ans. (i) 3-Seminal vesicles
4-Prostate gland
5-Scrotum

(ii) 2 is vas deferens that carries the sperms.
3 is seminal vesicle, its secretions serve as medium for the transportation of sperms.

(iii) Part labelled as 5 is scrotum sac.
Significance scrotal sac act as thermoregulator. The temperature in scrotal sac remains 2-3°C lower than that of body temperature which is suitable for maturation of sperm.

(iv) Testosterone.

(v)

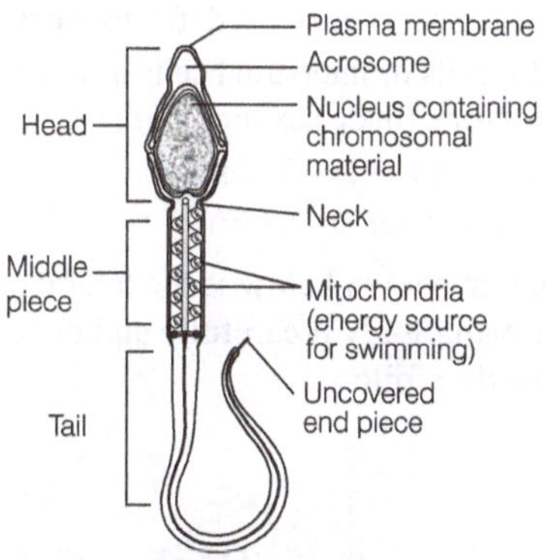

55. The diagram shown is the longitudinal section of a testis of man. Study it carefully and answer the questions that follows.

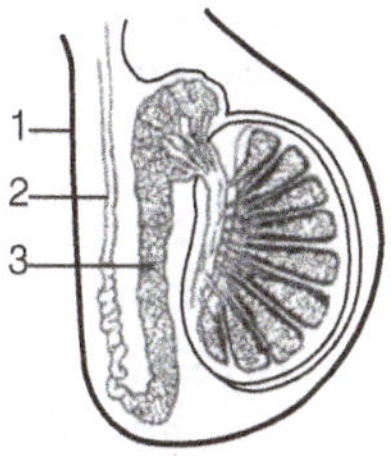

(i) Label the parts numbered 1 to 3 in the diagram.

(ii) In which part of the testis are the sperms produced?

(iii) State the functions of the parts labelled 1 and 3 in the diagram.

(iv) Name the cells that secrete testosterone.

(v) Draw a neat, labelled diagram of a sperm. **ICSE 2017 (5M)**

Ans. (i) 1 – Scrotum.
2 – Sperm duct (vas deferens).
3 – Epididymis.

(ii) Sperms are produced in seminiferous tubules.

(iii) 1 (Scrotum) It provides optimal temperature for developing sperms.
2 (Sperm duct) It carries sperms.
3 (Epididymis) Sperms are stored in epididymis, till they get matured and become motile.

(iv) **Interstitial cells** (Leydig's cells) secrete testosterone.

(v) Refer to answer no. 54 (v)

56. The diagram shown is the male urinogenital system of a human being. Study the diagram and answer the questions that follow.

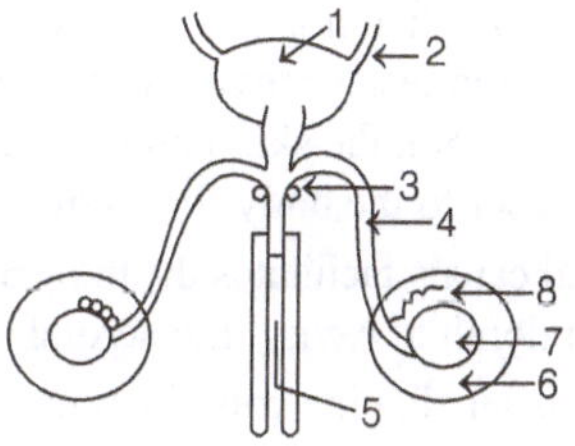

(i) Label the parts numbered 1 to 8.

(ii) Name the corresponding structure of part 4 in female reproductive system.

(iii) What is the role of part 7? **ICSE 2015 (3M)**

Ans. (i) 1 - Urinary bladder 2 - Ureter
3 - Prostate gland 4 - Vas deferens
5 - Urethra 6 - Scrotum
7 - Testis 8 - Epididymis

(ii) Fallopian tube

(iii) The testis forms the important part of male reproductive organ. It is responsible for the sperm formation and testosterone production.

57. Given below is a diagram of the lateral section of a testis of a man. Study the same and answer the questions that follow.

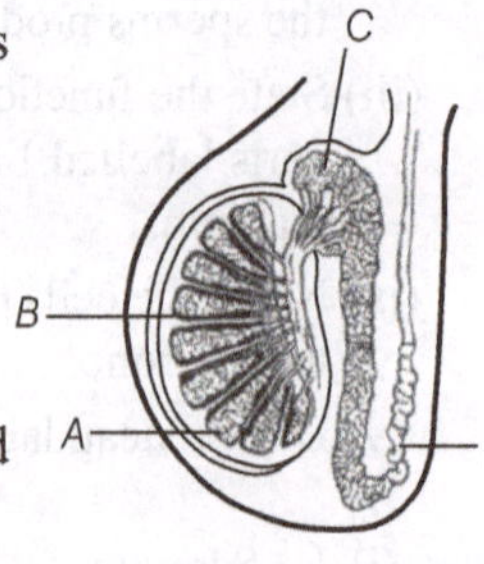

(i) Label the parts labelled as *A* and *B* in the diagram.

(ii) State the functions of the parts labelled as *A* and *C*.

(iii) What is the significance of the testes being located in the scrotal sac outside the abdomen?

(iv) What is the role played by the inguinal canal?

(v) What is semen? **ICSE 2013 (5M)**

Ans. (i) Parts labelled as *A* and *B* are

A – Seminiferous tubule. *B* – Testicular lobes.

(ii) **Function of Part *A*** (Seminiferous tubules) The cells of seminiferous tubules keep on dividing and produce sperms by the process called spermatogenesis.

Function of Part *C* (Epididymis) It helps in transportation of sperms from seminiferous tubules into vas deferens and it also helps the sperm to attain maturity.

(iii) Testes are located in scrotal sac because it provides 2-3°C less temperature than the normal body temperature, which is required for the maturation of sperms. So, when it is too hot the skin of scrotal sac get loose and testes move away from the body. When it is cold, the skin contracts and the testes move closer to the body for warmth.

(iv) Inguinal canals facilitates the movement of testis from abdominal cavity into scrotal sac or *vice-versa*.

(v) Semen is an alkaline combination of sperms and seminal fluid.

58. Study the diagram given below and answer the questions that follow.

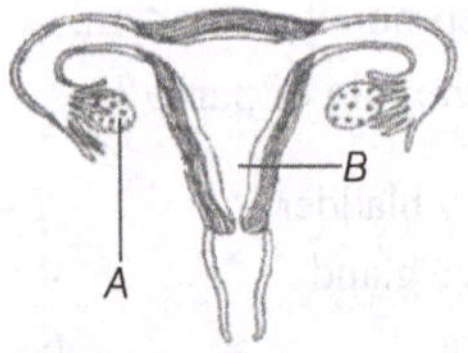

(i) Name the part labelled *A*. Name any two hormones produced by the labelled part *A*.

(ii) What happens to the part labelled as *B*,

(a) If fertilisation takes place?

(b) If fertilisation does not take place?

(iii) Where does fertilisation occur? **ICSE 2012 (5M)**

Ans. (i) Part *A* – Ovary

Two hormones produced by ovary are

(a) Oestrogen (b) Progesterone

(ii) (a) If fertilisation takes place, part *B*, (uterus) gets prepared to receive the embryo. The endometrial lining gets thickened and highly vascularised.

(b) If fertilisation does not take place in part *B*; the endometrial lining of uterus erodes out causing bleeding, known as menstruation or menstrual flow.

(iii) Fertilisation occurs in the Fallopian tube/oviduct.

59. Given below is the outline of the male reproductive system.

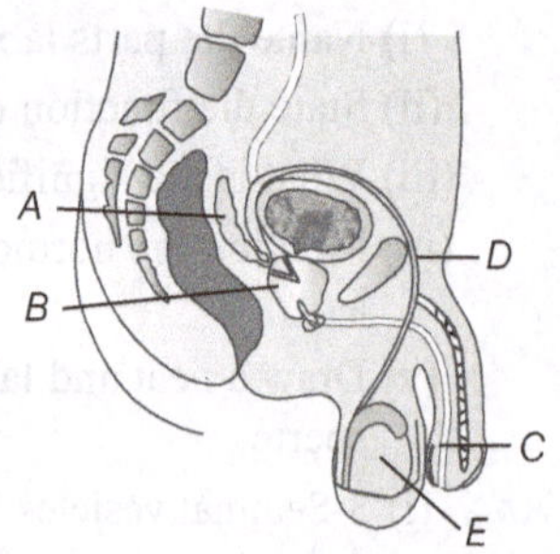

(i) Name the parts labelled as *A* to *E*.

(ii) State the functions of the parts labelled as *A* and *D*.

(iii) Name the cells of part *E* that produce testosterone.

(iv) Why is the structure *E* present outside the body in the scrotal sacs?

(v) What is semen? **ICSE 2010 (5M)**

Ans. (i) Parts labelled from *A* to *E* are as follows

A – Seminal vesicle *B* – Prostate gland

C – Urethra *D* – Sperm duct/vas deferens

E – Testis

(ii) Functions of different labelled parts are as follows

Part *A* : Secretion of seminal vesicle serves as a medium for the transportation of the sperms.

Part *D* : Sperm duct/vas deferens carry the sperms.

(iii) Leydig cells or interstitial cells of testis, produce testosterone (male sex hormone).

(iv) Refer to answer no. 57 (iii).

(v) Refer to answer no. 57 (v).

60. The diagram shown below is the lateral section of a testis of man. Study it carefully and answer the questions that follow.

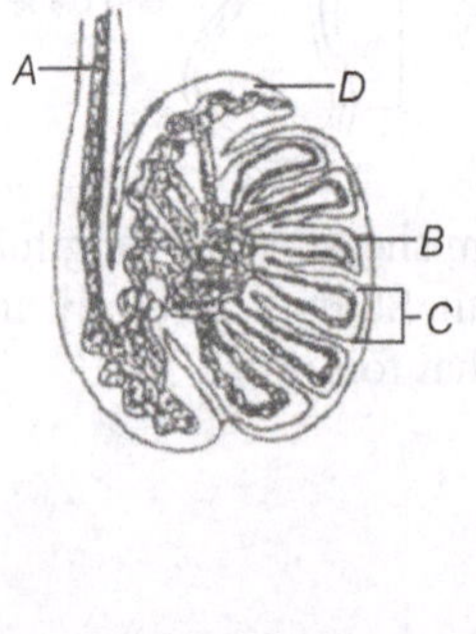

(i) Label the parts *A* to *D* of the diagram.

(ii) State the functions of the parts labelled as *A* and *B*.

(iii) Draw a labelled diagram of a sperm. **3M ICSE 2005**

Ans. (i) Parts *A* to *D* are as follows

A – Vas deferens

B – Seminiferous tubules

C – Lobule/segment

D – Epididymis

(ii) Functions of different parts are

A – **Vas deferens**. It passes the sperms from testes to penis.

B – **Seminiferous tubules**. It is responsible for the production of sperms (Spermatogenesis).

(iii) Refer to answer no. 54 (v).

61. Given below is the outline of the cross-section of the male reproductive system.

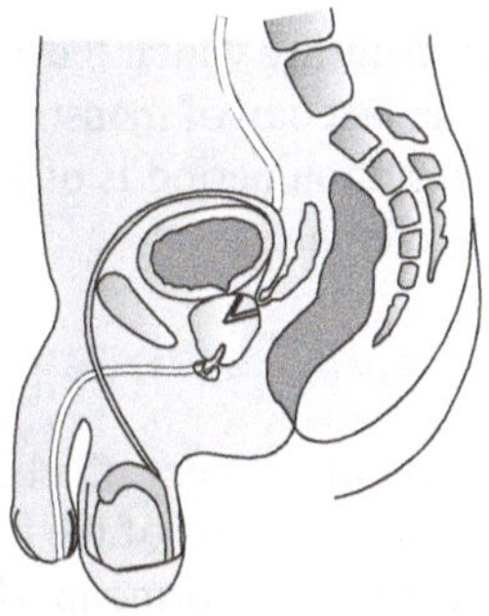

(i) Copy the outline on to your answer sheet in pencil and label the following parts– testis, epididymis, seminal vesicles, vas deferens.

(ii) Name the hormone produced by the testis.

(iii) Why are sperms produced in large numbers?

(iv) State the function of the seminal vesicles.

ICSE 2003 (4M)

Ans. (i) Different parts in the diagram are labelled as

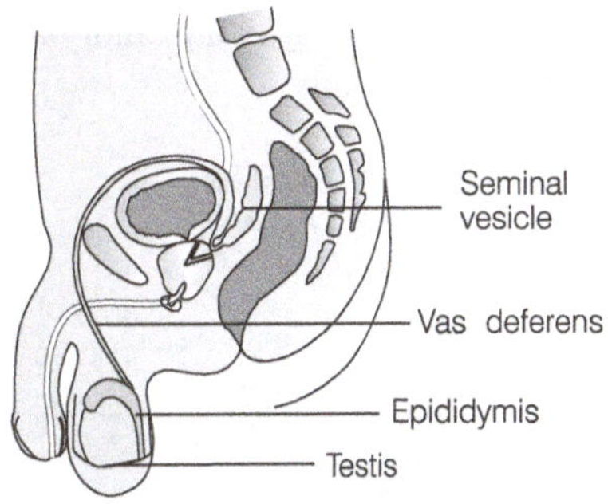

(ii) The hormone produced by testis is testosterone.

(iii) Sperms are produced in large numbers in order to ensure the fertilisation of the ovum.
Since, there are many obstacles like pH of vagina or short lifespan of sperm which restrict the fertilisation of egg and sperm. Production of sperms in large numbers is a natural process of ensuring fertilisation.

(iv) They are responsible for producing milky fluid known as semen.

TOPIC 2
Post-fertilisation Changes

Fertilisation

- It is the process of fusion of male gamete (sperm) and the female gamete (ovum) to produce a zygote. Process of fertilisation takes place in the Fallopian tubes of female reproductive organs.
- During copulation, the sperms are released by the male through penis into the vagina (near the cervix of the uterus) of the female. It is called **insemination**.
- Out of millions of sperms released, only few are able to climb to the upper parts of the oviducts, rest of them die on their way and get absorbed.
- The most active and motile sperm enters the uterus and reaches the Fallopian tube to fertilise the egg. In doing so, the tail is left outside and only the head part that contains nucleus enters the egg.

Implantation

- It is the phenomenon of attachment of developing embryo within the uterus. It leads to the state of pregnancy.
- The embryo continues to develop in the uterus and by the end of five weeks of pregnancy, its heart and circulatory system gets functional.

From seven weeks of gestation and onwards, the embryo is called **foetus**, as it looks like a baby.

Placenta

It is a disc-shaped organ, formed inside the female body attached to the uterine wall. It gives nutritive support to the developing embryo through a cord known as umbilical cord. It contains blood vessels which connect the placenta to the uterus through which a growing embryo or foetus gets its nutrition and O_2 supply.

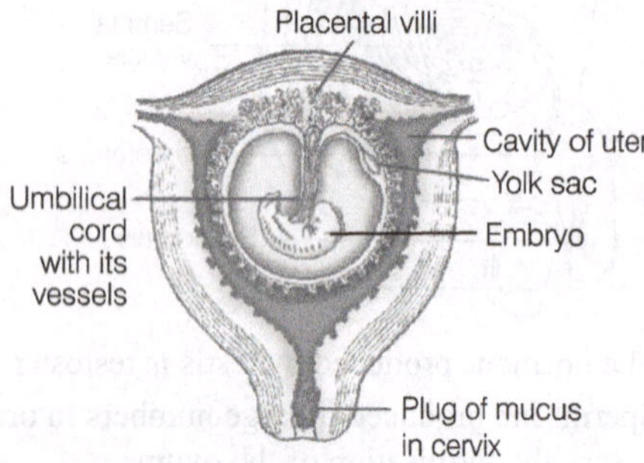

Fig. 11.6 The human foetus within the uterus

Placenta in human female performs the following main functions

Allows diffusion of substances such as O_2, nutrients, antibodies, minerals, etc. from mother to foetus.

Allows diffusion of waste products (excreted by foetus) such as urea, CO_2 and other waste products, into mother's body for elimination.

Prevents the entry of germs and other infectious agents that might enter into the foetus body through maternal blood.

Acts as an endocrine gland by producing certain hormones needed for embryonic development. It produces hormones like oestrogen and progesterone. These hormones help to maintain the pregnancy. The presence of progesterone in urine confirms pregnancy.

Foetal Membranes

The foetal membranes are called extraembryonic membranes because they are not a part of the body of the embryo. These include

(i) **Amnion** It is thin, double layered membranous structure enclosing an embryo. The space between the amnion and foetus in the embryo is filled with the amniotic fluid. This fluid helps in protecting embryo from mechanical shocks and physical damage. Fluid also allows only restricted movements of foetus and prevents the sticking of foetus to the amnion.

(ii) **Allantois** It is a tiny sausage-shaped pouch, which arises from the gut of the embryo near the yolk sac. It supplies the blood vessels to the placenta and is involved in nutrition and excretion.

(iii) **Chorion** It completely encloses the developing embryo and extraembryonic tissues. The chorion facilitates the transfer of nutrients, gases and wastes between the embryo and the mother's body.

(iv) **Yolk Sac** It is a membrane that surrounds the yolk. It is the first extraembryonic membrane to make appearance in mammal, but gets reabsorbed before the embryo is formed.

Gestation

It is the time period during which the embryo remains in the uterus (after the last day of menstruation to the day of childbirth). The gestation period is of about 9 months or 280 days in human females.

Parturition (Childbirth)

It is the phenomenon of delivery of a baby which occurs due to the vigrous contractions of the uterus at the end of pregnancy. **Oxytocin** is the hormone which is responsible for these contractions in human female resulting into the childbirth.

Twins

These are the offsprings produced by same pregnancy. Twins can be of two main types

1. Fraternal Twins (Produced From Two Eggs)

These are the twins produced when two eggs released from ovaries at a time get fertilised to produce two individuals. These twins may be either **both boys** or **both girls** or can be **one boy** and **one girl**.

Fraternal twins in all respects are like the normal sisters and brothers, but they are of the same age having been born within a few minutes of each other. This is the most common type of twins found.

- These twins are biologically known as **diovular** (means produced from two ova) or **dizygotic** (meaning produced from two zygotes, i.e. two fertilised eggs).

2. Identical Twins (Produced From One Egg)

- These are produced when a single fertilised egg, get splitted and separated into two parts during early stage of cell division.
- Each of these two split parts then behaves like an independent egg and produces one complete individual each.
- Identical twins being produced from a single egg, can either be **both boys** or **both girls**. Thus, they are very similar (identical) to each other except for certain things which are dissimilar, such as fingerprints, birth marks and even hand writings.

PYQs Previous Years' Questions

1 Mark Questions

Multiple Choice Question

1. Choose the correct answer to the following statement out of the choices given after statement.

   The technical term for the fertilised egg is **ICSE 2010**

   (a) placenta (b) zygote
   (c) morula (d) blastula

Ans. (b) zygote

Very Short Answer Type Questions

2. Name the following.
   The process of attachment of fertilised ovum to the wall of uterus. **ICSE 2024**

Ans. Implantation.

3. Mention the exact location of the amniotic fluid. **ICSE 2023, 2019**

Ans. **Amnion** is thin, double-layered membranous structure enclosing an embryo. The space between the amnion and foetus in the embryo is filled with the amniotic fluid.

4. Name the structure which connects the placenta and the foetus. **ICSE 2019, 2013**

Ans. Umbilical cord

5. Correct and rewrite the statement given below by changing the biological term that is underlined.

   The protective sac which develops around the developing embryo is called the pericardium. **ICSE 2019**

Ans. Amnion

6. Give appropriate biological or technical term for

   'The fluid which surrounds the foetus.' **ICSE 2018**

Ans. Amniotic fluid

7. Give biological explanations for

   'The placenta is an important structure for the development of a foetus.' **ICSE 2018**

Ans. Placenta is a disc-shaped organ formed inside the female body, which remains attached to the uterine wall. It gives nutritive support to the developing embryo through a cord known as **umbilical cord**. It contains blood vessels which connect the placenta to the uterus through which a growing embryo or foetus gets its nutrition and O_2 supply.

8. Given below are the sets of five terms each. Rewrite the terms in correct order in a logical sequence.

   Example Large intestine, Stomach, Mouth, Small intestine, Oesophagus.

   Answer Mouth → Oesophagus → Stomach → Small intestine → Large intestine.

   Uterus, Parturition, Fertilisation, Gestation, Implantation. **ICSE 2017**

Or Given below is the group of terms, arrange and rewrite the terms in the correct order. So, as to be in a logical sequence. **ICSE 2006**

Implantation, Fertilisation, Ovulation, Gestation.

Or Given below is the group of terms, arrange and rewrite the terms in the correct order. So, as to be in a logical sequence. **ICSE 2006**

Implantation, Fertilisation, Ovulation, Gestation.

Ans. Fertilisation → Uterus → Implantation → Gestation → Parturition (Mechanism of childbirth).

Or The correct logical sequence in the set is ovulation, Fertilisation, Implantation, Gestation, Parturition.

Or

The logical sequence in the set is
Ovulation → Fertilisation → Implantation → Gestation.

9. Give appropriate biological/technical terms for 'The kind of twins formed from two fertilised eggs.' **ICSE 2017**

Ans. Fraternal twins.

10. Name the structure formed by the villi of the embryo and the uterus of the mother. **ICSE 2015**

Ans. The structure formed by the villi of the embryo and the uterus of the mother is known as placenta.

11. Give the biological/technical term for

Fixing of developing zygote on the uterine wall. **ICSE 2015**

Ans. Implantation.

12. What is the significance of the amniotic fluid? **ICSE 2015**

Ans. Amniotic fluid is significant for the developing foetus in the mother's womb as it protects the foetus from jerks.

13. Give the exact location of amnion. **ICSE 2011**

Ans. Amnion is found around the embryo in the uterus.

14. State whether the following statement is true or false. If false, rewrite the correct statement by changing the first or last word only.

Gestation is the process of fixing of the zygote to the uterine wall. **ICSE 2011**

Ans. The statement is false. **Implantation** is the process of fixing of the zygote to the uterine wall.

15. Explain the term parturition. **ICSE 2009**

Ans. Parturition is the delivery of the foetus or childbirth.

16. Give the technical/biological term for the mucous membrane lining the uterus. **ICSE 2008**

Ans. The mucous membrane lining the uterus is called endometrium.

17. Account for the following briefly. **ICSE 2008**

Twins may or may not be identical.

Ans. Twins may not be identical as in the case of fraternal twins which are produced from two eggs.

In this case, two eggs are released from ovaries at the same time and both get fertilised to produce two individuals.

On the other hand, identical twins are produced from the same egg.

18. State whether the statement is true or false. If false, write the correct statement by changing the incorrect word only. Process of fusion of the sperm nucleus and the egg nucleus is termed implantation. **ICSE 2007**

Ans. The given statement is false. Process of fusion of the sperm nucleus and the egg nucleus is termed **fertilisation**.

Given below are the terms, in which the first pair indicates type of relationship that exists between the terms. Rewrite and complete the pair. **ICSE 2006**

Uterus : Implantation :: Fallopian tube : ....

Ans. Uterus : Implantation :: Fallopian tube : Fertilisation

19. Given below is the biological statement which is incomplete and hence incorrect. Rewrite the correct form of the statement by inserting a suitable word/words at the right place. Do not delete any word already given in the statement underline the inserted word/words. **ICSE 2004**

Fertilisation is the product of fusion of egg nucleus and sperm nucleus.

Ans. Zygote is the product of fusion of egg nucleus and sperm nucleus.

20. Complete the following statement by filling in the blank with the appropriate word in the choice given in the bracket.

The site of fertilisation in the human female is .... (vagina, oviduct, uterus) **ICSE 2001**

Ans. Site of fertilisation in human females is oviduct.

2 Marks Questions

21. Mention any two functions of the human foetal placenta. **ICSE 2023**

Ans. Functions of foetal placenta are as follows

- The placenta provides nutrients and oxygen to the embryo while also eliminating carbon dioxide and waste materials produced by the embryo.
- The placenta produces hormones such as oestrogens, human Chorionic Gonadotropin (hCG) and progesterone.

22. Mention two functions of amniotic fluid. **ICSE Specimen 2023, 2019**

Ans. Two functions of amniotic fluid are

(i) It acts as shock absorber and protects the embryo from mechanical jerks.

(ii) It also maintain even pressure all around the embryo.

23. Briefly explain the gestation. **ICSE Specimen 2019**

Ans. The period of time that a baby develops inside its mother's body is called gestation period. Average length of human gestation period is 280 days.

5 Marks Questions

24. Give the biological/technical terms for the following. **ICSE Specimen 2019**

(i) Period of complete intra uterine development of foetus.

(ii) The structure formed after the release of ovum from the Graafian follicle.

(iii) The surgical technique used in human females to prevent pregnancy.

(iv) The onset of menstruation in a young girl of 13 years.

(v) The canal through which testes descend into the scrotum just before birth in a human male baby.

Ans. (i) Gestation period (ii) Corpus luteum (iii) Tubectomy (iv) Menarche (v) Inguinal canal

25. Copy and complete the following by filling in the blanks (i) to (v) with appropriate words.
The human female gonads are ovaries. A maturing egg in the ovary is present in a sac of cells called ……… (i). As the egg grows larger, the follicle enlarges and gets filled with a fluid and is now called the ……… (ii) follicle. The process of releasing the egg from the ovary is called ……… (iii). The ovum is picked up by the oviducal funnel and fertilisation takes place in the ……… (iv). In about a week the blastocyst gets fixed in the endometrium of the uterus and this process is called ………(v). **ICSE 2014**

Ans. The human female gonads are ovaries. A maturing egg in the ovary is present in a sac of cells called (i) **ovarian follicle**. As the egg grows larger, the follicle enlarges and gets filled with a fluid and is now called the (ii) **Graafian** follicle. The process of releasing the egg from the ovary is called (iii) **ovulation**. The ovum is picked up by the oviducal funnel and fertilisation takes place in the (iv) **oviduct**. In about a week, the blastocyst gets fixed in the endometrium of the uterus and this process is called (v) **implantation**.

Diagram Based Questions

26. Given below are diagrams showing the different stages in the process of fertilisation of an egg in the human female reproductive tract.
Study the diagrams and answer the questions

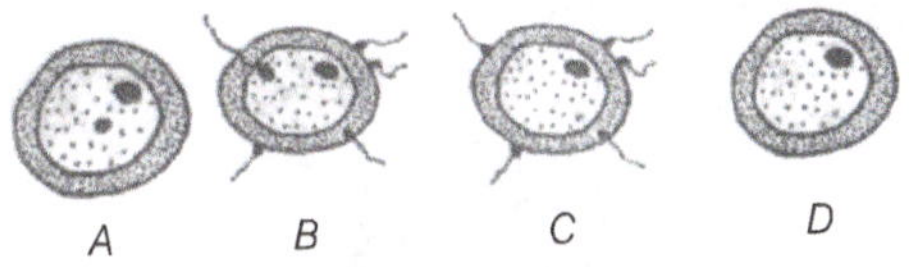

(i) Arrange the letters given below each diagram in a logical sequence to show the correct order in the process of fertilisation.

(ii) Where does fertilisation normally take place? What is 'implantation' that follows fertilisation?

(iii) Mention the chromosome number of the egg and zygote in humans.

(iv) Explain the term 'gestation'. How long does gestation last in humans?

(v) Draw a neat and labelled diagram of a mature human sperm. **ICSE 2018 (5M)**

Ans. (i) $D \rightarrow B \rightarrow C \rightarrow A$.

(ii) Process of fertilisation takes place in the Fallopian tube of female reproductive organs.
After fertilisation, implantation takes place. It is the phenomenon of attachment of developing embryo within the uterus. It leads to the state of pregnancy.

(iii) Human egg contains 23 chromosomes (haploid), while zygote contains 46 chromosomes (diploid).

(iv) Gestation is the time period during which the embryo remains in the uterus (after the last day of menstruation to the day of childbirth). It is of about 9 months or 280 days in human females.

(v)

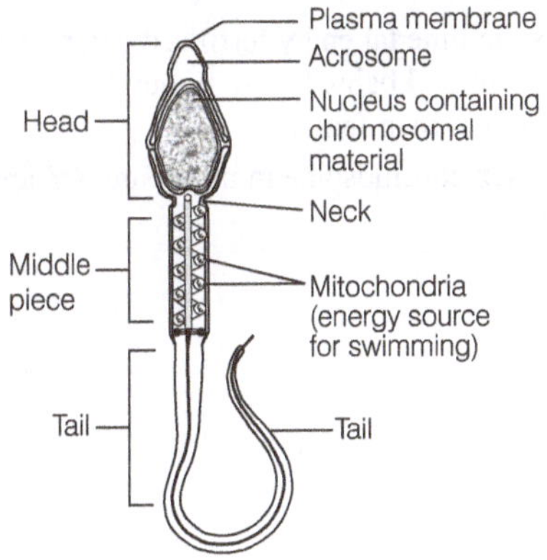

27. The diagram given below is that of a developing human foetus. Study the diagram and then answer the questions that follow.

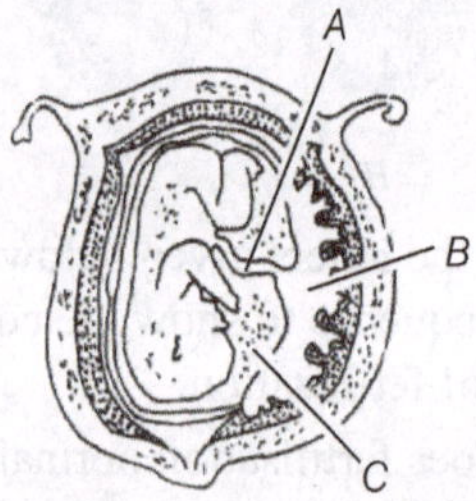

(i) Label the parts numbered *A* to *C* in the diagram.

(ii) Mention any two functions of the part labelled *B* in the diagram.

(iii) Explain the significance of the part labelled *C* in the diagram.

(iv) Define the term gestation. What is the normal gestational period of the developing human embryo?

(v) Mention the sex chromosomes in a male and female embryo. **ICSE 2016 (5M)**

Ans. (i) *A*-Umbilical cord *B* -Placenta
C -Amniotic fluid

(ii) Any two functions of placenta (*B*) are as follows

(a) Placenta supplies nutrition and oxygen to the developing foetus.

(b) It also produces endocrine hormone hCG needed for normal foetus growth.

(iii) Amniotic fluid act as shock absorber. It protects the foetus from physical damage by jerks or mechanical shocks.

(iv) It is the time taken by fertilised egg to develop into fully formed baby. It is of about 9 months or 280 days in human females.

(v) The sex chromosome in males are XY and in female XX.

28. Given below is the diagram showing the developing foetus inside the uterus.

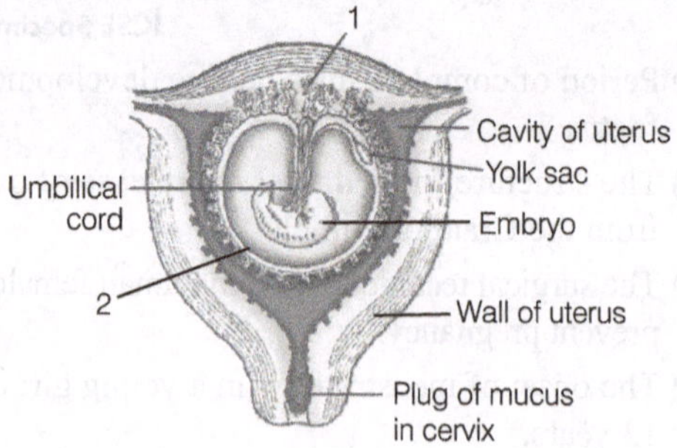

(i) Name the parts marked 1 and 2. State the functions of each part.

(ii) State any two functions of the amniotic fluid.

(iii) What is the role of the umbilical cord in the development of the foetus?

(iv) Name the part in the diagram which is endocrine in nature.

Ans. (i) 1–Placenta- It assists in nutrition, excretion and respiration of the embryo.
2– Chorion-It forms the placenta.

(ii) Refer to answer no. 22.

(iii) The umbilical cord makes the connection between placenta and foetus. It supplies the nutrients and O_2 with maternal blood to foetus and removes CO_2 and excretory wastes from foetal blood into maternal blood.

(iv) Placenta is endocrine in nature.

Concept Enhancer Placenta is endocrine in nature as it secretes a hormone named hCG (human Chorionic Gonadotropin). This hormone plays important role in pregnancy test. Presence of hCG in blood is an indicator that a female is pregnant.

CHAPTER TEST

Section-A

01 Mark Questions

1 Select the correct answers of question from the given options.

(i) Human sperm shows movement with the help of

(a) cilia (b) neutrophilis
(c) flagella (d) None of these

(ii) Name the hormone that is released from testes.

(a) Oestrogen (b) Vasopressin
(c) Testosterone (d) Progesterone

(iii) In human, fertilisation takes place in

(a) uterus (b) Fallopian tube
(c) ovary (d) testis

(iv) Another name of sex cells is

(a) eggs (b) urethra
(c) scrotum (d) gametes

(v) Which part of sperm contain mitochondria, thus provide energy for fertilisation?

(a) Head (b) Middle piece
(c) Tail (d) Axial filament

2 (i) Name the following.

(a) Permanent stoppage of menstrual cycle.
(b) The period during which immature reproductive organs of boys and girls mature and becomes capable for reproduction.
(c) Onset of menstruation in young female.
(d) The cord which contains blood vessel and connect the placenta with foetus.

(ii) Arrange and rewrite the terms in each group in the correct order so as to be in a logical sequence, beginning with the term that is underlined.

(a) Seminiferous tubule, Penis, Urethra, Epididymis, Vas deferens
(b) Ostium, Fallopian tube, Graafian follicle, Ovum, Uterus
(c) Menstrual phase, Luteal phase, Follicular phase, Ovulatory phase
(d) Zygote, Infant, Morula, Foetus, Embryo, Blastocyst

(iii) Match the items given in Column I with the most appropriate ones in Column II and rewrite the correct matching pairs.

	Column I		Column II
A.	Acrosome	1.	Produced from two eggs
B.	Site of implantation	2.	Enzyme (hyaluronidase)
C.	Fraternal twins	3.	Produced from one egg
D.	Ovulation	4.	Uterus
E.	Identical twins	5.	Luteinizing hormone

(iv) Choose the odd one out from the following terms and name the category to which others belong.

(a) Fallopian tube, Uterus, Ureter, Vagina
(b) Testosterone, Progesterone, Vasopressin, Oestrogen
(c) Prostate gland, Seminal vesicle, Corpus luteum, Bulbourethral gland
(d) Menstrual phase, Puberty phase, Follicular phase, Luteal phase, Ovulatory phase.

(v) State the exact location of the following structures.

(a) Site of maturation of human sperm
(b) Seminal vesicle
(c) Hymen in reproductive system
(d) Part of reproductive system where foetus develop

02 Marks Questions

3 State the main function of a sperm duct.

4 What is semen?

5 Define ovary.

6 State two changes which occur in human male and female during puberty.

7 Describe the function of placenta.

03 Marks Questions

8 Name and describe in brief, the stages of the development of human embryo.

9 Draw a neat and labelled diagram of human sperm.

10 Write difference between prostate gland and Cowper's gland.

11 Define parturition.

12 Write the components of female reproductive system.

Section-B

Diagram Based Questions

13 Given diagram represent the female reproductive system.

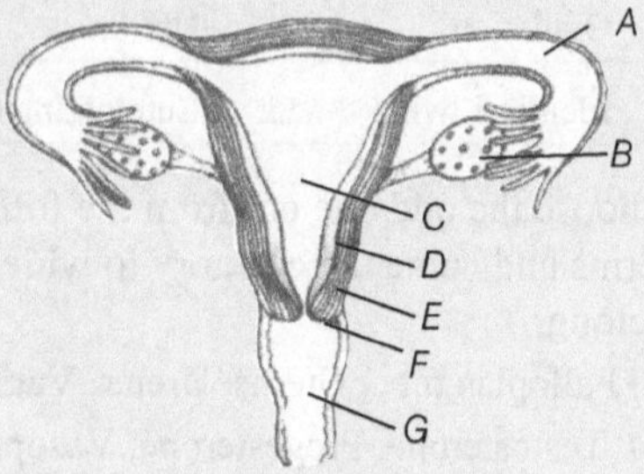

(i) Name the parts labelled as A-G.

(ii) Name the part where implantation occur.

(iii) Name the part which produces oestrogen hormone.

14 In the given diagram two reproductive cells *A* and *B* are shown.

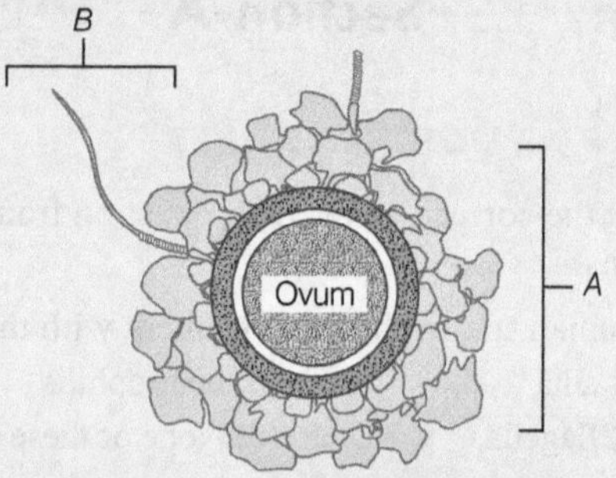

(i) Write the name of event which is shown in the diagram.

(ii) Name the cell formed after the fusion of both reproductive cells.

(iii) As soon as *'B'* enter into *'A'* cell, what prevent other *'B'* cells from entering in *'A'*?

Answers

1. (i) (c), (ii) (c), (iii) (b), (iv) (d), (v) (b)

12

Population and Its Control

TREND ANALYSIS 4 YEARS

Average No. of Questions Across all Sets

Topic	Types of Questions	2024	2023	2020	2019
TOPIC 01 Population and its Explosion	1 Mark	1	1	–	1
	2 Marks	1	1	–	–
	3 Marks	–	–	–	–
	4 Marks	–	–	–	–
TOPIC 02 Population Control and its Measures	1 Mark	1	–	–	–
	2 Marks	–	1	–	–
	3 Marks	–	–	–	–
	4 Marks	–	–	–	–

Presently, the population throughout the world has seen an alarming increase. The rising human population has become the most serious problem and put challenges for mankind by creating deficiency of the resources.

TOPIC 1

Population and its Explosion

Population is defined as summation of all living organisms of the same species or group of species in a geographical area, where they live and inbreed among themselves. Human population throughout the world, as well as in India, has been rising continuously at an alarming rate, which is one of the serious problems, the world is facing today.

Most animals maintain their population at fairly constant level by various means. But man, inspite of being most evolved, intelligent and equipped with scientific knowledge, has not been able to keep a check on the overgrowing population. To understand about the causes, effects and control of population explosion, one should know about the basic terms and definitions, which are discussed below

Terms Related to Population

- **Population density** It is the measurement of population per unit area or per unit volume, at a given time.
- **Growth rate of population** It is defined as the difference between the birth rate and death rate in a given population at a given time.

- **Population growth** It is the change in the population over a period of time. It is the collection of inter-breeding organisms of a particular species. Technically, population growth refers to any species, but is used always for humans. The population growth is affected by
  - **Emigration** The number of people moving out of a particular region or country.
  - **Immigration** The addition of new people to already existing population in a region from other areas or countries.
- **Demography** Population is the total number of individuals of species present in a particular area at a given time. The scientific statistical study of human population is called demography.
- There are five demographic factors in a population which works continuously to determine three phenomenon of demography, i.e. size, composition and distribution. These are literacy, mortality, marriage, migration and social mobility.

Population Explosion

A rapid increase in size of population of human because of certain factors is called population explosion. The combination of a continuing high birth rate and low death rate is the major cause of population explosion in several countries.

Terms Related to Population Explosion

Several terms related to the rate of population are given below

(i) **Carrying Capacity** It can be defined as the maximum number of individuals within a population, that can be supported by the optimum environmental resources for their healthy living. Beyond carrying capacity, no major increase can occur and population has zero growth rate when it reaches the carrying capacity.

(ii) **Birth Rate** (Natality) It is defined as the total number of live births per 1,000 individuals of a population per year. It results in increased population size and population density. The actual birth rate which is obtained under existing conditions is termed as realised natality or fertility rate. It is inversely related to environmental resistance.

(iii) **Death Rate** (Mortality) It is defined as the total number of deaths per 1,000 individuals of a population per year. It results in decrease in population size and population density. Decrease in death rate results in increased population growth rate.

(iv) **Vital Index** The percentage ratio of natality and mortality in a unit population in a unit time is called vital index. Formula for calculating vital index is

$$\text{Vital Index} = \frac{\text{Natality}}{\text{Mortality}} \times 100$$

Major Causes of Population Explosion in World

The factors responsible for the increase of population in world are

- Increased birth rate.
- Decreased death rate, due to better medical facilities.
- Abundance of food, due to advanced agricultural technology.
- Reduced infant mortality.
- The awareness about the reproduction related aspects, methods of disease prevention and hygiene has helped in the rise of population.
- Many steps have been implemented by government as in India to reduce the number of unnecessary deaths, which include clean public toilets, clean roads, proper drainage systems, regular check ups of all facilities, etc.

Major Causes of Population Explosion in India

The factors responsible for the increase in population in India are as follows

- Illiteracy due to which many people in rural areas do not know the functioning of reproductive system.
- High natality rate, i.e. high birth rate.
- Traditional belief that children are the gift of God and a sign of prosperity.
- Desire for a male child in the family as people believe that male child is usually of great help to the aged parents.
- Low economic conditions due to which children become helping hands for their parents which also affects their education.
- The high mortality rate in infants makes people think it is safer to produce more children.
- Religious and social customs make some families unable to accept family planning norms.

Consequences of Population Explosion

Overpopulation has lead to various serious problems. Some of these are given below as

(i) **Unemployment** Overgrowing population is main and the foremost reason for unemployment. As the number of people will increase, the job need will also increase. Therefore, more number of people will remain unemployed, if sufficient number of jobs are not available.

(ii) **Poverty** Family tends to become poor, if there are more persons in it and the income is less. Therefore, poverty increases with the birth of each child in the family.

(iii) **Pollution** The increased population leads to all kinds of pollution, i.e. land, air soil and water.

Effects of Population Explosion on Resources

Any material either natural or artificial used by humans for their growth, development and welfare is known as **resource**.

As human population is rising at an alarming rate, it is creating pressure on the resources because resources are limited. The six main resources which are under pressure in context of rise in population, are water, food, forest, land, energy and minerals.

These are described as below

(i) **Food** Many advance methods have been applied to increase the yield of good quality food, but they are not enough because population increases by geometric progression, i.e. 1,2,4,8... whereas food production occurs by an arithmetic progression, i.e. 1,2,3,4,5... . A level would therefore be reached where the entire world would suffer from food shortage.

(ii) **Water** The availability of clean, contamination free drinking water will become more scarce with the growing population.

(iii) **Forests** Vast areas of the forests have been already cleared for human settlements like housing, schools, hospitals, etc. Forests are reservoirs of many valuable resources and also maintains the balance in ecosystem.

(iv) **Land** It is required for building, farming, roads, etc. The area of land is fixed on the earth and will not increase as per our demand.

(v) **Energy** It is required for cooking, industrial processes, transportation, etc. Energy is obtained from fossil fuel which are non-renewable.

(vi) **Minerals** These are utilised by many industries to produce different materials required by us. Increased population has raised the utilisation of minerals like iron, copper, aluminium, etc. at a faster rate.

PYQs Previous Years' Questions

1 Mark Questions

Multiple Choice Question

1. Birth rate is the number of live births per thousand persons in **ICSE 2024**

(a) 1 year (b) 2 years (c) 10 years (d) 20 years

Ans. (a) 1 year

2. Give the biological/technical terms for the following.

Statistical study of human population. **ICSE Specimen 2023, 2014, 2012, 2009**

Or The statistical study of human population is called

(a) mortality (b) demography **ICSE 2023**
(c) natality (d) equality

Ans. (b) Demography

Very Short Answer Type Questions

3. Differentiate between the pair on the basis of what is mentioned in bracket. Demography and population density (Definition) **ICSE Specimen 2019, 2017**

Ans. Difference between demography and population density is

Demography	Population Density
The scientific statistical study of human population is called demography.	It is the measurement of population per unit area at a given time.

4. Give suitable biological reasons for the following statement.

The birth rate in India is very high. **ICSE 2019**

Ans. The reason behind the high birth rate in India is illiteracy, poor economic conditions, lack of awareness, high mortality rate of infants, desire for a male child, etc.

5. Give appropriate biological or technical terms for 'The difference between the birth rate and the death rate.' **ICSE 2018**

Ans. Growth rate

6. Explain the following terms.
Growth rate of population. **ICSE Specimen 2017**

Ans. Growth rate refers to difference between the birth rate and death rate in a given population at any time.

7. The number of individuals inhabiting per unit area. **ICSE 2016**

Or Give biological term for
'The number of persons living per square kilometre at any given time.' **ICSE 2015**

Ans. The number of individuals inhabiting per unit area is known as population density.

8. State two reasons for the increase of population in India. **ICSE 2015**

Or Write any two major reasons for the population explosion in India. **ICSE 2014, 2012, 2004**

Ans. The two reasons for the increase of population in India are
(i) High illiteracy rate (ii) Control over diseases

9. Explain the term natality. **ICSE 2015, 2009**

Or Explain the term birth rate. **ICSE 2006, 2003**

Ans. **Natality** It is defined as the total number of live births per 1000 individuals of a population per year. It is also termed as birth rate.

10. Write any two major reasons for the population explosion in the world. **ICSE 2013**

Ans. Two major reasons for population explosion in the world are as follows
(i) Abundance of food (ii) Decreased death rate

11. Differentiate between the natality and mortality. (Definition) **ICSE 2012**

Ans. Difference between natality and mortality is

Natality	Mortality
It is defined as the total number of live births per 1000 individuals of a population per year.	It is defined as the total number of deaths per 1000 individuals of a population per year.

12. Insert a key word in place of '^' in the statement given below and complete it.
Birth rate is the number of '^' births per thousand of the population per year. **ICSE 2008**

Ans. Natality or birth rate is the number of **live** births per thousand individuals of the population per year.

13. Explain the term death rate. **ICSE 2008**

Ans. Death rate is the total number of deaths per thousand individuals of the population per year.

14. State true or false. If false, write the correct statement by changing the incorrect word/words only. Mortality is the number of deaths per thousand of the population per decade. **ICSE 2007**

Ans. The statement is false. Mortality is the number of deaths per thousand individuals of the population per year.

15. Mention two reasons for the high birth rate in India. **ICSE 2007**

Ans. Two reasons for the high birth rate in India are
(i) Advancement of medical science, so there is low infant mortality.
(ii) Better healthcare facilities.

16. Given below is the biological statement which is incomplete and hence incorrect. Rewrite the correct form of the statement by inserting a suitable word/words at the right place.
Do not delete any word already given in the statement.
Death rate is the number of deaths of the given population per year. **ICSE 2004**

Ans. Death rate is the total number of deaths per 1000 individuals of a population per year.

17. Mention two reasons for the population explosion in India. **ICSE 2023**

Ans. Two reasons for the population explosion in India
(i) Illiteracy and lack of awareness about birth control measures.
(ii) Early age marriages.

18. Name any two resources which come under pressure due to rising population. **ICSE 2023**

Ans. (i) Food (ii) Land

2 Marks Questions

19. 'Birth rate in India is very high.' Mention two reasons in support of the statement. **ICSE 2024**

Ans. 'Birth rate in India is very high' due to the following reasons

(i) **Illiteracy** Most of the rural population which forms the bulk of our society are still illiterate, ignorant and superstitious. They also do not know the functioning of the human reproductive system.

(ii) **Traditional beliefs** Among the people from lower strata of society, children are regarded as a gift of God and a sign of prosperity. Therefore, they make no effort to avoid pregnancy.

(iii) **Mortality rate** Due to high infant mortality rate in our country, people from the economically weaker section think it safer to produce more children so that at least some may survive.

(iv) **Economic reasons** Children are considered to be helping hands to increase the family income.

(v) **Religious and social customs** India is a centre of various religious and social customs, and as such most people do not accept family planning norms.

(vi) **Desire for a male child** Most Indian families still hold the view that a male child is essential for keeping up the name of the family. Further, a male child is usually a great help to the aged parents.

These two reasons often contribute to getting several children before getting one son or sometimes not even that.

(vii) **Lack of recreation** Poor standard of living and poverty provide no recreation other than sex. (Any two)

20. Explain the terms.

(i) Population density **ICSE 2023**

(ii) Natality **ICSE 2010**

Ans. (i) **Population density** is the measurement of population per unit area or per unit volume, at a given time.

(ii) **Natality** is defined as the total number of live births per 1000 individuals of a population per year.

21. Give two reasons for a sharp rise in world human population. **ICSE Specimen 2023**

Ans. Two reasons for a sharp rise in world human population are

(i) Abundance of food.

(iii) Decreased death rate.

22. Mention three main reasons for the sharp rise in human population in the world. **ICSE 2008**

Ans. Three main reasons for sharp rise in human population in world are

(i) Decreased death rate due to advanced medical facilities.

(ii) Increase in the food availability due to advanced agricultural technology.

(iii) Fewer infant deaths.

23. Mention three reasons why the growth of population has not been appreciably checked in India. **ICSE 2008**

Ans. Three reasons due to which the growth of population has not been appreciably checked in India are as follows

(i) Illiteracy

(ii) Desire for a male child

(iii) Children are regarded as God's gift.

TOPIC 2

Population Control and its Measures

It is mandatory and necessary to control the increasing population for better future of mankind. The rise in population density causes many problems, such as decline in general health, per capita income and depletion of natural resources, etc.

Hence, to avoid all such problems steps should be taken to check the growth of population. This can be majorly done by planning a small family. The control of population add to many advantages such as better health care, better education, less burden on natural resources, etc.

Measures to Control Population Explosion

To prevent the adverse effect of overcrowding and population explosion, following measures must be taken

(i) **Improved Education Facilities** It is necessary for each person of the society to be well educated for understanding all the criteria and impacts of population explosion.

(ii) **Sex Education** Reproductive or sex education must be provided to the people at young age. People should be educated about the advantages of small family which can help in controlling population.

(iii) **Marriageable Age** In order to check the population growth, the age of marriage must be raised. It can be a more effective means for control of the population.

(iv) **Family Planning** It was introduced in 1951 in India. The department which plays a significant role in controlling population and is committed to provide advice and help about family planning is known as **Family Welfare Centre Department.** The inverted **red triangle** has become a popular sign in India for family welfare.

Contraception or Birth Control

The prevention or regulation of conception can be done by using different methods or devices so as to limit the number of offspring. This is called **birth control** or **contraception** methods.
Contraception can be achieved by one of the following methods

- Blocking sperms transport to ovum.
- Blocking ovulation.
- Blocking implantation of early embryo.

Methods of Contraception

The various methods are discussed in table below

Method	Example	Details
Natural contraception	Periodic abstinence	• Couples avoid intercourse from day 10-17 of the menstrual cycle.
	Coitus interruptus or withdrawal	• Male partner withdraws his penis from the vagina just before ejaculation.
(for both male and female)	Condom	• Rubber sheath worn over the penis to check the sperm entering the vagina. • Prevents transmission of STDs.
	Diaphragm	• Round rubber cup that is placed in the vagina over the cervix and prevent sperms to enter uterus.
	Spermicide	• Applied in vagina. • Kill sperms. • Only be used with condoms or diaphragm.
	Oral contraceptive pills	• Contain hormones, which prevent release of ovum. So that, fertilisation does not occur but it disturbs the hormonal balance of the body and can cause side effects also.

Reasons for Birth Control

Various reasons for birth control are

- To check increasing population.
- To maintain family health.
- For maintaining gap between successive children.
- To provide better education and care to the child.
- To provide good health for mother.
- To help the couples decide the number of children they want.

Steps Taken to Control Population

Population can be easily controlled by educating people and by taking the following steps

- By spreading information about ill-effects of population rise in rural areas.
- By removing the orthodox view of having atleast one son in the family.
- By making people aware of benefits of small families and also about the disadvantages of big families.
- The marriageable age of boys and girls has been increased which at present is 21 yrs for boys and 18 yrs for girls in India.
- By educating already married couples to delay the birth of their first child and to space the both of second child and strictly avoiding the third one.
- By advising people to adopt family planning methods to avoid pregnancy (contraception methods).

Method	Example	Details
Intra-Uterine Contraceptive Device (IUCD)	Copper-T	• It is placed in uterus by doctor or veined nurse.. • Used to prevent pregnancy by preventing implantation of blastocyst or embryo. • Can cause side effects due to irritation of uterus.
(a) Vasectomy	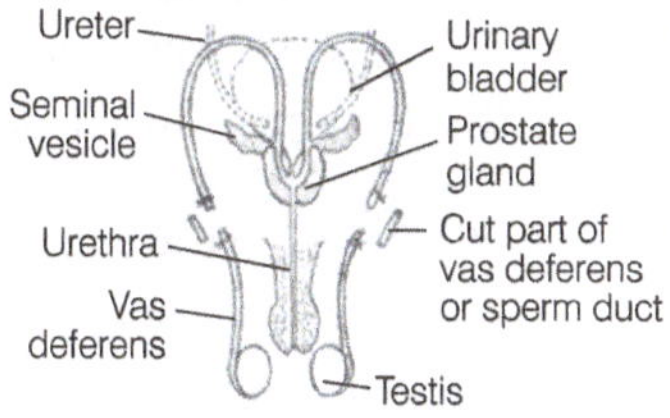	• A small portion of sperm duct or vas deferens is cut and tied properly. Therefore, the sperm transfer is prevented. • Performed surgically in males by doctors. • Irreversible process.
(b) Tubectomy	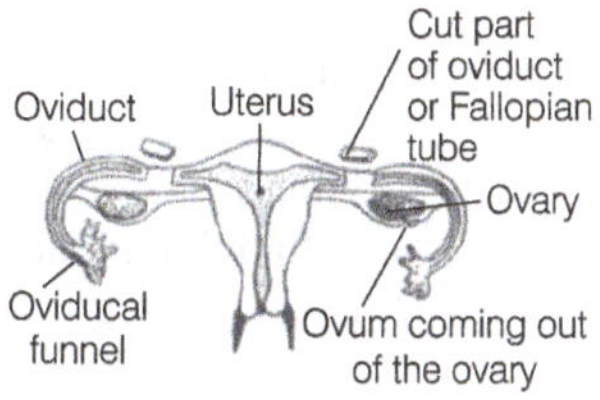	• Removal of a small portion of oviducts. The cut ends are tied properly. The Fallopian tube in the female is blocked and the egg will not be able to reach the uterus. Thus, fertilisation will not take place. • Prevents the egg from meeting the sperms. • Irreversible process.

PYQs Previous Years' Questions

1 Mark Questions

Multiple Choice Question

1. Surgical method of sterilisation in a woman involves cutting and tying of **ICSE 2017**

   (a) ureter (b) uterus
   (c) urethra (d) oviduct

Ans. (d) oviduct

Very Short Answer Type Questions

2. Give the biological terms for the surgical method of contraception in human females. **ICSE 2024**

Ans. Tubectomy.

3. Give the biological/technical terms for the following. The surgical technique used in human females to prevent pregnancy. **ICSE Specimen 2019**

Ans. Tubectomy.

4. What are the age restrictions for marriage for boys and girls in India. **ICSE Specimen 2019, 2009**

Ans. Age restriction for marriage for boys is 21 yrs and girls is 18 yrs in India.

5. Give biological explanations for the

   Education is very important for population control. **ICSE 2018**

Ans. Reproductive or sex education must be provided to the people at young age. People should be educated about the advantages of small family which can help in controlling population.

2 Marks Questions

6. Name the two surgical methods of population control. **ICSE 2023**

Ans. Vasectomy and tubectomy.

7. Write the three advantages of a small family. **ICSE Specimen 2019, 2010**

Ans. Three advantages of a small family are as follows

(i) It helps in the upgradation of the quality of life.

(ii) It maintains the natural resources like land, mineral, wood, fuel, etc., to use for longer time.

(iii) It increases the per capita income, i.e. reduces the economic pressure.

8. Differentiate between the following pair on the basis of what is mentioned within brackets.

   Tubectomy and vasectomy (Part cut and tied) **ICSE 2015**

Or Differentiate between the following pair on the basis of what is mentioned in bracket?
Vasectomy and tubectomy (Explain) **ICSE 2013**

Ans. Differences between vasectomy and tubectomy are

Vasectomy	Tubectomy
It is the sterilisation strategy in males.	It is the sterilisation strategy in females.
It involves surgical cutting of part of vas deferens in males and ligation of cut ends to prevent sperm transfer.	It involves surgical cutting of part of Fallopian tube of a woman and ligation of the cut ends to prevent fertilisation.

9. Give the technical term for a method of contraception in which the sperm duct is cut and ligated. **ICSE 2014**

Ans. The technical term for a method of contraception in which sperm duct is cut and ligated is **vasectomy**.

10. Answer the following questions as directed.
State whether the following statement is true or false. If false, rewrite the correct form of the statement by changing the first or last word only.
Tubectomy is the surgical method of sterilisation in males. **ICSE 2010**

Ans. The statement is false, vasectomy is the surgical method of sterilisation in males whereas tubectomy is the surgical method of sterilisation in females.

11. Give the appropriate term.
The surgical method of sterilisation in the human female. **ICSE 2006**

Ans. Tubectomy is the surgical method of sterilisation in the human female.

Concept Enhancer Tubectomy technique does not protect against sexually transmitted infections people, who are at higher risk should use barrier method even after sterilisation.

12. State whether the following statement is true or false. If false, rewrite the correct statement by changing the first or last word only.
Vasectomy is the surgical method of sterilisation in men. **ICSE 2005**

Ans. The statement is **true**.

13. What is meant by 'population density'? What is the operation done in women to prevent the flow of eggs into the oviduct? **ICSE 2001**

Ans. **Population density** is defined as the size of a population in relation to a particular unit area or unit volume at a given time.
The operation made in women to prevent the flow of eggs into the oviduct is called tubectomy.

5 Marks Question

14. (i) What are the age restrictions for marriage by law for boys and girls in India?
(ii) Name two surgical techniques (one for the human male and another for the human female) that can be used to prevent pregnancy.
(iii) Give two advantages of a small family. **ICSE 2003**

Ans. (i) Refer to answer no. 4.
(ii) Surgical techniques to prevent pregnancy in human are
In males, it is called vasectomy. In this process, the vas deferens of a male is cut and tied properly. Whereas in female it is called tubectomy. In this process, a female's Fallopian tubes are cut and tied with nylon thread.
(iii) Refer to answer no. 7.

Diagram Based Question

15. The diagram given below represents a surgical sterilisation method in males.
Study the same and then answer the questions that follow.

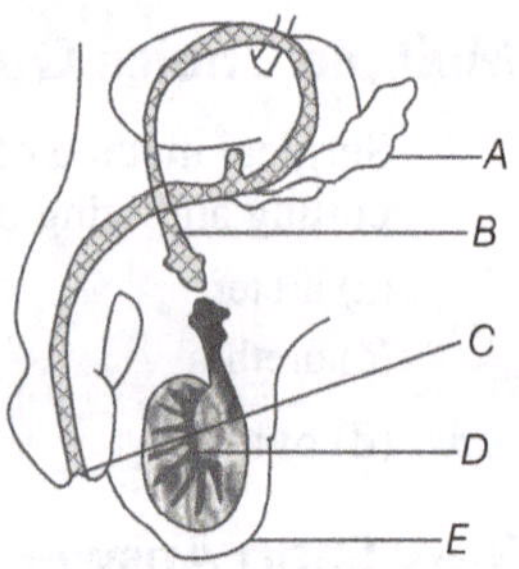

(i) Name the parts marked *A*, *B*, *C*, *D* and *E*.
(ii) Give the name of the surgical method represented in the diagram.
(iii) Which part is ligated or cut?
(iv) Name the corresponding surgical method conducted on females.
(v) Name the part which is ligated in females and why? **ICSE 2009 (5M)**

Ans. (i) Parts labelled from *A* to *E* are
A– Seminal vesicle. *B*– Sperm duct or vas deferens
C– Urethra *D*– Testis
E Scrotum
(ii) Vasectomy
(iii) Sperm duct or vas deferens is the part that is ligated and cut.
(iv) Refer to answer no. 11.
(v) Part ligated in females is oviduct (Fallopian tube) in order to prevent the fusion of egg with the sperms, thus avoiding pregnancy.

CHAPTER TEST

Section-A

01 Mark Questions

1 Select the correct answer to the questions from the given options. (Do not copy the question. Write the correct answer only).

(i) The inverted red triangle is popular sign for
(a) family planning
(b) dangerously increasing population
(c) dangerously decreasing population
(d) family welfare

(ii) In tubectomy what part is ligated?
(a) uterus (b) Ovary
(c) Vagina (d) Fallopian tubes

(iii) Which one is male contraceptive agent?
(a) Nirodh (b) Diaphragms
(c) Copper-T (d) Male condoms

(iv) Which of the following is not the reason for population explosion in India?
(a) Illiteracy
(b) The universalisation of marriage
(c) Upliftment in life style
(d) None of the above

(v) Demography refers to
(a) study of earth's graphical structure
(b) study of human population
(c) study of fossil fuel
(d) study of tree's age

2 (i) Name the following.
(a) One female contraceptive
(b) Maximum no. of individuals within a population that can be supported with optimal resources
(c) Difference between birth rate and death rate in a given population at anytime.
(d) Number of people moving out of a particular region

(ii) Define the following.
(a) Carrying capacity (b) Demography
(c) Family welfare (d) Deforestation

(iii) Match the items given in Column I with the most appropriate ones in Column II and rewrite the correct matching pairs.

	Column I		Column II
A.	Surgical method of contraception	1.	Oral pills
B.	Nirodh	2.	Interuterine device
C.	Copper-T	3.	Sperm billing agent
D.	Mala- D	4.	Condom
E.	Spermicidal	5.	Tubectomy

(iv) Choose the odd one out from the following terms and name the category to which the others belong.
(a) Vasectomy, Tubeectomy, Nirodh, Diaphragms
(b) Emigration, High birth rate, Low death rate, Abundance of food
(c) Carrying capacity, Natality, Mortality
(d) Unemployment, Poverty, Pollution, Malaria

(v) State the exact location of following structures.
(a) Mala - D
(b) Copper - T
(c) Diaphragms
(d) Vasectomy

02 Marks Questions

3 Define exhaustible resource.

4 What is total world population at present?

5 What is vasectomy?

6 Define population density.

7 Name two barrier methods of contraception.

03 Marks Questions

8 Write three advantages of small family.

9 Mention three reasons for rapid increase in population in India.

10 Write three common methods of contraception with example.

11 Write three differences between birth rate and death rate.

12 List three consequences of high population density.

Section-B

Diagram Based Questions

13 (i) Given below is a figure. Answer the following questions with reference to figure.

(i) What does this diagram represent?

(ii) Write some aspects of it.

(iii) Write the name of some places on which it is prominently displayed.

14 Given below is a figure. Answer the following question in reference to this figure.

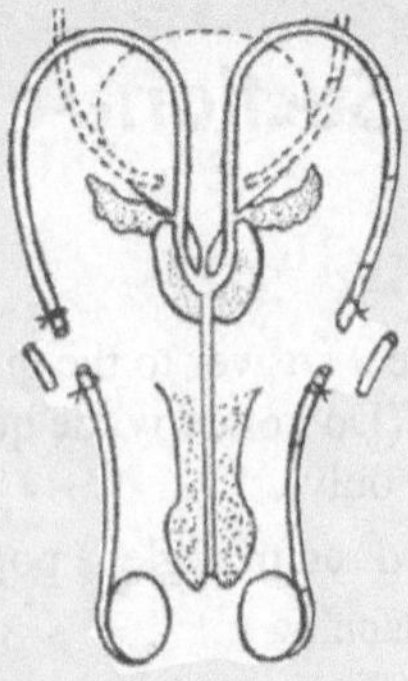

(i) Name this surgical method of contraception.

(ii) In which gender it is performed?

(iii) Which part is ligated in this method of contraception?

Answers

1. (i) (d), (ii) (d), (iii) (d), (iv) (c), (v) (b)

13

Human Evolution

TREND ANALYSIS 4 YEARS

	Average No. of Questions Across all Sets				
	Types of Questions	2024	2023	2020	2019
Human Evolution	1 Mark	2	–	–	–
	2 Marks	1	–	–	–
	4 Marks	–	–	–	–
	5 Marks	–	–	–	–

The origin of life is considered a unique event in the history of universe. Two important aspects of life are its origin and evolution and the branch of life science which deals with these two aspects is called **evolutionary biology.**

Evolution is the sequence of gradual changes from simple life forms to complex life forms, i.e. from primitive organisms that lived over millions of years ago to new organisms that exist today. Human beings are the most recent and most highly evolved among these organisms. In this chapter, we will study various theories of evolution and evolution of human.

Theories of Evolution

Organic evolution implies that the present day organisms are modified but lineal descendants of species that lived in former geological time and that the more complex and highly differentiated forms have evolved from the simpler organisms by gradual modifications.

Thus, it can be defined as orderly changes in living organisms over the course of generations.

A number of theories have been put forward to explain the pattern of evolution leading to formation of new species.

The important theories of evolution are described below

Lamarck's Theory of Evolution (Lamarckism)

- **Jean Baptiste de Lamarck** proposed his idea of evolution in 1809 in his book *Philosophie Zoologique*. It is popularly known as **the inheritance of acquired characters.**
- He proposed that the changes in structure or function of any organ acquired during the lifetime of an organism in response to changes in surrounding environment are inherited by its offsprings.
- These acquired characters keep on adding up over a period of time. These changes lead to the origin of new species.

Postulates of Lamarckism

It is based on following postulates

(i) **Tendency to increase in size** Organisms and their organs have natural tendency to continuously increase in size, generation after generation.

(ii) **Direct effects of the environment** Continuous changes in the environmental conditions directly influence the nature, habits, ways of living of an organism and their structural organisation.

(iii) **Use and disuse of organs** Changes in the environment create new needs in living organisms. To meet these new needs, certain organs are being used greatly and certain organs are lesser used or disused. The continuous use of an organ keeps it functional and makes it stronger and more efficient. Continuous disuse of an organ leads to gradual reduction in its size and finally disappear.

(iv) **Inheritance of acquired characters** The characters acquired by an organism during its lifetime are inherited by the next generation. In every generation some new characters were acquired and older characters kept on improving. After several generations, the species gets modified into a new one.

Evidences of Lamarckism

These are following evidences of Lamarckism

(i) **Evolution of long neck in giraffe** Lamarck postulated that the ancestors of giraffe had short neck and forelimbs who used to graze on grass. Due to changed environment, these areas became arid. The vegetation was gradually replaced by tall trees. To obtain leaves for food they had to stretch their neck and forelimbs which resulted in elongation of these parts.

Constant stretching led to the elongation of neck and forelimbs in giraffe. This change was transmitted to the next generation. This in due course of time resulted in present day long neck of giraffe.

(ii) **Vestigial organs** The organs which are present in reduced form and do not perform any function in the body are called vestigial organs.

They correspond to the fully developed functional organs of related animals. They are believed to be the remnants of organs which were complete and functional in their ancestors, e.g. nipples in male, splint bones in hindlimb of horse, etc.

In human beings, there are about 90 vestigial organs. Some of these are as follows

(a) **Wisdom teeth** The third pair of molars are vestigial in humans. They erupt late in life and sometimes they even fail to erupt.

(b) **Vermiform appendix** The human appendix is the remnant of caecum. The presence of non-functional appendix in man indicates that the ancestors of man had a diet rich in cellulose. The changed food habits over time led to the reduction of this organ in present day man.

(c) **Muscles of pinna** External ear of human is called pinna. Many mammals move their pinna for collecting sound waves from the atmosphere. This part is non-functional in humans.

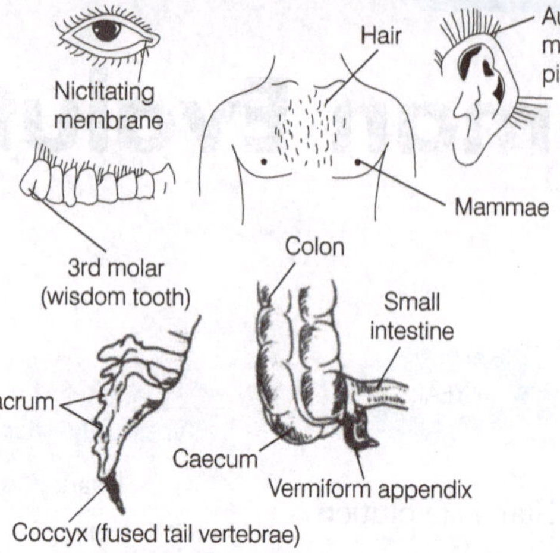

Fig. 13.1 Vestigial organs in human body

Criticism of Lamarckism

Theory of inheritance of acquired characters Lamarckism was discarded due to the following reasons

- Blind, deaf and lame parents do not produce abnormal (blind, deaf or lame) offsprings.
- Wounds of parents do not appear in their offsprings.
- Despite of use of iron shoes to keep their feet short by Chinese women, their young ones at birth have normal feet size.
- **Weismann** removed the tail of mice continuously for 22nd generations, but he failed to obtain tail-less mice till 22nd generation.

Darwin's Theory of Natural Selection (Darwinism)

- **Charles R Darwin** (1809–1882) was a British naturalist. He postulated the 'theory of origin of species by natural selection' which is based on several facts, observations and deductions. It is popularly known as Darwinism.
- Of the various theories, Darwinism is the most widely accepted theory because it provides a convincing explanation.
- During his voyage on **Galapagos Islands** by **HMS Beagle** ship, Darwin observed various types of plants and animals.

- The credit of 'Natural Selection Theory' goes to **Charles Darwin** and **Alfred Russel Wallace**.
- Wallace came to the same conclusions as Darwin regarding natural selection. In 1858, Wallace wrote a 20 pages essay outlining his theory and sent it to Darwin.
- In 1859, Charles Darwin published his observations and conclusions in a book '*Origin of Species*'.

Postulates of Darwinism

Darwin's theory of organic evolution by natural selection is based on following principles

(i) **Overproduction** (Rapid multiplication) All organisms possess enormous fertility. They multiply in a geometric proportion with some organisms producing very large number of species. Despite of this high rate of reproduction of a species, its number remains constant under fairly stable environment.

(ii) **Struggle for existence** The limited resources present in an environment are the main cause of struggle for existence, which may occur at following three levels

(a) **Intraspecific struggle** It is the struggle among the individuals of same species for their common requirements like food, shelter, mate, breeding places, etc.

(b) **Interspecific struggle** It is the struggle between the individuals of different species for their similar requirements like food and space.

(c) **Environmental struggle** It is the struggle of living forms against the environmental conditions like extreme heat, cold, drought, earthquakes, storms, disease, volcanic eruption, etc.

(iii) **Appearance of variations** All individuals are dissimilar in some of their characters except the identical twins. This dissimilarity is mainly due to the variations. These are the small or large differences among the individuals. Variations allow some individuals to better adjust with their environment.

(iv) **Natural selection or Survival of the fittest** Originally it was an idea of **Herbert Spencer** (1820-1903) who used the phrase 'survival of the fittest' for the first time, while **Darwin** named it natural selection.

Survival of the fittest refers to the idea that the natural selection tends to favour those organisms that are most fit to survive with the reproductive age in a particular environment and to produce offsprings. A popular example of natural selection is industrial melanism.

Evidences of Natural Selection

It has the following evidences

- Rate of reproduction, limitation of resources, competition and struggle for existence can be seen in nature normally.
- Abundance of variation is evident by the absence of two similar individuals except monozygotic twins, which also shows some environmental variations.
- Production of new varieties of plants and animals through artificial selection. These show evidences that the nature having vast resources can easily produce new species through the natural selection.

Industrial Melanism

- Peppered moth (*Biston betularia*) is an example of natural selection by industrial melanism.
- In England during1850s, before industrialisation there were more white-winged moths on trees than dark-winged or melanic forms. But after industrialisation, i.e. in 1920, dark-winged moths became more than white-winged moths.
- This is because during industrialisation, the tree trunks covered by white lichens became dark due to air pollution (dust and soot particles).
- Due to this, white winged moths could be easily seen and eaten by the predators as they failed in camouflaging (hide or disguise the presence of a person, animal or object).
- This shows that in a mixed population, those that can better adapt, survive and increase in population size.

Criticism of Darwin's Natural Selection Theory

Darwin's theory was widely accepted, but **Sir Richard Owen** and **Adam Sedgewick** criticised it due to following reasons

- Darwin emphasised on the **inheritance of small variations**, which are mainly non-heritable and useless for evolution.
- He could not explain the presence of vestigial organs and effect of their use and disuse.
- Darwinism failed to explain the survival of the fittest.
- Natural selection failed to explain the evolution of terrestrial animals from the aquatic organisms.
- Natural selection failed to explain some adaptations such as electric organs of fish, mimicry in Karama butterfly, etc.

- Darwin was unaware about the knowledge of heredity.
- Darwinism does not account for the degeneration of certain animal organs.

Human Evolution

- Human is the wisest creature on the Earth. Some people consider human beings as a supreme creation.
- **Carolus Linnaeus** placed man among the monkeys and apes.
- **Charles Darwin** stated that man was one more animal species whose origin and evolution could be traced just like that of any other species.
- He published his idea about human ancestry in the book '*Descent of Man*' and '*Selection in Relation to Sex*'.
- He suggested that man, apes and monkeys have a common ancestor. The unique qualities of human are language, advanced thoughts and culture evolved through the natural selection.
- Human beings belong to a single family (Hominidae), a single genus (*Homo*), a single species (*sapiens*), a single sub-species (*sapiens*) and four races (Mongoloid, Negroid, Caucasoid and Australoid).

Characteristics of Human

The modern man shows the following characteristic features, which were acquired during the course of evolution

(i) **Large brain and cranial cavity** Man has extra ordinary large brain and high intelligence. The volume of cranial cavity is more (1450 cc) in human than apes and monkeys.

(ii) **Upright posture** Upright posture is due to major changes in musculo-skeletal system. Consequently, legs became longer for balancing the body, abdominal region became short, thorax became broad and flat.

(iii) **Bipedal locomotion** Due to bipedal locomotion, forelimbs or hands are free to do other functions.

(iv) **Forelimbs** The forelimbs evolved into efficient grasping and manipulating devices for carrying things, making tools and hurling weapons.

(v) **Opposable thumb** (Dexterity) During evolutionary change in human, thumb (pollex) has been brought opposite to fingers enabling the hand for better grasping power.

(vi) **Orthognathous face** In *Homo sapiens,* face is orthognathous with protruding canines of the lower jaw, whereas ape's face is prognathous, i.e. protruded out into a short of muzzal.

(vii) **Binocular vision** Human beings possess binocular and stereoscopic vision, which enables the depth perception and distance estimation.

(viii) **Loss of body hairs** Body hairs are present as a vestigial form.

History of Human Evolution

- The study of living and fossil primates shows that the primates (including monkey and man) have descended from a common ancestor and separated from the main stock (of a homonisation) during Oligocene period.
- Fossil records are the best evidence which show intermediate steps between apes and man.
- The evolutionary history of man can be divided into following three steps only for the convenience of study
  - Prior to ape man.
  - Ape man (including prehistoric man).
  - True man (including the living modern man).
- The fossil records prior to ape man includes
  - ***Dryopithecus*** Common ancestor of man and apes.
  - ***Ramapithecus*** Earliest man-like primate or first hominoid.

- The various fossil records of ape man are as follows

Human Ancestors	Time of Origin	General Features	Cranial Capacity (cc)
Dryopithecus	20-25 mya	Ape-like, hairy, ate soft fruits and leaves. Arms and legs of same length, large brain.	325-500
Ramapithecus	14-15 mya	More man-like, walked more erect, teeth like modern man.	325-500

Australopithecus (This first ape man)	2 mya	Probably lived in East African grasslands and ate fruits, hunted with stones, weapons,	450-600
Homo habilis (Handy man)	1.2-1.5 mya	Fossils found in East Africa, first hominid, i.e. human being like, brain capacity 650-800 cc, did not eat meat.	650-800
Homo erectus (Java man)	1.5 mya	Fossils found in Java in 1891, probably ate meat.	750-1100
Homo sapiens neanderthalensis (Primitive man)	1,00,000-40.000 years ago	Known as neanderthal man. Fossils found in East and Central Asia, used hides to protect body buried their dead. They became extinct 25000 years ago.,	1300-1600
Homo sapiens fossilis (Cro-Magnon man)	35,000-11,000 years ago	More intelligent than modern man, omnivores, developed socially and become extinct 10000 years ago.	1660
Homo sapiens (Modern man)	75,000-10,000 years ago (ice age)	Arose in Africa, developed cave art around 18000 years ago, agriculture started around 10000 years back and thus human settlement and civilisation started.	1300-1600

PYQs Previous Years' Questions

1 Mark Questions

Multiple Choice Questions

1. Industrial melanism was observed in **ICSE 2024**

   (a) mice (b) peppered moth
   (c) house flies (d) crow

Ans. (b) peppered moth

2. The most primitive ancestor of man is **ICSE Specimen 2019**

   (a) *Homo habilis* (b) Cro-Magnon
   (c) Neanderthal (d) *Australopithecus*

Ans. (d) *Australopithecus*

Very Short Answer Type Questions

3. Arrange and rewrite the terms in each group in the correct order to be in a logical sequence beginning with the term that is underlined:

   Australopithecus, Cro-Magnon, *Homo erectus*, Neanderthal man. **ICSE 2024**

Ans. *Australopithecus*, *Homo erectus*, Neanderthal man, Cro-Magnon.

4. Briefly explain the following.
   Lamarck's theory of use and disuse of organs. **ICSE Specimen 2019**

Ans. It states that when certain organs become specially developed as a result of some evolutionary need, than that state of development is hereditary and can be passed on to progeny, e.g. giraffe's long neck.

5. Mention two features of Neanderthal man. **ICSE Specimen 2019**

Ans. The two features are as follows

(i) Their cranial capacity was 1400 cc.

(ii) They used for bury their dead.

Important Questions

6. What is evolutionary biology?

Ans. Evolutionary biology is the study of history of life forms on earth.

7. Define the term organic evolution.

Ans. Organic evolution can be defined as orderly changes in living organisms over the course of generations.

8. Name the book in which Lamarck published his idea of evolution.

Ans. The book in which Lamarck published his idea of evolution was *Philosophie Zoologique*.

9. Mention the name of postulates stated by Lamarck through which an organism acquires new characters.

Ans. The name of postulates stated by Lamarck through which an organism acquires new characters are
(i) Use and disuse of organs.
(ii) Inheritance of acquired characters.

10. Who proposed the concept of inheritance of acquired characters?

Ans. The concept of inheritance of acquired characters in support of evolution was proposed by Lamarck. New traits are acquired by organisms during their lifetime and are passed on to the next generation.

11. State one reason due to which Lamarck's theory was criticised.

Ans. Lamarckian theory is also known as theory of inheritance of acquired characters or theory of use and disuse of organs.
This theory cannot explain the reason of weak muscles in the son of a wrestler.

12. What was Lamarck's explanation for long neck of giraffe?

Ans. According to Lamarckism, long neck and high forelimbs of giraffe were well-developed due to their stretching for obtaining foliage (leaves, etc.) from the trees when ground vegetation became sparse.

13. Give the biological term used for organs present in reduced form and do not perform any function.

Ans. Vestigial organs.

14. Name a vestigial organ found in horse.

Ans. Splint bones in the hindlimbs are vestigial in horse.

15. Choose the odd one in the following series.
Wisdom tooth, nictitating membrane, vermiform appendix, vertebral column.

Ans. Vertebral column is the odd one. This structure is well-developed and functional in humans. Rest of the options represents vestigial organs that are non-functional.

16. What is fitness according to Darwin?

Ans. The fitness according to Darwin refers ultimately to reproductive fitness.

17. Name the scientist who also came to similar conclusion as Darwin. Where did he work?

Ans. The scientist who also came to similar conclusion as Darwin was Alfred Wallace. He worked in Malay Archipelago.

18. Mention the two key concepts of Darwinism.

Ans. The two key concepts of Darwinism are
(i) Branching descent.
(ii) Natural selection.

19. Explain the meaning of survival of the fittest.

Ans. The ability to survive and to reproduce in their respective environment is termed as survival of the fittest.

20. Differentiate the term on the basis of what is mention in the bracket. (Lamarckism and Darwinism-Definition)

Ans.

Lamarckism	Darwinism
Proposed by Lamarck.	Proposed by Darwin.
New individuals are formed due to the inheritance of acquired characters.	New individuals are formed by the accumulation of variations.

21. What are fossils?

Ans. Fossils are the remnants and/or impressions of the life forms that lived in the remote past.

2 Marks Questions

Important Questions

22. Differentiate between *Australopithecus* and Modern man based on body hair. **ICSE 2024**

Ans. Difference between *Australopithecus* and Modern man on the basis of body hair

Australopithecus	Modern man
Their body is covered with hair.	They have highly reduced body hair.

23. What does the inheritance of acquired characters mean? Who gave this idea?

Ans. Inheritance of acquired characters means that organs which are used more extensively would enlarge and become more efficient and such changed characteristics (acquired traits) would be transmitted to the offsprings. This idea was the central theme of Lamarckism.

24. Which traits are important for evolution?

Ans. Inherited traits are important for evolution because these traits are transferred from generation to generation. Accumulation of inherited traits with variations, for several generations can give rise to new species.

While retention of inherited traits of similarities for generations maintain integrity of an existing species.

25. Natural selection operates when nature selects for fitness. Explain.

Ans. Natural selection for fitness is based on the characteristics which are inherited. So, there must be a genetic basis for getting selected and to evolve; in other words, there are some organisms which are better adapted to survive in an otherwise hostile environment.

Adaptive ability is inherited and it has a genetic basis; hence, fitness is the end result of the ability to adapt and get selected by nature.

26. Explain Darwin's concept of natural selection.

Ans. According to Darwin's concept of natural selection, the organisms, which are provided with favourable variations would survive because they are fittest to face their surrounding, while the organisms, which are unfit for surrounding variations are destroyed.

27. State the reason for the increased population of dark coloured moths coinciding with the loss of lichens (on tree barks) during industrialisation period in England.

Ans. During post-industrialisation period, the tree trunks got dark because of industrial smoke and soot, so the dark coloured moths were able to hide without any risk of predation, survived and increased in population. White-winged moths did not survive due to increased predation. As they could be easily seen and eaten by predators.

3 Marks Questions

Important Questions

28. Describe Lamarck's theory of evolution.

Ans. **Lamarck's theory** It is known as theory of inheritance of acquired characters.

According to this theory, organisms undergo certain changes to adapt themselves to the environment.

These characters acquired by an organism during its lifetime, are passed on to the progeny, e.g. the long neck of giraffe was explained by Lamarck, as an outcome of these animals to stretch their necks constantly to eat the leaves on the upper branches of the trees.

Lamarckism is based on the following postulates

(i) Tendency to increase in size.

(ii) Direct effects of the environment.

(iii) Use and disuse of organs.

(iv) Inheritance of acquired characters.

29. Differentiate between inherited and acquired traits.

Ans. Differences between inherited and acquired traits are as follows

Inherited traits	Acquired traits
These are obtained from the parents.	These are developed during the life of an individual.
These are genetic variations.	These are somatic variations.
These develop due to crossing over phenomenon and mutations.	These develop due to use and disuse of organs and direct effect of environment.
These are passed on from one generation to the other.	These are lost with the death of the individual.

30. Explain how vestigial organs give an idea about evolution?

Ans. Those organs, which no longer have a function in our body are known as vestigial organs. These organs have reduced structurally as well as functionally.

It appears that these organs were once well-developed and functional in ancestors and later on due to their less use they became reduced, e.g. vermiform appendix in man is reduced and functionless while in herbivores vermiform appendix along with caecum is used for digestion of cellulose.

It gives an idea that human had herbivorous food habit and cellulose containing materials were major part of their food.

Concept Enhancer The human vermiform appendix is an example of it. It was used to store microbes which produced cellulase to break plant cell wall. Leaves are main diet of apes, but not of humans as cellulose cannot be digested by humans.

31. Name the ancestors of man based on the features given below.

(i) Human-like meat eater with 900 cc brain, lived in Java.

(ii) More human with brain size 1400 cc, lived in Central Asia, used hides and buried their dead.

(iii) Human-like, vegetarian, with brain capacity between 650 cc and 800 cc.

Ans. (i) *Homo erectus.*

(ii) Neanderthal man.

(iii) *Homo habilis.*

32. (i) When and where did Neanderthal man live?

(ii) What was his brain capacity?

(iii) Mention the advancements he showed over *Homo erectus*.

Ans. (i) Neanderthal man lived in near East and Central Asia, between 100000- 40000 years before.

(ii) His brain capacity was 1400 cc.

(iii) He used hides to protect the body. He buried the dead. His brain size was more (1400 cc) than that of *Homo erectus* which was 900 cc.

5 Marks Questions

Important Questions

33. (i) Who gave the theory of inheritance of acquired characters?

(ii) Which book he had written?

(iii) Write the main essence of his theory?

(iv) Why his theory was criticised?

Ans. (i) Jean Baptiste de Lamarck gave the theory of inheritance of acquired characters.

(ii) *Philosophie Zoologique*' was the book written by Lamarck.

(iii) The main essence of his theory is that environment keeps changing and creates new needs. Organisms acquire new habits (involving use and disuse of certain body structures) to meet these new needs for successful living.

Useful organs modify and enlarge and disused organs get reduced and gradually disappear. These acquired changes are inherited and give rise to new species.

(iv) Lamarck's theory was criticised because acquired characters are not inherited. Weismann showed that even after cutting the tails of white mice continuously for 21 generations, a tail-less mouse was never born. Thus, the idea of inheritance of acquired characters was not found to be true.

34. Compare Lamarck's and Darwin's theory.

Ans. Lamarck's theory says that according to environment, an organ can be used more while others can be useless. Useful organ grows and is inherited while useless organ is gradually lost, giving rise to new species devoid of that organ.

Darwin says that variations arise naturally in a population. Organism with variation best suited for environment survives, reproduces and forms new species while others become extinct.

These two theories can be compared using giraffe's evolution. According to Darwin, giraffes had different neck lengths.

Those with longer neck were better adapted to eat leaves from trees. Thus, naturally selected and those with shorter necks died out due to starvation. While Lamarck says, initially all giraffes had smaller necks. When leaves on lower branches of trees were all eaten up, they had to stretch their neck to eat from upper branches.

Continued stretching of neck resulted into modern long neck giraffes.

35. The evolutionary story of moths in England during industrialisation reveals, that 'evolution is apparently reversible' . Clarify this statement.

Ans. The peppered moth occurs in two forms, i.e. light coloured (*Biston betularia typoica*) and dark coloured (*Biston betularia carbonaria*).

Before industrial revolution only light coloured moths were prevalent. Light coloured moths camouflaged well with the lichens that covered tree trunks, on the contrary dark moths were easy prey on the tree trunks and were very rare.

During the industrial revolution the population of dark coloured moth increased, while that of light coloured moth decreased. This change was due to the burning of coal in factories. The smoke from the factories killed the lichens and the tree trunks turned black due to the deposition of soot.

The black moths had an advantage against soot, therefore, escaped predation by birds while on the other hand, white moths were identified in sharp contrast and become easy prey.

With the progression of industrial revolution the coal was replaced by oil and electricity.

This resulted in reduction of soot deposits on the tree trunk. Gradually, the population of black moth decreased and that of light moth began to increase.

Thus, it can be said that 'evolution is apparently reversible'.

36. (i) Name the primates that lived about 15 million years ago. List their characteristic features.

(ii) (a) Where was the first man-like animal found?

(b) Write the order in which Neanderthals, *Homo habilis* and *Homo erectus* appeared on the earth. State the brain capacity of each one of them.

(c) When did modern *Homo sapiens* appear on this planet?

Ans. (i) *Dryopithecus* and *Ramapithecus*

Characteristics

(a) They were hairy.

(b) They walked like gorillas and chimpanzees.

(c) *Ramapithecus* was more man-like while *Dryopithecus* was more ape-like.

(ii) (a) East African grasslands.

(b) *Homo habilis*, *Homo erectus* and Neanderthals had brain capacities of 650-800 cc, 900 cc and 1400 cc, respectively.

(c) During the ice age between 75000-10000 years ago.

Diagram Based Questions

37. Given below are two stages in the evolution of man. Study them and answer the questions that follows **ICSE 2019 (5M)**

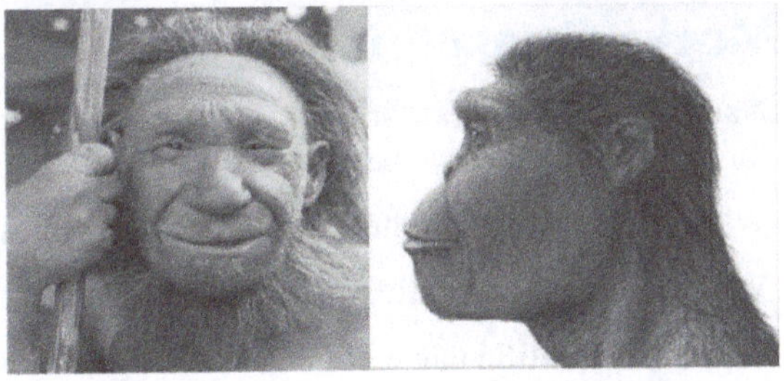

A B

(i) Identify *Australopithecus* and Neanderthal man from the above pictures.

(ii) Mention two characteristic features each for the two stages.

(iii) Who proposed the theory of 'natural selection'?

(iv) Name the organism used as an example to explain 'industrial melanism.'

(v) Give two examples of vestigial organs in humans.

Ans. (i) *A*- Neanderthal man *B*- *Australopithecus*

(ii)

Characteristic features of Neanderthal man	Characteristic features of *Australopithecus*
Large head	Protecting face.
Broad flat slopping forehead.	Chin absent.
Less hair on the body.	Prominent eyebrow ridges.
Cranial capacity (1500 cc)	Flat nose
	Projecting face
	Cranial capacity (450-600 cc)

(iii) Charles Darwin.

(iv) Peppered moth

(v) Pinna of ear, vermiform appendix.

Important Question

38. Given below are the few structures of human body.

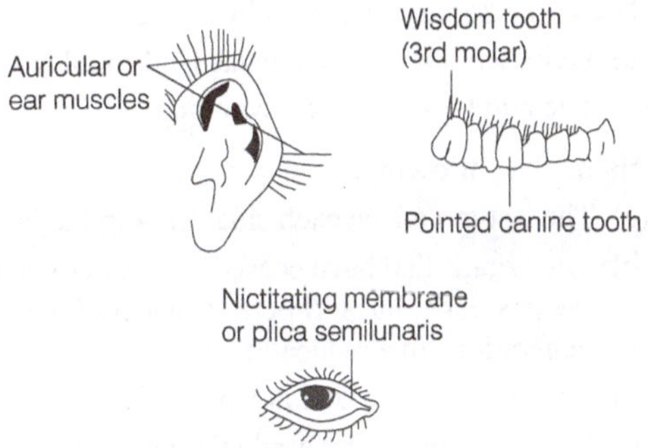

(i) What are these structures called?

(ii) Give any two characteristics of these structures.

Ans. (i) These structures are called vestigial organs.

(ii) These are present in reduced or ruminent form in human body. They do not perform any function. They correspond to the fully developed functional organs of related animals.

CHAPTER TEST

Section-A

01 Mark Questions

1 Select the correct answer to the questions from the given options.

(i) Grasping ability was completely lost in

(a) Java man (b) Neanderthal man
(c) first ape man (d) Handy man

(ii) The theory of natural selection was proposed by

(a) Wallace (b) Lamarck
(c) Darwin (d) Mendel

(iii) Average cranial capacity of modern man in cubic centimeter is

(a) 350 (b) 580 (c) 1100 (d) 1450

(iv) Who were called as 'handy man'?

(a) *Homo erectus* (b) *Homo sapiens*
(c) *Homo habilis* (d) None of these

(v) The evolutionary history of a species is called

(a) phylogeny (b) palaeoanthropology
(c) speciation (d) evolution

2 (i) Name the following.

(a) The last molars on each sides of both the jaws.
(b) The organs that have ceased to be of any use to the possessor but still persists generation after generations in a reduced form.
(c) The book written by Lamarck.
(d) Origin of species by gradual modification.
(e) The muscles of pinna which is non-functional in humans.

(ii) Fill in the blanks with suitable word.

(a) The modified natural theory of Darwin is called ....
(b) The dental arch of *Australopithecus* was a smoothly rounded ....
(c) The Neanderthals were found in Europe, North Africa and ....
(d) .... is the slowest breeder producing 6 young ones in its life of about 90 years.

(iii) State true or false.

(a) Industrial melanism took place in Manchester.
(b) Struggle for existence was given by Lamarck.
(c) Evolution of modern man is a discontinuous process.
(d) Cro-Magnon man had more cranial capacity compared to modern man.

(iv) Match items given in Column I with the most appropriate ones in Column II and rewrite the correct matching pairs.

	Column I		Column II
A.	Handy man	1.	*Australopithecus*
B.	First ape man	2.	*Homo sapiens fossils*
C.	More intelligent than modern man	3.	*Homo erectus*
D.	190 cm height full erect	4.	*Homo habilis*
E.	Java man	5.	Modern man

(v) Explain the following terms.

(a) Phylogeny (b) Speciation
(c) Lamarckism (d) Living fossil

02 Marks Questions

3 Name the six ancestral form in their correct sequence through which modern man has evolved.

4 What is speciation ? Write name of human species.

5 Write some characteristic features of modern man.

6 Write the scientific name of human. Who gave this term?

7 Write the name of some tools used by Cro-Magnon man.

03 Marks Questions

8 Mention the two principles through which Lamarck explained his ideas.

9 Explain evolution of giraffe's neck according to Darwin's theory of natural selection.

10 Give reasons for the following.
Offspring of blind couple are not blind.

11 Briefly discuss the theory of inheritance of acquired characters.

12 Industrial melanism provides a good example of natural selection. Discuss.

Section-B

Diagram Based Questions

13 The following figure is of ape man.

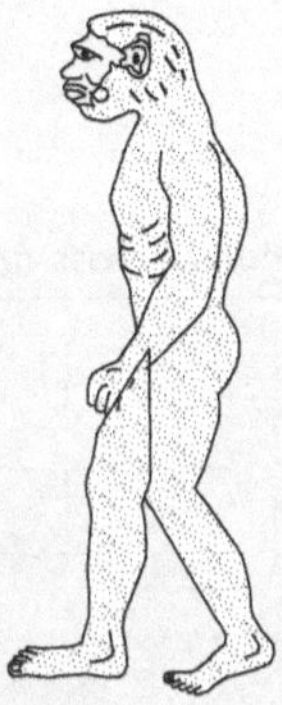

(i) Identify him.

(ii) What type of locomotion they showed?

(iii) Write the special feature of these ape man

14 The diagram shows human pinna and muscles named as *X*.

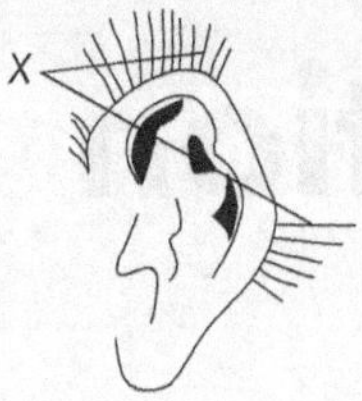

(i) What is *X*?

(ii) Why is it called vestigial organ in human?

(iii) According to Lamarck what make this organ vestigial?

Answers

1. (i) (c), (ii) (c), (iii) (d), (iv) (c), (v) (a)

14

Pollution

TREND ANALYSIS 4 YEARS

Average No. of Questions Across all Sets

Topic	Types of Questions	2024	2023	2020	2019
TOPIC 01 Pollution and its Types	1 Mark	1	1	–	–
	2 Marks	1	–	–	–
	3 Marks	–	–	–	–
	5 Marks	–	–	–	1
TOPIC 02 Effects of Pollution	1 Mark	2	–	–	5
	2 Marks	2	1	–	–
	3 Marks	–	–	–	–
	4 Marks	–	–	–	–

TOPIC 1

Pollution and its Types

Pollution is any undesirable change in the physical, chemical or biological characteristics of air, water, land or soil. It is due to addition of any unwanted substance to the environment that may adversely affect the organisms.

The agents that cause pollution and bring undesirable changes in the environment are known as **pollutants**. These are classified into two main types

(i) **Biodegradable pollutants** are the substances which can be degraded by the action of microorganisms, e.g. food and kitchen waste, paper, plant waste, etc.

(ii) **Non-biodegradable pollutants** are the substances which cannot be degraded by the action of microorganisms, e.g., polythene bags, metals, electric components, pesticides (DDT), etc.

Based on the component of the environment being affected, pollution can be categorised into following main types

Air Pollution

The degradation of the quality of air affecting the living organisms and objects is called air pollution. It occurs due to undesirable changes in the physical, chemical or biological characteristics of air.

Air pollutants are of following two main types

(i) **Particulate Pollutants** These constitute harmful particles such as dust particles, metallic particles, smoke, mining, stone drilling, wearing of rubber tyres, etc., which remain suspended in the air.

(ii) **Gaseous Pollutants** These constitute the harmful gases such as CO_2, H_2S, CO, SO_2, NO_2, etc., that are given out from a variety of sources.

Sources of Air Pollution

Air pollution can be caused by either of the following sources

- **Natural sources** include volcanic eruptions, fumes from forest fires, dust from storms, pollens, etc.
- **Man-made sources** include excessive use of automobiles, garbage, industries, brick kilns, etc.

Some of the man-made sources of air pollution are described below:

(i) **Vehicular Air Pollution** All vehicles whether car, two-wheelers, buses, tractors, railway engines, etc., run on either petrol or diesel. These vehicles liberate harmful gaseous pollutants mainly as CO_2, NO_2, SO_2 and CO.

Apart from this, rubber particles released from the wearing of rubber tyres of automobiles and dust particles that rise into the air are also causes of vehicular pollution.

These can be easily controlled by the use of lead free petrol, use of CNG over petrol, efficient engines, good quality automobiles, etc.

(ii) **Industrial Air Pollution** Various small scale industries (like pottery, carpet weaving units, etc.) to large scale industries (such as textiles, automobiles manufacturing units, sugar and food industries, oil refineries, etc.) expel out gaseous and particulate pollutants that are responsible for air pollution.

The chief industrial gaseous pollutants are CO_2, SO_2, CO and oxides of nitrogen.

(iii) **Burning Garbage** Wastes from homes and kitchen include items such as vegetable and fruit peels, polythene bags, etc.

These wastes are either used in making manures for agricultural purposes or are burnt in enclosures. On burning garbage, harmful gases such as CO_2, etc., are released which causes air pollution.

(iv) **Brick Kilns** These are fire-heated enclosures used for making bricks that are used in construction purposes. The wastes produced by these enclosures are large quantity of ash and broken small pieces of bricks, which cause air pollution.

Water Pollution

Any change in the water quality that makes it unsuitable for use by humans and other living organisms is known as water pollution.

Source of Water Pollution

The major sources of water pollution are given below

(i) **Sewage** The liquid waste released out from domestic activities is called sewage.

- It includes toilet waste, kitchen and other household wastes and water.
- It is necessary to remove dirty part of water and release clean water into the nearby water bodies and rivers.
- For this purpose, many big cities have sewage treatment plants, but small cities and rural areas do not have such facilities thus, they discharge sewage waste directly into a nearby water body such as rivers and lakes thereby, polluting it.
- This is inturn causes the pollution of water at major level.

(ii) **Household Detergents** Soaps or detergents used for household purposes, i.e. for washing clothes, utensils and for bathing. They release dirty water that is also a cause of water pollution.

(iii) **Industrial Wastes** Water released both by small scale and large scale industries contain various types of chemical pollutants and other wastes. These industries discharge dirty water directly into the rivers, lakes, etc., and cause water pollution.

(iv) **Oil Spills** Accidental discharge of petroleum and its products by oil refineries, overturned oil tanks, offshore oil mining into seas, oceans and estuaries are called oil spills. Due to oil pollution, many aquatic life forms such as fishes, etc., are killed.

(v) **Thermal Pollution** Water used in oil refineries, nuclear power plants and other thermal power plants is released into the nearby streams. The water released by industries is warmer than the normal water of streams. Due to this temperature change, the aquatic life forms and aquatic plants get affected.

Soil Pollution

It is defined as any undersirable change in the soil profile thereby, affecting its productivity. Water and air pollution can spread to long distances but soil pollution is largely localised.

Sources of Soil Pollution

The major sources of soil pollution are given below:

(i) **Industrial Wastes** Various industries release certain solid wastes in addition to gaseous air pollutants and other chemicals. The solid wastes from industries are thrown out in the form of flyash, metallic ash, chemical residues, etc., which gets settled on the surface of soil, thus polluting it.

(ii) **Urban and Domestic Wastes** Solid waste is also produced from our homes, shops, restaurant, etc. These include plastic bottles, polythene bags, bulbs, kitchen wastes, etc. which is collected and disposed off by kabadiwalas and municipal workers.

These people dispose these wastes into nearby areas rather than disposing it properly to avoid pollution. The proper disposal method includes sanitary landfills etc, where these wastes are disposed and dumped in ground depressions and are covered with a layer of soil.

(iii) **Biomedical Wastes** Wastes produced by hospitals, clinics, laboratories, etc., are also one of the major causes of soil pollution. Numerous items such as syringes, needles, unused or discarded tablets, research material, wound dressings, etc., are discarded and disposed off carelessly in the municipal garbage, due to which soil gets polluted.

(iv) **Chemical Fertilisers** These are used for increasing crop yield and are proven to be harmful in excess amount. Rainwater washes away the chemical fertiliser to reach the lakes, rivers, etc., where they get accumulated and affect the aquatic life.

(v) **Pesticides** DDT which are used to kill pests and other insects in agricultural farms and fields, also act as major pollutants responsible for soil pollution. The insects, pests and other microorganisms which are killed by these pesticides alter the basic structure of soil.

This later reaches the living beings such as humans and animals through the food grown in such soils and get concentrated in food chains at various levels.

Noise Pollution

- Any unwanted and disturbing sound beyond the normal level is known as noise pollution.
- **Major sources of noise pollution** include high intensity sound produced by trains, heavy machines, jet crafts, automobiles, loudspeakers at road side and in residential areas. A normal person can hear 20dB sound and feels discomfort with sound of 85dB.
- Noise pollution has harmful effects on human beings such as it interferes in communication, lowers the efficiency of work, interferes with the concentration of thoughts and disturb the sleep thus leading to nervous irritability and sometimes damages eardrum.
- Noise pollution can be easily controlled by restricting the use of loudspeakers after a fixed time, banning blowing of horns and by planting more and more trees along the roadside and near schools, hospitals, etc.

Radioactive Pollution

- Radiation is the form of energy which consists of high energy particles such as photons, X-rays, etc. Radiations are used in laboratory equipments in the field of medicines and other researches.
- **Sources of radiations** are mainly X-rays and radioactive rays released from nuclear power plants. X-rays contain a huge amount of energy particles which may damage the body cells.
- The person who is exposed to X-rays frequently has much more chances of getting serious health hazards such as mutations in chromosomes, bone cancer, genetic variations, etc.
- Apart from this, nuclear radiations leaked out of nuclear power plants are also major cause of radioactive pollution.
- The chief radioactive pollutant during explosion in Japan and Chernobyl was **Iodine-131,** which was responsible for haemorrhaging and even cancers. It also raises the risk of thyroid cancer. Thus, radioactive material should be discarded and disposed off carefully, so as to avoid the serious damage, to environment and mankind.

PYQs Previous Years' Questions

1 Mark Questions

Multiple Choice Questions

1. Which one of the following is a biodegradable waste? **ICSE 2023**

(a) Metal cans (b) E-waste
(c) Plastic (d) Flowers

Ans. (d) Flowers

2. Choose the correct option

An example of a biodegradable substance is **ICSE Specimen 2023**

(a) aluminium (b) paper
(c) plastic (d) stal

Ans. (b) Paper

3. Which one of the following is non-biodegradable? **ICSE 2018**

(a) DDT
(b) Vegetable peel
(c) Cardboard
(d) Bark of trees

Ans. (a) DDT is a non-biodegrdabale insecticide.

Very Short Answer Type Questions

4. Leaves, Styrofoam, Grass, Cow dung **ICSE 2024**

Ans. **Odd term** Styrofoam

Category Others are biodegradable wastes

5. Choose the **odd one** out from the following terms and name the **category** to which the others belong.
Dust, Smoke, Carbon monoxide, Effluents **ICSE Specimen 2023**

Ans. **Odd term** Effluents

Category Others are industrial air pollutants.

6. Give the biological/technical terms for the following

The constituents which cause the natural quality of the environment to deteriorate. **ICSE Specimen 2019**

Ans. Pollutant.

7. Choose the **odd** one out from the following terms given and name the **category** to which the others belong

Example Nose, tongue, arm, eye
Odd term-Arm

Category - Sense organs Detergents , X-rays, sewage, oil spills **ICSE 2018**

Ans. **Odd term** X-rays

Category Pollutants

8. The statement given below is incorrect. Rewrite the correct statement by changing the underlined words of the statement.
Deafness is caused due to the rupturing of the pinna. **ICSE 2017**

Ans. Deafness is caused due to the rupturing of the **eardrum** (tympanic membrane).

9. Give appropriate biological/technical term for the following

The type of waste generated in hospitals and pathological laboratories. **ICSE 2017**

Ans. Biomedical waste

10. Explain the following term. **ICSE Specimen 2017**

Pollutant

Ans. The agents that couse pollution and bring undesirable changes in environment are known as pollutant.

11. Mention three causes of soil pollution. **ICSE Specimen 2017**

Ans. Causes of soil pollution

(i) Soil pollution is caused by non-biodegradable waste.
(ii) Urban and domestic waste dumped into the soil.
(iii) Agriculture and chemical pesticides are used in soil.

12. Name the pollutants that cannot be broken down in to simple and harmless products. **ICSE 2016**

Ans. Non-biodegradable pollutants

13. In each set of terms given below, there is an odd one and cannot be grouped in the same category to which the other three belong. Identify the odd term in each set and name the category to which the remaining three belong.

Example Ovary, Fallopian tube, Ureter, Uterus

Odd term-Ureter.

Category-Part of female reproductive system

Sewage, Newspaper, Styrofoam, Hay **ICSE 2016**

Ans. **Odd term**–Styrofoam is non-biodegradable pollutant.

Category–Biodegradable pollutant.

14. Give the biological/technical term for the process causing an undesirable change in the environment. **ICSE 2016**

Ans. Pollution

15. Give one example of water pollutant. **ICSE 2014**

Ans. Domestic sewage is an example of water pollutant.

16. Briefly explain the term biomedical waste. **ICSE 2014**

Ans. Biomedical wastes consist of the waste produced by hospitals, i.e. wastes containing dressing, amputated body parts, used surgical instruments, etc. These spread diseases if left unmanaged.

17. Name the non-biodegradable pesticide. **ICSE 2013**

Ans. DDT is an example of non-biodegradable pesticide.

18. A constituent that causes pollution. **ICSE 2013**

Ans. A constituent that causes pollution is pesticide.

19. A non-degradable pollutant is .... **ICSE 2007**

Ans. A non-degradable pollutant is **plastic.**

20. A group is given with four examples in that group. There is one example which does not fit into the category, write down the category of the group and identify the odd one.

Sulphur dioxide, carbon monoxide, oxygen, nitrogen dioxide. **ICSE 2003**

Ans.

Odd	Category
Oxygen	Rest all are pollutants

21. Define the term noise pollution. **ICSE 2002**

Ans. Refer to text on page no. 218.

22. Define the pollutants with example. **ICSE 2001**

Ans. Pollutants are the substances/materials that cause pollution and bring undesirable changes in the environment, e.g. chemicals, industrial wastes, etc.

2 Marks Question

23. Give two examples of water pollutants. **ICSE 2024**

Ans. (i) Sewage or Industrial wastes.

(ii) Household detergents.

4 Marks Question

24. The diagram given below refers to the following account of an investigation and a graph of the results obtained. In 1986, a large city experienced a dense fog from 4th-9th December. During this time there was an increase in the number of deaths. In answering the following questions use the graph which shows how deaths per day were related to the amount of sulphur dioxide in the air. Select the best answer out of the five available choices given under each questions. **ICSE 2000**

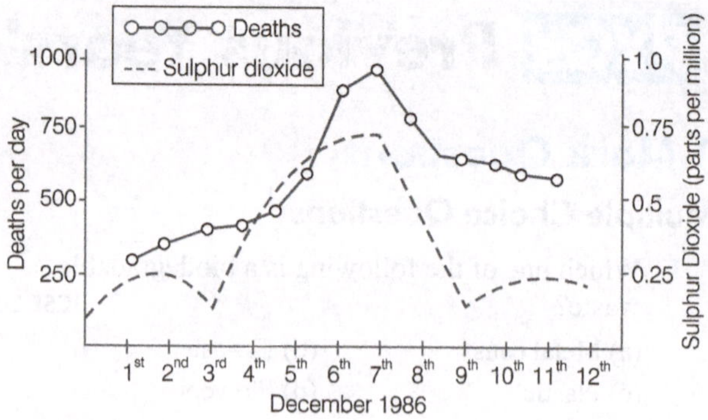

(i) On which day was the increase in sulphur dioxide greatest?

(a) 4th December (b) 5th December
(c) 6th December (d) 7th December
(e) 8th December

(ii) How many deaths occurred on the day following the highest sulphur dioxide concentration?

(a) 350 (b) 575 (c) 700 (d) 875
(e) 925

(iii) The graph shows the deaths per day were not

(a) lower before the fog than during the fog
(b) higher after the fog than before fog
(c) highest at the time of fog
(d) decreasing after fog
(e) increasing throughout the fog

(iv) Clean air prevents the occurrence of fog. Which of the following will help to ensure a clean environment?

(a) Air pollution (b) Education
(c) Legislation (d) Population control
(e) Ventilation

Ans. (i) (d) (ii) (e) (iii) (e) (iv) (b)

Diagram Based Questions

25. Study the picture given below and answer the following questions

(i) Identify the type of pollution.

(ii) Name one pollutant that causes the above pollution.

(iii) Mention the impact of this pollution on human health.

(iv) State one measure to control this pollution.

(v) What is a pollutant ? Explain the term.

Ans. (i) Water pollution **ICSE 2019 (5M)**

(ii) Sewage or Industrial waste

(iii) Effects of water pollution on human health

- Pollution of water may cause many water borne diseases such as typhoid, dysentery, etc.
- Aquatic animals and sea birds may be killed due to oil spills. Oil does not dissolve in water and it forms layer on water which prevents the oxygenation of sea water, which affects the aquatic organisms.
- Discharge of excessive nutrients through sewage into the static water leads to death of aquatic life. The organic matter increases growth of algae that consumes a lot of O_2. This decreases the O_2 causing problem for water organisms. This phenomenon is known as **eutrophication**. It refers to the natural ageing of lake by the nutrient enrichment of its water.

(iv) Water pollution can be controlled by introducing sewage treatment plants.

(v) **Pollutants** The agent that cause pollution and bring undesirable changes in the environment are known as pollutants. These are classified into two main types

- **Biodegradable pollutants** are the substances which can be degraded by the action of microorganisms, e.g. food and kitchen waste, paper, plant waste, etc.
- **Non-biodegradable pollutants** are the substances which cannot be degraded by the action of microorganisms, e.g. polythene bags, metals, electric components, pesticides (DDT), etc.

26. Given below is a representation of a type of pollution. Study the picture and answer the questions that follows

(i) Name the type of pollution shown in the picture.

(ii) Name one source of this pollution.

(iii) How does this pollution affect human health?

(iv) Write one measure to reduce this pollution.

(v) State one gaseous compound that leads to the depletion of the ozone layer and creates 'Ozone holes'. **ICSE 2018 (5M)**

Ans. (i) The type of pollution shown in the picture is air pollution.

(ii) One source of this pollution is forest fires, automobile exhaust, etc.

(iii) It causes various diseases in humans such as asthma, cancer and can also damage the CNS.

(iv) Air pollution can be reduced by using unleaded petrol and CNG over petrol and diesel as it is environment friendly.

(v) Chlorofluorocarbons (CFCs) are gaseous compounds responsible for the depletion of ozone layer.

27. Given below is a representation of a kind of pollution. Study the same and answer the questions that follows.

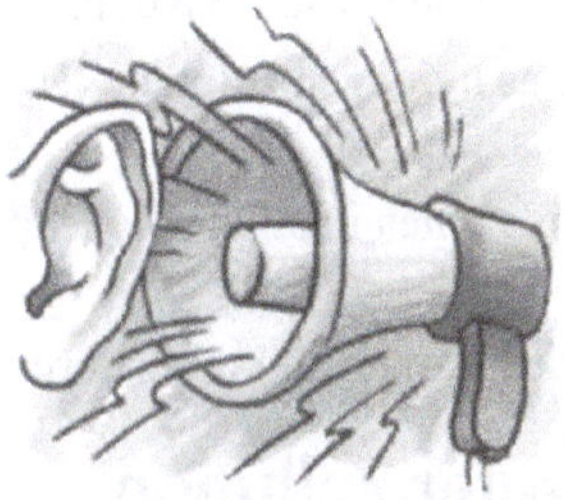

(i) Name the kind of pollution.

(ii) List any three common sources of this pollution.

(iii) Mention three harmful effects of this pollution on human health.

(iv) Explain the term 'Pollutant'.

(v) Name two soil pollutants. **ICSE 2017 (5M)**

Ans. (i) The given figure is showing noise pollution.

(ii) The three common sources of noise pollution are

- Trains
- Loudspeakers
- Jet crafts

(iii) The three harmful effects of noise pollution on human health are as follows

- Nervous irritability.
- Damage to eardrum.
- Interferes with the concentration of thoughts.

(iv) **Pollutant** The agents that cause pollution and bring undesirable changes in the environment are known as pollutants.

(v) Two soil pollutants are

- pesticides e.g. DDT.
- biomedical wastes like syringes, etc.

TOPIC 2

Effects of Pollution

It affects the life of organisms thereby, influencing the whole environment and climate ultimately.

Effects of Pollution on Human Beings and other Organisms

Various types of pollution affect the life of human beings in the following ways

Effects of Air Pollution

- Increased susceptibility to diseases due to several respiratory or lung disorders.
- It causes various diseases such as asthma, cancer and can also damage the CNS.
- Carbon monoxide released as pollutant can combine with haemoglobin thus, preventing the supply of O_2 to the cells and causing death due to asphyxiation.
- Pollutants such as hydrogen sulphide (H_2S) may cause headache, nausea, etc.
- Carbon monoxide when inhaled may lead to damage of the brain.
- In plants, reduced growth and premature death occurs.

Effects of Water Pollution

- Pollution of water may cause many water borne diseases such as typhoid, dysentery, etc.
- Aquatic animals and sea birds may be killed due to oil spills. Oil does not dissolve in water and it forms layer on water which prevents the oxygenation of sea water, which affects the aquatic organisms.
- Discharge of excessive nutrients through sewage into the static water leads to death of aquatic life. The organic matter increases growth of algae that consumes a lot of O_2. This decreases the O_2 causing problem for water organisms. This phenomenon is known as **eutrophication**. It refers to the natural ageing of lake by the nutrient enrichment of its water.

Effects of Soil Pollution

- Pesticides and insecticides may lead to loss of soil fertility.
- Accumulation of pesticides in increasing concentration in the body of living beings through food chain results in biomagnification or biological magnification.
- Non-target organisms are killed in the soil.

Effects of Radioactive Pollution

- Radiation may cause cancer and mutation in reproductive cells.
- Overdoses of radiation may be lethal and may even cause death.

Effects of Pollution on Climate and Environment

Pollution may adversely affect the climate and environment in many ways. The three major ways are as follows

1. Acid Rain

When the rain water contains large quantities of acids like HNO_3 and H_2SO_4 formed by dissolution of oxides of N and S in water, it is called acid rain. The pH of normal rain is about 6, while that of the acid rain is less than 3 or 4, i.e. highly acidic. Acid rain is harmful to the environment in many ways which are as follows

- It damages the fish and other aquatic life by increasing acidity of water.
- It damages the vegetation by killing the useful soil microbial community.
- Acid in the rain reacts with the calcium of statues, sculpture and ancient monuments and damages them. (e.g. Damage to Taj Mahal).
- Fine particles of sulphates and nitrates are also harmful for humans.

2. Greenhouse Effect and Global Warming

- Greenhouses are small houses made up of glass for the purpose of growing plants mainly in chilly winters.
- The glass allows the sunlight to enter the glass panel, but does not allow the heat to escape out from the glass. Therefore, warming the environment inside the glass house.
- In the same way **greenhouse effect** is a naturally occurring phenomenon that is responsible for heating earth's surface and atmosphere (without the effect of greenhouse, the average temperature on the surface of the earth would have been chilly-18°C rather than the present average of 15°C).

- **Global warming** is the phenomenon of gradual increase in the average temperature of the surface of the earth. This occurs due to the following reasons:
  - Release of more CO_2 due to burning of fossil fuels.
  - Less utilisation of CO_2 in photosynthesis due to decrease in the vegetation cover by deforestation.

3. Ozone Layer Depletion

- Ozone is a triatomic molecule (O_3) of oxygen found in the stratosphere layer of atmosphere. In the stratosphere, it helps in absorbing harmful UV radiations coming from the Sun.
- Various gaseous compounds such as chlorofluorocarbons (CFCs) from the refrigerators, packing material styrofoam, etc., are released into the atmosphere cause its breakdown into chlorine atoms. These Cl atoms break O_3 into O_2 and O. Thus, O_3 layer gets depleted or becomes thin.
- Ozone depletion is particularly marked over the Antarctic region. This led to formation of a large area of thinned ozone layer, called as **Ozone hole**.
- International Ozone Day is celebrated on **16th September** to create awareness for ozone layer protection.
- If the ozone layer gets depleted continuously, it would not prevent the entry of UV-rays to reach the earth. This will lead to various skin cancer, sunburn, genetic disorders, reduced productivity of forests, seas, etc.

Measures to Control Pollution

We cannot stop pollution from our environment completely but by taking few major steps we can easily prevent it from increasing with each passing day. Some of the steps that we should follow to control or to remove pollution are as follows

- By using unleaded petrol and CNG (Compressed Natural Gas) over petrol and diesel as they are environment friendly.
- By introducing and setting up sewage treatment plants.
- By switching off the engines of the vehicles at traffic signals, when they are not in use.
- By using organic substances instead of chemical fertilisers and pesticides.
- By planting more and more trees by the roadside, waste land and mountain slopes, so as to absorb more and more CO_2 that is released. This improves the quality of air.
- By avoiding throwing food wastes into open areas or into the drains.

> - **Organic farming** is a zero-waste procedure. It operates in the form of a cycle, where waste from a process is cycled as nutrients to the next process. It leads to maximum utilisation of resources and higher efficiency.
> - **Social forestry** refers to the planting of trees in barren and deforested lands. It aims at environmental, social and rural development.

Euro/Bharat Stage : Standard for Vehicles to Reduce Air Pollution

- The main goal of this standard is to reduce sulphur and nitrogen oxides from the automobile exhausts. Any motor vehicle running on the road has to follow emission norms in order to reduce pollution.
- These standards are based on European regulations and these were first introduced in 2000 and have been upgraded since then as BS-II, BS-III and now BS-IV. The BS numbers are based of European emission norms *viz*. Euro 4, Euro 5, Euro 6, etc.

Table Showing the Latest Mass Emission Standards in India

Types of Vehicle	Norms	Cities of Implementation
4 Wheelers	Bharat Stage III	Throughout the country since October, 2010
4 Wheelers	Bharat Stage IV	13 Mega cities (Delhi and NCR, Mumbai, Kolkata, Chennai, Bengaluru, Surat, Kanpur, Agra, Lucknow and Sholapur) since April, 2010 and it has been enforced to entire country since April 2017.
3 Wheelers	Bharat Stage III	Throughout the country since October, 2010
2 Wheelers	Bharat Stage III	Throughout the country since October, 2010

In 2016, the Central Pollution Control Board of Indian government announced that the country would skip the BS-V norms altogether and adopt BS-VI norms by 2020.

Swachh Bharat Abhiyan : A National Campaign for Clean India

"A clean India would be the best tribute, we Indians could pay to Mahatma Gandhi on his 150th birth anniversary in 2019". This was quoted by our Prime Minister Shri Narendra Modi before launching the Swachh Bharat Abhiyan officially on 2nd October 2014. This campaign is a significant drive for undertaking cleaning of cities, towns and villages of India.

PYQs Previous Years' Questions

1 Mark Questions

Multiple Choice Questions

1. Which one of the following is a greenhouse gas?
(a) Oxygen (b) Methane **ICSE 2018**
(c) Sulphur dioxide (d) Nitrogen

Ans. (b) Methane

2. The primary source of chlorofluorocarbons is **ICSE 2017**
(a) vehicular emissions (b) industrial effluents
(c) domestic sewage (d) refrigeration equipments

Ans. (d) Refrigeration equipments

Very Short Answer Type Questions

3. Write any two objectives of 'Swachh Bharat Abhiyan'. **ICSE 2024**

Or Mention any two objectives of 'Swachh Bharat Abhiyan'. **ICSE 2014, 2019**

Ans. The objectives of this campaign are as follows
- Elimination of open defecation and construction of house and commercial toilets.
- Cleaning the streets, roads and infrastructure of our country's towns and cities.
- Efficient management and disposal system to be developed for solid and liquid wastes.

4. Name one gaseous compound which depleted the ozone layer. **ICSE 2019**

Ans. Chlorofluorocarbons (CFCs).

5. Give suitable biological reasons for the following statement. Carbon monoxide is dangerous when inhaled. **ICSE 2019, 2014**

Ans. Carbon monoxide when inhaled in a large quantity, combines with the haemoglobin in blood with greater affinity which decreases the capacity of the blood to carry and transport oxygen in body. Thus, resulting in death of a person.

6. Give suitable biological reasons for the following statement.
Acid rain is harmful to the environment. **ICSE 2019**

Ans. **Acid Rain** contains large quantities of acids like HNO_3 and H_2SO_4. Due to high acidic content, it damages the fish and other aquatic life, vegetation, etc. and also proves harmful for humans in certain ways.

7. Identify the **odd** term in the set and name the **category** to which the remaining three belong.

Example Glucose, starch, cellulose, calcium
Odd term : Calcium
Category : Others are different types of carbohydrates.

Polythene bag, Crop residue, Animal waste, Decaying vegetables. **ICSE 2019**

Ans. **Odd term** - Polythene bag
Category - Others are agriculture wastes and rich in nitrogen and carbohydrates which have potential to produce renewable bio-based energy and chemical products.

8. Give biological reason for the statement.
Cutting of trees should be discouraged. **ICSE 2017**

Ans. Cutting of trees should be discouraged because plants utilise atmospheric CO_2 during photosynthesis and release O_2.
This maintains the balance of O_2 and CO_2 in the environment which is helpful in reducing pollution.

9. Rewrite the statement by changing the underlined word. <u>CNG</u> is mainly responsible for the formation of acid rain. **ICSE 2015**

Ans. SO_x and NO_x is mainly responsible for the formation of acid rain.

10. Rewrite and complete the sentence by inserting the correct word in the space indicated. .... causes corrosion of the marble or brick surface. **ICSE 2015**

Ans. Acid rain causes corrosion of the marble or brick surface.

11. Give the biological/technical term for the following A mixture of smoke and fog. **ICSE 2015**

Ans. Smog

12. Explain the term of greenhouse effect. **ICSE 2015**

Ans. **Greenhouse effect** is the warming up of the Earth's atmosphere due to increasing concentrations of various greenhouse gases like CO_2, methane, etc.

13. Give scientific reasons. Why use of CFC is banned in many countries? **ICSE 2014**

Ans. Chlorofluorocarbons (CFCs) are banned in many countries because they are one of the major cause for ozone layer depletion.

14. State two harmful effects fo acid rain on environment. **ICSE 2024**

Or

State any two harmful effects of acid rain. **ICSE 2013**

Ans. Two harmful effects of acid rain are as follows

(i) It damages the fish and other aquatic life by increasing acidity of water.

(ii) Acid in the rain reacts with the calcium of statues, sculpture and ancient monuments and damages them.

15. Answer briefly why carbon dioxide is considered as an air pollutant. **ICSE 2007**

Ans. CO_2 is responsible for the greenhouse effect or global warming. Rise in CO_2 level causes enhanced greenhouse effect which leads to raise in temperature following many harmful effects as raising sea level, melting of glaciers, extinction of species at faster rate, etc.

16. Define ozone hole. When is the International Ozone Day observed? **ICSE 2004**

Ans. Ozone hole is the thinning of ozone layer due to increased use of CFCs. International Ozone Day is celebrated on 16th September every year.

17. Name the pollutant largely responsible of acid rain. **ICSE 2002**

Ans. Sulphur dioxide is the pollutant largely responsible for acid rain.

2 Marks Questions

18. Carbon monoxide is dangerous when inhaled in excess. Comment on the statement **ICSE 2024**

Ans. Carbon monoxide is a poisonous gas. It is produced due to incomplete combustion of fuels such as petrol and diesel. It reduces the oxygen-carrying capacity of haemoglobin in our blood.

In the presence of carbon monoxide, instead of binding with oxygen, haemoglobin combines with carbon monoxide as it has more affinity for carbon monoxide resulting in the formation of carboxyhaemoglobin which is more stable than oxyhaemoglobin (formed when oxygen combines with haemoglobin). It causes headache, nausea, dizziness and may even result in death of the person.

19. Mention two harmful effects of nose pollution.. **ICSE 2024**

Ans. Harmful effects of noise pollution are as folllows

(i) It interferes in communication.

(ii) It interrupts concentration of thought and disturbs peace of mind.

(iii) It lowers efficiency of work.

(iv) It disturbs sleep and leads to nervous irritability. (Any two)

18. Excessive use of fertilisers in agricultural fields reduces the yield of crops. Justify the statement. **ICSE 2023**

Ans. The excessive use of fertilisers in agricultural fields can actually have a negative impact on crop yields in the long run. This is because excessive fertiliser use can lead to a number of problems, including

- Overuse of nitrogen-based fertilisers can cause the soil to become more acidic, which can ultimately reduce the soil's ability to support healthy plant growth.
- Overuse of a particular type of fertiliser can lead to imbalances in soil nutrients, which can cause some nutrients to become unavailable to the plant, while others are present in excess. This can lead to stunted growth and reduced yields.

CHAPTER TEST

Section-A

01 Mark Questions

1 Select the correct answer to the question from the given options.

(i) On which day International Ozone Day is celelebrated?

(a) 15 August (b) 16 May
(c) 24 June (d) 16 September

(ii) Which one of the example of radiation pollutant?

(a) SO_2 (b) O_3
(c) I-131 (d) UV-B

(iii) pH of 'Acid rain' is

(a) less than 5 (b) less than 9
(c) less than 2 (d) more than 7

(iv) 'Swachh Bharat Abhiyan' was officially launched on

(a) 15th August 2016
(b) 2nd October 2014
(c) 26th January 2018
(d) 8th November 2017

(v) 'X' rays' are a potential source of

(a) radiation pollution (b) noise pollution
(c) water pollution (d) air pollution

2 (i) Name the following.

(a) A pollutant which is responsible for causing radiation pollution.
(b) A chemical which caused minimata disease in Japan.
(c) Ozone layer prevent us from which rays.
(d) A gaseous pollutant.

(ii) Fill in the blanks and with suitable words.

(a) Sewage is the liquid waste from .... activities.
(b) .... fertiliser help in faster and increased crop yield.
(c) The chief industrial gaseous pollutants again consist of .... and .... gases.
(d) Radioactive pollutant .... raise the risk of thyroid cancer.

(iii) Match the items of Column I with those in Column II and rewrite the correct matching pair.

	Column I	Column II
A.	Soil pollution	1. CO_2 and methane
B.	water pollution	2. Cobalt-60
C.	Radiation pollution	3. H_2N,NO_2
D.	Air pollution	4. Eutrophication
E.	Greenhouse gases	5. Biomagnification

(iv) State true or false

(a) Soil pollution is largely localised ....
(b) Pollution and pollutant are same thing ....
(c) CO_2 and ethane are directly contribuiting to global warming ....
(d) Disease like cholera and jaundice are the result of water pollution ....

(v) Write full forms.

(a) DDT (b) CNG
(c) CFC (d) UV

02 Marks Questions

3 Define pollution. Write major types of pollution.

4 List the major sources of water pollution.

5 What is thermal pollution?

6 Define smog.

7 List the sources of soil pollution.

03 Marks Questions

8 Differentiate between biodegradable and non-bio degradable waste.

9 Write short note on 'Swachh Bharat Abhiyan.

10 Write the effects of ozone layer depletion on human health.

11. Write a short note on greenhouse effect.

12. Write the steps to control pollution.

Section-B

Diagram Based Questions

13. With the reference of given figure answer the following questions.

(i) What does this figure representing?

(ii) Write its harmful effects.

(iii) Write some measure to minimise it.

14. With the reference of given figure. Answer the following question.

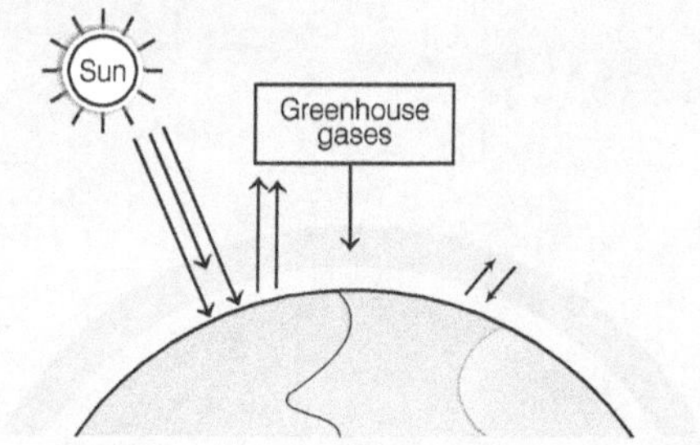

(i) What does this phenomenon representing for its?

(ii) Which gases are responsible for it?

(iii) Define 'global warming.

Answers

1. (i) (d), (ii) (c), (iii) (a), (iv) (b), (v) (a)

ICSE

CHAPTERWISE - TOPICWISE
QUESTION BANK

Sample Papers
(1-3)

ICSE Unsolved

SAMPLE PAPER 01

Time : 2 hrs
Marks : 80

Biology

General Instructions

1. You will not be allowed to write during the first 15 minutes. This time is to be spent in reading the question paper.
2. The time given at the head of this paper is the time allowed for writing the answers.
3. **Section-A** is compulsory. Attempt **any four** questions from **Section-B**.
4. The intended marks for questions or parts of questions are given in brackets [].

Section - A

(Attempt **all questions** from this section)

1. Choose the correct answer to the questions from the given options. (Do not copy the question write the correct answer only.) **[15]**

(i) **Assertion** (A) The roots of plants absorb water through osmosis.

Reason (R) Osmosis is the movement of water molecules from a region of their higher concentration to a region of their lower concentration through a semipermeable membrane.

(a) A is true, but R is false
(b) A is false, but R is true
(c) Both A and R are true
(d) Both A and R is false

(ii) The secretion of Antidiuretic Hormone (ADH) is inhibited by

(a) nicotine (b) morphine
(c) emotion and stress (d) alcohol

(iii) The middle piece of the sperm provides

(a) gene (b) energy
(c) chromosomes (d) food

(iv) When the level of thyroxine concentration exceeds the normal level in blood then it

(a) inhibits the secretion of TRH by anterior pituitary gland
(b) inhibits the secretion of TSH from the hypothalamus
(c) inhibits the secretion of TRH by hypothalamus
(d) stimulate the scretion of TSH from pituitary gland

(v) Birth rate is the number of live births

(a) per 100 people per year
(b) per 100 people per decade
(c) per 1000 people per year
(d) per 1000 people per decade

(vi) **Assertion** (A) A plant cell placed in a hypotonic solution get deplasmolysed.

Reason (R) Hypotonic solution causes endosmosis.

(a) A is true, but R is false
(b) A is false, but R is true
(c) Both A and R are true
(d) Both A and R is false

(vii) The rate of transpiration is less when

(a) atmosphere is dry
(b) temperature is high
(c) humidity is high
(d) atmosphere is dry and temperature is high

(viii) **Assertion** (A) Chromosomes are visible during cell division in the before of chromatids.

Reason (R) Chromatids are formed by the condensation of chromatin fibres or threads during cell division.

(a) A is true, but R is false
(b) A is false, but R is true
(c) Both A and R are true
(d) Both A and R is false

(ix) How much litres of blood by volume are contained in the body of a normal adult individual?
(a) 3-4 litres (b) 5-6 litres
(c) 7-8 litres (d) 9-10 litres

(x) Kidneys do not play any significant role in the removal of
(a) water (b) ammonia (c) urea (d) uric acid

(xi) **Assertion** (A) Homozygous individuals for a particular trait have two identical alleles for that trait.
Reason (R) In heterozygous individuals, the alleles for a particular trait are different from each other.
(a) A is true, but R is false
(b) A is false, but R is true
(c) Both A and R are true
(d) Both A and R is false

(xii) A human eye can focus objects at different distance by adjusting the focal length of the eye lens. This is due to
(a) accomodation (b) far-sightedness
(c) near-sightedness (d) presbyopia

(xiii) Vasopressin causes rise in blood pressure. Which of the following reasons are correct regarding the mechanism of action of vasopressin?
P. It increases reabsorption of water from the kidneys.
Q. It causes contraction of blood vessels.
R. Secretion of water to kidneys.
(a) Only P (b) Only Q (c) P and Q (d) Q and R

(xiv) Richmond Lang effect is associated with ....
(a) auxin (b) gibberellin
(c) cytokinin (d) ethylene

(xv) A biology teacher asked her students to provide two examples of forces responsible for the ascent of sap in plants. Four students gave the following examples.
Student 1 Root pressure and transpirational pull
Student 2 Capillary action and root pressure
Student 3 Only cohesion
Student 4 Only adhesion
Who gave the most suitable examples?
(a) Students 1 and 2 (b) Students 2 and 3
(c) Students 3 and 4 (d) Students 4 and 1

2. (i) Name the following.
(a) The type of cell division which does not occur in the reproductive cells of organisms.
(b) The statistical study of the human population of a region.
(c) The biological term used for the protective membranes of the brain.
(d) The phase of cardiac cycle in which the auricles contract.
(e) Hormone whose under secretion in the body of an adult cause myxoedema. **[5]**

(ii) Arrange and rewrite the terms in each group in correct order so as to be in a logical sequence beginning with the term that is underlined.
(a) Ovary, Uterus, Oviduct, Cervix, Vagina
(b) Receptor, Sensory neuron, Effector, Association neuron, Motor neuron
(c) Cornea, Lens, Aqueous humour, Pupil, Yellow spot
(d) Xylem, Substomatal space, Intercellular space, Stoma, Mesophyll cells
(e) Soil, Water, Endodermis, Xylem, Cortical cells, Root hair **[5]**

(iii) Fill in the blanks with suitable words.
To test the leaf for starch, the leaf is boiled in water to (a) .... It is next boiled in methylated spirit to (b) .... The leaf is placed in warm water to soften it. It is then placed in a dish and (c) .... solution is added. The region which contains starch, turns (d) .... and the region, which does not contain starch, turns (e) .... **[5]**

(iv) Given below is a structure of nephron. Match the structures marked (*A*) to (*E*) with their correct functions. **[5]**

Structure of neuron	Functions
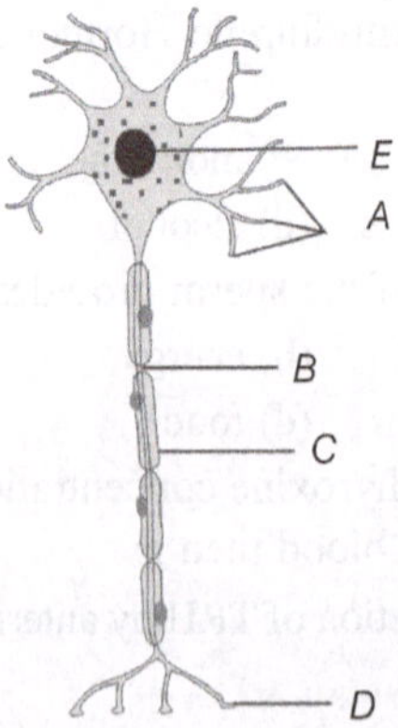	1. Provides insulation
	2. Controls the cell's activities, including growth, metabolism and protein synthesis.
	3. Transmit signals to other neurons.
	4. Receive signals from other neurons.
	5. Transmit impulses away from the cell body.

[5]

(v) Given below is the structure of human sperm. Read the information below the diagram and fill in the blanks.

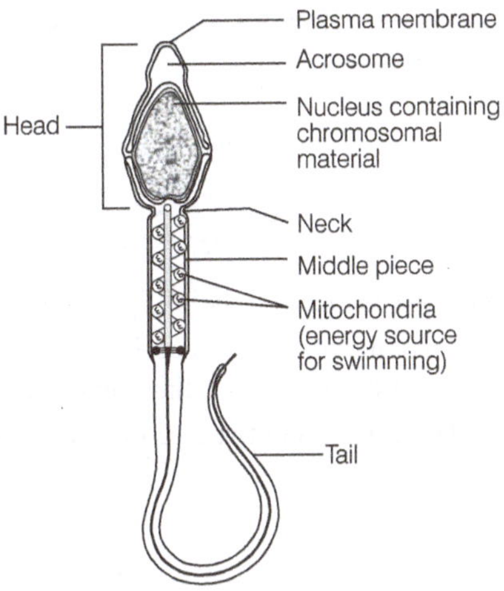

A mature sperm cell or spermatozoa is a microscopic, tadpole-shaped structure of about 2-5 mm in diameter and 60 mm long. It comprises of three main parts.

The head of sperm is composed of a large nucleus and a small cap-like structure known as .....(a)....., which secretes .....(b)..... enzymes. The neck consists of funnel-shaped basal body and a pair of .....(c)..... lying at the right angle to each other. Middle piece is cylindrical in shape and is known as ....(d).... of the sperm cell because it possesses .....(e)..... . **[5]**

(a) Cowper's gland (b) stirrup
(c) stroma (d) uterus
(e) ciliary body **[5]**

Section - B

(Attempt any **four questions** from this section.)

3. (i) How does CNS receive the signals when there is an urge to pass urine? **[1]**

(ii) State Mendel's law of independent assortment. **[2]**

(iii) What is meiosis? Give its significance. **[2]**

(iv) Differentiate between light and dark reaction. **[2]**

(v) Draw a neat, labelled diagram of male reproductive system. **[3]**

4. (i) Mention the exact location of stomata. **[1]**

(ii) Name two vestigial organs of human body. **[2]**

(iii) Differentiate between oogenesis and spermatogenesis. **[2]**

(iv) Mention any two adaptations found in plants to overcome the excessive rate of transpiration. **[2]**

(v) Study the diagram given below and answer the questions that follows.

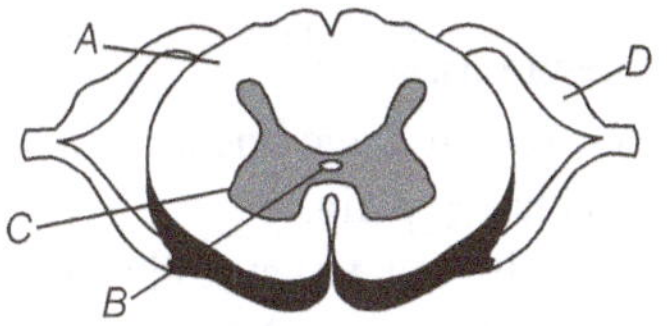

(a) Name the structure shown in the given figure.

(b) Where would you find cell bodies and myelinated axons?

(c) List any two functions performed by the given structure. **[3]**

5. (i) Define birth rate. **[1]**

(ii) Explain the significance of α-cells of pancreas. **[2]**

(iii) State two functions of chordae tendineae. **[2]**

(iv) Name one hormone released by thyroid gland. State its functions. **[2]**

(v) Given below is the outline of the male reproductive system.

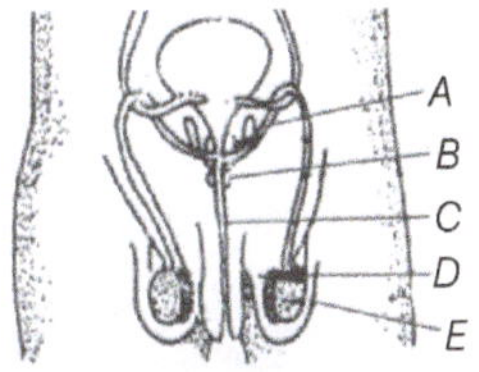

(a) Name the parts labelled *A* to *E*.

(b) Name the cells of part *E* that produce testosterone.

(c) State the functions of the parts labelled as *A* and *D*. **[3]**

6. (i) Give the exact location of adrenal gland. **[1]**

(ii) Differentiate between myopia and hypermetropia with reference to cause of the defect. **[2]**

(iii) State the main function of lymphocytes. **[2]**

(iv) Education is very important for population control. Explain. **[2]**

(v) Draw a neat diagram of a chloroplast and label its parts. **[3]**

7. (i) Explain the term plasmolysis. **[1]**

(ii) Give two reasons why photosynthesis is considered as a life supporting process on earth? **[2]**

(iii) Give one function of each, medulla oblongata and cerebellum. **[2]**

(iv) What is the difference between diffusion and osmosis. **[2]**

(v) Draw a neat labelled diagram of a Malpighian capsule. **[3]**

8. (i) Define uterus. **[1]**

(ii) Some women have facial hair like beard and moustache. Explain. **[2]**

(iii) Mention the value of systolic BP and diastolic BP of a normal human adult. **[2]**

(iv) State two harmful effects of chemical fertilisers. **[2]**

(v) Given below is a schematic diagram showing Mendel's experiment on sweet pea plants having axial flowers with round seeds (AARR) and terminal flowers with wrinkled seeds (aarr). Study the same and answer the questions that follows

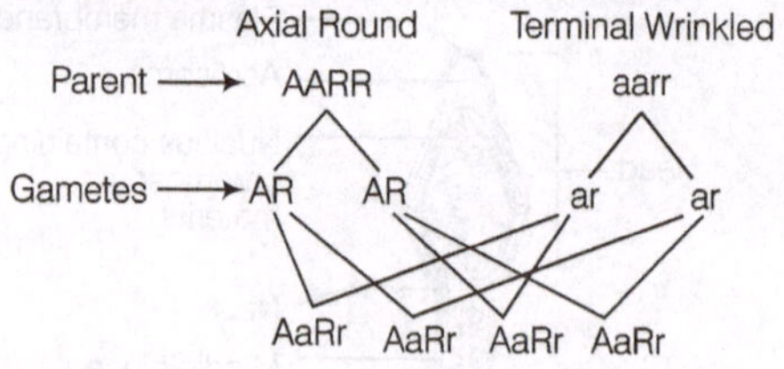

(a) Give the phenotype of F_1-progeny.

(b) Give the phenotypes of F_2-progeny produced upon by the self-pollination of F_1-progeny.

(c) Give the phenotypic ratio of F_2-progeny. **[3]**

Answers

1. (i)-c, (ii)-d, (iii)-b, (iv)-d (v)-c, (vi)-c, (vii)-c, (viii)-a, (ix)-c, (x)-b, (xi)-c, (xii)-a, (xiii)-c, (xiv)-c, (xv)-a

ICSE Unsolved

SAMPLE PAPER 02

Time : 2 hrs
Marks : 80

Biology

General Instructions

1. You will not be allowed to write during the first 15 minutes. This time is to be spent in reading the question paper.
2. The time given at the head of this paper is the time allowed for writing the answers.
3. **Section-A** is compulsory. Attempt **any four** questions from **Section-B**.
4. The intended marks for questions or part of questions are given in brackets [].

Section-A

(Attempt **all questions** from this section)

1. Choose the correct answers to the questions from the given options. (Do not copy the question, write the correct answers only) **[15]**

(i) Which of the following is not a type of transpiration observed in plants?
(a) Stomatal transpiration
(b) Mitochondrial transpiration
(c) Lenticular transpiration
(d) Cuticular transpiration

(ii) A higher concentration of the gaseous hormone ethylene is found in
(a) green banana (b) fresh potato tuber
(c) green apple (d) ripe banana

(iii) **Assertion** (A) Transpiration helps in cooling the plant.
Reason (R) As water evaporates from the surface of the leaves, it absorbs latent heat from the leaf.
(a) A is true and R is false
(b) A is false and R is true
(c) Both A and R are true
(d) Both A and R are false

(iv) Which of the following is associated with the regulation and coordination of muscular contraction and body balance?
(a) Spinal cord (b) Cerebellum
(c) Cerebrum (d) Medulla oblongata

(v) Which of the following acts as a life support system where fertilised ovum receives nourishment and further development proceeds.
(a) Ovaries (b) Oviduct
(c) Uterus (d) Fallopian tube

(vi) **Assertion** (A) Dominant allele is an allele whose phenotype expresses even in the presence of another allele of that gene.
Reason (R) It is represented by capital letter, e.g. T.
(a) A is true, but R is false
(b) A is false, but R is true
(c) Both A and R are true
(d) Both A and R are false

(vii) The blood is primarily composed of
(a) plasma
(b) cellular elements
(c) blood plasma and cellular elements
(d) None of the above

(viii) Mr. Sharma asked his students about the metaphase stage of cell division.
Riya said: During metaphase, chromosomes align at the cell's equatorial plane.

Amit said: Metaphase is the phase where DNA replication occurs.

Sneha said: In metaphase, spindle fibres attach to the centromeres of chromosomes.

Kunal said: Metaphase is the phase where the cell membrane divides.

Who gave the correct answer? Choose the correct option given below.

(a) Riya and Sneha
(b) Amit
(c) Kunal
(d) Riya and Kunal

(ix) The process in which the living or dead plant cells absorb water through surface attraction is called

(a) osmosis (b) swelling
(c) absorption (d) imbibition

(x) **Assertion** (A) Photosynthesis occurs in the chloroplasts of plant cells.

Reason (R) Chloroplasts contain chlorophyll, which captures light energy required for photosynthesis.

(a) A is true, but R is false
(b) A is false, but R is true
(c) Both A and R are true
(d) Both A and R are false

(xi) The other name of sex chromosomes is

(a) autosomes
(b) allosomes
(c) somatic chromosomes
(d) None of the abvoe

(xii) Liver plays a very important role in detoxify ammonia by transforming it into

(a) creatinine (b) urea
(c) bile pigments (d) None of these

(xiii) A biology teacher asked her students to give two significances of meiosis. Four students provided the following answers.

Student 1 "Meiosis helps in growth and development."

Student 2 "It maintains the chromosome number in a species."

Student 3 "Meiosis is important for asexual reproduction."

Student 4 "It introduces genetic variation through crossing over."

Who provided the correct significance of meiosis?

(a) Student 1 and student 2
(b) Student 3 and student 4
(c) Student 1 and student 4
(d) Student 2 and student 4

(xiv) Light independent phase is also known as

(a) biosynthetic phase (b) photochemical phase
(c) reduction phase (d) fixation phase

(xv) **Assertion** (A) Cytokinins promote the growth of roots in plants.

Reason (R) Cytokinins stimulate root development when the auxin concentration is high.

(a) A is true, but R is false
(b) A is false, but R is true
(c) Both A and R are true
(d) Both A and R are false

2. (i) Name the following.

(a) Part of the chloroplast where dark reaction occurs.
(b) Organ in man concerned with maintaining water balance in the body.
(c) Nerve which transmits impulses from the eye to the brain.
(d) Smallest blood vessel.
(e) Chemical used to test starch. **[5]**

(ii) Arrange and rewrite the terms in each group in correct order so as to be in a logical sequence beginning with the term that is underlined.

(a) <u>Cell wall</u>, Nuclear membrane, Nucleolus, Cytoplasm, Cell membrane, Nucleoplasm
(b) Water molecules, Oxygen, Grana, Hydrogen and hydroxyl ions, <u>Photons</u>
(c) Implantation, Fertilisation, <u>Ovulation</u>, Gestation
(d) Ear ossicles, Oval window, Tympanum, Cochlea, <u>Auditory canal</u>
(e) Uterus, Parturition, <u>Fertilisation</u>, Gestation, Implantation **[5]**

(iii) Given below is the diagram, showing a section of human brain. Read the information below the diagram and fill in the blanks.

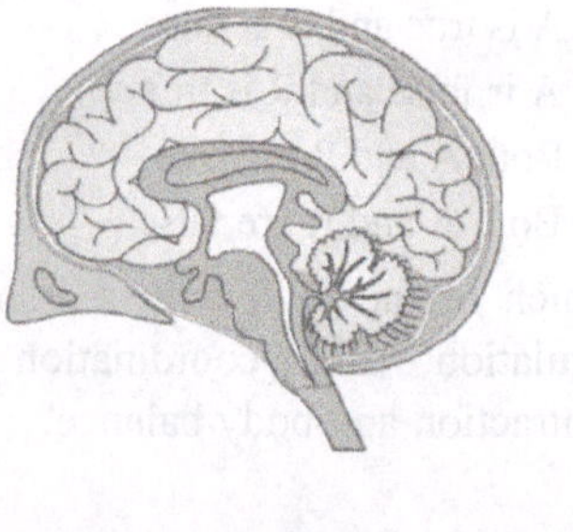

The brain is the central information processing organ of our body and acts as the 'command and control system' of all body activities. It is anterior most part of the central neural system, which is located in the cranium of the skull.

Human brain is divided into .....(a)....., ...(b)..... and hindbrain. .....(c)..... is the largest part of the brain and is divided into olfactory lobe, ...(d)..... and cerebrum. Cerebrum is considered as the seat of intelligence and is divided into two main parts known as .....(e)...... . **[5]**

(iv) Read the explanation given below and name the structure. **[5]**

(a) Name the gland located in front of the neck region, just below the larynx.

(b) The part of brain associated with memory.

(c) Thin, flattened membrane-bound sac found within the chloroplast.

(d) Name the endocrine cells found in the pancreas that secrete hormones.

(e) Name the part of the human brain concerned with the coordinates muscular activity. **[5]**

(v) Given below is a human excretory system. Match the structures marked *A* to *E* with their correct functions. **[5]**

Human Excretory System	**Functions**
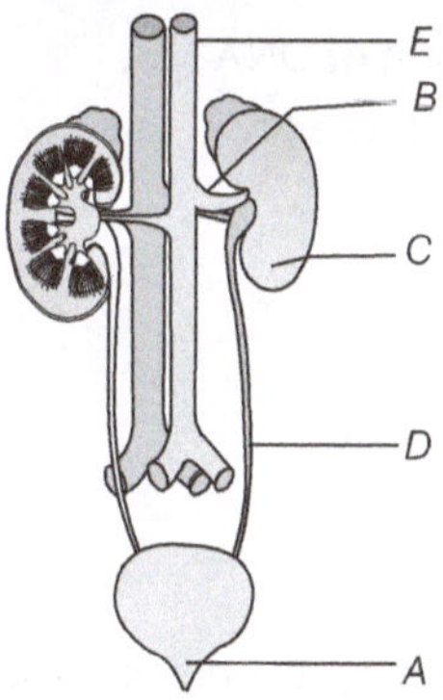	1. **Ureter:** Carries urine from the kidneys to the urinary bladder.
	2. **Dorsal Aorta:** Distributes oxygenated blood from the heart to the lower regions of the body.
	3. **Renal Artery:** Supplies oxygen-rich blood to the kidneys for filtration.
	4. **Posterior Vena Cava:** Filters blood to remove waste products and excess substances, producing urine.
	5. **Urethra:** Transports urine from the bladder to the outside of the body during urination.

[5]

Section-B

(Attempt any **four questions** from this section.)

3. (i) Write the overall chemical equation for cellular respiration. **[1]**

(ii) Mention any two functions of WBC. **[2]**

(iii) Differentiate between meiosis and mitosis. **[2]**

(iv) Name the hormone secreted by adrenal gland. **[2]**

(v) Draw a neat and labelled diagram of human neuron. **[3]**

4. (i) Mention the exact location of aqueous humour. **[1]**

(ii) What is passive transport? **[2]**

(iii) Mention the role of abscisic acid in stress condition. **[2]**

(iv) State Mendel's law of segregation. **[2]**

(v) Study the diagram given below and then answer the questions that follows.

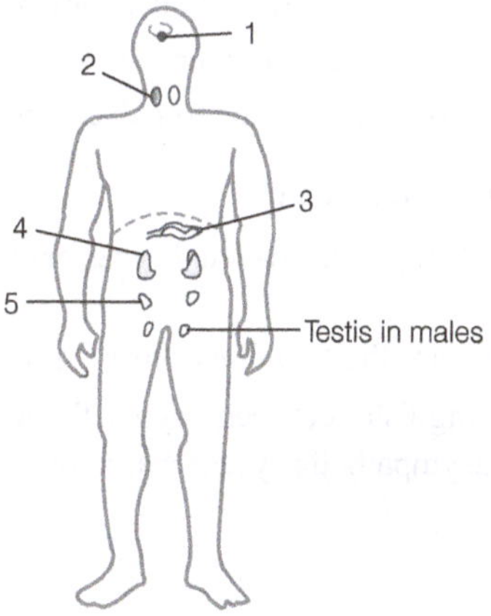

(a) Name the glands marked 1 to 5.

(b) Which hormone secreted by 2? Give one important function of this hormone.

(c) The cells present in part 3 are alpha and beta cells which secrete .... and .... , respectively. **[3]**

5. (i) Give the exact location of malleus. **[1]**

(ii) Differentiate between G_1-phase and G_2-phase. **[2]**

(iii) Mention the two functions of liver. **[2]**

(iv) What is the significance of variation? **[2]**

(v) Draw a well-labelled diagram of nephron. **[3]**

6. (i) Explain the term 'mortality'. [1]
(ii) Name the two hormones secreted by posterior lobe of pituitary. [2]
(iii) Mention the two factors majorly responsible for air pollution. [2]
(iv) Name any two surgical techniques that can be used to prevent pregnancy. [2]
(v) Given below is a representation of a type of pollution.

(a) Name the type of pollution shown in the figure.
(b) Mention the one source of this pollution.
(c) Write one measure to reduce this pollution. [3]

7. (i) What is reflex arc? [1]
(ii) Pituitary gland is called the master gland. Explain. [2]
(iii) What are the two functions of spinal cord? [2]
(iv) Distinguish between sympathetic system and parasympathetic system based on the functions. [2]
(v) Draw neat and labelled diagram showing the oxygen diffuses into the tissue fluid around cells.

8. (i) What is semen? [1]
(ii) Explain the reason why some plants show wilting of their leaves during mid day even when the soil is well watered. [2]
(iii) What is tendril? Name any two types of tendrils. [2]
(iv) What is vitreous humour? Name the part of eye responsible for maintaining the shape of the eyeball. [2]
(v) There is a diagram of a double helical structure of DNA.

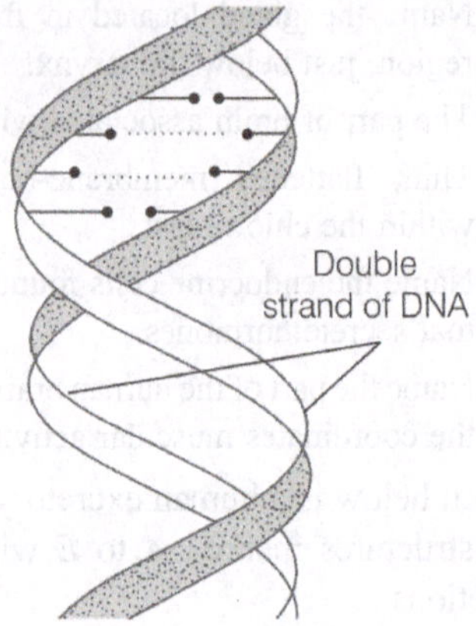

(i) Name the four nitrogenous bases that forms a DNA molecule.
(ii) Give the full form of DNA.
(iii) Name the unit of heredity. [3]

Answers

1. (i)-b, (ii)-d, (iii)-c, (iv)-b (v)-c, (vi)-c, (vii)-c, (viii)-d, (ix)-d, (x)-c, (xi)-b, (xii)-b, (xiii)-d, (xiv)-a, (xv)-b

ICSE Unsolved

SAMPLE PAPER 03

Time : 2 hrs
Marks : 80

Biology

General Instructions

1. You will not be allowed to write during the first 15 minutes. This time is to be spent in reading the question paper.
2. The time given at the head of this paper is the time allowed for writing the answers.
3. **Section-A** is compulsory. Attempt **any four** questions from **Section-B**.
4. The intended marks for questions or part of questions are given in brackets [].

Section- A

(Attempt **all questions** from this section)

1. Choose the correct answer to the questions from options (Do not copy question write the correct answer only). **[15]**

(i) Anterior lobe of pituitary secretes
(a) growth hormone (b) luteinizing hormone
(c) prolactin (d) All of these

(ii) Part of ear that collects sound waves
(a) pinna (b) temporal bone
(c) eardrum (d) cochlea

(iii) **Assertion** (A) The heart has four chambers; two atria and two ventricles.

Reason (R) The four chambers helps in keeping oxygenated and deoxygenated blood separate to ensure efficient circulation.

(a) A is true, but R is false
(b) A is false, but R is true
(c) Both A and R are true
(d) Both A and R are false

(iv) AIDS is caused by infection of HIV (virus) which can be transmitted through
(a) sexual contact
(b) through blood transfusion
(c) contaminated syringes or needles
(d) All of the above

(v) Dhara tried to match Mendel's laws with their definitions.

She tabulated the pairs as follows

Laws	Definitions
U	Two alternative forms of traits are present in an organism, only one factor expresses itself in F_1-progeny and others remain suppressed.
V	Two factors or alleles controlling one character segregate independently, without influencing each other, i.e. each gamete receives one factor for each character.

Identify the correct pair.
(a) *U*- Law of dominance, *V*- Law of independent assortment
(b) *U*- Law of independent assortment, *V*- Law of dominance
(c) *U*- Law of dominance, *V*- Law of segregation
(d) *U*- Law of segregation, *V*- Law of dominance

(vi) **Assertion** (A) Mitosis is also known as equational division.

Reason (R) In mitosis, two daughter cells with equal number of chromosomes (as of parent cell) are formed.

(a) A is true, but R is false
(b) A is false, but R is true
(c) Both A and R are true
(d) Both A and R are false

(vii) Which one of the following is the phenotypic monohybrid ratio in F_2-generation?

(a) 3 : 1 (b) 1 : 2 : 1
(c) 2 : 2 (d) 1 : 3

(viii) Root hair absorbs water from the soil with the help of

(a) suction pressure
(b) turgour pressure
(c) osmotic pressure
(d) None of the above

(ix) **Assertion** (A) Urea is the primary nitrogenous waste excreted by humans.

Reason (R) Humans are uricotelic organisms.

(a) A is true, but R is false
(b) A is false, but R is true
(c) Both A and R are true
(d) Both A and R are false

(x) Dark reaction

(a) is independent of light
(b) occurs in dark
(c) requires product of light reaction
(d) All of the above

(xi) Which of the following growth regulators is known as stress hormone?

(a) Abscisic acid (b) Ethylene
(c) GA_3 (d) Auxin

(xii) The forebrain consists of

(a) cerebrum (b) thalamus
(c) hypothalamus (d) All of these

(xiii) **Assertion** (A) Thyroid Stimulating Hormone (TSH) directly affects the secretion of thyroid hormones.

Reason (R) TSH is secreted by the anterior pituitary, which stimulates the thyroid gland to produce thyroxine.

(a) A is true, but R is false
(b) A is false, but R is true
(c) Both A and R are true
(d) Both A and R are false

(xiv) Which of the following is used as an atmospheric pollution indicator?

(a) Lepidoptera
(b) Pollutant
(c) Plants and animals
(d) Lichens

(xv) In an experiment on the endocrine system, a teacher asked students to identify the correct components and their functions. The following responses were given.

Garima said : The thyroid gland regulates metabolism and produces thyroid hormones.

Ayushi said : The pituitary gland is called the "master gland" because it controls other endocrine glands.

Simran said : The pancreas secretes insulin and glucagon, which help regulate blood sugar levels.

Malika said : The adrenal glands produce hormones like adrenaline, which control stress responses.

Who gave the correct response?

(a) Ayushi and Garima
(b) Malika and Simran
(c) Ayushi and Malika
(d) All of the students

2. (i) Name the following.

(a) Two organelles that are present in plant cell but not in animal cell.
(b) Type of cells in which meiosis occurs.
(c) Two major types of mutation.
(d) Part which contribute majorly in the process of transpiration.
(e) Most active and motile constituent of blood that possess nucleus. **[5]**

(ii) Arrange and rewrite the terms in each group in correct order so as to be in a logical sequence beginning with the term that is underlined.

(a) Light, Thylakoids, Oxygen, Chloroplast, Water
(b) Lungs, Right auricle, Left ventricle, Left auricle
(c) Glomerulus, Afferent arteriole, Bowman's capsule, Urinary bladder, Renal tube
(d) Dorsal root ganglion receptor, Effector, Ventral root ganglion, Associated neuron

(e) <u>Hypothalamus</u>, TSH, Anterior pituitary, Thyroid hormone, TRH Thyroid gland **[5]**

(iii) Fill in the blanks with suitable words.

Reflexes are initiated by some (a) ……… they are mainly (b) ……… due to environment. Commands originate mostly in the (c) ………… and (d) ……… and a few in the brain as well. They involve (e) ……… and glands. **[5]**

(iv) Choose the odd one out from the following terms and name the category to which the other belong.

(a) A^+, B^+, O^+, Rh^+

(b) Thromboplastin, Fibrin, Prolactin, Thrombin

(c) Tonsils, Spleen, Lymph nodes, Bowman's capsule

(d) Neurophils, Basophils, Monocytes, Eosinophils

(e) Capillaries, Glomerulus, Artery, Vein **[5]**

(v) The following paragraph is related to cell division. Complete the following paragraph by giving the answers.

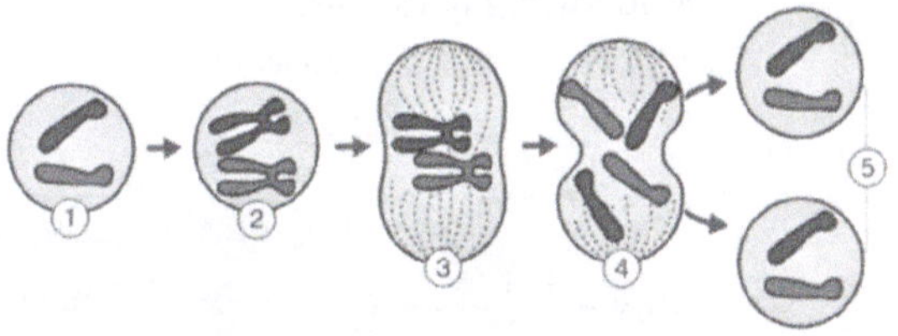

A biologist was studying cell division. One day he observed a dark coloured stain under a microscope. These structures represented chromosomes.

Chromosomes are made up of long strands of DNA and histone proteins known as …..(i)….. during …..(ii)….., chromosomes duplicate and form …..(iii)….., which are held together by a centromere. As the cell divides, the chromosomes align at the equator of the cell during, …..(iv)….. and then move to opposite poles during …..(v)….. . **[5]**

Section - B

(Attempt any **four questions** from this section.)

3. (i) Define endocrine gland. **[1]**

(ii) Give two differences between biodegradable and non-biodegradable wastes. **[2]**

(iii) Mention any two functions of human ovary. **[2]**

(iv) Why do plants die in excess water? **[2]**

(v) Draw a neat, labelled diagram of nephron. **[3]**

4. (i) Give the exact location of guard cells. **[1]**

(ii) What is the significance of ozone layer. **[2]**

(iii) Write about two sex-linked diseases in humans. **[2]**

(iv) How are modern humans and Neanderthals related? **[2]**

(v) A well-watered healthy potted plant with variegated leaves was kept in darkness for about 24 hours.

It was then set up as shown in the diagram below and exposed to light for about 12 hours. At the end of this time, leaf *X* and leaf *Y* were tested for starch. Study the diagram and answer the questions that follows.

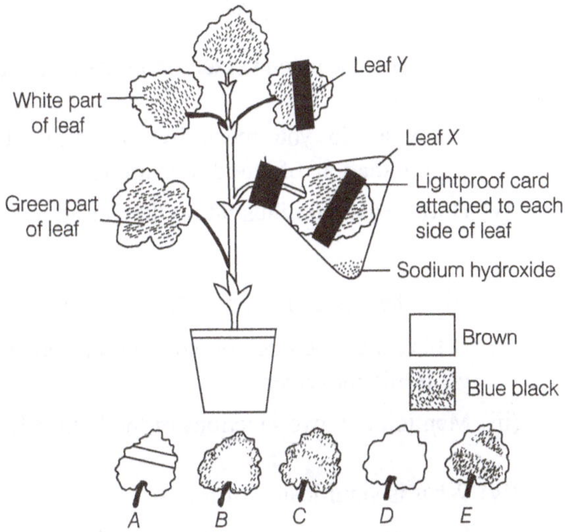

(a) Why was the plant initially kept in darkness for 24 hours?

(b) What is the function of sodium hydroxide solution in the flask?

(c) Select the correct leaf from the five available choices shown in the diagrams *A*, *B*, *C*, *D* and *E*. Rewrite the correct answer by filling the appropriate letter for the questions that follows.

(i) After the starch test, leaf *X* would look like …… .

(ii) After the starch test, leaf *Y* would look like …… . **[3]**

5. (i) Explain the term epididymis. [1]

(ii) Name the hormones released by anterior lobe of pituitary. [2]

(iii) What is the cause of dwarfism? [2]

(iv) Given below is a simple diagram of the circulation of blood in a mammal showing the main blood vessels, the heart, lungs and body tissues. The blood vessels, labelled *F*, contain deoxygenated blood and the valve leading to it has three semi-lunar pockets.

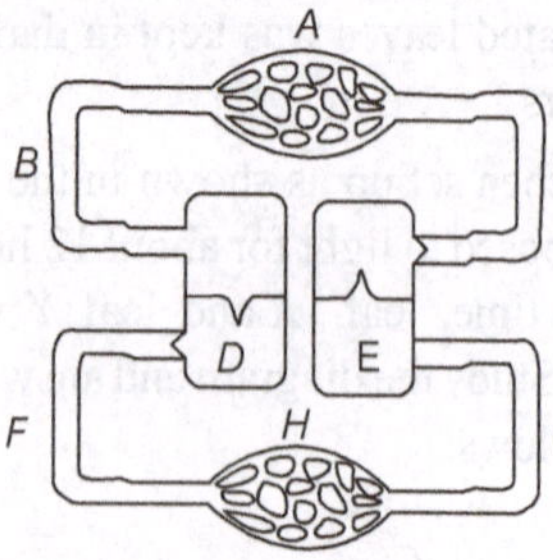

(a) Name the blood vessels or organs labelled as *A* to *G*.

(b) What do you mean by the term 'double circulation' of blood in mammals?

(v) Draw a diagram illustrating the closed and open stoma.

6. (i) Give the exact location of 'amniotic fluid'. [1]

(ii) Differentiate between phototropic movement and geotropic movement. [2]

(iii) Mention any two functions of the human kidney. [2]

(iv) What is significance of mitosis? [2]

(v) Draw a neat diagram of the longitudinal section of a human kidney and label the renal cortex and renal medulla on the diagram. [3]

7. (i) What is sex-linked inheritance? [1]

(ii) Give reason for plants growing in fertilised soil are often found to wilt if the soil is not adequately watered. [2]

(iii) What are the two functions of stomata? [2]

(iv) Distinguish between auricle and ventricle on the basis of site of occurrence. [2]

(v) Draw a flow chart explaning the mechanism of blood clotting. [3]

8. (i) Define the term mitosis. [1]

(ii) Explain why root hair become flaccid, when fertilisers are added to the moist soil around it? [2]

(iii) What is dihybrid cross? Explain by giving suitable example. [2]

(iv) What is permeable membrane? Name the permeable membrane in plants. [2]

(v) Study the diagram given below and then answer the following questions.

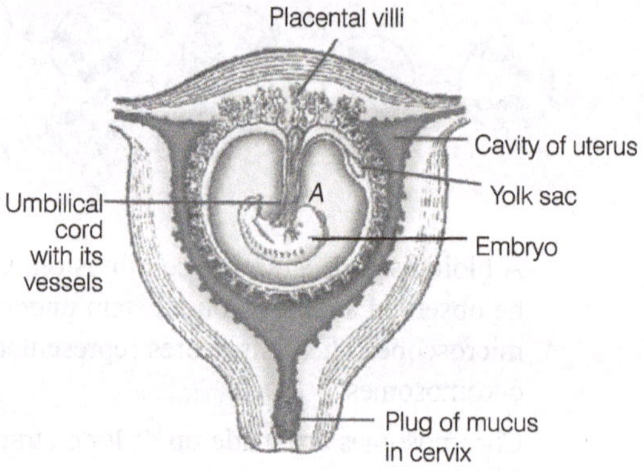

(a) Label the part *A*.

(b) State any one function of the amniotic fluid.

(c) What is the role of the umbilical cord in the development of the foetus? [3]

Answers

1. (i)-d, (ii)-a, (iii)-c, (iv)-d (v)-c, (vi)-c, (vii)-a, (viii)-c, (ix)-a, (x)-d, (xi)-a, (xii)-d, (xiii)-c, (xiv)-d, (xv)-d

ICSE Fully Solved

LATEST SPECIMEN PAPER

Time : 2 hrs
Marks : 80

Biology

General Instructions

1. You will not be allowed to write during the first 15 minutes. This time is to be spent in reading the question paper.
2. The time given at the head of this paper is the time allowed for writing the answers.
3. **Section-A** is compulsory. Attempt **any four** questions from **Section-B**.
4. The intended marks for questions or part of questions are given in brackets [].

Section-A

(Attempt **all questions** from this section)

1. Choose the correct answer to the questions from the given options.
(Do not copy the questions, write the correct answer only.) **[15]**

(i) The loops of Henle lie in **[1]**
(a) renal cortex (b) renal medulla
(c) renal pelvis (d) renal artery

(ii) The antiseptic present in tears **[1]**
(a) iodine (b) hydrogen peroxide
(c) lysozyme (d) lysosome

(iii) **Assertion** (A) The foetus respires, but does not breathe.
Reason (R) The maternal blood supplies oxygen to the foetus through placenta. **[1]**
(a) A is true, but R is false
(b) A is false, but R is true
(c) Both A and R are true
(d) Both A and R are false

(iv) During ventricular systole, the atrioventricular valves (*P*) and semilunar valves (*Q*). **[1]**
(a) *P*-close, *Q* - open
(b) *P*-close, *Q* - close
(c) *P*-open, *Q* - close
(d) P-open, *Q* - open

(v) The two cerebral hemispheres are joined by a sheet of fibres called **[1]**
(a) pons (b) corpus luteum
(c) hypothalamus (d) corpus callosum

(vi) The onset of menstruation in a human female is called **[1]**
(a) menopause (b) menarche
(c) ovulation (d) oogenesis

(vii) **Assertion** (A) Rods and cones are photoreceptors in the sclera of eyeball.
Reason (R) Rods are sensitive to dim light. **[1]**
(a) A is true, but R is false
(b) A is false, but and R is true
(c) Both A and R are true
(d) Both A and R are false

(viii) Priya tried to match the hormones with their effect on the human body. She tabulated the pairs as follows: **[1]**

Hormones	Effect on the body
P	Stimulates conversion of glycogen to glucose
Q	Reabsorption of water by the nephrons.

Identify the correct pair of hormones.

(a) *P*-Insulin, *Q*-Glycogen
(b) *P*-Adrenaline, *Q*-Oxytocin
(c) *P*-Glucagon, *Q*-Vasopressin
(d) *P*-Vasopressin, *Q*-Adrenalin

(ix) While studying the stages in the evolution of man, a well-developed chin is observed in **[1]**

(a) *Homo habilis* (b) *Homo erectus*
(c) *Homo sapiens* (d) *Australopithecus*

(x) A pair of corresponding chromosomes of the same shape, size and one from each parent is called **[1]**

(a) autosomes
(b) allosomes
(c) analogous chromosomes
(d) homologous chromosomes

(xi) **Assertion** (A) We urinate more in summer.
Reason (R) Sweat glands are more active in summer. **[1]**

(a) A is true, but R is false
(b) A is false, but R is true
(c) Both A and R are true
(d) Both A and R are false

(xii) Rahul inserted a hairpin into his right ear to remove ear wax. He felt a sudden sharp pain with loss of hearing. This was due to **[1]**

(a) rupture of eardrum
(b) rupture of vestibule
(c) rupture of cornea
(d) rupture of pinna

(xiii) **Assertion** (A) All food chains begin with herbivores.
Reason (R) Green plants are heterotrophs. **[1]**

(a) A is true, but R is false
(b) A is false, but R is true
(c) Both A and R are true
(d) Both A and R are false

(xiv) A biology teacher asked her students to give two examples of vestigial organs in the human body.

Raj said: Wisdom teeth and Pinna
Sonu said: Body hair and large intestine
Lata said: Vermiform appendix and wisdom teeth
Abhay said: Pinna and Ossicles

Who were correct? **[1]**

(a) Abhay and Sonu (b) Sonu and Lata
(c) Raj and Lata (d) Abhay and Raj

(xv) During a practical exam, a plant cell in a particular solution was placed under a compound microscope. Students were told to observe the cell and name the tonicity of the solution and mention the process that occurred in the cell. **[1]**

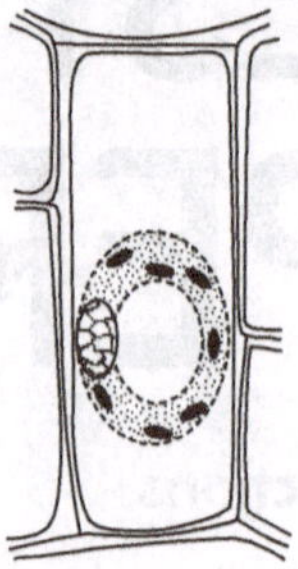

(a) Isotonic, endosmosis
(b) Hypotonic, active transport
(c) Hypertonic, endosmosis
(d) Hypertonic, exosmosis

2. (i) Name the following **[5]**

(a) The basic units of heredity.
(b) The undesirable change in the environment leading to its deterioration
(c) The structure that connects placenta and the human foetus.
(d) The statistical study of human population.
(e) The nitrogenous base that pairs with adenine.

(ii) Given below is the transverse section of the spinal cord. Read the information below the diagram and fill in the blanks: **[5]**

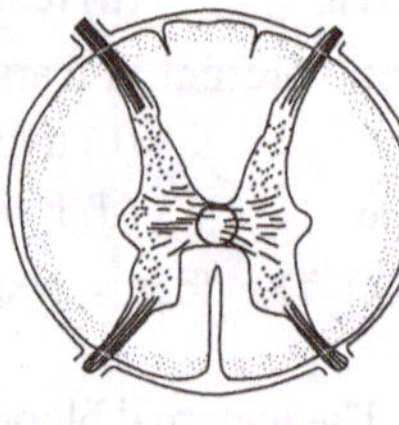

The spinal cord extends from the medulla oblongata of the brain and runs down through the whole length of the vertebral column. The spinal cord is covered by the meninges. It conducts impulses from the skin and muscles to the brain. It also conducts impulses from the brain to the muscles of the trunk and limbs.

The spinal cord is a part of the (a)……… nervous system. The grey matter in the picture given above consists of (b)……… the white matter consists of (c)……… The spinal cord is concerned with the (d)……… actions below the neck. (e)……… is the bony structure that protects the spinal cord.

(iii) Arrange and rewrite the terms in each group in the correct order so as to be in a logical sequence beginning with the term that is underlined. **[5]**

(a) Apical meristem, Positive phototropism, Auxins, Cell elongation.

(b) Urethra, Urinary bladder, Ureter, Kidney.

(c) Auditory canal, Organ of Corti, Stapes, Malleus.

(d) Cell membrane, Chromatin fibres, Cell wall, Cytoplasm.

(e) Lungs, Right auricle, Inferior vena cava, Pulmonary artery.

(iv) Read the explanations given below and name the structure: **[5]**

(a) Food conducting tissue in vascular plants.

(b) A cell formed by the fusion of gametes.

(c) The smallest blood vessels in the human body.

(d) A tubular passage that connects the pharynx and the middle ear.

(e) The openings on the barks of trees through which transpiration occurs.

(v) Given below is a cross section of the human eye. Match the structures marked (*a*) to (*e*) with their correct functions: **[5]**

Cross section of Human Eye	Functions
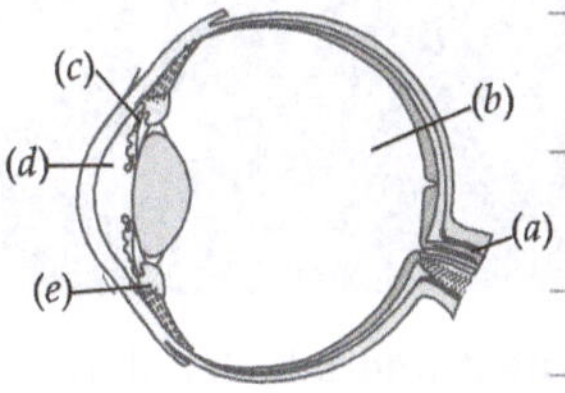	1. Protects retina
	2. Regulates the size of the pupil
	3. Alters the shape of the lens
	4. Keeps the lens moist
	5. Transmits nerve impulses to brain

[5]

Section-B

(Attempt any **four questions** from this Section.)

3. (i) Explain the term active transport. **[1]**

(ii) Name the structures through which transpiration and guttation occur in a plant. **[2]**

(iii) How does the rate of transpiration differ when there is

(a) high temperature?

(b) high humidity? **[2]**

(iv) Write the overall chemical equation for photosynthesis. **[2]**

(v) Sam observed a slide containing the lower epidermis of a leaf under a microscope. A number of tiny openings between the epidermal cells were present as shown below in the diagram: **[3]**

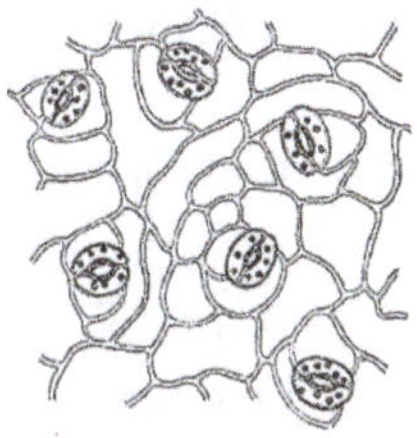

(a) What are these tiny openings called?

(b) Name the cells that regulate the opening and closing of these structures.

(c) Which ion is responsible for the opening and closing of these openings?

4. (i) Why is adrenaline called the 'Emergency Hormone'? **[1]**

(ii) Expand the abbreviation ADH. Give one example of a diuretic substance. **[2]**

(iii) Mention the significance of the following minerals

(a) Iodine in our food.

(b) Magnesium in green plants. **[2]**

(iv) State two objectives of Swachh Bharat Abhiyan. **[2]**

(v) Draw a neat and labelled diagram of a root hair. **[3]**

5. (i) Mention one characteristic of roots for absorbing water from the soil. **[1]**

(ii) What is parthenocarpy? Give one example. **[2]**

(iii) State the difference between micturition and parturition. **[2]**

(iv) Write any two functions of lymph. **[2]**

(v) Study the picture given below and answer the questions: **[3]**

(a) How does water get polluted?

(b) What is the effect of water pollution on human life?

(c) Mention one control measure to stop the pollution of water bodies.

6. (i) State Mendel's law of segregation. [1]

(ii) What are tropic hormones? Give one example. [2]

(iii) Differentiate between the terms phenotype and genotype. [2]

(iv) What is the significance of testes being placed in scrotal sacs? [2]

(v) Draw a neat and labelled diagram of a human sperm. [3]

7. (i) What is the scientific name of the pea plant that Mendel used for his experiments? [1]

(ii) Mention the surgical methods of contraception in

(a) men (b) women [2]

(iii) Name two harmful effects of noise pollution. [2]

(iv) Which parts of a plant exhibit

(a) negative geotropism?

(b) positive hydrotropism? [2]

(v) Kathak is an Indian classical dance which involves a lot of spinning by the dancers. The learners of this dance experience dizziness in the beginning while spinning. [3]

(a) Name the part of the membranous labyrinth responsible for this dizziness.

(b) Give a suitable reason for your answer.

(c) Mention the nerve that carries the impulse for dizziness to the brain.

8. (i) How does transpiration help in the uptake of water from the soil? [1]

(ii) Given below are two statements which are incorrect. Rewrite the correct statements.

(a) Fresh water fish when placed in hypertonic salt solution absorb water and burst.

(b) Seminiferous tubules secrete testosterone. [2]

(iii) During mitosis, what is the position of chromatids in

(a) Metaphase?

(b) Anaphase? [2]

(iv) Chris was watching the display of fireworks in the sky. [2]

(a) Trace the path of the light rays using the following terms: Fovea, Lens, Conjunctiva, Pupil, Cornea

(b) Name the nerve that carries the impulse for vision to the brain.

(v) Draw a neat and labelled diagram of a Malpighian body. [3]

Answers

1. (i) (b) renal medulla
   (ii) (c) Lysozyme
   (iii) (c) Both A and R are true.
   (iv) (a) *P*-close, *Q*-open
   (v) (d) Corpus callosum
   (vi) (b) Menarche
   (vii) (b) A is false, but R is true. A can be corrected as
   Photoreceptors (rods and cones) are specialised light-detecting cells on the retina, at the back of eyes
   (viii) (c) *P*-Glucagon, *Q*- Vasopressin.
   (ix) (c) *Homo sapiens*
   (x) (d) Homologous chromosomes
   (xi) (b) A is false, but R is true. A can be corrected as
   We urinate more in winter. Due to more perspiration in summer, there is more water loss from the body.
   (xii) (a) rupture of eardrum
   (xiii) (d) Both A and R are false. These can be corrected as
   - All food chains start with a producer.
   - Green plants are autotrophs.

   (xiv) (c) Raj and Lata
   (xv) (d) Hypertonic, Exosmosis

2. (i) (a) Genes (b) Pollution
   (c) Umbilical Cord (d) Demography
   (e) Thymine (T)
   (ii) (a) central (b) cytons/nerve cell bodies
   (c) Axons/nerve cell fibres
   (d) reflex
   (e) Vertebral column
   (iii) (a) Auxins, Apical meristem, Cell elongation, Positive phototropism.
   (b) Kidney, Ureter, Urinary bladder, Urethra.
   (c) Auditory canal, Malleus, Stapes, Organ of Corti.
   (d) Chromatin fibres, Cytoplasm, Cell membrane, Cell wall.
   (e) Inferior vena cava, Right auricle, Pulmonary artery, Lungs.
   (iv) (a) Phloem (b) Zygote
   (c) Capillaries (d) Eustachian tube
   (e) Lenticels
   (v) (a) 5 (b) 1 (c) 2 (d) 4 (e) 3

3. (i) Active transport is the movement of salt or ions across a cell membrane from lower to higher concentration by the use of energy.
   (ii) Transpiration in plants occurs through stomata, lenticels and cuticle, while guttation occurs through hydathodes.
   (iii) (a) The rate of transpiration increases when there is high temperature.
   (b) The rate of transpiration decreases in the case of high humidity.
   (iv) Photosynthesis is a physiological process in which living plant cells that contain chlorophyll, synthesise food in the form of glucose and starch from CO_2 and water, using light energy.
   Overall reaction of photosynthesis can be summarised as follows

$$\underset{\text{Carbon dioxide}}{6CO_2} + \underset{\text{Water}}{12H_2O} \xrightarrow[\text{Chlorophyll}]{\text{Sunlight}} \underset{\text{Sugar}}{C_6H_{12}O_6} + \underset{\text{Water}}{6H_2O} + \underset{\text{Oxygen}}{6O_2} \uparrow \text{ (By product)}$$

   (v) (a) These tiny openings are called as stomata.
   (b) Guard cells regulate the opening and closing of the stomata.
   (c) K^+ /potassium ions are responsible for the opening and closing of the stomata.

4. (i) Adrenaline is called as the 'Emergency Hormone' because it is secreted under conditions of stress like anger, fear, excitement. It prepares the body to face the emergency situation.
   (ii) ADH stands for Antidiuretic Hormone. One example of a diuretic substance is alcohol.
   (iii) (a) For synthesis of thyroxine by thyroid gland.
   (b) For synthesis of chlorophyll.
   (iv) The two objectives of Swachh Bharat Abhiyan are as follows
   - To clean streets, roads, cities and towns.
   - To eliminate open defecation by constructing toilets.

   (v) Diagram of a root hair.

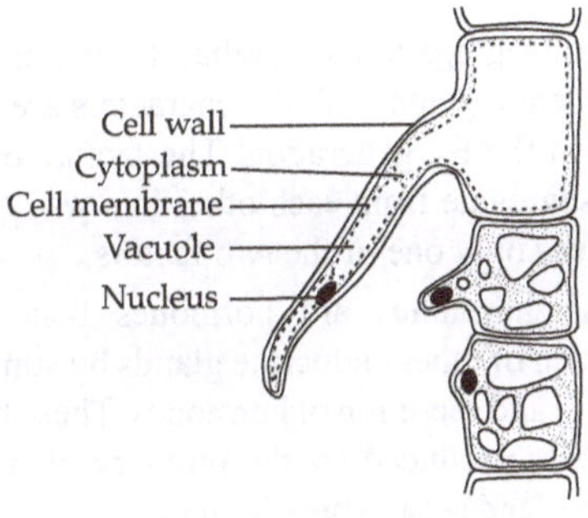

5. (i) One characteristic of roots for absorbing water from soil is the presence of root hairs. Root hairs increase the surface area of a root, enhancing its ability to absorb water and nutrients from the soil.

(ii) Parthenocarpy is the development of fruits without fertilisation of the ovules, resulting in seedless fruits. One example of parthenocarpy is banana.

(iii) Differences between micturition and parturition are as follows

Micturition	Parturition
Expulsion of urine from the urinary bladder.	It is the expulsion of fully developed foetus from the uterus at the end of gestation.
Involves urinary system.	Involves the reproductive system.
Removal of waste products in the form of urine.	Delivery of a baby from the mother's womb.

(iv) The function of lymph are as follows

Transport of nutrient and waste - Lymph help to transport nutrients, oxygen and hormones to cells through out the body and removes metabolic waste products and toxins from tissues.

Immune function - Lymph plays a crucial role in the immune system by transporting white blood cells, especially lymphocytes, which help to fight infections.

(v) (a) Water pollution occurs through various means including sewage, waste water, industrial effluents, oil spills and agricultural run off.

(b) Water pollution has significant impact on human life, including health risks from waterborne diseases such as diarrhoea, cholera, typhoid and reduced access to clean drinking water.

(c) Implementing strict sewage treatment regulations and ensuring proper waste water management, to prevent untreated sewage from being discharged into water bodies are crucial measures to stop water pollution.

6. (i) Law of segregation states that the alleles do not show any blending and both the characters are recovered as such in the F_2 generation. The factors or alleles of a pair segregate from each other in a way that a gamete receives only one of the two factors.

(ii) Tropic hormones are hormones that regulate the function of other endocrine glands by stimulating their growth and secretion of hormones. These hormones are typically produced by the pituitary gland and act on target glands else where in the body.

One example of tropic hormone is thyroid-stimulating hormone (TSH), which is produced by the anterior pituitary gland.

(iii) Differences between genotype and phenotype are as follows

Genotype	Phenotype
Genetic makeup of an organism.	Observable physical traits.
Complete set of gene an organism carries.	Physical expression influenced by genes and environment.
Example : TT, tt	Example : tall and dwarf

(iv) The scrotal sac allow testes to be positioned outside the body, maintaining their temperature at about 2-2.5°C lower than the internal body temperature. This cooler environment is crucial for optimal sperm production (spermatogenesis) and ensure sperm quality and viability, thereby supporting male reproductive functions.

(v) Diagram of human sperm.

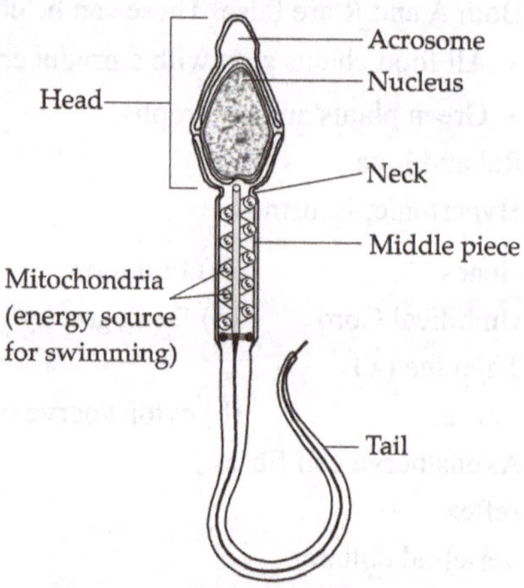

7. (i) The scientific name of pea plant that Mendel used for his experiment is *Pisum sativum*.

(ii) (a) The surgical method of contraception in men is vasectomy. In vasectomy, a small part of the vas deferens is cut and tied up through a small incision in the scrotum.

(b) The surgical method of contraception in female is tubectomy. In tubectomy, a small part of Fallopian tube is cut or tied up through small incision in the abdomen or vagina.

(iii) The two harmful effects of noise pollution are as follows

- Prolonged exposure to loud noises can damage the eardrums and may permanently impair the hearing ability of humans.

- Chronic noise exposure can lead to increased stress levels which can elevate blood pressure and the risk of heart diseases.

(iv) (a) The part of a plant that exhibit negative geotropism is shoot. Negative geotropism refers to the growth of the plant part in the direction away from the force of gravity.

(b) The part of a plant that exhibit positive hydrotropism is the root. Positive hydrotropism refers to the growth response of plant towards water.

(v) (a) Semicircular canals.

(b) The semicircular canals in the inner ear detect rotational movements of the head *via* fluid movement and hair cell.

When these canals signal rapid head motion to the brain, it can cause sensation of dizziness due to sensory inputs.

(c) Vestibular nerve carries the impulse for dizziness to the brain.

8. (i) Transpiration creates a negative pressure in the leaves as water evaporates, pulling water up from the roots through the xylem. This process facilitates the continuous uptake of water and nutrients from the soil.

(ii) (a) Fresh water fish when placed in hypertonic salt solution lose water and shrink. While, marine fish when placed in hypotonic salt solution absorb water and burst.

(b) Seminiferous tubules produce sperms, while Leydig cells secrete testosterone.

(iii) (a) During metaphase of mitosis, chromatids are aligned at the cell's equatorial plane, also known as the metaphase plate. This alignment ensures that each daughter cell receive an identical set of chromosome when chromatids are separated during anaphase.

(b) During anaphase of mitosis, the sister chromatids are separated and pulled towards the opposite poles of the cell. This movement is facilitated by the shortening of the spindle fibres attached to chromatids centromere.

(iv) (a) Conjunctiva, Cornea, Pupil, Lens, Fovea.

(b) Optic nerve carries the impulse for vision to the brain.

(v) Diagram of Malpighian body

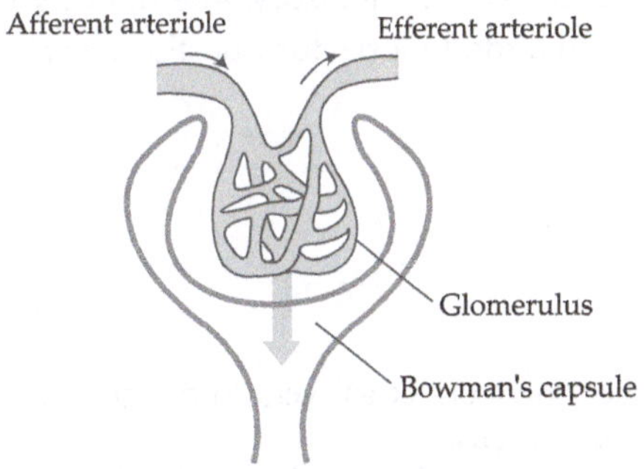

ICSE

Examination Paper 2025

Time : 2 hrs
Marks : 80

Biology

General Instructions

1. You will not be allowed to write during the first 15 minutes. This time is to be spent in reading the question paper.
2. The time given at the head of this paper is the time allowed for writing the answers.
3. **Section-A** is compulsory. Attempt **any four** questions from **Section-B**.
4. The intended marks for questions or part of questions are given in brackets [].

Section-A

(Attempt **all questions** from this section) **[40 Marks]**

1. Select the correct answers to the questions from the given options.
(Do not copy the question, write the correct answer only) **[15]**

(i) The number of live births per thousand people per year is called
(a) mortality
(b) population density
(c) population growth rate
(d) natality

(ii) The structure that lies at the junction of the choroid and the iris and is itself a part of the choroid is called
(a) ciliary body (b) suspensory ligament
(c) pupil (d) lens

(iii) **Assertion** (A) Seminal vesicles pour an alkaline secretion into the semen as it passes through the ureter.
Reason (R) The female vagina is acidic and needs to be neutralised for sperm survival.
(a) A is true, but R is false.
(b) A is false, but R is true.
(c) Both A and R are true.
(d) Both A and R are false.

(iv) The hormone that induces vigorous contractions of the uterus in a pregnant mother is
(a) oestrogen
(b) prolactin
(c) oxytocin
(d) progesterone

(v) A scientist wanted to conduct a genetic experiment on mice. He cut the tails of all the mice and made them reproduce. What will be the phenotype of the offsprings?
(a) All the offsprings will be tailless.
(b) There will be a mix of tailed and tailless offsprings.
(c) All the offsprings will have tails.
(d) Tail of the offsprings cannot be predicted.

(vi) **Assertion** (A) A turgid plant cell is in a balanced state.
Reason (R) In a turgid cell, turgor pressure and wall pressure are equal and in the same direction.
(a) A is true, but R is false.
(b) A is false, but R is true.
(c) Both A and R are true.
(d) Both A and R are false.

(vii) The optimum temperature for photosynthesis is
(a) 10 - 15 °C
(b) 60 - 65 °C
(c) 40 - 45 °C
(d) 25 - 35 °C

(viii) Ajay and Vijay are siblings. Ajay can roll his tongue while Vijay cannot.
What is the genotype of their parents?
(a) Both the parents are homozygous dominant.
(b) Both the parents are homozygous recessive.
(c) One parent is homozygous dominant and the other is homozygous recessive.
(d) Both the parents are heterozygous dominant.

(ix) **Assertion** (A) Deficiency of antidiuretic hormone causes an increase in urination.
Reason (R) Antidiuretic hormone acts on the kidney to reabsorb water from the kidney tubules.
(a) A is true, but R is false.
(b) A is false, but R is true.
(c) Both A and R are true.
(d) Both A and R are false.

(x) A phase of cell division where the spindle fibres disappear is
(a) telophaseop
(b) prophase
(c) metaphase
(d) anaphase

(xi) **Assertion** (A) Arachnoid layer helps in speeding up the transmission of nerve impulses along the axons.
Reason (R) Axon endings at the synapse secrete acetylene.
(a) A is true, but R is false.
(b) A is false, but R is true.
(c) Both A and R are true.
(d) Both A and R are false.

(xii) Many nuclear power plants are constructed near water sources. They use water for cooling their machinery and release it back into the water stream. Identify the kind of pollution caused
(a) radiation pollution
(b) water pollution
(c) industrial pollution
(d) thermal pollution

(xiii)

Owls are nocturnal animals. They are active at night and hunt small animals for food. Owls have large eyes and can see well at night. This is due to
(a) cones and rhodopsin
(b) rods and iodopsin
(c) rods and rhodopsin
(d) cones and iodopsin

(xiv) Sunil tried to match the tropic movements in plants with the stimulus they respond to. The tabulation is given below:

	Tropism	Stimulus
P	Thigmotropism	Touch
Q	Geotropism	Water
R	Chemotropism	Chemicals
S	Phototropism	Gravity

Identify the correct pair.
(a) P and R
(b) Q and S
(c) R and S
(d) P and R

(xv) Observe the following picture, identify the defect and the cause of the defect.

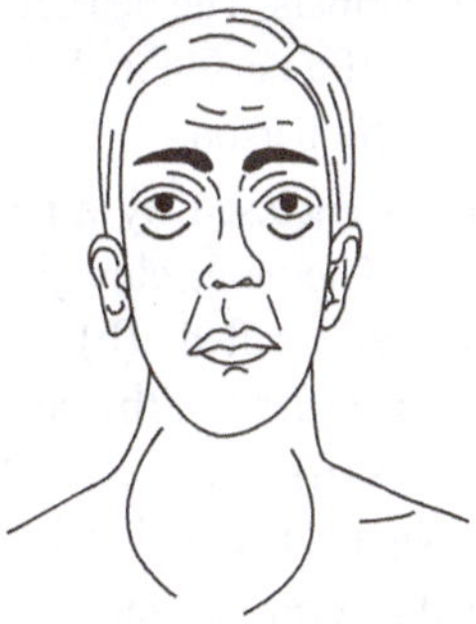

(a) Simple goitre, under secretion of thyroxine.
(b) Ex-ophthalmic goitre, over secretion of thyroxine.
(c) Simple goitre, over secretion of thyroxine.
(d) Ex-ophthalmic goitre, under secretion of thyroxine.

2. (i) Name the following: **[5]**

(a) The fully developed part of the ovary containing a mature ovum.

(b) A waxy layer on the upper epidermis of leaves meant to reduce transpiration.

(c) The ear ossicle which opens into the oval window of cochlea.

(d) The physiological process which is the starting point of all food chains.

(e) An insect which is a classic example of natural selection due to industrial melanism.

(ii) Given below is the diagram of a human heart. Read the information below the diagram and fill in the blanks: **[5]**

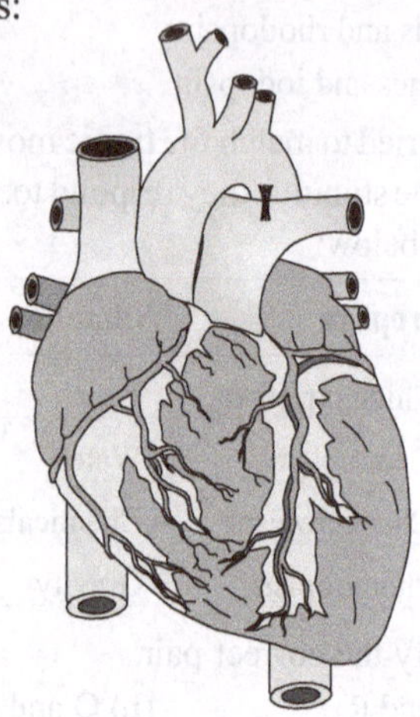

The human heart pumps blood throughout the body. It is the size of a large fist. The heart is located between the lungs in the thoracic cavity. It has four chambers. The heart functions all through the lifespan of a person and is responsible for the survival of the person.

The heart is enclosed by a membrane called (a) .... The ventricles give rise to two large blood vessels called (b) .... and (c) .... The flaps of the cuspid valves are kept in position by (d) .... (e) .... arteries supply oxygenated blood to the walls of the heart.

(iii) Arrange the terms in each group in the correct order. Write them in a logical sequence beginning with the term that is underlined. **[5]**

(a) Palisade cells, Cuticle, Upper epidermis, Spongy cells.

(b) Hepatic portal vein, Stomach, Hepatic vein, Liver.

(c) Cyton, Dendrites, Synaptic cleft, Axon endings.

(d) Insulin release, High blood sugar, Lowers blood sugar, Stimulates glucose uptake from blood.

(e) Sperm duct, Seminiferous tubule, Epididymis, Efferent ducts.

(iv) Read the explanations given below and name the structures. **[5]**

Example The tubules which produce sperms.

Answer Seminiferous tubules

(a) The canal through which the testes descend down into the scrotum just before the birth of a male baby.

(b) The part of the brain that regulates the peristaltic movement of the alimentary canal.

(c) A structure that collects the soundwaves and conducts them through the external auditory canal.

(d) The point of attachment of two chromatids of a chromosome.

(e) Regulation of the opening and closing of stomata.

(v) Given below is an outline of the human body showing the important endocrine glands. Match the glands marked (a) to (e) with their correct functions. **[5]**

Example (*f*) 6. Secretes testosterone.

Endocrine glands

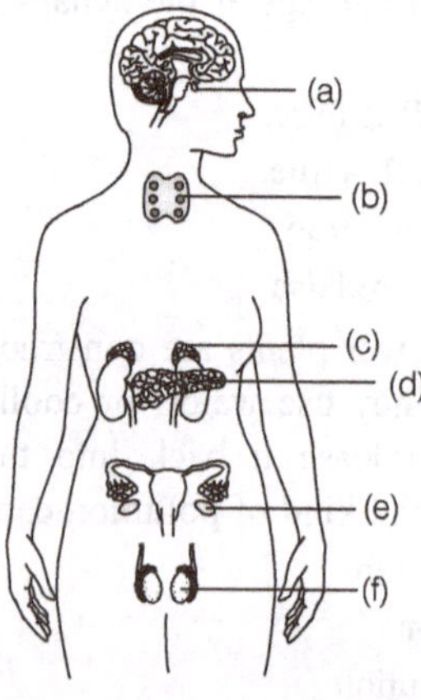

	Functions
1.	Prepares the body to face stress.
2.	Secretes tropic hormones
3.	Secretes oestrogens
4.	Maintains blood sugar level
5.	Regulates basal metabolism
6.	Secretes testosterone.

Section-B

(Attempt any **four questions** from this Section.)

3. (i) Write the overall chemical equation for photosynthesis. **[1]**

(ii) Ramesh is a farmer who has a vineyard and cultivates grapes. To improve the shape of the grapes and make them elongated he sprays particular phytohormone at the time of fruiting. **[2]**

(a) Name the phytohormone that Ramesh sprays on the plant at the time of fruiting.

(b) These grapes are said to be seedless. What is the technical term for the formation of such fruits?

(iii) Mention the two pairs of nitrogenous bases that are present in a DNA strand and pair with each other by hydrogen bonds. **[2]**

(iv) State any two disadvantages of living close to an airport. **[2]**

(v) Draw a neat, labelled diagram of an animal cell showing metaphase with four chromosomes. **[3]**

4. (i) What is the structure of DNA as proposed by Watson and Crick? **[1]**

(ii) Name the white blood cells that

(a) show phagocytosis.

(b) produce antibodies. **[2]**

(iii) Complete the food chain by mentioning the names of the organisms in (c) and (d): **[2]**

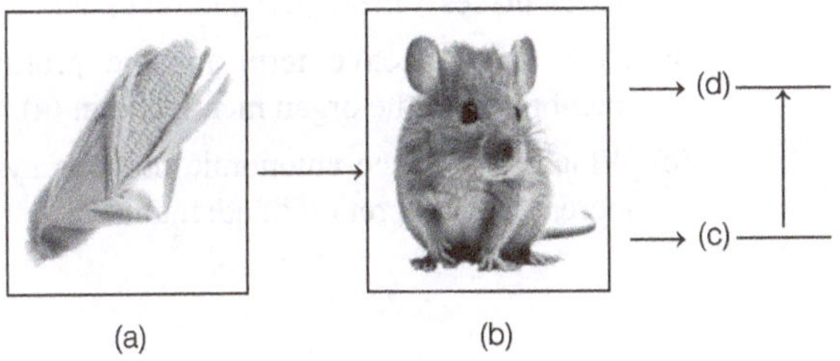

(iv) State any two harmful effects of acid rain. **[2]**

(v) Given below is a picture of a tree. Mention the scientific phenomena occurring in the parts labelled (a), (b) and (c). **[3]**

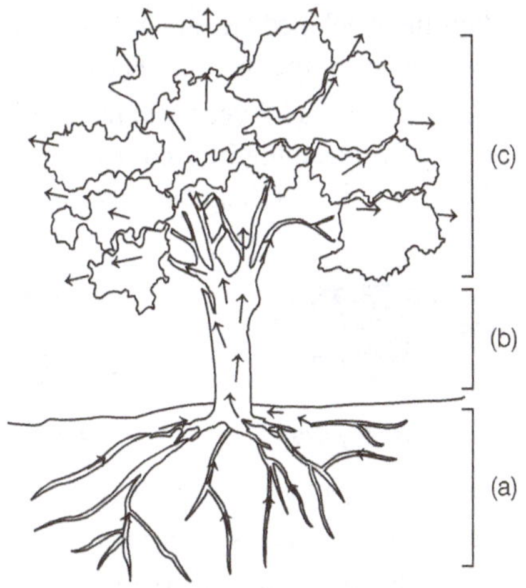

5. (i) What is micturition? Explain. **[1]**

(ii) What are biomedical wastes? Give an example. **[2]**

(iii) Differentiate between the functions of urethra and uterus. **[2]**

(iv) Rachna is an expert gymnast on the balance beam. She has been vigorously practising for the Olympic games. Lately, she has been experiencing dizziness and losing her balance during the practise sessions. **[2]**

(a) Which part of the membranous labyrinth is responsible for maintaining the body balance on the beam?

(b) Which type of balance is maintained by the structure mentioned in (a)?

(v) Draw a neat, labelled diagram to show that oxygen is released during photosynthesis. **[3]**

6. (i) Where are hydathodes located? [1]

(ii) What are vestigial organs? Give one example of a vestigial structure in the human mouth. [2]

(iii) Ahmed had a severe throat infection. After a few days he developed an earache too. What could be the reason for the pain in his ears? Explain. [2]

(iv) Mr. Sharma is a 76 years old man. His vision was gradually becoming blurred. He consulted an eye doctor and it was diagnosed as cataract. [2]

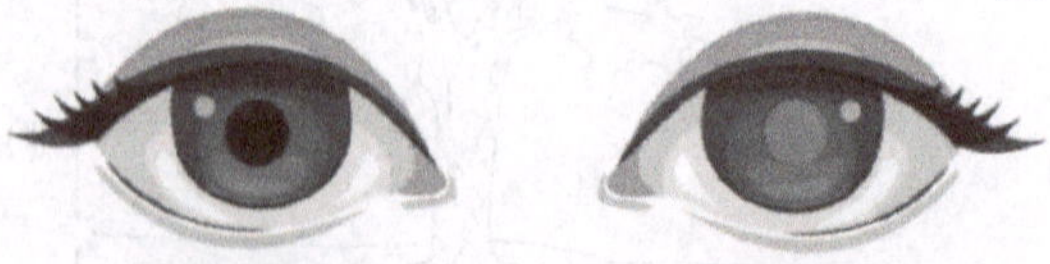

(a) Which part of the eye does cataract affect?

(b) Why does the vision become blurred?

(v) Given below is the diagram of a plasmolysed cortical cell of a root. [3]

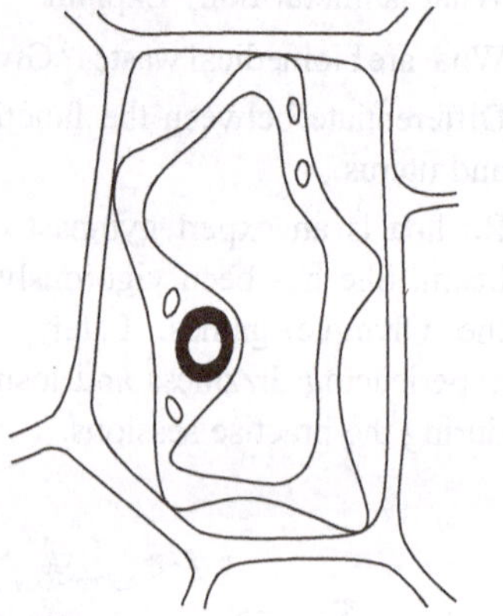

Copy the diagram and label the following parts in the diagram.

(a) Cytoplasm

(b) Hypertonic solution

(c) Plasma membrane

7. (i) Define the term allele. [1]

(ii) In the last century, the human population has increased tremendously. Death rate has reduced and life expectancy has increased. This rapid growth has placed significant pressure on resources. Global cooperation is needed for environmental preservation. [2]

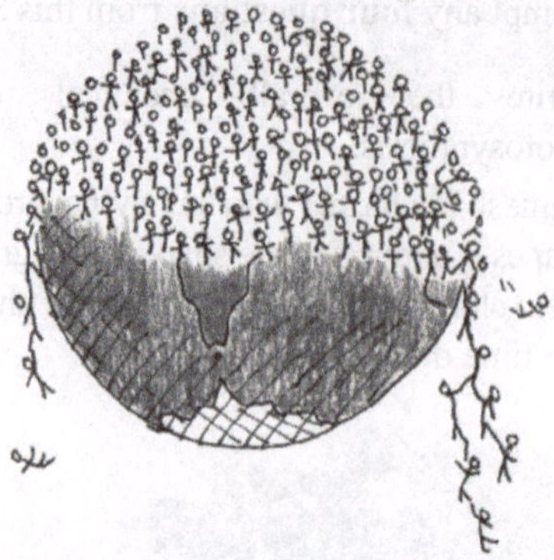

(a) Mention any one reason for reduction in the death rate.

(b) Name any one resource that is under pressure due to population explosion.

(iii) Mention any two functions of amniotic fluid. [2]

(iv) Expand the following abbreviations. [2]

(a) CFC (b) CNG

(v) Vineet's day begins with a cup of piping hot coffee. Caffeine is a stimulant present in coffee which increases the circulation of adrenaline in the body. Vineet feels refreshed, alert and focussed. [3]

(a) Name the organ that is stimulated by caffeine which makes Vineet alert and focussed.

(b) Give the collective term for the protective membranes of the organ mentioned in (a).

(c) Which part of the autonomic nervous system increases the secretion of adrenaline?

8. (i) Explain the term excretion. [1]

(ii) State the difference between nephron and neuron. [2]

(iii) Mention any two objectives of Swachh Bharat Abhiyan. [2]

(iv) Give any two characteristic features of a Cro-Magnon man. [2]

(v) A farmer cultivates a unique species of tomato plants. The two traits selected for breeding were: Colour of the fruits and height of the plants. The farmer initially crosses a homozygous tall planf bearing red fruits (TTRR) with a dwarf plant bearing yellow fruits (ttrr) and the genotype of all the offsprings of the F_1-generation was TtRr. Next, he crosses two F_1-generation plants (TtRr). [3]

Tall plant with red fruits　　Dwarf plant with yellow fruits

(a) Explain the phenotype of the offsprings of the F_1-generation obtained from the initial cross.

(b) Mention the phenotypic ratio of the F_2-generation offsprings.

(c) State Mendel's law of independent assortment.

Answers

1. (i) (d) Natality

(ii) (a) Ciliary body

(iii) (b) A is false, but R is true. The seminal vesicles do secrete an alkaline fluid rich in fructose, but semen does not pass through the ureter. The ureter is the tube that carries urine from the kidneys to the bladder in males.

(iv) (c) Oxytocin

(v) (c) All the offsprings will have tails . This is because the length of a tail in mice is determined by genes, not by acquired traits.

(vi) (c) Both A and R are true

(vii) (d) 25- 35 °C

(viii) (d) Both parents are heterozygous dominant

(ix) (c) Both A and R are true

(x) (a) Telophase

(xi) (d) Both A and R are false . The arachnoid layer is one of the three meninges (protective coverings of the brain and spinal cord), but it does not play a direct role in nerve impulse transmission. And the correct neurotransmitter is acetylcholine (ACh), not "acetylene".

(xii) (d) Thermal pollution

(xiii) (c) Rods and rhodopsin

(xiv) (a) *P* and *R*

(xv) (b) Exophthalmic goiter, over secretion of thyroxine.

2. (i) (a) Graafian follicle

(b) Cuticle

(c) Stapes

(d) Photosynthesis

(e) Peppered Moth (*Biston Betularia*)

(ii) (a) Pericardium

(b) Pulmonary artery and Aorta

(c) Chordae tendineae

(d) Coronary

(iii) (a) Cuticle, upper epidermis, Palisade cells, Spongy cells

(b) Stomach, hepatic portal vein, liver, hepatic vein.

(c) Dendrites, cyton (cell body), axon endings and finally, the synaptic cleft.

(d) High blood sugar, stimulates glucose uptake from blood, Insulin release, lowers blood glucose sugar.

(e) Seminiferous tubules, Efferent duct , Epididymis, Sperm duct (Vas deferens)

(iv) (a) Inguinal canal

(b) Medulla oblongata

(c) Pinna

(d) Centromere

(e) Guard cells

(v) a- 2, b- 5, c -1 , d- 4, e- 3

3. (i) $6CO_2 + 6H_2O + \text{Light} + \text{Energy} \rightarrow C_6H_{12}O_6 + 6O_2$

(ii) (a) Gibberellin

(b) Parthenocarpic fruits

(iii) Adenine and Thymine

(iv) Two disdvantages are :

(a) Airports generate constant loud noise from aircraft takeoff, landing, and taxiing.

(b) expose residents to air pollution affecting health and overall well-being.

(v)

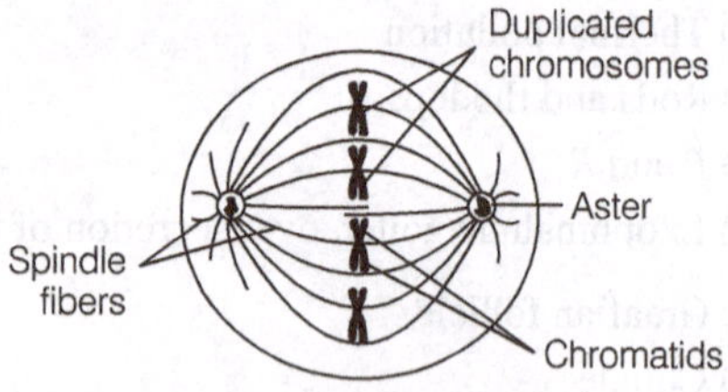

Metaphase stage of mitosis

4. (i) Double helical structure of DNA

(ii) (a) Macrophage

(b) B-lymphocytes

(iii) (c) Eagle

(d) Snake

(iv) Harmful effects of Acid rain are

(a) It damages the fish and other aquatic life.

(b) It also damages the vegetation by killing the useful soil community

(v) (a) Absorption of water and minerals from soil

(b) Ascent of sap

(c) Transpiration

5. (i) The process of expelling out of urine is known as micturition. This process is done under the impulse of nervous system.

(ii) The wastes produced by the hospitals, clinics, laboratories are known as biomedical wastes. These are the major causes of soil pollution. For, e.g. Wound dressings.

(iii) Urethra- Transports urine (and semen in males) out of the body

Uterus- Supports fetal development during pregnancy

(iv) (a) Semicircular canal

(b) Static balance

(v)

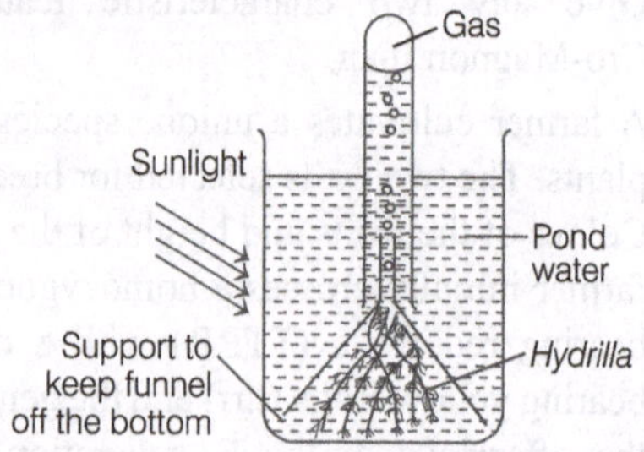

6. (i) At the tips and margins of leaves

(ii) The organs that are present in reduced for and do not perform any function in the body are called vestigial organs. For eg, The third pair of molars are the vestigial organ present in the mouth of the human. These are known as wisdom tooth.

(iii) The malleus (or hammer) of the middle ear on its one end is attached to the eardrum and other free end is attached to the oval window of the inner ear. It opens into Eustachian tube that connects with the pharynx and maintains the pressure on each sides of the ear drum. This is the reason, an infection in the throat may lead to the ear infections due to this connection.

(iv) (a) Cataract affects the lens of the eye

(b) The vision becomes blurred because the crystalline lens of the eye becomes milky or cludy due to the growth of a membrane over it.

(v)

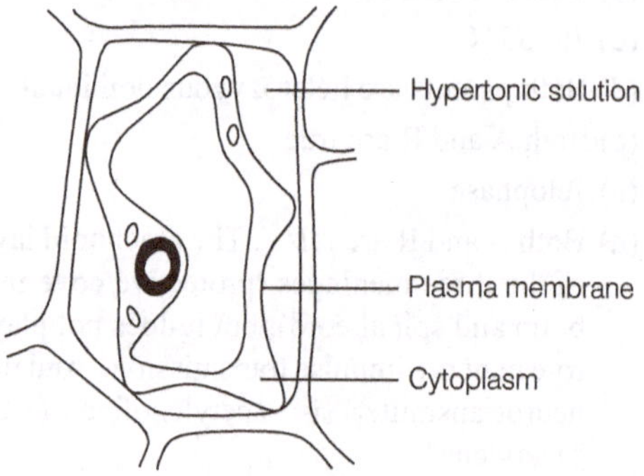

7. (i) Alleles are the alternative forms or varieties of gene in a particular gene pair.

(ii) (a) The one reason for the reduction in death rate is improved medical facilities

(b) Food resources as increased population may lead to shortage of food supply.

(iii) Amniotic fluid perform following functions:

(a) It provides an aqueous environment in which the embryo is protected from shocks and keep even pressure all around the embryo.

(b) It also restricts foetal movements and prevents sticking foetus to the amnion.

(iv) (a) CFC- Chloroflurocarbon

(b) CNG- Compressed Natural gas

(v) (a) Brain

(b) Meninges.

(c) The sympathetic nervous system (SNS) of the autonomic nervous system (ANS) increases the secretion of adrenaline.

8. (i) The process of removal of harmful metabolic waste products from the body is called excretion.

(ii) **Nephron**- The structural and functional unit of the kidney, responsible for filtration and urine formation.

Neuron- The structural and functional unit of the nervous system, responsible for transmitting nerve impulses.

(iii) Two objectives of Swachh Bharat Abhiyan are :

(a) To Eliminate open defecation

(b) To improve waste management & cleanliness

(iv) Two major features of Cro- Magnon man are:

(a) Broact and arched forehead

(b) Strong jaws

(v) (a) The phenotype of F_1 generation obtained by the initial cross is Tall red (TtRr)

(b) The phenotypic ration of F_2 generation is – 9:3:3:1

(c) The law of Independent assortment states that when two pairs of contrasting traits or characters are combined in a hybrid, segregation of one pair of character is independent of the other pair of character at the time of gamete formation.